THE GOSPEL OF LUKE

Sacra Pagina Series

Volume 3

The Gospel of Luke

Luke Timothy Johnson

Daniel J. Harrington, S.J.
Editor

A Michael Glazier Book
THE LITURGICAL PRESS
Collegeville, Minnesota

Cover design by Don Bruno.

A Michael Glazier Book published by The Liturgical Press.

4   5   6   7   8   9

Library of Congress Cataloging-in-Publication Data

Johnson, Luke Timothy.
    The Gospel of Luke / by Luke Timothy Johnson.
       p.   cm. — (Sacra pagina series ; 3)
    ''A Michael Glazier book.''
    Includes bibliographical references and index.
    ISBN 0-8146-5805-9
    1. Bible. N.T. Luke—Commentaries. I. Title. II. Series.
BS2595.3.J64 1991
226.4'077—dc20   91-12956
                                                    CIP

CONTENTS

III. Preparing a Leadership for the People

IV. The Prophet Journeys to Jerusalem

V. The Prophet in Jerusalem

VI. The Suffering of the Prophet

VII. The Prophet Is Raised Up

Indexes

EDITOR'S PREFACE

Sacra Pagina is a multi-volume commentary on the books of the New Testament. The expression *Sacra Pagina* ("Sacred Page") originally referred to the text of Scripture. In the Middle Ages it also described the study of Scripture to which the interpreter brought the tools of grammar, rhetoric, dialectic, and philosophy. Thus *Sacra Pagina* encompasses both the text to be studied and the activity of interpretation.

This series presents fresh translations and modern expositions of all the books of the New Testament. Written by an international team of Catholic biblical scholars, it is intended for biblical professionals, graduate students, theologians, clergy, and religious educators. The volumes present basic introductory information and close exposition. They self-consciously adopt specific methodological perspectives, but maintain a focus on the issues raised by the New Testament compositions themselves. The goal of *Sacra Pagina* is to provide sound critical analysis without any loss of sensitivity to religious meaning. This series is therefore catholic in two senses of the word: inclusive in its methods and perspectives, and shaped by the context of the Catholic tradition.

The Second Vatican Council described the study of "the sacred page" as the "very soul of sacred theology" (*Dei Verbum* 24). The volumes in this series illustrate how Catholic scholars contribute to the council's call to provide access to Sacred Scripture for all the Christian faithful. Rather than pretending to say the final word on any text, these volumes seek to open up the riches of the New Testament and to invite as many people as possible to study seriously the "sacred page."

DANIEL J. HARRINGTON, S.J.

PREFACE

Like other commentaries in the series, this one on Luke's Gospel provides for each section an original translation from the Greek, a set of detailed notes, an interpretation, and a short bibliography. An introduction presents the principles governing this reading of the Gospel and provides a general bibliography.

My translation aims at clarity and readability. Since this translation is meant for private study rather than liturgical reading, I felt free occasionally to give an idiosyncratic reading to the Greek. The notes are a wonderful luxury for the translator, allowing a fuller explanation of obscurities and alternatives. The reader should be aware from the start that I have deliberately eliminated many of Luke's biblicisms, even some treasured ones. I did this in the hope of providing a freshness to the language, but it may have resulted in the loss of some beauty as well. I have also struggled to provide a translation that is gender inclusive so far as that is possible within the limits of the Greek syntax and biblical symbolism.

When I began my formal work on Luke-Acts some fifteen years ago, it could fairly be said that there was no good contemporary English commentary on the Gospel. As the bibliography indicates, the situation has changed. The recent commentaries by Danker and Talbert each offer distinctive pleasures, especially since each has a distinctive point of view. Marshall's commentary is valuable above all for its careful discussion of the options provided by the Greek text. But Fitzmyer's two-volume commentary in the Anchor Bible is the most complete and best commentary now available. Exhaustive alike in its treatment of subjects and its dialogue with scholarship as well, it is both precise in its discussion of exegetical problems and insightful into Lukan themes. I consulted Fitzmyer on each passage only after completing my own work. Sometimes he alerted me to something I had missed; other times I found him arguing a position quite different from my own. But I found his companionship to be both a constant challenge and a comfort.

Why, then, another commentary? What does this one provide that the others do not? The main thing is that from beginning to end this is a literary analysis. I do not take up issues concerning the origin of a story in the life of Jesus, or the development of a tradition before it reaches Luke. Nor do I engage in long discussions of scholarly positions concerning those questions. My concern is only with what Luke is saying and how he goes about saying it. I have tried to provide a sense of Luke's compositional techniques—how he accomplishes his effects and creates his themes. Above all, I have tried to overcome the inherent atomism of the commentary format by giving a sense of narrative development, including some grasp of how each part fits into the whole.

Because I do not take up all the other questions (each in its own way important) that increasingly distend major commentaries, I am actually able within a limited space to give proportionately greater attention to literary analogies from the ancient world, and to the background or development of biblical themes. As the notes will demonstrate, the concordances to the Septuagint and New Testament have been given a rather thorough going-over. All these citations will be only useless ornament, of course, if the reader does not follow them through the actual text. But if they are used, the reading of Luke provided here should prove to be a rich one.

The first book I read that made me see that Luke was up to something special was Adrian Hastings' *Prophet and Witness in Jerusalem.* Over the intervening twenty-five years many other scholars have taught me. I hope that even though their names may not be mentioned in the text, their insights are fairly represented. The main lines of the reading are, of course, my own.

Because of the pressure of other commitments, this commentary was written over a six-month period. My wife Joy and my daughter Tiffany were gracious in their support of a husband and father who spent more time than is healthy, hunched over lexica. My thanks to them, as always, for their love and generosity.

1 January 1990

ABBREVIATIONS

AER	American Ecclesiastical Review
AnBib	Analecta Biblica
ASNU	Acta Seminarii Neotestamentici Upsaliensis
ATR	Anglican Theological Review
BETL	Bibliotheca Ephemeridum Theologicarum Lovaniensium
Bib	Biblica
BJRL	Bulletin of the John Rylands Library
BK	Bibel und Kirche
BZ	Biblische Zeitschrift
BWANT	Beiträge zur Wissenschaft vom Alten und Neuen Testaments
BZNW	Beihefte zur ZNW
CBQ	Catholic Biblical Quarterly
EBib	Etudes Bibliques
ETL	Ephemerides Theologicae Lovanienses
EvQ	Evangelical Quarterly
ExpTim	Expository Times
HeyJ	Heythrop Journal
HTR	Harvard Theological Review
HTS	Harvard Theological Studies
Int	Interpretation
JBL	Journal of Biblical Literature
JSNT	Journal for the Study of the New Testament
JTS	Journal of Theological Studies
NovT	Novum Testamentum
NovTSupp	Novum Testamentum, Supplements
NRT	La Nouvelle Revue Theologique
NTS	New Testament Studies
RB	Revue Biblique
RevScRel	Revue des Sciences Religieuses
RHPR	Revue d'Histoire et de Philosophie Religieuses
RSR	Recherches de Science Religeuse
SANT	Studien zum Alten und Neuen Testaments
SBLDS	Society of Biblical Literature Dissertation Series
SBLMS	Society of Biblical Literature Monograph Series
SBT	Studies in Biblical Theology

ScEccl	Sciences Ecclesiastiques
SNT	Studien zum Neuen Testament
SNTMS	Studiorum Novi Testamenti Societas, Monograph Series
ST	Studia Theologica
TDNT	Theological Dictionary of the New Testament
TS	Theological Studies
TU	Texte und Untersuchungen
ZNW	Zeitschrift für die Neutestamentliche Wissenschaft

INTRODUCTION

The Gospel according to Luke is the first volume of a single two-volume writing. In the New Testament canon it is separated from the Acts of the Apostles by the Gospel of John. Although ancient manuscripts do not place them together, virtually all contemporary scholars think that the Gospel and Acts were conceived and executed as a single literary enterprise, which they have come to call Luke-Acts.

So clearly do the writings invite this appraisal that the long delay in formal recognition is surprising. Each volume is introduced by a prologue directed to the same reader, Theophilus, who is obviously a Christian and quite possibly the patron who sponsored the composition. The prologue to Acts (Acts 1:1-2) is simply a short summary of the first volume. The Gospel prologue is more elaborate and provides important clues to the author's purposes in writing (Luke 1:1-4). In addition to the prologues, the volumes are joined by an intricate skein of stylistic, structural, and thematic elements which demonstrate convincingly that the same literary imagination was at work in both.

The decision to read these separate texts as a single literary work means deliberately to adopt a literary-critical approach to the New Testament, and to rely upon a contemporary literary designation in preference to a traditional perception of the texts or even their canonical placement. Although formal acknowledgement of Luke-Acts' literary unity is today almost universally given, few commentaries (if any) have yet taken that decision seriously in their treatment of the respective volumes. The present commentary intends systematically to exploit the implications of the designation "Luke-Acts."

Luke-Acts occupies fully one quarter of the NT canon. It is pivotal both for the history of earliest Christianity (indeed our indispensable source for even attempting such a history) and for the development of Christian theology. It can be read as a historical source and as a theological resource. But not every sort of question can be asked simultaneously. The present commentary will touch on historical and theological questions only as they are required for the intelligent reading of the text. The main focus of this

1

commentary, instead, is on the literary shape of Luke's writing. It seeks to clarify not only what the writing says but also how it speaks.

A. *Circumstances of Composition*

With the partial exception of Paul's letters, placing any of the earliest Christian writings in time and place is a matter of guesswork. We have few external guideposts. Conclusions must be based on internal evidence which can be (and has been) construed in widely divergent ways. The best guesses are those avoiding a vicious circularity while giving a decent account of the composition in question. The main reason for entering into a discussion of the circumstances of Luke-Acts is the opportunity it provides for an initial description of important features of the text.

Ancient manuscripts attribute the Gospel to a certain Luke, whom patristic writers identify as a companion of Paul (Phlm 24; Col 4:14; 2 Tim 4:11), an identification found also in early canonical lists such as the Muratorian Canon. The supposition seems to find support in the so-called "we passages" of Acts (16:10-17; 20:5-15; 21:1-18; 27:1–28:16), where the text shifts suddenly to first-person narration, suggesting the presence of an eyewitness to the events.

Critical scholarship has frequently challenged the traditional attribution. The tone, perspective, and purposes of Luke-Acts are, it is argued, better suited to a "second-generation" composition; in light of this, a companion of Paul would probably not be the author. "Second generation," however, is hardly a precise designation, and attempts to place Luke-Acts as late as the second century are clearly excessive. In fact, nothing in the writing prohibits composition by a companion of Paul who was eyewitness to some events he narrates. If a thirty-year-old man joined Paul's circle around the year 50, he would still be only sixty in the year 80, young enough to do vigorous research, yet old enough and at sufficient distance to describe the time of beginnings with a certain nostalgia.

The fact that Luke does not use Paul's letters or even mention that Paul wrote letters obviously argues for an earlier rather than a later date. It is far more likely for Paul's letters to be ignored before their collection and canonization than after. Some scholars turn the authorship question the other way: they attribute some of Paul's letters (the Pastorals) to Luke, possibly even as a third volume after Acts. These hypotheses fall far short of proof and are less convincing than the traditional attributions of authorship for Luke-Acts and Paul's letters.

To conclude that a companion of Paul could before the end of the first century have written this work (probably between 80 and 85 but possibly earlier) does not, however, determine either the character of the writing or its historical value. That the author admires Paul is obvious from the text anyway, and the author himself could in any case have witnessed only a few of the many events "fulfilled among us." For the rest, the author acknowledges his dependence on other witnesses and written sources (Luke 1:1-2).

Neither is this attribution automatically informative about the author, who like the other evangelists recedes modestly behind his story. Attempts to discover in Luke-Acts the distinctive style or outlook of a physician, for example, have repeatedly been refuted. More helpful insight into the author is provided by the character of his composition. His stylistic fluency is demonstrated by his facile use of several Greek styles. His Hellenistic education is shown by his use of rhetorical conventions. His wide reading in Torah is manifested by his dense scriptural allusions and by the very structure of his narrative. His storytelling ability is revealed in his many striking vignettes and parables. Most of all, Luke-Acts shows us an author of synthetic imagination, who was able to make the story of Jesus (already current in the Church's tradition) and the story of Christianity's beginnings into one coherent and interconnected narrative which continued the ancient biblical story of God and his people.

We are unable to determine precisely the place of Luke's writing or his readership. Ancient tradition wavers on the place of composition, and the text itself gives no reliable clues. Neither can we have any confidence concerning the first readers of this narrative. Certainly, Luke's readers were Greek-speaking and sufficiently acquainted with scriptural traditions to grasp at least the gist of his many allusions. They were also obviously Christian; Luke wrote to confirm teachings already held (Luke 1:4). His readers were in all likelihood Gentiles; a great deal of Luke-Acts, in fact, would not make sense if its readers were not Gentile.

But did Luke write in response to some local crisis or confusion? It is not likely. Given the length, complexity, and literary sophistication of his work, it is more likely that Luke intentionally addressed a more general readership, and did so with a larger ambition than the resolving of a local dispute. If there is a crisis addressed by Luke-Acts—and there certainly is—it is not occasioned by momentary circumstance, but by the very nature and historical development of the Christian movement itself.

B. *Genre and Purpose*

Luke's literary *métier* is the story. He is, simply, a gifted storyteller. His composition is filled with short, sharply defined, vignettes. Each of them summons for the reader an entire imaginative world. Only in Luke's Gospel do we find the parable of the rich fool (12:16-21), of Lazarus and Dives

(16:19-31), of the good Samaritan (10:30-35), and perhaps most memorable, the lost son (15:11-32). All of these parables are placed in the mouth of Jesus, but much of their shaping may be due to Luke himself. Luke's infancy and resurrection accounts have an almost folkloric quality. In Acts, there are also the wonderful stories of Ananias and Sapphira (5:1-11), Simon Magus (8:9-24), Peter's release from prison (12:6-17), and Paul's shipwreck (27:1-44), each of them small masterpieces of narration.

Luke is more than a miniaturist. He forges these short stories (many of them already circulating in some form) into a single narrative which draws the reader imaginatively from the mists of antiquity all the way to a rented apartment in Rome, and in the short space of 52 chapters communicates an impressive sense of historical movement. Luke had at least one predecessor for his Gospel story, and he used Mark extensively. But he had no example to follow for extending that story to the time of his readers. Luke's original contribution to Christian literature was connecting the events of the early Church to those of Jesus' ministry, and to the whole story of God's people, indeed of humanity, all the way back to Adam (Luke 3:38).

Luke is quite conscious of the literary form he has chosen. He associates his work with earlier attempts at a "narrative" (*diēgēsis*, 1:1), and emphasizes that he is relating events "in sequence" (*kathexēs*, 1:3). From his use of this last term elsewhere, it appears that Luke considers the narration of events "in order" to have a distinctively convincing quality (see e.g., Acts 9:27; 11:4; 15:12-14). The development of the plot itself has a persuasive force. Luke shares the perception of Hellenistic rhetoric that the *narratio* ("narration") is critical to historical argument or personal defense. Notice, for example, the construction of Paul's "defense speeches" (Acts 22:3-21; 24:10-21; 26:2-23).

Some implications for the interpretation of Luke-Acts follow immediately from his deliberate use of the narrative form. To regard Luke-Acts as a *story* means, at the least, that we do not read it as a systematic treatise. Rather, we must seek Luke's meaning through the movement of the story. It is of primary importance to locate *where* something occurs in Luke's narrative. The connection between individual vignettes are as important as their respective contents. The sequence itself provides the larger meaning.

Luke-Acts must also be read as a *single* story. Acts not only continues the story of the Gospel but provides Luke's own authoritative commentary on the first volume. Any discussion of Luke's purposes, or the development of his themes, must take into account the entire two-volume work. One should not, for example, describe the "Christology of Acts" as though that stood in isolation from Luke's portrayal of Jesus in his Gospel. Luke sustains some themes through both volumes, develops others, and allows still others to drop. Any discussion of "the poor" in Luke-Acts, for example, must take seriously the effective disappearance of that terminology after chapter 16 of the Gospel, which suggests that Luke used such language for a special literary function in his first volume. The interpretation of *what* Luke says on any subject must take into account *where* in his story he says it.

The category of story reminds us also of the importance of plot and characters—the constitutive elements of narrative. Characters motivate and enact the plot. The plot reveals the characters in action. The most important character of all in Luke-Acts may be God, who never directly appears but who in various ways directs the action, and with reference to whom the entire narrative unfolds. Special attention as well should be paid to Luke's way of describing his characters (especially Jesus and the apostles) in stereotypical terms, and to the interactions between Luke's heroes and the people who are less vividly described but whose positive and negative reactions are critical to Luke's narrative purposes.

It is appropriate to ask further whether Luke's narrative fits into the conventional literary forms of antiquity. Determining genre is difficult, but important. If literary genre has a function, it is to create expectations in readers, and program certain responses. When genre works, function truly follows form. We know that Hellenistic culture, unlike our own, made use of and prized conventional literary forms. If we can determine the generic character of Luke-Acts, therefore, we are provided important clues as to how it would have been read and understood by its first readers—or at least, how Luke would have wanted it to be understood.

Our task once again is to ask the generic question of Luke-Acts as a whole, leaving aside debates whether "Gospel" is a separate genre or whether "Acts" becomes one, as in the many later "Acts" of various apostles. It has been suggested that Luke-Acts resembles the Hellenistic romance or novel. The similarities are mostly stylistic and superficial. In Luke-Acts, more than aesthetic delight is operative, even in formal terms. More serious candidates for the genre of Luke-Acts are Hellenistic history or biography, and Jewish apology. Deciding between them demands a careful consideration of the text, and leads further into the character of Luke's narrative.

There are good reasons for considering Luke-Acts as a form of Hellenistic history. First, his Gospel prologue looks like those prescribed for Greek historians (cf. Lucian, *How to Write History*, 47-54) as well as like contemporary examples of such prologues (as in Josephus, *Antiquities of the Jews*). He tells his reader that he uses earlier oral and written sources (Luke 1:1-2), but has also done personal and accurate research (1:3), which implies that he can handle his sources critically. He states further that he is writing a "sustained and sequential" narrative (*kathexēs*), whose purpose is to give his reader certainty rather than surmise concerning the events of the past (1:4) and even of the present (1:1).

Second, Luke places the story of Jesus and the Church in the context of world history. He connects it not only to the story of Israel (Luke 1:5), but also to the larger *oikoumenē*, the civilized world of Hellenism. Thus he alone of the evangelists provides chronological references for key events (see Luke 1:5; 2:1-2; 3:1-2; Acts 18:12). He identifies rulers and powerful figures in Palestine (Acts 12:20-21), Asia Minor (Acts 19:31), and in Europe (Acts 18:12-17).

Above all, Luke has the historian's instinct for causality. His narrative is essentially linear, moving the reader from one event to another. The term "in order" (*kathexēs*) in his prologue is an important key to his composition. Luke draws connections between events, so that a thread of purpose runs through his entire narrative.

A full discussion of Luke's accuracy as a historian is not needed here, but a few comments are required because the question of genre demands consideration of what sort of historian Luke might be. To a considerable extent, historians rely on their sources. Luke tells us he had some reports from eyewitnesses who became ministers of the word (Luke 1:2). Perhaps his unusually full information about Herod's household came from such a source (see Luke 8:3; 23:6-12; Acts 12:20-23). The "we" source of Acts could also have come from an eyewitness, but since the first person plural was sometimes used conventionally for travel narratives, we cannot be certain.

Luke also used written sources (Luke 1:1). For the Gospel, he used Mark, materials from the written source scholars have designated Q (meaning materials shared with Matthew not found in Mark), and the materials distinctive to his Gospel that scholars designate L. We are able to check his use of these sources only in the case of Mark. Q gives no real help since the shape of this hypothetical source must be abstracted from both Matthean and Lukan versions.

Luke uses Mark differently than Matthew does. When Luke follows Mark's narrative, he does so more closely, although he tends to eliminate blatant doublets, such as the feeding stories, whereas Matthew increases them. And rather than insert great blocks of discourse material into the narrative, thereby interrupting its flow (as Matthew does), Luke more subtly interweaves the deeds and sayings of Jesus (e.g., Luke 9–19). Luke uses Mark with reasonable fidelity. The larger problem is determining where Luke has a source. If Matthew and Mark were not available for comparison it would be hard to detect where Luke is using Mark and where he is not.

The difficulty in detecting Luke's sources is twofold. Luke follows the perfectly respectable Hellenistic practice of rewriting his sources (cf. Josephus, *Against Apion*, 1:53). We can observe how he modifies Mark's Greek to bring it closer to his own liking. Luke also has the ability to write in a variety of styles. If we excerpted and compared the Greek of his Gospel prologue, the infancy accounts, Peter's Pentecost sermon and Paul's defense speeches, we might think they were from different writers. The reason is that Luke follows the Hellenistic literary ideal of *prosōpopoieia*, which means writing in a style appropriate to character and circumstance. The Paul who addresses philosophers in Athens is therefore much more "Greek" than the Paul who preaches in the synagogue.

Similarly, the Greek of the infancy narratives has a distinctive Semitic coloration. Some have therefore concluded that Luke was using Hebrew or Aramaic sources in those stories. But we can observe elsewhere that Luke shows a flair for imitating biblical language, and in particular that of the Greek translation of Torah called the Septuagint (LXX). These factors make the determination concerning Luke's use of sources in the Gospel difficult.

In Acts, the search for Luke's possible sources is even more frustrating. We have no way to check his usage. Certainly, Luke would have had fewer sources for his second volume than for his first, and therefore much more literary freedom. Apart from the "we" sections—which are in fact stylistically consistent with the material around them—we can identify no certain sources for Acts. Attempts to allocate material in Acts 1–15 to a "Jerusalem" or an "Antioch" source have proven illusory.

If we ask how factually accurate Luke is as a historian, the answer is mixed. He disagrees with other ancient sources on matters such as the timing of the census (Luke 2:2) or the appearance of messianic pretenders (Acts 5:36-37). On the other hand, his account of Paul's movements (where we can check them against the letters) is not far out-of-line. By the standards of Hellenistic historiography, Luke seems reasonably accurate in what he tells us. The phrase "what he tells us," however, is critical, for Luke is obviously selective. He omits portions of Mark (the so-called "great omission" of Mark 6:45–8:27). He mentions no Galilean appearances of Jesus (cf. Mark 16:7; Matt 28:16). In Acts, Luke either does not know or chooses not to relate things otherwise known to us. He describes no Galilean mission (note the conspicuous silence in Acts 1:8 and 15:3). He tells us nothing of an eastward or rural evangelization. Of the first missionaries, he concentrates on Peter and Paul to the virtual neglect of others. Paul's arrival in Rome is the climax of Acts, for example, yet Luke does not inform us when the Christian movement itself reached the capital city (see Acts 28:14-16).

Indeed, Luke's concentration on Jesus and a few of his followers makes some scholars consider his work less a history than a Hellenistic biography. Biographies of Hellenistic philosophers (such as the collection by Diogenes Laertius, *Lives of Eminent Philosophers*, or *The Life of Pythagoras* by Iamblichus) are thought by some to provide the best formal analogy to Luke-Acts: first the life of the founder is related, with a focus on his wondrous birth, his deeds, and his teachings; there follows a succession narrative, which recounts the deeds and teachings of the philosopher's school.

The suggestion is both attractive and illuminates important aspects of Luke-Acts. The way Luke adds infancy and appearance accounts certainly moves the Markan Gospel closer to the standard Hellenistic biography, as does also his placement of sayings material. The portrait of Jesus and his followers is also shaded to resemble the Hellenistic *sophos* (philosopher). Thus, Jesus is found teaching at banquets, which resemble the *symposia* of the sages (see esp. Luke 14:1-24; 22:14-38). During his passion and trial, Jesus' innocence and courage are emphasized (see Luke 22:39-53; 23:39-47). The disciples after his death show "boldness" (a philosophical trait) in their preaching (Acts 4:13), and like Socrates, they obey God rather than human authorities (Acts 4:19).

Extant Hellenistic biographies, however, do not offer convincing evidence that Luke-Acts fits that genre. The hypothesis must also leave out the clear indications of the prologue that Luke himself considered his work to be a history. He writes not only of Jesus and his successors, but also of the "matters (*pragmata*) accomplished among us." His narrative reaches beyond Jesus and his "school." In fact, one of the most important characters in Luke's narrative is Israel, considered as God's people. Because Jesus and his disciples are placed within this broader story, Luke's writing is properly categorized as a form of history.

But what sort of history did he set out to write? Luke was committed to the movement he described. If, as the very fact of a prologue suggests, Luke's composition was intended for publication, perhaps he meant it to influence the wider world, and composed in effect the first Christian *apologetic* literature.

The fact that Luke has a positive view of Gentiles and of Roman officials in particular has led some to suggest that Luke wrote an apology for the Christian movement as such. The Christians were politically harmless, and should be allowed the same freedom given by Rome to "other Jews." In this light, Luke's rooting of Christianity in Judaism serves a definite political end. The proconsul Gallio's decision in Acts 18:14-15 should be taken by all civil leaders as exemplary: in matters of dispute between "Jews," magistrates need not concern themselves. Luke's positive attitude toward the Empire can also be turned the other way. It has been suggested that he is writing an apology for the Empire, (somewhat in the manner of Josephus in *The Jewish War*), encouraging politically restive fellow Christians to a non-apocalyptic and cooperative stance toward Rome.

Other scholars make Luke's concentration on Paul in the latter part of Acts (13–28) the key to his apologetic intentions. He is writing an apology for Paul and his teaching, perhaps even for his trial. A variant of this approach has Luke appeasing a significant and theologically vocal minority of Jewish believers, who need to be reassured that Paul is not opposed to Torah or a renegade from Judaism, but teaches in agreement with Pharisees (see Acts 23:6; 28:17-20). Paul's critical role in Acts certainly demands interpretation. But Luke's extensive and complex narrative is not likely to have been composed for such a narrow and specific function. We need to account for Luke-Acts as a whole.

As helpful as such suggestions are for throwing light on aspects of Luke's text, they depend on too narrow a definition of apologetic. They isolate one theme or emphasis and make it determinative for the entire narrative, directing it to specific insider or outsider audiences. In fact, however, Jewish apologetic literature contemporary to Luke-Acts (which would include such writings as *The Letter of Aristeas* as well as Philo's *Hypothetica, Against Flaccus* and *Embassy to Gaius,* Josephus' *Against Apion, The Jewish War* and *Antiquities of the Jews,* as well as the fragments of Artapanus and Eupolemus), had a dual function. Ostensibly, it defended Jews against misunderstanding and persecution. But it had an equally important function for its Jewish readers.

Apologetic enabled them to understand their own traditions within a pluralistic context, by bringing an outsider perspective to bear on them. In Philo, for example, the symbols of Greek philosophy and history provide the categories for the interpretation of Moses (see his *Life of Moses*). Apologetic literature could thus provide "security" or "reassurance" to Jewish readers by demonstrating within a pluralistic cultural context the antiquity and inherent value of their traditions.

Something very similar is happening in Luke-Acts. To a possible outside Hellenistic reader, the Christian movement is presented as a philosophically enlightened, politically harmless, socially benevolent and philanthropic fellowship. But its more immediate purpose is to interpret the Gospel for insiders within the context of a pluralistic environment composed of both Jews and Gentiles.

The Gospel prologue (Luke 1:1-4) again provides us important clues to Luke's purposes. Luke addresses a Christian readership. Theophilus has already been "instructed" (*katēcheō*) in the Christian story (1:4). Why, then, does he require still another version of it? Luke writes, he says, to give his reader "security" (*asphaleia*, 1:4) in his knowledge of "the things brought to fulfillment among us" (1:1). Not only the distant past, therefore, but also present circumstances require interpretation: the "among us" reaches up to Luke's own day. The expression "brought to fulfillment," is in the passive voice, and in the biblical idiom means: "realities which God has brought to fulfillment."

Luke's narrative, therefore, is expressly concerned with the fulfillment of God's promises up to his own day. But why is "security" required? and how will a narrative written "in sequence" (*kathexēs*) provide that security? Here we come to the key element in discerning Luke's purpose for his composition as a whole.

Everything about Luke's narrative confirms that it was directed to Gentile Christians. He may have had some Jewish readers, but the Jewish mission, which Acts repeatedly shows failing, is less than vigorous. In contrast, the outlook for the Gentile world is entirely positive. The closing statement in Acts about them is that "they will listen" (28:28). Indeed, Luke's readers are themselves the proof that Paul's prophecy was fulfilled. But the two historical facts of Jewish rejection of the Gospel and the Gentile acceptance of it combine to create a severe "uncertainty" for thoughtful Gentile Christians.

The problem is simple but profound. In Torah (the Scripture shared by messianist and nonmessianist Jews alike), God's promises had been made to Israel, that is the *Jewish* people, through Abraham (Gen 12:1-3). If that historical people was now not in possession of the blessings, and other people were, what did that imply about God's faithfulness to his promises? Had God utterly betrayed his people? And in so doing, had he also proven himself faithless? The difficulty here is as acute for Gentiles as for Jews. How could they rely on the things "accomplished among them?" If God had failed the Jews, could he not betray the Gentiles even more easily?

The issue addressed by Luke's narrative is one of *theodicy*. He seeks—as Paul did in Romans 9–11—to defend the word and work of God in history. How does his shaping of the narrative accomplish this apology (defense) of God, and therefore of the Christian movement? By telling how events happened 'in order" (*kathexēs*), Luke shows how God first fulfilled his promises to Israel, and only then extended these blessings to the Gentiles. Because God had shown himself faithful to the Jews, therefore, the Word that reached the Gentiles was also trustworthy. Thus we see how important "order" or consecutiveness is for Luke's narrative. The saving of Israel was necessary for the security of Gentile faith.

Luke is therefore an apologetic historian of a very special sort. He sets himself to write the continuation of the biblical story, not alone to defend the Christian movement, but above all to defend God's ways in the world. By showing that the story of Jesus was rooted in that of Israel, and by demonstrating how God kept his promise by restoring Israel, Luke assured his Gentile readers that they could have confidence in "the things in which they were instructed" (Luke 1:4). Luke's purposes are not determined by a momentary crisis or by doctrinal deviance, but by the very existence of a messianic sect in the Gentile world. So successfully did Luke address this problem that his narrative became the aetiological myth of Gentile Christianity.

C. *Literary Dimensions of Luke-Acts*

Our discussion of genre and purpose may have been misleading in one respect. If we determine what shaped Luke's narrative as a whole, we do not thereby determine the reasons for the inclusion of any specific passage, or its placement. Nor do we thereby exhaust all of the Lukan emphases and interests. The way the narrative works as a whole is not the only level of meaning. Each part of Luke-Acts can have separate but complementary functions. Each smaller unit of narrative has something to say on its own terms, as well as by its part in the larger story.

Precisely the way the smaller parts of the story speak and the issues they address will take up the larger part of this commentary. But because of the way commentaries are constructed (with each unit being looked at separately) the biggest problem for most readers is to maintain the sense of the whole as they study the details of each part. It is important, therefore, as a preparation for our more detailed and atomistic analysis, to remind ourselves of some of the consistent literary techniques Luke uses throughout his long narrative to accomplish his overarching goals. We will consider here in turn aspects of Luke's style, his narrative techniques, and his structuring of the two volumes into a single narrative. With these in mind, we will be better readers of Luke-Acts as a whole and of each of its parts.

1. *Style*

For the reader of this commentary, a technical discussion of Luke's Greek diction and syntax are less helpful than an indication of his characteristic concerns. These can be indicated by his use of Mark and of the Old Testament (Torah).

a) *Use of Mark*

As stated earlier, Luke tends to follow the *order* of Mark's narrative rather closely. His corrections to this source, furthermore, fall within a framework of fundamental agreement. Luke's use of Mark suggests a far deeper level of agreement than of disagreement. Nevertheless, Luke consistently amends Mark in the direction of correctness, clarity, and consecutiveness. Even a reader who knows no Greek can get some sense of these changes by comparing the Markan and Lukan versions of the same story. I have tried to demonstrate this throughout, but give special attention to it in the discussion of 8:22-39, "Two Wonders," in the commentary section.

By correctness, of course, we mean correct by Luke's estimation. He found some of Mark's vocabulary and characterizations either vulgar or inaccurate or perhaps even offensive. He therefore upgrades Mark's diction, grammar, and syntax, while retaining as much as possible of his source's original flavor. Luke is also concerned with clarity. Mark is not overly concerned with consistency in tenses, or number, or the antecedents of pronouns and adjectives. These grammatical niceties, however, are not irrelevant, for they can cause confusion. Luke tries to tidy up Mark's often messy version. Luke's concern for consecutiveness is shown by his avoidance of narrative surprises. Mark will introduce a character or an action without prior warning. Luke improves Mark by inserting earlier on in the story the proper preparation for a later development. He not only solves difficulties for his reader but establishes a more logical order to the narrative. At the same time, he reveals something of his larger preoccupation: by preparing the way for every subsequent plot development, Luke in effect creates a literary "prophecy and fulfillment" pattern within his narrative.

b) *Biblical Imitation*

Luke's character as a Hellenistic author is revealed by his fondness for archaizing. In apologetic literature, the claim to antiquity is enhanced by language derived from ancient scriptures. In great stretches of his narrative, Luke imitates the Greek of the Septuagint. It is a diction wonderfully suited to his purposes. That Luke consciously adopts this "biblical mode" is shown by his easy use of other styles when it suits him: Paul's speech at the Areopagus (Acts 17:16-31) could have come from Dio Chrysostom; the riot of the silversmiths in Ephesus (Acts 19:23-41) could have been lifted from the pages of Lucian of Samosata. It is in fact one of the subtle pleasures in reading the Greek of Luke-Acts to observe how the style becomes less "biblical" and more "Hellenistic" as the Gospel makes its way into the Gentile world.

In addition to direct citations from Torah (which will be discussed below), Luke uses biblical diction in various ways. In the Stephen speech (Acts 7:2-53), he excerpts and fits together pieces from a very long section of Torah so artfully that the result appears both as a seamless and spontaneous speech by Stephen, and a straightforward recital of the biblical story. In fact it is neither, but rather a literary construction by Luke which provides an interpretation of his entire two-volume work (cf. below). Similarly, the Magnificat (Luke 1:46-55) has Mary declare words inspired by and to some extent derived from the song of Hannah in 1 Sam 2:1-10, yet with a remarkable freshness and originality.

Luke also employs a range of allusions which reveal a thorough knowledge of biblical cadences. The annunciation scene (Luke 1:28-38) builds on previous biblical annunciations (such as Judg 13:2-7), but overlays them with a dense texture of other allusions. The angel's greeting to Mary, for example, echoes Zeph 3:14 and Zech 2:10. Likewise, the conclusion of the Transfiguration account, which has the voice from heaven declare "listen to him" (Luke 9:35) suggests that Jesus is the prophet like Moses of Deut 18:15, to whom the people should listen.

Luke can use biblical prototypes to build entire scenes. In both volumes, stories which are unique to Luke appear to depend on biblical models, either for details of their language or for their structure. The death of Ananias and

Sapphira (Acts 5:1-11), for example, is strikingly reminiscent of the stoning of Achan in Josh 7:1-26. Luke especially uses the Elijah-Elisha cycle, both in smaller vignettes (compare Luke 9:54 to 2 Kgs 1:9-16, and Luke 9:61 to 1 Kgs 19:20), and in more elaborate combinations. Luke 7:1-16, for example, "fulfills" the allusion to Elijah and Elisha made earlier in Luke 4:25-27, by having Jesus perform deeds which mirror theirs in 2 Kgs 5:1-14 and 1 Kgs 17:17-24.

The use of the Elijah-Elisha cycle is most obvious in the distinctive Lukan rendering of the ascension and giving of the Spirit. The prophet Jesus departs and leaves his prophetic followers with a "double-share" of the Spirit so that they can do deeds as great as or even greater than his, just as Elijah did for Elisha when he departed in a fiery chariot (cf. Luke 24:51-53; Acts 1:9-11; 2:1-13, with 2 Kgs 2:1-14).

2. Narrative Devices

The impression of amplitude given by Luke's narrative owes less to an abundance of materials than to literary artistry. Luke creates a sustained and coherent narrative by extending and amplifying the traditions available to him.

a) He extends his narrative by means of *summaries*. These take details of specific stories and generalize them, giving the reader an impression of repeated or customary occurrence. Mark had already used such summaries (cf. e.g., Mark 1:39; 3:7-12). Luke takes them over and increases their number (Luke 1:80; 2:52; 4:14-15; 7:21-22; 8:1-3; 13:22; 19:47; 21:37). In Acts, where Luke had far fewer materials available to him, the use of summaries is even more important. In the first chapters of Acts, there are three "major summaries" (2:42-47; 4:32-35; 5:12-16). They provide critical spacing for the narrative, and give the reader a sense of elapsed time. They also offer a "typical" if highly idealized insight into the life of the community in its formative stages. In the later sections of Acts, Luke again uses smaller summary statements to advance his narrative (see 5:42; 6:7; 9:31; 12:24; 19:20).

b) An even more important device is the use of *speeches*. In the first eight chapters of Acts (where Luke had at best a handful of traditional stories available to him) there are nine speeches of greater or lesser length (Acts 1:4-8; 16-22; 2:14-36; 3:12-26; 4:8-12, 24-30; 5:35-39; 6:2-4; 7:2-53). As a whole, these constitute fully half the narrative. Luke uses these speeches exactly as any Hellenistic historian would. They may retain some traditional elements, but in their present form, they are Luke's handiwork, and reflect his perspective rather than that of the original speaker. The speeches tell us what Luke thought should have been said on a particular occasion. In *How to Write History* 58, Lucian of Samosata recognizes that speeches give the historian the chance "to play the orator and show your eloquence," but he recommends that in such speeches the historian must respect character: "let his language suit his person and his subject." Luke follows this advice admirably.

As a narrative device, the speeches also *interpret* the story for the reader. Peter's Pentecost speech (Acts 2:14-36), for example, is addressed far more directly to Luke's readers than to the Diaspora Jews in Jerusalem. In the Gospel, the speeches of Jesus have the same interpretive function. Luke arranges Jesus' sayings so that they both reflect and interpret the narrative events surrounding them (see e.g., Luke 4:16-30; 14:7-24; 15:1-32).

c) Like other Hellenistic historians, Luke also uses *journeys* as a narrative device. His treatment of Paul is dominated by a series of journeys, climaxing with the long sea voyage to Rome (Acts 27:1-44). The central portion of the Gospel is taken up entirely by a great "travel narrative" that extends from chapters 9 to 19. When this section of the Gospel is analyzed, it becomes clear that Luke created this dramatic stage of his story out of a variety of sayings materials and a series of travel notices (see 9:51, 53, 56, 57; 10:1; 13:22, 31, 33; 14:25; 17:11; 18:31, 35-36; 19:1, 11; 28). By careful editing, he made them into a coherent and satisfying sequence.

d) Luke makes extensive use of *parallelism* in his story. He matches persons and events in different parts of his narrative. As Mary is overshadowed by the Holy Spirit in Luke 1:34-35, for example, so are Mary and the disciples overshadowed by the Holy Spirit at the beginning of Acts (1:13-14; 2:1-4). Peter and Paul work similar miracles (3:1-10 and 14:8-11; 9:36-40 and 20:7-12) which in turn mirror those performed by Jesus (Luke 5:17-26; 8:40-56). Peter and Paul face similar threats (Acts 8:9-13 and 19:13-19) and enjoy similar miraculous escapes (Acts 12:6-17 and 16:25-34). The trial of Stephen in Acts 6:8-15 echoes that of Jesus in Luke 22:66-71, and the connection between them is made unmistakable by Acts 7:56 (cf. Luke 22:69). The "passion" of Paul bears some resemblance to that of Jesus (see esp. Acts 21:1-14). By using the device of parallelism, Luke accomplishes two things. First, he makes connections between his main characters; second, he creates a dynamic tension between discrete parts of his narrative.

3. *Literary Structure*

Luke uses two structural components to give shape to his overall narrative: geography and literary prophecy. Each ultimately points in the same direction and serves his overall purposes.

a) *Geography*

Luke uses geography to structure his story and to advance his literary and theological goals. The center of his story is the city of Jerusalem and the events that take place there. In the Gospel, the narrative moves *toward* Jerusalem. The infancy account leads to the presentation of Jesus in the

Temple (2:22) and his discovery there as a young boy (2:41-51). In the Lukan temptation account, the order of the last two temptations in Matthew is reversed, so that the climax is reached in Jerusalem (4:9). At the end of the Galilean ministry, the transfiguration account explicitly prepares for the journey to Jerusalem and Jesus' death there (9:31). The journey itself begins with a solemn announcement (9:51), and continues with multiple references to Jesus' destination (13:22, 33-34; 17:11; 18:31; 19:11, 28). Luke has all of Jesus' resurrection appearances take place in the environs of the city, and in the last of them, Jesus instructs the disciples, ''stay in the city'' (24:49).

In Acts, the geographical movement is *away from* Jerusalem. Jesus' announcement in 1:8, ''You shall be my witnesses in Jerusalem and in all Judea and Samaria and to the ends of the earth,'' is carried out within the narrative itself. The ministry in Jerusalem (Acts 1-7) is followed by the evangelization of Judea and Samaria (8-12), then Asia Minor and Europe, ending in Rome (13-28). Each outward movement, however, also circles back to Jerusalem (see Acts 12:25; 15:2; 18:22; 19:21; 20:16; 21:13; 25:1).

In spatial terms, therefore, Jerusalem is the *center* of Luke's narrative. The middle twelve chapters of the two-volume work narrate events exclusively in that place. Why does Luke make Jerusalem so central? The city and its Temple (which Luke treats as virtually identical) were of obvious historical importance both for Judaism and the nascent Christian movement. But more than historical recollection is involved. For Luke, city and Temple stand as symbols of the people Israel. The death of Jesus and the beginning of the Church in Jerusalem provide the paradigmatic expression of the Jewish people's acceptance or rejection of God's visitation. Jerusalem, in short, is the place of pivot in Luke's story of the Prophet and the people.

b) *Prophecy*

In early Christian apologetic, proof from prophecy was a standard element. Texts from Torah were claimed to have been ''fulfilled'' by events in Jesus' life, death, and resurrection. Matthew uses a sophisticated form of such proof in his so-called ''formula citations'' (e.g., Matt 1:22-23; 2:5-6). Luke expands and refines the concept of prophetic fulfillment. He shows that not only events in Jesus' ministry fulfill Scripture, but also stages of the Church's life and mission. They are among ''the things fulfilled among us'' (Luke 1:1; cf. e.g., Acts 3:24; 13:40; 15:15; 28:25-27). Luke does not align texts and events in the mechanical fashion favored by Matthew. His references are both more general and inclusive. He often uses the term ''it must (*dei*)'' of various situations, suggesting thereby that events were determined by prophecies: these include the suffering and subsequent glorification of the messiah (Luke 9:22; 17:25; 24:7; Acts 3:21; 17:3), the apostasy of Judas and the election of Matthias (Acts 1:16-22), the sufferings of Paul (Acts 9:16) and of all Christians (Acts 14:22). Luke also extends and refines proof from prophecy by making it his most important literary device.

1) *Literary Prophecy*

Specifically Lukan is the use of literary prophecy. Not texts from Torah, but statements of characters *within the narrative* are explicitly shown to find fulfillment. Only Luke takes pains to show how Jesus' passion predictions (Luke 9:21; 44; 18:32-33) were in fact fulfilled (24:6-8, 44). Likewise, Jesus' prediction of his followers' tribulations (Luke 21:12-15) is literally fulfilled in the narrative of Acts (4:3-5, 14; 5:17-42). His instruction for the proper behavior toward unbelieving cities (Luke 9:5; 10:11) is carried out by the missionaries in Acts (13:51). Jesus says the Twelve are to be judges over Israel (Luke 22:30) and indeed they are in Acts (5:1-11). The prophet Agabus predicts sufferings for Paul (Acts 21:10-14) which speedily come true (21:30-35).

2) *Programmatic Prophecy*

Luke uses such prophecies at critical junctures in his narrative as a means of interpreting for the reader the story which follows. The reader is to understand the plot development as a fulfillment of the prophecy. The most obvious example is Jesus' statement in Acts 1:8 which provides an outline for the plot of Acts. In similar fashion, Paul states at the end of Acts, "the salvation of God has been sent to the Gentiles, they will listen," and the prophecy has in fact clearly reached fulfillment among Luke's readers. Prophecies at the end and beginning of the Gospel are equally important as clues to the narrative's meaning. Jesus' promise of a "power from on high" (Luke 24:49) enables the reader to perceive the ascension (Luke 24:50-53; Acts 1:9-11) not as an absolute departure but as a transformed presence, and to see the outpouring of the Spirit (Acts 2:1-4) as fulfilling Jesus' saying, "I am sending the promise of my Father upon you" (Luke 24:49). At the start of the Gospel, the saying of Simeon, "This child is destined to cause the rise and fall of many in Israel and to be a sign that is disputed" (Luke 2:34) prepares the reader to see the entire Gospel narrative as the story of a prophet whose ministry creates a division among God's people.

3) *Speech-Narrative Prophecy*

Luke even arranges speech and narrative in a prophetic pattern. He places speeches so that the narrative immediately following them fulfills their point, often with considerable irony. Thus, Jesus declares that a prophet is not acceptable in his own country, and his townspeople immediately reject him who is a prophet (Luke 4:16-30). Likewise Stephen, described as a prophet filled with the Holy Spirit, accuses the Jewish leadership of rejecting prophets and resisting the Holy Spirit; they respond by killing him (Acts 7:51-60)! Luke uses this pattern with great frequency, enabling him to make speech and narrative mutually interpretive.

D. *The Prophetic Structure of Luke-Acts*

On the basis of these observations, we can suggest that Luke-Acts has as a whole a definite "prophetic" structure, and that the two volumes can best be understood in the light of this overarching literary framework. The prophetic structure of Luke's entire work is established first by the relationship between the two volumes. The Book of Acts both continues the story of the Gospel and also confirms it. In Acts, Luke himself shows how the Gospel story is to be understood. The perspective given by Acts is all the more important since in that volume, Luke had greater freedom to shape it.

In addition, the two volumes together form a two-stage prophetic narrative. This second point requires more demonstration. We must move from a consideration of the prophetic image of the main characters in Acts, to the implications of Luke's portrayal of Moses.

1. *The Apostles as Prophets*

Acts can appropriately be called the "Book of the Holy Spirit." The Spirit actively intervenes in the story, impelling and guiding it (cf. Acts 8:29, 39; 10:19; 11:15; 13:2; 15:28; 16:6; 20:23). Indeed, Luke includes five separate accounts of the Spirit's dramatic "outpouring" on believers (2:1-4; 4:28-31; 8:15-17; 10:44; 19:6). For Luke, all Christians manifestly "have" the Holy Spirit.

But Luke's most important characters are described as "men of the Spirit" in a very special way, which begins to lead us to Luke's distinctive shaping of his story. The characters in Acts who fundamentally advance the plot (Peter, John, Philip, Stephen, Barnabas and Paul) are not *called* prophets; in Acts, that designation is reserved for relatively minor actors (see 11:27; 13:1; 15:32; 21:10). Instead, Luke describes his main characters in stereotypical language which clearly demarcates them as prophets.

Each of these characters is described as "filled with the Holy Spirit" (Acts 4:8; 5:32; 6:3; 7:55; 11:24; 13:9). Each is "bold" in proclamation (4:13; 13:46; 28:31). Each proclaims "Good News" (5:42; 8:4, 12, 25, 40; 11:20; 13:32; 14:7; 15:35), or "the Word of God" (4:29; 8:14; 13:5). Each is a "witness" (2:32; 10:41; 13:31; 22:20). Each works "signs and wonders" (*sēmeia kai terata*, 4:30; 6:8; 8:6; 14:3; 15:12). Each preaches and performs these wonders "among the people" (*laos*), the Jewish population considered as the people of God (3:12; 4:1; 6:8; 13:15). Taken together, these characteristics point unmistakably to one image in the biblical tradition, that of the prophet.

2. *Jesus Is the Prophet like Moses*

When Peter interprets the outpouring of the Spirit at Pentecost, he cites the prophecy of Joel 2:28-32 that the Spirit would be poured out on all flesh (Acts 2:17-21). Luke makes three small but significant changes in the Joel citation. He changes "after these things" to "in the last days," thereby defining Pentecost as an eschatological event. He adds the words, "and they shall prophesy" in verse 18, accentuating the *prophetic* character of the Spirit that the original citation had already suggested. He also adds the words "and signs on the earth below" in verse 19, to form the combination "signs and wonders."

By these changes, Luke draws together three elements—an eschatological Spirit of prophecy manifested by signs and wonders—which in the biblical tradition were associated above all with Moses, the first and greatest of the prophets (see e.g., LXX Ps 77:11-12, 32, 43). In fact, the text of Deut 34:10-12 had given rise to a messianic expectation of a "prophet like Moses":

> There has not arisen a prophet since in Israel like Moses, whom the Lord knew face to face, none like him for all the signs and wonders which the Lord sent him to do in the land of Egypt . . . and for all the mighty power and all the great and terrible deeds which Moses wrought in the sight of all the people.

This expectation remained alive in contemporary Judaism (cf. *4QTestim* 1–5 and John 1:21; 4:19; 6:14), despite the clear statement of Deut 34:9 that "Joshua (in Greek, Jesus) son of Nun was full of the Spirit of wisdom, for Moses had laid his hands on him."

The notion that God would "raise up a prophet" obviously had great potential for interpreting a resurrected Messiah like Jesus. Immediately after the Joel citation, in fact, we find Peter referring to Jesus in just this fashion (Acts 2:22-24):

> Jesus of Nazareth, a man attested to you by God with mighty works and wonders and signs which God did through him in your midst . . . this Jesus you crucified . . . but God raised him up.

Jesus is described in terms which in this connection cannot but recall the prophet Moses.

When he describes the wondrous activities of the apostles, in turn, Luke makes perfectly clear that the power active in their prophetic witness is the Spirit of Jesus (Acts 2:33; 3:13; 4:10; 13:30-33). As Elijah gave a twofold portion of the Spirit to Elisha, we are to understand, so have the apostles received a manifest bestowal of Jesus' prophetic Spirit. The specific imagery is Mosaic, but then so, of course, was the portrayal of Elijah and Elisha modelled on that of Moses and Joshua.

The rejection of the apostles, in turn, is foreshadowed and interpreted by the passages which recall the rejection of Jesus by humans and his vindication by God (2:23, 36; 10:39). The longest of these statements (3:13-18) relieves the people of some of the responsibility for this rejection because of their "ignorance" (3:17). And when, in this speech, Peter offers a chance of repentance to the ordinary people, he draws an explicit connection between Jesus and Moses (Acts 3:22-23; cf. Deut 18:15, 18-19):

> Moses said, "the Lord God will raise up a prophet among your brethren as he raised me up. You shall listen to him in whatever he tells you. And it shall be that every soul that does not listen to that prophet shall be destroyed from the people."

Both the apostles and Jesus, therefore, are portrayed in terms that evoke Moses. The connection is made emphatically in Stephen's speech, a large portion of which is devoted to Moses (Acts 7:17-44). Comparison with Torah itself shows that Luke here selected and structured his account of Moses so that it matches precisely the story of Jesus and his successors.

3. The Mosaic Pattern

In Stephen's speech, the story of Moses has two main stages with an interlude. He is sent a first time and rejected; he is given power; he is sent and rejected a second time. At the time when the promises to Abraham were about to be fulfilled (7:17), Moses is sent by God to "visit" the people and "save" them. They, however, are "ignorant" of his identity and role, so they reject him a first time. Moses is forced to go away in exile (7:23-29). While in exile, Moses encounters God and is empowered to return to the people a second time (7:30-34). Moses then leads the people out of Egypt with "signs and wonders," but the people reject him and his words a second time, preferring an idol made with their own hands. Those who reject Moses this second time are themselves to be rejected (7:39-43).

Moses is therefore sent twice, the first time in weakness, the second time in power. There are two offers of salvation to the people. The first is rejected out of ignorance, and leads to a second chance. When this is refused despite the overwhelming evidence of signs and wonders, God rejects the people. These elements strikingly parallel Luke's account of Jesus. He makes the connection between Moses and Jesus absolutely clear, furthermore, by placing at the heart of the Moses story precisely the sort of statement made elsewhere about Jesus (Acts 7:35-37):

> This Moses, whom they refused, saying "who made you ruler and judge?" God sent as both ruler and deliverer by the hand of the angel that appeared

to him in the bush. He led them out, having performed wonders and signs in Egypt and at the Red Sea and in the wilderness for forty years. *This is the Moses who said to the Israelites, ''God will raise up for you a prophet from your brethren as he raised me up.''*

Did Luke's perception of Jesus' death and resurrection shape his portrayal of Moses, or did the influence go the other way? We cannot know. It is, however, abundantly clear that Luke in his portrayal of Moses has given us the essential clue for understanding his overall story. This understanding of Moses shows the ''necessity'' of a prophet's suffering before glory, and why the scriptural demonstration of that necessity must begin with ''Moses and all the prophets'' (Luke 13:33-34; 24:25-27, 44-46).

The Mosaic pattern also establishes a typology and succession of spiritual authority that serves Luke's goals. Jesus is the prophet like Moses. But Jesus was not ''raised up'' simply in the sense of being ''chosen.'' He was ''raised up'' as Lord in the resurrection (LXX Ps 109:1; Acts 2:34-36). Moses ''received the living words and gave them'' to the people (7:38), but Jesus receives the Holy Spirit from God and pours it out on his followers (2:33). And in the proclamation of these witnesses, the saving message of Jesus is filled with prophetic power, bearing an equally powerful threat: those not listening to the voice of ''this prophet'' will be ''cut off from the people'' (3:23).

We have seen in this introduction that Luke shapes the image of Jesus as a philosopher, and as a prophet. The commentary on the Gospel will show how important still another image is, that of the king (1:33; 4:43; 10:9; 19:11-27, 38; 22:29-30; 23:42). It must not, however, be thought that Luke's first readers would find these images in any sense contradictory. Since the time of Plato, the ideal of the philosopher-king combined the images of the righteous person and righteous ruler (*Republic* 473D; 540D-E). Popular moral teaching, in turn, made every true wise person (*sophos*) into a king (cf. Epictetus, *Discourses* III, 22, 67-72). It is not surprising, therefore, to find Jewish apologetic literature, which provides the best analogy to Luke's composition, applying the same sort of categories to Moses, not artificially, but completely naturally, since the Jews who were writing thought of him just this way. So Josephus, when he describes the death of Moses, uses the categories of the *general,* the *sophos,* and the *prophet* to define his greatness (*Antiquities of the Jews* 4:327-331). Even more elaborately, Philo in his *Life of Moses* (written with a definite apologetic intention) combines the images of king (1:148), lawgiver (2:8-65), high priest (2:66-186) and prophet (2:187-291). In just this fashion does Luke combine into one compelling portrayal of the messiah the symbols attached to the philosopher, the king, and—most critically—the prophet.

4. *The Gospel in the Light of Acts*

The pattern of the Moses story provides the basic framework for Luke's two-volume work. The Gospel is the story of God's first sending of the prophet Jesus to "visit" the people for their "salvation" (see Luke 1:68; 7:16; 19:44); of their initial rejection of this salvation, out of ignorance; and of Jesus' being "raised up" out of death. Acts recounts Jesus' establishment in power, manifested by the gift of the Holy Spirit; the sending out of his witnesses empowered by that Spirit; and the second offer of salvation to Israel "in His name" (Acts 4:12; 5:41). This time, however, the cost of refusal is separation from the people God is forming.

This pattern explains why Luke's geographical structure places Jerusalem in the center. In Jerusalem, the first rejection, the empowerment, the second offer, and the issue of acceptance or rejection by the people, are all played out. The geographic structure serves the story of the prophet and the people.

Luke was freer to shape his story in Acts than he was in the Gospel. But if Acts provides Luke's understanding of the Gospel, we can expect to find within the first volume's tighter literary constraints, intimations of this image of Jesus and his relationship to the people, and in fact, we do (see 7:11-16; 9:35; 24:19). Indeed, one of the main preoccupations of this commentary on the Gospel will be showing the multiple ways in which Luke, while handing on traditions about Jesus (each of which also has its own point), was constructing an "orderly account" that already anticipated the story of Acts.

E. *Literary-Religious Themes*

It would be a mistake, however, to read a work as rich as this in terms of a single preoccupation. Within the story line that is concerned primarily with showing God's fidelity to the people, other literary and religious subthemes are developed, not independently but within that larger pattern. Here are a few:

1. *World-Affirmation*

Luke-Acts is positive toward the world, not only as God's creation but also as the arena of history and human activity. It is perhaps the least apocalyptic of the NT writings, and the least sectarian. Not only is Luke relatively unconcerned about the end-time, his historical narrative bestows value on time itself. Luke is also generally approving of those outside the Christian movement. Outsiders—not counting the Jewish opponents who are not "outsiders" at all—are generally regarded as reasonable and open-minded, which is the high compliment paid by apologetic literature.

The Roman Empire does not appear as the instrument of Satan, but as the condition for the safety and spread of the Gospel. Gentiles can be converted, and many are already "God-fearers." Even the unconverted show intelligence and kindness (see Acts 28:2-10). The perception that outsiders are enlightened corresponds to the portrayal of the Jesus and his successors as self-controlled, courageous, just, law-abiding, and reasonable—the farthest thing from fanatics.

Luke-Acts also affirms the value of human culture simply by taking care to shape the story beautifully. He uses the forms of Hellenistic literature deftly and creatively. He thereby implies the compatibility of Christianity and culture. Human symbols are adequate vessels of the Good News about God.

2. The Great Reversal

To affirm the world does not mean to approve all human conduct or structures. The prophetic imagery of Luke-Acts is joined to a prophetic critique of human religious expectations and social values. In the "visitation of the people" by the Prophet, a great reversal is proclaimed and enacted. Human security and complacency are challenged by the Gospel. Those who are powerful, rich, and "have consolation" within society and who seek on that basis to "justify themselves" respond to this prophet with "testing" and rejection. They themselves are "cast down" or "lowered" and in the end, "cut off from the people." In contrast, those ordinarily deemed unworthy, lowly, marginal, or even outcast, are accepted by God. They are "raised up" and become part of the restored people of God.

Here we find the significance of Luke's language about "the rich" and "the poor" (1:53; 4:18; 6:20-24; 7:22; 14:13, 21; 16:19-31). The rich stand for those who have their consolation already in society and have no need of God's consolation; they therefore reject the Prophet. The poor stand for all those who have been rejected on the basis of human standards, but are accepted by God; they in turn accept the Prophet. Among them are the crippled, the lame, the blind and deaf, the sexually mutilated, and all those ritually excluded from full participation in the life of the people. The religiously unrighteous are also included, the "sinners and tax-agents," as well as those women who by virtue of their gender always took a second place within the ritual life of the Jewish community. Luke's portrayal of Mary is emblematic of how God reverses the poverty and powerlessness of the human condition. And throughout his narrative, Luke pays particular and positive attention to the role of women. The theme of reversal is expressed as well by the inclusion within the people of God of Samaritans and Gentiles.

3. *Salvation*

Human values are reversed by God not for the destruction of the wicked but for the saving of the lost. God's "visitation" is for their salvation (cf. Acts 7:25). Luke emphasizes the salvific aspect of the Good News more than any of the other Gospels. He does this first in the image of Jesus. The Prophet is not only Philosopher and King; he is as well Savior (2:11), who brings salvation (1:69; 19:9), and works saving acts (7:50; 8:48, 50). He has "come to save the lost" (19:10). What is said of Jesus in the Gospels applies to the apostles in the Book of Acts. The message of God delivered by these prophetic successors is one of salvation (Acts 15:11; 28:28). The theme of salvation is prominent in distinctively Lukan parables, above all in those of the lost sheep (15:3-6), the lost coin (15:8-10) and the lost son (15:11-32).

4. *The Word of God*

The theme of God's Word is of course intimately connected to that of the Prophet and the people. It is through the prophetic word that God addresses the people. Luke emphasizes the power of this Word in Acts by showing it as deriving from the Holy Spirit and accompanied by signs and wonders. Indeed, the mission itself can be described as the Word of God expanding and growing (Acts 6:7; 8:14; 10:36; 11:1; 12:24; 19:20). In the interpretation of the parable of the sower, Luke has Jesus identify the seed explicitly as "the Word of God" (8:11) and the human response of faith is correspondingly defined in terms of "hearing" and "obeying" the Word of God (Luke 5:1; 6:47; 8:13-15, 21; 11:28).

5. *Conversion*

The Word of God demands the acceptance of the prophetic critique and a "turning" of one's life. Conversion is an important theme in Luke-Acts, closely joined to the pattern of the prophet and the people. Jesus' ministry is preceded by the Word of God spoken through the prophet John, which called people to repentance (conversion; Luke 3:7-14). Acts opens with the preaching of Peter which also calls for repentance (Acts 2:37-40). Those who enter the people that God forms around the prophet must "turn around" (Luke 5:32; 10:13; 11:32; 13:3-5; 15:7-10; 24:47; Acts 3:19; 5:31; 8:22; 11:18; 17:30; 20:21; 26:20). The most impressive example of all is the "turning" of Paul from persecutor to apostle, whose conversion/call is so important that it is repeated three times (Acts 9:1-9; 22:6-11; 26:12-18).

6. *The Response of Faith*

God's restored people answer the challenge of his visitation with "fruits worthy of repentance" (Luke 3:8; Acts 26:20). The first of these is faith. God requires faithfulness in return for his fidelity. In Luke-Acts, "faith" combines obedient hearing of the Word and patient endurance. It is not a momentary decision but a commitment of the heart that can grow and mature (Luke 8:15; 17:5-6). Essential to the response of faith is the practice of prayer. Jesus prays throughout his ministry (Luke 3:21; 5:16; 6:12; 9:28-29; 11:1; 22:41-44) and teaches his disciples to pray (11:2-4; 18:1; 22:46). Luke also provides splendid samples of prayer, showing a people for whom life is defined first of all by its relationship with God (cf. Luke 1:46-56, 68-79; 2:29-32; 10:21-22; 22:42; Acts 1:24-25; 4:24-30).

Conversion demands that people change their social behavior in imitation of God. As God welcomes all people, so are Christians expected to show hospitality. The opening of home and heart to the stranger is explicitly connected to the theme of accepting or rejecting the prophet (Luke 9:3-5; 10:2-16). Luke provides concrete examples of the proper response of hospitality (Luke 10:38-42; Acts 16:11-15). In the same way, as the Messiah showed leadership as a kind of table-service (Luke 22:27), so is leadership in the messianic community to be one of service (22:24-26) spelled out in the simple gestures of practical aid (9:16; 12:41-48; Acts 4:32-34; 6:1-4).

Likewise Luke's instructions on the use of possessions have their logic within the pattern of prophetic visitation. Those who accept the prophet share their possessions with the needy, whether through almsgiving (Luke 12:32-34; 16:1-13) or the total donation of what they possess in a community of goods (Acts 4:32-37). Finally, as God's visitation of the people for salvation was a revelation of his loving-kindness above all to the outcast (Luke 1:50, 54, 58), so are his people to reach out in love to all without thought of repayment (6:32-36; 10:27-37). In such daily and specific modes of fidelity is the following of the Messiah spelled out. In Luke, the "carrying of the cross" is to take place "every day" (9:23; 14:27).

These are not all the literary and religious themes of Luke-Acts, but the listing demonstrates how the rich subthemes find coherence within the story of the prophet and the people by which Luke seeks to convince his Gentile readers that God's fidelity to his promise should give them confidence in their commitment to him.

BIBLIOGRAPHY

It is impossible to provide a complete bibliography for Luke-Acts, and the principles of selection for any shorter version are difficult. Since the present list is intended to be useful for a range of readers wider than professional scholars, I will list only works in English (although the short bibliographies for individual passages often include German and French works as well). Up to the dates of publication, Fitzmyer's bibliographies are exhaustive and reliable. I will provide here only a selection of works that might be useful for pursuing the literary and religious dimensions of Luke-Acts, with particular attention to the Gospel, since another list will be provided for the volume on Acts.

Barrett, C. K. *Luke the Historian in Recent Study*. London: Epworth, 1961.

Brawley, R. L. *Luke-Acts and the Jews: Conflict, Apology, and Conciliation*. SBLMS 33; Atlanta: Scholars Press, 1987.

Brown, R. E. *The Birth of the Messiah*. Garden City, N.Y.: Doubleday, 1979.

Brown, S. *Apostasy and Perseverance in the Theology of Luke*. Analecta Biblica 36; Rome: Pontifical Biblical Institute, 1969.

Cadbury, H. J. *The Style and Literary Method of Luke*. HTS VI; Cambridge: Harvard University Press, 1920.

_____. *The Making of Luke-Acts*. New York: Macmillan Co., 1927.

Cassidy, R. *Jesus, Politics and Society: A Study of Luke's Gospel*. Maryknoll, N.Y.: Orbis Press, 1978.

Conzelmann, H. *The Theology of St. Luke*. Trans. G. Buswell. New York: Harper and Row, 1961.

Dillon, R. J. *From Eyewitnesses to Ministers of the Word: Tradition and Composition in Luke 24*. Analecta Biblica 82; Rome: Biblical Institute, 1978.

_____. "Previewing Luke's Project from his Prologue." *Catholic Biblical Quarterly* 43 (1981) 205–227.

Dupont, J. *The Salvation of the Gentiles*. Trans. J. Keating (New York: Paulist Press, 1979) 11–34.

Hastings, A. *Prophet and Witness in Jerusalem: A Study of the Teaching of St. Luke*. Baltimore: Helicon, 1958.

Jervell, J. *Luke and the People of God*. Minneapolis: Augsburg Press, 1972.

Johnson, L. T. *The Literary Function of Possessions in Luke-Acts*. SBLDS 39; Missoula: Scholars Press, 1977.

_____. "On Finding the Lukan Community: A Cautious Cautionary Essay." *1979 SBL Seminar Papers*. Ed. P. Achtemeier (Missoula: Scholars Press, 1979) 87–100.

_____. *The Writings of the New Testament: An Interpretation*. Philadelphia: Fortress Press, 1986.

Karris, R. J. "Missionary Communities: A New Paradigm for the Study of Luke-Acts." *Catholic Biblical Quarterly* 41 (1979) 80–97.

Keck, L. and J. L. Martyn, eds., *Studies in Luke-Acts*. Nashville: Abingdon, 1966.

Lampe, G. W. H. "The Holy Spirit in the Writings of St. Luke." *Studies in the Gospels*. Ed. D. E. Nineham (Oxford: Basil Blackwell, 1955) 159–200.

_____. "The Lukan Portrait of Christ." *New Testament Studies* 2 (1955–56) 160–175.

Maddox, R. *The Purpose of Luke-Acts*. Ed. J. Riches. Edinburgh: T&T Clark, 1982.

Marshall, I. H. *Luke: Historian and Theologian*. Exeter: Paternoster Press, 1970.

Minear, P. *To Heal and to Reveal: The Prophetic Vocation according to Luke*. New York: Crossroads, 1976.

Moessner, D. P. *Lord of the Banquet: The Literary and Theological Significance of the Lukan Travel Narrative.* Minneapolis: Fortress Press, 1989.

Neyrey, J. *The Passion according to Luke: A Redaction Study of Luke's Soteriology.* New York: Paulist Press, 1985.

O'Toole, R. F. *The Unity of Luke's Theology: An Analysis of Luke-Acts.* Good News Studies 9; Wilmington: Michael Glazier, 1984.

Schubert, P. "The Structure and Significance of Luke 24." *Neutestamentliche Studien für R. Bultmann.* Ed. W. Eltester (Berlin: A. Töpelmann, 1954) 165–186.

Talbert, C. H. *Literary Patterns, Theological Themes and the Genre of Luke-Acts.* Missoula: Scholars Press, 1974.

_____, ed. *Perspectives on Luke-Acts.* Danville, Va.: Association of Baptist Professors of Religion, 1978.

_____, ed. *Luke-Acts: New Perspectives from the SBL Seminar.* New York: Crossroads, 1984.

Tannehill, R. C. *The Narrative Unity of Luke Acts: A Literary Interpretation.* Vol I: *The Gospel according to Luke.* Philadelphia: Fortress Press, 1986.

Teeple, H. *The Mosaic Eschatological Prophet.* SBLMS 10; Philadelphia: Society of Biblical Literature, 1957.

Tiede, D. *Prophecy and History in Luke-Acts.* Philadelphia: Fortress Press, 1980.

Van Unnik, W. C. "The 'Book of Acts' the Confirmation of the Gospel." *Novum Testamentum* 4 (1960) 26–59.

Walasky, P. W. *"And So We Came to Rome": The Political Perspective of St. Luke.* SNTMS 49; Cambridge: Cambridge University Press, 1983.

Wilson, S. G. *The Gentiles and the Gentile Mission in Luke-Acts.* SNTMS 23; Cambridge: Cambridge University Press, 1973.

_____. *Luke and the Law.* SNTMS 50; Cambridge: Cambridge University Press, 1983.

Commentaries on the Gospel of Luke:

Danker, F. W. *Jesus and the New Age: A Commentary on St. Luke's Gospel.* rev.ed. Philadelphia: Fortress Press, 1988.

Ellis, E. E. *The Gospel of Luke.* The New Century Bible Commentary; Grand Rapids: Eerdmans, 1974.

Fitzmyer, J. A. *The Gospel according to Luke I–IX.* The Anchor Bible 28; Garden City, N.Y.: Doubleday, 1981).

_____. *The Gospel according to Luke X-XXIV.* The Anchor Bible 28A; Garden City, N.Y.: Doubleday, 1985.

Marshall, I. H. *Commentary on Luke.* New International Greek Testament Commentary; Grand Rapids: Eerdmans, 1978.

Schweizer, E. *The Good News according to Luke.* Trans. D. E. Green. Atlanta: John Knox, 1984.

Talbert, C. H. *Reading Luke: A Literary and Theological Commentary on the Third Gospel.* New York: Crossroads, 1989.

TRANSLATION, NOTES, INTERPRETATION

1. *Prologue* (1:1-4)

1. Since many have tried to arrange a narrative about the matters that have been brought to fulfillment among us 2. just as the eyewitnesses who also became ministers of the word handed them on to us from the beginning, 3. I too decided, since I have examined everything carefully from the start, to write for you, excellent Theophilus, an orderly account, 4. so that you might have full confidence concerning the words in which you have been instructed.

NOTES

1. *Since many have tried*: The opening word in Greek (*epeidēper*) is very formal, having the official tone of "inasmuch," or "whereas." Similarly, "tried" is literally "put their hands to," which can be read either neutrally or as a negative evaluation. Compare Polybius, *History* 1, 15, 11-12. The problem is connecting the *causative* character of this opening clause to Luke's own decision to write (1:3). See the discussion below.

   the matters brought to fulfillment: This could be rendered "accomplished," but the biblical resonance of "fulfillment" is deliberate and unmistakable. In the passive voice, it means *God* brought them to fulfillment (see Luke 4:21; 22:37; 24:44; Acts 1:16; 3:18).

   among us: Since the prologue to the Gospel introduces both volumes, this qualification is important. The events he relates extend to the time of his readers: all of them are in fulfillment of God's promises. This simple phrase extends Luke's statement of purpose to include the narrative of Acts.

2. *just as . . . handed on*: Luke's exact point here is difficult. He wants to emphasize a connection to eyewitness accounts "from the beginning" (see Acts 1:21). But is he subtly criticizing previous narratives for being too dependent on the form of those traditions (with an emphasis on the "just as"), and too little "ar-

ranged"? The necessity of rearranging one's sources is recognized by Lucian in *How to Write History*, 47.

eyewitnesses . . . ministers of the word: "Eyewitness" is found only here in the Bible, and reflects Luke's historical interests. Although the Greek could be read either way, it is more likely that Luke has in mind one rather than two groups, that is, eyewitnesses *who became* ministers of the word (see Acts 1:21-22 and 26:16). Luke therefore claims access to a) eyewitness accounts, b) written narratives, and c) his own careful research. Here and throughout Luke-Acts (as also in 1:4), "word" has theological significance (e.g., Luke 4:32; 5:1; 8:11, 21; 11:28; Acts 4:4; 6:2, 7; 8:4; 19:10).

3. *I too decided*: Also can be rendered, "it seemed good to me"; for the idiom, cf. Acts 15:25. Because the phrase also occurs in Acts 15:28, some copyists added "and the Holy Spirit" to their manuscripts (MSS).

   an orderly account: The word "account" is implied by the use of "narrative" in 1:1. The adverb "orderly" (*kathexēs*) is critical. Does it mean only "in succession," as in Acts 3:24; 18:23? Or is there special emphasis on the *order* in which events are related, as in Acts 11:4? Clearly, the "order" of Luke's work is its distinguishing characteristic in contrast to those who "tried to arrange (1:1)." Lucian declares that the main task of the historian is "arrangement and exposition," to "give a fine arrangement to events" (*How to Write History*, 50-51).

   since I have examined everything carefully: The Greek verb could mean "follow" in the literal sense, but here it means "examine." Because he "followed everything" that happened "from the top" Luke is able to write "accurately" and "in order." He thereby characterizes himself as a careful and critical historian; for the virtue of "painstaking examination," cf. Lucian, *How to Write History*, 47.

   excellent Theophilus: The person to whom a work was dedicated was often the financial patron who sponsored publication. Theophilus is Luke's "intended reader" (1:4), whether or not his name has a symbolic resonance ("Lover of God") or he represents a wider Gentile-Christian readership. For the title *kratiste* ("excellent"), see Josephus, *Life* 430; *Against Apion* 1:1.

4. *might have full confidence*: Literally, "that you might know (or recognize) assurance." Luke's narrative gives the reader knowledge or recognition. But of what? The key word is *asphaleia*. It does not mean "truth" as opposed to "falsehood," as though Luke's predecessors had their facts wrong. *Asphaleia* refers rather to a mental state of certainty or security (Acts 5:23, and for the idiom 21:24). Luke's narrative is intended to have a "convincing" quality. In his treatise, *How to Write History* 9, Lucian affirms that the usefulness of history lies in its quality of truthfulness.

   in which you were instructed: The term (*katēcheō*) might be used simply to mean "being informed" as though Theophilus were an outsider (see e.g., Acts 21:21, 24), but the stronger translation, referring to initiation into the community (see Acts 18:25) is much to be preferred; in the same way, "words" is obviously awkward in English, and "things" (see 1:1) might be preferable, but the theme of God's Word is too obvious to gloss over completely (see note on 1:2).

Interpretation

The fact that Luke-Acts begins with a formal prologue in which the author states his intentions would seem to be of great importance for assessing Luke's composition. Yet although the prologue is written carefully in a style notably more elegant than normal in the NT, it remains sufficiently obscure to stimulate vigorous discussion by scholars, all of whom recognize its significance without agreeing on its meaning.

Some read the prologue in a minimalist fashion, as though Luke simply and without much reflection used conventional formulae. Others find deep theological significance in each word. As so often, the middle ground is the surest. The present discussion distinguishes between the clear and the obscure, placing an interpretive emphasis on the cumulative force of the clear elements.

Certainly, the prologue indicates an explicit literary self-consciousness. He knows the form for historical prologues and follows it (cf. e.g., Lucian of Samosata, *How to Write History,* 23; Josephus, *Antiquities of the Jews* 1:1-17). The fact of such self-awareness is important for assessing literary intentionality in the rest of his narrative. There is every reason to think that his composition as a whole is as deliberate and considered as his prologue. We do not betray the author, then, when we observe the signs of literary artifice in the text.

A second implication is the possibility that the prologue was addressed to Luke's financial patron, Theophilus, which by the conventions of that world would signify publication. In principle, Luke-Acts would be available for reading by outsiders to the Christian movement, even though its patron—and other implied readers—were surely themselves Christian. The prologue signaled the movement of the Gospel into the wider world of Hellenistic literature. No matter if outsiders would not have bothered to read it; Luke brought the peculiar sensitivity of apologetic literature ("to see ourselves as others see us") to the story of Jesus and the early Church. His Christian audience can read its own story as shaped by sensitivity to the pluralistic world outside the community.

The prologue shows that Luke understood his composition as a form of history. His references to earlier written sources, to eyewitness accounts, and to his own careful research, together with his characterization of his work as a "narrative" concerning "matters accomplished among us," as well as his insistence that he treats these matters "in order," all point in the same direction. Much harder to determine is his attitude toward the earlier narratives, and the precise reason for writing his own. The two questions are related.

The syntax of this elaborate sentence connects the fact that others had "tried to arrange a narrative" with Luke's own decision to write. On one hand, the earlier efforts legitimate Luke's own effort: they wrote, so could he. But why should he, if their attempts were satisfactory? What distinguishes his own effort? Luke's language suggests dissatisfaction with the earlier attempts. Many had "put their hand to arranging," which suggests they did not quite succeed. Why? We must take seriously the force of the phrase "just as the eyewitnesses . . . handed on." Perhaps efforts such as Mark's were regarded by Luke as rhetorically ineffective because, too dependent on the way materials were transmitted by communities, they lacked a convincing sort of order. We remember the complaint by the second-century author Papias about Mark's lack of order (Eusebius of Caesarea, *Ecclesiastical History* 3, 39, 15). What this means—if we can judge from the improvement Luke himself made—is that they did not make sufficiently clear "connections" between events (cf. Lucian, *How to Write History,* 55). This was, in any case, the way that Eusebius understood Luke's prologue (*Ecclesiastical History* 3, 24, 14–16).

Luke's purpose in writing, therefore, is to provide "security" to his Gentile readers by establishing a more explicit and deliberate "order" to his narrative. He is able to do this, he says, because of his own personal research of all things "from the top."

The Introduction suggested the reason why Luke's readers would need such security. The success of the Gentile mission and the failure of the Jewish mission raised an issue of theodicy. If Jews were rejected from the good news, how could God be considered faithful to his promise? And if God was not faithful to his own people, how could Gentiles have confidence in their faith? God could abandon them as well!

Luke therefore sets out to write the continuation of the biblical story, showing how the Gentile Church of his own day emerged in continuity from a faithful and restored Israel, organizing his narrative as a whole into the pattern of the Prophet and the people.

FOR REFERENCE AND FURTHER STUDY

Brown, S. "The Role of the Prologues in Determining the Purpose of Luke-Acts." *Perspectives on Luke-Acts.* Ed. C.H. Talbert (Danville, Va.: Association of Baptist Professors of Religion, 1978) 99–111.

Cadbury, H. J. "Commentary on the Preface of Luke." *The Beginnings of Christianity,* Part I. *The Acts of the Apostles.* Ed. F. J. Foakes-Jackson and K. Lake. Vol. II (London: Macmillan and Co., 1920) 489–510.

Dillon, R. J. "Previewing Luke's Project from his Prologue." *CBQ* 43 (1981) 205–227.

Klein, G. "Lukas 1:1-4 als theologisches Programm." *Zeit und Geschichte.* Ed. E. Dinkler (Tübingen: JCB Mohr, 1964) 193–216.

Schneider, G. "Zur Bedeutung von *kathexēs* im lukanischen Doppelwerk." *ZNW* 68 (1977) 128–131.

Van Unnik, W. C. "Once More, St. Luke's Prologue." *Essays on the Gospel of Luke and Acts* (Neotestamentica 7; New Testament Society of South Africa, 1973) 7–26.

I. BIRTH AND CHILDHOOD OF THE PROPHET

2. *The Prophecy of John's Birth* (1:5-25)

5. In the days of Herod, King of Judea, there was a priest named Zechariah. He served in the priestly division of Abia. His wife's name was Elizabeth. She was descended from Aaron. 6. Both were righteous in the sight of God. They walked blamelessly in all the commandments and requirements of the Lord. 7. But they had no child, for Elizabeth was barren and both had grown elderly. 8. When Zechariah was acting as priest before God during his allotted time of service, 9. he drew the duty of offering incense, and went into the temple of the Lord. 10. At the time of incense-offering, the whole populace was praying outside. 11. An angel of the Lord appeared to Zechariah. The angel stood at the right side of the incense altar. 12. When Zechariah caught sight of him, he became agitated and overcome with fear. 13. The angel said to him: "Fear no longer, Zechariah, for your prayer has been heard. Your wife Elizabeth will provide you with a son. You will give him the name John. 14. You will experience joy and gladness. Many will rejoice because of his birth. 15. He will be great in God's sight. He will never drink wine or strong drink. Even from his mother's womb he will be filled with the Holy Spirit. 16. He will turn many children of Israel back to the Lord their God. 17. He will go before the Lord with the spirit and power of Elijah, to turn fathers' hearts toward their children, and faithless people to the perceptions of the righteous, in order to make ready a people prepared for the Lord." 18. Zechariah said to the angel, "How will I know this? I am an old man. My wife has grown elderly." 19.. The angel answered, "I am Gabriel. My place is in God's presence. I have been sent to speak to you and announce this good news. 20. Behold, you will fall silent. You will be unable to speak until the time these things happen, because you did not believe my words, which will reach fulfillment each in its appointed time." 21. The people were waiting for Zechariah. They were astonished at the time he spent in the Temple. 22. But when he came out, he could not speak to them. They understood that he had a vision in the temple. Meanwhile he kept signalling to them, but remained mute. 23. When his

period of service was completed, he returned to his home. 24. After some days, his wife Elizabeth became pregnant. She withdrew privately for five months. 25. She declared, "Thus has the Lord done for me. He has now looked on me, to relieve me of human reproach."

NOTES

5. *in the days*: This is the first of many Semitisms in this section by which Luke deliberately imitates the Septuagint; cf. also "it happened that" (1:8); "and behold" (1:20), and many others; this sort of shift in style between prologue and narration is disapproved by Lucian, *How to Write History*, 16.

   Herod King of Judea: This is Herod the Great, whose magnificent and sometimes mad enterprises are entertainingly related in Josephus, *Jewish War* 1:203–669. By naming him, Luke connects the narrative both to the biblical story and to wider world history. In contrast to Herod's extensive and bloody activity in Matt 2:1-23, this is his only appearance in Luke.

   priestly division: The Greek word *ephēmeria* is used in LXX 1 Chr 23:6 for the 24 priestly cohorts who handled the daily service in the Temple on a rotating basis (cf. 1 Chr 24:1-19); for Abia's cohort, see 1 Chr 24:10 and Neh 12:4. John's parents, we see, are both of the priestly class.

6. *righteous in the sight of God*: Another Semitism. All of Luke's characters in the infancy account have the simple piety associated with the "poor of Yahweh" (Zeph 3:12-13) whose faith enabled them to be open to God's revelation.

7. *Elizabeth was barren*: The echo of a classic biblical motif. The great exemplar of infertility and the shame it engenders is Sarah (cf. Gen 16–21); cf. in this light the force of Jesus' prophecy to the women of Jerusalem in 23:29.

   both had grown elderly: As elsewhere, the translation chooses the prosaic sense rather than the more "biblical" cadence of "advanced in their days." The age of the parents heightens their human hopelessness and the wonder of the divine intervention (see 1:18, and Rom 4:19).

8. *when Zechariah was acting as priest*: The offering of incense twice daily in the Temple is mandated by Exod 30:1-10.

9. *drew the duty*: Literally, "it fell to him by lot." The use of lots to determine God's will is found also in Acts 1:26.

10. *the whole populace*: It is characteristic of Luke to focus on "the people" (*laos*). The fate of Israel is one of his main concerns. Here, it is a faithful and prayerful people, expectant of God's visitation.

11. *angel of the Lord*: Literally, a "messenger from the Lord," but by the time of Luke's writing, the conception of "angels" as "ministering spirits" (see Heb 1:14) was well advanced in Jewish apocalyptic literature (e.g., *I Enoch* 3:1; 4:1-2; 5:1). The angel is identified as Gabriel in 1:19. This angel appeared also to Daniel at the time of evening incense offering, to prophesy a seventy-week period required "to seal both vision and prophet, and to anoint a most holy place" (Dan 9:20-27).

Many scholars detect the influence of Daniel's apocalyptic vision in Luke's infancy account. Note, for example, the effect of "each in its appointed time" in 1:20.

13. *your prayer has been heard*: A motif running through all of Luke-Acts. The righteous are those who pray, and their prayer is answered (see e.g., Acts 1:14; 4:24; 10:31, and especially Luke 18:7-8).

    you will give him the name: The first words spoken by any character in Luke-Acts are in the form, first, of a message from God, and second, of a prophecy. Its fulfillment, of course, is found in 1:57-66.

14. *you will experience joy*: The terms "joy and gladness" have definite eschatological and messianic overtones (see e.g., Isa 12:6; 25:9; 29:19; 49:13). John's birth is not merely a family affair: "many" (or: "all") will celebrate his birth. John's significance is for all the people (see 3:2-18; 7:24-28; Acts 13:24-25).

15. *he will be great*: First of all in his dedication to the Lord, and then in what he will do. Abstinence from strong drink was required of Aaron's sons for worship (Lev 10:9), but as a way of life defined the Nazarite, one who by vow was "set apart for the Lord" (Num 6:3). Compare the annunciation of Samson's birth in Judg 13:5. That John "fulfills" this prediction is typically noted by Luke in 7:33.

    filled with the Holy Spirit: The essential mark of the prophet for Luke (cf. Introduction). Like Jeremiah (Jer 1:5) before him, and Paul after him (Gal 1:15), John is a prophet "from the womb," a fact demonstrated literally by his leaping in Elizabeth's womb in recognition of Jesus in 1:41.

16. *he will turn . . . to the Lord*: Luke shows this function dramatically fulfilled in his fuller than usual depiction of John's preaching ministry, 3:3-18.

17. *the spirit and power of Elijah*: Luke does not make the straightforward *identification* of John with Elijah (cf. Mark 9:11-13 and especially Matt 17:10-13), but does agree that John plays the role assigned to Elijah of preparing the people (Sir 48:10; Mal 4:5). In Luke's eyes, of course, "going before the Lord" meant being the precursor to Jesus, a specification uncongenial to non-Christian messianic expectations based on Malachi (see Justin, *Dialogue with Trypho*, 49).

    the perceptions of the righteous: Is difficult in Greek, although the basic sense is clear: as (hostile) fathers are turned to their children, so are faithless people turned to righteous thoughts. It is typical of Luke to emphasize the *social* and *spiritual* aspects of the restoration of Israel (see Acts 2-4).

    a people prepared: In the larger sense, this is what the entire Gospel narrative tries to show, how a people within historic Judaism was prepared to become the restored Israel of God.

19. *this good news*: In Luke-Acts, "preaching good news" (*euangelizomai*) is thematic. It is carried out by John himself (Luke 3:18), by Jesus (4:18; 7:22; 20:1) and by the apostles (Acts 5:42; 8:4; 10:36; 13:32). Here and in Luke 2:10, the good news is directly announced in the most authoritative fashion, by messengers from God. John, in turn, is thoroughly integrated into what Luke conceives of as "this good news" (see Acts 1:5, 22; 11:16; 13:24-25), that is, God's "visitation" of the people (Luke 1:68).

20. *you will fall silent*: For a similar pedagogic hardship, assigned this time by Paul, see Acts 13:11.

    will reach fulfillment: The prophecy-fulfillment pattern is legitimated by the angelic messenger: God fulfills his promises! The phrase "in its appointed time" suggests an "orderly" progression of events under the control of God, which is precisely the point Luke is trying to establish by his narrative. In this case, the "fulfillment" is immediate (1:21-22).

24. *Elizabeth became pregnant*: The angel's prophecy is fulfilled, despite the human odds against it. Luke has Elizabeth herself draw the clear moral (v. 25): "thus has the *Lord* done for me."

INTERPRETATION

The facts that Mark's Gospel lacks an infancy account and that between them, Matthew and Luke share no specific stories but only some bare information (the names of Mary, Joseph and Jesus, the place-names Nazareth and Bethlehem), and that each takes quite a different tack in his infancy narrative, all support the conclusion that in this part of his Gospel, Luke was largely free to shape the narrative according to his own perceptions. These chapters are, therefore, like Acts, of particular importance in showing the reader how Luke intended his story to be understood.

Luke's infancy account has a complex internal structure, in which stories concerning John are matched with those about Jesus, in each case showing Jesus' superiority. These stories of prophecy (John, 1:5-25; Jesus, 1:26-38) and birth (John, 1:57-66; Jesus, 2:1-20) are supplemented by the story of Mary's visit to Elizabeth (1:39-45) and the account of Jesus' presentation by his parents in the Temple (2:21-38). The canticles of Mary (1:46-55), Zechariah (1:68-79), and Simeon (2:29-32) serve to interpret these events. Finally, the story of Jesus as a boy in the Temple (2:41-52) provides an almost novelistic expansion of the notice about John's growth to manhood in 1:80, and makes an "orderly" transition to the ministry narrative, in which the respective prophetic missions of John and Jesus are again matched, with the same emphasis: Jesus succeeds and supercedes John (Luke 3:1-4:14). John's importance as a prophetic figure, however, is shown by Luke's constant pairing of him with Jesus, not only in the Gospel (7:18-35; 11:1; 16:16; 20:4-6) but also in Acts (1:5, 22; 10:37; 11:16; 13:24-25; 18:25; 19:3-4).

Luke's intention of continuing the biblical narrative is shown by the dramatic shift from the balanced, complex sentence of the prologue (1:1-4) to the more plodding rhythms of the Greek Bible (LXX) in 1:5. His language suddenly is filled with Semitisms. These do not suggest that Luke was using Hebrew or Aramaic sources, but that he was imitating biblical language. So skillful is he that the reader is plunged into the world of Ruth, the Judges, and Samuel. Imaginatively, then, the reader begins in the biblical world of Temple and Torah, and instinctively feels, "this is part of *our* story."

Such stylistic archaizing was widely practiced in Hellenistic literature. Luke also shows himself thoroughly a Hellenistic author by providing for his heroes John and Jesus both portents and predictions at their birth. These were standard accompaniments to the conception and birth of immortals and philosophers (see e.g., Philostratus, *Life of Apollonius of Tyana* 1:4–7; Plutarch, *Parallel Lives*, Alexander 2:1–3:2). But the symbolic world he himself inhabits and the traditions he exploits are those of Torah. The events of Israel's past, and the language used to describe those events, shape his own narrative. He does not, like Matthew, line up story and Scripture in a one-to-one correspondence (cf. Matt 1:22-23; 2:5-6, etc.). Luke composes a kind of haggadic midrash, a narrative that in its very language echoes a variety of biblical precedents. By this highly allusive style he roots the origins of Jesus and the Church in the story of Israel.

Luke's infancy stories also point forward. By means of programmatic prophecies they anticipate later plot developments. Luke uses prophecy and fulfillment to structure his entire narrative. In the story before us, we can see how a speech is followed by an immediate fulfillment (Zechariah's muteness) and a delayed fulfillment (Elizabeth's pregnancy), but also provides a perspective on everything else later said about John: that he is a prophet, that he is to prepare a people for the Lord. John is not specifically Elijah *redivivus*, but has the imagery of Elijah applied to him, just as it is applied to Jesus as well (see Luke 4:25-26; 7:11-16). John also has symbolism associated with Jeremiah applied to him (1:15). Luke uses prophetic imagery freely and without systematization. The main point he wants to establish is that John stands in a succession of prophetic figures through whom God "visits his people" (1:68), just as Moses before him (Acts 7:23) and Jesus after him (Luke 19:44).

Finally, we can observe in this passage some Lukan concerns that are developed throughout his narrative: the geographical concentration of Jerusalem and its Temple (1:9); the activity of "the whole people" (1:10, 17); the importance and efficacy of prayer (1:13); the way God reverses human expectations and perceptions (1:25); the understanding of conversion in terms of a change of heart (1:17); the voice given to women to interpret their own experience (1:25).

FOR REFERENCE AND FURTHER STUDY

Benoit, P. "L'Enfance de Jean-Baptiste selon Luc 1." *NTS* 3 (1956–57) 169–194.
Brown, R. E. *The Birth of the Messiah* (Garden City, N.Y.: Doubleday & Co., 1979) 235–495.

Laurentin, R. *Structure et Théologie de Luc I–II.* Etudes Bibliques; Paris: J. Gabalda, 1957.

Minear, P. "Luke's Use of the Birth Stories." *Studies in Luke-Acts.* Ed. L. Keck and J. L. Martyn (Philadelphia: Fortress, 1966) 111–130.

Talbert, C. H. "Prophecies of Future Greatness: The Contribution of Greco-Roman Biographies to an Understanding of Luke 1:5–4:15." *The Divine Helmsman.* Ed. J. L. Crenshaw and S. Sandmel (New York: KTAV, 1980) 129–141.

Turner, N. "The Relation of Luke I and II to Hebraic Sources and to the Rest of Luke-Acts." *NTS* 2 (1955–56) 100–109.

3. The Prophecy of Jesus' Birth (1:26-38)

26. In the sixth month, the angel Gabriel was sent from God to a town of Galilee named Nazareth. 27. He was sent to a virgin betrothed to a man named Joseph. He was descended from David. The virgin's name was Mary. 28. When the angel had approached her, he said, "Hail, Gifted Lady! The Lord is with you!" 29. She was utterly confused by this speech. She wondered what the greeting might mean. 30. The angel said to her, "Fear no longer, Mary. You have found favor with God. 31. Behold, you will conceive and will bear a son. You will give him the name Jesus. 32. He will be great. He will be called son of the Most High. The Lord God will give him the throne of his father David. 33. He will rule over the house of Jacob forever. His kingdom will never end." 34. Mary said to the angel, "How will this be, since I have no knowledge of a man?" 35. The angel answered her, "The Holy Spirit will come over you and the power of the Most High will overshadow you. Because of this, your child will be holy. He will be called son of God. 36. Look, Elizabeth your kinswoman is called barren. And she has conceived a son in her old age, and is in her sixth month! 37. Nothing is impossible for God!" 38. Mary said, "Behold the servant of the Lord. Let it happen to me as you say." The angel then withdrew from her.

NOTES

26. *the sixth month*: By using this phrase here and in 1:36, Luke connects the two miraculous pregnancies. He calls Nazareth a "city" (*polis*) but reality demands the translation "town."

27. *a virgin betrothed*: The word *parthenos* is used in the LXX for the "maiden (*alma*) shall conceive" passage in Isa 7:14, quoted in Matt 1:23. In general Greek usage, the term can refer to any unmarried woman without specific reference to sexual experience, but in early Christian apologetic, the text in its LXX version was vigorously defended against Jewish objections (cf. Justin, *Dialogue with Trypho* 43, 66, 71, 77). Luke's phrase here recalls Deut 22:23 in which it is clear that

"betrothal" is already a binding commitment, so that the term "wife" is appropriate for the woman (Deut 22:24; Matt 1:20), although Luke resists that step. He repeats in 2:5 that Mary was Joseph's "betrothed (*emnēsteumenē*)."

descended from David: Literally, "of David's house." Luke like Matthew (1:1, 6, 17, 20) uses his infancy account to emphasize Jesus' connection to David (Luke 1:27, 32, 69; 2:4, 11), even if it is through Joseph (see 3:23, 31) that the descent must be traced.

28. *Hail, Gifted Lady*: No translation can capture the alliteration of *chaire kecharitōmenē*. Getting the right sense of the perfect passive participle of *charitoō* is particularly difficult. The present translation tries to catch something of the formality of the address, "Hail, Lady," while avoiding the possible theological overloading that is invited by the term "grace." Notice that the Vulgate has *gratia plena*, "full of grace," which has stimulated a great deal of speculation concerning Mary's special status among other humans. The plain sense of the greeting (which Luke says confused her, too) is given by the angel: Mary has found favor with God. The evidence and expression of that favor is her being enabled to bear the Messiah. The scene as a whole resembles Judg 13:2-7, with verbal allusions from Zech 9:9 and Zeph 3:14, each of which has strong messianic overtones: Mary has the Lord "within her" even as the eschatological Zion would have the presence of the Lord within it. Not for the last time, Mary represents Israel.

29. *utterly confused*: Tries to convey the strengthening Luke obviously sought with *diatarassō* rather than the *tarassō* he used of Zechariah's response (1:12). One is tempted to translate "terrified" because the angel tells her not to "go on fearing" (1:30).

32. *Son of the Most High*: The title *ho hypsistos* ("Most High") is a favorite Lukan designation for God (see 1:35, 76; Acts 7:48; 16:17). Of particular interest is its use by a demoniac who calls Jesus, "Son of God the Most High" (8:28, following Mark), and in a statement unique to Luke, Jesus telling his followers that if they have selfless love they will be "sons of the Most High" (6:35).

throne of his father David: This is a clear allusion to 2 Sam 7:12-13, where Nathan promises a Davidic dynasty. The text was used messianically at Qumran (see 4QFlor 10-13). In Luke's Gospel, Jesus is emphatically descended from David (1:69; 2:4, 11; 3:31; 6:3; 18:38-39), but as 20:41-44 shows, his relationship to David is above all defined by the resurrection, when Jesus assumes his "seat at the right hand" (LXX Ps 109:1), a theme naturally developed in Acts (see 2:25-34; 13:22, 34).

33. *rule over the house of Jacob*: A somewhat archaic designation for Israel, found e.g., in Gen 46:27; Exod 19:3; Isa 8:17. That Jesus will "rule as king" is an important motif (see esp. 19:11-27, 38; 22:29-30; Acts 1:3, 6), even though the relationship between Jesus' "rule over the house of Jacob" and the "kingdom of God" is not altogether clear. Certainly for all of 1:32, the text in Acts 15:16, "I will rebuild the dwelling of David which is fallen" (Amos 9:11-12) is important.

34. *no knowledge of a man*: Mary's statement is straightforward, and enables the angel to clarify the true origin of the child. Luke obviously thinks of Mary as virginal in the biological sense (he resists calling her Joseph's "wife," 2:5), but his main

interest is in the miracle of God's power that overcomes human incapacity, quite unlike the obsessive encratism reflected in later infancy gospels, such as the *Protevangelium of James* 8:3; 20:1, or the *Arundel Manuscript* 69.

35. *the Holy Spirit will come over you*: This is similar to the phrase Jesus uses in his promise of the Spirit after his resurrection (Acts 1:8). The "overshadowing" occurs also with the cloud in the transfiguration story (Luke 9:34), and is clearly an allusion to the cloud of God's presence in the Exodus (Exod 40:35; cf. also Ps 90:4; 139:7 [LXX]). By such subtle signals does Luke connect parts of his story.

    holy . . . called Son of God: Jesus is called "Holy One" again in Acts 3:14, and "Holy Child" (of God) in Acts 4:27, 30. Obviously, for Luke, Jesus was not only *a* son of God, of which the Greek world had plenty (such as Heracles, in Epictetus, *Discourses* 2, 16, 44), but the Son of God in a unique fashion (Luke 3:22; 9:35; 22:70), above all because of his resurrection (see Acts 9:20; 13:32-33).

37. *nothing is impossible with God*: The angel's statement is given a slightly different twist by Jesus in 18:27; it also echoes the declaration made about the birth of Isaac to the barren Sarah in Gen 18:14.

38. *behold the servant*: The translation avoids the feminine equivalent, "handmaiden" since that might obscure the text's obvious implication that Mary is also a "Servant of Yahweh" (cf. Isa 49:3; 50:4, 10; 52:13). She is the woman of faith whose "yes" is unequivocal (see also 1:48 and Acts 2:18).

INTERPRETATION

The prophecy of Jesus' birth would have made excellent sense to any Hellenistic reader, who was accustomed to miraculous events accompanying the birth-accounts of extraordinary people. In its specific structure and symbolism, however, Luke's story is patterned on the annunciation scenes in the Bible, above all that in Judg 13:2-7. Luke also has this scene match the preceding one announcing John's birth. Many of the elements are shared: the angelic visitor, the proclamation, the overcoming of a human deficiency (age and barrenness in the first instance, youth and virginity in the second), and a sign to legitimate the prophecy. The points of contrast to the earlier story are therefore all the more striking.

Because the form of the angel's statement in each case is so similar, the difference in content concerning the identity and role of the respective children attracts the reader's eye (or ear in its original rendering and continued liturgical articulation). John will be great before the Lord (1:15), but Jesus will be great and Son of the Most High (1:32). John will prepare a people (1:17), but Jesus will rule the people (1:33). John's role is temporary (1:17), Jesus' kingdom will never end (1:33). John is to be a prophet (1:15), but Jesus more than another prophet: he is Son of God (1:35). John will be "filled with the Holy Spirit" as a prophet (1:15), but the overshadowing of the Spirit and Power will make Jesus "the Holy One." The full meaning of these epithets become clear only in the course of Luke's narrative, but from the start the reader is prepared to see in Jesus something far more than a Davidic king.

Another obviously deliberate contrast is that between Zechariah and Mary. Remarkable in any case is Luke's concentration on Mary. In Matthew's infancy account, Joseph is the central figure (Matt 1:16, 19, 20, 24, 25; 2:13-14, 19, 23). Luke's focus on Mary is striking not only in light of the patriarchal character of his biblical tradition (and social world) but also because it is through Joseph that Jesus receives his Davidic legitimacy "according to the flesh." At our distance, it is impossible to say whether historical reminiscence, special tradition, or Luke's predilection for presenting positive women figures (evident throughout his narrative) dictated his choice. The results, however, are clear: his narrative has exercised an incalculable influence in shaping Marian piety in subsequent Christian tradition.

In contrast to Zechariah, we notice, Mary holds no official position among the people, she is not described as "righteous" in terms of observing Torah, and her experience does not take place in a cultic setting. She is among the most powerless people in her society: she is young in a world that values age; female in a world ruled by men; poor in a stratified economy. Furthermore, she has neither husband nor child to validate her existence. That she should have found "favor with God" and be "highly gifted" shows Luke's understanding of God's activity as surprising and often paradoxical, almost always reversing human expectations.

Mary's mode of response is more positive than Zechariah's. Instead of his "how shall I know," which is a demand for proof, Mary simply asks how the promise might come true in the light of its obvious roadblock, her virginity. It is almost as though she had heard only the "you will conceive and bear a son" part of the message. When the angel makes clear that not human actions but divine power will effect this birth, she responds in obedient faith as powerful as those spoken later by her son in the garden before his death (Luke 22:42), "let it happen to me as you have said."

Finally, there is the contrast in signs. Zechariah is struck mute. But Mary is told of the *fulfillment* of an earlier prophecy. For the first time, we see a favorite device of Luke's found most extensively displayed in Acts 10-15: one character's experience of God's fidelity is used to give confidence to another character. The pertinence of this for revealing Luke's overall narrative purposes is patent (see also Luke 24).

For Reference and Further Study

Audet, J.-P. "L'Annonce à Marie." *RB* 63 (1956) 346-374.

Brown, R. E. "Luke's Method in the Annunciation Narrative of Chapter One." *No Famine in the Land: Studies in Honor of J. L. McKenzie.* Eds. J. W. Flanagan and A. W. Robinson (Missoula: Scholars Press, 1975) 179-194.

Brown, R. E. et.al., eds. *Mary in the New Testament* (Philadelphia: Fortress Press, 1978) 105–134.

Lyonnet, S. "St. Luke's Infancy Narrative." *Word and Mystery: Biblical Essays on the Person and Mission of Christ.* Ed. J. C. Donovan (Glen Road, N.J.: Newman, 1968) 143–154.

Schaberg, J. *The Illegitimacy of Jesus: A Feminist Theological Interpretation of the Infancy Narratives* (San Francisco: Harper and Row, 1987) 78–144.

Smith, D. M. "Luke 1:26-38." *Interpretation* 29 (1975) 411–417.

4. *Mary Visits Elizabeth* (1:39-56)

39. At this time, Mary set out in haste to a town in the hill country of Judea. 40. She entered Zechariah's house and greeted Elizabeth. 41. As soon as Elizabeth heard Mary's greeting, the infant in her womb leaped. Elizabeth was filled with the Holy Spirit. 42. She cried out in a loud voice, "You are blessed among women! And the fruit of your womb is blessed! 43. How do I deserve to have the mother of my Lord visit me? 44. No sooner had your greeting reached me than, look, the infant within me leaped with gladness. 45. How blessed is the woman who has believed, because the things said to her by the Lord will reach fulfillment." 46. Mary said, "My soul extols the Lord, 47. my spirit rejoices in God, my savior. 48. He has considered the lowliness of his servant. Behold, from now on all generations will declare me blessed, 49. because the Mighty One has accomplished great things for me. His name is holy. 50. He shows his mercy to those who fear him generation after generation. 51. He has shown power in his right arm! He has scattered those who are arrogant in their understanding. 52. He has pulled the mighty from their thrones. He has exalted the lowly. 53. He has filled the hungry with good things. He has sent the rich away empty. 54. He has taken Israel his child by the hand, remembering his mercy 55. to Abraham and his descendants forever just as he said to our fathers." 56. Mary stayed with her for three months, then returned to her home.

NOTES

39. *Mary set out in haste*: The entire passage is filled with Semitisms; literally, "she rose up and went," which imitates the biblical locution of passages such as Gen 19:14; 22:3, etc. As in 1:26, the translation reduces Luke's *polis* to a "town."

41. *the infant . . . leaped*: The verb *skirtaō* suggests an eschatological recognition (cf. Ps 113:4, 6 [LXX] and Mal 4:2), and alludes to the jostling of Rebecca's children which foretold their later destinies (Gen 25:22). John is thus shown to be a prophet in accord with the angel's prediction in 1:15.

filled with the Holy Spirit: Elizabeth too has the prophetic spirit in order to interpret the significance of her experience and that of Mary as well.

42. *you are blessed*: Elizabeth's prophetic insight is amazing. She knows that Mary has been specially chosen by God, and that her child is special; knows indeed without being told that Mary is pregnant and that Jesus will have a significance even greater than John's.

43. *mother of my Lord*: This is Elizabeth's most dramatic statement, dropped almost casually. "Lord" is a title first of all for God (as already in Luke 1:6, 9, 11, 15, 16, 17, 25). Of Jesus, it is used most properly as a resurrection title (see Acts 1:21; 2:34-36; 4:26, 33; 8:16, etc.). But Luke, even more than Matthew, uses it for Jesus not only as a greeting but also as a title (see Luke 2:11; 7:13; 10:1; 11:39; 12:42; 17:6; 18:6; 19:8, 31; especially 24:3 and 34). At the very least, Elizabeth recognizes the infant as "master," but a deeper dimension is surely implied.

44. *leaped with gladness*: A classic Lukan device is using dialogue to reveal the fuller dimensions of what the narrative has already revealed. Here, the "gladness" of John's leap picks up the note of eschatological "gladness (*agalliasis*)" promised by the angel to greet John's birth (1:14). John, in turn, will announce the eschatological "coming of the Lord" in 3:4-17.

45. *how blessed*: In contrast to verse 42, Luke here uses *makaria* rather than *eulogoumenē*. It can mean "happy," but that misses the resonance of the biblical tradition, which uses the word to denote the condition of righteous existence before God (cf. e.g., Pss 1:1; 2:12; 83:4; 93:12 [LXX]), so that the term becomes almost technical as a "macarism" or "Beatitude"; this is the term used by Jesus in his Beatitudes (6:20-22). Of particular interest is the contrast in Luke 11:27 between "blessed is the womb that bore you" and Jesus' correction, "rather blessed are those who hear the word of God and keep it." In Luke's view, of course, Mary is blessed on both counts.

because: Could also be translated "that." Is Mary praised for the *content* of her faith ("that they would be fulfilled"), or is the fulfillment itself the blessing? Despite 11:27, which would argue the other way, the translation takes the context as stronger support for "because."

reach fulfillment: Literally, "perfection" (in the sense of completion). Notice that in Jdt 10:9 it is used precisely of the fulfillment of a promise.

46. *Mary said*: Some MSS attribute the song to Elizabeth or omit any name, but the majority of MSS support the attribution to Mary, as does the content: notice, for example, how the "all generations will call me blessed" (1:48) picks up the "blessed is the woman" of 1:45.

my soul extols the Lord: Mary's prayer (1:46-55) is called the "Magnificat" because of the Latin translation of the first word. It takes the form of a hymn. Notice the distinguishing mark of Hebrew poetry, the parallelism of members (already in "my soul"/"my spirit"). A framework is provided by Hannah's song in 1 Sam 2:1-10, but Luke enriches the language by allusions to other sources, such as the psalms. .

47. *rejoices in God, my savior*: The term is "gladness" as in 1:14 and 1:44. Luke here introduces the theme of *salvation* which is central to his composition: Jesus also is Savior (2:11), and brings salvation (2:30; 19:9); the message about Jesus preached by the apostles is also salvation (Acts 13:26; 28:28). Although the language of "salvation" is thoroughly at home in Torah (see e.g., Deut 32:15; Ps 34:3 [LXX]), Luke's use of it would have been particularly appreciated by Hellenistic readers, for whom both gods and sages could wear the title *sotēr* (see e.g., Dio Chrysostom, *Oration* 12:74; 32:18).

48. *lowliness of his servant*: The term "servant" (*doulē*) picks up Mary's self designation in 1:38. "Lowliness" is not simply a mental attitude ("humility") but an objective condition: like those enumerated in her song, Mary occupied a position of poverty and powerlessness in her society. On the other hand, she does also display the "lowliness" that is the opposite of the "arrogance" that God opposes.

49. *great things for me*: Could also be "in me," referring to the conception of the Messiah, but the allusion to Deut 10:21 supports the translation.

51. *power in his right arm*: A dramatic anthropomorphism for God's activity (see Exod 6:6 and Ps 88:11 [LXX]). Together with the previous verse, this statement marks a transition from what God has done with Mary to what he has done in history. The use of past tenses is less a problem than endless scholarly discussions of it might suggest: as God did in the past, he continues to do—age after age.
    arrogant in their understanding: Is a complex phrase in Greek, "arrogant in the understanding of their hearts." Luke uses "heart" to mean the realm of human thought and intention (see e.g., Luke 10:27). If it did not sound so contemporary, "arrogant in their attitude" might best capture what he intends. In Luke's narrative, such arrogance blocks the perception of God's visitation (e.g., Luke 5:21-22, 30; 6:8; 7:39; 13:14; 14:1; 16:15; 18:9). The arrogant are the opposite of the "lowly" (cf. Prov 3:34; Jas 4:6). The pattern of reversal that is here begun corresponds to the "fall and rise of many in Israel" (2:34) fundamental to Luke's narrative.

54. *Israel his child by the hand*: The translation tries to capture the original sense of Israel as God's "child" (*pais*), corresponding to Jesus the child (*huios*), and to continue the metaphoric force of "God's right arm" in 1:51, by emphasizing the "taking hold of" aspect of *antilambanō*, which here means the way he "looks after" or "takes care of" Israel.
    remembering his mercy: Picks up 1:50, and is another anthropomorphism frequently used of God in Torah (e.g., Gen 8:1; 9:15; 19:29, etc.) for the idea of "remembering mercy," see Pss 24:6-7; 97:3 [LXX]).

55. *to Abraham and his descendants*: The translation takes "just as he said" as a parenthetical statement, although in the Greek it comes between "remembering mercy" and "to Abraham," making the syntax complicated. The significance of God's promise to Abraham and "his seed" (the literal rendering) is considerable in Luke-Acts (see 1:73; 3:8; 19:9, and esp. Acts 3:25; 7:2-17). The "forever" picks up the "generation after generation" in 1:50. That God does in fact fulfill his promises "just as he spoke" long ago (in this case to Abraham in Gen 12:2-3;

15:5; 17:7-8; 18:18; 22:17) is the essential message of Luke's narrative for Gentile Christian readers.

INTERPRETATION

Several aspects of Luke's literary art are displayed in this lovely encounter between two strong women. The first is the way Luke can take short vignettes and work them into a longer, sustained narrative. Here he brings characters from the two annunciation accounts together. There is no significant action (Mary goes and returns), only dialogue, but the result is a sense of amplitude in a narrative otherwise episodic. The passage shows us as well how Luke uses dialogue to advance the story, or, more properly, to advance the reader's understanding of the story. Notice how Elizabeth knows (and reveals to the reader as she speaks to Mary) dimensions of Mary's condition and Jesus' status previously undisclosed. The resumptive character of such dialogue also enables Luke to emphasize how previously stated prophecies have been fulfilled, and future ones will be (1:41, 45).

This passage is dominated by the song of Mary, which shows us another important Lukan compositional technique, one he shares with all Hellenistic historians, namely the use of speeches (cf. Lucian, *How to Write History*, 58). In his *Peloponnesian War*, Thucydides would report not a verbatim account of what a particular Greek general said before battle, but rather an idealized version of what he should have said to properly represent Hellenic virtues (cf. e.g., I, 5, 139–46; IV, 14, 126–127). In similar fashion, Luke uses speeches to proclaim what was appropriate to a particular event. By *prosōpopoeia*, we notice, he has Mary's canticle imitate a scriptural prototype. But he also uses the speech to interpret the meaning of narrative events.

In the Magnificat, Mary's praise for what God had done to her personally widens out to include what God does for "all who fear him" in every age, including what God is doing for Israel by the birth of its Messiah. As God "showed power in his right hand" by his mighty works in the past, so does he now "take Israel by the hand." The song moves in stages from the reversal of Mary's condition from lowliness to exaltation (1:46-49), then to a general statement of God's mercy to those who fear him (1:50), then to a recital of his past and present reversals (1:51-53), finally to the statement of how that mercy is now being shown to Israel in fulfillment of God's promise to Abraham (1:54-55).

As the song moves outward, it also unfolds a density of symbolism. One cannot avoid the sense that Mary is here made the representative if not the personification of "Israel." The mercy shown her reflects and exemplifies the mercy shown to the people. The representative symbolism of Mary is stated even more clearly later in the infancy account (in 2:34). We notice as well that the epithets applied to God in the song are attributes as well of the son she is carrying. God is called "Lord" and "Savior" and "Holy." So Jesus has already been called "holy" (1:34), and "lord" (1:43), and will shortly be termed "savior" as well (2:11). As with name, so with function: God reverses human status and perception: in a downward movement, he scatters the arrogant, pulls down the mighty, sends the rich away empty. But God also, in an upward movement, exalts the lowly, fills the hungry, and takes the hand of Israel. Precisely such a reversal is announced by Jesus in his Beatitudes and woes (6:20-26), and is enacted by him in the narrative of his ministry.

FOR REFERENCE AND FURTHER STUDY

Dahl, N. A. "The Story of Abraham in Luke-Acts." *Studies in Luke-Acts*. Ed. L. Keck and J. L. Martyn (Philadelphia: Fortress, 1966) 139–158.
Jones, D. "The Background and Character of the Lukan Psalms." *JTS* 19 (1968) 19–50.
Tannehill, R. "The Magnificat as Poem." *JBL* 93 (1974) 263–275.
Winter, P. "Magnificat and Benedictus—Maccabean Psalms?" *BJRL* 37 (1954) 328–347.

5. *Prophecy Fulfilled: John's Birth* (1:57-80)

57. Elizabeth completed her pregnancy and gave birth to a son. 58. Her neighbors and relatives heard that God had shown her great mercy, and they celebrated with her. 59. On the eighth day they came to circumcise the little boy. They were already calling him by the name of his father Zechariah. 60. But his mother responded, "No, he will be called John." 61. They said to her, "None of your relatives is called by this name." 62. They made gestures to his father to find out what he wanted the child called. 63. He asked for a tablet. He wrote on it, His name is John. Everyone was astonished. 64. Immediately his mouth was opened, and his tongue loosened. He broke into speech, praising God. 65. Their neighbors felt fear. All these events were discussed through the entire hill country of Judea. 66. Everyone who heard took it to heart. They said, "What, then, will this child be?" And the hand of the Lord was with him. 67. His father Zechariah was filled with the Holy Spirit, and gave this prophecy: 68. "Blessed be the Lord the God of Israel, because he has visited and redeemed his people. 69. In the house of David his child he has raised a horn for our salvation 70. just as from long ago he spoke through his holy prophets: 71. to save us from our enemies and from the power of all who hate us, 72. thereby showing mercy toward our ancestors and remembering his holy covenant 73. which he swore by oath to Abraham our father; and, to give us this gift: 74. that having been delivered from the grasp of our enemies, we might worship him

fearlessly 75. in holiness and righteousness before him all our lives. 76. And you, child, will be called a prophet of the Most High. You will go before the Lord to prepare his ways, 77. in order to give his people knowledge of salvation by the forgiveness of their sins 78. through the merciful compassion of our God. By his compasssion also a dawning from on high will visit us, 79. to shine light on those sitting in darkness and the shadow of death, and to guide our feet onto the path of peace." 80. The child grew and became strong in the spirit. He stayed in desert places until the time of his manifestation to Israel.

NOTES

59. *on the eighth day*: As in 1:6 and 2:22-23, Luke shows the parents of John and Jesus as observant of Torah; see Gen 17:12 and Lev 12:3.

    already calling him: The "already" is supplied, taking the imperfect tense of the verb as continuous rather than conative ("they wanted to call him"), in order to give substance to Elizabeth's "response."

62. *made gestures*: Notice the deference shown the father in this patriarchal setting! The imperfect tense suggests an elaborate pantomime. Luke is expert at these small humorous touches; cf. Rhoda at the door in Acts 12:13-16.

64. *was loosened*: Is added by the translation to compensate for the truncation of the Greek: "his mouth was opened and his tongue."

65. *felt fear*: As we have seen already (1:12, 30), the response of fear (or perhaps better, "awe") to a marvelous event is standard in Luke-Acts (see 2:9; 5:10, 26; 7:16; 8:25, 35; 9:34; Acts 2:43; 5:5, 11; 9:26; 19:17).

    events were discussed: Another standard Lukan response. News of wonders spreads quickly throughout the Gospel (see 2:17-18, 38; 4:37; 5:15; 7:17; 8:36, 39; 24:18), which accords with Luke's portrayal of Jesus' ministry as one carried out "before all the people" (Acts 2:22).

    hand of the Lord: Another anthropomorphism (cf. "the right arm" in 1:51), for God's power and guidance (see e.g., Exod 6:1; 7:4; Ps 74:8 [LXX]). Note the subtle difference in what is said of Jesus in Acts 10:38, "God was with him."

67. *gave this prophecy*: Literally, "prophesied," which he is able to do because he is "filled with the Holy Spirit." What follows is a classic example of a "programmatic prophecy": it guides the reader's understanding of the narrative to follow.

68. *Blessed be*: Verses 68–75 follow the pattern of the Jewish blessing prayer, the *berakah*. An initial statement of praise is followed by the reasons for the praise. Often this is followed by another blessing formula, but here there is a shift to the direct address of the child (verses 76–79).

    visited and redeemed his people: The focus, as we have seen before, is on "Israel" as the people of God. The term "visit" (*episkeptein*) occurs in Torah for God's historical interventions (see Gen 21:1; 50:24; Exod 4:31; Ruth 1:6; Ps 105:4 [LXX]), and is used by Luke in the same sense (see Luke 1:78; 7:16; 19:44; Acts 7:23;

15:14); the number of citations is not large, but they all occur in critical places. The religious meaning of "redemption" derives from the ransoming of a slave, or the paying off of a pledge. In contrast to the "liberation" of the people from Egypt under Moses, however (Acts 7:35), Luke here defines it in apolitical, cultic terms.

69. *raised a horn for our salvation*: At the literal level, one is tempted to render this, "lifted a trumpet to announce salvation," but the biblical precedents for *keras* make it likely that "horn" here means a symbol of power (like a sceptre), as in Ps 17:3 (LXX), where "horn of salvation" is in apposition to "rock" and "refuge" and "strength." The Greek of 1 Sam 2:10 clinches the matter. And since this horn is raised "in the house of David" the allusion is clearly also messianic.

70. *as he spoke through his holy prophets*: The theme of fulfillment is struck again: what is happening now is an enactment of God's promising word in the past. The wording here is similar to that in Acts 1:16; 3:18, and especially—because of its awkwardness—4:25. From this point on the translation of the canticle is difficult because the clauses of a single long sentence are interrelated in a way hard to render gracefully in English.

73. *by oath to Abraham*: The covenant remembered by God is not the one through Moses, but through Abraham in Gen 22:17, and appeal to it is critical in Acts 3:25, for it makes the first Christians in effect the "seed of Abraham" to whom the blessings are delivered. As with Paul in Gal 3:6-18, the covenant with Abraham is more fundamental than the Mosaic covenant. For the importance of the "oath," cf. Heb 6:13-18.

and to give us this gift: Literally only "to give us." The canticle has defined liberation negatively as "freedom from enemies" and now turns to the positive content of salvation.

74. *worship him fearlessly*: Such a sentiment would fit a priest like Zechariah, so the verse shows *prosōpopoeia*. But it also corresponds with Luke's own view of the Church as a worshipping community, as in Luke 24:52-53; Acts 2:42-47; 4:23-31; 13:1-3; 20:7-12.

75. *in holiness and righteousness*: These terms show that worship means internal dispositions as well as ritual actions; so does the qualification "all our lives." *Hosiotēs* has the sense of "piety" rather than that of "separateness," and as elsewhere, Luke means "righteousness" (*dikaiosynē*) less in the "strong" Pauline sense than as a virtue (cf. e.g., Acts 10:35; 24:25). His use of "righteous" on the other hand, is more flexible.

76. *and you, child*: Zechariah communicates to the baby what he (and the readers) learned in 1:15-17, but with a significant addition. This is a favorite Lukan technique, to expand through recapitulation (cf. Acts 10–15).

77. *knowledge of salvation*: The meaning of a "prepared people" in 1:17 is specified in terms of the "forgiveness of sins." Luke prepares the reader for the ministry of John in 3:3. More than any other NT author, Luke makes "forgiveness of sins" a concomitant and sign of salvation (Luke 3:3; 4:18; 5:20- 21, 23-24; 7:48-49; 11:4; 17:4; 23:34(!); Acts 2:38; 5:31; 10:43; 13:38; 26:18(!).

78. *the merciful compassion of our God*: This phrase awkwardly bridges two Greek phrases. The translation tidies a messy syntax by dividing into separate sentences. The thought is clear enough: all is accomplished by God's mercy (see 1:58 above). The term "visitation" is the same as in 1:68, but this time is in the future rather than the past, suggesting it is the Messiah who is meant.

    a dawning from on high: A clumsy rendering of a dense and poetic phrase. "From on high" means simply "from God" as the phrase which so closely parallels this one in Luke 24:49 makes clear. The term "dawn" (*anatolē*) occurs three times in the LXX of the prophets to translate the Hebrew term "branch" or "scion," in each case with a messianic connotation, most clearly in Jer 23:5, "I will raise up for David a righteous branch" (see also Zech 3:8; 6:12). Luke may well be making a messianic allusion, and if so the reference for Luke would obviously be to the birth of Jesus, in which also "light from on high" is seen (2:9). *Anatolē* most frequently is used as "dawn" and as such propels the metaphor which is carried into the next phrases.

79. *those sitting in darkness and the shadow of death*: The entire phrase comes from LXX Ps 106:10, 14, a thanksgiving psalm in which the reversal worked by God holds a prominent place. For "feet onto the path of peace," see Isa 59:8, and for the theme of "peace" (*eirēnē*) in Luke-Acts, see 2:14, 29; 7:50; 8:48; 19:38, 42; Acts 7:26; 10:36.

80. *the child grew*: With this short phrase, Luke prepares the reader for the reappearance of John "in desert places" in 3:2.

INTERPRETATION

The passage provides a hinge in the infancy narrative. It has the fulfillment of one prophecy and the declaration of another. The birth of John gives Luke the chance to compose one of the delightful scenes for which he is rightly renowned. The entire point is that the prophecy of the angel Gabriel was fulfilled, and was so despite human resistence. Despite the charm of the village scene, an important Lukan perception of history is conveyed: God and humans sometimes work at cross-purposes, but what God wills reaches accomplishment in the end (cf. e.g., Acts 5:35-39). In this case, the social pressure to name the child after his father is resisted by Elizabeth, and then by Zechariah. When he finally consents to God's instruction, his punishment is lifted, and he is free to speak. His first words are in praise of God. Luke has thereby made the experience of Zechariah a miniature enactment of his canticle: God's mercy liberates the people to worship fearlessly; Zechariah's release from muteness is expressed in praise.

The second half of the passage is entirely taken up by the canticle. Although it could have been placed in verse 64, Luke skillfully moves it to a place of emphasis, so that it points forward to the story that follows.

In contrast to Mary's canticle which moved out from her experience to the work of God in history, Zechariah's begins with the visitation of the people and then focuses on the specific role of John as "prophet of the Most High." In his words to John, we see again Luke's technique of expanding the point of his narrative through dialogue: Zechariah basically repeats what he had been told by the angel, but adds greater detail.

The canticle gives the reader the first sure sense of what "liberation" means for Luke. It is defined in specifically "religious" rather than political terms. Negatively defined, freedom means release from the power of enemies. But its positive content is worship and holiness of life. Thus John's role in preparing the people for "restoration" involves the forgiveness of sins rather than the rallying of troops. Likewise the Messiah's role is not one of violent revolt but rather of leading the people "in the path of peace."

If the "dawning from on high" is—as seems most likely—a reference to Jesus as Messiah, it is a marvellous metaphor. It balances the brute force suggested by the "horn of salvation." The horn is "raised," in an upward movement; the dawn is "from on high," in a downward movement. The horn is within the house of David, and could be understood as a political force. But the dawn is "from on High" which denotes the power of God for a salvation greater than freedom from enemies, freedom from the "shadow of death" itself.

The last statement implies a certain universality and ultimacy with respect to the Messiah. But this part of Luke's story remains deeply rooted in the ethos and symbolism of Judaism. The parents of John are punctilious in observing the Law, as their performance of the ritual of circumcision demonstrates. How fitting for Zechariah to celebrate "the oath sworn to Abraham" on the occasion of a circumcision! And how appropriate that the "hope for salvation" be expressed by the symbols of the people. Only when Luke has shown how this salvation has in fact been accomplished (in his account of the first community in Jerusalem) can he develop the world-wide scope of the salvation God intends. If Luke cannot show that "the God of Israel visited and redeemed his people," then the hope of the Gentiles is groundless.

For Reference and Further Study

Benoit, P. "L'Enfance de Jean-Baptiste selon Luc 1." *NTS* 3 (1956–57) 169–194.
Comblin, J. "La Paix dans la Théologie de Saint Luc." *ETL* 32 (1956) 439–460.
George, A. "Israël dans l'Oeuvre de Luc." *RB* 75 (1968) 481–525.
Winter, P. "Some Observations on the Birth and Infancy Narratives of the Third Gospel." *NTS* 1 (1954–5) 111–121.

6. *Prophecy Fulfilled: Jesus' Birth* (2:1-20)

1. During that time a decree was issued by Caesar Augustus to have the whole empire registered. 2. This was the first registration. It happened while Quirinius was governor of Syria. 3. Everyone went to be registered in one's own city. 4. Since he was from the house and lineage of David, Joseph also went up from Galilee to Judea, from the town of Nazareth to the city of David called Bethlehem, 5. to be registered with Mary, his betrothed. She was pregnant. 6. While they were there, the time for her delivery arrived. 7. She gave birth to her first-born son. She wrapped him in cloth strips. She placed him in a manger because they had no place in the lodging area. 8. There were shepherds in the same area. They were in the open fields keeping watch at night over their flock. 9. An angel of the Lord came and stood by them. The glory of the Lord shone around them. They were terrified. 10. The angel said to them, "Fear no longer! I am announcing to you good news that will be a great joy for all the people. 11. Today in the city of David a savior was born for you. He is Lord Messiah. 12. Here is a sign for you: you will find an infant wrapped in cloth strips and lying in a manger." 13. Immediately a crowd of the heavenly army joined the angel, praising God. They said, 14. "Glory in the highest places to God! On Earth, peace for God's favored persons!" 15. As the angels withdrew into heaven, the shepherds said to each other, "Let us go to Bethlehem and see this accomplished word that the Lord made known to us." 16. They went quickly. They found Mary and Joseph, and the infant lying in the manger. 17. When they had seen, they spoke publicly concerning the word that had been spoken to them about this little child. 18. Everyone who heard was astonished at the things told them by the shepherds. 19. Mary preserved all these words, pondering them in her heart. 20. The shepherds went back, glorifying and praising God for everything they had heard and seen, just as had been spoken to them.

Notes

1. *the whole empire*: As in 1:5, Luke connects his drama to the wider world-stage. The term *oikoumenē* can mean "known world" but the context demands the translation "empire." Luke's attempt at synchronism is not entirely successful, as endless technical discussions have made clear. Herod died in 4 B.C.E., and Augustus was emperor from 27 B.C.E. to 14 C.E. So far, so good. But Quirinius was governor in Syria from 6–7 C.E., and the gap can't be filled. Luke simply has the facts wrong. For another reference to the census (and another disputed sequence) cf. Acts 5:37.

4. *house and lineage of David*: The translation rearranges the clauses with greater than usual liberty. As in 1:27, 32, 69 and 2:11, David is drawn into the account at every opportunity, giving an important clue to the point of the passage. "Lineage" is *patria*, which in Tob 5:12 and Jdt 8:2 appears as a subdivision of the *phylē*, or tribe.

5. *with Mary his betrothed*: Luke avoids calling Mary Joseph's wife, even though the state of betrothal allowed that designation (see note on 1:27). The placement of this phrase could modify "went up" but more naturally goes with "was registered"; we cannot, on this account, draw conclusions about Mary's Davidic lineage.

7. *first-born son*: The term *prōtotokos* does not demand more than one child. Here, the designation sets up the presentation of Jesus as Mary's first child in 2:22-24. For the religious resonances of "first-born" with reference to Israel, cf. Exod 4:22-23; Jer 31:9.

   wrapped him in cloth strips: It is almost impossible to dislodge the "swaddling clothes" of the KJV. Strips or bands of cloths were wrapped around a newborn to keep the limbs straight by means of restraint. The *pannus* used in the Vulgate seems to suggest "rags."

   placed him in a manger: This could be an open feeding area, or a feeding trough for animals. As for the "lodging area" (*kataluma*) it is used in Luke 22:11 for space in a house, but it could also refer to the area where travellers and their animals gathered in the open. In either case, the transient condition of the parents is clear. The tradition of the animals at the crib derives from Isa 1:3, and is reflected in apocryphal infancy accounts.

9. *glory of the Lord*: Luke exploits the sense of splendor in the Greek word *doxa* which was used to translate the Hebrew *kabod*; see Exod 16:10; 24:17; Ps 101:16 [LXX]. Here is the fulfillment of the "dawning from on high" promised by Zechariah's canticle (1:78).

   they were terrified: A not unnatural response. For the fear engendered by the "glory of God," see Isa 6:1-5 and Luke 8:34.

10. *announcing good news*: See the note on 1:19 for the way Luke uses the term *euangelizomai* thematically throughout Luke-Acts. "For all the people" here means Israel, not "all peoples"; Luke uses *laos* in the sense it usually has for him.

11. *Lord Messiah*: To the title of Savior (see note on 1:47), Luke adds *Christos* and *Kyrios*. Neither is given the definite article, which makes the precise rendering of them problematic. The translation reverses the order of the Greek to put the English emphasis on Messiah, making "Lord" something of an honorific, like "master." This might better capture the sense appropriate to the birth narrative. Notice that after the resurrection, Luke himself reverses the titles to "Lord and Messiah" in Acts 2:36. Even in the present passage, of course, Luke himself probably took both terms in their full valence.

12. *a sign for you*: The sign here is not the child's circumstances as such but the fact that the angel's description of the circumstances will prove accurate. The fulfillment of this small prophecy helps validate the prophecy about Jesus' future significance for the people.

13. *the heavenly army*: For the phrase, see 2 Chr 33:3; Neh 9:6; Jer 8:2.

14. *glory in the highest places*: The echo of this refrain is sounded in Luke's account of Jesus entering Jerusalem proclaimed as king, but with a significant alteration: "in heaven peace and glory in the high places" (19:38).

peace for God's favored persons: That the Messiah would lead the people on the "paths of peace" was prophesied by Zechariah in 1:79. The term *eudokia* ("good will" or "favor") is variously in the nominative or genitive cases in ancient manuscripts. In either case, it clearly refers not to a human quality ("good-will") that generates peace, but to a disposition of God toward humans; see Luke 3:22 and 10:21 for other examples. In spite of its awkwardness, the translation uses "persons" for two reasons. The first is to avoid needless exclusionary language (as in "men of good will"); the second is to make clear that "people" here does not use Luke's word *laos*, in contrast to 2:10.

15. *accomplished word*: A better English rendering would be, "the thing that happened." The translation is over-literal to capture two nuances. The first is that Luke uses *rhēma* here and later in the passage (2:17, 19). It can mean both "thing" and "word" (see also 1:37-38), but in this case, the *verbal* aspect predominates and is essential to the prophecy-fulfillment pattern Luke is using. The second nuance is the perfect use of *ginomai*, which in this place seems to demand the sense of "accomplished" (compare Luke 8:34-35; Acts 4:21; 5:7).

17. *they spoke publicly*: Literally, "they made known," using the same word, *gnōrizō*, as in 2:15. For the thoroughly public character of Luke's narrative, see note on 1:65, and Paul's statement in Acts 26:26, "None of this happened in a corner."

19. *Mary preserved all these words*: The term *rhēma* is used here as in 2:15, and with the same ambiguity.

    pondering them: The term *symballō* means literally to "throw together" and is used variously, e.g., "discussing" or "comparing." Luke uses it later in the sense of "debate" or "discuss" (see 11:53; Acts 4:15; 17:18; 18:27). A mental process is clearly intended here, as in 2:51.

INTERPRETATION

For a variety of quite natural reasons, this passage is one of the most over-interpreted in the New Testament, making it difficult to sort out what comments are helpful to the reader who wants to understand how Luke constructs his overall story in order to accomplish certain religious goals.

To obsess over Luke's chronological accuracy in dating the birth of Jesus, for example, is to miss the point of his attempt at synchronism, and is of real importance only if factual accuracy in every detail were critical to a narrator's overall credibility. Certainly, on the basis of exhaustive research, Luke's dates seem out of kilter: Quirinius and the census under him do not match the other dates. Luke should not, on that account, be read out of court as a historian. He could not, in the first place, have had available to him the materials that exhaustive research has made accessible to contemporary historians.

More importantly, an obsession with accuracy leads the reader astray. Luke needs the emperor and a census in the picture, because he needs to get Joseph and Mary to Bethlehem. He needs to get them to Bethlehem both because a shared tradition placed Jesus' birth there in the time of Herod (cf. Matt 2:1-6), and because birth in the city of David was important as a messianic credential. We are dealing, in other words, not with a scientifically determined chronology, but with purposeful storytelling.

When we read the story as Luke's literary creation, we are better able to appreciate its deceptively simple depth. No need to dwell overlong on the prophecy-fulfillment motif, although Luke employs it again here with almost metronomic predictability: what the angel announces, the shepherds see, what they see they report, and it is all as "was spoken to them" (2:20). As in the annunciations to Zechariah and Mary, the angelic presence and prophecy gives a divine legitimation not only to the events but to the interpretation of them in the narrative itself. The opening of the heavens and the disclosure of the angelic worship (2:13) establish for the reader both that this is a narrative with transcendental dimensions (events in heaven and earth impinge each on the other), and that traffic can move both ways between these realms (as with Jesus' ascension, Acts 1:9-11).

The portrayal of Mary and Joseph is consistent with the earlier narrative. They belong, through Joseph, to the house of David—in which the "horn of Salvation" will arise (1:69)—so that Jesus is certifiably "son of David," as well as "son of God." They are simple people who are obedient to authority. The command of the empire does not stir them to join revolt; rather they obey the decree, in contrast to Luke's mention of Judas the Galilean who revolted "at the time of the census" (Acts 5:37). They are also portrayed as being among the poor of the land. However we construe the manger and the lodge and the wrapping bands put on the baby and the visit by shepherds, there is no doubt concerning Luke's portrayal of the economic or social level of Jesus' first companions. Perhaps the shepherds are not to be assessed as "sinners" as they are in the later rabbinic materials (cf. e.g., *m.Qidd.* 4:14; *m.Bab.Qam.* 10:9), but they are certainly among the lowest-esteemed laborers. Mary and Joseph, in turn, are transients, equivalent to "the homeless" of contemporary city streets, people who lack adequate shelter.

The contrast, then, between the angelic panoply and the earthly reality is sharp; no wonder Mary "turned these events over" in her heart, seeking to understand them. Nothing very glorious is suggested by the circumstances of the Messiah's birth. But that is Luke's manner, to show how God's fidelity is worked out in human events even when appearances seem to deny his presence or power. The reader is correct, therefore, to see subtle intimations of a greater reality in this humble recital. Certainly the choice of shepherds is not accidental; they gather to see the "son of David" who was in tradition the shepherd of the flock of Israel (1 Sam 16:11; 17:15; 2 Sam 5:2), as was also to be his messianic successor (Jer 3:15; Ezek 34:11-12; Mic 5:4).

The reader might even be moved to reflect over the deeper dimensions of the "sign" given by the angel (2:12). In the notes I suggest it is not the circumstances of the child but the angel's description of them that functions as the sign. Yet, is there perhaps another dimension to the odd details enumerated by Luke? Can the threefold, deliberate phrasing in the Greek of, "wrapped him in cloth strips, placed him in a manger, because there was no place" perhaps anticipate the same threefold rhythm of "wrapped him in linen cloth, placed him in a rock-hewn tomb, where no one had yet been laid" (23:53) so that birth and burial mirror each other?

For Reference and Further Study

Brown, R. E. "The Meaning of the Manger; the Significance of the Shepherds." *Worship* 50 (1976) 528–538.

Fitzmyer, J. A. "Peace upon Earth among Men of His Good Will." *TS* 19 (1958) 225–227.

Giblin, C. H. "Reflections on the Sign of the Manger." *CBQ* 29 (1967) 87–101.

Legrand, L. "L'évangile aux bergers: Essai sur le genre Littéraire de Luc, II, 8–20." *RB* 75 (1968) 161–187.

Meyer, B. F. " 'But Mary Kept all these Things . . .' (Luke 2:19, 51)." *CBQ* 26 (1964) 31–49.

Moehring, H. R. "The Census in Luke As an Apologetic Device." *Studies in New Testament and Early Christian Literature; Essays in Honor of Allen P. Wikgren.* Ed. D. Aune (NovTSupp. 33; Leiden: Brill, 1972) 144–160.

7. Jesus Is Presented to the Lord (2:21-40)

21. After eight days, the child was circumcised and called Jesus, the name given by the angel before he was conceived. 22. When it came time for their purification as the Law of Moses commanded, they brought him up to Jerusalem to present him to the Lord, 23. according to the prescription in the Lord's Law that "every first-born male will be called holy to the Lord," 24. and to offer a sacrifice according to the statement in the Lord's Law, "a pair of turtledoves or two young pigeons." 25. In Jerusalem, there was a man named Simeon. He was a righteous man and pious. He was awaiting a comfort for Israel. The Holy Spirit was upon him. 26. It was revealed to him by the Holy Spirit that he would not die before seeing the Lord's Messiah. 27. Under the influence of the Spirit, he came into the temple grounds. When he met the child Jesus' parents as they were performing the customary legal obligations concerning him, 28. Simeon took the child in his arms. He blessed God in this fashion: 29. "Now, Master, you re-

lease your servant in peace, according to your word, 30. for my eyes have seen the salvation 31. you have prepared in the sight of all the peoples: 32. a light for revelation to the Gentiles, and a glory for your people Israel." 33. His father and mother were astonished at the things being said about him. 34. Simeon blessed them. He said to Mary his mother, "Behold, this child is destined to cause the fall and the rise of many within Israel, and to be a sign that is disputed 35. —indeed, a sword will cut through your very life—so that the calculations of many hearts will be revealed." 36. There also was Anna, a prophetess, a daughter of Phanuel of the tribe of Aser. She had grown very elderly. She had lived seven years with a husband after her marriage, 37. and as a widow some eighty-four years. She never left the temple grounds. She worshipped night and day with fastings and prayers. 38. She arrived at that very moment, and offered up praises to God. She kept speaking about him to all those awaiting a liberation for Jerusalem. 39. When they completed everything demanded by the Lord's Law, they returned to Galilee and their own town, Nazareth. 40. The child grew and continued to grow strong. He was full of wisdom, and God's favor was upon him.

NOTES

21. *was called*: Another match between Jesus and John (see 1:59). The naming this time goes smoothly, according to the portrayal of Jesus' parents as obedient to God's directions.

22. *their purification*: Actually, the law for purification after childbirth in Lev 12:2-5 applies only to the woman; for this reason, some MSS change "their" to "her." Although Luke has previously mentioned the "commandments" (1:6), this is the first time he mentions the "Law of Moses" or the "Lord's Law." Remarkably, of his nine uses of the term in the Gospel, five occur in this passage (2:22, 23, 24, 27, 39; see also 10:26; 16:16-17; 24:44).

23. *first-born male*: Literally, "every male opening the womb"; the prescription of Exod 13:2 is worked into the narrative of the people's liberation, in which the role of "first-borns" is obviously important (see also Exod 13:12, 15).

   holy to the Lord: As the angel had said in 1:35, "he will be called holy." Luke clearly understands this at a level other than that of ritual dedication.

24. *a pair of turtledoves*: According to Lev 12:6, the woman is to offer a year-old lamb and either a turtledove or pigeon for her purification, but if she is poor (according to Lev 12:8) she can make the offering described by Luke. The parents are again portrayed as among the poor of the land.

25. *he was awaiting a comfort*: Like the other characters in the infancy account, Simeon is described as righteous and "pious" (*eulabēs*; for Luke's understanding of it, see Acts 22:12). He is also "expectant," a term Luke uses in his narrative for those positively disposed and open to God's visitation (see 2:38; 23:51; Acts 24:15). The terms "comfort" or "consolation" is *paraklēsis*, which Luke uses in two other significant contexts, 6:24 and 16:25.

the Holy Spirit: As throughout the infancy account, this is the spirit of prophecy (cf. 1:15, 17, 41, 67). Luke makes Simeon's prophetic role unmistakable: he has the Spirit upon him (v. 25), receives revelations from the Spirit (v. 26), and comes into the temple "in the Spirit" (v. 27); for a similar sequence applied to Jesus, see Luke 4:1, 14.

26. *revealed to him*: The term *chrēmatizō* is found frequently in Hellenistic literature for oracles; it is used of the revelations to Joseph in Matt 2:12, 22, and of an angelic revelation in Acts 10:22.

    the Lord's Messiah: Luke retains an archaic sense of "anointed" for the title of Messiah, as can be seen in 4:18, and in Peter's confession, "the Messiah of God" (8:20). The similarity of the present phrase to that in the angel's proclamation of "Lord Messiah" (2:11) probably accounts for the textual variants in that place.

27. *the temple grounds*: Luke uses the term *hieron*, which includes the entire temple area, instead of *naos*, which means the sanctuary accessible only to priests (see Luke 1:9, 21, 22). Simeon could have met a woman only in these outer precincts; cf. Lev 12:6, "she shall bring to the priest at the door of the tent."

    customary legal obligations: the use of "customary" is an important clue to Luke's view of the continuing role of the Law vis-à-vis Jew and Gentile, as his story develops through Acts.

29. *now you release*: The "now" is emphatic, pointing to the moment of receiving Jesus in his arms. "Servant" (*doulos*) is correlative to "master" (*despotēs*, here and Acts 4:24). The image, therefore, is one of manumission.

    in peace . . . your word: For the theme of peace in Luke-Acts, see note on 1:79 In this case, Simeon is one of those "favored by God" to whom the Messiah's birth brings peace, as the angel announced (2:14); thus, "according to your word" not only by personal revelation but also in the narrative.

30. *the salvation*: Another important theme in Luke-Acts; for the texts, see the note on 1:47. In this case, the child Jesus *is* the salvation (cf. 1:69 and 2:11), as the etymology of Joshua/Jesus suggests: "Yahweh Saves."

32. *light of revelation for Gentiles*: *Ethnōn* could mean nations but is being distinguished from the "people Israel" so must mean Gentiles as people. This is a programmatic prophecy, using the language of Isa 42:6 and 49:6 originally applied to the Servant of the Lord. Luke applies the epithet to Paul as he begins his explicit move to the Gentiles in Acts 13:47.

    glory for your people Israel: Another citation from Isaiah's Servant Songs, this time 46:13, "I will put my salvation in Zion, for Israel my glory." The term "glory" connotes both the presence and splendor of God rather than the "reputation" of Israel.

34. *this child is destined*: Literally, "this one lies (*keimai*)," which suggests the placing of an object.

    to cause the fall and the rise: The image is that of the stone of stumbling in Isa 8:14-15, which is appropriated by Luke in 20:17-18. The spatial movement of falling and rising is the same as in the Magnificat (1:51-53).

a sign that is disputed: The verb *antilegō* is used by Luke of those who "resist" or "oppose" (see 20:27; Acts 13:45; 28:19, 22). The prophetic image here suggested, therefore, is this: Jesus is within the people a stone of stumbling, a sign to create opposition, and in response to him the people will be divided, some falling and some rising.

35. *sword through your very life*: The noun *psychē*, ("life,") can also mean "soul." The syntax here is difficult. The translation retains the structure of the Greek, with the personal statement to Mary (with singular and feminine pronouns) interrupting the broader proclamation concerning Jesus. This sandwich effect makes the two statements mutually interpretive.

    calculations of many hearts: With the exception of 1:29 and 3:15, the term *dialogismos* and its verbal equivalent defines the mental process of those actively opposed to Jesus (see 5:21-22; 6:8; 9:46-47; 12:17; 20:14; for the oddness of 24:38, see the note on that verse). That a prophet can read people's hearts is axiomatic, as we learn in Luke 7:39-40.

36. *Anna, a prophetess*: It is Luke's habit to pair a female character with a male character even when, as in this case, her testimony adds nothing specific to what has already been established.

    marriage: Literally, "her time of virginity."

37. *never left the temple grounds*: May be hyperbole and need not suggest that Anna lived there. For such a practice in legend, cf. the *Protevangelium of James* 7:1-8:2. "Fastings and prayers" are classic expressions of piety, as in Acts 13:3; 14:23; see also Matt 6:5, 16.

38. *a liberation for Jerusalem*: Notice that Luke sees "Israel" (2:32, 34) and "Jerusalem" as symbolically synonymous; for "liberation" (*lytrōsis*) see 1:68 ("the people") and esp. 24:21 ("Israel").

40. *the child grew*: This mirrors the statement about John in 1:80, and will be amplified in the story which follows in 2:41-52. The description of Jesus parallels that of Moses in Acts 7:22. For the distinctive note of "grace" with respect to Jesus, see 2:52 and 4:22.

INTERPRETATION

In Luke's story, the Messiah will emerge from within a family and social world deeply enmeshed in the traditions of Israel, a pious and expectant "people of God." His parents observe the laws regarding circumcision, purification, and presentation of the first born as dedicated to the Lord, and do so within the symbolic heart of the people, Jerusalem and its Temple.

The special role of this child is also defined by the encounter with Simeon. Not only is the old man elaborately designated as a reliable prophetic spokesperson, but his actions and words together enact Luke's distinctive prophecy-fulfillment literary pattern. Luke establishes first that Simeon was expecting the "consolation" of Israel, and that he was promised to see the

Messiah before death. He takes the child in his arms. At that moment he praises God for "keeping his word." The child himself, we are to understand, *is* the consolation that Simeon was awaiting.

Simeon's prophetic song, like those of Zechariah and Mary, extends this personal gift to a proclamation concerning Jesus' significance for the wider world. In this case the prophecy is programmatic for the entire subsequent narrative, and therefore is of particular importance for guiding the reader's understanding of the story.

In his blessing, Simeon enunciates the positive, overall significance of Jesus. This is the salvation prepared by God "before all the peoples." Here this means all the people of the earth. The statement of "salvation" (using *sōtērion*) is resumed at the very end of Acts, when Paul states that "this salvation (*sōtērion*) of God has been sent also to the Gentiles, and they will listen" (Acts 28:28). Simeon therefore presents an overview of the entire story, although in the opposite order. Jesus will be the "glory" for Israel before the message about him is proclaimed as "light of revelation for Gentiles."

The positive picture appropriate to the prayer of blessing is modified in the abrupt declaration to Jesus' mother. As in the Magnificat, Mary is here portrayed as a personification of the people Israel. Israel will be divided, and so will Mary's life be run through by a sword. The statement is highly elliptical, and is developed no further; it is not susceptible to psychological analysis. Its awkward syntactical placement demands that we take it as a stark symbolic representation. At the level of human drama, the revelatory significance of Jesus will not be obvious to all, nor accepted by all. Jesus will be a sign of contradiction. He is destined to create a division within the people Israel, so that some fall and some rise. Together these positive and negative prophecies shape the reader's perception of Luke's Gospel narrative.

We learn at once, furthermore, that Luke is making a fundamental alteration to the model of prophetic rejection that he displays in the story of Moses and that structures his two-volume work. According to that model, the first visitation by the prophet to the people is one that ends in complete rejection. But Luke will instead show the reader a divided people. Some Jews will receive gladly this first visitation. Indeed, Simeon and Anna symbolize precisely such a welcoming "people of God." From such as these the prophet Jesus will call together the authentic people of God, those who will "rise" within Israel.

FOR REFERENCE AND FURTHER STUDY

Bachmann, M. *Jerusalem und der Tempel: Die geographisch-theologischen Elemente in der lukanischen Sicht des jüdischen Kultsentrums.* BZWANT; Stuttgart: W. Kohlhammer, 1980.

Benoit, P. " 'Et Toi-même, un glaive te transpercera l'âme,' (Luc 2,35)." *CBQ* 25 (1963) 251–261.

Brown, R. E. "The Presentation of Jesus (Luke 2:22-40)." *Worship* 51 (1977) 2–11.

Dodd, C. H. *According to the Scriptures* (London: James Nisbet and Co., 1952) 41–43.

Grelot, P. "La cantique de Simeon (Luc II, 29-32)." *RB* 93 (1986) 481–509.

Kilpatrick, G. D. "*laoi* at Luke ii.31 and Acts iv.25-27." *JTS* 16 (1965) 127.

8. *Jesus Teaches in the Temple* (2:41-52)

41. His parents were accustomed to travel every year to Jerusalem for the feast of Passover. 42. When he was twelve years old, they went as usual for the feast. 43. But when the festival days were over and they turned for home, the boy Jesus stayed in Jerusalem without his parents' knowing it. 44. They went on the road for a day thinking that he was in their group. They kept seeking him among relatives and acquaintances. 45. When they could not find him, they turned back to Jerusalem to search for him. 46. Three days later, they found him in the temple precincts. He was sitting among the teachers. He was listening to them and questioning them. 47. All those who heard him were amazed at his understanding and his responses. 48. When his parents spotted him, they were utterly astonished. His mother said to him, "Child, why have you treated us this way? Look, your father and I, filled with pain, have been seeking you." 49. He said to them, "Why is it that you have been seeking me? Did you not know that I must involve myself in my father's affairs?" 50. They did not grasp what he said to them. 51. But he went back down with them to Nazareth and remained subject to them. His mother kept all things in her heart. 52. Jesus made progress in wisdom and stature and in favor both with God and with people.

NOTES

41. *were accustomed to travel*: The imperfect tense denotes repeated action. The next verse's "as usual" strengthens the sense of customary practice.

    feast of Passover: Also "unleavened bread" (Luke 22:1), was celebrated for a week in the spring, beginning on 14 Nisan. It is, with Booths and Pentecost, one of the three pilgrimage feasts that pious Jews wished to celebrate in Jerusalem (Deut 16:16; Exod 23:14-15). For the crowds in Jerusalem on such feasts, cf. Josephus, *Jewish War* 6:425-426.

42. *twelve years old*: The age is probably intended to mark Jesus' time to accept adult religious responsibility. According to *Pirke Aboth* 5.21, a child was fit for mishnah at ten and at thirteen for the fulfilling of the commandments, and *m.Nid.* 5:6

says a twelve-year-old boy is responsible for the vows he makes. These texts are late, but Luke's story helps confirm that they reflect traditional perceptions.

43. *stayed in Jerusalem*: The boy remained behind because of his own choice not because of his parents' neglect.

44. *their group*: The term *synodia* suggests a pilgrimage party made up of relatives and neighbors from the same village.

46. *three days later*: Suggests an allusion to the resurrection, even though Luke uses *tritē hēmera* in his passion predictions (9:22; 18:33; cf. 24:7) rather than the phrase used here. See the interpretation section for the argument.

    among the teachers: The title is applied to Jewish teachers only here. Otherwise, Luke applies it to John (3:12) and above all to Jesus (7:40; 8:49; 9:38; 10:25; 11:45; 12:13; 18:18; 19:39). Notice especially its use for his activity in the Temple before his passion (20:21, 28, 39; 21:17; 22:11).

47. *amazed*: The term *existēmi* is a favorite of Luke's to describe a variety of strong emotional responses, as in 8:56; 24:12; Acts 2:7, 12; 8:9, 11, 13; 9:21; 10:45; 12:16.

48. *utterly astonished*: Like *existēmi*, but with perhaps a bit stronger force, the term *ekplessomai* denotes an emotional response (see 4:32; 9:43; Acts 13:12). The translation tries to capture the surprise, shock, and stupefaction suggested by Mary's question and subsequent lack of comprehension.

    filled with pain: Luke uses *odynaomai* for both physical and mental suffering (16:24-25; Acts 20:38). In this case, "filled with anxiety" would certainly be appropriate to the context. Although it is tempting to treat this as the immediate fulfillment of the prophecy made to Mary in 2:35, this event involves both parents and is, perhaps, too personal in scope to function for the sort of "dividing" that the prophecy foretold. But it is possible.

    have been seeking: Here and in the next verse, the translation follows the text of the 26th ed. of Nestle, rather than the present tense found in some ancient MSS. The content of this exchange resembles that at the empty tomb, Luke 24:5.

49. *did you not know*: Has the suggestion that they should have known; cf. the use of *ouk oidate* in 1 Cor 3:16; 6:2.

    my Father's affairs: The point of the statement remains frustratingly obscure. In the Greek, *en tois tou patros mou* is "in the [plural *things* understood] of my Father." What things? What idiom? An argument can be made for three renderings: "My Father's things (i.e., affairs or business)"; "my Father's house"; or "my Father's associates (e.g., relatives)." The argument for the translation is taken up in the interpretation section.

50. *they did not grasp*: The failure to understand during the time of the Messiah's first visitation is thematic (see 8:10; 9:45; 18:34; Acts 3:17; 7:25).

51. *remained subject*: The translation picks up the durative force of the imperfect. For *hypotassomai*, see Luke 10:17, 20; 1 Cor 16:16, and in households, Col 3:18–4:1.

    kept all things: Here and in 2:50 the term *rhēma* recurs, with the same polyvalence as seen earlier in 2:15-17, so that both "words" and "things" are possible translations. The verb "kept" (diatērein) has about the same sense as that used in 2:19, syntērein.

52. *Jesus progressed*: Among moral philosophers, the term *prokoptein* had technical force for growth in the moral and intellectual life (cf. e.g., Lucian, *Hermotimus*, 63; also Gal 1:14 and 1 Tim 4:15). The term "stature" (hēlikia) can also mean "age," but Luke uses it for size in 19:3. For the favor (or grace, *charis*) enjoyed by Jesus with God and humans, see the note on 2:40, and also the description of the first Christian community in Jerusalem, "having favor (grace) with all the people" (Acts 2:47) and "great favor (grace) was upon them all" (Acts 4:33).

INTERPRETATION

This story of Jesus' youth is unparalleled in the canonical Gospels, although it forms the conclusion of the apocryphal infancy *Gospel of Thomas*, 19:1-5. A Hellenistic reader of biographies would not, however, be suprised at an account concerning the hero's youth that gave a glimpse of his future significance. Such stories can be found, for example, in Philostratus' *Life of Apollonius of Tyana*, 1:7-8, and in Philo's *Life of Moses*, 1:21.

The story serves an especially important function for a writer who is concerned about "sequence" in his narrative. Without it, Luke's account has a lamentable thirty-year hiatus. This small vignette at least enables him to make a somewhat less abrupt transition between the birth and the ministry of Jesus. In 1:80, Luke devoted a single line to summarizing John's life in the desert awaiting the time for his ministry. In this story, Luke gives the reader a far more extensive insight into the kind of "progress" Jesus made before assuming his prophetic mantle.

Read simply as a story, the account shows Luke's artistry: the loss of a child at the festival with the resulting wrench in the heart of his parents; the frantic search; the distancing speech by the adolescent; the parents' incomprehension of a mandate obvious to the young man; these are all sketched with economy and psychological penetration unusual in ancient religious literature. What readers cannot identify with the shock, anguish, and confusion of the parents, or the tension felt by the adolescent between piety owed parents and the pull of a higher vocation?

The domestic drama gives Luke the chance to express some of his characteristic religious perceptions. We see again the centrality of Jerusalem and its Temple. When Jesus arrives in Jerusalem in chapter 19, he does not come as a stranger. Once more, we see the piety of Jesus' family that draws them each year on a difficult pilgrimage for Passover. Most of all, Luke reveals to the reader his distinctive equation of "finding" with saving (Luke 19:10). For Luke, "being lost" is like "being dead," and "being found" is like "being made alive." This is stated most dramatically at the end of the parable of the prodigal son, "your brother was dead and is alive; he was lost and is found" (15:32).

The most difficult part of the passage to interpret is the statement of Jesus in 1:49. What did he mean, and why should his parents not grasp it? As the notes to 1:49 indicate, the Greek is particularly difficult and capable of being read in several ways. Any specific construal must therefore take the context into account, and recognize as well that another reading is possible. This much is clear: Jesus states that he lies under a necessity of some sort. Luke uses here the term *dei*, "it is necessary," which elsewhere in his narrative directs the reader to critical aspects of the story, for example, that "the Messiah must suffer" (24:26; Acts 17:3). Luke therefore has Jesus take up some part of the task God has ordained for him.

But what aspect of his destiny, and why is it unintelligible to his parents, who had been given extravagant clues to the fact that this was a child with a special identity and mission? The translation "to be in my Father's house" does not work as well as "to be involved in my Father's affairs." The first translation would emphasize the place rather than Jesus' activity, but unlike John 2:16, Luke never has Jesus call the Temple "my Father's house," and although the Temple plays an important role in his narrative, it is as a place of activity.

This points us to the second translation. The "affairs" must mean the sort of activity Jesus was engaged in, discoursing with the Jewish teachers. Because the amazement of the crowd focuses on his "answers," he is in effect teaching the teachers. In fact this is precisely the activity of Jesus that Luke emphasizes at the climax of his ministry. From 20:1-45, Jesus responds to the questions put him in the Temple precincts by Jewish leaders, and this activity Luke calls "teaching in the Temple" (19:47; 20:1; 21:37; 22:53). This activity is continued by Jesus' prophetic successors in Acts (4:2; 5:21, 25).

Why should this cause incomprehension? His parents had been told that he would be Lord and Messiah and Savior and assume the throne of his father David. But nothing was said about this being accomplished through question and answer sessions! A certain amount of cognitive dissonance would be natural. No matter how much they had been told of the child's special character, having the young man himself denominate God as his Father would come as a shock. But the incomprehension of the parents also serves a broader literary function. It is the first note in the theme of "ignorance" that plays such an important role in Luke-Acts. Luke shows the reader how even the most faithful of the people "did not understand" in the time of the prophet's first visitation. The reader is also reminded that just as Jesus must "progress" in wisdom, so must those who follow his story, who, like Mary, "keep these words in their heart."

As the narrative of Jesus' birth subtly intimated his burial, so does this account anticipate his resurrection. Remember, Luke identifies being lost with being dead, and being found with coming back to life (15:32). Once this is granted, then a number of details remind us of the empty tomb story in Luke 24:1-8. The time notice "after three days" is an important but not the sole clue (2:46; 24:7). There is the seeking of one who is lost (2:44-45), and the sharp question put to the seekers, "why have you been seeking" (2:49), and "why do you seek the living among the dead" (24:5). There is the response of "keeping all the words in her heart" by Mary (2:51), and "remembering his words" by the women at the tomb (24:8).

The story provides an anticipation as well of the appearance of the risen Lord to the two disciples on the road to Emmaus (24:19-34). In the present story, those who love Jesus are filled with anxiety because of his "absence," his "being lost." In the appearance story, there is anguish and sorrow among those who had "hoped in" Jesus, because he was now "gone." But in the present story, although Jesus is "found" by his parents, he already begins the process of withdrawal from them. In the resurrection account, Jesus' presence is discovered to be even more powerful as he withdraws from sight.

For Reference and Further Study

Brown, R. E. "The Finding of the Boy Jesus in the Temple: A Third Christmas Story." *Worship* 51 (1977) 474–485.

deJonge, H. J. "Sonship, Wisdom, Infancy: Luke 11. 41-51a." *NTS* 24 (1977–78) 317–354.

Elliott, J. K. "Does Luke 2:41-52 Anticipate the Resurrection?" *ExpTim* 83 (1971–72) 87–89.

Kilgallen, J. J. "Luke 2, 41-50: Foreshadowing of Jesus, Teacher." *Bib* 66 (1985) 553–559.

Ruddick, C. T. "Birth Narratives in Genesis and Luke." *NovT* 12 (1970) 343–48.

Temple, P. J. " 'House' or 'Business' in Luke 2:49?" *CBQ* 1 (1939) 342–52.

II. THE PROPHETS JOHN AND JESUS

9. *The Prophetic Ministry of John* (3:1-20)

1. In the fifteenth year of Tiberius Caesar's reign, when Pontius Pilate was prefect of Judea and Herod tetrarch of Galilee, Philip his brother tetrarch over the territories of Ituraea and Trachonitis, and Lysanias tetrarch of Abilene, 2. under the chief priesthood of Annas and Caiaphas, the word of God came to John the son of Zechariah in the desert. 3. He went into the area all around the Jordan. He announced a baptism for conversion leading to the forgiveness of sins, 4. as it is written in the book of the words of the prophet Isaiah: "A voice of one crying out in the desert, Prepare the Lord's Way! Make straight his paths! 5. Every gulley will be filled. Every mountain and hill will be leveled. Crooked ways will be made straight, rough ways smooth. 6. All flesh will see the salvation that comes from God." 7. John accordingly was telling the crowds that came out to be baptized by him, "Offspring of vipers! Who warned you to flee the wrath that is approaching? 8. Produce therefore deeds appropriate to conversion. Do not start saying to yourselves, 'Abraham is our father.' I tell you, God can raise up children for Abraham out of these stones! 9. Already, indeed, trees have the axe laid to their roots. Any tree that does not produce good fruit is being cut off and thrown into the fire." 10. The crowds would ask him, "What, then, should we do?" 11. He answered them, "The person who has two tunics should share with the person who has none. The person who has food should do the same." 12. Tax agents also came to be baptized. They said to him, "Teacher, what should we do?" 13. He said to them, "Stop demanding more than what is owed you." 14. Even soldiers asked him, "What should we do?" He said to them, "Don't extort anyone, don't practice blackmail. Be satisfied with your pay." 15. The people had expectations concerning John. They wondered inwardly whether he might be the messiah. 16. John answered all of them, "I am baptizing you with water. But the one stronger than me is coming. I am not fit to loose the straps of his sandals. He himself will baptize you with a Holy Spirit and with fire. 17. He has his winnowing fan ready to clear his threshing floor. He will gather the wheat into his barn. But the chaff he will burn in an unquenchable fire." 18. With many other such exhortations, he continued preaching good news to the people. 19. But Herod the tetrarch, because he was convicted by John concerning Herodias his brother's wife and all the evil things he had done, 20. added this to everything else, that he shut John up in prison.

NOTES

1. *Tiberius Caesar's reign*: His imperial rule is usually dated from 14 C.E., which would make Luke's reference ca. 28–29 C.E. This is the third example of Luke's syn-

chronism (cf. 1:5 and 2:1). He begins with the empire, works through regional authorities and ends with the religious leadership. As in the other instances, putting the chronological pieces together is difficult but ultimately irrelevant to Luke's *literary* purpose, which is to attach his story to the wider world culture.

Pilate was prefect: The term Luke uses is *hēgemeneuō*, the same as for Tiberius' "governing" (*hēgemonia*). Pilate was prefect in Judea from 26–36 c.e. (cf. Josephus, *Jewish War* 2:169-174) and plays an important role later in the narrative (13:1; 23:1-6, 13-52; Acts 3:13; 4:27; 13:28).

Herod tetrarch of Galilee: This is Herod Antipas, son of Herod the Great (Luke 1:5). He was nominal ruler in Galilee until 39 c.e. (cf. Josephus, *Jewish War* 2:94), and also plays a role in the later narrative (3:19; 9:7-9; 13:31) interacting with Pilate in the passion account (23:7-15; cf. Acts 4:27). Philip (except in a ms variant for 3:19) and Lysanias do not reappear in Luke's story.

2. *Chief priesthood of Annas and Caiaphas*: The difficulty, reflected in the Greek, is that custom dictated only one chief priest at a time. Annas was chief priest from 6-15 c.e., and was eventually succeeded by his son-in-law Caiaphas (18–36 c.e. [cf. Josephus, *Antiquities of the Jews* 18:26; 35; 95]). Luke puts them together again in Acts 4:6. Matthew makes Caiaphas alone the high priest (26:3, 57), as does John (11:49; 18:13-28), but John also attests to Annas' continuing influence and importance (John 18:13, 24).

   word of God: Is thematic in Luke-Acts; see note on 1:1-4, and for the importance of "word of God" for the portrayal of prophets, see introduction, pp. 17, 23.

3. *announced a baptism*: Luke uses the term *kērysso*, which takes on the technical meaning of proclaiming the good news (see e.g., 4:18-19, 44; 8:1, 39; 9:2; 12:3; 24:47; Acts 8:5; 9:20; 10:37, 42; 19:13; 20:25; 28:31). Deciding how the words go together is difficult; perhaps "conversion-baptism" would be most accurate.

   conversion: Translates *metanoia*, which literally means changing one's mind or outlook. Although the lxx does not use it to translate the Hebrew *teshubah*, something of that sense of "turning back" resides in the nt appropriation of *metanoia* (see Luke 3:8; 5:32; 15:7). "Forgiveness of sins" as a result of conversion fulfills Gabriel's prediction concerning John (1:77), and is for Luke a constant element of the good news (see 24:47; Acts 5:31; 10:43; 11:18; 13:38; 26:18).

5. *every gulley will be filled*: The image in this citation is of a road engineer, shouting out orders for the construction of the "royal road" of the Lord. Luke shares the citation from Isa 40:3 with Matthew, Mark, and John, but he alone adds these lines from Isa 40:3-5. He omits, somewhat puzzlingly, "the glory of the Lord will be revealed" in Isa 40:5.

7. *offspring of vipers*: Is literally "children of snakes," but Acts 28:3 pictures the *echidna* as a viper. The expression seems to be traditional (cf. Matt 3:7; 12:34; 23:33).

   wrath that is approaching: The term *orgē theou* ("wrath of God") occurs in the nt for God's eschatological judgment, which sinners will experience as "wrath" (see Rom 1:18; 2:5; 5:9; 1 Thess 1:10; Matt 3:7). Luke uses it again in 21:23.

8. *produce deeds*: Is literally, "bear fruit," a common way of designating human behavior whether good or bad (see 6:43-44; 8:8; and, in parable, 13:6-9; 20:10). "Appropriate to conversion" translates the literal phrase "worthy of repentance."

   Abraham is our father: The claim is to be part of the people blessed by the Lord; see also Luke 13:16; 16:24; Acts 7:2, and Paul's address in the synagogue (Acts 13:26), "Men, brethren, sons of the family of Abraham" (cf. also John 8:33-56; Rom 4:1; Gal 3:7, 29; Jas 2:21).

   God can raise up children: This is hyperbole, but barely: it reflects the conviction that resurrection of the dead and creation from nothingness are both within God's power: "Nothing is impossible for God" (Luke 1:37; cf. Rom 4:17). The "people of God" for Luke will not be one defined by biological descent but by God's gift of the Spirit and by faith.

9. *is being cut off*: The note sounded in 3:8 of "bearing fruit" is continued. Judgment on the basis of one's deeds is axiomatic; see e.g., Rom 2:6-8. What is striking here is the progressive nature of the judgment and its criterion: the way people respond to the visitation of God through the prophet (see also Luke 7:29-30). Acts 3:23 will apply this idea directly to the "cutting off" of the people.

10. *what should we do*: The three-fold question is echoed in Acts 2:37 in the response to Peter's Pentecost sermon; 3:10-14 are unique to Luke, and serve to fill out John's prophetic mission.

11. *two tunics*: The *chitōn* was an undergarment for the *himation* (see Acts 9:39). In Luke 9:3, itinerant missionaries are forbidden two tunics. For the sharing of clothing and food as basic expressions of faith, cf. Jas 2:15-17.

12. *tax agents*: Translates *telōnai*, often rendered as "publicans" or "tax collectors." In this period in Palestine, they seemed to have been largely collectors of indirect taxes through tolls (see the *telōnion* or tollbooth in Luke 5:27) under the supervision of "chief tax agents" such as Zacchaeus (*architelōnēs*, 19:2), and imperial regulation. The scorn directed at them by the religiously committed is patent (see 15:1-2; 18:10-11). They form one of the groups who accept both the prophet John and the prophet Jesus (see Luke 5:27, 29-30; 7:29-30, 34; 15:1-2; 19:2).

13. *stop demanding more*: The verb *prassō* has the sense of "exacting payment" and the exhortation is not to extort more than the legal (*diatasso*) tolls.

14. *don't extort*: The literal translation of the verb *diaseiō* would fit the contemporary idiom perfectly, "don't shake down anyone." This verb is found with *sycophanteō* (as here) in reference to harassment by officials. Soldiers, like police, see a great deal of human experience, and are in the position to practice the vices of extortion and blackmail (the threat to inform).

15. *people had expectations*: As does John 1:24-25, Luke 3:15 supplies the motivation for John's disavowal of the messianic role. Luke reports his self-relativizing statement like Matthew and Mark, except that he omits "after me" (*opisō mou*). He does, however, use it in Acts 13:25!

16. *Holy Spirit and fire*: Both Luke and Matthew add "and fire" to Mark's "Holy Spirit." This carries on the symbolism of fire in 3:9 (Matt 3:10), and is continued in turn by 3:17 (Matt 3:12). In Luke-Acts, of course, the reference is to Pentecost. There both spirit and fire appear (Acts 2:3, 19), in a "baptism in the Spirit" explicitly contrasted to that of John (Acts 1:5; 11:16).

18. *with many other such exhortations*: This is a typical Lukan summary and transition statement. It enables him to suggest that John's ministry took place over some time (notice also his use of imperfect verbs throughout to suggest repeated actions), that he was a prophet "among the people," and that his message had a Gospel character.

20. *shut John up in prison*: Luke omits completely the vivid account of John's beheading (Mark 6:17-29; Matt 14:3-12) which the other Synoptists place much later in Jesus' ministry. For Josephus' account concerning the event, which gives it a slightly different twist than the Gospels, cf. *Antiquities* 18:116-119. By placing the note of John's imprisonment here, Luke is able to establish a succession between prophets and shift attention completely to Jesus. The two prophets will have their last interaction at long distance in 7:18-19.

INTERPRETATION

With the baptism preached by John, Luke's narrative begins to follow his main written source, the Gospel of Mark. The importance of John's ministry for Luke's story is indicated by its solemn introduction by means of Luke's third and most elaborate synchronism (3:1-2), as well as by the way in which John marks a "beginning" (*archē*) of the good news that can be confirmed by eyewitnesses (Acts 1:21-22; see also 13:24-25). By observing Luke's editorial and compositional touches in this passage, the reader gains insight into his literary methods and his religious concerns.

Luke's interest in what he thinks is proper sequence is shown by his alteration of Mark's order. He does not use the mixed citation from Mal 3:1 and Exod 23:20 found in both Mark 1:2 and Matt 3:3, preferring to employ it much later in Jesus' discourse about John in 7:27. Even more strikingly, he shifts the notice about John's imprisonment to a place immediately prior to Jesus' baptism (3:19-20) rather than later in Jesus' ministry as in Mark 6:17-18 and Matt 14:3-4.

Luke freely omits and adds material. He drops the notice about John's clothing and diet (Mark 1:6; Matt 3:4-6) and the term "after me" from John's declaration concerning the Stronger One (cf. Mark 1:7; Matt 3:11). More impressive, however, are Luke's additions. From Q (material shared with Matthew), Luke adds John's message on repentance (3:7-9; cf. Matt 3:7-10), and the saying on the winnowing fan (3:17; cf. Matt 3:12). Much of the new material comes from Luke himself. The posing and answering of questions in 3:10-14 could possibly come from a source, but the perspective on possessions is completely consonant with Luke's own. As for the synchronism of 3:1-2, the lengthened citation from Isaiah in 3:4-6, and the transition sentences of 3:18-19, these all derive immediately from Lukan composition.

The effect of these compositional touches is to highlight John's ministry, give it a distinctive character, and locate it in what Luke considers the proper sequence.

John's ministry is highlighted because the chronological drumroll of 3:1-2 makes John's prophetic call ("the word of God came to John") as important for history as the birth of the Messiah, and because the expansion of materials devoted to John leads the reader to perceive him as carrying out an extended ministry of his own (3:18), relatively independent of—although surely pointing forward to—that of Jesus. Luke reminds us in Acts 19:3 that John still had disciples in Ephesus some twenty years later.

A distinctive character is given to John's ministry. By calling him son of Zechariah (3:2), of course, Luke connects the ministry narrative to the infancy account, and also reminds the reader of all that was prophesied about John by Gabriel and his father—prophecies which this narrative shows are being fulfilled. John is designated as a prophet who speaks the "word of God" (3:2), which is a form of "good news" for the "people" (3:18). By this description, Luke has placed him in the sequence of prophetic figures (cf. Introduction, pp. 17, 23). Luke supplies content for John's prophetic ministry: he is a teacher of morals who calls for deeds appropriate to conversion. In his admonitions to the crowd, we recognize Luke's characteristic perception that the use of possessions symbolizes one's response to God's visitation. To give up extortion, blackmail, gouging and acquisitiveness, and to begin sharing with those more needy, is to enact in body language the response of faith. John is indeed in the process of "preparing a people ready for the Lord" (1:17).

However important John's own message, Luke follows Mark in defining John's role primarily as the precursor to the Messiah. Luke has him explicitly eschew that designation for himself, and point to a stronger than himself whose baptism would be in spirit and fire (3:16), a literary prophecy that will reach fulfillment only in Luke's account of Pentecost. John describes himself as an unworthy servant of the one to come (3:16). Most of all, by having John imprisoned before Jesus' public emergence, Luke establishes a sequence between the prophets. Jesus' anointing with the Spirit is perceived by the reader as following after John's ministry rather than overlapping it.

Salvation and judgment are equally emphasized in this passage. The expanded citation from Isaiah 40 enables the reader to hear again the pattern of reversal, of rising and falling (see 1:51-53; 2:34). And as Simeon had foretold a "light of revelation for the Gentiles" (2:32), so here the reader learns that "all flesh will see the salvation of God" (3:6). The universal extension of "this word of salvation" (Acts 28:28) is slowly being unfolded. If God can "raise up children for Abraham from these stones," then he surely can also from among Gentiles. The theme of judgment occurs in this: a positive response of faith in the prophet is required. Otherwise, even those who belong to the historical people will be like unfruitful trees that are cut off at the roots (3:9), or like chaff that is thrown into an endless fire (3:17).

For Reference and Further Study

Benoit, P. "Qumran and the New Testament." in *Paul and Qumran: Studies in New Testament Exegesis*. Ed. J. Murphy-O'Connor (London: Chapman, 1968) 1–30.
Brown, S. " 'Water-Baptism' and 'Spirit-Baptism' in Luke-Acts." *ATR* 59 (1977) 135–151.
Robinson, J. A. T. "Elijah, John, and Jesus: An Essay in Detection." *NTS* 4 (1957–58) 263–281.
Wink, W. *John the Baptist in the Gospel Tradition* (London: Cambridge University Press, 1968) 42–86.

10. *The Baptism and Genealogy of Jesus* (3:21-38)

21. It was when all the people were being baptized, and when Jesus had been baptized and was praying, that heaven was opened, 22. and the Holy Spirit descended on him with the physical shape of a dove. There was a voice from heaven, "You are my beloved son. I am pleased with you." 23. At this beginning, Jesus was himself about thirty years old. He was the son, as it was supposed, of Joseph, son of Heli, 24. son of Matthat, son of Levi, son of Melchi, son of Jannai, son of Joseph, 25. son of Mattathias, son of Amos, son of Nahum, son of Esli, son of Naggai, 26. son of Maath, son of Mattathias, son of Semein, son of Josech, son of Joda, 27. son of Joanan, son of Rhesa, son of Zerubbabel, son of Shealtiel, son of Neri, 28. son of Melchi, son of Addi, son of Cosam, son of Elmadam, son of Er, 29. son of Joshua, son of Eliezer, son of Jorim, son of Matthat, son of Levi, 30. son of Simeon, son of Judah, son of Joseph, son of Jonam, son of Eliakim, 31. son of Melea, son of Menna, son of Mattatha, son of Nathan, son of David, 32. son of Jesse, son of Obed, son of Boaz, son of Sala, son of Nahshon, 33. son of Amminadab, son of Admin, son of Arni, son of Hezron, son of Perez, son of Judah, 34. son of Jacob, son of Isaac, son of Abraham, son of Terah, son of Nahor, 35. son of Serug, son of Reu, son of Peleg, son of Eber, son of Shelah, 36. son of Cainan, son of Arphaxad, son of Shem, son of Noah, son of Lamech, 37. son of Methuselah, son of Enoch, son of Jared, son of Mahalaleel, son of Cainan, 38. son of Enos, son of Seth, son of Adam, son of God.

NOTES

21. *when all the people were being baptized*: The whole verse is elaborately periphrastic; Luke extends the distance between John's baptism and Jesus by omitting John's name and using adverbial participle clauses.

was praying: An element of the account found only in Luke. Prayer is a constant motif in Luke-Acts, and the critical moments of Jesus' ministry are punctuated by prayer (3:21; 5:16; 6:12; 9:18, 28-29; 11:1; 22:41, 44-45; 23:46). Luke omits "coming out of the water," and therefore disrupts the ascent/descent pattern found in Mark 1:10 and Matt 3:16. Instead, the event is a prayer experience, as is also Luke's version of the transfiguration (cf. Luke 9:28-29).

heaven was opened: See the note on 2:13, and compare Luke 24:51; Acts 1:9-11; 7:55. In Acts 10:11, we find the same pattern: the heaven opens, a great sheet descends, and a voice is heard, all as an experience of Peter in prayer (10:9).

22. *Holy Spirit descended*: Mark 1:10 has "the Spirit," and Matt 3:16, "the Spirit of God." For Luke, it is the same "Holy Spirit" that has already been at work earlier in the story (1:15, 35, 41, 67; 2:25, 26). See also "the Spirit will come upon you" in Acts 1:8 for the same spatial movement. The implications of this anointing with the Spirit for Luke's understanding of messiahship will unfold in the narrative to follow (see esp. 4:18).

with the physical shape of a dove: The dove is a feature of Mark's story, where the syntax suggests an adverbial sense: "the spirit descended as a dove would descend," perhaps referring to the movement. Luke omits the "he saw" of Mark 1:10 and Matt 3:16, and emphasizes the physical reality of the event. The symbolism is at once evocative and obscure. Does it refer to the "hovering" of God's Spirit over the deep in Gen 1:2? But in the LXX, *epephereto* does not suggest a bird. Does it refer to the dove over the waters in Gen 8:8 at the end of the flood? Other NT connections between baptism and the flood could support this (e.g., 1 Pet 3:21), but remotely. These and other suggestions are not persuasive, yet—such is the nature of symbols—all are possible.

a voice from heaven: The notion of God speaking from heaven is widely enough attested in the LXX to make an appeal to the Rabbinic concept of the *bath kol* unnecessary; see e.g., Exod 19:3; 20:22; Deut 4:12, 36, and especially John 12:28-30. The voice will be heard again in the transfiguration with a similar declaration (Luke 9:35-36).

you are my beloved son: Luke follows Mark in making this a direct address to Jesus. The omniscient author allows us to share Jesus' prayer experience. The first part of the declaration is directly from LXX Ps 2:7 with only a change in word order. The verse is applied as a whole, including "this day I have begotten you" to Jesus by Paul in Acts 13:33, but with reference to the resurrection. The first verses of the psalm are also exploited by Luke in Acts 4:25-26. The word "beloved" (*agapētos*) possibly bears the nuance of "only son," since the LXX uses it several times to translate *yahid* (Gen 22:2, 12, 16; Amos 8:10; Zech 12:10).

I am pleased with you: Luke follows Mark in using *eudokeō*. A MS variant "this day I have begotten you" derives from the inertial effect of Ps 2:7, even though it is attested several times by early writers (e.g., Justin, *Dialogue with Trypho* 88, 103). It is possible that Luke alludes to the servant song of Isaiah 42:1 even though the LXX version provides no verbal basis for thinking so. Matt 12:18 reports a version of Isa 42:1 like Luke's, and the possibility is strengthened by Luke's use of *eklegomai* in 9:35. See also the use of *eudokia* in 2:14.

23. *at this beginning*: Literally, "was beginning." Luke uses *archō* mainly as an introductory verb, so some supply "to teach" in this place (cf. Acts 1:1), or, as the RSV, "began his ministry." The thought is certainly correct.

    as it was supposed: With no exceptions, Luke uses *nomizō* to mean a false apprehension (see 2:44; Acts 7:25; 8:20; 14:19; 16:13, 27; 17:29; 21:29).

23–27. *Heli . . . Rhēsa*: These names are unknown to the Old Testament. The only name in even partial agreement with Matthew is that of Matthat (Matt 1:15 has Matthan).

27. *Zerubbabel, Shealthiel*: Are found in 1 Chr 3:19 and 3:17, among the sons of David through Solomon.

28. *Nēri . . . Mattatha*: Are likewise unknown to the Old Testament, and have no point of contact with Matthew's genealogy.

31. *Nathan*: In 2 Sam 5:14 and 1 Chr 3:5, he is one of the children born to David in Jerusalem. Matt 1:5 traces the genealogy through David's son Solomon instead.

31–34. *David . . . Abraham*: In this section, Matthew and Luke share twelve names, with Luke adding Admi and Arni (3:33). The names used by each evangelist are found together with many others in the genealogies of 1 Chr 1:34–2:15.

34–38. *Terah . . . Adam*: Since Matthew stops his birth list at Abraham, he lacks these names. They can be found in 1 Chr 1:1-27, as well as Gen 4:25-26; 5:9-32; 11:10-26.

35. *Son of God*: Is the deliberate climax of the genealogy, forming a bracket to 3:22, "you are my beloved son."

INTERPRETATION

With the baptism account, Luke shifts attention completely to Jesus, and to what "he began to do and teach" (Acts 1:1). He uses Mark for the baptism (3:21-22), and shares with Matthew the material from Q for the story of Jesus' testing (4:1-13). But by joining these accounts with his distinctive version of the genealogy (3:23-38), and by following them with his elaborate presentation of Jesus' first proclamation in 4:14-30, Luke is able to answer three questions he thinks important to resolve if the reader is to properly understand the narrative of Jesus' deeds and words which begins in 4:31: Who is Jesus? He is God's son (3:21-38). What sort of son is he? An obedient son (4:1-13). What kind of Messiah is he to be? A prophetic Messiah (4:14-30). The baptism and genealogy should be read together, therefore, as making a single emphatic statement.

Luke's version of the baptism deviates from the other Synoptists in several respects. We can note first his distinctive way of dealing with the possible misunderstandings that could be caused by having Jesus baptized by John. Mark appears unaware of the problem. But Matthew's dialogue between Jesus and John concerning who is greater and the need for righteousness (Matt 3:13-15) tells us the two possible implications to be drawn from Jesus being baptized by John: that John was greater than Jesus, and that Jesus was a sinner who required repentance. Luke has no dialogue of this sort. Instead, he virtually removes John from the scene. He notes his imprisonment in 3:19, and then extends the distance between him and Jesus by means of a series of adverbial clauses. As a result, the reader does not see Jesus acted on by John, but John in prison and Jesus baptized amid a crowd of people.

Another distinctive Lukan touch is to have Jesus praying after his baptism. The act of praying would seem to perdure through the descent of the Spirit and the audition of the voice. Luke's version is therefore neither so public as Matthew's nor so private as Mark's. As in the transfiguration story, the reader is provided access to an empowerment and declaration that takes place between God and Jesus in the communication that is prayer.

As in the Pentecost story (Acts 2:1-4), we observe Luke's rather heavy emphasis on the physical manifestation of the Spirit. There it is wind and tongues of fire; here it is the "physical appearance of a dove." In both cases, nevertheless, the reader recognizes that this is symbolism put to the difficult task of giving narrative expression to an essentially interior transformation or confirmation. Rather than seek the meaning of the dove in biblical precedents, the reader may do better by observing the structural similarity between this scene and that of the annunciation (1:35) and the angelic song (2:14) in the infancy account. In the annunciation, the Spirit comes down and the child will be called son of God; furthermore, the power will "overshadow" Mary—the word, we saw, recalled the "hovering" in passages such as Ps 90:4 (LXX). In the angelic song, we find the heavens open, and the declaration of peace to people "of God's favor"—the same word used here of Jesus. In the baptism, perhaps, the dove is the "hovering" symbol that enables the reader's imagination to pull these elements into a single focus.

The problems of Luke's genealogy for the historian are obvious, and stated most briefly by noting the ways in which it disagrees with Matt 1:1-17. The fact that they give the names in opposing directions is not important, nor that they use a different genealogical formula, nor even that Matthew uses an explicit three-fold structural organization lacking in Luke. The critical problem is that Luke has 76 names to Matthew's 42, and that they agree so rarely. From Jesus to David (where no biblical texts can guide either author), they share only five names. In contrast, from David to Abraham (where both are controlled by biblical precedents) they share all but the two names added by Luke. Obviously, since Luke continues on to Adam, whereas Matthew stops with Abraham, those names also (to be found in biblical genealogies) are not shared. The two NT genealogies for Jesus are simply different and cannot be reconciled, not even by making Luke's a line traced through Mary; Luke emphatically connects Jesus to David's line through Joseph (1:27; 2:4).

The question of historicity is in this case futile and even fatuous. A better question concerns the function of the birth list. The use of genealogies in Hellenistic biographies and histories is well attested, including some that trace a hero back to a divine parent (cf. Diogenes Laertius, *Life of Plato* 3:1-2; Plutarch, *Parallel Lives,* Alexander, 2:1). The obvious purpose of such genealogies is to establish the pedigree of the hero, and, in some cases, to establish the basis for the divine *dynamis* (power) at work in the hero or sage. As the sources used by both Matthew and Luke attest, genealogies (such as those in Genesis and Chronicles) play an important role also in biblical narratives. The clear function of Luke's genealogy of Jesus is therefore, like that of the infancy account as a whole, to root his narrative in the story of the entire people as recorded in the birth records of Torah.

Several aspects of Luke's version, however, are noteworthy. In contrast to Matthew, he extends the genealogy past Abraham all the way back to Adam. By so doing, he touches again the note of universality sounded by 3:6: the significance of Jesus is not only for the "children of Abraham," but for all the descendants of Adam, all the nations of the earth. By placing the genealogy where he has, furthermore, Luke points less to Jesus' human ancestry and more to his status as "God's son," and this is to be understood above all as a "sonship" mediated by the Holy Spirit.

FOR REFERENCE AND FURTHER STUDY

Abel, E. L. "The Genealogies of Jesus *ho Christos.*" *NTS* 20 (1973–74) 203–10.

Feuillet, A. "Le Baptême de Jésus." *RB* 71 (1964) 321–52.

Johnson, M. D. *The Purpose of the Biblical Genealogies with Special Reference to the Setting of the Genealogies of Jesus.* SNTSMS 8; Cambridge: University Press, 1969.

Keck, L. E. "The Spirit and the Dove." *NTS* 17 (1970–71) 41–67.

Kurz, W. S. "Luke 3:23-38 and Greco-Roman and Biblical Genealogies." *Luke-Acts: New Perspectives from the SBL Seminar.* Ed. C.H. Talbert (New York: Crossroad, 1984) 169–187.

Williams, G. O. "The Baptism in Luke's Gospel." *JTS* 45 (1944) 31–38.

11. *The Testing of the Prophet* (4:1-13)

1. Full of the Holy Spirit, Jesus returned from the Jordan, and was led by the Spirit in the desert 2. for forty days in order to be tested by the devil. He ate nothing during that period. When it was over, he was hungry. 3. The devil said to him, "If you are God's son, tell this stone to become bread." 4. Jesus answered him, "It is written, 'A human being will not live on bread alone.' " 5. The devil led him higher and, in a second, showed him all the kingdoms in the empire. 6. The devil said to him, "I will give you all this power and all the glory that goes with it. It has been given to me. I grant it to whomever I wish. 7. It will all be yours if you prostrate yourself before me." 8. Jesus answered him, "It is written, 'You will prostrate yourself before the Lord your God, and you will serve only him." 9. The devil took him to Jerusalem. He stood him on the pinnacle of the temple. He said to him, "If you are God's son, throw yourself down from here. 10. For this is written, 'He will give his angels a command concerning you, that they should protect you,' 11. and also this: 'They will lift you up with their hands to keep you from stubbing your foot on a stone.' " 12. Jesus answered him, "It has been said, 'You will not test the Lord your God.' " 13. When the devil had exhausted every sort of testing, he withdrew from him for a time.

NOTES

1. *full of the Holy Spirit*: Is Luke's characteristic way of designating the prophetic figures in his narrative (see 1:15, 41, 67; Acts 2:4; 4:8, 31; 6:3, 5; 7:55; 11:24; 13:9); and, like Simeon, (2:27), Jesus is led by the Spirit.

2. *in order to be tested*: The Greek participle is here read as a purpose clause, which the sequence seems to demand. Luke conveys a sense of deliberateness to the whole process, unlike Mark's "driven out into the desert" (Mark 1:12). The verb "test/tempt" (*peirazō*) is used in the LXX for the testing of the people by Yahweh in the wilderness, and of their testing of him (e.g., Exod 16:4; 17:2; Deut 8:2; Ps 94:9 [LXX]). In Luke it has this sense of "testing" only in 11:16; Acts 5:9; 15:10.

   by the devil: With Matthew, Luke uses *diabolos* in contrast to Mark's *satanas* (cf. 8:12; Acts 10:38; 13:10), although Luke also uses *satanas* elsewhere in an equivalent sense (10:18; 11:18; 13:16; 22:3, 31; Acts 5:3; 26:18), as also *beelzeboul* (11:15, 18, 19). Satan gains his reputation as the tester from Job 2:3. This chief opponent is viewed by Luke as the suzerain of a counter-kingdom within which the *daimonia* (demons) and *pneumata akatharta* (unclean spirits) are his minions (see esp. 11:14-20).

   he was hungry: Luke notes that Jesus went without food, but avoids calling this "fasting" as Matt 4:2 does. In Luke, the testing begins at the end of the period, when Jesus is weak from hunger.

3. *stone to bread*: In Luke's version, this challenge parodically echoes the declaration of the Baptist that God could raise up "children for Abraham from these

stones" (3:8). Jesus is challenged to reveal the theurgic powers of divine *dynamis* (power) associated with the "sons of gods" in the Hellenistic world, and to mimic the power of God to give "bread in the wilderness" to the people (Exod 16:14-21). The stone/bread combination recurs again in 11:11.

4. *on bread alone*: The best MSS lack the reading "but on every word that comes from the mouth of God," which is in Matt 4:4 and completes Deut 8:3, the source of Jesus' citation. The Deuteronomic passage stresses the dependence of the people on God during their wanderings.

5. *in a second*: Found only in Luke, it clarifies the visionary nature of the experience. *kingdoms in the empire*: Luke uses *oikoumenē* rather than Matthew's *kosmos* ("world"). It means "inhabited world," but as in 2:1, seems to bear in this highly political context the meaning of "empire." Notice that when Luke uses *kosmos*, he refers to the natural, created order (9:25; 11:50, and esp. 12:30; Acts 17:24), but when he means the social or political order, he uses *oikoumenē* (2:1; 21:26; Acts 11:28; 17:6; 19:27; 24:5; the only exception is Acts 17:31). The vision is of an empire with suzerainty over kingdoms (*basileia*) which in turn control cities, exactly Luke's perception of imperial arrangements (cf. e.g., Luke 19:12-27). Although Luke usually uses "kingdom" with reference to "kingdom of God," the discussion in Luke 11:17-18 shows us the devil as ruler in a counter-kingdom. Note that the devil has power to "bestow," just as Jesus claims to have been "given a rule" by God in 22:29. The fact that Jesus has *exousia* (power/authority) in the kingdom of God is demonstrated by his power to drive out the ministers of the other kingdom, the unclean spirits (see 4:36 and esp. 11:20).

7. *prostrate yourself*: The term *proskyneō* is used of the obeisance made in the East to rulers. Luke uses it straightforwardly as "worship" in 24:52; Acts 7:43; 8:27; 10:25; 24:11.

8. *serve*: The verb *latreuō* ("serve") is also used by Luke in the cultic sense of "worship" (Luke 1:74; 2:37; Acts 7:7, 42; 24:14; 26:7; 27:23). The devil asks for more than political fealty; he wants worship. Jesus' response derives from Deut 6:13, a command that has as its context the rejection of other gods than Yahweh.

9. *to Jerusalem*: Matt 4:5 has instead "the holy city." Luke's geographical interest makes this the climactic temptation.

10. *protect you*: Luke adds these words from Ps 90:11 [LXX] which Matt 4:6 omits. Including the complete command provides a better context for the next citation.

11. *stubbing your foot*: There is a cunning implicit *qal wahomer* (lesser to the greater) argument in the devil's citation. If God commands the angels to protect David (Ps 90:1, LXX) from stubbing his foot, how much more would God protect the Messiah who is "God's Son" if he throws himself headlong from the Temple height?

12. *it has been said*: The MS evidence supports this reading, which shifts from the form of the first two responses and from the parallel in Matt 4:7, which retains "it is written." The citation from Deut 6:16 follows immediately on that quoted in 3:8. It applies to both Jesus and the devil.

13. *withdrew . . . for a time*: Luke adds this phrase. The term *kairos* has the sense of "particular season" (see note on 1:20), but in Acts 13:11, the exact same phrase means simply, "for a time." Although the devil re-emerges forcefully in the passion narrative (22:3, 31, and possibly 22:53), excessive periodization of the ministry should be avoided. The conflict between the rival kingdoms continues throughout Jesus' ministry (see esp. 11:14-20).

INTERPRETATION

The tradition that Jesus was tested had wide currency in early Christianity. It is emphatically stated by Heb 2:14-18 and 4:15. Mark summarizes the testing in two curt sentences (1:12-13). John sprinkles references to testings throughout Jesus' active ministry (John 6:14-15; 7:1-9; 12:27-28). Matthew and Luke take the elaboration of this tradition in Q, and following Mark's narrative placement, use the vivid account of Jesus' scriptural debate with the devil as a means of revealing the inner character of Jesus' sonship as one of simple obedience.

Luke's version is consequently close to Matthew's, differing only with respect to the order of the temptations (he places Jerusalem in last place), and in some minor additions or omissions. It is Luke's *framing* of this episode by the genealogy on one side (3:23-38) and by Jesus' inaugural preaching on the other (4:14-30) that gives his version its particular interest. Having been so clearly assured that Jesus is through the Holy Spirit God's Son, the reader is now allowed to learn the quality of that sonship. The sequence of temptations and of Jesus' responses give credibility to the good news as "release of captives" (4:18), and of his proclamation of the kingdom of God as "healing all those oppressed by the devil" (Acts 10:38, and especially Luke 13:16).

The passage shows us Luke's construal of the struggle between God and the powers of evil as one between two kingdoms. The devil has real "authority" (*exousia*) over those he rules. And his shadow-kingdom parodies that of God, enabling him in his challenges to this Messiah to counterfeit the coinage of God's realm, offering seductions all too real for a messianic ambition in that troubled place and time. The reader is to understand that by winning this most fundamental battle of the heart, the Messiah's subsequent words and deeds are in effect a mopping-up operation, "If by the finger of God I cast out demons, then the kingdom of God is upon you" (Luke 11:20). The point of the encounter therefore is that Jesus is true minister of God's kingdom, obedient to the one who commissioned him (Luke 10:16), so that in all he does "God is with him" (Acts 10:38).

No more need be said about the threefold structure of the story except that it is typically folkloric, and that it is ominously echoed by the threefold betrayal by Peter in 22:54-62 and the threefold taunting of Jesus at the Cross (23:35, 37, 39). As to the content of the temptations, each involves a seizure of palpable power: the theurgic ability to change the elements of creation, the political and military control of humans, the capacity to force God's protection. The tests would suggest to the Hellenistic reader the threefold categories of vice: love of pleasure, love of possessions, love of glory (see e.g., Dio Chrysostom, *Oration* 4:84). Jesus' refusal of these lures would identify him as a righteous person, a sage truly capable of teaching virtue.

Within biblical symbolism, of course, other and deeper signals are generated by the demonic challenges. The forty days of wandering in the desert without food recall the wanderings of the prophet Elijah (1 Kgs 19:8) and of his prototype Moses, who fasted for forty days before writing the words of the covenant (Exod 34:28). But the motif of testing recalls above all the wandering of Israel in the wilderness of Sinai for forty years (Deut 8:2; Ps 94:10 [LXX]; Acts 7:36). That people had been designated as "God's son" (Exod 4:22; Hos 11:1), but it "tested the Lord" repeatedly (Num 11:1-3; 14:1-3; Acts 7:39-41), longing for its more pleasurable past or demanding for itself a more secure future. As Deut 8:2 makes clear, however, the wilderness experience was also God's way of "testing you to know what was in your heart, whether you would keep his commandments or not."

Both Matthew and Luke show that Jesus is, in the heart, truly an obedient Son. In the wilderness, where no one could observe and where the inner dispositions laid bare by true hunger were challenged, Jesus chose not self but service of God. Jesus quotes Deut 8:3 and 6:13 to the devil's first two suasions, using Torah itself to assert first that human life is defined by reference to more than physical subsistence (even if miraculously sustained), and second, that service is owed only the ultimate source of all life, the creator God (and not the flashier surrogate of idolatry).

Luke's placement of the Jerusalem temptation in third place reveals not only his geographical concern, but even more a delicate spiritual sensitivity. The third testing is most severe, for in it the very support for Jesus' stand is subverted. On that high place of the Temple, the devil takes the texts of Torah (Ps 90:11-12 [LXX]) to offer the dizzying suggestion that Jesus test his sonship against the promise of God to protect him. How clever, for what is the radical obedience of the servant except something very close to just such a blind leap? But Jesus does not succumb to this spiritual vertigo. He returns to the central text of Deut 6:13, "You will not test the Lord your God" not only to rebuke the tempter but also to state the conviction of authentic faith. Jesus will not force the Father's hand. He will be the servant who "hears as those who are taught" (Isa 50:4), and who "walks in darkness yet trusts in the name of the Lord" (Isa 50:10), so that from a subsequent high place he can cry out while leaping, this time with his own choice of words from the Psalm, "Father, into your hands I commend my spirit" (Ps 30:6 [LXX]).

We can read this entire account against the backdrop of first-century Palestinian political upheaval and popular messianic expectation, and recognize that, in Luke's understanding, Jesus eschewed the option of a violent, military, zealot vision of God's kingdom in Israel. But the meaning of the testings go far deeper for Luke's Christian readers, who learn something of their own path from the conscious decision of the "Lord Christ" to choose another than a violent way to be Messiah, who rejected power over nature to serve his appetite, over humans for the sake of glory, over God for his own survival, in favor of the "path of peace" (1:79; 2:14, 29; Acts 10:36!) of the Isaianic servant/prophet, as his first words to the people next reveal.

FOR REFERENCE AND FURTHER STUDY

Feuillet, A. "Le récit lucanien de la tentation (Lc 4, 1-13)." *Bib* 40 (1959) 613–31.

Kirk, J. A. "The Messianic Role of Jesus and the Temptation Narrative: A Contemporary Perspective." *EvQ* 44 (1972) 11–29, 91–102.

Pokorny, P. "The Temptation Stories and their Intention." *NTS* 20 (1973–74) 115–127.

Swanston, H. "The Lukan Temptation Narrative." *JTS* 17 (1966) 71.

Taylor, A. B. "Decision in the Desert: The Temptation of Jesus in the Light of Deuteronomy." *Int* 14 (1960) 300 309.

12. *The Prophetic Messiah* (4:14-30)

14. Jesus returned to Galilee in the power of the Spirit. News of him spread through all the surrounding territory. 15. He was teaching in their synagogues and was praised by everyone. 16. He came to Nazareth where he had been raised. According to his custom, he entered the synagogue on the Sabbath. He stood up to read. 17. He was given the book of the prophet Isaiah. He unrolled the scroll and found the place where it was written, 18. "The Spirit of the Lord is upon me, for he has anointed me. He has sent me with the commission to announce good news to the poor, to proclaim release to captives and recovery of sight to the blind; to send off the oppressed with liberty, 19. to proclaim an acceptable year of the Lord." 20. He rolled up the scroll, handed it back to the minister, and sat down. Everyone in the synagogue gazed at him attentively. 21. He proceeded to tell them, "Today this scripture which you have heard is being brought to fulfillment." 22. Everyone witnessed it and was amazed at his graceful words. They were saying, "Isn't he Joseph's son?" 23. He said to them,

"You will surely tell me this proverb, 'Doctor, Heal yourself!' Perform also in your homeland here the many things we heard have been done in Capernaum." 24. He continued, "Amen, I tell you: no prophet is acceptable in his own country. 25. I tell you truly, in Elijah's time there were many widows in Israel. This was when heaven was closed for three and a half years, so that there was a great famine throughout the land. 26. But Elijah was not sent to any of them. Instead, he was sent to a widow of Sarepta in the region of Sidon. 27. Many lepers lived in Israel at the time of the prophet Elisha. None of them was cleansed, but Naaman the Syrian was." 28. When those in the synagogue heard these things, they were all filled with rage. 29. They stood up, and drove him out of the town. They took him up to the edge of the mountain on which their town was built, intending to throw him off. 30. But passing right through them, Jesus went on his way.

NOTES

14. *in the power of the Spirit*: Luke uses this generalizing summary to provide a transition to Jesus' inaugural preaching. Jesus' possession of the Spirit has been stated in 3:22; 4:1 (twice), and now again. The reader is prepared to appreciate the self-application of the Isaiah passage by Jesus.

15. *he was teaching*: For teaching as a characteristic activity of the ministry, see 4:31; 5:3, 17; 6:6; 13:10, 22; 19:47; 20:1, 21; 21:37; 23:5; Acts 1:1.

    was praised: The imperfect verbs are deliberate to establish the sense of repeated action; Jesus was making a circuit of local communities before he came to his own. The term *doxazō* (praise) is used of a positive response to Jesus' work in 5:25-26; 7:16; 18:43; 23:47. The "everyone" is important, for it sets up the contrast to Jesus' townspeople's rejection of him.

16. *where he had been raised*: The term *trephō*, "nourish" (often as with food, see Luke 23:29) refers to the nurturing of childhood. The textual variant, *anatrephō* is often used technically of education (as with Moses in Acts 7:20-21 and Paul in 22:3). Luke has repeatedly established Nazareth as Jesus' hometown (1:26; 2:4, 39, 51; see also Acts 10:38).

    according to his custom: Like his parents (2:42), Jesus is portrayed as a pious Jew who worships in the synagogue regularly (cf. 4:15 and 31). His activity in the synagogue will recur in 4:33, 44; 6:6; 13:10. In Acts, the synagogue will be an important locus for early Christian preaching (13:5, 14; 14:1; 17:10; 18:4, 26; 19:8). The origins of this institution are not entirely clear, but by the first century, it existed throughout Palestine and the Diaspora as a focus for Jewish life: meeting hall, place of prayer, house of study (cf. Acts 15:21). The present passage is important for the evidence it provides concerning early synagogal liturgical practice.

17. *the prophet Isaiah*: As in Luke's first extended citation from Scripture in 3:4-6 (from Isa 40:3-5), we see the importance of the later Isaiah for early Christians, and Luke in particular. This citation and Jesus' interpretation fundamentally alter

Luke's source (Mark 6:1-6a; cf. Matt 13:53-58). In the synagogue, a sequence of readings from the prophets (*haptarah*) followed the assigned readings from Torah proper (cf. Acts 13:15: "law and prophets"). Luke offers here a mixed citation from the LXX of Isa 61:1; 58:6 and 61:2, leaving out "to heal the broken-hearted," and replacing Isaiah's "call" with "proclaim" (in 4:19).

unrolled the scroll: Before the development of the codex (forerunner of the book), scriptures were written on parchment or vellum, rolled on two spindles; to find a place, a spindle was held in either hand, one hand unrolling, the other rolling back up.

18. *for he has anointed me*: Luke's context strongly suggests that this anointing is the baptism (3:21-22). The verb "anoint" (*chriō*) is cognate with *Christos* (Messiah), so that Luke's notion of Messiah is quite literal (cf. 9:20).

    a commission to announce good news: The verb *euangelizomai* is thematic in Luke-Acts for the prophetic message; see the note on 1:19. Typically, Luke will pick this up immediately in 4:43 and then echo it in 7:22. The translation gives full value to the sense of *apostellō* as "send with a commission," because Jesus is imaged as the prophetic spokesperson or representative of God (see esp. Luke 10:16).

    to the poor: As in Mary's canticle (1:52), the "poor" represent not only the economically impoverished but all those who are marginal or excluded from human fellowship, the outcast. This theme is a major one in the first half of the Gospel (see 6:20; 7:22; 14:13, 21; 16:20, 22).

    release to captives: Both here and with "send off oppressed with liberty," Luke uses the same Greek word, *aphesis*, which is used also of the "forgiveness of sins" (1:77) and "debts" (11:4). The term occurs in Deut 15:2 of the "release" from debt and slavery every seventh year in Israel (Deut 15:1-7). In Lev 25:8-12, a fiftieth "year of Jubilee" is idealistically sketched in which all debts would be "released." The terms "captive" and "oppressed" (also: "downtrodden") are found only here in Luke-Acts.

19. *acceptable year of the Lord*: The term *dektos* is translated "acceptable" because the echo of it in 4:24 is deliberate. Some translators prefer "year of the Lord's favor" to capture the sense of the Jubilee year, even though the term *dektos* is not used by the LXX in that connection.

20. *the minister*: Luke uses the same term as in 1:2 for Christian "ministers of the word." It is probably the synagogue functionary known as the *ḥazzan*.

    everyone gazed at him: The translation simplifies the Greek. The term "gaze attentively" (*atenizō*) is a favorite of Luke's (see 22:56; Acts 1:10; 3:4, 12; 6:15; 7:55; 10:4; 11:6; 13:9; 14:9; 23:1).

21. *you have heard*: Is literally, "in your ears." The translation problem is deciding whether the fulfillment takes place "in their hearing," or the "scripture in their ears" is being fulfilled. This translation picks the latter, but they ultimately amount to the same thing.

22. *witnessed*: Despite Luke's fondness for using *martureō* with religious connotations, this case has the straightforward sense of "they confirmed it." In the same

way, the literal "words of grace" should not be taken with excessive theological weighting.

Joseph's son: See 3:23. Luke greatly reduces the reaction of the townspeople in contrast to Mark 6:2-3 and Matt 13:54-56. In the other Synoptists, the contrast between Jesus' wisdom and his local origin provides the point of scandal; Luke makes this a minor note within a more powerful theme.

23. *this proverb*: The term *parabolē*, which elsewhere will be translated "parable," is here being used in the sense of *mashal*, or proverb, as in the LXX 1 Sam 10:12. Variations of the proverb itself are found in both Greek and Jewish writings; cf. e.g., "Physician, physician, heal thine own limp!" in *Genesis Rabbah* 23:4.

   things . . . done in Capernaum: Because he displaces the passage from its sequence in Mark, this reference does not make sense; Jesus does not come to Capernaum until 4:31. Luke's preoccupation with "order" is not always seamlessly successful!

24. *amen, I tell you*: The locution is peculiar to Jesus. The term "amen" would ordinarily respond to the speech of another ("so be it," "yes"), and come at the end. The Gospels show Jesus validating his own speech beforehand; an unmistakable sign of prophetic self-consciousness. The translation, "I assure you" would be more idiosyncratic, but since the Greek carries over the Hebrew as a recognition of Jesus' distinctive speech, so can the English (see also 12:37; 18:17, 29; 21:32; 23:43).

   no prophet: In Luke, Jesus' discourse *generates* the rejection. Here we find the typical Lukan pattern of speech finding its immediate fulfillment in the narrative that follows, for the townspeople immediately do reject Jesus the prophet. The saying is found in slightly different form in the other Synoptists, John 4:44, and *The Gospel of Thomas* 31. In Luke, the word *dektos* deliberately plays on 4:19: the prophet who announces a message acceptable to the Lord is not acceptable.

25-26. *in Elijah's time*: Refers to the story in 1 Kgs 17:1-16. Sarepta in the Old Testament's Hebrew is Zarephath. It was located near Sidon on the Phoenician coast, making the widow a Gentile.

27. *Naaman the Syrian*: The story alluded to is in 2 Kgs 5:1-14. Naaman also is a Gentile. Luke 7:1-16 will provide allusions to these two prophets.

28. *filled with rage*: The other Lukan use of this term occurs when another crowd reacts to a threat to its local prestige (Acts 19:28).

30. *passing right through them*: Is literally, "passing through their midst"; a similar ability to elude lethal danger is found in Philostratus, *Life of Apollonius of Tyana* 8:5.

INTERPRETATION

The story of Jesus' rejection by his neighbors is of particular importance for grasping Luke's literary and religious intentions. He has exercised considerable editorial and compositional control in adapting a conflict story found in the other Synoptists (Mark 6:1-6a; Matt 13:53-58). In their versions, the rebuff occurs after an extended period of ministry. Luke moves it to the very beginning of Jesus' work with only the smallest of transition statements in 4:14-15 to provide a point of contrast. In addition to emphasizing the importance of the event by moving it to first place in the ministry, Luke transforms the account by the addition of the citation from Isaiah and the speech of Jesus. The passage is made into a programmatic prophecy which guides the reader's understanding of the subsequent narrative.

The passage answers the third of the questions concerning Jesus: what kind of Messiah was he to be? Luke's answer is unequivocal. He is a *prophetic* Messiah. This is stated at once by the citation from Isaiah (4:18-19) in which the herald of good news is "anointed with the Spirit," just as later at Pentecost, the spirit of prophecy would be "poured out" on Jesus' followers (Acts 2:33). What was said by the prophet Isaiah about the "servant of the Lord," Jesus declares to be "fulfilled" that day in him (4:21). Jesus also applies to himself the title of prophet (4:24), and appropriates to himself the examples of the prophets Elijah and Elisha (4:25-27).

The Isaiah citation also defines the *character* of Jesus' ministry. He will announce good news to those who are poor, blind, in captivity, and oppressed. Luke's narrative will show this messianic program carried out in the specific stories told about Jesus, and by later thematic propositions (see esp. 6:20 and 7:22). The language of "release" and "year of the Lord" has suggested to some readers that Luke wishes to portray Jesus as announcing the eschatological Jubilee year, when all debts would be remitted and all slaves manumitted (cf. Lev 25:10-18). This is possible, but the Gospel does not offer further support for this being Luke's point. Rather than picturing Jesus' work in terms of a political or economic reform, Luke portrays his liberating work in terms of personal exorcisms, healings, and the teaching of the people. The radical character of this mission is specified above all by its being offered to and accepted by those who were the outcasts of the people.

The passage also announces the theme of prophetic rejection that had been adumbrated by the prophecy of Simeon (2:34). Jesus declares that no prophet is acceptable in his own country, and his townspeople's vivid rage and murderous intentions fulfill his prophecy. But why do they turn on Jesus? Many readers are puzzled by the apparent shift from 4:22, where the response of the listeners is if not admiring at least neutral, to 4:28, where wrath spills over into attempted manslaughter. Translations which overweigh 4:22 with theological nuance make the transition even sharper, but even when (as here) the first response is rendered more circumspectly, the mood visibly turns ugly in 4:28.

The provocation is given by the comparison of Jesus' ministry to that of Elijah and Elisha. The stories are bound together only by the fact that in both the prophetic visitation was extended to Gentiles—outside the boundaries of the people Israel. The reader has already been told by Simeon's prophecy in 2:32 and the citation of Isaiah in 3:6 that the salvation brought by Jesus would extend to all nations. But this is the first that any of the Jewish characters in the narrative have heard of it. The comparison's equations are simple: as Jesus = a prophet, and Nazareth = Israel, so Capernaum = the Gentiles.

It is this veiled intimation that the prophet would be for all and not just for them—and in the reader's understanding, that God's visitation and salvation were to be for the poor and oppressed of all nations and not just for Jews—that arouses the neighbors' wrath, impelling them to fulfill Jesus' statement: he is not acceptable in his own country because his mission extends beyond his own country. Luke thus provides the last part of the prophetic pattern, that of rejection by the people. As Simeon foretold, this will be worked out in the subsequent narrative in terms of a division within Israel between those who do and those who do not accept this prophet. But this ominous opening already suggests a reason why many Jews later on in Acts reject the Gospel, precisely because it is meant for all (cf. e.g., Acts 13:44-52).

FOR REFERENCE AND FURTHER STUDY

Anderson, H. "The Rejection at Nazareth Pericope of Luke 4:16-30 in Light of Recent Critical Trends." *Int* 18 (1964) 259-274.

Bajard, J. "La Structure de la Pericope de Nazareth en Lc iv. 16-30." *ETL* 45 (1969) 165-171.

Gils, F. *Jésus Prophète d'après les évangiles Synoptiques.* Orientalia et Biblica Lovaniensia II; Louvain: Publications Universitaires, 1957.

Lampe, G. W. H. "The Holy Spirit in the Writings of St. Luke." *Studies in the Gospels.* Ed. D. E. Nineham (Oxford: Basil Blackwell, 1955) 159-200.

Von Baer, H. *Der Heilige Geist in den Lukasschriften.* BZWANT 39; Stuttgart: W. Kohlhammer, 1926.

13. *First Signs and Wonders* (4:31-44)

31. He went down to Capernaum, a Galilean town. On Sabbath days, he taught people. 32. They were impressed by his teaching, for his speech had authority. 33. There was a man in the synagogue who had the spirit of an unclean demon. He shouted loudly, 34. "Ah! What is there between us, Jesus of Nazareth? Have you come to destroy us? I know who you are, the Holy One of God!" 35. Jesus rebuked him by saying, "Silence! Come out from him!" The demon threw the man down in front of them, and departed from him without hurting him. 36. Everyone was amazed. They said to one another, "What sort of speech is this? With authority and power he gives commands to the unclean spirits and they depart." 37. News about him spread to every place around there. 38. He left the synagogue and went to Simon's house. Simon's mother-in-law was in bed with a high fever. They approached him concerning her. 39. Standing over her, he rebuked the fever and it left her. She immediately got up and attended to their needs. 40. At sunset everyone who had sick folk with any sort of ailment brought them to him. Placing his hands on each one of them, he cured them. 41. Demons also departed from many. They would shout and say, "You are the Son of God!" He rebuked them and did not allow them to go on speaking, for they knew that he was the Messiah. 42. When it was day, he went out to a deserted place. But the crowds continued to seek for him. They came up to him and tried to keep him from leaving them. 43. He told them, "I must preach the good news about the kingdom of God in other towns as well. I have been commissioned for this task." 44. He continued preaching in the synagogues of Judea.

Notes

31. *on Sabbath days*: The ambiguous Greek plural comes from Mark and can refer either to a single or multiple Sabbaths. Luke's deliberate use of the imperfect tense denotes an ongoing ministry of teaching.

32. *speech had authority*: Luke uses the word *logos* ("word") here, and it has thematic significance (see the note on 1:2). For *exousia* (authority), see also 4:6, 36; 5:24; 20:2, 8.

33. *spirit of an unclean demon*: Luke adds to Mark 1:23 the qualifying words, which make clear for the rest of his narrative that the "unclean spirits" and "demons" are to be taken synonymously; it will be remembered that in the Greek world, a *daimōn* was not necessarily a bad thing (cf. Plutarch, *On the Sign* [*daimōn*] *of Socrates* 10–13 [*Mor.* 580D–582C]).

34. *ah, what is there between us*: The phrase *ti hēmin kai soi* (literally, "what to us and to you") idiomatically expresses identity of interest, as in John 2:4. The expletive here translated "Ah," could also, depending on the punctuation, be read as the imperative of the verb *eaō*, and thus mean roughly, "let us be."

holy one of God: Luke takes this from Mark 1:24, but he prepared for it earlier in 1:35 and 2:23. The theme of the demoniac recognition of Jesus recurs in 8:28.

35. *silence*: The verb *phimoō* means literally "to place a muzzle," therefore, "be muzzled!" (as in Deut 25:4).

   in front of them: The translation supplies the personal pronoun; Luke uses *eis to meson* to make clear that what happened was in the sight of all. Luke also adds to his Markan source the benign note, "without hurting him."

36. *what sort of speech*: Is literally, "what sort of word (*logos*)," which again continues the theme of word established in 1:2 and carried forward by 4:32.

   with authority: The reader remembers that the devil had promised an *exousia*. The fact that Jesus has authority over the minions of that counter-kingdom of the devil reveals that he is the emissary of the "kingdom of God," (4:43), the "Stronger One" prophesied by John (3:16). This same authority he will give, in turn, to those he sends out as his prophetic emissaries (see Luke 9:1; 10:19).

37. *news about him*: Is literally, "sound" or "echo"; for Luke, this spread of Jesus' reputation helps account for the crowd that appears with its sick folk in 4:40.

38. *Simon's house*: Luke has not yet introduced Simon into his narrative (see 5:4). The lapse is caused by his shifting the order of the stories he found in Mark. Luke also eliminates mention of Jesus' other companions that are listed by Mark 1:29.

39. *he rebuked*: Luke uses the same word (*epitimaō*) here as in 4:35, so that the exorcism and the healing are linked; like the demon as well, the fever "departs." Luke omits the physical gesture of grasping the woman's hand from Mark 1:31, displacing it to Jesus' healing of the many in 4:40.

   attended to their needs: Is literally, "served them" (*diakoneō*), but the context of domestic hospitality justifies the more idiomatic translation.

40. *at sunset*: As with 4:42, ("when it was day"), Luke tidies up Mark's rather awkward wordiness. He omits as well the exaggeration that the whole city was at the door (Mark 1:33).

41. *Son of God . . . Messiah*: Mark 1:34 has only that the demons knew who he was. Luke adds the titles Son of God and Messiah. Apart from Mary (1:35), only Jesus himself (3:22) and the demons know him as "God's son" (4:3, 9, 41). Likewise, this recognition of Jesus as Messiah is the only one prior to Peter's in 9:20.

42. *to a deserted place*: Luke follows Mark, but—oddly, since this is an important theme for him otherwise—he omits Mark's note that Jesus was praying (Mark 1:35). Further Lukan touches: if we read only his version, it would appear clearly that Jesus had spent the entire night healing and only withdrew at dawn; Luke also has the whole crowd seek out Jesus and try to restrain him, rather than have Peter report that wish second-hand. We are given a sense of the *public* nature of Jesus' ministry in Luke's Gospel.

43. *preach the good news about the kingdom of God*: This programmatic statement considerably expands Mark's "to preach" (Mark 1:38), and is of critical importance for assessing Luke's understanding of this sequence.

44. *in the synagogues of Judea*: The summary statement generalizes the incidents reported. But why does Luke have Judea, since he has had Jesus preaching in Galilee (4:16, 31) as does also his source (Mark 1:39)? This reading should be preferred as the harder one (that is, less likely to have been brought into conformity by scribes). The MSS that read "Galilee" bring Luke into line with Mark, Matthew, and his own prior narrative. Is this an example of Luke's geographical ignorance? Is he using "Judea" for the whole of Palestine inclusively, as "the land of the Jews"? Or is he simply nodding? In any event, the next verse puts us again in Galilee (see 5:1 and 7:1).

INTERPRETATION

After the leisurely presentation of Jesus' programmatic preaching in Nazareth (4:16-30), this rapid series of vignettes is a bit jarring. Luke picks up Mark's narrative and with it, his staccato rhythm. He follows Mark with exceptional closeness through the exorcism in Capernaum (4:31-37), the healing of Peter's mother-in-law (4:38-39), the healing of the sick in the evening and through the night (4:40-41), and the decision to preach elsewhere (4:42-44). Luke decided, however, to defer Mark's story about the calling of Peter to discipleship from its place at the head of this sequence (Mark 1:16-20) until its end (Luke 5:1-11).

Luke's rearrangement causes some inadvertent awkwardness. Jesus is forced in 4:23 to refer to events in Capernaum before they appear in the narrative in 4:31. Similarly, Simon's mother-in-law is healed in 4:38 before Simon himself enters the story in 5:4. The anomalies are absent in Mark. Luke reveals his use of Mark both when he follows him, and in the consequences of his changing Mark's order!

To what motivation can we attribute Luke's rearrangement? Nothing in the character of the stories themselves provides a clue. Because of the chronological notes in 4:40 and 4:42, we are in effect given the sense of "a day in the life of the Messiah" intended already by Mark to be taken as paradigmatic for Jesus' activity, and taken over in that form by Luke. Like his source as well, Luke draws the closest possible connection between Jesus' authority to teach, and his activities of exorcism and healing. Indeed, Luke tightly binds the two forms of wonderworking, by using the verbs "rebuke" both for the unclean spirit and the fever, and having both inhabitants "depart." The announced program of the Prophet to "free captives" begins to be carried out in these "liberations" of those captive to spiritual and physical sickness.

But why does Luke delay the call of the first disciples until after this sequence? The answer must be that, as in the case of John the Baptist's ministry (Luke 3:1-20), Luke wished to provide a profile of the prophet Jesus' ministry before drawing any attention to the recruitment of the next generation of prophets. By delaying Peter's call, Luke enables the reader to pause over Jesus' personal prophetic ministry of liberation. Among other things, this helps make clear that it is the divine *dynamis* (power) that works, not a team of healers. In the power of the Spirit Jesus heals and exorcises. Notice that it is Luke alone who identifies these activities as "preaching the good news of the kingdom of God." When Jesus later sends out the twelve on their first mission, he will in turn give them *exousia* (authority) to perform these same deeds of healing and exorcism, again in connection to "preaching the kingdom of God" (Luke 9:1-2).

In sharp contrast to the post-enlightenment Western world that finds itself embarrassed by talk of miracles, the Hellenistic world (which was not without its skeptics in these matters, see Lucian of Samosata's *The Lover of Lies*, 16), was in general persuaded that a divine *dynamis* (power) worked among philosophers and heroes, enabling them to perform extraordinary deeds (cf. e.g., Philostratus, *Life of Apollonius*, 3:38–39). The wonders worked by the prophets in the biblical tradition (in particular Elijah and Elisha) had a slightly different religious underpinning, but were understood within the same broad perception of the human realm as one in which transcendent forces were at work. Luke is entirely unapologetic therefore in his presentation of Jesus as *thaumaturge*, for it validates the Messiah's message and his prophetic identity, showing that in his deeds God was truly visiting the people (cf. e.g., Luke 24:19; Acts 2:22). In fact, it is by such "signs and wonders" that prophetic authority is defined (see introduction).

For Reference and Further Study

Achtemeier, P. J. "The Lukan Perspective on the Miracles of Jesus: A Preliminary Sketch." *Perspectives on Luke-Acts.* Ed. C. H. Talbert (Danville, Va: Association of Baptist Professors of Religion, 1978), 153–167.

Bultmann, R. *The History of the Synoptic Tradition.* Rev.ed. Trans. J. Marsh (New York: Harper and Row, 1963), 209–244.

Busse, U. *Die Wunder des Propheten Jesus: Die Rezeption, Komposition und Interpretation der Wundertradition im Evangelium des Lukas.* Forschung zur Bibel 24; Stuttgart: Katholisches Bibelwerk, 1977.

Kee, H. *Miracle in the Early Christian World.* New Haven: Yale University Press, 1983.

Lamarche, P. "La guérison de la belle-mère de Pierre et le genre littéraire des évangiles." *NRT* 87 (1965) 515–526.

14. *Jesus Calls His Disciples* (5:1-11)

1. The crowd was pressing on him to hear the word of God while he was standing by the lake of Gennesaret. 2. He saw two boats lying on the shore. The fishermen who had disembarked from them were cleaning their nets. 3. Stepping onto one of the boats, that belonging to Simon, Jesus asked him to push off from the land a bit. He sat down and taught the crowds from the boat. 4. When he finished speaking, he said to Simon, "Go out into the deep water and lower your nets for a catch." 5. Simon answered, "Master, despite laboring through the whole night we caught nothing! But at your word I will lower the nets." 6. When they had done so, they caught so great a number of fish that their nets were beginning to burst. 7. They signalled to their partners in the other boat to come and assist them. They arrived and filled both boats, so that they were about to sink. 8. When he saw this, Simon fell at Jesus' knees. He said, "Depart from me, Lord! I am a sinner!" 9. He said this because amazement had overcome him and all his companions at the catch of fish they had made, 10. as it did also James and John, sons of Zebedee who were Simon's partners. Jesus said to Simon, "Fear no more! From now on you will be one who nets people." 11. They hauled their boats onto land, they left everything, they followed him.

NOTES

1. *to hear the word of God*: By having the crowd press on Jesus, Luke better motivates his movement to the boat. The translation reverses the relationship of the Greek clauses, but without affecting the meaning. The "word of God" is thematic; see the note on 1:2. As a prophetic characteristic, see Introduction pp. 17, 23. The "crowd" (*ochlos*) is Luke's generalized audience throughout the Gospel (as in 5:3; see also 3:7, 10; 4:42; 5:15, 19, 29; 6:19, etc). When they respond positively, they can become part of the "people" (*laos*) forming around the prophet.

   by the lake of Gennesaret: Luke minimizes the body of water the other Synoptists call a "sea" (*thalassa*), reserving that term for the Mediterranean (Acts 10:6, 32; 17:14; 27:30, 38, 40; 28:4). Despite the reference to Judea in the previous verse (4:44), the setting here is Galilee near Capernaum.

2. *on the shore*: In the Greek, this is the same phrase as "by the lake" in the previous verse. By focusing the reader's attention on the "two boats," Luke prepares for the story's development.

   cleaning their nets: This small detail indicates the men had finished their long night's work. In the parallel versions, Jesus encounters Simon and Andrew in the act of fishing (Mark 1:16; Matt 4:18), and James and John shortly thereafter "mending" their nets (Mark 1:19; Matt 4:21).

3. *sat down and taught*: As in 4:15 and 4:31, Jesus' early ministry is portrayed predominantly in terms of teaching. As in 4:16, "sitting" is the posture for the teacher (although see Paul in Acts 13:16).

5. *Simon answered "Master"*: The command to push off is in the singular, that to lower the nets in the plural, suggesting others in the boat. Simon is characteristically the spokesperson as he is throughout the Gospel (as Simon in 6:14; 22:31; 24:34; and as Peter in 6:14; 8:45, 51; 9:20, 28, 32-33; 12:41; 18:28; 22:8, 34, 54-61; 24:12) and throughout Acts 1-12. The term "Master" (*epistatēs*) as its etymology suggests means one who "stands over" as an authority. Luke is the only evangelist to use the term. He reserves it to disciples (8:24, 45; 9:33, 49) and people seeking help (17:13). The awkwardness of the Greek has led in this and the following verses to a number of scribal corrections in the manuscripts.

6. *beginning to burst*: The translation turns the Greek parataxis into a result clause, and makes the imperfect tense (lit. "were breaking") inceptive, and will do so again in verse 7. The detail emphasizes the magnitude of the catch. In John 21:11, the wonder is that the 153 fish do *not* break the net!

7. *they signalled to their partners*: The term "partner" translates *metochos* here as it does also *koinōnos* in verse 10. Luke pictures Simon and the sons of Zebedee as business associates. By using terms suggesting a pooling of interests and possessions, Luke also prepares the reader for the Galilean community in Jerusalem (Acts 2:41-47; 4:32-37).

   so that they were about to sink: Here the Greek itself supplies the result clause that had to be supplied in verse 6. The imperfect is again read as inceptive.

8. *fell at Jesus' knees*: A characteristic Lukan turn (see 22:41; Acts 7:60; 9:40; 20:36; 21:5). The body-language is clear. Peter's designation of Jesus as "Lord" (*kyrios*) is equivalent here to "Master" in verse 5, but the reader naturally detects the deeper resonance of resurrection power throughout this story (see the note on 1:43).

   depart from me: The response of fear before the revelation of transcendent power is a staple of religious phenomenology. What is remarkable here is that the phrase used by Peter repeats the command of Jesus to demons in 4:35: "depart from him!" By being designated as a "sinner" (*hamartōlos*), Peter is placed in the line of prophets like Isaiah who responded to the sight of the glory of the Lord in a similar fashion (see Isa 6:5 LXX), and represents as well the "sinners" who in Luke's narrative respond positively to the prophet Jesus (5:30, 32; 7:34, 39; 15:1-2, 7, 10; 18:13; 19:7). "Amazement" (*thambos*) is to be understood as religious awe before the Holy, as also in Acts 3:10.

10. *fear no more*: After the mention of James and John, attention shifts back to Peter. For the command to cease fearing, see 1:13 and 2:10.

    one who nets people: Luke omits the "fishers of men" pun of Mark 1:16-17 and Matt 4:18-19. The translation aims at the sense of *zōgreō* as "capturing alive" in the sense of "snaring" (compare 2 Tim 2:26), while retaining the piscatory metaphor.

11. *they left everything*: The staccato rhythm of the translation tries for the abruptness of the Greek. Jesus addressed his words to Simon, but the partners also respond. Luke follows Mark 1:18 and 20 more closely than at any other part of the story, but adds his distinctive note that they "left everything." For the

disposition of possessions as symbolic of response to God's visitation, see note on 3:11. Those within the narrative who are called to follow Jesus on his way signal their obedience by leaving all (see 5:28; 14:33; 18:22-23).

they followed him: The verb *akoloutheō* is used in all the Gospels for more than a physical act; it denotes the spiritual allegiance of the disciple (see e.g., 5:27-28; 9:23, 49, 57, 59, 61; 18:22, 28, 43; 22:39, 54). In Luke, the notion of "following" will take on special significance because of the importance of Jesus' journey toward Jerusalem.

INTERPRETATION

Luke had delayed the story of the disciples' call until he sketched the beginning of Jesus' own ministry in 4:14-44. Now, as with the Nazareth pericope, Luke expands the account available to him in Mark, making it reveal something of Jesus' prophetic power, as well as of Peter's faith and future role.

Determining exactly what Luke took from previous sources and what he constructed himself is not easy. Mark 1:16-20 is a highly compressed account of Jesus' passing by the sea, calling first Peter and Andrew, then later James and John. Matt 4:18-22 follows Mark's version closely. But Luke weaves the call of the disciples into the account of a miraculous catch of fish. This part of the story bears a strong resemblance to the resurrection story found in John 21:1-11 which also involves a great catch of fish. And both stories have some points of resemblance to the fish story told about Pythagoras in Iamblichus' *Life of Pythagoras* 36. Each account also has its distinctive elements. There is no more reason to think that Luke made use of a resurrection tradition than to think that John used a Pythagorean tradition. Each explanation is possible, but neither leads us anywhere in understanding Luke's distinctive version of the prophet's call of his first followers.

Jesus is once more portrayed as a teacher whose power is demonstrated by his deeds. But whereas earlier he had performed exorcisms and healings, in this case he effects a dramatic but quite personally directed display of the *dynamis* at work in him: following his instruction, an unexpected and almost disastrous abundance of fish is caught. Jesus is a prophet who knows what will happen beforehand. The fact that this prediction is so overwhelmingly fulfilled provides surety for his prediction concerning Peter, that he would be a netter of people. Unlike the other Synoptists who show Peter and companions responding only to the naked command of Jesus as he passes by, Luke builds a context and motivation for their commitment of faith.

In Peter's objection and acquiescence (5:5), we find a consistent Lukan perception. The fishermen had labored all night in vain. But at Jesus' command, Peter will lower the nets again. The careful reader will detect in this sequence an echo of Mary's objection that she did not know man (1:34) yet would accept the word of the Lord (1:38), as well as the lesson pointed out in that passage by the angel concerning the barrenness and surprising fertility of Elizabeth: "nothing is impossible for God" (1:37). The contrast between a lack of human potential and the reality of divine fulfillment is essential to Luke's theme of the "Great Reversal" and finds its paradigmatic expression in the suffering and raised Messiah. The attentive reader therefore may legitimately hear in Peter's designation of Jesus as "Master" and "Lord" hints of a fuller resurrection resonance to this story.

Simon enters Luke's narrative for the first time, (although his name identified the mother-in-law healed in 4:38), and will prove to be one of Luke's dominant and most engaging characters. This vignette offers a number of clues for deciphering Peter's narrative significance. Like the other Synoptists, Luke has Jesus foretell Peter's future role as "netter of people," but it is only Luke's extended narrative in Acts that will show Jesus' prophecy reaching fulfillment (see especially Peter's response to the crowd's question, "what shall we do" at Pentecost: "save yourself from this crooked generation," Acts 2:40).

Other details are also revealing. Peter is a "sinner" and thus represents one of the categories of people who respond with faith to the prophet's visitation. This enables Luke to portray Peter as one who is "saved," and to declare in Acts 15:11, "we believe that we are saved by the gift of the Lord Jesus just as they are." The declaration that he is a sinner should be understood not primarily in moral terms but as an expression of awe before the power of the Holy, the *mysterium tremendum ac fascinosum*. It is characteristic of Luke (and a point of contrast to Mark) that the "fascinating"—that is, attractive—aspect of Jesus' power is emphasized more than its "fearful"—and repelling—quality. Thus, although Peter asks Jesus to "depart," he ends up by "following."

Peter's sharing of possessions with his business partners is a subtle anticipation of the later Jerusalem community in Acts 2 and 4. More significantly, he and his fellows symbolize their *metanoia*, change of life, by "leaving all and following him." The disposition of possessions in Luke-Acts consistently symbolizes self-disposition.

Peter emerges here at once as the spokesperson for the disciples. Luke focuses the reader's attention on Peter throughout. He accomplishes this by melding the separate call of James and John to the account of Peter's call, and reducing this important pair to subordinate clauses, almost as an afterthought!

Most of all, Peter is portrayed as a person of faith. We may be allowed as readers to think that the character Simon may have heard of what Jesus had done for his mother-in-law, and therefore would be receptive to this teacher's power. But Jesus' present command confronted Peter's personal experience of a night's long work for nothing. Despite appearances to the contrary, however, he places his trust in the word of the prophet. His following Jesus on a path unknown is therefore a logical progression for one who had already "put out into the deep" on the basis of a word only.

FOR REFERENCE AND FURTHER STUDY

Brown, R. E. et.al. eds. *Peter in the New Testament* (New York: Paulist Press, 1973) 83–101.

Delorme, J. "Luc v.1-11: Analyse structurale et histoire de la rédaction." *NTS* 18 (1971–72) 331–350.

Leaney, R. "Jesus and Peter: the Call and Post-Resurrection Appearances (Luke v. 1-11 and xxiv. 34)." *ExpT* 65 (1953–54) 381–82.

Smith, C. W. F. "Fishers of Men: Footnotes on a Gospel Figure." *HTR* 52 (1959) 187–203.

Wuellner, W. H. *The Meaning of "Fishers of Men."* Philadelphia: Westminster Press, 1967.

15. *Two Healings* (5:12-26)

12. When Jesus was in one of the cities, a man filled with leprosy saw him. He fell on his face and begged him, "Lord, if you will it, you can cleanse me." 13. He stretched out his hand and touched him, saying, "I do will it. Be cleansed!" At once the leprosy left him. 14. Jesus commanded him, "Tell no one, but go show yourself to the priest and offer the sacrifice for your cleansing as Moses decreed, as a testimony to them." 15. Still, the word about him spread even more. Many crowds would gather to listen and to have their illnesses healed. 16. But he would withdraw into desert places and pray. 17. One day he was teaching while Pharisees and teachers of the Law who had come from every village of Galilee and Judea and Jerusalem were sitting there. The power of the Lord was enabling him to heal. 18. Some men arrived, carrying on a stretcher a man who was paralyzed. They were trying to bring him in and place him before Jesus. 19. Because of the crowd, they could find no way in, so they went up on the roof. They lowered him down through the tiles on his pallet to the space in front of Jesus. 20. When he saw their faith, he said, "Man, your sins are forgiven." 21. The scribes and Pharisees began to question, "Who is this person who speaks blasphemies? Who but God alone can forgive sins?" 22. Jesus knew their thoughts. He responded to them, "Why are you debating in your hearts? 23. What is easier, to say, 'Your sins are forgiven,' or to say, 'Rise

and walk?' 24. But so that you might know that the Son of Man has authority on earth to forgive sins"—he said to the paralytic, "I say to you, Rise! Pick up your pallet! Go to your house!" 25. Immediately he got up before them, picked up the pallet on which he had been lying, and went off to his house, glorifying God. 26. Astonishment seized them all and they gave glory to God. They were filled with fear. They said, "Today we have seen marvelous things!"

NOTES

12. *in one of the cities*: It is typical of Luke to supply this detail, so that the concluding note of Jesus withdrawing to desert places (v. 16) has some point.

    filled with leprosy: Is a correction of Mark's "leper," so that the leprosy can "depart" in verse 13. The sickness is described extensively in Lev 13–14 as a skin disorder that rendered a person "unclean" (Lev 13:3), and therefore removed from the common life of the people so long as the disfigurement lasted.

    fell on his face and begged: As with Peter's prostration in the previous story, a dramatic recognition of authority. The word "beg" (*deomai*) is a favorite of Luke's (8:28, 38; 9:38, 40; 10:2; 21:36; 22:32; Acts 4:31; 8:22, 24, 34; 10:2; 21:39; 26:3). With Matt 8:1, Luke adds the title "Lord" to Mark 1:40. On the other hand, he removes the element of "moved with compassion" in Mark 1:41.

14. *commanded him*: The translation adds "Jesus," to make clear the subject of the sentence. Luke makes the verb more specific than Mark 1:44 and Matt 8:4, but, like Matthew, he omits the rather startling comment by Mark that Jesus "snorted" (Mark 1:43).

    tell no one: This first phrase is in indirect discourse. The translation changes it to an imperative like those which follow. The contrast in the story is between this command to silence and the spread of fame which takes place despite it.

    show yourself. . . sacrifice: It was the priest's duty to examine persons to determine whether they were leprous or clean (see Lev 13:3, 10, 13, etc.). Lev 14:1-32 specifies a series of ritual actions including sacrifices for one certified as clean.

    as a testimony: Or, "as a proof for them." The term *martyrion* does not occur in LXX Lev 13–14. Luke uses it both positively (Acts 4:33) and negatively, as "witness against" (Luke 9:5; 21:13). Here he takes the phrase from Mark 1:44, and it could be read either way: as a testimony to the priests that the man was clean, or as a witness against whoever objected to Jesus as miracle-worker. Neither option is entirely satisfactory.

15. *word about him*: Whereas Matthew finishes the story with Jesus' command (Matt 8:4), Luke continues to follow Mark but with significant alterations. The first is to make the spread of rumor about Jesus an impersonal process rather than the result of the "preaching" of the healed leper, which in Mark is a direct disobedience of Jesus' command.

    crowds would gather: In Mark, Jesus is isolated in the desert, but in Luke he continues to meet with crowds, teach and heal.

16. *he would withdraw*: As in the previous verse, the imperfect tense is taken as re-
    peated action. Rather than being forced into the desert, Jesus is pictured as peri-
    odically withdrawing for the purpose of prayer (as in 9:28 and 11:1). For prayer
    as thematic in Luke-Acts, see the note on 3:21.

17. *Pharisees and teachers of the Law*: Luke typically establishes the scene more
    thoroughly than the other Synoptists. Mentioning them now prepares for the
    intervention of Jesus' opponents in verse 21. The Pharisees were one of the sects
    within first-century Judaism, whose strict observance of Torah—especially in mat-
    ters of purity and tithing—led them to form fellowships of "associates," and
    to develop the concept of "oral Torah," an expansion of the Law by means of
    midrash (interpretation) that sought applications to new circumstances (cf.
    Josephus, *Jewish War* 2:162-166; *Antiquities* 13:293-298). Their natural allies (with
    whom the NT constantly connects them) were professional interpreters, in He-
    brew *ha sopherim* ("men of the book") and in the NT, "scribes" (*grammateis*).
    Luke retains the title "scribe" in verse 21 (as also in 5:30; 6:7; 9:22; 11:53; 15:2;
    19:47; 20:1, 19, 39, 46; 22:2, 66; 23:10; Acts 4:5; 6:12; 23:9), but here uses the
    term *nomodidaskalos* ("teacher of law"), which recurs otherwise only in Acts 5:34
    with reference to Gamaliel. Luke also uses the term "lawyers" (*nomikoi*) syn-
    onymously with scribes (cf. Luke 7:30; 10:25; 11:45, 46, 52, 53; 14:3). Contrary
    to an often stated position, Luke is *not* more positive than the other Synoptists
    in his portrayal of the Pharisees and scribes. Particularly in the Galilean minis-
    try, they represent the chief opponents to the Prophet.

    power of the Lord: The term *dynamis* here appears almost as a force working im-
    personally through Jesus; see also 1:35; 4:14, 36. The same note will be sounded
    in 6:19 and 8:46. See the characterization of Jesus in Acts 2:22 and 10:38.

18. *on a stretcher*: Luke offers a number of clarifications to the Markan source. He
    specifies that "men" carry a "man who was paralyzed" and "on a stretcher."

19. *on his pallet*: Once more, Luke makes the whole process clearer: they lower the
    man on a pallet (*klinidion* is the diminutive of *klinē* in v. 18), right in front of
    Jesus; for *eis to meson* ("in the middle"), see the same phrase in 4:35.

20. *he saw their faith*: This is the first occurrence of *pistis* ("faith") in the Gospel,
    although Luke has previously used the verbal form *pisteuō* in 1:20 and 1:45. He
    takes it here from Mark 2:5, and bears the obvious sense of hope, trust, and
    perseverance. The theme of faith is central to Luke-Acts; it is the basic positive
    response to the visitation of God (see e.g., 7:9, 50; 8:12, 13, 25, 48, 50; 16:11;
    17:5, 6, 19; 18:8, 42; 20:5; 22:32, 67; 24:25; Acts 2:44; 3:16; 4:4, 32; 5:14, etc.).
    Man, your sins are forgiven: Rather than "child" as in Mark 2:5, Luke has "man,"
    as in 5:18. The Greek is literally, "your sins are forgiven for you," with the per-
    fect passive indicating at once an accomplished fact, and (in biblical idiom) that
    it was done by God. For forgiveness of sins as thematic, see note on 1:77. For
    the popular connection between sin and sickness, cf. John 9:2.

21. *began to question*: The same Greek word (*dialegomai, dialogismos*) is translated here
    successively as "question," "thoughts" and "debating." For the ability of the
    prophet to reveal the *dialogismoi* of hearts, see the prophecy of Simeon, 2:35.

blasphemy: Slanderous speech (*blasphēmia*) when directed against a divine being becomes in a monotheistic religion like Judaism a fundamental rebellion against God. Here, the declaration of sins forgiven is read as an arrogation of authority belonging to God "alone" (Luke has *monos*). Outside this passage, Luke-Acts uses "blasphemy" exclusively as slander against Jesus or Christians (Luke 12:10; 22:65; 23:39; Acts 13:45; 18:6; 19:37; 26:11).

23. *what is easier*: The heart of the controversy section of this story is taken entirely from Mark 2:8-11, and followed by Luke with only small alterations.

24. *that you might know*: This statement so awkwardly interrupts the natural flow of the Greek that it is often taken as an interjection reflecting a community apologetic. In this case, the "you" would be those opposing claims made about Jesus by Messianists. Within the narrative, the "you" refers to the opponents of Jesus himself.

    the Son of Man has authority: This is Luke's first use of the mysterious title *ho huios tou anthrōpou*, and he takes it from Mark 2:10. The ultimate source of this phrase (in Hebrew, *ben adam*, in Aramaic, *bar enosh*) and its significance for the understanding of the historical Jesus, are much debated in scholarship. The term is applied to the prophet Ezekiel by God in Ezek 2:1, 3, etc.; in Dan 7:13, one "like a Son of Man" plays a role in an apocalyptic scenario, and is further developed in writings such as *1 Enoch* 46:2-4, etc. In Luke, as in the other Synoptists, the phrase occurs only in the mouth of Jesus, and is self-referential. It is used in three contexts: Jesus' present ministry (5:24; 6:5; 7:34; 9:56, 58; 19:10), the suffering of the Messiah (9:22, 26, 44; 18:31; 22:22, 48; 24:7), and the future role of judging (11:30; 12:8, 10, 40; 17:22, 24, 26, 30; 18:8; 21:27, 36; 22:69). Acts 7:56 uses the title for Jesus as resurrected. Given the use in Ezekiel and Luke's appropriation in contexts such as the present one, the title can be understood as part of his prophetic imagery. For Jesus' "authority" (*exousia*), see 4:6, 32, 36.

25. *before them*: A characteristic Lukan touch to emphasize the public character of Jesus' ministry.

    glorifying God: In Luke, this is a regular response to a wonder or revelation (2:20; 4:15; 7:16; 13:13; 17:15; 18:43; 23:47; Acts 4:21; 11:18; 13:48; 21:20). Here, the healed man is joined by the bystanders (5:26) in correcting the misapprehension of the opponents: it is the "power of the Lord" who is at work in the prophet, and therefore "God is glorified."

26. *marvelous things*: The term *paradoxos* has the sense of the unexpected as well as the wonderful. It is used only here in the NT.

INTERPRETATION

After recounting the call of the first disciples (5:1-11), Luke picks up Mark's sequence once more, following him closely from 5:12 to 6:11 (Mark 1:40–3:6), where he will again deviate more substantially. Throughout this section, Luke's alterations of his source are minimal, consisting mainly of clarifications, but a few thematic interests find their way into the stories. As in Mark, the sequence of stories focuses on Jesus' working of wonders and the response they engendered among the populace. The first two stories are healings of a leper (5:12-16) and of a paralytic (5:17-26). Both stories retain the pattern of typical healing stories as these were handed on in the oral tradition. The story of the paralytic, however, is more complex, with a controversy story woven into the account of a healing.

The reader can note some of the distinctive touches Luke puts to the Markan portrayal of Jesus. He heightens the impression of a Hellenistic thaumaturge. Like other Greek sages, Jesus' teaching and working of wonders are closely joined (5:17). Through him, the divine *dynamis* is at work (5:17), enabling him to heal with a word (5:13, 20) and a touch (5:13). His deeds draw great crowds to him (5:15), and his *paradoxa* (marvels) generate fear and amazement (5:26). Even the note that he withdrew into desert places is not inconsistent with the image of the sage (*Life of Apollonius*, 1:16).

Luke also retains the biblical shading of the Markan portrait. Jesus is one who knows and commands observance of the commands of Moses concerning the purification from leprosy, even if his motivation for sending the healed man to the priest is obscure (5:14). He is identified as the Son of Man, who has *exousia* (authority) to declare sins forgiven even on earth (5:24). This cluster of symbols makes sense only in the context of Torah and the covenantal relationship with the "only" (*monos*) God, as Luke puts it (5:21).

The fact that Jesus can read the thoughts of his opponents takes on added significance in Luke's Gospel, where such an ability is axiomatic for one who is a true prophet (7:39). Precisely this aspect of Jesus' work was foretold by Simeon in 2:35: "the thoughts (*dialogismoi*) of many will be revealed." In light of this story, the reader is now better able to grasp the sort of "liberation" (*aphesis*, 4:18) proclaimed by the Prophet-Messiah. As God's spokesperson he has the authority to declare the "forgiveness" of sins, which is expressed in the "liberation" of the paralyzed limbs so that the person can move freely. The conclusion of the story, where both the healed man and the bystanders "glorify God," therefore, serves also to correct the opponents: through his *dynamis* in the Messiah, God is the one at work.

In Jesus' response to the opponents' objection, "what is easier, to say . . .," we find that a physical "rising" and a spiritual "forgiveness" are attached to the same power, which is able to accomplish both with equal ease. The same connection will recur in Luke's version of the resurrection and Pentecost: the "rising from the dead" of the Messiah is the source of the transforming Spirit which accompanies the proclamation by the apostles of the "forgiveness of sins" (Acts 2:32, 37).

The two stories also continue the theme of the division within the people caused by the Prophet. In Jesus' actions, we detect the characteristic concern for those who are ritually outcast from the people of Israel and therefore from full participation in its life. By touching the leper, Jesus restores him to human community; the paralytic he restores to his own home. Such is the reversal of human status announced by the prophet. We also see the positive response among the ordinary people to these gestures of invitation: the leper declares Jesus' capacity to cleanse, the crowds seek Jesus to "listen" as well as to be healed (5:15), and the friends of the paralytic demonstrate remarkable "faith" (5:20). On the other side, we meet for the first time the Pharisees and scribes. They hold positions of authority among the people. But although they too gather to observe this prophet at work—sitting, as do judges (5:17), they reject his words as blasphemous (5:21). This split between the ordinary folk and their leaders will be developed ever more explicitly by Luke.

FOR REFERENCE AND FURTHER STUDY

Boobyer, G. H. "Mark II, 10a and the Interpretation of the Healing of the Paralytic." *HTR* 47 (1954) 115–120.

Dupont, J. "La paralytique pardonné (Mt 9, 1-8)." *NRT* 82 (1960) 940–58.

Feuillet, A. "*L'exousia* du fils de l'homme (d'après Mc II, 10-28 et parr.)." *RSR* 42 (1954) 161–192.

Marshall, I. H. "The Synoptic 'Son of Man' Sayings in Recent Discussion." *NTS* 12 (1965–66) 327–351.

Mead, R. T. "The Healing of the Paralytic—A Unit?" *JBL* 80 (1961) 348–54.

16. *Call and Controversy* (5:27-39)

27. After this he went out. He noticed a tax-agent named Levi sitting in his toll station. He said to him, "Follow me!" 28. Leaving everything, the man stood up and followed him. 29. Levi provided a great reception in his house for Jesus. A large crowd of tax-agents and others associated with them were reclining at table. 30. The Pharisees and their scribes began to complain to his disciples. They said, "Why are you eating and drinking with tax-agents and sinners?" 31. Jesus answered them. He said, "Healthy people don't need a doctor, sick people do. 32. I have not come to invite righteous people to repentance, but sinners." 33. They in turn said to him, "John's disciples fast frequently and pray. So do the disciples of the Pharisees. But yours are eating and drinking." 34. Jesus said to them, "Can you force the members of a wedding party to fast while the bridegroom is with them? 35. But days are coming when the bridegroom is taken from them, then in those days they will fast." 36. He also told them a parable: "Nobody

takes a patch off a new garment to put it on an old piece of clothing. In that case, both the new garment is ripped, and the patch from the new garment will not match the old. 37. Nor does anyone put new wine into old wineskins. In such a case, the new wine will burst the wineskins. The wine itself will be spilled and the wineskins destroyed. 38. One must put new wine into new wineskins. 39. Also, no one drinking old wine prefers new wine, for he says, 'The old wine is good.' "

NOTES

27. *a tax-agent named Levi*: Luke follows Mark 2:14 here (although he leaves out the identifying phrase "of Alphaeus"), rather than Matt 9:9 which supplies the name "Matthew" for the tax-agent. Levi does not recur in the story apart from the scene which immediately follows. For the significance of the *telōnēs* ("tax-agent") in Luke's narrative, see note on 3:12.

28. *leaving everything*: As in the case of Peter, James and John (5:11), Luke adds this to Mark 2:14, reflecting his concern for the disposition of possessions as symbolizing the response to God's visitation. Its formal character is indicated at once by the fact that Levi can provide a feast in his home.

29. *Levi provided*: Luke creates one story by making Levi a point of continuity. The *dochē* is a reception or banquet; Luke uses the same expression again in 14:13. Guests at such banquets "reclined" in the Hellenistic manner (cf. Luke 7:36-37; 9:14-15; 14:8; 24:30).

    others associated with them: Luke uses periphrasis here rather than the "tax-agents and sinners" employed by Mark 2:15 and Matt 9:10, but he has their phrase in 5:30 as well as in 7:34 and 15:1.

30. *Pharisees and their scribes*: Whereas Matt 9:11 simplifies Mark's confusing "scribes of the Pharisees," (2:16) to "Pharisees," Luke's alteration is less drastic. More significantly, he has their complaint addressed to the disciples directly, rather than in reference to Jesus. Jesus' response thereby becomes a defense of his followers.

31. *healthy people . . . sick people*: Luke makes the contrast between sickness and health more explicit. The image of the doctor (*iatros*) was used earlier in 4:23, and as noted there, is standard in Hellenistic moral teaching as part of an elaborate medical imagery: the philosopher is the doctor, vice is sickness, and virtue is health (cf. Dio Chrysostom, *Oration* 32:14-30; Epictetus, *Discourses* 3:23, 30). In this case, Jesus is doctor, sickness is sin, and health is righteousness.

32. *invite . . . to repentance*: The translation treats the prophetic "call" (*kaleo*; cf. e.g., Isa 42:6; 61:2) as an "invitation," since this accords with Luke's own development of the theme in chapter 14. Repentance (*metanoia*) is a major theme in Luke-Acts (3:3, 8; 15:7; 24:47; Acts 5:31; 11:18; 13:24; 19:4; 20:21; 26:20). The call of God through the prophet demands a change of life: as with John, so with Jesus, so with the apostles.

33. *they in turn said to him*: Rather than a fresh start which tends to separate the pericopes (cf. Mark 2:18; Matt 9:14), Luke has the Pharisees respond to Jesus' last statement, thereby forming a single controversy story. He adds "make prayers" to the statement about the disciples of John. For fasting and prayer in Jewish piety, see note on 18:12 (and Luke 2:37; Acts 13:2-3; 14:23; 27:9).

34. *can you force*: The form of the Greek question demands the response, "of course not!" The image of the bridegroom was applied by prophets to the relationship of Yahweh to Israel (see Isa 61:10; 62:5; Hos 2:16-23; Jer 16:9). In the *Gospel of Thomas* 104, the image is again joined to the practice of prayer and fasting.

35. *days are coming*: Luke adjusts Mark's concluding "in that day" to have an agreement in number in both clauses, but thereby creates a redundancy.

36. *told them a parable*: Luke alone identifies Jesus' words as a parable. As in 4:23, the meaning is close to that of *mashal*, a proverb or riddle, rather than a metaphoric narrative.

    nobody takes a patch: Luke considerably clarifies these comparisons so that the new/old contrast is more intelligible. The *Gospel of Thomas* 47 combines these same comparisons with the one between two masters found in Luke 16:13.

38. *one must put*: Translates the verbal adjective (gerundive) of "they put" (*ballō*), which has the force of an imperative. The conclusion that "new should go with new" stands as the moral for both comparisons.

39. *the old wine is good*: Only Luke has this verse, which has a superficial resemblance to John 2:10. Some MSS change *chrēstos* ("sweet") to the comparative, but the comparison is clear enough without the correction: "the old wine is better."

INTERPRETATION

The note of conflict that was sounded in the healing of the paralytic now becomes explicit in a series of controversy stories. Such stories are among the most common building blocks deriving from the oral tradition used by each evangelist. They reflect the disputations between the early messianists and their (largely Jewish) opponents over the identity and claims of Jesus, and the validity of their own practices within the symbolic world of Judaism. The controversies tend to fall into set forms, and resemble the kind of disputes that took place all over the Hellenistic world between philosophical schools (both Jewish and Gentile).

Luke again follows Mark's order in this section, and makes only minor adjustments within the stories. It need not be emphasized that this represents a tacit approval of his source. Luke has, however, deftly woven three originally separate pericopes into a single extended scene. Jesus calls Levi (5:27-28); the banquet provided by Levi is the occasion for the objection concerning table companions (5:29-32); and the issue of fasting follows as a continuation of the same conversation (5:33-35), with three parabolic statements providing an interpretation of the entire sequence (5:36-39).

When Peter responded to Jesus' call, a "sinner" joined the Prophet; when Levi follows Jesus, a "tax-agent" becomes part of the small messianic fellowship. Issue is therefore immediately joined with the religious elite in Judaism concerning the nature of this "kingdom" proclaimed by Jesus. It was axiomatic in the ancient world that table fellowship, like hospitality, symbolized spiritual unity (cf. 2 John 11). What did it signify for Jesus and the "kingdom of God" he proclaimed if tax-agents and sinners were part of his fellowship? A similar point is raised by the question concerning fasting. John's fellowship and the *haburah* of the Pharisees each practiced the forms of traditional Jewish piety; but Jesus' fellowship engaged in banqueting. This contrast between the ascetic John and the libertine Jesus will be picked up again in Luke 7:33-34. How can a serious religious claim and such apparent frivolity be reconciled?

The response Jesus makes to these objections (intervening in defense of his followers) combines elements from the tradition in an original way: answering the first attack, Jesus uses the standard medical imagery of the Hellenistic philosopher. He is the physician who calls the sick to health. Like the physician, therefore, he must be where the sick are. His fellowship, we learn, is not one in which the "righteous" are separated from the sinners, as healthy people seek to protect themselves from the diseased, but one in which the service orientation of the physician defines the community as such as one of accessibility and availability. Answering the second attack, Jesus applies to himself the biblical image of the bridegroom. In the prophetic background of this imagery, there is the clear note of eschatological unity between God and people. Although days will come when the bridegroom is not around, and the companions will fast (as the disciples are shown doing in Acts), the time of Jesus with his disciples is symbolized as a wedding banquet.

The three parabolic aphorisms, so much more clearly stated in Luke than in Mark, all point in the same direction. They illustrate the distance between the kingdom proclaimed by Jesus and the religious perceptions of his contemporaries. His message, we understand at once, is the new garment and new wine. Worse than useless to try to match it to the old forms of piety and politics. Such a compromise between this *novum* and the conventional leads to the loss of what is new and the destruction of what is old. Specifically, one cannot fit this Gospel to the outcasts with its accessibility for all humans, within the perceptions and precepts of a separatist piety. Rarely in the New Testament do we find a statement of the Gospel so radical as in these short vignettes, which bear so striking a sense of having come from Jesus with only the lightest of evangelical shaping.

The final parabolic statement—found only in Luke—reminds us again of the capacity of this message to repel as well as to attract, and the way in which the visitation of the prophet creates a division within the people. Those who are most accustomed to the old wine will not even taste the new; the old, they say, is good enough. To drink the new wine offered at Jesus' banquet, to wear the new garment for his wedding feast, one must have a new heart, go through *metanoia,* a change of mind, such as that shown by tax-agents and sinners.

For Reference and Further Study

Bultmann, R. *History of the Synoptic Tradition.* Rev. ed. Trans. J. Marsh (New York: Harper and Row, 1963) 11–27.

Daube, D. "Responsibilities of Master and Disciples in the Gospels." *NTS* 19 (1972–73) 1–15.

Dupont, J. "Vin vieux, vin nouveau." *CBQ* 15 (1963) 286–304.

Jeremias, J. *The Parables of Jesus.* Rev.ed. Trans. S. H. Hooke (New York: Charles Scribner's Sons, 1962) pp. 20, 104.

Kee, A. "The Question about Fasting." *NovT* 11 (1969) 161–173.

_____. "The Old Coat and the New Wine." *NovT* 12 (1970) 13–21.

17. *Two Controversies and a Choice* (6:1-16)

1. On a Sabbath day he was passing through a field of grain. His disciples began to pluck the grain. They would rub the ears of grain in their hands and eat them. 2. Some of the Pharisees said, "Why are you doing what is not allowed on the Sabbath?" 3. Jesus answered them. He said, "Have you not even read what David did when he and his companions were hungry? 4. He entered the house of God, took the presentation loaves that only the priests were allowed to eat, ate them, and gave some to his companions." 5. He said to them, "The Son of Man is Lord of the Sabbath." 6. On another Sabbath he went into the synagogue and taught. There was a man there whose right hand was withered. 7. The scribes and Pharisees watched closely to see if he would heal on the Sabbath. They sought an accusation they could make against him. 8. He knew their thoughts, yet he said to the man with the withered hand, "Get up and stand here before us." The man rose and stood. 9. Jesus said to them, "I put this question to you: is it allowed to do good on the Sabbath or to do evil? To save a life or to destroy it?" 10. Gazing around at them, Jesus said to the man, "Stretch out your hand." The man did so and his hand was restored. 11. But they were beside themselves with anger. They began to discuss with

each other what they might do to Jesus. 12. During that time, he went off into the mountains to pray. He spent the entire night in prayer to God. 13. When it was day, he summoned his disciples. He chose from among them the Twelve, whom he also named apostles: 14. Simon whom he also called Peter, his brother Andrew, James, John, Philip, Bartholomew, 15. Matthew, Thomas, James Alphaeus, Simon called the Zealot, 16. Judas son of James, and Judas Iscariot, who became a traitor.

Notes

1. *on a Sabbath day*: Sets up the conflict; some MSS add an odd adjective "second-first" which apparently resulted from scribal attempts to sort out Luke's sequence of Sabbaths; the shorter reading is adopted here.

2. *some of the Pharisees*: Luke has only "some" rather than the absolute "the Pharisees" in Mark 2:24 and Matt 12:2. For the Pharisees as the opponents of Jesus, see note on 5:17.

   not allowed on the Sabbath: The Sabbath rest was a major preoccupation for pious Jews; since the command to "keep holy the Sabbath" (Exod 20:8-11; Deut 5:12-15) was, like the command to honor parents, a positive rather than a negative command, it invited elaborate midrashic expansion intended to "place a hedge around Torah" (*Pirke Aboth* 1:1). Hardest to determine was what constituted "work" rather than "rest." Thus, although what the disciples did was not stealing (it was explicitly allowed by Deut 23:25), it was, in the Pharisees' eyes, a breaking of one of the forty categories of activities determined to constitute "work" (cf. *m.Shab.* 7:2).

3. *Jesus answered*: As in the previous controversy, the charge is laid against the disciples but Jesus answers in defense of them. Thus, the declaration that he is "Lord of the Sabbath" is not merely a Christological claim, but legitimates the community practice of the first Christians who handed on stories such as these in the oral tradition.

   not even read: Luke sharpens the implied rebuke by his use of *oude*; these interpreters of Torah should have remembered their biblical precedents.

   what David did: The comparison of Jesus and his disciples to David and his companions is provocative, and the first narrative echo of the angel's promise to Mary that Jesus would inherit the "throne of his father David" (1:32).

4. *entered the house of God*: The story occurs in 1 Sam 21:1-6, and it names Ahimelech as the priest (21:1); Luke therefore omits Mark's identification, "when Abiathar was priest" in 2:26.

   presentation loaves: The phrase *artoi protheseōs* in all three Synoptists derives from the LXX translation for the bread placed before the Lord in the Temple, as in 1 Sam 21:6 (see Exod 25:30; 1 Chr 9:32).

   took . . . ate, gave: Luke alters the word order of Mark 2:26 and adds the word "took." As a result, Jesus' action anticipates the gestures of the Last Supper, when he "takes, gives thanks, breaks, gives" (Luke 22:19).

5. *Son of Man is Lord*: Like Matt 12:8, Luke omits the prior statement about the Sabbath being made for humans in Mark 2:27. He also omits the emphatic "even" (*kai*) in Mark. Nor does he have the "for" (*gar*) of Matthew, which makes the Christological point more explicit. His conclusion is no less emphatic, however, for being abrupt. For the Son of Man and his *exousia*, see note on 5:24.

6. *and taught*: A characteristic Lukan addition. Luke has consistently joined Jesus' wonders to his teaching ministry (4:15, 31; 5:3, 17).

7. *watched closely*: The term *paratēreō* is used by Luke of hostile observation in 14:1 and 20:20; see also 17:20.

   sought an accusation: Is literally "to find a charge." The term *katēgoreō* is understood by Luke in its full forensic sense of a legal charge brought against someone (see 11:54; 23:2, 10, 14 and Acts 22:30; 24:2, 19). This early Luke prepares for the trial of Jesus (23:2).

8. *he knew their thoughts*: As in 5:22, the fact that Jesus knows the *dialogismoi* of his opponents certifies that he is a prophet; cf. 7:39; 2:35.

   stand here before us: As in 4:35 and 5:19, *eis to meson* signifies "in the middle" of the assembled group.

9. *I put this question*: Luke adds this opening rubric and thereby shifts the initiative to Jesus; the testers are being tested.

   save a life or to destroy it: Luke changes Mark 3:4 from "kill" to "destroy." Jesus' question shifts the issue from ritual observance (however important) to moral discourse. A priority of obligation implicitly counter to the Pharisaic premise concerning Torah is thereby established. Note how *Aboth de Rabbi Nathan* 31 aligns "saving life and destroying life" *with* the observance or nonobservance of the Sabbath.

10. *gazing around at them*: This is the only time Luke retains the characteristic Markan expression (see Mark 3:5, 34; 5:32; 9:8; 10:23; 11:11). Luke omits Mark's note that the opponents were silenced, and that Jesus' gaze was one of anger at their hardness of heart.

11. *beside themselves with anger*: Is literally, "filled with senselessness" (*anoia*). In contrast to Mark 3:6, where the Pharisees and Herodians form a plot (*symboulion*) to "destroy" Jesus, Luke's version is milder: the Pharisees [no Herodians are mentioned] discuss what to do "about" or "with" or "to" Jesus.

12. *he went off . . . to pray*: As observed earlier (see note on 3:21) Luke has Jesus pray before major turning points in the narrative. The choosing of the Twelve is clearly such a moment, since Jesus "prays through the night to God" before making his choice.

13. *he chose from among them the twelve*: Luke makes several important changes to Mark 3:14-15. He emphasizes that this was a selection (*eklegomai*) from a larger group; he omits any mention of the function of the Twelve, deferring that until 9:1-2; and he has Jesus name them apostles (but not "twelve apostles" as in Matt 10:12). In Luke-Acts, the Twelve play a particularly important symbolic

role as the basis and leadership of the restored Israel called by the prophet (see 8:1; 9:1, 12, 17; 18:31; 22:3, 30, 47; Acts 6:2); see esp. Acts 1:15-26.

whom he named apostles: Luke has already made clear his understanding of *apostellō* as "sending with a commission" in 1:19, 26; 4:18, 43. Now the noun formed from this verb designates Jesus' chosen Twelve. Jesus will also "send them out" (11:49) not only during his ministry (9:1) but also, through the Spirit, as his prophetic successors in the narrative of Acts (1:2, 26; 2:37, 42-43; 4:33, 35, 36, 37; 5:2, 12, 18, 29, 40; 6:6; 8:1, 14, 18; 9:27; 11:1; 14:4, 14; 15:2, 4, 6, 22, 23; 16:4).

14. *Simon whom he also called Peter*: Luke has already identified him this way in 5:8. He tells no story of the naming like that in Matt 16:16-19.

    his brother Andrew: This way of putting it is particularly striking since Luke omitted Andrew from the call of the disciples (although he was present in the source, Mark 1:16). Andrew appears in Mark's narrative again in 13:3, as well as in John 1:40, 44; 6:8; 12:22, but plays no further role in Luke-Acts except to appear in Luke's second apostolic list (Acts 1:13).

    James, John: Of the four lists of the Twelve in the NT (Mark 3:13-19; Matt 10:1-4; Luke 6:12-16; Acts 1:13), there is complete agreement on the first eight names, with only a small change in order between Andrew and the sons of Zebedee, and between Matthew and Thomas. The last four names show greater variation. Luke (in both lists) has: James of Alphaeus, Simon the Zealot, Judas of James, and Judas Iscariot. Mark and Matthew have James of Alphaeus, Thaddaeus, Simon the Canaanite (perhaps the same as the Zealot), and Judas Iscariot. The only major discrepancy, therefore, is between Thaddaeus and Judas of James. James and John will reappear in Luke's story in 8:51; 9:28, 54 and the apostolic list of Acts 1:13. James will appear otherwise in Acts only at his death (12:2); John appears in Acts 3:1, 3, 4, 11; 4:13, 19; 8:14.

15. *Judas Iscariot*: Is naturally the last name in all the lists. Luke's clause, "who became a traitor," is somewhat subtler than the parallels. The apostasy of Judas (Luke 22:3, 47-48) is important for Luke because it breaks the circle of the Twelve (see Acts 1:15-26).

INTERPRETATION

Luke continues to follow Mark closely in these two Sabbath controversies, but deviates from Mark's order at the end of the sequence. Luke reverses the summary of Jesus' healings (Mark 3:7-12) and the appointment of the Twelve (Mark 3:13-19). The result is that the choosing appears a more direct response to the increasingly hostile reactions of the Jewish leadership to Jesus.

The Pharisees (and to a lesser extent the scribes) emerge even more clearly as the arbiters of piety, particularly with regard to the Sabbath. The first controversy continues the pattern established in the previous story: the disciples are charged with an offense, but it is Jesus who springs to their defense. In the process he reveals himself not only as authoritative interpreter of Torah (by appealing to the narrative example of David in 1 Sam 21:1-6), but also as Son of Man who is Lord of the Sabbath.

The second story raises the stakes. The Pharisees now are watching Jesus for a slip, so that they can bring a charge against him. Jesus, however, takes the initiative, challenging his challengers. They claim to protect the integrity of Torah by placing all observance on an equal plane of obligation and seriousness. But Jesus establishes a priority for moral activity above ritual. The doing of good or evil, the saving or taking of life, these are matters which are trivialized by being subordinated to the demands of ritual observance. The resolution of both conflicts points in the direction of an understanding of the kingdom of God that places high valuation on human life and needs, as well as on the ability to respond flexibly and freely to both.

To ask whether Luke's portrayal of the Pharisees here is historically accurate is to ask the wrong question. It is obvious that these stories reflect the conflicts of the first messianists with non-messianist Jews after the death of Jesus, in a time when the ''scribes and Pharisees'' represented the burgeoning rabbinic movement that was the chief rival within Judaism to the nascent messianic movement. In Luke's narrative, these leaders stand for those who resist the prophet. As with all polemic in the Hellenistic world, the portrayal involves a considerable amount of stereotyping. All opponents in that world were rapacious, lovers of pleasure and glory; no surprise that Luke pictures Jesus' opponents that way.

On the other hand, the portrayal should not, for that matter, be dismissed as utterly without historical merit. The picture of the Pharisees as effectively controlling the piety and politics of the Palestinian populace is surely an exaggeration, but there is supporting evidence that in the first-century, they already had a militant concern for matters such as purity, tithing, and the Sabbath observance (see *m. Demai* 2:3), and were willing to harass those of whom they disapproved (cf. Josephus, *Life*, 191, 198–203).

But it is Luke's literary presentation, rather than the historical facts, which demands the reader's attention, because in the interplay between Jesus and these Jewish leaders we find one of the important plot mechanisms of his story. In this case, we observe how Luke has deliberately set the appointment of the Twelve as a response to the rejection of Jesus (and the beginning of the plan to eliminate him) by the Jewish leaders. Jesus turns to those who have responded positively to his prophetic visitation. From among them, he chooses twelve. They symbolize, form the basis of, and become the leaders of the restored Israel. They and their successors will extend the prophetic mission to the nations. Already this early in the narrative, therefore, the pattern of the division within the people is established, and the way toward a new leadership anticipated.

FOR REFERENCE AND FURTHER STUDY

Cerfaux, L. "Pour l'histoire du titre *apostolos* dans le Nouveau Testament." *Receuil Lucien Cerfaux* (BETL; Gembloux; Duculot, 1954) 2: 185–200.

Hultgren, A. J. "The Function of the Sabbath Pericope in Mark 2:23-28." *JBL* 91 (1972) 38–43.

Lohse, E. "Jesu Worte über den Sabbat." *Judentum—Urchristentum—Kirche: Festschrift für Joachim Jeremias*. Ed. W. Eltester (BZNW 26; Berlin: A. Töpelmann, 1960) 79–89.

Rengstorf, K. H. "Apostolos." *TDNT* I: 407–445.

Schnackenburg, R. "Apostles before and during Paul's Time." *Apostolic History and the Gospel*. Eds. W. W. Gasque and R. P. Martin (Grand Rapids: Eerdmans, 1970) 287–303.

18. The Prophet's Public Preaching (6:17-35)

17. When he had come down with them he stopped on a level place with a large crowd of his disciples and a great multitude of the people from all Judea and Jerusalem and the coastal region of Tyre and Sidon, 18. who came to hear him and to be cured of their diseases. Those tormented by unclean spirits were being healed 19. and the crowds were trying to touch him, because power was going out from him and he was healing them all. 20. And when he had looked up at his disciples he began to say: "Blessed are you poor, for yours is the kingdom of God. 21. Blessed are you who are hungry now, for you will be filled. Blessed are you who are weeping now, for you will laugh. 22. Blessed are you when people hate you, and when they set you aside, and scorn you and cast out your name as an evil thing for the sake of the Son of Man. 23. Rejoice in that day and dance, for look! your reward is great in heaven! In just the same way your ancestors dealt with the prophets. 24. But woe to you rich people, for you are receiving your consolation. 25. Woe to you who are now filled, for you will be hungry. Woe to you who are now laughing, for you will mourn and weep. 26. Woe to you when all people speak well of you. In just the same way your ancestors treated the false prophets. 27. But I declare to you who are listening: Love your enemies. Act well toward those who hate you. 28. Bless those who curse you. Pray for those who abuse you. 29. To the one who strikes you on the cheek, offer your other cheek as well. Do not hold back even your shirt from the one who takes away your coat. 30. Give to everyone who asks you, and do not demand restitution from one who takes what is your own. 31. Just as you want people to act toward you, act in the same way toward them. 32. If you love those who love you, what sort of credit is that to you? Even sinners love those who love them. 33. And if you do good to those who do good to you, what sort of credit is that to you? Even

sinners do the same. 34. And if you lend to someone from whom you expect a return, what sort of credit is that to you? Even sinners lend to sinners so that they can get back an equal amount. 35. Instead, love your
enemies! Do good and lend without expecting a return! Your reward will
be great. You will be children of the Most High, for he himself is kind to
those who are without kindness and are evil.''

NOTES

17. *come down with them*: That is, from the mountain where Jesus had prayed and
chosen the Twelve.

    stopped on a level place: Is literally ''stood,'' but the sense is of a stage on a jour-
ney. Luke uses the summary of Mark 3:7-12 but transposes its location and uses
the gathering of people to set up Jesus' sermon. For the provenance of the crowd,
compare 5:17. Matt 4:24-25 has a similar summary but a reverse spatial movement: Jesus sees the crowd, then goes up on the mountain to teach (Matt 5:1).

18. *to hear him and to be cured*: Luke uses the same combination as in 5:15. The comment that ''power (*dynamis*) was going out of him'' echoes 5:17. For the crowd's
attempt to touch healing power, compare 8:44-47 and Acts 5:14-15.

19. *healing them all*: As has been his consistent practice, Luke joins the ministry of
exorcism and healing to that of teaching (4:36, 40, 43; 5:15), and will make the
same connection for the apostles (9:1-2).

20. *looked up at his disciples*: Luke again reverses Matt 5:1, where Jesus ''sees the
crowds'' and speaks to the disciples. In Luke, the disciples are the specific audience of the sermon, although the ''multitude of the people'' (6:17) form part
of the implied audience, as do also Luke's Christian readers: ''I say to you who
are listening'' (6:27).

    blessed are you poor: For the meaning and use of the macarism (from *makarios*,
''blessed''), see note on 1:45. In contrast to Matthew's nine Beatitudes, Luke
has four; other differences are discussed in the interpretation. The ''poor''
(*ptōchoi*) are not spiritualized. They are the economically impoverished. But in
Luke's narrative, they also represent all those who are marginalized in God's
people (see 4:18; 7:22; 14:13, 21; 16:20-22).

    yours is the kingdom of God: Jesus' mission has been summarized as preaching
the good news of the kingdom of God (4:43), and in 4:18 it has been defined
as ''good news to the poor.'' To say that the kingdom is ''yours'' does not imply rule within the realm (which is to be given to the Twelve, 22:29), but acceptance by God within the restored people.

21. *hungry now, for you will be filled*: As the poor echo the ''lowly'' in the Magnificat
(1:52), so do the hungry (*peinōntes*) recall the ''hungry filled with good things''
in 1:53. Hunger, like poverty, is a sign of need and neglect. The term for ''being
filled'' (*chortazō*) will be used in the multiplication of the loaves (9:17) and the
parable of Lazarus (16:21). The two middle Beatitudes of 6:21 continue Luke's

theme of divine reversal; a present condition ("now") will be turned around in the future.

weeping now, for you will laugh: The term *klaiō* can mean any loud expression of pain or sorrow. In the prophets (LXX), it is often associated with sorrow at disaster caused by apostasy and as a sign of repentance (cf. e.g., Joel 1:5, 18; Isa 22:4; 30:19; 33:7; Jer 9:1; 13:17). In Luke, its use is similar (7:32, 38; 8:52; 19:41; 23:28). The verb *gelaō* ("laugh") is found only in this passage in the NT. The LXX uses it in contexts where a derisive nuance is evident; as in "laughing over" someone (cf. e.g., Gen 17:7; 18:12, 13, 15; Esth 4:17; Ps 51:6; Jer 20:8; Lam 1:7).

22. *hate you . . . set you aside, and scorn you*: Three terms for the experience of rejection. Zechariah described God's visitation as a "salvation from the hand of those who hate us" (1:71), but Jesus promises in 21:17 that his followers would be "hated by all on account of my name." The term *aphorizō* ("set aside") is used only here in the Gospel, but recurs neutrally in Acts 13:2 and 19:9. Here, it has the sense of being segregated. In contemporary parlance, this is what we mean by "marginalization." The final term, "scorn" (*oneidizō*) means a verbal reproach (see e.g., Luke 1:25; I Pet 4:14; Heb 13:13). The three verbs therefore move from attitude (hate) to action (setting apart), to speech (scorn).

cast out your name as an evil thing: The phrasing suggests an exorcism applied to the Christians! In biblical parlance, the "name" (*onoma*) defines identity. The name with which Christians are associated in their mission is that of Jesus (9:48-49; 10:17; Acts 2:38; 3:6, 16; 4:7, 10, 12, 30; 8:12, 16; 9:27, 28; 10:43, 48; 16:18; 19:5; 22:16; 26:9), and it is for this same name that they will experience suffering (21:8, 12, 17; Acts 4:17-18; 5:28, 40; 9:14, 16).

for the sake of the Son of Man: The parallel in Matt 5:11 has "on my account." Luke here connects the fate of the Christians to the narrative development of the figure of the Son of Man in 5:24 and 6:5; see also 7:34.

23. *rejoice . . . dance*: For "rejoicing" as a response to God's visitation see 1:14 and esp. 10:20. The verb translated "dance" (*skirtaō*) was translated in 1:41, 44 as "leap"; the eschatological connotations of the word are noted there.

your reward is great in heaven: Luke uses the term "reward" (*misthos*) of the wages due a laborer in 10:7, or payment for a deed (Acts 1:18). The use in this passage (see also 6:35) is close to his phrase "treasure in heaven" (12:33; 18:22). The main difficulty is understanding "heaven": is it a periphrasis for God, so that Luke means "God will reward you?" (see e.g., 15:7, 18, 21), or does it refer to inscription in a heavenly book (as in 10:20)? It is not possible to infer automatically from either option that "heaven" means also a "place" where the reward will be enjoyed.

ancestors dealt with the prophets: Matt 5:12 has "persecuted the prophets," showing that this is not a uniquely Lukan emphasis. It does, of course, entirely accord with Luke's understanding of the disciples as the prophetic successors of Jesus and facing the same rejection by the people. The idea of the suffering of the prophet is therefore touched on for the first time in Luke's narrative (see esp. 13:33-34). The conviction is stated most emphatically by Stephen: "which of the prophets did not your ancestors persecute?" (Acts 7:52).

24. *woe to you rich people*: Only Luke has these four woes, which match the Beatitudes precisely in form and content. The term "woe" (*ouai*) is especially associated
with the prophets in the LXX, an expletive for disfavor or calamity either described
or desired; for a series of woes similar to these in Luke, see Isa 5:8-22. For Luke's
other uses of the expletive, see 10:13; 11:42, 43, 44, 46, 47, 52 (see the parallel
in Matt 23:13-23); 17:1; 21:23; 22:22. The "rich" play a thematic role in the Gospel
as opposites of the poor. The term denotes economic well-being and security.
It connotes belonging and power within the people, and, in the narrative, a sense
of arrogance that does not require the visitation of God (see 1:53; 12:16, 21; 14:12;
16:1, 19, 21-22; 18:23, 25; 19:2; 21:1).
   receiving your consolation: The term *paraklēsis* has the sense of an aid or help one
leans on. The "consolation" of the rich is their wealth. It is contrasted to the
consolation of the poor which is the kingdom of God (see Luke 2:25; 6:20, and
above all 16:25).

25. *now filled*: These middle woes exactly reverse the two middle Beatitudes; a present condition will be reversed (by God) in the future. The only addition occurs
with the term "mourn" (*pentheō*) which is also used in the LXX for response to
disaster (Hos 4:3; 10:5; Amos 8:8; Isa 24:4; Jer 4:8, etc.). A NT passage remarkably similar to this is Jas 4:9, "your laughter (*gelōs*) will be turned to mourning
(*penthos*)."

26. *treated the false prophets*: Luke does not (in contrast to Matt 7:15; 24:11, 24) use
the term *pseudoprophētēs* with reference to contemporary troublemakers in the
Church, but of figures in the past, using the biblical tradition of the false but
popular prophet who tells people what they want to hear (see Acts 13:6; LXX
Jer 6:13; 33:7, 8, 11, 16; 34:9; 35:1; 36:1, 8; also Zech 13:2).

27. *love your enemies*: The wording of this oxymoronic command is exactly the same
in Matt 5:43, but is there placed in one of Matthew's characteristic antitheses.
Like the other evangelists, Luke prefers to think of this characteristic Christian
attitude in terms of a verb (the noun *agapē* is used only in 11:42). In the NT, it
appears as an attitude and mode of action rather than an emotion. It means to
will the good for another, as Luke's own exegesis immediately makes clear: "act
well (*kalōs*) toward those who hate you." The radical nature of this command
remains as fresh and paradoxical as when it was first uttered.

28. *bless . . . pray*: Luke continues to elaborate what "doing well" means when dealing with an enemy. Jesus calls for the reversal of the universal urge for retaliation. By so doing, he also turns the attitudes of outsiders toward the community
(6:22) around. To bless rather than curse not only recalls the deuteronomic pattern of blessings and curses (see Deut 30:1-7), but more pertinently, the fact that
Jesus was cursed for being crucified (Gal 3:10, 13; 1 Cor 12:3), and his followers
could expect the same, as when "their name is cast out as an evil thing" (6:22).
Similarly, they are to "pray" for those who "abuse" (*epēreazō*) them." The term
has the same sense as *oneidizō* in 6:22. Matt 5:44 has "pray for those who persecute you."

29. *offer . . . do not hold back*: Both commands are found in Matt 5:39-41 within an
antithesis; Luke's version is considerably simpler. The progression has been from

attitude (love) to speech (blessing, praying), to action. Luke has Jesus reject the *do ut des* logic of ancient reciprocity (and benefaction), and inserts the element of "going beyond" what is demanded or required. The offer to give undergarment as well as outer garment is a particularly dramatic example.

30. *give to everyone*: The two commands in this verse make even clearer the absolute character of the prophetic charter. Luke adds "everyone" to the parallel in Matt 5:42, so that the disciple's response is completely nondiscriminatory. The force of the present imperative (*didou*) suggests "keep on giving." Likewise, even from one who "takes what is your own" they are not to "demand a return" (*apaiteō*).

31. *act in the same way toward them*: Luke's version of the "golden rule" is paralleled in Matt 7:12. The command is a version of Lev 19:18, "Love your neighbor as yourself," a text which Luke does not explicitly cite in his version of the "great commandment" in 10:27. The negative form of this principle of ethical reciprocity is widely attested in the ancient world (Tob 4:15; Hillel in *bTShab* 31a), but the positive form is found as well (Pseudo-Isocrates, *Demonicus*, 14; *Nicocles*, 61). Luke's version is sharpened by the interpretation he proceeds to give.

32. *what sort of credit is that to you*: This phrase is repeated three times (6:32, 33, 34). In the Matthean parallel we find "what reward (*misthos*) will you have" (Matt 5:42), and that is the main sense here (cf. Luke's use of *misthos* in 6:35). There is an added nuance given by using the word *charis*, however, and that is the "gift" quality of what Jesus demands. He wants them to go *beyond* mere reciprocity into gift-giving; one is almost tempted to translate, "what sort of gift is that?"

even sinners love: The "sinners" also provide the point of contrast three times in verses 33-34. The kingdom calls "sinners" (5:8, 30, 32), but they are required to "repent of their sins," and follow this new standard of behavior.

34. *lend to someone*: In all three rhetorical questions, the norm of the "sinners" is strict reciprocity in love, doing good, and lending. But Luke goes beyond "the golden rule" in his understanding of relations in the community. It is characteristic of him to focus on the use of possessions as an expression of relationship.

35. *love your enemies*: Only in Luke do we find this dramatic recapitulation of the command of 6:27, spelled out in terms of "doing good" and "lending."

without expecting a return: The use of the word *apelpizō* here has created confusion. The obvious meaning "expect a return" is otherwise unattested in extant Greek literature, and the verb ordinarily means "give up hope." Thus the Vulgate translated *nihil desperantes* ("despairing in nothing"). That led in turn to the need for the MS emendation *mēdena*, "no one" rather than "nothing." Thus, "losing hope in no one." But the translation given here is obviously correct in context.

you will be children of the Most High: This is similar to Matt 5:48 where the disciples are to be "perfect as your heavenly Father is perfect." God's behavior toward humans is positive even when they are undeserving. The divine measure for human activity will become more explicit in the next verse (treated in the next segment of this commentary).

INTERPRETATION

Proof that a decisive turn had been taken when Jesus chose the Twelve is the present discourse addressed to a "large crowd of his disciples" as well as a "great multitude of the people," as soon as Jesus comes down off the mountain to a level patch of ground. The prophet formally enunciates the principles of inclusion within the kingdom he has been proclaiming, and for those who have already joined him, he states clearly the norms of behavior that govern life within the messianic community. The reader is allowed to overhear the "teaching" that Jesus had already been doing in the synagogues but that now, with the Twelve before his eyes, he states as publicly as possible. The summary of Mark 3:7-12 has been transferred by Luke to 6:17-19 in order to set the stage for the prophetic discourse. He draws the crowds together—shows Jesus healing and exorcising. And, since the people also "came to hear" (6:18), the Messiah begins to teach.

This "Sermon on the Plain" is much shorter than the parallel account in Matt 5-7, and is thematically more integrated. Matthew's has 111 verses to Luke's 29. Both evangelists make considerable use of Q material, but unequally. Much of what Matthew has in this sermon, Luke distributes through his great journey narrative in chapters 9-19; and Luke includes some Q material here that Matthew places in later polemical contexts. The major difference in the two discourses is that Luke lacks entirely the distinctively Matthean material dealing with "Law and Prophets" and their interpretation, a concern that clearly reflects the situation of Matthew's Church vis-à-vis the developing rabbinic tradition. As a result, Luke's sermon is notably more spare and focused, with an ethical emphasis entirely intelligible to Gentile readers. The discourse moves smoothly from the opening Beatitudes and woes (6:20-26) to the measure of life before God (27-40) to the demand for action and not just speech (41-49). For the sake of digestible discussion, the present commentary splits the sermon in two; the reader is encouraged to take it all in one swallow.

The literary prototype for both sermons is provided by the delivery of Torah to the people by Moses (cf. Exod 19:20-23:33; Deut 4:44-26:19). In Matthew, the opening scene dramatically recalls the ascent of the mountain by Moses and the giving of the Law, a theme that is carried through not only in such statements as 5:17-21, but above all in the antitheses which follow. In Luke, it is not so much Moses as lawgiver, but Moses the prophet and sage of whom a reader would be reminded.

The opening Beatitudes provide the greatest point of similarity between Matthew's and Luke's sermons, as well as each evangelist's difference in perspective. Matthew has only the nine blessings, with no corresponding woes. His blessings are in the third person and have the air of general propositions concerning membership in the kingdom. They have, furthermore, a tendency toward an individual's spiritual attitudes. In contrast, Luke has Jesus proclaim contrasting sets of blessing and woe. The contrast reminds the reader of the "blessings and curses" of Deuteronomy, but the use of the "woe" also echoes the speech of the prophets. His statements address the hearers (and readers) directly, "yours is the kingdom of heaven," and "*you* rich people." Finally, instead of speaking of internal dispositions which yield specific results (as in Matthew), Luke describes objective conditions that will be or are being reversed by God.

Luke's Beatitudes and woes have the same internal structure. The middle two members of each set describe present conditions of need or comfort that will be turned about in the future. The outer statements in each set describe *present* realities which are paradoxically transformed by the perspective of the kingdom. The rich who represent the secure and powerful are rejected by the prophetic "woe," but the poor who represent the outcast and needy are said to possess the kingdom. This pattern of acceptance and rejection is mirrored (with of course a reverse image) in the final blessing and woe. Those who are rejected by humans are being accepted by God. Those who are accepted by humans are in the position of "false prophets."

The connection established between Jesus and his followers is therefore powerful. As the Son of Man has been shown to be rejected by the leaders of the people, yet is known by the readers to be God's "beloved Son," so are his followers, when rejected on his account, to rejoice, "for their reward is great in heaven." The Beatitudes and woes continue the Lukan literary pattern of reversal. God is at work in this prophetic visitation, transforming values, challenging perceptions: the mighty are being cast down, the lowly are being lifted up.

These opening statements also fit within the narrative pattern of the prophet and the people. Jesus' woes recall the prophetic oracles; his disciples are compared to the prophets; but most of all, Jesus is shown to fulfill the programmatic prophecy of 4:18. The prophetic Messiah was to proclaim "good news to the poor." Now, in this formal public address, we in fact see the Messiah proclaiming, "blessed are you poor." And lest we miss the point, it will be made again in 7:22.

After the Beatitudes and woes demarcate those to whom the kingdom pertains, the following exhortations are directed to those who have heeded the voice of the prophet and "repented." With the transition sentence in 6:27, "I declare to you who are listening," Luke shows Jesus as the teacher of morality for the restored people of God. From verses 27-35, Jesus develops the proper understanding of the law of love by which this community lives. The ethical standard set by these commands is remarkably high, and they take on added significance by following so closely the final blessing and woe. The command to love enemies, do good to those who hate, bless those who curse and pray for those who scorn is not, we are to understand, hypothetical, but is to be taken as the norm for those who are in fact hated, scorned, set aside, reviled and cursed.

As in Matthew's sermon, but with a different set of symbols, Luke has Jesus demand of his followers a standard for human relationships that involves a "going beyond" or "more" than the norm of reciprocity, of *do ut des*. The "golden rule" of "do as you would want done" is not the ultimate norm here, but rather, "do as God would do." The repeated reproach, "what sort of credit is that to you," is aimed at the minimalism of an ethics of "tit for tat," as is also the repeated comparison to "the sinners" who live by just such a norm rather than by the standard of excellence demanded of this people by its prophet. Ultimately, of course, Luke grounds this morality in the covenantal attitudes and actions of God. As God is kind toward all creatures, even those who are not themselves kind, even wicked, so are these disciples to be. The reward is itself the reality of being "children of the Most High," who can imitate in the world the kindness of God toward the world.

FOR REFERENCE AND FURTHER STUDY

Dupont, J. *Les Béatitudes.* 3 vols. Louvain: Nauwerlaerts, 1958, 1969, 1973.

Grundmann, W. "Die Bergpredigt nach der Lukasfassung." *Studia Evangelica* I. Ed. K. Aland, F. Cross (TU 73; Berlin: Akademie-Verlag, 1959) 180–89.

Jeremias, J. *The Sermon on the Mount.* Facet Books, Biblical Series 2; Philadelphia: Fortress, 1963.

May, E. " '. . . for Power Went forth from Him . . .' (Luke 6, 19)." *CBQ* 14 (1952) 93–103.

Percy, E. *Die Botschaft Jesu.* Lund: C. W. K. Gleerup, 1953.

19. *Prophetic Wisdom* (6:36-49)

36. "Become compassionate as your father is compassionate. 37. Do not judge and you will not be judged. Do not condemn and you will not be condemned. Forgive and you will be forgiven. 38. Give and it will be given to you. A fine measure, one pressed down and shaken up and overflowing, will be poured into your lap. By the measure you use to measure, you will be measured in return." 39. He also told them a parable: "Can a blind person be a guide for another blind person? Won't they both fall in a ditch? 40. A disciple is not above the teacher. But when fully trained, every disciple will be like his teacher. 41. Why do you spot the splinter in your brother's eye, but not notice the log in your own eye? 42. How can you

say to your brother, 'Brother, allow me to extract the splinter from your eye,' when you yourself don't see the log in your eye? Hypocrite! First extract the log from your eye! Then you can see clearly enough to extract the splinter from your brother's eye. 43. A sound tree does not produce rotten fruit, nor does a rotten tree produce good fruit. 44. For each tree is known by its own fruit. People don't harvest figs from brambles or grapes from thornbushes. 45. The good person draws the good deed from the good storehouse of the heart, and the wicked person draws the evil deed from a wicked storehouse. Each person speaks from the overflow of the heart. 46. Why do you call me Lord, Lord, and do not do what I say? 47. I will show you what every person who comes to me and hears my words and does them is like. 48. Such a person is like someone building a house. He dug a deep hole and built a foundation on bedrock. When a flood came and a torrent beat against that house, it was not powerful enough to shake it, for the house was well built. 49. But the person who hears and does not do is like someone who built a house right on the ground without a foundation. The torrent dashed against it, and it fell at once, and the collapse of that house was a great one."

NOTES

36. *become compassionate*: The word *oiktirmōn* can be translated also as "merciful," and has much the same range (cf LXX Zech 1:16; Isa 63:15), but is used more rarely in the NT (cf. Rom 12:1; 2 Cor 1:3; Phil 2:1; Col 3:12; Jas 5:11). The term "compassion" captures something of the emotional aspect of the attitude suggested by such LXX passages as Pss 50:1; 102:13; 111:5; Hos 2:19. This command follows directly on that in verse 35, and provides a transition to the next directives.

37. *judge . . . condemn . . . forgive*: With each of these commands, the word "others" is to be understood. The corresponding phrase, "you will not be," on the other hand, is in the passive, which in biblical parlance means action by God. Such retributive formulas are frequent in the NT (cf. e.g., 9:26; 14:38). For the prohibition of judging, see Matt 7:1; Rom 2:1; 14:4, and most remarkably, Jas 4:12; 5:9. The verb translated "forgive" here (*apoluō*) is more properly rendered "release" in the sense of "dismiss" (see 2:29).

38. *give and it will be given*: The passive again means "God will give"; the phrase puts a twist on the more common, "ask and it will be given" (Matt 7:7; Jas 1:5), which Luke also has in another passage (11:9). This positive exhortation is lacking in Matthew, as is its extravagant imaging that follows.

    a fine measure: The *metron* is exactly that: a standard or rule used for measuring other things. But the image here is of a "measure" basket filled with grain, which is pressed down (to make more room), shaken up (to make the grain settle and create more room), and still "overflowing." Thus, a "fine" measure, and the one by which God responds to those who give and forgive.

    you will be measured: The play on the term *metron* continues. The passive again signifies: "God will thus measure you." A truly radical notion, that God adopts for the judgment of humans the standard they use in their relations with each other. The saying is paralleled by Mark 4:24 and Matt 7:2, and is given expression by the Lord's Prayer (Luke 11:4; Matt 6:12).

39. *a parable*: As in the two earlier uses of this term by Luke (4:23; 5:36), the meaning is "proverb." The singular, however, is a bit puzzling, for the rest of the discourse is dominated by a series of comparisons (39, 41, 43, 44, 47). The best rendering might be, "he began to speak parabolically."

   blind person be a guide: The parallel in Matt 15:14 is directed polemically against the Pharisees. The *Gospel of Thomas* 34 also has a version of this saying. The image is given pertinence here by the teacher/disciple context; the teacher should be one who is a "guide to the blind, a light to those in darkness" (Rom 2:19).

40. *a disciple is not above the teacher*: Is found also in Matt 10:24 but put to a different use, as is the double use in John 13:16 and 15:20. In Luke, the disciple can become "fully trained" and thus able to teach as the teacher does. For the saying *qualis dominus talis et servus*, cf. Petronius, *Satyricon* 58.

41. *spot the splinter*: The image of "seeing" follows naturally from the proverb about blind guides; the subject remains that of judging between "brothers" (i.e., fellow members of the community or people, which would also include "sisters"; see 12:13; 17:3; 22:32; Acts 1:15-16; 2:29, 37; 3:17, etc.). The entire saying is found in Matt 7:1-5 and in the *Gospel of Thomas* 26; there is also a close parallel in Petronius' *Satyricon* 57.

42. *hypocrite*: The term *hypokritēs* derives from drama and oratory as "one who responds," that is, an actor. In the Gospels, the term is always derogatory and refers to dissimulation and lack of sincerity. Luke uses the term "hypocrisy" in 12:1 of the Pharisees, and uses "hypocrite" of Jesus' opponents in 12:56 and 13:15, but is more sparing in his application than Matthew.

   first extract: The attention to one's own faults first is a commonplace in Hellenistic moral exhortation; see e.g., Epictetus, *Discourse* 3:22, 9-15.

43. *a sound tree*: The next verses give emphatic expression to a universal conviction in the ancient world, that character precedes action. A person's deeds therefore revealed the state of the "heart." The fact that this natural progression could be camouflaged, of course, is what gives "hypocrisy" its sting.

45. *the good person*: This verse makes the point of the prior comparisons explicit. Jesus is speaking about moral actions and the character that produces them. Matt 12:33-35 places the same sayings in a polemical context; see also *Gospel of Thomas* 45.

46. *not do what I say*: The phrasing nicely illustrates how the discourses of the Gospels reach out to early Christian readers. In the narrative to this point, only Peter and the leper have called Jesus "Lord" (5:8, 17), so the rebuke cannot be addressed to them; it is obviously aimed at Christians who profess faith but don't live it out. Luke derives the saying from Q (cf. Matt 7:21-23) but gives it a distinctive ethical edge. The motif of "saying and not acting" is a common one in Hellenistic philosophy (see e.g., Seneca, *Moral Epistles* 20:1 and *Sentences of Sextus*, 177). The New Testament's fullest treatment of the theme is in Jas 2:14-26.

47. *I will show you*: The term *hypodeiknymi* is used frequently in Greek paraenetic literature to introduce an example (*hypodeigma*). Luke adds this expression to the example he shares with Matt 7:24-27. In both Gospels it closes the sermon.

comes to me and hears: Luke adds "comes to me" and thereby ties this closing message to the setting of the sermon in which the people "came to hear him" (6:18).

48. *building a house*: Luke does not have Matthew's contrast between the "prudent" and the "foolish"; he also simplifies and clarifies the wording. He uses another building analogy in 14:28-30.

INTERPRETATION

The opening section of Luke's sermon had a strongly prophetic character. The prophetic Messiah, anointed with the Spirit, announced good news to the poor and pronounced woes against the rich. He issued a radical commandment of love as the norm for the restored people of God. He concluded by stating that the measure for human relationships is God's graciousness shown toward all.

The next section of the discourse picks up with the same point: Christians are to become compassionate just as God is compassionate. But the exhortation which follows has more a sapiential than prophetic tone. Indeed, if this section were excerpted, it would not seem—with the exceptions to be noted—out of place in the writings of many Hellenistic moralists, at least in its major concerns. We find here typical stylistic elements: the alternating of negative and positive commands; the use of apostrophe and rhetorical questions; the employment of examples. And we see the typical concerns for actions flowing from a certain character or "heart," of action not speech defining convictions, of teaching and learning as a matter of guidance and mutual correction.

These elements can be found with equal concentration in such paraenetic texts as those of Pseudo-Isocrates (*Demonicus*), Epictetus (*Discourses*), and Dio Chrysostom (*Orations*). Because of this flavor, Luke's sermon offers itself far more intelligibly to a Gentile audience than does Matthew's.

The major distinguishing feature is the essential one. As in the first part of the sermon, the ethics of the kingdom is not defined simply by reason or character; it is based in a covenantal relationship with the living God. The "imitation of God", therefore,—which is not absent from Greek philosophy (as in Plato, *Phaedrus* 248A, or Epictetus, *Discourse* 1:12, 8)—is here by way of response to initiative taken by God in history, and enlivened by the conviction that God takes human freedom into account. Thus, the prohibitions of judging and condemning are not based on excellence of character or prudential evaluation of consequences. The drawback of condemning others is not that they will condemn us in return, but rather that *God* will condemn us. Likewise, giving and forgiving are answered by the generosity of God. The most thought-provoking proposition is that God uses as the measure for the response to humans the measure they use in their relations with each other (37-38). Finally, of course, it is not only God who is to be obeyed, but also the words of the prophet himself. The acting out of his teaching will dig the deep foundation that enables the disciples to resist the floods of opposition they inevitably will face (see 6:22).

For Reference and Further Study

Furnish, V. *The Love Commandment in the New Testament* (Nashville: Abingdon, 1972) 54–59, 84–90.

Horn, F. W. *Glaube und Handeln in der Theologie des Lukas.* Göttingen: Vandenhoeck & Ruprecht, 1983.

Kahlefeld, H. *Der Jünger: Eine Auslegung der Rede Lk 6, 20-49.* Frankfurt: Knecht, 1962.

Spicq, C. *Agape in the New Testament.* 2 vols. St. Louis: B. Herder, 1963.

Van Unnik, W. C. "Die Motivierung der Feindesliebe im Lukas vi. 32-35." *NovT* 8 (1966) 284–300.

Verhey, A. *The Great Reversal: Ethics and the New Testament.* Grand Rapids: Eerdmans, 1984.

20. *Two Prophetic Wonders (7:1-17)*

1. Since he had finished all his words to the people, he entered Capernaum. 2. A certain centurion had a slave whom he highly valued. The slave was ill and approaching death. 3. The centurion had heard about Jesus. He sent Jewish elders as a delegation to him. They were to ask him to come save his slave. 4. When they reached Jesus, they implored him earnestly. They said, "He deserves to have this done for him, 5. since he loves our nation and has himself built the synagogue for us." 6. Jesus went with them, but when he had reached a point not far from the house, the centurion sent friends to say to him, "Master, don't trouble yourself any more. I am not fit for you to come under my roof. 7. And for the same reason, neither did I judge myself worthy to come to you. But say a word and let my servant be healed. 8. I also am a man subject to authority, and I have soldiers under me. I say to this one, 'Go!' and he goes. And I say to another, 'Come!' and he comes. And I say to my slave, 'Do this!' and he does it." 9. When Jesus heard this, he marvelled at him. He turned to the crowd that was following him. He said, "I tell you, not even in Israel have I found faith

like this!'' 10. Those who had been sent returned to the house. They found the slave in good health. 11. Jesus went the next day to a town called Naim. His disciples and a large crowd were travelling with him. 12. As he approached the town gate, a dead man was being carried out. He was his mother's only child, and she was a widow. A substantial crowd from the town accompanied her. 13. When the Lord saw her, he felt compassion toward her. He said to her, ''Weep no more.'' 14. He went forward and touched the coffin. Those who were carrying it stopped. He said, ''Young man, I tell you, Arise!'' 15. The dead man sat up. He began to speak. Jesus presented him to his mother. 16. Fear took hold of everyone. They gave glory to God. They said, ''A great prophet has been raised up among us!'' and, ''God has visited his people!'' 17. This account concerning him spread through the whole of Judea and all the surrounding region.

NOTES

1. *words to the people*: Literally, ''in the hearing of the people,'' a Semitism (cf. LXX Exod 15:26; Deut 11:3). The reference to the people reestablishes the narrative connection to 6:17-18.

2. *a certain centurion*: In Matthew's version (8:5-13) we find the same character and situation; the partial parallel in John 4:46b-54 has a ruler and a sick son. The centurion was in charge of a hundred men. It is clear from 7:5 that this soldier was a ''God-fearing'' Gentile. In Acts 10:1, 22, we meet Cornelius, another well-disposed Gentile centurion. A Gentile soldier seeking help from an Israelite prophet reminds us of Naaman the Syrian general who sought help from Elisha (2 Kgs 5:1-14; cf. Luke 4:27).

3. *Jewish elders as a delegation*: Each synagogue had its *gĕrousia* or board of elders which administered the community's affairs. We see here local Galilean leaders, not the ''elders of the people'' who sat in the Sanhedrin and created such problems for Jesus and the first Christians (Luke 9:22; 20:1; 22:52; Acts 4:5, 8, 23; 25:15). The centurion appears as the benefactor of the community; we are to understand therefore that the elders went not under order but as grateful patrons. The note of Jewish intercession is peculiar to Luke's version and reminds us of the role of the Jewish girl in 2 Kgs 5:3.

5. *loves our nation*: The term *agapaō* (''love'') shows itself as an attitude of benevolence that is translated into specific acts. ''Our nation,'' of course, refers to Israel as a people; compare Luke 23:2; Acts 24:17.

   built the synagogue for us: That is, provided the funds for its construction; inscriptions from the period memorialize such benefactions.

6. *sent friends*: For those powerfully placed in Hellenistic society, ''friends'' were often political allies or associates (cf. Luke 23:12) or the patrons of a powerful benefactor (cf. Luke 14:10-12; Acts 10:24; 19:31). Luke's Hellenistic perceptions are revealed in his flexible uses of the language of friendship.

master, don't trouble yourself: The centurion uses the title *kyrios,* which is at the least a sign of respect, and by the Christian reader would be regarded as a sign of faith. Only Luke has this interjection.

7. *for the same reason:* Although both Luke and Matt 8:8 have "I am not fit to have you come under my roof," only Luke adds this revealing rider. The sending of emissaries, we are to understand, is not a sign of arrogance but of humility; in effect, another compliment to an even greater benefactor.

say a word: Is literally "say by a word," and the following phrase is put in the imperative as though it were such a command, "let the servant be healed." In fact, Jesus does not even speak such a word. But the centurion's recognition that his power does not require his physical presence is an impressive tribute.

8. *subject to authority:* The entire section is paralleled by Matt 8:9-10, but is lacking in John 4:49. The statement demonstrates the understanding of *exousia* (authority) held by those higher on the social pyramid, and helps us understand passages like 4:6-8.

9. *faith like this:* Is literally, "such faith"; in contrast to the case of the paralytic (5:17-19), the centurion's faith is not left implicit in his deeds. It is made explicit by his message. At this point in the story, Matthew 8:11-13 adds sayings on the acceptance of outsiders and the rejection of insiders (which Luke uses in another place, 13:28-29). John 4:50-54 adds a certifying colloquy concerning the time of the healing.

11. *the next day:* The Greek here (*en tǫ hexēs*) is unusual (compare Luke 9:37; Acts 21:1; 25:17; 27:18, and Luke 8:1). No great significance attaches to the temporal transition. The story is found only in Luke and he deliberately pairs it with the previous one.

disciples and a large crowd: The crowd (*ochlos*) has circled Jesus from the start (4:42; 5:1, 3, 15, 19, 29; 6:17, 19; 7:9), but Luke increasingly shows "the disciples" (*mathētai*) as a group discernible from the mass (5:30; 6:1, 13, 17, 20). They will steadily become the focus for Jesus' instruction.

12. *and she was a widow:* The phrase echoes the biblical prototype for Luke's story, Elijah's raising of the son of the widow of Sarepta (1 Kgs 17:20; cf. Luke 4:25). Luke does not state the obvious consequence of a widow's losing an only son, which is that she would have no economic support.

13. *Lord saw her:* This is the first time in the narrative that Luke himself has identified Jesus as *ho kyrios,* ("the Lord"), but not the last. It is a distinctive feature of his Gospel to use the title so extensively in the narrative itself (see 7:19; 10:1, 39, 41; 11:39; 12:42; 13:15; 17:5-6; 18:6).

felt compassion: The verb *splanchnizomai* (see also 10:33; 15:20) is used in the LXX Prov 17:5 of the inner emotion accompanying mercy. Jesus here shows the compassion he enjoins on his disciples in 6:36.

14. *young man . . . arise:* The verb "rise" (*egeirō*) was used also for the paralytic (5:23-24) and the man with the withered hand (6:8). But this literal resuscitation sets up the thematic statement in 7:22, "the dead are being raised."

15. *presented him to his mother*: The phrase *edōken auton tē mētri autou* is exactly that found in 1 Kgs 17:23.

16. *a great prophet has been raised up*: This is the first explicit application of the title prophet to Jesus in the narrative, although Jesus' prophetic ministry has been abundantly demonstrated. The present response echoes LXX Deut 18:15, "The Lord God will raise up (*anhistēmi*) for you a prophet like me." In Acts 3:21, this text is applied to the resurrected Jesus. In this case, the verb has the sense of "appointed" or "selected" (by God) as in Judg 2:16; 3:9; Deut 13:1 (and see the "raising up of the Teacher of Righteousness" at Qumran [CD 1:11]), although the Lukan reader will pick up the deeper resonances. The phrase, "among us" is significant, for the prophet's role is within the people (see Acts 2:22; 3:22). One should also compare the response of the widow of Sarepta to Elijah's deed: "Behold, I know that you are a man of God and the word of the Lord is truly in your mouth" (1 Kgs 17:24).

    God has visited his people: For the biblical background to "visitation," see the note on 1:68. What Zechariah said by way of prophecy is shown to be fulfilled in the narrative. Note also the important use of this language again in Luke 19:44 and Acts 15:14.

17. *this account*: Is literally "this word"; for the thematic implications, see the note on 1:2. This summary statement provides a transition to the message delivered to and sent by John in the following passage.

INTERPRETATION

This entire section of the Gospel bears the marks of vigorous and independent redaction. Luke abandoned Mark's order in 6:20 in order to present Jesus as the prophetic proclaimer of good news to the poor, and will return to Mark's sequence again only in 8:4, in the meantime providing what is sometimes called the "little interpolation" (the large one being his travel journey of chs. 9–19). Luke combines material from Q—that is, shared with Matthew—such as the healing of the centurion's slave (7:1-10; Matt 8:5-13) and the discourse on John the Baptist (7:18-35; Matt 11:2-19) together with material unique to his Gospel, such as the raising of the widow's son (7:11-17) and the forgiving of the sinful woman (7:36-50). His way of putting these pieces together clearly reveals his overall compositional interests. He brings together the prophets John and Jesus, and shows how they are rejected or accepted by the people. Once he has stated this theme fully, he can then move on in chapters eight and nine to the formation of the people and its leadership.

These first two stories in the sequence serve to certify Jesus' status as a prophet through whom God is visiting the people. In order to grasp this function, the reader must consider the stories not only individually but also as a set, and one that responds to an earlier part of Luke's story.

The healing of the centurion's slave is substantially the same as Matthew's version. Jesus heals in response to a Gentile's request, and compares his faith favorably to that found in Israel. Already the structure of the story recalls the narrative of 2 Kgs 5:1-14 about Naaman the Syrian. Luke's redactional touches are slight. He adds the Jewish delegation and the intervention of friends. These elements show the good will of the soldier toward Judaism as well as his power, but most of all, they make the story resemble even more that of Naaman the leper, in which we find the intercession of a young Jewish girl, and the encouragement of servants. The fit is not exact, of course, but Luke has moved the story received from a source identifiably in that direction.

In the second story, Jesus raises the only son of a widow from the dead. This resuscitation is unparalleled in the Gospel tradition. In Greek literature, the story of Apollonius of Tyana raising a young bride from the dead (Philostratus, *Life of Apollonius*, 4:45) has a number of superficial resemblances. The most obvious source Luke used for his own composition was the raising of the widow of Sarepta's son from the dead by the prophet Elijah (1 Kgs 17:20-24). In this case there is both a structural similarity, and a number of deliberate verbal echoes (7:12, 15).

Taken as a set, the stories represent the narrative fulfillment of the programmatic prophecy of Luke 4:25-27. The Sermon on the Plain showed how, in fulfillment of 4:18, Jesus "proclaimed good news to the poor." Now Luke has Jesus perform wonders that closely resemble those performed by those "prophets of old" (see Luke 9:19). In reverse order, we see Jesus perform a healing similar to that done by Elisha, and a resuscitation even more strikingly reminiscent of that performed by Elijah. And since this arrangement is entirely due to Luke's redaction (he is not following any source's sequence at this point), it must be attributed to Luke's intentions rather than coincidence. The purposefulness of his arrangement is shown by the concluding response by the people. By calling him "the great prophet raised up for us," they identify Jesus as the prophetic Messiah. In the second declaration, "God has visited his people," they state the meaning of this prophet's ministry. It is entirely consistent with the pattern that Luke has already established that this visitation reaches those who are outcast because they are a Gentile or a woman.

FOR REFERENCE AND FURTHER STUDY

Brodie, T. L. "Towards Unravelling Luke's Uses of the Old Testament: Luke 7:11-17 as *imitatio* of 1 Kgs 17:17-24." *NTS* 32 (1986) 247-267.

Dubois, J. D. "La figure d'Elie dans la perspective lucanienne." *RHPR* 53 (1973) 155-176.

Gils, F. *Jésus Prophète d'après les évangiles synoptiques* (Orientalia et Biblica Lovaniensia 2; Louvain: Publications Universitaires, 1957) 26–27.

Johnson, L. T. *The Literary Function of Possessions in Luke-Acts* (SBLDS 39; Missoula: Scholars Press, 1977) 96–99.

Lindars, B. "Elijah, Elisha and the Gospel Miracles." *Miracles: Cambridge Studies in Their Philosophy and History.* Ed. C. F. D. Moule (London: Mowbray, 1965) 63–79.

Minear, P. *To Heal and to Reveal: The Prophetic Vocation according to Luke.* New York: Crossroad, 1976.

21. *John, Jesus, and the People* (7:18-35)

18. John's disciples told him about all these things. Summoning two of his disciples, 19. John sent them to the Lord to ask, "Are you the one who is coming, or must we wait for another?" 20. When the men reached him they said, "John the Baptist sent us to ask you, 'Are you the one who is coming or must we wait for another?'" 21. At that hour he healed many people from illnesses and wounds and evil spirits, and he granted sight to many blind persons. 22. He answered them, "Go tell John what you have seen and heard: blind people see, lame people are walking, lepers are being cleansed and deaf people are hearing again, dead people are being raised, poor people are being told good news. 23. Blessed is the person who does not find me reason to falter." 24. After John's messengers left, Jesus spoke to the crowds about John. "Why did you go out into the desert? Did you go to watch a reed shaken by a wind? 25. But why did you go out? To see a man clothed in delicate garments? Look, people with splendid garments and luxurious lives are found in palaces! 26. But why did you go out? To see a prophet? Yes, I tell you, and something more than a prophet. 27. He is the one of whom it is written, 'Look, I am sending my messenger ahead of me. He will prepare my way before me.' 28. I tell you, no one ever born of woman is greater than John. But the least person in the kingdom of God is greater than him." 29. All the people and the tax-agents had heard and justified God by being baptized with John's baptism. 30. But the Pharisees and the lawyers rejected God's plan for them by not being baptized by him. 31. "To whom shall I compare the people of this age? Who are they like? 32. They are like children in the marketplace. They sit and yell at each other. They say, 'We piped for you and you didn't dance! We wailed in lament, and you didn't weep!' 33. John the Baptist has come neither eating bread nor drinking wine and you say, 'He has a demon!' 34. The Son of Man has come eating and drinking, and you say, 'Look! A glutton and drunkard, a friend of tax-agents and sinners!' 35. But wisdom is justified by all her children."

Notes

18. *John's disciples*: John's disciples were mentioned in 5:33. In Acts 19:1, Paul finds disciples of John in Ephesus years after the death of Jesus. John 3:25–4:1 suggests some period of interaction between the followers of Jesus and John during Jesus' ministry. The present story is a vestige of a similar tradition. Luke has John's disciples travel in pairs (v. 19) as he does also the emissaries of Jesus (10:1; 19:29). Luke omits mention of John being in prison, a point made explicitly by the parallel, Matt 11:2.

19. *the one who is coming*: The title *ho erchomenos* is found also in Matt 11:3 and picks up the language about "coming" in such passages as 3:16; 4:34; 5:32. John 6:14 uses the expression "the Prophet who is coming into the world." In the present passage, the Baptist's question refers to "the Stronger One" he had predicted in 3:16.

    wait for another: The term *prosdokaō* denotes expectation as well as waiting, and echoes the initial response to the Baptist's own preaching (3:15).

20. *sent us to ask*: This whole stage in the story is lacking in Matthew. Luke uses this and the next sentence to establish a solemn atmosphere for a proclamation.

21. *at that hour*: Luke uses a phrase like this one to signal particularly important moments in the narrative (see 2:38; 10:21; 12:12; 13:31; 20:19; 22:53; 24:33); remarkably, he uses it only once in Acts, in a passage recalling the name of Jesus (Acts 16:18).

    wounds and evil spirits: Luke adds this whole sentence, which enables the thematic statement which follows to be literally true. The term translated "wounds" (*mastix*) can also mean "plagues," but the more common sense seems better here. Notice again how Luke joins physical and "spiritual" healing (as in 4:36; 6:17-18). Luke uses the word *charizō* ("to gift") for the healing of the blind.

22. *what you have seen and heard*: In Matt 11:4, the present tense is used; Luke has the witnesses present for the events and therefore able to report to John what they "saw and heard."

    blind . . . poor: Exactly the same listing is found in the parallel, Matt 11:5. Making "good news to the poor" even more climactic than "raising the dead" has particular force in Luke, where the resuscitation story had just been told (7:11-17).

23. *blessed is the person*: Matt 11:6 has the same macarism; for the usage, see the note on 1:45. With one exception (17:1-2), this is Luke's only use of the term *skandalizō* from which we derive "scandalize." The idea, however, is certainly present in passages about the "sign of contradiction" in 2:34 and the "rock of stumbling" in 20:18. Here, the statement asks that the works of healing and preaching be accepted as signs of the prophetic Messiah through whom God is visiting the people.

25. *delicate garments*: Verses 24–28 are matched by Matt 11:7-11, with only small changes. Luke adds "garments" for clarification in this sentence, and in the next characterizes further the clothing and lifestyle of those who live in palaces. The term translated "luxurious lives" (*tryphē*) is often used in Hellenistic moral teach-

ing for a corrupt voluptuousness (cf. *Sentences of Sextus*, 73). Luke's animus toward the rich and powerful accounts for these small details.

26. *more than a prophet*: John's prophetic status has been known to the reader since the canticle of Zechariah (1:76), and his function as precursor from 3:4, 16.

27. *I am sending my messenger*: The passage appears to be a mixed citation from LXX Exod 23:20 and Mal 3:1. The Malachi passage could also be based on that in Exodus. The citation is found in the same form in Mark 1:2 as well as Matt 11:10.

28. *least . . . is greater*: The contrast is not between John and Jesus, but between the old and new order. The translation takes the comparative *mikroteros* "smaller" as the superlative, "least." Matt 11:12-15 follows this with the logion concerning the Law and the kingdom (deferred by Luke to 16:16) and the explicit identification of John as Elijah.

29. *all the people*: This sentence is an interjection by Luke which is lacking in Matthew. It is of considerable thematic importance, for it distinguishes the response by the tax-agents and sinners from that of Pharisees and lawyers.

    justified God: The verb *dikaioō* means to "regard as righteous." Those who accept the prophet thereby "recognize the righteousness from God." Note the use again in 7:35 (Wisdom's children) and 18:14.

30. *rejected God's plan for them*: A very strong statement, in which the same verb *atheteō* (to put aside) is used as in 10:16: those who reject Jesus' emissaries reject him and by rejecting him reject God. The "will of God" (*boulē tou theou*) is a favorite term of Luke's, denoting God's plan for history (see Acts 2:23; 4:28; 13:36; 20:27). Contrasted to it is the "will of man" in Acts 5:38. Likewise, those "justifying themselves" in Luke 10:29 and 16:15 stand in opposition to this who "justifies God."

31. *people of this age*: Verses 31-35 are paralleled closely by Matt 11:16-19. The phrase "to what (in this case "whom") shall I compare" frequently introduces a parable (cf. Mark 4:30; Matt 7:24-26; 13:24; 18:23; 25:1). Luke uses it also in 13:18, 20. The term "age" or "generation" (*genea*) can be used neutrally (Luke 21:32; Acts 13:26; 15:21), but Luke uses it increasingly of those opposed to the prophet's message (Luke 9:41; 11:29, 30, 31, 32, 50, 51; 16:8; 17:25; Acts 2:40).

32. *sit and yell at each other*: The image is wonderfully vivid. Matt 11:16 has "yell to others," but Luke makes the shouting reciprocal.

    we piped: In Luke's version, the whole point is that whatever is done by one group displeases the other. Thus, no matter what the style of the prophets John and Jesus, there will be cause for complaint.

33. *neither eating bread nor drinking wine*: The asceticism of John's disciples was noted in 5:33, and in 1:15 John was portrayed as one who would not drink strong drink.

    he has a demon: The charge is otherwise unattested in the Gospels, except as applied to Jesus in John 7:20; 8:48, 52. The idea is present in passages such as Mark 3:21-30.

34. *glutton and drunkard*: There may be some sense of allusion here to the passage in Deut 21:18-21 concerning the "stubborn and rebellious son," although the

LXX does not support the suggestion of a verbal allusion. More to the point in Luke is the charge that Jesus is "friend" (*philos*) of tax-agents and sinners, since in the ancient world friendship meant spiritual sharing of the most profound kind (cf. Aristotle, *Nichomachean Ethics*, 9). The narrative basis for the charge is in 5:27-29, 30, 32.

35. *wisdom is justified*: The same verb is used as in 7:29 (*dikaioō*); consistent with that, Luke has personalized the statement in contrast to Matthew's "wisdom is justified by her works" (Matt 11:19). In Luke, the point has to do with the formation of the people of God. Those who are "children of Wisdom (God)" will respond positively to the prophetic visitation; cf. the "wisdom of God" in Luke 11:49, and especially the story which follows this one.

INTERPRETATION

This substantial discourse is shared almost entirely with Matt 11:2-19. The distinctive Lukan point is communicated by small but significant editorial adjustments, and most of all by the placement of the discourse after the two stories of 7:1-17, and before the story of 7:36-50. The rule of thumb for interpreting Luke-Acts—that *where* something is said is as significant as *what* is said—is appropriately applied here.

Now, Luke's inclusion of the messages sent and received by John and Jesus through their disciples, which serve to reassure John (and the reader) that Jesus is indeed "the Coming One" whom John had announced (3:16), as well as Jesus' discussion of John as a prophet who did not receive universal acceptance from his hearers, are to be read against the narrative backdrop of two stories in which Jesus has been portrayed as "the great prophet who has been raised up" and doing the deeds of Elijah and Elisha among the people.

In similar fashion, what Jesus says about John will also be understood by the careful reader in light of Luke's extensive attention to the Baptist earlier in his narrative. Thus John's asceticism (7:33) has been prepared for by Gabriel's announcement to Zechariah (1:15) and the conflict with the Pharisees (5:33). Similarly, John's role as the "messenger going before the face" of the Messiah (7:27) was announced before (1:17) and after his birth (1:76), and shown narratively in Luke's account of John's preaching (3:4-6, 15-16). Luke had not, however, spoken of John's clothing (in contrast to Matt 3:4), so he takes this opportunity to twice add the word "garments" in 7:25 in the description of John's lack of "delicacy." He heightens the picture of John's asceticism as well by adding the terms "splendid" and "luxurious" for those dwelling in palaces. By so doing, Luke includes John with Jesus among the poor opposed by the rich and powerful.

While Luke subscribes entirely to the perception of John as prophet, and more than a prophet, he reminds the reader as well that the "great prophet" is Jesus. The exchange between John and Jesus in 7:18-23 provides a fine example of how Luke builds a scene. In verse 20, he has the messengers from John repeat verbatim the message they had been given by John. The repetition serves only to increase the dramatic tension. But his addition in verse 21 serves to provide a link between this scene and those immediately preceding it. The messengers in effect are made witnesses of the sort of deeds Jesus was doing "in that hour" and which the reader heard in the two preceding stories. The statement therefore that "the dead are being raised" is confirmed by the narrative itself. By combining physical healings with the proclamation of good news, furthermore, Luke continues to make the point noted earlier, that the ministry of healing involves most of all the "healing" or the "restoration" of the people of God.

By his arrangement of materials, Luke has also established connections to more distant parts of his story. He shares with Matthew the list of wonders that concludes with "the poor have good news told them." But only in Luke does this solemn announcement echo the programmatic preaching of Jesus in 4:18, and its narrative fulfillment in 6:20. The prophecy/fulfillment pattern is for Luke a literary mechanism. Notice as well that in the statement, "blessed is the person who does not find me reason to falter," Luke anticipates not only the authorial comment of 7:29-30, but also the story that follows in 7:36-50.

Because 7:29-30 interrupts the flow of Jesus' discourse, is absent from the Matthean parallel, and so clearly reflects Lukan vocabulary and thematic interests, we are justified in regarding it as his own authorial commentary rather than as a report of Jesus' words. It is one of Luke's most important interjections, enabling the reader to put together diverse strands in the story up to this point. The sinners and tax-agents accepted John and by so doing justified God. The Pharisees and lawyers rejected John and by so doing rejected God's plan in their regard. The statement makes explicitly thematic the "division in the people" that had been prophesied by Simeon. It also shows us that the statements concerning the divine reversal, in which the categories of rich and poor played such an important role (as here in 7:22) will be enacted in the story by these characters, so that "rich" in Luke effectively equals "Pharisee/lawyer," and "poor" equals "sinner/ tax-agent." The language about possessions is not simply about money, but about power and position, about openness and closedness. The reader will see an immediate exemplification of it in the story that follows in 7:36-50.

For Reference and Further Study

Cotter, W. J. "The Parable of the Childen in the Market-Place, Q (Lk) 7:31-35: An Examination of the Parable's Image and Significance." *NovT* 29 (1987) 289–304.

Dupont, J. "L'Ambassade de Jean-Baptiste (Matthieu 11, 2-6; Luc 7, 18-23)." *NRT* 83 (1961) 805–21; 943–59.

Feuillet, A. "Jésus et la sagesse divine d'après les évangiles synoptiques." *RB* 62 (1955) 161–96.

Linton, O. "The Parable of the Children's Game: Baptist and Son of Man (Matt xi, 16-19= Luke vii, 31-35): A Synoptic Text—Critical, Structural, and Exegetical Investigation." *NTS* 22 (1975-6) 159–79.

Schubert, P. "The Structure and Significance of Luke 24." *Neutestamentliche Studien für Rudolf Bultmann* (BZNW 21; Berlin: A. Töpelmann, 1954) 165–86.

22. The Friend of Sinners (7:36-50)

36. One of the Pharisees invited Jesus to eat with him. He went into the Pharisee's house and reclined at table. 37. There was a woman in the city who was a sinner. She learned that he was dining in the Pharisee's house. She carried in an alabaster jar of perfumed oil. 38. She stood behind him near his feet. She wept and her tears began to wet his feet. She dried his feet with her hair, she kissed his feet and anointed them with the perfumed oil. 39. The Pharisee who had invited him said to himself, "If this fellow were a prophet he would know who and what kind of woman it is who touches him, that she is a sinner." 40. Jesus answered him by saying, "Simon, I have something to say to you." He said, "Teacher, speak!" 41. "A certain moneylender had two debtors. One owed five hundred denarii, the other owed fifty. 42. Since neither had the funds to repay, he forgave both debts. Now which of them will love him more?" 43. Simon answered, "I suppose the one to whom more was forgiven." Jesus told him, "You have decided rightly." 44. Turning toward the woman, he said to Simon, "Do you see this woman? I came into your house. You did not give me water for my feet. But she bathed my feet with her tears and dried them with her hair. 45. You gave me no kiss. But from the moment I entered she has not ceased kissing my feet. 46. You did not anoint my head with oil. She anointed my feet with perfumed oil. 47. On this basis, I tell you, her many sins have been forgiven, since she has shown so much love. The person forgiven little loves only a little." 48. He said to her, "Your sins have been forgiven." 49. Those who were reclining at table began to say to themselves, "Who is this who even forgives sins?" 50. But he said to the woman, "Your faith has saved you. Go in peace."

NOTES

36. *one of the Pharisees*: The literary link to the previous passage is established at once by the introduction of the characters; "Pharisee" is repeated four times in verses 36-39.

reclined at table: The translation supplies "at table" here and below; Luke uses *kataklinō* here and *katakeimai* in verse 37; the meaning is the same. They were dining in the Hellenistic manner which was to lounge on one's side, with the feet pointing away from the table. Thus the woman can stand "behind him at his feet."

37. *who was a sinner*: This second character matches the "sinners" in verse 29. We do not know the nature of her sinfulness, but it was sufficiently public to be known by Jesus' host; the indefinite relative pronoun *hētis* also suggests "the sort of woman in the city who was a sinner."

    perfumed oil: *Myron* is an oil with a pungent scent (see John 12:3). Although myrrh was used for the burial of Jesus (Luke 23:56), there is no emphasis on this anointing having any such proleptic significance (against Mark 14:8; Matt 26:12), or on the oil being expensive (as in Mark 14:3-5; Matt 26:7; John 12:3).

39. *if this fellow were a prophet*: The designation of Jesus as "prophet" connects the story once more to the thematic statement in 7:29-30. That a prophet can see the heart is axiomatic (see John 4:19). The irony here is not only that Jesus *does* know the woman's heart, but also shows that he can read Simon's thoughts! The prophecy of Simeon in 2:35 is again fulfilled.

    who touches him: As with table fellowship, the separation between the pure and impure had much to do with what could be touched and what not (see Lev 5:2-3; 6:18, 27; 7:20; 22:4-9). For the touching of an unclean woman, see Lev 15:19-32.

40. *teacher, speak*: The use of the title *didaskalos* ("teacher") does not indicate a positive response to Jesus (cf. e.g., 11:45; 20:21, 28).

41. *two debtors*: The parable is straightforward and perfectly intelligible. It serves the classic function of clarifying a real-life situation. The link between analogy and life is provided by the concept of "forgive" applied respectively to debt and to sin. Both sums of money were substantial, since the *denarius* equalled a day's wage (Matt 18:28; 20:2).

42. *forgave both debts*: Both here and in verse 43, the term *charizomai* is used, which has the nuance of "graciously" or "by way of gift" attached to it. Certainly, to release a debt simply because of an inability to pay is unusually kind behavior in a moneylender!

    love him more: The term *agapaō* ("love") should not be given a specifically religious or ethical connotation in this place. In context, it means gratitude. The term is used here, one suspects, because of its use in the application to follow.

44. *do you see this woman*: For Jesus' parable to work, he must argue in reverse from the "love" shown by the woman as a demonstration of how she must have been forgiven.

    you did not give me: The phrase is repeated for each of the ways Simon failed in hospitality: water for cleansing (v. 44), a kiss of greeting (v. 45), oil for anointing (v. 46). By the logic of the parable, the woman's actions showed her state of forgiveness. Simon's refusal, likewise, indicates a lack of forgiveness. There is an edge, here.

47. *on this basis*: The impersonal construction *hou charin* points backward: "on the evidence of what she has done."

   her many sins have been forgiven: As in 5:20, 23, Luke has Jesus use the perfect passive form, rather than the present. Her sins "have been forgiven by God." Jesus declares what has been done for her.

   since she has shown so much love: In line with Jesus' argument, the "since" is to be understood not as the basis for the forgiveness but as the demonstration of it. Only this reading makes sense of Jesus' extended exposition of her deeds. And the trailer makes it clear: the one who is forgiven little loves little.

48. *sins have been forgiven*: Luke uses *aphiēmi* here as in the previous and following verses (47, 49). The phrasing recalls 5:13, and the response of the observers recalls 5:21.

50. *faith has saved you*: This is the first time in the ministry account that "faith" and "saving" have been explicitly joined, but it will not be the last (see 8:12, 48; 17:19; 18:42, and above all, Acts 15:11). For the theme of salvation in Luke-Acts, see the note on 1:47 and on 1:77, where salvation and forgiveness of sins are first joined.

   go in peace: This is a traditional farewell (see 1 Sam 1:17; 20:42) found also in Luke 8:48; Acts 16:36 (cf. also Jas 2:16). The reader recalls that the gift of salvation would lead people on the path of peace (Luke 1:79), and Acts 10:36 summarizes Jesus' ministry in terms of "preaching good news of peace."

INTERPRETATION

This wonderful story—with its encapsulated parable—is unique to Luke's Gospel and admirably serves his compositional purposes. Not all readers agree that the story is unique to Luke. They point out the resemblance between this story and the anointing story found in Mark 14:3-9, Matt 26:6-13, and John 12:1-8, and posit at least a shared tradition. But Luke's story takes place in a completely different place in the narrative. The anointing in the other Gospels takes place immediately before the passion account. Luke's version is inconceivable apart from its present context. There are, furthermore, so few points of specific contact that it is difficult to defend even the hypothesis that a shared tradition is being used.

The facts can be stated simply. Of some 23 possible points of contact in all four accounts, Luke agrees with the other three on only four: a woman, myrrh (perfumed oil), anointing, rebuke. Luke also agrees with Matthew and Mark on two other small details: the oil was carried in an alabaster jar, and the host's name was Simon. This last point loses its force, however, when we realize that in Matthew and Mark, Simon is identified as "the leper," whereas in Luke, he is designated as a Pharisee, a point critical to the story's meaning.

In contrast, the versions of John, Matthew and Mark agree on nine critical points: 1) location at Bethany, 2) the woman, 3) the myrrh, 4) anointing of Jesus' *head*, 5) the cost of the ointment, 6) the objection, 7) the note about the poor, 8) the rebuke by Jesus, 9) the anointing for burial. Finally, there are twelve points found *only* in Luke, and these are critical to the very structure of the story: 1) the Pharisee (mentioned four times); 2) the woman is a sinner; 3) she cries; 4) the tears wash the feet; 5) she dries the feet; 6) she kisses the feet; 7) she anoints the feet; 8) the parable of the debtors; 9) the words on love; 10) the forgiveness of sins; 11) objection to forgiveness; 12) the farewell, "go in peace." These massive differences justify the position that Luke is telling quite another sort of story from the other evangelists, all of whom tell one story with small variations.

Luke's story of the sinful woman has stronger resemblances, in fact, to his earlier healing of the paralytic (5:17-26). In both, Jesus is surrounded by Pharisees; someone enters the house and demonstrates faith by an extravagant gesture; the Pharisees object and Jesus reads their hearts; there is the forgiveness of sins; the power to forgive is questioned; the person is dismissed.

What distinguishes this story, however, are the distinctive points of Lukan thematic interest: the language of possessions used to symbolize human relationships; the reading of hearts by the prophet; the forgiveness of sins; faith as saving; salvation leading to peace. Most of all, in the sinful woman we recognize again a member of the outcast poor, rejected by the religious elite as an untouchable, but like the poor throughout this Gospel, showing by her acts of hospitality that she accepts the prophet Jesus. In contrast, the Pharisee invites Jesus to table, but violates all the rules of hospitality, and thereby shows (as he does also by his thoughts) that he does not accept Jesus as God's prophet.

The specific placement of this story makes it a striking example of Luke's practice of having story fulfill saying in a prophecy/fulfillment pattern (cf. introduction, pp. 16–17). In 7:29-30, the people were divided between sinners and tax-agents who accepted prophets and justified God, and the lawyers and Pharisees who rejected prophets and also God's plan. In 7:34, furthermore, Jesus was pilloried as a "friend of sinners" and one who "ate and drank." Here we find him eating and drinking at table, showing himself a friend to a sinner, who in turn accepts him as a prophet, while the Pharisee rejects him. The ending of this story, in turn, prepares for the next development, in which Luke will show more fully how "faith saves."

FOR REFERENCE AND FURTHER STUDY

Delobel, J. "L'Onction de Jésus par la pécheresse: la composition littéraire de Lc vii, 36-50." *ETL* 42 (1966) 415-75.

Donahue, J. J. "The Penitent Woman and the Pharisee: Luke 7:36-50." *AER* 142 (1960) 414-21.

Elliott, J. K. "The Anointing of Jesus." *ExpT* 85 (1973-74) 105-107.

Orchard, R. K. "On the Composition of Luke vii, 36-50." *JTS* 38 (1937) 243-45.

Ravens, D. A. S. "The Setting of Luke's Account of the Anointing: Luke 7:2-8:3." *NTS* 34 (1988) 282-292.

23. *Gathering the People of Faith* (8:1-21)

1. Soon afterwards he made his way through city and village. He was preaching and proclaiming the good news of the kingdom of God. The Twelve were with him, 2. and certain women who had been healed from evil spirits and sicknesses. Mary, who was called Magdalene, had seven demons depart from her. 3. There were also Joanna the wife of Chusa—an administrator for Herod—and Susanna, and many others. These women were supporting them from their own possessions. 4. Since a considerable crowd was gathering from the people who came to him in each town, he spoke to them by means of a parable. 5. "The sower went out to sow his seed. As he was sowing, some seed fell beside the path and was stepped on. Birds flew down and ate it up. 6. Other seed fell on rock. When this grew it dried up because it lacked moisture. 7. Other seed fell among thorn bushes, and as they grew up together, the thorns choked it out. 8. Other seed fell on good soil. When it grew, it produced fruit a hundredfold." As he was saying this he shouted, "Let the one who has ears to hear, hear this!" 9. His disciples asked him what this parable might mean. 10. He said, "To you has been given knowledge of the secrets of the kingdom of God, but to the rest they remain parables, so that 'although they see they might not see, and although they hear they might not understand.' 11. This is the parable. The seed is the word of God! 12. Those beside the path are people who have heard but then the devil comes and takes the word from their hearts, lest by believing they might be saved. 13. Those on the rock are people who when they hear accept the word gladly. But they have no roots. They continue in faith for a time, but in a season of testing they fade away. 14. That which fell into thorns? These are people who have heard, but as they go along they become encumbered by anxieties and wealth and the pleasures of life, so that they bring nothing to maturity. 15. But that which is in good soil? These are the people who having heard the word with a generous and good heart, protect it. They will bear fruit because of their endurance. 16. No one who has lighted a lamp hides it in a jar or puts it under a bed. Instead it is put on a lampstand so that those who come in can see the light. 17. Likewise, there is nothing hidden that will not be revealed, nothing secret that will not become known and brought into the

light. 18. Look therefore to how you hear! Whoever has will receive. Whoever does not have will be deprived even of what one thinks one has." 19. His mother and his brothers approached him, but they could not reach him because of the crowd. 20. He was told, "Your mother and your brothers are standing outside wishing to see you." 21. He answered them, "My mother and my brothers are those who hear the word of God and do it."

NOTES

1. *preaching and proclaiming*: For the third time (see 4:18, 43-44), Luke connects these two terms by which he defines Jesus' prophetic mission, and sets up the parable of the sower who "sows the word of God" (v. 11).

   Twelve were with him: The phrase (*syn autǭ*) recalls Mark's first mandate for the Twelve, that they "be with him" (Mark 3:14).

2. *evil spirits and sicknesses*: This recalls 7:21, where Jesus was said to be healing from sicknesses and evil spirits; we have noted before how Luke consistently links Jesus' preaching and healing (e.g., 6:18-19).

   Mary, who was called Magdalene: The name Magdalene refers to the town of Magdala. Luke's emphasis on women has been noted before. This group is particularly important. They will witness Jesus' death (23:49) and burial (23:55). Mary Magdalene and Joanna are also the first to be told of Jesus' resurrection (24:10, 22). Although Mary had "seven demons driven from her," the text gives us no reason to connect her to "the sinful woman" of the previous story, although the harmonizing tendency of Church tradition has done so.

3. *an administrator for Herod*: An *epitropos* is a manager, and is often translated as "steward" (cf. Matt 20:8; Gal 4:2). We learned in 3:1 that Herod was tetrarch of Galilee; he will reappear in the narrative in 9:7-9; 13:31 and 23:7-12. Another connection between Herod's household and early Christians is noted in Acts 13:1. Nothing else is known of the other woman named, Susanna.

   supporting them from their own possessions: The verb *diakoneō* is used by Luke in 4:39; 10:40; 12:37; 17:8; Acts 6:2 in the sense of "waiting at table" or "seeing to hospitality." Here the imperfect tense and the explicit reference to "possessions" (*hyparchonta*, as in 11:21; 12:15, 33, 44; 14:33; 16:1, 14; 19:8; Acts 3:6; 4:32, 34, 37; 5:4) suggests that the women financially supported Jesus and the Twelve (*autois*).

4. *a considerable crowd*: As in 6:17-19, the summary statement serves to provide Jesus with an audience for his discourse. Notice that it is drawn from all the towns; Jesus is gathering followers from throughout Galilee.

5. *went out to sow his seed*: The parable is paralleled in Mark 4:1-9 and Matt 13:1-9, with still another version in *Gospel of Thomas* 9. Luke keeps the singular (collective) "seed" throughout, rather than Matthew's plural "seeds." The ancient method of sowing had the seeds scattered broadly, before plowing the soil; it was natural therefore that some seeds would fall in the places stated.

birds flew down: This is a very free translation of "birds of heaven," which is only in Luke and adds nothing to Mark 4:4.

6. *it lacked moisture*: Luke changes the "had no roots" of Mark 4:6 and Matt 13:6 in favor of this more precise statement.

8. *a hundredfold*: Each seed of corn or wheat that reaches maturity obviously produces in its head many more seeds. Luke avoids the "thirty-sixty-hundred-fold" escalation of Mark 4:8, as well as the distributive version of Matthew, which places an emphasis on individual responses. Luke wants to note only the impressive yield that maturity brings.

9. *what this parable might mean*: In sharp contrast to Matthew and Mark, where the disciples ask *why* Jesus speaks in parables, the disciples in Luke seek only the meaning of this parable; compare Mary's question in 1:29.

10. *knowledge of the secrets*: Luke is closer here to Matt 13:11 with its emphasis on secrets and knowledge, rather than Mark 4:11 which has the singular "mystery" (meaning Jesus himself). The disciples are given an explanation, but the rest must be content with the coded language of the parables. The motif of secrecy is only vestigial in Luke.

    of the kingdom of God: Since he began this passage with Jesus' "preaching of the kingdom of God" (8:1), the parable is obviously going to function as an interpretation of Jesus' ministry.

    they might not see: As in the parallels, an allusion to Isa 6:9 (LXX), but Luke lacks the extensive citation in Matt 13:14-15 and the sharp note of distancing and rejection in Mark 4:12. In Luke, it simply means that without an interpretation, "the others" don't understand what they heard.

11. *this is the parable*: Meaning, "the parable's interpretation," in response to the disciples' question, "what this parable might mean." Compare "these are my words" in Luke 24:44.

    the seed is the word of God: In contrast to Mark's "the word" (4:13) and Matthew's "word of the kingdom" (13:19) Luke uses the phrase that most fits the model of the prophet; for the theme of the word of God, see the note on 1:2, as well as 8:21, below.

    believing they might be saved: The translation supplies "people" throughout this section. Only Luke makes the note of saving faith explicit, while lacking the element of "understanding" in Matt 13:19. For the devil as opponent, see 4:2-12.

13. *season of testing*: Again, Luke makes the acceptance of the word a matter of "faith." The use of *kairos* here demands the translation "season," especially in a horticultural context. Rather than the "tribulation" (*thlipsis*) and "persecution" (*diōgmos*) of Mark 4:13 (and Matt 13:21), terms which Luke lacks entirely in his Gospel (although he uses them in Acts 7:10-11; 8:1; 11:19; 13:50; 14:22; 20:23), he uses "testing," which makes the experience of the disciples like that of Jesus himself (4:2, 13).

    they fade away: The translation tries to capture the image of etiolation proper to plant life, rather than the "stumbling" (*skandalizomai*) of Mark 4:17 and Matt 13:21.

14. *bring nothing to maturity*: Luke stresses the plant's ability to bring fruit to maturity, rather than simply "bearing" as in Mark 4:20; Matt 13:23. The causes of "encumbrance" (literally: "suffocation") are slightly altered. Luke drops "of the world" from anxieties, as well as "deceit" from wealth, but adds "the pleasures of life." The effect is to make the danger the charm of life rather than its worrisomeness. The same point is made by the exhortation to eschatological readiness in Luke 21:34.

15. *generous and good heart*: A wonderful example of Luke's Hellenistic sensibility is this combination which as *kalokagathia* expresses what Greek culture regarded as nobility of character (cf. e.g., Aristotle, *Nichomachean Ethics* 1, 8, 13).

    protect it: The verb *katechō* suggests holding something close as a prized possession. This is to be understood with *en hypomonē* ("with endurance") as expressing fidelity; cf. Luke 21:19, "in your endurance (*hypomonē*) you will gain your lives."

16. *who has lighted a lamp*: The three discrete sayings in verses 16-18 are taken with small alterations from Mark 4:21-25; Matthew scatters them to other places in his Gospel.

    can see the light: Only Luke makes this point, which is fairly obvious, but helps connect these sayings thematically to the motif of secrecy/disclosure found in parables.

18. *look therefore to how you hear*: Luke drops the saying about measurement in Mark 4:24 (cf. Luke 6:38), as well as the apocalyptic "if anyone has ears to hear" in Mark 4:23.

    thinks one has: Rather than an real dispossession as in Mark, Luke makes this the loss of an illusory possession.

19. *mother and his brothers approached*: This is taken from Mark 3:31-35 which Luke has transferred from its Markan position before the parable of the sower. And by separating it from Mark 3:22, Luke also avoids any implication that Jesus' family was hostile to him, or he toward them.

21. *hear the word of God and do it*: The story now forms the perfect moral to the parable of the sower. For Luke, Mary *does* hear the word and keep it (1:45 and 11:28). In contrast, 7:29-30 indicates that the leaders did not, for John spoke God's word (3:2), and his baptism was "from heaven" (20:4).

INTERPRETATION

Luke now begins to show the reader how the restored people of God is to be formed around the prophet. He returns to Mark as his basic source, following him closely in the parable of the sower (8:4-8; cf. Mark 4:1-9; Matt 13:1-9) and the explanation of the parable (8:11-15; Mark 4:13-20; Matt 13:18-23), making however some significant editorial changes. He considerably shortens and simplifies the bridge between parable and its interpretation (Luke 8:9-10; cf. Mark 4:10-12; Matt 13:10-17). Unlike Matthew, he also follows Mark closely in the sayings of 8:16-18 (Mark 4:21-25). But Luke has fundamentally transformed this section by the way he has framed it. He alone precedes the parable with a summary of Jesus' preaching success rather than rejection (8:1-3). And he has transferred the story of Jesus' family seeking him from before the parable (as in Mark 3:22-35) to after it (Luke 8:19-21).

As a result, this part of Luke's composition becomes a statement on the internal meaning of Jesus' prophetic ministry. His sayings perform the classic function of speeches in Hellenistic histories of interpreting the meaning of the narrative. Here, we have learned that the people is divided in response to the visitation of God through the prophet. Some accept it, some do not. Now, Luke shows what the response of acceptance means. He focuses on three elements: the preaching of the prophet as the word of God; the diverse responses to the word of God in terms of hearing and faith; the character of God's people as constituted by faith that acts and endures.

In 8:1-3, Jesus is shown proclaiming the good news of the kingdom from town to town, accompanied by the Twelve and supported by the women he had helped. With this small note, Luke not only anticipates the critical role the women will play later (as witnesses of Jesus' death and resurrection), but shows a people *in nuce* gathering around the prophet, and sharing their lives and possessions, a picture that foreshadows that of the Galilean community of believers in Acts 1:13-14 and 2:41-47.

In the process, Luke gathers as well a crowd for Jesus to address in his second major sermon after that of 6:20-49. In the Synoptic parallels, Jesus starts speaking in parables as a reaction to the experience of rejection in his public ministry (cf. Mark 3:20-35; Matt 12:24-50). He teaches in parables as a way of communicating to insiders and of repelling outsiders (Mark 4:10-12; Matt 13:10-17). The difference between insider and outsider is spelled out by understanding and the lack of it.

Luke's version goes in another direction. He has already shown Jesus speaking in parables some four times (4:23; 4:31-32; 5:41-42; 6:39), so there is no transition to a new mode of speaking or a secret ministry. Consequently, rather than an extended bridge between parable and interpretation, in which the stress is on the distinction between insiders and outsiders, Luke shifts attention to the sayings that follow the interpretation, in which the stress is on the need to act on faith—Look to how you hear! The lesson of the parable is that it is possible to lose what one has initially been given or thinks one has (vv. 12-13). Protection of the word and perseverance in it mean everything (vv. 14-15).

Luke's interpretation of the parable is therefore remarkable only for its clarity and consistency. In contrast to Matthew, who makes "understanding" thematic (Matt 13:19, 23), Luke puts his emphasis on faith as a response of obedience and fidelity to the word of God (8:11). As in the parallels, faith begins in "hearing" (all readers recognize how strained is the application of soil-condition to seed-response in all three versions). In Luke, everyone "hears the word" (8:12, 13, 14, 15). But it is only "faith" that "saves" (8:12). This obviously picks up from Jesus' assurance to the sinful woman in the story just preceding that her "faith had saved her" (7:50).

But Luke means by faith more than a momentary decision. Its distinguishing characteristic is fidelity and perseverance. It does not fade away in times of testing (8:13); it does not become suffocated by the distractions and delights of worldly existence (8:14); it is protected in patience and thus comes to maturity (8:15).

If such is the basis for membership in God's people, then the story of Jesus' family seeking him becomes, not a tale of rejection, but one of straightforward affirmation for all who seek him: this is a people that consists of those who "hear the word of God and do it."

FOR REFERENCE AND FURTHER STUDY

Brown, S. *Apostasy and Perseverance in the Theology of Luke.* AB 36; Rome: Pontifical Biblical Institute, 1969.

Crossan, J. D. "The Seed Parables of Jesus." *JBL* 92 (1973) 244–66.

Dupont, J. "La parabole du semeur dans la version de Luc." *Apophoreta: Festschrift für E. Haenchen* (BZNW 30; Berlin: A. Töpelmann, 1964) 97–108.

Hastings, A. *Prophet and Witness in Jerusalem* (Baltimore: Helicon, 1958) 38–49.

Robinson, W. C. "On Preaching the Word of God (Luke 8:4-21)." *Studies in Luke-Acts.* Ed. L. Keck and J. Martyn (Nashville: Abingdon, 1966) 131–138.

24. *Two Wonders* (8:22-39)

22. One of those days he got into a boat with his disciples. He told them, "Let us cross to the other side of the lake." And they set sail. 23. As they were sailing, they fell asleep. A violent wind-storm hit the lake. They began taking on water and were in danger. 24. They came to him and roused him. They said, "Master, Master, we are perishing!" He got up and rebuked the wind and the turbulent water. They ceased and there was a calm. 25. He said to them, "Where is your faith?" They were fearful and wondered. They said to each other, "Who is this, then, that commands even the winds and the water and they obey him?" 26. They came to land in the territory of the Gerasenes, which is opposite Galilee. 27. As he stepped onto land, a man from the city met him. He had demons. For some time he had not worn clothes. He did not stay in a house but among the tombs. 28. When he saw Jesus he shouted, fell on his face, and cried in a loud voice, "What

is there between us, Jesus Son of God Most High? I beg you, do not torture me!'' 29. He said this because Jesus was ordering the unclean spirit to go out of the man. He had seized on him many times, and although the man was kept under guard with chains and fetters, he would burst his bonds and be driven into deserted places by the demon. 30. Jesus asked him, ''What is your name?'' He said, ''Legion!'' In fact many demons had entered him, 31. and they began begging Jesus not to order them off into the abyss. 32. A large herd of pigs was there, grazing on the mountainside. They begged him to allow them to enter the herd. He did allow them. 33. The demons left the man and entered the pigs. The herd plunged down the cliff into the lake and was drowned. 34. When the pig-keepers saw what happened, they fled. They told the story in the city and countryside. 35. People came out to see what had happened. They went up to Jesus. They saw the man from whom the demons had departed seated at the feet of Jesus, clothed and in his right mind, and they grew afraid. 36. Those who had seen told them how the demoniac was saved. 37. The whole assembly of the Gerasene region asked him to depart from them, for they were seized by a great fear. Getting into the boat, he was about to return. 38. But the man from whom the demons had departed began begging to go with him. Jesus dismissed him. 39. He said, ''Go back to your house and relate everything that God has done for you.'' He went away, preaching throughout the whole city everything Jesus did for him.

NOTES

22. *with his disciples*: Unlike the parallels (Mark 4:35-41; Matt 8:23-27), Luke does not make the trip a matter of withdrawal from the crowd. Luke also eliminates from the story the ''other boats'' of Mark 4:36.

23. *they fell asleep*: Luke has everyone fall asleep, not only Jesus (compare Mark 4:38; Matt 8:24). Their panic at being so overtaken is therefore more understandable.
    taking on water: Is literally ''filling up'' (*symplēroō*). Luke adds the note that they were therefore ''in danger'' (*kinduneuō*).

24. *master, we are perishing*: All three Synoptists use the perfect tense of ''perish'' (*apollymi*). In Mark, the disciples rebuke Jesus for his lack of concern (Mark 4:38). In Matt 8:25, Jesus is called ''Lord'' and the element of ''saving'' is made explicit. As noted earlier, Luke uses the term *epistatēs* (''Master'') only in the disciples' address to Jesus (see note on 5:5).
    rebuked the wind and the turbulent water: The verb ''rebuke'' (*epitimaō*) recalls the exorcisms of 4:35, 41. The translation ''turbulent water'' tries to account for the redundant ''of water'' Luke adds to *kludon* (but cf. also Jas 1:6).

25. *where is your faith*: In contrast to Mark 4:40 which questions whether the disciples have faith, and Matt 8:26 where they are called ''men of little faith,'' Luke has Jesus ask why their faith was not effective.
    who is this: Is basically the same question in all three Synoptists, echoing the question raised by Jesus' first exorcism (4:36).

26. *territory of the Gerasenes*: The textual variants in the MSS of all three Gospels attest to the difficulties this place-name posed. This is the best attested reading; other MSS have either "of the Gadarenes," or "of the Gergesenes." None of the names matches a city this close to the sea of Galilee. The geographical fact, luckily, is not necessary for appreciating the story.

27. *a man from the city*: Although the man stayed among the tombs, Luke says he is from the city in order to make sense of 8:34 and 39. A similar concern for literal consistency is reflected in his supplying of "stepped on land" which avoids the possible impression from Mark of stepping off the boat into the water (cf. Mark 5:2). With some transpositions and corrections, Luke follows Mark much more closely here than Matthew does.

    not worn clothes: Once more this detail is supplied now in order to prepare for the reclothing later in verse 35.

28. *what is there between us*: The demon's cry resembles that in Jesus' first exorcism, 4:34, except for the addition of "Son of God Most High." And whereas in the first story the demon asked whether Jesus had come to destroy them, here he begs not to be tormented; the term *basanizomai* is used for "testing" in the sense of cross-examining, hence, "torturing."

29. *said this because*: The translation provides a full reading of the small Greek connective *gar* ("for"). All of verse 29 is parenthetical, describing the man's condition. Luke has transferred this from its original place in Mark 5:3-5, and it is not clear he has improved things. He has certainly missed Mark's deliberate emphasis on "the tombs."

30. *Legion*: This is a Latin loan word in the Greek. The military unit called the *Legio* consisted of between four and six thousand soldiers, so a large number of demons is present! One must, however, strain to find a political statement embedded in this name. Once more, Luke uses a parenthesis which makes the following indirect discourse even more difficult to render consistently. This translation has supplied plural pronouns throughout.

31. *they began begging*: The verb *parakalō* is used in its meaning of "implore" or "beseech." Mark has the demons fear being sent out of the region, but Luke makes them fear being dismissed to what we must understand as their place of origin: *abyssos* in Rev 11:7 and 17:8 is the place of the beast, and in 20:3 the place where Satan is consigned. The image comes from the LXX translation of *tehom*, or "the deep" (Gen 1:2; 7:11), a place where "sea monsters" lived (Ps 148:7). In Luke, the demons end up in deep water anyway.

35. *people came out to see*: Luke does not note his grammatical subjects in this section. The translation supplies "people," meaning those from the city and countryside (literally: "fields"), whereas in verse 36 "those who had seen" refers again to the pig-keepers.

    clothed, and in his right mind: The term *sophrōnounta* denotes sobriety and clear-sightedness (compare Rom 12:3; 2 Cor 5:13; Titus 2:6; 1 Pet 4:7). As a virtue, *sophrosynē* had the sense of self-control and was very highly esteemed (cf. Aristotle, *Nichomachean Ethics* 3, 10-12).

36. *how the demoniac was saved*: Luke reduces the rambling paraphrasis of Mark 5:16 to this terse and thematically significant summary. He also exchanges Mark's "narrate" (*diēgeomai*) here with "announce" (*apangelō*), but will reverse them in verse 39.

37. *the whole assembly*: The translation takes *plēthos* not as a loose gathering, but (in the sense it sometimes has) an assembly of the people (cf. e.g., Luke 23:1, 27; Acts 6:2).

    about to return: The aorist tense here is taken as ingressive. Jesus begins the act but is interrupted by the man's begging. The syntax of Mark 5:18 is in this case smoother.

39. *go back to your house*: Mark 5:19 has "go back to your own people"; Luke has prepared for this command by noting in 8:27 that he had not lived in a house for some time.

    relate everything that God has done: Luke has shifted the term *diēgeomai* to this place, which may reflect his perception of narrative as an "ordered account."

    throughout the whole city: Rather than the Decapolis (Mark 5:20), Luke has the man return to his own city (see 8:27), but he retains the note of "preaching" from Mark.

INTERPRETATION

In these two miracle stories, Luke follows Mark 4:35–5:20 closely both in sequence and substance. Jesus stills a storm (8:22-25) and drives many demons out of a man (8:26-39). Precisely because Luke follows Mark so closely and edits so lightly, these stories show in their small deviations how the evangelists are up to quite different things.

In the calming of the sea, Luke moves the emphasis away from the failure of the disciples to the power of Jesus. He omits the charge of cowardice against the disciples (Mark 4:40 and Matt 8:26). He has them sleeping along with Jesus, which makes their panic more intelligible. Jesus does not ask why they do not have faith but "where" is their faith. The final question, "who is this" recalls in both versions the first exorcism of Jesus. But the impact is quite different. In Mark, the disciples have just been declared insiders who have been given the mystery of the kingdom (4:11). They are supposed to know who this is! The story of the stilling functions in Mark as part of his portrayal of "insiders" who are not really so.

But in Luke, that "insider/outsider" motif does not work the same way. Luke does not work his irony against the disciples. And in their question, "who is this" we hear the echo of that earlier question, "what is this speech (*logos*), that he commands even unclean spirits and they obey." As with demons, so with winds and waves. But the disciples are to learn from this that Jesus speaks "The word of God" as the previous discourse has made plain (8:11). The question "where is your faith" therefore is to be understood against the backdrop of the same discourse: faith means "hearing the word of God and doing it" (8:21). It is the lack of effectiveness of the disciples' faith which is challenged.

Luke works over Mark's version of the Gerasene demoniac much more fully and with mixed results. He apparently finds his source stylistically and structurally deficient. He works first at correctness. He does not find it appropriate to have the demoniac "adjure" (*orkizō*) Jesus, for example, (as in Mark 5:7), so he changes it to "beg" (8:28). He corrects the confusion in number that he detected in Mark 5:9-10 and the tense sequence in Mark 5:14 (cf. Luke 8:30-31, 35). Second, Luke tries to provide clarifications. He tells where the territory of the Gerasenes was (8:26) and assures the reader that Jesus stepped on land not into the water (8:27). He has the pig-keepers see the events before they report them (8:34) and supplies a motive for the assembly's request that Jesus leave (8:37). Mark's diffuse report in 5:16 is condensed into an admirable summary and interpretation in 8:36. Third, Luke puts the story into what he thinks is a more logical order. He especially dislikes narrative surprises. Mark 5:14 has the pig-keepers go to the city without ever having mentioned a city being in the area; Luke anticipates the later passage by mentioning the city at once in 8:27; he is also thereby able to have the man preach "throughout the city" in 8:39. He does the same with the clothes. Mark has the demoniac reclothed without ever stating that he was naked (Mark 5:15). Luke supplies this information from the beginning (8:27).

What is the result of Luke's editing? He has effectively eliminated those elements which are critical to Mark's own use of the story. Mark put such emphasis on the strength of the demoniac, and his living among the tombs, and his being clothed in his right mind, and his preaching in Gentile territory rather than travelling with Jesus, because in *his* story, this passage represents the "real ending" of the Gospel, deliberately held in tension with the ambiguous empty-tomb account in Mark 16:1-8. Luke does not grasp what Mark is up to compositionally; for him, Mark is simply an awkwardly written source.

Luke's editing also enables us to perceive some of his own characteristic concerns. His preoccupation with "order" in narrative is obsessive. Two aspects of this deserve comment. The first is that his constantly providing precedent for later plot developments creates something of a "prophecy/fulfillment" pattern even within the compass of a single story: every note is echoed, every question answered. The second aspect is his understanding of the role of "narrative" (*diēgēsis*). Surely it is not by accident that he defers the use of the term *diēgeomai* until the end of the story. The man is to "relate all that God had done for him" after the sequence of events was over. For Luke, as his own narrative shows, this is now the shape of preaching the good news: relating "in order" what God/Jesus had done.

Finally, in Luke's terse reduction of Mark 5:16, "how the man was saved," we see his characteristic understanding of what the meaning of the story is: God's visitation is for salvation. Now, when we see two stories (of the stilling and the demoniac), we perceive not only that they both demonstrate the power of the prophet over winds and spirits, but that they join the elements of "faith" and "salvation," and thereby provide a link between Luke's version of the parable of the sower, where hearing the word and doing it is "believing that they might be saved" (8:12), and the story of the two daughters in which saving faith is the entire point.

FOR REFERENCE AND FURTHER STUDY

Cave, C. H. "The Obedience of Unclean Spirits." *NTS* 11 (1964–65) 93–97.
Craghan, J. "The Gerasene Demoniac." *CBQ* 30 (1968) 522–36.
Van der Loos, H. "The Stilling of the Storm." *The Miracles of Jesus* (NovTSupp 9; Leiden: Brill, 1965) 638–649.

25. *Saving Faith* (8:40-56)

40. When Jesus returned the crowd welcomed him, for they were expecting him. 41. A man named Jairus who was a ruler of the synagogue came up and fell at Jesus' feet. He implored him to come to his house, 42. because his only daughter, about twelve years old, was dying. As he went, the crowd closed about him. 43. There was a woman who had a flow of blood for twelve years. She had spent all her money on physicians but no one was able to cure her. 44. Approaching from the rear, she touched the hem of his robe. Immediately the flow of blood stopped. 45. Jesus asked, "Who has touched me?" Everyone was denying it, but Peter said, "Master, the crowds are pressing on you and crushing you." 46. But Jesus insisted, "Someone touched me. I knew that power was going out from me." 47. The woman saw that she was discovered. She came up, trembling. She fell down before him. She announced before all the people why she had touched him and how she had been immediately healed. 48. He said to her, "Daughter, your faith has saved you. Go in peace!" 49. While he was still speaking, someone came from the ruler of the synagogue's house and said, "Your daughter has died. Trouble the teacher no more." 50. Jesus heard this and said to him, "Don't be afraid. Only have faith and she will be saved." 51. When he arrived at the house, he allowed no one to enter with him except Peter, John, James, and the child's father and mother. 52. Everyone was weeping and mourning her. He said, "Stop crying! She is not dead. She is sleeping." 53. They mocked him, since they knew that she had died. 54. But he took hold of her hand. He called out, "Get up,

little girl!" 55. Her spirit returned, and she suddenly got up. He ordered that she be given something to eat. 56. Her parents were astounded. He commanded them to tell no one what had happened.

NOTES

40. *crowd welcomed him*: This transition sentence is lacking in the parallels (Mark 5:21-43; Matt 9:18-26). With it, Luke connects his stories and reminds the reader of the positive response engendered by the prophet among the Galilean populace. For "expectation," cf. 3:15; 7:19-20.

41. *ruler of the synagogue*: The name Jairus is taken from Mark 5:22. In 7:1-10 we met "elders" from the *gĕrousia* of a local synagogue. The head of the board of elders was the *archisynagōgos*, often found in inscriptions as leader and/or financial patron. Here again, we are to understand a leader of a local community who seeks the prophet's help, not a member of the religious elite who tend to reject him.

    fell at Jesus' feet: As with the Gerasene demoniac, the position "at the feet" of someone means a recognition of authority; it is a favorite expression in Luke-Acts (7:38, 46; 8:35; 10:39; 17:16; 20:43; Acts 2:35; 4:35-37; 5:2, 10; 10:25; 22:3).

42. *only daughter, about twelve years old*: Luke alone notes that this was an "only daughter" (*monogenēs*), which makes the situation resemble that of the widow of Naim (7:12). Luke puts the age here rather than at the end of the story (cf. Mark 5:42).

    crowd closed about him: The term used is *sunpnigō*, cognate to the term used in the parable of the sower describing the "suffocating" of seed among thorns.

    flow of blood: The term *rhysis haimatos* comes from Lev 15:25-27, used for a gynecological bleeding outside the menstrual period, and extending the "period of impurity." Such a hemorrhage would have made the woman ritually unclean for twelve years, therefore ritually separated from the people. See the elaborate discussion in *m.Niddah*.

43. *spent all her money*: Some of the best early MSS lack this phrase which is a masterful abbreviation of Mark 5:26. Editors often deal with their indecision concerning the phrase by including it in brackets.

44. *hem of his robe*: Luke uses *kraspedon* only here. In Matt 23:5, Jesus attacks the Pharisees for "multiplying the fringes," referring to the ritual tassels commanded by Num 15:38-39 and Deut 22:12. In Luke, the meaning may be simply "hem." The term "immediately" (*parachrēma*) is a favorite in Luke-Acts (1:64; 4:39; 5:25; 8:55; 13:13; 18:43; 19:11; 22:60, etc.).

45. *who has touched me*: Luke eliminates the internal dialogue found in Mark 5:29-30. Whereas in Mark 5:31 the disciples respond to Jesus somewhat sardonically, Peter's response here is a mild observation.

46. *power was going out from me*: Luke shifts this awareness from the omniscient author (Mark 5:30) to Jesus' speech. For the use of *dynamis* in contexts of healing, see Luke 5:17 and 6:19.

47. *saw that she was discovered*: Is literally, "she could not hide (*lanthanō*)"; in Mark 5:32, Jesus sees her, whereas in Luke she recognizes that she is seen.

why she had touched him: The word order here is unusual and Luke is uncharacteristically wordier than Mark 5:33, where she only "tells the whole truth."

48. *daughter, your faith has saved you*: This line remains consistent in all three versions (cf. Mark 5:34; Matt 9:22). In Luke, the statement replicates, even to the final exhortation to "go in peace," the declaration of Jesus to the sinful woman in 7:50. The designation "daughter" connects the woman to the child of the synagogue leader; see also 13:16.

49. *trouble the teacher no more*: The intervention resembles that in the healing of the centurion's servant (7:6). Jesus' response, "only have faith" is paralleled by Mark 5:36, with two alterations: a) Luke has the aorist tense rather than the present (so the command does not have the sense "go on believing"); b) he makes the note of salvation explicit: "she will be saved."

51. *child's father and mother*: Luke follows Mark 5:37 in having Peter, John and James enter with Jesus; for these characters elsewhere, see the notes on Luke 5:1-10. By adding the parents here, Luke avoids Mark's later awkward enumeration.

52. *weeping and mourning her*: The verb *koptomai* means to strike oneself as a gesture of mourning; Luke uses it again as a response by the populace to Jesus' death in 23:27.

53. *they mocked him*: The verb *katagelaō* is cognate with the verb used in the Beatitudes and woes (6:21, 25). Luke adds the motivation, "for they knew she had died." In Luke's redaction, it should be noted, the logical subjects of "mocking" would be the disciples and parents, but this may be accidental.

    took hold of her hand: This is the only time Luke has Jesus use this gesture which is more characteristic of Mark's Gospel (1:31; 5:41; 9:27).

54. *get up, little girl*: Luke uses the noun *pais* with the feminine article, avoiding the Aramaic *talitha koum* of Mark 5:41, as well as the diminutive *korasion* (Mark 5:41; Matt 9:25), possibly because of its unsavory connection in the Salome story, which Luke also omits (Mark 6:22; Matt 14:11).

55. *her spirit returned*: A small note, but revealing Luke's understanding of life and death. When Jesus dies, he gives up his spirit (*pneuma*, 23:46), and his resurrection life is signalled by his giving the *pneuma* to others (Acts 2:33). So the departure and return of the girl's *pneuma* signals her death and life.

    be given something to eat: This is also in Mark 5:42, but Luke uses the motif in the resurrection appearances of Jesus as a sign of the reality of his new life (24:30, 41-43; Acts 10:41).

56. *tell no one what had happened*: Luke retains a vestige of the Markan secrecy motif (see 4:41 and 5:14) but does not develop it.

INTERPRETATION

The series of miracles following the parable of the sower concludes with the complex story of the two daughters. Luke takes the account from Mark

5:21-43, where it already appears as a story-within-a-story. So much is this sort of intercalation Mark's literary habit that the form of the present account is undoubtedly due to his artistry. The slightness of Luke's redaction indicates his approval of the narrative.

More than a mechanical sandwiching links the raising of Jairus' daughter and the healing of the hemorrhaging woman. Both women are called "daughter." The girl is twelve years old, an age traditionally associated with menarche (cf. *Protevangelium of James* 8:3); the woman has had a "flow of blood" (obviously gynecological in origin) for twelve years. The older woman has not been able to be cured; the younger woman is known to have died; the situation of each seems hopeless.

The stories are joined most explicitly by the healing power of Jesus and the saving response of faith. In the first healing, Jesus is touched by the woman, and feels *dynamis* going out from him; in the second, he takes the hand of the girl and calls to her. Although the power of the prophet appears almost impersonal, Luke stresses the personal character of the healings. Many in the crowd pressed on Jesus, but he knew that one had touched him with faith and was healed. He calls out to the girl, and orders that she be fed. The woman is told explicitly by Jesus that her faith had saved her. And Jairus is told by Jesus to have faith and his daughter would be saved. The theme of saving faith that Luke worked through the previous two miracles is here brought emphatically to an explicit point.

In terms of Luke's overall narrative, these stories continue the demonstration (the "fulfillment") of the programmatic statements in Jesus' interpretation of the parable of the sower (8:11-15). Faith saves. The people who belong to Jesus are those who hear the word of God and do it. Before preparing a new leadership for this people, therefore (9:1), Luke has shown how the restored people of God is constituted by faith. In both stories, we notice, the person who is saved is restored to community. The young girl is returned to her family. More impressive still is the woman with the hemorrhage who for twelve years was excluded from the common life of the people because of purity regulations. By the measure of these remarkably complex strictures which had the effect of effectively marginalizing the woman, as long as she was bleeding, she rendered "unclean" anyone who touched her. Simply entering a crowd was therefore a bold act of faith, perhaps born of desperation. She was impoverished as well because of spending all her possessions on doctors. This woman was enabled to "declare before all the people the reason for what she had done and how she was immediately healed."

When we look back over this sequence of stories, we see how Luke has emphasized the call and saving of the outcast. The sinful woman shows hospitality to the prophet and is told her faith has saved her (7:36-50). The disciples, who after all include a sinner and tax-agent, are saved from perishing and rebuked for their ineffective faith (8:22-25). The Gerasene demoniac is the most dramatically outcast of all, in the tombs, naked, bound with chains—he is "saved" and is told to proclaim what God had done back in the city from which he had been separated (7:36, 39). Finally, these two women joined by the isolation of sickness, death and impurity, are addressed as daughter, and saved by faith (8:40-56). With such delicate touches Luke has taken over stories from his source yet shaped them to his narrative purposes.

For Reference and Further Study

Kermode, F. *The Genesis of Secrecy* (Cambridge: Harvard University Press, 1979) 131-134.

Kertelge, K. *Die Wunder Jesu im Markusevangelium: Eine Redaktionsgeschichtliche Untersuchung* (SANT 23; Munich: Kösel, 1970) 110-120.

Van der Loos, H. "The Healing of the Woman with the Issue of Blood." and "Jairus' Daughter." in *The Miracles of Jesus* (NovTSupp 9; Leiden: Brill, 1965) 509-519, 567-573.

III. PREPARING A LEADERSHIP FOR THE PEOPLE

26. *The Apostolic Tasks* (9:1-17)

1. He called the Twelve together. He gave them power and authority over all demons and to heal diseases. 2. He sent them out with the commission of proclaiming the kingdom of God and healing. 3. He said to them, "Take nothing on the road, not staff or purse or bread or coin. Don't take two tunics. 4. When you enter a house, remain there and leave from there. 5. Whenever people don't receive you, as you depart from that town shake the dust from your feet as a sign against them." 6. They left and went through the villages preaching the good news and healing in every place. 7. Herod the tetrarch heard about all this. He was confused because he was being told by some people that John was raised from the dead. Others told him that Elijah had appeared, and others that a certain prophet of old had arisen. 9. Herod said, "I myself beheaded John. Who is this man of whom I hear such things?" And he sought to see him. 10. The apostles returned and recounted to Jesus all they had done. Taking them with him he withdrew in private to a city called Bethsaida. 11. But the crowd knew of it.

They followed him. He welcomed them and spoke to them concerning the kingdom of God. Those having need of healing he cured. 12. When the day was nearing an end the Twelve approached him. They said, "Dismiss the crowd. Let them go into the villages and farms near here to find lodging and provisions, for here we are in a deserted place." 13. He said to them, "You give them something to eat." They said, "We have no more than five loaves of bread and two fish, if we don't go purchase food for all this people." 14. There were in fact about five thousand men present. He said to his disciples, "Have them recline in groups of about fifty." 15. They did so, and everyone reclined. 16. He took the five loaves of bread and two fish. He looked up to heaven. He blessed and broke them. He gave them to the disciples to serve the crowd. 17. Everyone ate and was satisfied. Twelve baskets of leftover fragments were collected.

NOTES

1. *power and authority*: These terms are used repeatedly of Jesus' own ability to rebuke both demons and disease (see 4:36; 5:17; 6:19; 8:46).

2. *sent them out with the commission*: The verb *apostellō* must be taken here at full strength, since these Twelve have already been designated as *apostoloi* (= "those sent out on a commission," 6:13), and will be given that title again immediately in 9:10. Luke defers the "two-by-two" of Mark 6:7 to the sending of the seventy [-two] in 10:1.

   proclaiming . . . healing: Some MSS add "sicknesses" which is in any case understood. Luke's understanding of prophetic succession is clearly expressed by having the Twelve carry on exactly the same activities performed by Jesus. For the combination of preaching and healing, see 4:18, 40-44; 6:17-18; 8:1-2.

3. *take nothing on the road*: In these instructions, Luke is closer to Mark 6:8-9 than he is to Matt 10:9-10. Matthew lacks the blanket command to take nothing and adds both silver and gold to Mark's copper coin. Luke in contrast simply replaces the copper with silver, forbids the staff allowed by Mark, and says nothing about sandals.

4. *remain there and leave from there*: Matthew 10:11 has "city or village" rather than house. This rather strange command has the intention of preventing the sort of gadding about from house to house associated with charlatans (cf. e.g., 2 Tim 3:6).

5. *don't receive you*: In contrast to Mark 6:11 and Matt 10:14, Luke says nothing about hearing their words; the acceptance and rejection is entirely of the prophetic persons.

   shake the dust from your feet: An apotropaic gesture found also in Mark 6:11 and Matt 10:14, a sign of rejection for those rejecting the apostles. In this case, "as a witness" (*eis martyrion*) is surely understood negatively (see the note on 5:14). Only Luke has this command of Jesus "fulfilled" in the narrative of Acts (13:51).

7. *Herod . . . was confused*: This is the tetrarch identified in 3:1. Notice how the passing comment of 8:3 has served the narrative function of working Herod back into the story. He will reappear in 13:31. The verb translated "confused" (*diaporeō*) reflects perplexity and indecision. In contrast to Mark 6:14-16 and Matt 14:1-2, Luke has Herod trying to decide between conflicting reports rather than jumping to conclusions himself.

8. *John . . . Elijah . . . prophet*: These three opinions will recur in 9:18 as "popular views" of Jesus. The expectation concerning John was reported in 3:15. Jesus compared himself to Elijah in 4:26 and worked a miracle recalling that prophet in 7:11-16, which led to the cry that a "great prophet has been raised" (7:16) making the identification of Jesus with a "prophet raised up" plausible. Luke omits Matthew's wonderful note that Jesus could do wonders because he was John raised from the dead (14:2), but he undoubtedly shares the perception: the resurrected Jesus will work even more powerfully through his successors in Acts.

9. *I myself beheaded John*: This is Luke's only report (after the fact) of John's death. He omits the extensive account found here in Mark 6:17-29 (and more briefly in Matt 14:3-12). Herod's eagerness to see Jesus is found only in Luke and prepares for 13:31 as well as Herod's unique role in Luke's passion account (23:8).

10. *recounted . . . all they had done*: Luke again uses the term *diēgeomai* "to narrate" as he does in 8:39; the term is cognate to the term describing his own composition (*diēgēsis*, Luke 1:1).

    withdrew in private: Luke takes *kat'idian*, ("in private") from Mark 6:31-32, where it reflects a more elaborate withdrawal from the crowd (cf. also Matt 14:13). Mark uses the phrase seven times, but Luke has it only here and in 10:23.

    Bethsaida: Only Luke has the identification here, rather than following the feeding account (cf. Mark 6:45). The transposition is not successful, for it creates a conflict with the "desert place" described by the disciples in the feeding (9:12). Some MSS try to relieve the problem by substituting for this name "a village" or even "a desert place," but Luke may simply have been careless. Bethsaida reappears for a prophetic rebuke in 10:13.

11. *he welcomed them*: The verb *apodechomai* is unique to Luke in the NT. In 8:40, we saw that the crowds "welcomed him" (see also Acts 2:41; 18:27; 21:17; 24:3; 28:30). The theme of hospitality struck in 9:5 is here continued in the prophet's reception of the people. Luke omits Jesus' emotional response of compassion and the messianic allusion of Mark 6:34 (cf. Matt 14:14).

    spoke to them . . . cured: Luke has the same combination here as in 9:2 and 9:6 in order to show the continuity of authority between Jesus and the Twelve. Mark 6:34 has "he taught much" and Matt 14:14 has "he healed their sick"; only Luke has the combination of preaching and healing.

12. *the Twelve approached him*: In all three Synoptics the disciples initiate the dialogue by posing the problem of the desert place. In John's version of this story, Jesus begins with a question to Philip (John 6:5) in full knowledge of what he was planning to do (6:6). Only Luke identifies the disciples again as "the Twelve"

in order to connect the story to 9:1-6 and to make the symbolism of 9:17 unmistakable. For the exchange, compare 2 Kgs 4:42-44.

13. *if we don't go purchase food*: Luke's editorial work on Mark 6:37-38 is admirable; he remains basically faithful to his source but subtly rearranges the order. Notice especially how he now identifies the crowd as "this people," and how he shifts the note about the number of men from the end of the story (as in Mark 6:44; Matt 14:21) to verse 14, in order to put an emphasis on the number twelve at the conclusion (cf. also John 6:10).

14. *groups of about fifty*: Luke's use of *klinas* in the sense of "groups" lacks the picturesque quality of Mark's *symposia symposia* ("drinking party by drinking party"). There is no discernible symbolism in the multiples of five (loaves, groups and total crowd).

16. *took . . . blessed . . . broke . . . gave*: The sequence of verbs anticipates the Eucharistic gestures of the Last Supper (22:19; see also the note on 5:4).

    to the disciples to serve: The verb *paratithēmi* is literally "to set beside," but is used often for table service. In all three Synoptists the disciples are involved in the feeding, but in Luke the symbolism of authority as table service is thematic (22:24-27; Acts 6:1-6).

17. *everyone . . . was satisfied*: All three versions use *chortazō* ("satisfy," Mark 6:42; Matt 14:20), but only in Luke does the story of the feeding thus become a narrative fulfillment of the Beatitude: "blessed are those who are hungry now, for they shall be filled (*chortasthēsesthe*)" (6:21); see also 1:53.

    twelve baskets of leftover fragments: In addition to providing a fairly obvious symbol of Israel ("the twelve tribes") whom the Twelve are to serve, the collection of fragments is a sign of abundance, putting the reader in mind of the "fine measure" of 6:38 that is "pressed down and running over" in fulfillment of Jesus' promise, "give and it shall be given to you." It is, therefore, an anticipation of the eschatological banquet as well (cf. 13:23-30). The ritual meals of the Qumran sect appear to have anticipated the eschatological banquet in similar fashion (see *1QSa* 2).

INTERPRETATION

The prophet Jesus has by his deeds and words created a divided response within historical Israel: the outcasts from the people have accepted him and his message, and have become disciples. A restored Israel based on repentance is starting to gather around this prophet. At the same time, however, the prophet is being rejected by the religious elite, the leadership of Israel. This creates a leadership vacuum. Who will be the leaders of this people? Before the prophet begins his great journey to Jerusalem and his death, he begins to prepare a new leadership for the restored Israel.

From now to the start of Jesus' journey (9:51), Luke keeps our attention fixed on the relationship between Jesus and his closest followers, the Twelve, who in the narrative of Acts will assume the role of leaders over the people. He begins with the sending of the Twelve on mission (9:1-6), the response of Herod to the deeds they were performing (9:7-9), and the feeding of the multitude (9:10-17). Although Luke follows Mark 6:6-16 and 6:32-44 (omitting the story of John's beheading in Mark 6:17-29), his careful editing of the three scenes shows the reader how consciously he has shaped this part of the narrative around the future role of the Twelve as the prophetic successors of Jesus.

The first scene is focused entirely on the authority of those Jesus sends out to represent him, and their reception. Luke carefully connects their authority to that of Jesus. They have the same authority over demons and disease. As with Jesus, such authority is connected to the preaching of the kingdom (9:1-2). Luke then has the Twelve explicitly fulfill their commission (9:6), and after they have reported "all they had done" to Jesus (9:10), he has Jesus in turn immediately "speak concerning the kingdom of God and heal" (9:11).

In the instructions to the missionaries, we recognize the ideals of the ancient philosopher, especially the wandering Cynic who was identifiable by his rough cloak and staff and wallet (cf. Epictetus *Discourses* 3, 22, 9–12), except that the commands of Jesus are more severe. They are not allowed even these basics. The point is not asceticism but a function of prophetic acceptance and rejection. Travelling without any provisions makes these missionaries totally dependent on the hospitality of their listeners. At the Last Supper, Jesus will recall this command and ask the Twelve whether they had suffered any deprivation as a result. They will answer that they lacked nothing (Luke 22:35). Luke wants the reader to understand, therefore, that they were received by the people as Jesus was, with welcome and hospitality. Only later will the instructions concerning the taking of provisions require revision (Luke 22:36) and the need to carry out the sign of rejection against rejectors (Acts 13:51) become real.

In the second scene, Luke seems to shift our attention from Jesus and the Twelve by allowing us to overhear Herod's interior monologue, but in fact they are also what is preoccupying the tetrarch. He has heard what the Twelve had been doing (9:7), and he puzzles over its significance. He has also received reports concerning Jesus, and these will serve Luke later for the foil to Peter's confession (9:20), but the purpose of Luke's cutting away to Herod's state of mind is to let the shadow of political opposition fall in an anticipatory way over the Twelve as also over Jesus. It is not only households who will reject them (9:5) but powers that seek to kill (13:31). Herod will reappear in the trial of Jesus (23:6-15) and will later be included in the blame for Jesus' death (Acts 4:27). Still another Herod (Agrippa) will persecute the apostles and put James to death (Acts 12:1-3).

In the third scene Jesus provides food for the multitude in a deserted place.

Luke shares the story not only with the other Synoptists but also John. In all these versions, the feeding of the people cannot but recall the miraculous manna which fed Israel in its wilderness wanderings (see Exod 16:4-36), and therefore helps shape Luke's portrayal of Jesus as a "Prophet Like Moses," even though he (unlike John 6:14) does not specifically develop this connection. The scene also recalls Elisha's feeding his followers (2 Kgs 4:42-44).

Several aspects of Luke's distinctive treatment, however, deserve attention. We saw how he connects the feeding to the sending of the Twelve by the overlap of preaching and healing. We now notice that he focuses on the *deeds* of Jesus by eliminating the element of Jesus' compassion and the messianic allusion in Mark 6:34. The wonderful abundance of food stands as a double lesson to the Twelve: abundance is found not in the power to purchase with money, but in the power of the Lord; and, those who give receive back even more extravagantly. Both lessons reinforce what they were to have learned on their own journey.

Like the other evangelists, Luke has the feeding miracle point forward to the Last Supper of Jesus with his disciples (22:19). But his account has another element of anticipation. Jesus here appears as one who provides food for the people. His authority to preach and heal, in other words, is symbolized by table service. This is made explicit at the Last Supper, when he tells the Twelve, "Am I not among you as the one who serves?" (22:27).

The same symbolization of authority as service applies to the Twelve as well. They are later compared to stewards (12:41-48), and will see to the table needs of the faithful (Acts 4:35; 6:1-2). In this story, Luke involves the disciples in the feeding, as do also Mark and Matthew. But in Luke the choice of words is instructive; the disciples are to "spread the table before the people." Luke further emphasizes the role of the Twelve by eliminating the account of John's beheading and thus more closely connecting the apostolic authority to preach with table service. He alone identifies those who approach Jesus in 9:12 as "the Twelve." And he has arranged the conclusion so that the story ends with the symbolism of the twelve baskets (9:17). The number "twelve" stands for Israel and also for its new leadership the prophet is preparing (see Acts 1:15-26). Thus, only in Luke do the disciples, when asking what they should do, refer not to the "crowd" but to "this people" (*laos*, 9:14).

FOR REFERENCE AND FURTHER STUDY

Beare, F. W. "The Mission of the Disciples and the Mission Charge: Matthew 10 and Parallels." *JBL* 89 (1970) 1-13.

Fitzmyer, J. A. "The Composition of Luke, Chapter 9." *Perspectives on Luke-Acts.* Ed. C. H. Talbert (Danville, Va.: Association of Baptist Professors of Religion, 1978) 139-52.

Hahn, F. *Mission in the New Testament* (SBT 47; Naperville, Ill.: Allenson, 1965) 41–46.
Iersel, B. M. F. "Die Wunderbare Speisung und das Abendmahl in der synoptischen Tradition." *NovT* 7 (1964) 167–194.
O'Toole, R. F. "Luke's Message in Luke 9:1-50." *CBQ* 49 (1987) 74–89.

27. *Recognizing Jesus* (9:18-36)

18. The disciples were with him while he was praying privately. He questioned them, "Whom do the crowds say I am?" 19. They answered, "John the Baptist; others say Elijah, others that one of the prophets from of old has arisen." 20. He said to them, "But who do you say that I am?" Peter answered, "The Messiah of God!" 21. But he rebuked them. He ordered them to tell no one this. 22. He said, "The Son of Man must suffer many things, and be rejected by the elders and high priests and scribes, be killed, and be raised on the third day." 23. He said to them all: "If anyone wishes to come after me, that person must deny the self, take up one's cross every day, and follow me. 24. In fact, whoever wishes to save one's life will lose it, but whoever loses one's life for my sake will save it. 25. What use is it for a person to purchase the whole world but lose or be fined one's self? 26. Whoever is ashamed of me and my words, of that person will the Son of Man be ashamed when he comes in his glory and that of the Father and the holy angels. 27. I tell you truly, there are some of those standing here who will not die before they see the kingdom of God." 28. About eight days after saying these words, taking Peter and John and James, he went up onto the mountain to pray. 29. As he was praying, the appearance of his face was altered, and his clothing became dazzlingly white. 30. And look, two men were speaking with him. They were Moses and Elijah. 31. They appeared in glory. They spoke of his departure which he was about to fulfill in Jerusalem. 32. Peter and those with him had been overcome with sleep. When they woke up, they saw his glory and the two men standing with him. 33. As they began to withdraw from him, Peter said to Jesus, "Master, it is a fine thing for us to be here. Let us make three tents, one for you and one for Moses and one for Elijah." He did not know what he was saying. 34. And as he said these things, a cloud appeared and overshadowed them. They were terrified as they entered into the cloud. 35. A voice came from the cloud. It said, "This is my son, the chosen one. Listen to him!" 36. When the voice stopped, Jesus was found alone. They were silent. They told no one during that period of time anything of what they had seen.

NOTES

18. *praying privately*: This is another occasion when Jesus prays before a significant development (see the note on 3:21). The phrase *kata monas* ("privately") does not exclude "being with the disciples" (see Mark 4:10). Luke does not identify the place of Peter's confession (unlike Mark 8:27; Matt 16:13).

19. *John . . . Elijah . . . prophets of old*: The opinions presented to Herod in one scene previous to this are now reported to Jesus, dropping the note of John being "raised from the dead" or Elijah "appearing" (cf. 9:7-8), but retaining the qualifying note of "raised up" for the prophet from of old, which is consistent with Luke's way of thinking about Jesus (7:16; Acts 3:22).

20. *Messiah of God*: Or, "God's anointed," which picks up the use of *chriō* in 4:18. For Jesus' anointing with the Spirit and God's "being with him," see Acts 10:38. The Gospel is much more chary of giving the title *Christos* to Jesus than is Acts, where it occurs frequently. Apart from the infancy accounts, which identify Jesus' significance for the reader (2:11, 26), the two uses of the term before this one are ambiguous. John denies being the Messiah (3:15), and the demons are silenced because they recognize Jesus as the Messiah (4:41). After this point, the title is used only in polemic (20:41; 22:67; 23:2, 35, 39). Only after the resurrection is the title found in Jesus' own mouth, when he says, "the Messiah must suffer" (24:26). A version of the confession is found in *Gospel of Thomas* 13.

21. *to tell no one*: Luke lacks the elaborate blessing of Peter found in Matt 16:17-19. He also alters Mark's "tell no one about him" to "this thing" (*touto*), which makes his subsequent (and syntactically continuous) saying about the Son of Man a sharper qualification: if Jesus is to be known as Messiah at all, it must be as the one who will suffer (24:26).

22. *the Son of Man must suffer*: This is the first of three passion predictions (see 9:43b-45; 18:31-34) that Luke has taken over from Mark. The form of the saying is close to Mark 8:31. Both, for example, include "be rejected" (*apodokimazō*) which is omitted by Matt 16:21. Luke will return to this note of rejection again in 17:25 and 20:17, as well as in Acts 4:11. For the uses of "Son of Man," see the note on 5:24.

    elders and high priests and scribes: The "rejection" is specifically by these parties. They make up the Sanhedrin which was the court of the "Jewish nation" sitting in Jerusalem and exercising religious authority at Rome's leave (cf. Josephus, *Against Apion* 2:184-87). In the Jerusalem narrative, they will actively oppose Jesus, and they are blamed for his death in 24:20.

23. *said to them all*: Luke skips the objection by Peter to Jesus' suffering, and Jesus' counter-rebuke of Peter. The portrait of Peter is thus enhanced, and the sayings on discipleship appear less as a correction. In Mark 8:34 and Matt 16:24, these remarks are made "to the disciples," and in context, Luke would have "all the disciples" as the audience. But, as in the Sermon on the Plain, these commands open themselves to all who read them (see Luke 6:19-20, 27; 7:1).

    if anyone wishes to come after me: The translation here struggles to make the language inclusive at the expense of elegance. Luke alters Mark 8:34 slightly by replacing the aorist *elthein* with the present tense *erchesthai*, which emphasizes the ongoing character of discipleship.

deny the self: The verb *arneomai* has a wide-range of meanings, all amounting to "saying no" to something, whether a truth (see 1 John 2:22) or a person (see 1 John 2:23). Compare Luke 8:45; 12:9; 22:57; Acts 3:13-14; 4:16; 7:35). What the opposition did to Jesus leading to his crucifixion (Acts 3:13-14), the disciple is to do with regard to the self.

take up one's cross: Luke adds *kath' hēmeran* ("daily" or "day by day") which again stresses the continuing response of imitating the Messiah; see also 14:27. The way of the disciple continues the path walked by the teacher: first there is suffering, then glory (Luke 24:26). For the "cross" as the central symbol for this reality, see 1 Cor 1:17-18, 23; Gal 2:19-20. For "following," see the note on 5:11.

24. *for my sake will save it*: The phrase *heneken emou* ("for my sake") shifts the loss of life or self-denial from masochism to witness. In Luke, because of the theme of "salvation," the idea of "saving" one's life takes on particular force.

25. *what use is it*: The verbs frequently translated "gain" (*kerdainō*) and "forfeit" (*zēmioō*) both have specifically financial connotations (cf. Jas 4:13). Given Luke's penchant for "possessions" language to symbolize relationships, the translation seeks to capture that sense; compare 12:15.

26. *ashamed of me . . . the Son of Man*: The form of the statement is discussed in the note to 6:37-38. For the notion of "shame," cf. Rom 1:16; Heb 2:11. Both Luke and Matthew omit reference to "this sinful and adulterous generation" in Mark 8:38, thus generalizing the proposition.

in his glory: By a slight shift in word order, Luke has altered the meaning. Rather than "in the glory of his Father" as in Mark 8:38, Luke has "in *his* glory and that of the Father . . ." He thereby makes the transfiguration an immediate fulfillment of this prediction (see 9:31-32), while leaving open a future return "with the angels" (12:9; Acts 1:11).

27. *before they see the kingdom of God*: For the form of this statement, compare the promise made to Simeon (2:26), which was similarly fulfilled in the narrative. Notice that Luke omits "coming in power" from Mark 9:1, and the specific connection to the parousia in Matt 16:28.

28. *to pray*: More significant than the change from Mark's "six days" to Luke's "eight days" (the significance of either remaining obscure) is Luke's making the transfiguration a prayer experience of Jesus, ("as he was praying," v. 29), just as he had of the baptism epiphany (3:21-22).

29. *appearance of his face*: Luke avoids the verb *metamorphoreō* ("change of form = transfigure") in Mark 9:2 and Matt 17:2. For "appearance" (*eidos*) see the glory of the Lord before Moses (Exod 24:17), and especially Luke 3:22.

dazzlingly white: The participle form of *exastraptō* is here translated as an adverb; the LXX uses it for spectacular kratophanies (Ezek 1:4, 7; Dan 10:6). White garments are symbols of joy and celebration in LXX Qoh 9:8 and Cant 5:10. In Dan 7:9 the Ancient of Days had garments white as snow (cf. the "Son of Man" in the present Lukan context). Luke has "men" (angels?) in white garments at the ascension (Acts 1:10) and in "dazzling" clothes at the resurrection (Luke 24:4).

30. *Moses and Elijah*: Luke and Matt 17:3 reverse Mark's order of the names, probably just to get the chronological sequence right. The importance of Moses for Luke-Acts has often been stressed (see Introduction, pp. 19–20). The image of Elijah (4:26; 7:16) and the "prophet from of old raised up" (9:8, 19) recalls Deut 18:15-18 and 34:10, which promise a "prophet like Moses" whom "God will raise up." Both Moses (Exod 24:15-18) and Elijah (1 Kgs 19:8-13) had experiences of God's presence on the holy mountain. Each also anointed a successor prophet with the Spirit (Joshua in Deut 34:9, Elisha in 1 Kgs 19:16-19; 2 Kgs 2:9-15).

31. *appeared in glory*: This note is unique to Luke, and is repeated in verse 32. It connects the transfiguration to Jesus' prediction concerning the Son of Man in "his" glory. The reader has already associated "glory" with the person of Jesus in Luke 2:9, and especially in 2:32, where Simeon designates him as the "glory of your people Israel."

    his departure: The term *exodos* here can only be taken as a deliberate allusion to Moses, and therefore to Jesus as the prophet like Moses. In this case, the "passing over" includes the entire movement of the Prophet's death, resurrection, and ascension, which enables Jesus to bestow the Spirit on his followers.

    about to fulfill: The verb *plēroō* (see 1:20; 4:21) points us to the motif of "fulfillment" of prophecy; see esp. Luke 24:44, "It was necessary to fulfill everything about me in the Law of Moses and the Prophets and the Psalms." See also the use of *symplēroō* immediately in 9:51.

32. *had been overcome with sleep*: The sequence is different in Mark and Matthew. As at the agony of Jesus (22:45) the disciples sleep, so that they miss the topic of conversation. And they see the vision (of glory) only as it "withdraws from them."

33. *let us make three tents*: Peter's suggestion is an attempt to fix the experience before it completely "withdraws." The tents (*skēnai*) are an allusion to the feast of Booths (Tents, *sukkoth*) called in LXX Deut 16:13 *heortēn skēnōn*. The ancient harvest festival had become one of the three pilgrimage feasts to Jerusalem, and had over time taken on eschatological overtones (see Zech 14:16-21).

    did not know what he was saying: The slighting qualification is retained from Mark 9:6 but without the element of "fear," which Luke transfers to verse 35. Luke has Stephen tell us clearly in Acts 7:48-50 that "The Most High does not dwell in houses made with hands," so Peter's plan is a foolish one.

34. *they were terrified*: There is much movement here: the vision is withdrawing; the cloud approaches and overshadows; they enter into the cloud. The cloud (*nephelē*) recalls the one enveloping Moses on the mountain (Exod 24:15-18) as well as the one leading the people in the desert signalling God's presence (Exod 13:21). Elijah, too, saw a cloud from Mt. Carmel (1 Kgs 18:44-45). So also did the "Son of Man" come on the "clouds of heaven" in Dan 7:13 when he received from the Ancient of Days "glory and kingdom." The verb *episkiazein* ("overshadow")

also recalls the tent of meeting in the wilderness (Exod 40:35) as well as the annunciation in Luke 1:35.

35. *my son, the chosen one*: The voice from the cloud is God's, as at the baptism (3:22). In this case the term "chosen" (*eklegomai*) is used rather than "beloved" (*agapētos*), which emphasizes the sense of "selection" (see Luke 6:13). See also Num 16:7; LXX Ps 32:12, and esp. the "Servant of the Lord" in Isa 41:9; 43:10; 44:1.

listen to him: That this is an allusion to Deut 18:15 (LXX) is probable in Mark 9:7 and Matt 17:5, but is certain in Luke because of the explicit use of that passage applied to Jesus in Acts 3:22.

36. *they were silent*: The ending of the story is simpler than in Mark 9:9-10 and Matt 17:9, avoiding the explicit reference to Jesus' resurrection. The reason is the development of the theme in Acts. Silence (*sigē*) is frequently associated with initiation into the Mysteries in Hellenistic literature (cf. e.g., Plutarch, *On Talkativeness*, 17 [*Mor.* 510E], and Philo, *On the Cherubim* XII, 42).

INTERPRETATION

The deliberate character of Luke's composition is shown by his daring excision of Mark 6:45-8:26. Through a series of feedings, water-crossings, and discourses, as well as symbolic healings (7:31-37; 8:22-26), Mark develops the theme of the disciples' incomprehension of Jesus. Luke does not like repetition, and has quite a different understanding of the disciples to develop. He connects the sequence here directly to the sending of the Twelve and the multiplication of the loaves, thereby compressing the narrative and fixing its focus on the Twelve as the new leaders of the restored Israel. This section again falls into three scenes: Peter's confession of Jesus as the Messiah with the first prediction of the passion (9:18-22); sayings on the cost of discipleship (9:23-27); and the transfiguration (9:28-36). Taken together, they lead the disciples (and the reader) into a deeper understanding of Jesus' identity and their call.

In Luke, Peter's confession is both less dramatic than in Matthew and Mark, and less ironic. In those Gospels, this recognition marks a turn in the narrative, and shows both the insight and blindness of Peter, who rejects the notion that the Messiah must suffer. Since Luke drops the objection by Peter and Jesus' rebuke, both the confession and the prediction of the passion move more deliberately toward the sayings on discipleship and the transfiguration. The recognition scene itself resembles that on the road to Emmaus after the resurrection (24:19-26): there is the report of popular opinion, the view of the disciples, and the clarification by Jesus concerning the need to suffer.

In this case, Jesus himself gathers the threads of the earlier narrative concerning the growing resistance to him (5:21, 30, 33; 6:2, 11; 7:29-30, 39, 49) into this solemn announcement that serves as narrative summary and structuring device. Indeed, Jesus' passion predictions are echoed in Luke's resurrection accounts (24:6, 26, 44). The reader therefore perceives that Jesus is a prophet who not only knows people's hearts but who also can foretell his own future death and resurrection.

Since Luke omits the objection and rebuke of Peter, the sayings on discipleship appear less as a correction than as a logical development of Jesus' self-designation as a suffering Son of Man. In context, we would think that the Twelve formed the audience for these sayings, but Luke notes that they were said "to all," allowing these sayings on the cost of discipleship apply directly to the readers of the Gospel. The path the disciple is to "follow" must be that already travelled by the Messiah. The necessity of suffering for wisdom or service to humanity was not unknown to Hellenistic philosophy (cf. e.g., Epictetus, *Discourses* 3, 22, 54-57; Dio, *Oration* 77/78, 41-42). What is striking here is that the demand for self-denial applies not simply to the extraordinary person, the sage, but "to all." Here is the essential pattern for Christian identity. That Luke understands by this *imitatio Christi* something more than a momentary decision or surviving occasional external testing is clear. In his interpretation of the parable of the sower, he stressed coming to "maturity" and bearing fruit "in patience" (8:14-15). In this passage, he uses the present tense, "continue following," and adds the words "every day" to "taking up the cross." Luke moves the sayings of Jesus in the direction of a Christian spirituality.

The sayings conclude with the warning concerning shame. Luke uses it to make a transition to the transfiguration. It is the Son of Man who will suffer. If Christians are ashamed of him *and his words*, then neither can they share in the glory that is to follow his suffering (24:26). So Luke makes the text read "his glory," which he will have three of his followers ("some of those standing here") witness in the prayer experience which follows. Although the dominant imagery of the transfiguration points us in the direction of the prophets, it should be noted as well that the elements of white clothes, clouds, glory, and kingdom all recall Dan 7:9-13, where the Son of Man receives a kingdom.

The basic structure and meaning of the transfiguration account are shared by all three Synoptists: the symbolism of cloud and light and voice and mountain gathers about the figures of Moses and Elijah (see notes). But what is their significance in the story? It has been suggested that they represent the Law and the Prophets, or figures who have ascended into heaven, or eschatological figures who were expected to return. Any or all of these possibilities may be present in this extraordinarily dense passage. What is most clear is that they serve as support and foil to Jesus. Peter's suggestion is regarded as wrong-headed for two reasons. The first is obviously that he wanted to capture and routinize the presence of God's glory. The second is that by assigning a tent apiece, he treated Jesus as the equal of Moses and Elijah. God's voice from the cloud therefore corrects the misapprehensions: Jesus only is God's Son and chosen one; and they are not to control the holy but respond to it: "listen to him."

Luke's version is distinctive not only because it casts the entire event as a prayer experience, and downplays the theme of the disciples' noncomprehension, but because it sharpens elements concerning Jesus' identity, glory, and suffering.

With regard to the suffering, Luke alone supplies the topic of conversation between Jesus, Moses and Elijah: they discuss the "departure" he is to fulfill in Jerusalem. Luke thereby places the suffering into the very middle of the vision of glory. The vision thereby confirms Jesus' own prediction that he would be rejected and suffer, and at the same time prepares the way for the journey narrative and all the events of the passion.

Concerning the glory, by twice using this term in the story (9:31-32), Luke deliberately makes his version of the transfiguration the direct and immediate fulfillment of Jesus' prediction in 9:26-27 that the Son of Man would come in "his glory." The notions of "glory" and "kingdom of God" are closely tied by Luke to the person and words of Jesus. Jesus has already been identified (2:32) as the "glory of Israel," and Luke will extensively develop the theme of Jesus as king at the end of the journey to Jerusalem (see 19:11ff).

The identity of Jesus as prophet is here made explicit. Whatever the significance of Moses and Elijah in the other Synoptists, their presence in Luke's story serves to confirm Jesus' identity as the prophet "raised up by God" to "visit the people" (7:16). Luke's account makes earlier narrative hints explicit and directs the reader toward Jerusalem, where Jesus will accomplish his "exodus." The concluding command, "listen to him," cannot be anything but a deliberate allusion to Deut 18:15 as Luke reads it, and certifies Jesus not only as God's Son and the chosen servant, but the "prophet like Moses."

Finally, we can observe that Luke concludes this account with an elaborate statement which stresses the silence of the witnesses. They told no one "in those days" what they had seen. Two points are made by this. The first is that the disciples are shown to be obedient to Jesus' command in 9:21 that they should keep silence. The second is that it is only after the "exodus" of the Prophet has been accomplished and these witnesses had been given the Spirit could they become "ministers of the word" (1:2).

FOR REFERENCE AND FURTHER STUDY

Brown, R. E. et.al. *Peter in the New Testament* (New York: Paulist, 1973) 64–69; 111–112.
Feuillet, A. "Les perspectives propres à chaques évangeliste dans les recits de la transfiguration." *Bib* 39 (1958) 281–301.

Fletcher, D. R. "Condemned to Die: the Logion on Cross-Bearing: What Does It Mean?" *Int* 18 (1964) 156–164.

Kenny, A. "The Transfiguration and the Agony in the Garden." *CBQ* 19 (1957) 444–52.

Manek, J. "The New Exodus in the Books of Acts." *NovT* 2 (1958) 8–23.

Moessner, D. "Luke 9:1-50: Luke's Preview of the Journey of the Prophet like Moses of Deuteronomy." *JBL* 102 (1983) 575–605.

Riesenfeld, H. *Jésus Transfiguré: L'arrière-plan du récit évangélique de la transfiguration de Notre-Seigneur.* ASNU 16; Copenhagen: Munksgaard, 1947.

28. *Flawed Followers* (9:37-50)

37. The next day as they were coming down from the mountain, a large crowd met him. 38. Suddenly a man from the crowd yelled, "Teacher, I beg you to consider my son. He is my only child. 39. A spirit seizes him, and at once he screams, goes into convulsions and foams at the mouth. The child is battered before it finally withdraws. 40. I asked your disciples to cast it out but they were unable." 41. Jesus answered, "O faithless and twisted generation! How long must I be with you and put up with you? Bring your son here." 42. Even while they were bringing him, the demon tore at him and convulsed him. Jesus rebuked the unclean spirit. He healed the child and gave him to his father. 43. Everyone was overwhelmed by the majesty of God, and while they all were marvelling at all the things he was doing, he said to his disciples: 44. "Pay close attention to these words: the Son of Man is about to be handed over to human power." 45. But they did not understand this saying. Its meaning was hidden from them so that they could not grasp it. And they were afraid to ask him about it. 46. Instead, they entered into a discussion concerning who might be the greater among them. 47. Jesus knew the calculations of their hearts. He took a child and placed him beside himself. 48. He said to them, "Whoever receives this child in my name receives me. Whoever receives me receives the one who sent me. For the one who is least among you all, this one is great." 49. But John responded, "Master, we saw someone in your name casting out demons. We stopped him because he is not following with us." 50. Jesus said to him, "Don't stop him. Whoever is not against you is for you."

NOTES

37. *a large crowd met him*: Luke alters Mark 9:14 by eliminating the dispute between the (remaining) disciples and the scribes.

38. *suddenly a man . . . yelled*: The adverb seeks to translate the phrase *kai idou*, "and behold" which is so common in Luke-Acts, and is part of Luke's biblical diction.

    consider my son: The verb *epiblepō* has the sense of "look at attentively." Only Luke identifies the boy as *monogenēs* ("only-begotten"), thereby tying this story to that of the widow of Naim (7:12) and the ruler of the synagogue's daughter (8:42).

39. *a spirit seizes him*: Luke differs considerably from Mark's description of a "dumb spirit" (Mark 9:17). Luke gives symptoms that fit a *grand mal* seizure. The translation "foams at the mouth" amplifies the Greek "with foam." The suddenness and violence of such seizures made them appear in the ancient world to be caused—as were other forms of psychological dissociation—by spirit possession rather than neurological disorder.

    child is battered: The translation brings the Greek into line with the other symptoms; literally, "it scarcely departs from him and crushes him."

41. *faithless and twisted generation*: The term *genea* here has the sense of "people." In Mark 9:19 it repeats the phrase Jesus had used in 8:38, but in Luke the exclamation seems less at home. "Twisted" (*diastrephō*) is sometimes translated as "perverse" (see Acts 2:40 and esp. Phil 2:15). For Luke's use of "faithless," see 12:46.

    must I be with you: The verbs here are both in the future, but require the translation given; "put up with" (*anechō*) means to endure or bear up under something.

42. *rebuked the unclean spirit*: Luke omits a large portion of his Markan source (9:21-25), in which the dialogue between Jesus and the father teaches a lesson on faith.

    gave him to his father: The gesture is found also in the raising of the widow of Naim's son (7:15); Luke again considerably simplifies Mark's version at this point.

43. *the majesty of God*: The noun *megaleiotēs* is rare (see Dan 7:27; Acts 19:27); here it means, "the might God had shown in this deed." Luke omits Mark's concluding logion on prayer and fasting (Mark 9:29).

44. *pay close attention*: Is literally: "place these words in your ears." Luke intentionally joins this second passion prediction (cf. 9:22) to the previous story by the participle, "while they were all marvelling" (v. 43b), rather than the more general introduction used by Mark 9:30 and Matt 17:22.

    handed over to human power: Since the issue in context is one of power and its manifestations, this translation of "into the hands of men" is appropriate. Compared to Mark 9:31 and Matt 17:22-23, Luke both shortens and generalizes this prophecy.

45. *its meaning was hidden from them*: Is a free translation of "it was veiled (*parakekalummenon*) from them." And the concluding clause, "so they did not grasp it" treats a *hina* construction as a purpose rather than a result clause. Notice that the disciples' "ignorance" concerns the necessity of the Messiah to suffer. Luke invokes "ignorance" as an excuse for the death of Jesus in Acts 3:17 and 13:27. Likewise, Luke has the disciples' "fear to question" apply not to Jesus but to the content of the saying, in contrast to Mark 9:32.

46. *instead, they entered into a discussion*: The translation takes the conjunction *de* seriously. Luke intends a real contrast between the disciples' unwillingness to discuss Jesus' suffering and their eager participation in a debate about their rank. Luke joins these pieces much more closely than either Mark 9:33 or Matt 18:1.

47. *calculations of their hearts*: The translation makes the singular "heart" plural; it is not a good sign that the disciples have such thoughts; for *dialogismoi* and the detection of them, see 2:35; 5:21-22; 6:8 and 7:39-40.

    took a child: The way Luke has structured the story this could even be the exorcised boy, in which case the issue of authority and power would be even more dramatically displayed. Luke has another sort of lesson in mind than becoming small (Mark 9:35), or as Matthew puts it explicitly, "becoming like children" (18:3-4).

48. *receives . . . in my name*: The phrase *epi tǭ onomati* ("in my name") has the same sense as "in my behalf" (*heneken emou*) in 9:24. For the "name" as an identification for Christians, see the note on 6:22. Both sending and receiving are understood to be "in his name," that is, as representing him.

    this child: The demonstrative is deliberate. It is not any child, or "all children," as though this were a moral lesson. In Luke it refers to any one, however insignificant, sent out on mission.

    receives the one who sent me: We could add "with a commission" here, for the strong meaning of *apostellō* is again demanded. Jesus was sent out by God to preach the kingdom (4:18, 43). He sends out *apostoloi* with the same commission (9:1-2). The acceptance or rejection of emissaries indicates the acceptance or rejection of the prophet, and ultimately of God's visitation (see esp. 10:16).

    least . . . is great: The lesson is not directly one of humility (although that might apply), but rather that it is the prophetic commission rather than the person that gives significance. See the interpretation which follows.

50. *don't stop him*: The incident clearly echoes Num 11:26-30, where the same words are used by Moses to Joshua. Luke has once more considerably simplified Mark 9:38-41, and reduced it to the simple point that it is the acceptance or rejection of the prophet that matters.

INTERPRETATION

Luke's narrative intentions are demonstrated in this section by what he omits from his Markan source, and by the way he stitches vignettes together. He omits the exchange concerning Elijah as Jesus and the disciples come down the mountain (reported by Mark 9:11-13 and Matt 17:10-13). Luke has already made the connection between that prophet and John (1:17) and has no need to make it again. Instead, it is the resemblance between *Jesus*, Elijah and Moses that he most wants to develop. In keeping with his purpose for this stage of his story, moreover, he wants to keep his readers' attention fixed on Jesus and the disciples as the new leadership being prepared for the people. Unlike the other Synoptists, Luke creates a single long scene in which all the dialogue between Jesus and his followers (9:43b-50) follows immediately on the healing of the epileptic boy (9:37-43a).

In contrast to the previous two sections, however, Luke now concentrates on the inadequacy of the disciples, both in charism and character. They had been given authority and power over *all* demons and to heal (9:1-2), but they are unable to exorcise this man's only child of an unclean spirit. Jesus must exorcise the spirit and heal the boy (9:42). In Mark's version, the story teaches the necessity of faith expressed in prayer and fasting (Mark 9:21-24, 28-29). Luke eliminates any trace of that teaching. As a result, the reader focuses completely on the incapacity of the disciples despite Jesus' commission. They are the obvious object of Jesus' lament, "O faithless and twisted generation" (9:41), a complaint all the more striking for being unanticipated and otherwise addressed to people who do not belong to the Prophet the way they do (7:31; 11:29, 30, 31, 32, 51; 16:8; 17:25).

The disciples had also been clearly told that Jesus was to suffer, and that to follow him meant denying the self and taking up one's own cross every day (9:22-25). These instructions were concluded by the statement that whoever was ashamed of the Son of Man *and his words*, would in the future find the Son of Man ashamed of that person (9:26). But now what do we find? After the transfiguration in which Jesus' death was as surely proclaimed as his glory, and the disciples were told, "Listen to him," and after Jesus prefaces another prophecy of his suffering by the injunction, "Pay close attention to these words," they not only do not grasp the saying, they engage immediately in a discussion concerning their own greatness (9:46). The Prophet whom they are supposed to follow will be "handed over to human power," but they are arguing rank!

There is nothing sentimental therefore in Jesus' saying about the child received in his name. Neither is there (in contrast to the parallels) a direct moral lesson about becoming small, although one might be deduced. Luke's point is more directly derogatory of the disciples' pretensions. Jesus could pick *anybody* to do what he has picked them to do. They have not shown the power, and they have not understood the mission. The very powerlessness of a child makes the point dramatically. The "greatness" of any of them derives not from themselves but from the mission of representation (of the prophet and of God) on which they have been sent.

The response by John (9:49) echoes the complaint made by Joshua to Moses in Num 11:26-30. Some men in the Israelite camp had been prophesying in the spirit even though they had not been selected or approved by Moses. Joshua wanted to stop them. Moses retorted that he wished all God's people had the gift of prophecy. John's attempt to control the charism reveals how little he understood Jesus' last point. He wanted to prevent someone from "casting out demons" (which his cohorts had *not* been able to do, we remember!), even though it had been "in the name" of Jesus (which points us back to the saying on the child!). His grounds for prevention? Because the man was not "following with us." Jesus recalls him to a prophetic consciousness. As God had sent Jesus, so Jesus sends them; as God sent them, God can send others. Indeed, Jesus himself will immediately send out other emissaries (9:52; 10:1). These would-be leaders of the people still have much to learn: they are not in charge but under a charge.

For Reference and Further Study

Leaney, R. "Jesus and the Symbol of the Child." *ExpT* 66 (1954–55) 91–92.

Légasse, S. *Jésus et l'enfant: 'Infants', 'Petits', et 'Simples' dans la tradition synoptique.* EBIB; Paris: Gabalda, 1969.

Van der Loos, H. *The Miracles of Jesus* (*NovT* 9; Leiden: Brill, 1965) 397–405.

Wilkinson, J. "The Case of the Epileptic Boy." *ExpT* 79 (1967) 39–42.

IV. THE PROPHET JOURNEYS TO JERUSALEM

29. *Turning Toward Jerusalem* (9:51-62)

51. When the time for his being taken up was approaching, he deliberately set himself to travel to Jerusalem. 52. He sent messengers before him. As they travelled they entered a Samaritan village to prepare for his arrival. 53. But they did not welcome him because he was heading toward Jerusalem. 54. When his disciples James and John saw this, they said, "Lord, do you want us to order fire to fall from heaven and destroy them?" 55. He turned and rebuked them. 56. They went on to another village. 57. As they were travelling on the road, someone said to him, "I will follow you wherever you go." 58. Jesus told him, "Foxes have holes and the birds of the sky have nests. But the Son of Man has no place to lay his head." 59. He said to another, "Follow me." But the man answered, "Allow me first to bury my father." 60. Jesus said to him, "Let the dead bury their own dead. But you go announce the kingdom of God." 61. Still another said, "I will follow you, Lord. But allow me first to say good-bye to those in my family." 62. Jesus said to him, "No one who has once grasped the plow yet keeps looking backward is fit for the kingdom of God."

Notes

51. *time . . . was approaching*: The syntax is convoluted and biblical; literally: "it happened in the coming to fulfillment of the days of his being taken up and he himself . . ." Luke uses the verb *synplēroō* again for Pentecost in Acts 2:1. The passage 9:51-56 is found only in Luke and relies heavily on imagery associated with the Elijah cycle.

    for his being taken up: The noun *analēmpsis* is used only here in the NT, but Luke uses the verb form *analambanō* in Acts 1:2, 11, 22, which makes it clear that Jesus's *exodos* and *analēmpsis* refer not simply to his death but to the whole sequence of events, climaxing in his ascension. Notice the similarity to 2 Kgs 2:1: "When the Lord was about to take Elijah up to heaven by a whirlwind . . ."

    deliberately set himself: Is literally: "he hardened his face to go"; the verb *sterizō* with *prosōpon* is used most frequently in the OT in Ezekiel (6:2; 13:17; 14:8; 15:7; 20:46). Especially important is Ezek 21:7-8. There the "Son of Man" is told to "set his face against Jerusalem," and to "prophesy against the land of Israel." The language here, in other words, is unmistakably prophetic.

52. *he sent messengers*: This echoes what was said of John the Baptist in 7:27, which in turn depended on Exodus 23:20.

    to prepare for his arrival: Unlike the Twelve who were sent out to preach and to heal, these emissaries are a sort of advance party of scouts who prepare places of hospitality; in Greek the phrase "to prepare" is a bit unusual, *hōs hetoimasai*.

53. *he was heading toward Jerusalem*: The ancestral antipathy between Judeans and Samaritans is reflected in this verse. It was based on the rivalry between the shrines of Mt. Gerizim and Mt. Zion, and on a whole cluster of disputes concerning the right way to read the sacred books, messianism and above all, who was a real Israelite. See e.g., Josephus, *Antiquities of the Jews* 20:118-138; John 4:9-20.

54. *fire to fall from heaven*: A clear reference to 2 Kgs 1:10, when Elijah threatens fire to fall on his enemies and then delivers on the promise. James and John want to practice similar vengeance on their opponents. Some ancient scribes recognized the allusion, and their gloss, "as Elijah did," found its way into some MSS.

55. *rebuked them*: This short version of the text is to be preferred to the MSS that supply: "you do not know of what spirit you are," and those that add further, "for the Son of Man did not come to destroy souls but to save them" (compare Luke 19:10).

57. *I will follow you*: These verses (9:57-62) are Q material, shared with Matt 8:18-22. The threefold call and offer remind the reader of the threefold willingness of Elisha to follow Elijah in the period before his ascension (2 Kgs 2:1-6). Here and in verse 61 are the only places in the Gospel where someone volunteers to follow. In contrast to the would-be disciples who place prior conditions, this one's offer is open-ended, "wherever you might go." In Matt 8:19, it is a scribe who offers, but Luke includes them among the leaders who do not respond positively to the Prophet.

58. *place to lay his head*: The saying is close to that in Matt 8:20 and the *Gospel of Thomas* 86 (without narrative context). That the life of a philosopher can demand homelessness is made clear by Epictetus, *Discourse* 3, 22, 18-20, and Dio Chrysostom, *Oration* 6, 18-20.

59. *bury my father*: This is not a trivial excuse, but the fulfillment of the obligation to "honor father and mother" as is made clear in Tobit 4:3-4; 6:13-14; 14:11-13.

60. *bury their own dead*: The meaning here depends on the understanding of conversion as a "new life," with those not sharing the new life being in effect "dead." With the reference to "kingdom of God," here and in verse 62, we return to the apostolic commission (9:2, 6) as a share in the work of Jesus (9:11).

61. *good-bye to those in my family*: Is literally, "those in my house." For the verb *apotassomai* ("say good-bye"), cf. Acts 18:18, 21, and especially Luke 14:33 where it is applied to one's possessions rather than family. The sense of this saying is the same as Luke 14:26, "unless someone hates ones father and mother . . .''

62. *fit for the kingdom of God*: The adjective *euthetos* describes not a moral category but one of aptitude, so that for "kingdom" here we should understand a shorthand way of saying "preaching the kingdom of God." For this, a sense of direction and concentration is required. The image of the plow recalls Elisha who was called while plowing, and begged leave to "kiss my father and mother and then I will follow you" (1 Kgs 19:19-21). Elijah allowed him; Jesus' demand is stricter.

Interpretation

Luke begins in 9:51 the great middle section of his Gospel. He stops following Mark, returning to it as his main source again only in 18:15. The material in this long section comes from Q (shared with Matthew) or L (Luke's own source or composition).

Some readers profess to find a sense of structure in these chapters elusive. Other readers find an intricate literary structure. Some, for example, have thought to discover in these chapters a careful imitation of the narrative of Deuteronomy. But as persuaded as this commentary is by the parallel between the prophet Jesus and the prophet Moses, that thesis seems overly restrictive: Luke's imagery is more wide ranging. The same can be said—more cautiously—by the analyses which hope to demonstrate that the entire journey narrative describes a great *chiasm*, in which parallel stories radiate outward in a careful and deliberate balance from a central point. There are such points of balance to be discovered, obviously, otherwise such theories would be impossible. But the points of resemblance often result as much from the definitions given by scholars as from the stories themselves.

This commentary works with an understanding of the journey as having a structure that is relatively simple but which serves Luke's narrative purposes well.

His major organizing device is obviously the journey to Jerusalem. At the transfiguration, Jesus discussed with Moses and Elijah the *exodos* he was to fulfill in Jerusalem (9:31). Now, with great solemnity, Jesus "sets his face to go to Jerusalem" in order to accomplish his "lifting up" (9:51). From this point until Jesus' arrival in the city (19:28), the reader is constantly reminded that Jesus is "on the way" (9:52, 56, 57; 10:38; 13:33), and specifically "on the way to Jerusalem" (9:53; 10:1; 13:22, 31; 14:25; 17:11; 18:31, 35; 19:1, 11, 28). Luke 9:51 functions both as a key element in Luke's geographical structure, and also as a programmatic prophecy for the narrative spanning the next nine chapters.

The presentation of Jesus as a prophet is also intensified in this section of the Gospel. Nothing so stylistically matches the deliberate announcement concerning Jesus' "lifting up" in 9:51 as the statement about Elijah's ascension in 2 Kgs 2:1. Another dimension of the presence of Moses and Elijah at Jesus' transfiguration becomes clearer in this light: Moses and Elijah are both figures who in the tradition were regarded as having ascended into heaven; both, furthermore, appointed successors who acted in the Spirit.

Now, in these first gestures of Jesus as he begins his journey we can detect subtle allusions to the prophets Moses and Elijah. Jesus' sending of "messengers before his face" obviously recalls Exodus 23:20 and the Moses story, just as the desire of the disciples to stop a rival prophet in 9:49-50 echoed the confrontation between Moses and Joshua in Num 11:26-30. In the section now being analyzed, the question of James and John about whether they should bring fire on the Samaritans is a verbal allusion to 2 Kings 1:10 when Elijah brought fire on his enemies. Likewise, the request of the would-be disciple to bid farewell to his family echoes the request made by Elisha to Elijah in 1 Kings 19:19-21. Finally, the language of 9:51 deliberately recalls that used of Ezekiel as "Son of Man" who turned his face toward Jerusalem to "prophesy against Israel" (Ezek 21:7-8). The reader is told clearly that it is as the prophet that Jesus makes his way to Jerusalem.

As the prophet who travels toward Jerusalem, Jesus speaks the word of God. The great bulk of material in this section is made up of sayings. Jesus does perform some wonders: an exorcism (11:14), the healing of a bent woman (13:10-13), the man with dropsy (14:1-6), ten lepers (17:11-19), and a blind man (18:35-43). But the rest of the time, he is speaking. And as he speaks, the Prophet is shown to be surrounded by three carefully distinguished groups. Journeying with him are the disciples who increasingly emerge as significant hearers of the word. The term *mathētēs* ("disciple") occurs more frequently in these nine chapters than anywhere else in the Gospel, and eight times the expression "Jesus said to his disciples" is used, followed by a body of teaching. Another group to whom Jesus speaks is "the crowd" (*ochlos*). This term occurs some eighteen times in these chapters, while the term "people" (*laos*) is used only three times. Finally, Jesus has repeated confrontations with his opponents, the Pharisees and lawyers.

Luke is very careful to note Jesus' audience in every instance. To each group, furthermore, Jesus speaks quite different sorts of words: to the crowd, he issues warnings and calls to conversion. To those who convert and become disciples, he gives positive instructions on discipleship. Finally, to those who resist his prophetic call, he tells parables of rejection.

Luke gives dramatic structure to these sayings by carefully alternating the audiences. Throughout the journey (as the notes will indicate), Luke has Jesus turn from one group to the other, from crowd to disciples to Pharisees. The narrative that results from this "arrangement" is therefore filled with unexpected tension: the Prophet makes his way to Jerusalem, to his death and "lifting up." As he goes, he speaks the word of God to those around him. Some hear and become part of the people. Others reject the word and are themselves in process of being rejected from the people. The climax is reached when Jesus reaches the city and is greeted, now not by a handful of followers (cf. 8:1-3) but by a "whole multitude of disciples" (19:37) prepared to hear the teaching of the Prophet in the precincts of the Temple.

FOR REFERENCE AND FURTHER STUDY

Evans, C. F. "The Central Section of St. Luke's Gospel." *Studies in the Gospels.* Ed. D. E. Nineham (Oxford, Blackwell, 1955) 37–53.

Johnson, L. T. *The Literary Function of Possessions in Luke-Acts* (SBLDS 39; Missoula: Scholars Press, 1977) 103–109.

Moessner, D. *Lord of the Banquet: The Literary and Theological Significance of the Lukan Travel Narrative.* Philadelphia: Fortress, 1989.

Miyoshi, M. *Der Anfang des Reiseberichts Lk 9:51–10:24: Eine redaktionsgeschichtliche Untersuchung.* AnBib 60; Rome: Biblical Institute, 1974.

Reicke, B. "Instruction and Travel in the Travel Narrative." *Studia Evangelica* I. Eds. K. Aland, F. Cross (TU 73; Berlin: Akademie-Verlag, 1959) 206–216.

Robinson, W. C. "The Theological Context for Interpreting Luke's Travel Narrative (9:51ff)." *JBL* 79 (1960) 20–31.

30. *Acceptance and Rejection* (10:1-24)

1. After this the Lord appointed seventy others and sent them before him in pairs to every city and place where he himself was about to go. 2. He said to them, "The harvest is rich but there are few workers. Therefore ask the Harvest Master to send workers to the harvest. 3. You go! Look, I am sending you like lambs among wolves. 4. Don't carry a purse or bag or wear sandals. Don't greet anyone on the road. 5. Whenever you enter a house, say at once, 'Peace to this household.' 6. If a child of peace is there, your peace will rest on that person. Otherwise it will return to you. 7. Stay in that house. Eat and drink what they provide, for the worker deserves a reward. Don't travel from house to house. 8. Whenever you enter a city and it welcomes you, eat whatever is set before you. 9. Heal the sick people there. Say to them, 'The kingdom of God has reached you!' 10. Whenever you enter a city and it does not welcome you, walk out on its streets and say, 11. 'For you, we wipe off even the dust that has stuck to our feet from your city! But know this: The kingdom of God has arrived!' 12. I tell you, in that day it will go easier for Sodom than for that city. 13. Woe to you, Chorazin! Woe to you Bethsaida! For if the powerful deeds done among you had been performed for Tyre and Sidon, they would long since have repented, sitting in sackcloth and ashes. 14. Indeed it will be easier for Tyre and Sidon in the judgment than for you. 15. And you, Capernaum! Will you be lifted up as high as heaven? You will be cast down as far as Hades! 16. The one who listens to you listens to me. The one who rejects you rejects me. The one who rejects me rejects the one who sent me." 17. The seventy returned joyfully. They said, "Lord, even the demons are submissive to us in your name!" 18. He said to them, "I was watching Satan fall like a bolt of lightning from the sky! 19. Look, I have given you the authority to walk over snakes and scorpions, over every power of the enemy. He will in no way get back at you. 20. But don't rejoice because spirits are subjected to you. Rejoice instead because your names are written in heaven." 21. At that moment he exulted in the Holy Spirit. He said, "I praise you Father, Lord of heaven and earth, because you have hidden these things from wise and intelligent people and revealed them to infants. Yes, my Father, for this has pleased you. 22. All things have been given to me by my father. No one knows who the son is except the father. No one knows who the father is except the son, and the one to whom the son chooses to reveal him." 23. He turned to the disciples and said to them privately, "Blessed are the eyes that see the things you are seeing! 24. I tell you, many prophets and kings wanted to see the things you are seeing, and they did not see; wanted to hear the things you are hearing, and did not hear."

NOTES

1. *seventy others*: For the narrative use of *kyrios* ("Lord"), see the note on 7:13. The text-critical problem here is nearly insoluble. The MSS are evenly divided between

"seventy" and "seventy-two" both here and in verse 17. Arguments from context can be made for either number. Many editions deal with the impasse by placing [-two] in brackets. This translation chooses "seventy" because it coincides with the image of Jesus as the prophet like Moses which is so important thematically for Luke. Moses picked seventy elders (Num 11:16-17) to share his work with the people, and they shared the spirit of prophecy (Num 11:25). In Exod 24:1, 9-14 the seventy elders also accompany Moses on the mountain. In light of the clear allusion to Num 11:26-30 in Luke 9:49, so close to the present passage, the choice for seventy seems reasonable.

in pairs: The Greek has "two by two," and the presence of these extra "two's" certainly affected the confused state of the text.

where he himself was about to go: The Twelve were sent to preach and heal without Jesus (9:1-2); the messengers of 9:51 were sent to prepare hospitality for Jesus; the seventy combine both functions: they preach and heal, but do so in preparation for Jesus' arrival.

2. *harvest is rich*: The saying is found in Matt 9:37-38 before the sending of the Twelve, and a similar saying is found in John 4:35. The image of the harvest lying ready corresponds to the parable of the sower of the seed (8:5). There is some awkwardness in the transition between verses 2-3; one is tempted to treat the statement almost as proverbial: "whenever . . . one should pray . . . that he send . . .", but the syntax does not allow it.

3. *lambs among wolves*: Note that Jesus uses here the verb *apostellō*, to send with a commission: they represent the prophet. The comparison to lambs is also in Matthew's instructions to the Twelve (Matt 10:16) with a moral teaching attached. In Luke there is no moralization: the comparison points to the dangers they face, and the reason for travelling light. The context established by 9:53 gives this urgency.

4. *carry a purse or bag*: Compare the instructions to the Twelve (note on 9:3). The redundancy of purse and bag here matches that of purse and silver in the earlier passage. The sandals are a new item. The instructions seem a bit *ad hoc*, as though Luke wanted to refer the reader to the earlier version without repeating it.

don't greet anyone on the road: There is a good narrative reason for this new element which is unique to Luke. In contrast to the mission of the Twelve in a Galilee receptive to Jesus, the present mission is in dangerous Samaria, which has already been shown in the narrative (9:53) to be hostile.

6. *peace will rest on that person*: That is, there will be peace between you and that person (see also Matt 10:12-13). The reciprocity here fits the pattern of acceptance/rejection dominating this section. For "peace" as a greeting, see 24:36; 3 John 15. "Child (literally: son) of peace" means, simply, a peacefully inclined person.

7. *the worker deserves a reward*: The saying is unusually well attested in the NT: compare Matt 10:10; 1 Cor 9:14; 1 Tim 5:18. For the prohibition of moving from house to house, see the note on 9:4.

9. *heal the sick people*: As in 9:1-2, 6, 11, the preaching of the kingdom of God is signalled by the power to heal (cf. also Matt 10:7-8 for the same combination at this point).

11. *we wipe off even the dust*: The brief command of 9:5 is here turned into a moment of drama by the use of direct speech. Luke here shifts from the household (*oikia*) to the city (*polis*). Distinctive to this version is the assertion (matching that in v. 9) that "the kingdom of God has arrived."

12. *in that day*: Clearly refers to the day of God's judgment (see "judgment" in v. 14, below). The NT uses various terms for the eschatological judgment, e.g., "day of wrath" (Rom 2:5), "day of the Lord" (1 Cor 1:8), and in Luke, "day of the Son of Man" (17:24, 30).

    go easier for Sodom: The wickedness of Sodom was proverbial (see Gen 13:13; Isa 3:9; Ezek 16:48, 56), but its great sin was the betrayal of hospitality to God's messengers (Gen 19:1-23). Its consequent overthrow became a warning for succeeding generations (Deut 29:23; Isa 1:9; 13:19; Jer 23:14; Lam 4:6), an example used as well by NT writers (Jude 7; 2 Pet 2:6; Rom 9:29), and once more by Luke in 17:29.

13. *woe to you*: For the use of *ouai*, see 6:24-26 and 11:42-52. The town Chorazin appears only here and in the parallel of Matt 11:21. Bethsaida is a locus for Jesus' ministry in Mark 6:45 and 8:22. In Luke, we have noted its rather odd appearance in 9:10. We have been given no narrative reason for its condemnation.

14. *Tyre and Sidon*: Are towns on the Phoenician seacoast mentioned in 6:17. Tyre is also part of Paul's journey in Acts 21:3, 7. They are not part of Jesus' ministry, which is exactly the point. Sackcloth and ashes are traditional symbols of repentance (see Jonah 3:6 [LXX]; Isa 58:5; Dan 9:3 [LXX]). Matt 11:21 supplies the reason for this attack: "because they did not repent." Luke leaves it implicit. Conversion/repentance (*metanoia*) becomes a more prominent theme (11:32; 13:3, 5; 15:7, 10; 16:30) as Jesus calls the crowd.

15. *and you, Capernaum*: Luke places Jesus in this Galilean town in 4:31 and 7:1. From 4:23 we infer that the things he had done in Capernaum enjoyed a reputation in Nazareth, and perhaps were a source of local boasting. The threat is paralleled in Matt 11:23a, with an appended logion against Sodom (Matt 11:23b-24). The language about "being lifted up" and "being cast down to Hades (*hadēs*)" is used in Isa 14:11, 13-15 against the Babylonian king. Hades is the Greek place of the dead, the nether world of shades, equivalent to the Hebrew *sheol* (cf. LXX Gen 37:35; Ps 6:5).

18. *Satan fall like a bolt of lightning*: This is Luke's first use of the name Satan for the chief of the demons; he earlier used "the devil" (4:2-13; 8:12). Through the rest of the Gospel, *Satanas* is his usual designation (11:18; 13:16; 22:3, 31). The role of Satan as tester is established by Job 1:6-12; 2:1-7; Zech 3:1-2; 1 Chr 21:1. The image of falling like lightning may continue the allusion to Isa 14:15 (see the note on v. 15 above). For the use of "in the name," see the note on 9:49.

19. *over snakes and scorpions*: The two creatures appear together again in Luke 11:11-12.

Protection from snakes is guaranteed by the risen Jesus in the longer ending of Mark's Gospel (16:18).

get back at you: The verb *adikeō* here has the sense of taking revenge for a hurt done (cf. Acts 7:24-27). The translation "in no way" combines the force of *ouden* and *ou mē* in the Greek.

20. *names are written in heaven*: The notion of a heavenly book in which the names and deeds of the righteous are recorded is found in Exod 32:32-33; Ps 69:28; 138:16 [LXX]; Phil 4:3; Heb 12:23; Rev 3:5. For a similar idea, see "merit in heaven" (note on 6:33) and Luke's later use of "treasure in heaven" (12:33; 18:22).

21. *exulted in the Holy Spirit*: The expression is the same used of Mary at the beginning of the Magnificat (1:47). See also Acts 2:26 and 16:34. The expression "in the Holy Spirit" here means "under the influence of" the Holy Spirit (cf. 2:27).

    I praise you Father: Is literally "I acknowledge you" (*exhomologeomai*, cf. Acts 19:18). Jesus' prayer follows the pattern of the Jewish synagogue prayers such as the *Berakah Yozer*: a) opening praise, b) reasons for the praise, c) affirmation of assent or repetition of praise. Luke's version is very close to that in Matt 11:25-26.

    hidden . . . revealed: There is a double contrast here; for that between "hidden" and "revealed," see Luke 8:17. The contrast between the wise and children is exploited by 1 Cor 3:1 and Heb 6:13-14. The "pleasure of God" (*eudokia*, cf. 2:14) toward the poor and lowly has been thematic throughout the Gospel, and infants certainly qualify. For the paradoxical nature of the Christian revelation, see esp. 1 Cor 1:18-31.

22. *no one knows . . . the Father*: The double repetition of "Father" (*patēr*) in verse 21 leads naturally to this solemn declaration concerning the unique relationship of Jesus as Son (*huios*) to God ("my Father"). Such explicit relational language is unusual in the Synoptics, but found much more often in John (see 3:35; 7:29; 10:14-15; 13:3; 17:2, 25, 29). Luke's logion is close to that in Matt 11:27.

23. *said to them privately*: By this transition clause (cf. also 9:1 and 9:18), Luke binds the macarism to the previous statement on revelation. Matt 13:16-17, in contrast, places the saying immediately after the parable of the sower.

    blessed are the eyes that see: This is now the seventh macarism of the Gospel (see 1:45; 6:20, 21 [2]; 22; 7:23). Here the emphasis is on seeing; in verses 24 and 28, it is on hearing. We are reminded of 8:18, "watch how you hear."

24. *prophets and kings*: Matt 13:17 has "prophets and righteous people." For the disciples' continuity with the prophets, see Luke 6:23. The "kings" helps continue the contrast between the mighty and the lowly.

INTERPRETATION

The sending and return of seventy additional emissaries (10:1-12) is unique to Luke's Gospel. The commission and sending resemble 9:1-6 and the Synoptic parallels, but also contain distinctive touches. To this scene, Luke has added a prophetic denunciation of cities (10:13-15) and a pronouncement on acceptance and rejection (10:16) that come from Q (cf. Matt 11:22-24; 10:40). After the account of the missionaries' return (10:17-20) which is unique to him, he adds a prayer of thanksgiving (10:21-22) and a macarism (10:23-24) that are again derived from Q (Matt 11:25-27; 13:16-17). The effect of his redactional work is the creation of another three-scene sequence similar to that found in the sending of the Twelve: the commission, an interlude, the return.

An author who otherwise so sedulously avoids doublets must have a good reason for adding one. Most readers seek a clue in the number 70 (or 72). The number 12 for the first sending was obviously symbolic of Israel as the restored people of God. What does this number signify? The text-problem makes the issue more difficult (see the note on 10:1). That Luke intends the reader to understand this appointment as analogous to Moses' choosing of seventy elders is quite clear. The action therefore adds further to his presentation of Jesus as the prophet like Moses. Beyond that, there would seem to be some merit in the suggestion that this sending anticipates the later spread of the Gospel beyond Judaism to the Gentiles. Certainly, the Samaritan mission in Acts 8 represents an important stage in the spread of the mission in fulfillment of the prophecy of Jesus (1:8). It is less clear, however, that the Samaritans represent "Gentiles." It is more likely that Luke saw the Samaritans as "outcasts of the people" who also were given the opportunity to join the restored people forming around the Prophet.

By placing discourse material within the context of a journey to Jerusalem, Luke is able to give biographical verisimilitude to certain sayings. The desire of would-be disciples to "follow" him, for example, is more dramatic. In the present section, the setting in the larger narrative also highlights some of Luke's distinctive features. Thus, the instructions to the seventy to travel light and to greet no one on the way make sense in the context of a Samaria whose hostility was established in 9:53. The same context gives added point to the sayings on hospitality and rejection. Indeed, the main difference between these instructions and those given to the Twelve is the greater emphasis on rejection. Here is the possibility that peace will *not* rest on someone in a household. The disciples might need to shout out their apotropaic challenge in the streets. The prophet therefore speaks a woe against the cities that reject his delegates, himself, and the one who sent him (10:16). At the same time, whether it is accepted or rejected, the messengers are to proclaim the same message: the kingdom of God has come!

Finally, we observe the further development of Luke's theme of the divine reversal, which is expressed in God's "pleasure" (*eudokia*) to reveal "these things" to the lowly and the simple, not to kings or the wise. Notice how in verse 23 Luke has Jesus "turn to the disciples" with his macarism, "Blessed are the eyes that see." The turning is characteristic of the journey narrative, which alternates messages and audiences. As in the Sermon on the Plain but in reverse order, a declaration of woe is followed by a blessing. Now it is becoming clearer who within the populace is receiving what.

FOR REFERENCE AND FURTHER STUDY

Cerfaux, L. "L'Evangile de Jean et 'le logion Johannique' des synoptiques." *L'Evangile de Jean: Etudes et Problèmes.* Ed F.-M. Braun (RechBib 3; Bruges: Desclée de Brouwer, 1958) 147–159.

Cullmann, O. *The Christology of the New Testament.* Rev.ed. Trans. S. Guthrie (Philadelphia: Westminster, 1959) 286–289.

Feuillet, A. "Jésus et la sagesse divine d'après les évangiles synoptiques." *RB* 62 (1955) 161–196.

Grelot, P. "Etude critique de luc 10, 19." *RSR* 69 (1981) 87–100.

Jeremias, J. *New Testament Theology* I. *The Proclamation of Jesus* (New York: Charles Scribners, 1971) 56–61.

Metzger, B. M. "Seventy or Seventy-Two Disciples?" *NTS* 5 (1958–59) 299–306.

31. *Rejection and Acceptance* (10:25-42)

25. A certain lawyer stood up to test him. He said, "Teacher, what must I do to inherit eternal life?" 26. He said to him, "What stands written in the Law? How you do you read it?" 27. He answered, " 'You must love the Lord your God with your whole heart and your whole soul and your whole strength and your whole mind, and your neighbor as yourself.' " 28. Jesus said to him, "You answered correctly. Do this and you will live." 29. But wishing to justify himself he said to Jesus, "But who is my neighbor?" 30.. Jesus took this up and said, "A certain man was travelling down from Jerusalem to Jericho. He fell among bandits. They stripped him. They beat him. They left him half dead. 31. By chance a certain priest was travelling down that same road. He saw the man but passed by on the other side. 32. In the same way a Levite came to the spot, saw him, and passed by on the other side. 33. But a certain Samaritan travelling on the road came up to him. He saw him and felt compassion. 34. He approached him. He bandaged his wounds. He poured oil and wine on them. He put the man on his own beast. He led him to an inn and took care of him. 35. The next day, he pulled out two silver pieces and gave them to the innkeeper. He said, 'Take care of him. When I return I will repay you whatever else you must spend.' 36. Which of these three do you think turned out to be a neighbor to the one who fell among bandits?" 37. He said, "The one who treated him with mercy." Jesus said to him, "You go and do the same." 38. As Jesus was travelling, he entered a certain village. A woman named Martha

welcomed him. 39. She had a sister named Mary who sat at the feet of Jesus and listened to him speak. 40. But Martha was overwhelmed by so much serving. She came up and said, "Lord, does it not concern you that my sister left me alone to serve? Tell her to help me!" 41. The Lord answered her, "Martha, Martha, you are anxious and troubled by many things. 42. But there is need for only one. Mary chose the good part. It won't be taken away from her."

NOTES

25. *stood up to test him*: Luke thus identifies the intent of the question as hostile rather than neutral; note the use of *ekpeirazō*, "put to the test" in 4:12.

    inherit eternal life: The same question recurs later in Luke 18:18, paralleled by Matt 19:29 and Mark 10:17. The combination of terms does not occur in Torah. The "inheritance" (*klēronomia*) promised the people is the land (Gen 28:4; Deut 1:8; 2:12; 4:1; cf. Acts 7:5). Ps 15:5 [LXX] speaks of the Lord as one's inheritance, and Ps 36:18 [LXX] of an eternal inheritance (see also Esth 4:7), but this is not connected to "eternal life." In Dan 12:2 [LXX] on the other hand, the just will rise to "eternal life." In the NT, the idea of an "eternal inheritance" is found only in Heb 9:15 although it is suggested by I Pet 1:4. But the idea of "eternal life" is frequently found (see e.g., Rom 2:7; 5:21; 6:22-23; Gal 6:8; Jude 21; and esp. John 3:15-16, etc.). The other Synoptists use it only once, but Luke has it in 18:18, 30; Acts 13:46, 48.

26. *stands written in the Law*: Remarkably, this is Luke's first reference to "the Law" (*nomos*) since the frequent use in the infancy account (although cf. 6:3).

27. *you must love the Lord your God*: With minor variations in the prepositions (all of which are suppressed in this translation), Luke substantially reproduces Deut 6:5 [LXX], adding the fourth phrase "your whole mind (*dianoia*)." Matt 22:37 and Mark 12:30 place this citation in response to a question about "the greatest commandment" during Jesus' Jerusalem ministry.

    your neighbor as yourself: An exact citation from Lev 19:18. The commandment of love of neighbor is widely attested in the NT writings (Mark 12:31; Matt 22:39; Rom 13:9; Gal 5:14; Jas 2:8; John 15:12). Luke's version is distinctive because he collapses the two commandments into one.

29. *justify himself*: There is irony here. Rather than "do this and live," that is, "love the neighbor," (in this case Jesus), the lawyer continues to test Jesus in order to assert himself. Notice the contrast to "justifying God" in the thematic statement about teachers of the law in 7:29-30 (see the note there) and the recurrence of this identifying tag in 16:15.

    who is my neighbor: Lev 19:18 makes "sons of your own people" (i.e., fellow-Israelites) as equivalent to "neighbor." Later, in Lev 19:33-34, this is extended to the *ger* ("stranger" or "sojourner") in the land. Since the LXX translated this as *prosēlytos* ("proselyte"), the attitude of love was still rather restricted. Among sectarians like those at Qumran, the division between love for the sons of light and hate for all others was absolute (cf. *1QS* 1:9-10). For the Pharisees, discussion of the limits of interaction with non-Jews was extensive, as e.g., *m.Abodah Zarah* 1:1; 2:1-2; 4:9-10.

30. *took this up*: The verb *hypolambanō* is used for the understanding of a point, or, as here, responding to it.

   a certain man: Is understood to be, from the structure of the story, himself Judean. Jerusalem is some 2,500 feet above sea level and Jericho 700 feet below it, so travelling between them is indeed downward.

   fell among bandits: The term *lēstēs* is used by Josephus for organized bands of highwaymen who made travel perilous; cf. *Jewish War* 2:228-230. Luke uses the term again in 19:46 and 22:52.

31. *a certain priest*: The indefinite pronoun *tis* with each of the characters indicates their representative status in the story. The priests and Levites were not among the wealthy aristocracy, but did symbolically represent the leadership of the people (cf. e.g., *1QS* 1:8ff; 5:1-4); they were restricted by purity regulations which limited their contacts with others. The point of the story is not a contrast between "Jews" and "Samaritans" to the advantage of the latter, but a contrast between those who were established and recognized as part of the people and those who were not.

33. *a certain Samaritan*: For the rivalry between Judeans and Samaritans, see the note on 9:53. The force of this identification is all the more powerful because of the Samaritan hostility to Jesus' own ministry mentioned in 9:53. Another Samaritan is mentioned positively in 17:16, and the mission to Samaria is an important stage in the spread of the good news in Acts (1:8), enjoying great success there (Acts 8:1-14; 9:31; 15:3).

   felt compassion: This is the emotion attributed to Jesus in 7:13. The Samaritan's involvement began with his choice to "approach" rather than pass on the other side. Then he saw, felt compassion, and came even closer.

36. *turned out to be a neighbor*: Jesus reverses the question from one of legal obligation (who deserves my love) to one of gift-giving (to whom can I show myself neighbor); and of this the despised *Samaritan* is the moral exemplar!

38. *Martha welcomed him*: In Luke's Gospel she appears only here. In John 11:1-39 and 12:2, Martha and Mary are sisters with a brother named Lazarus. The other Synoptics lack this story as well as any mention of these characters. The name Mary is so common that it is not necessary to connect this one to Mary Magdalene in 8:2.

39. *listened to him speak*: Is literally, "listened to his word (*logos*)." She was attentive to what he was saying and therefore received him as he was, a prophet who spoke "the word of God" (8:11). Throughout Luke-Acts, sitting at the feet indicates acknowledgement of authority (7:38; 8:35, 41; 17:16; Acts 4:35, 37; 5:2; 22:3).

40. *overwhelmed by so much serving*: The verb *perispaō* has the sense of "being distracted." The reason is that there was too much to do. It should be noted that the narrator indicates this as an objective fact (*pollēn diakonian*), and not as a neurotic obsessiveness on her part.

Lord, does it not concern you: Compare the question posed Jesus in Mark's account of the stilling of the storm (4:38). Martha's "question" is in fact an accusation against her sister: "she abandoned me to do all the work."

tell her to help me: Jesus will again be asked to intervene in a domestic dispute, this time over property, in 12:13; as here, he responds with a pronouncement. We are reminded as well of the complaint of the resentful elder brother in 15:28-29.

41. *anxious and troubled*: The term "anxious" (*merimnaō*) is used elsewhere for the entanglements of life in the world (Matt 6:25-34; 1 Cor 7:32-34; Luke 12:26). The second term, *thorubazomai*, is more often used in the active rather than the middle voice, of "making an uproar," as a crowd would in an assembly. The verb is not attested elsewhere in the NT and some scribes tried to replace it with a more common verb. But this one is colorful, "you are putting yourself in an uproar."

42. *there is need for only one*: The failure to grasp this short phrase in context led to various scribal emendations. Thinking that Jesus was recommending the preparation of fewer dishes, some copyists replaced "one" with "a few," and still others combined the two phrases to accomplish total confusion. Jesus refers rather to the essential note of hospitality which is to pay attention to the guest; only that is necessary; the rest is optional.

Mary chose the good part: Or perhaps better, "Mary made the right choice" of what was necessary. Luke uses *agathos* rather than *kalos*, so there is a moral dimension to her choice: by her listening, she has received the person of the Prophet, for the Prophet is defined by his "word."

INTERPRETATION

The Prophet travels to Jerusalem and on the way interacts with three groups: the amorphous crowd, the eager disciples, the watchful and increasingly hostile adversaries. Jesus has just addressed his disciples with a blessing (10:21-24) and is immediately confronted by a lawyer (10:25). We have been instructed by the thematic statement in 7:29-30 to recognize in the "teachers of the Law" those who reject prophets and reject God's will for them, failing to justify God. We are not surprised, therefore, to find a lawyer "testing him" by asking how to gain eternal life, and when given an answer, not accepting it but "seeking to justify himself," trying to trap Jesus in a classic casuistic puzzler.

In the other Synoptic Gospels also Jesus is asked about the "greatest commandment" and responds by citing as the most important Deut 6:5 on the whole-hearted love of God, and in second place Lev 19:18 on love for the neighbor (Mark 12:28-34; Matt 22:34-40). Luke's version is distinctive on several counts. Rather than make one commandment first and the other second, he combines them into a single unified command so that "love of neighbor" has the same force as "love for God." And rather than a scholastic opinion on Torah, Jesus in Luke's version responds with a command to the questioner: "do this and you shall live." Instead of a debate taking place in Jerusalem, this hostile questioning takes place in dangerous Samaria. Finally, the lawyer's trap question, "who is my neighbor" (v. 29) is "taken up" by Jesus (v. 30) and turned on his opponent in one of the most beautiful of all the Gospel parables, the moral tale (unique to Luke's composition) of the compassionate Samaritan (10:30-35).

The parable itself is intended to provoke. The violence done to the travelling Judean is overt: he is stripped, beaten, left half dead. This is not a sentimental tale. A deeper level of shock, however, is the recognition that Jews esteemed for their place in the people and dedicated to holiness before the Lord would allow considerations of personal safety or even concern for ritual purity (a corpse defiled) to justify their not even crossing the road to look. They "pass by on the other side." If love for neighbor meant anything, it meant to care for the "sons of your own people." But they cannot be bothered. A third shock is the discovery that a despised Samaritan, himself most at risk in this dangerous no man's land of deserted territory, takes the chance of stopping, looking, and—increasing his own vulnerability— leading the man on his beast to an inn. It is the hated enemy who is the hero with a human heart.

More stunning still is the use to which Jesus turns the parable. The point, we learn, is not who deserves to be cared for, but rather the demand to become a person who treats everyone encountered—however frightening, alien, naked or defenseless—with compassion: "you go and do the same." Jesus does not clarify a point of law, but transmutes law to gospel. One must take the same risks with one's life and possessions that the Samaritan did!

Luke follows this hostile encounter with a vignette in which the Prophet is received with hospitality by the two sisters (10:38-42), a story which is again found only in Luke and clearly expressive of his thematic interests. The sisters together represent the proper response to the Prophet of receiving him in the home; an itinerant mission depended on such support and safety. We have seen earlier in the narrative how the women of Galilee (8:1-3) supported Jesus and the Twelve in their travel. Now in this more hostile territory Jesus finds another receptive household. The story also refines the understanding of hospitality. Jesus' response to Martha makes clear that the "one thing necessary" for hospitality is attention to the guest, rather than a domestic performance. If the guest is a prophet, the appropriate reception is listening to God's word! The lesson extends by implication of course to every guest received. Jesus nicely turns the point from one of providing a service to receiving a gift: the other who comes into our space is a messenger of grace.

Martha's anxiety and concern are understandable enough. But her self-preoccupation and resentment led her to break the rules of hospitality far more radically than did her sister, for she asked a stranger to intervene in a family rivalry.

One cannot read these stories without appreciating Luke's deftness and skill. They stay as fresh for readers thousands of years after their composition, resisting even bad translations. It is obvious that Luke understands something about human psychology. The pattern of avoidance exhibited by the priest and Levite, the self-justifying bluster of the lawyer, the irritation of the "dutiful daughter" Martha. These are people like us. Less familiar perhaps is what goes beyond psychology into gospel: the compassion that is not simply a feeling but translates itself into the self-giving that takes risks, that disposes of the self and one's possessions and then allows the other to leave without clinging; the hospitality that receives the other as the other wishes to be received, that listens.

FOR REFERENCE AND FURTHER STUDY

Baker, A. "One Thing Necessary." *CBQ* 27 (1965) 127–137.
Crossan, J. D. "Parable and Example in the Teaching of Jesus." *NTS* 18 (1971–72) 285–307.
Crossan, J. D., ed. "The Good Samaritan." *Semeia* 2 (1974)—entire issue.
Furnish, V. P. *The Love Commandment in the New Testament* (Nashville: Abingdon, 1972) 34–45.
Sellin, G. "Lukas als Gleichniserzähler: Die Erzählung von barmherziger Samariter (Lk 10:25-27)." *ZNW* 65 (1974) 166–189; 66 (1975) 19–60.

32. *Teaching on Prayer* (11:1-13)

1. He was in a certain spot praying. When he stopped, one of his disciples said to him, "Lord, teach us to pray just as John taught his disciples." 2. He said to them, "Whenever you pray, say, 'Father, may your name be holy! May your kingdom come! 3. Give to us every day the bread we need! 4. Forgive us our sins, for we ourselves also forgive everyone who owes us! Do not lead us into testing!' " 5. He said to them, "Suppose one of you has a friend and goes to him in the middle of the night, saying, 'Friend, I need three loaves of bread 6. because a friend of mine has come off the road and I have nothing to offer him.' 7. And he answers from within the house: 'Stop bothering me! The door is shut. The children are in bed with me! I can't get up and give it to you.' 8. I tell you, even if he does not get up and give it to him as a friend, because of the man's shamelessness he will get up and give him whatever is needed. 9. So I say to you, Ask and

it will be given to you. Seek and you will find. Knock and the door will be opened for you. 10. For everyone who asks receives. The one who seeks finds. The one who knocks will have the door opened. 11. Which father among you whose son asks for a fish will give him a snake rather than a fish? 12. Or if he asks for an egg will give him a scorpion? 13. Now if you, wicked as you are, know how to give good gifts to your children, how much more your father will give the Holy Spirit from heaven to those who ask him."

NOTES

1. *in a certain spot praying*: It is typical of Luke to place instruction in a biographically plausible setting; contrast Matthew's version (6:9-13) which comes in the Sermon on the Mount. For the role of prayer in Jesus' ministry, see the note on 3:21.

   John taught his disciples: Luke has told us some details of John's ministry: he preached (3:18) and himself fasted (7:33); his disciples both fasted and "prayed" (5:33).

2. *whenever you pray*: The construction suggests a general pattern for prayer. In addition to the parallel in Matthew, the prayer is found as well in the early Christian handbook, *Didache* 8:2. Luke's version is the simplest, with five members. Matthew's is both more elaborate in wording and has seven members. The *Didache* follows Matthew's version and adds the doxology, "for yours is the kingdom . . ."

   Father, may your name be holy: The simple greeting *patēr* makes the community prayer close to that of Jesus himself (10:21). Matthew has "our Father in heaven," and some Lukan MSS have assimilated that reading. The "sanctification of the name" is an ancient feature of Jewish prayer. The doxology called the *kaddish* began "Magnified and sanctified be his great name," and one of the Eighteen Benedictions (*shemoneh esre*) was called *Kedushat ha shem* ("Sanctification of the Name"). The prayer recognizes God's absolute difference from all created things (see Ezek 36:22-28) and takes on the obligation to "be holy as [he is] holy" (Lev 11:45). Cf. esp. John 17:17-19.

   may your kingdom come: Is a prayer for the rule of God to be made effective in the world of humans; the prayer is again paralleled in the *kaddish*. The wording is the same as in Matthew, and fits perfectly within Jesus' ministry of proclaiming the arrival of the kingdom of God, a theme which has become more pressing in this section (9:2, 11, 27, 60, 62; 10:9, 11). Luke does not have the next clause in Matt 6:10 "your will be done," which in effect explicates the previous petition. Instead a petition for the Holy Spirit enjoyed a limited circulation in the early Church, as some MS versions show.

3. *the bread we need*: The hardest part of this petition is the phrase shared by Matthew and Luke, *ton arton ton epiousion*. The word *epiousios* is not found anywhere else in Greek literature, so interpretation depends on the shaky grounds of etymology and context. Least likely is "supernatural bread," favored by some

patristic writers. The three likely options are: 1) "daily," 2) "future," and 3) "necessary." In light of the narrative context which emphasizes going without provisions and depending on hospitality for provisions, the translation "the bread we need" is appropriate. Matthew has "today," while Luke has *kath'hēmeran* "day by day" or "every day." In line with this, he uses the present tense of *didōmi* (in contrast to Matthew's aorist), to emphasize repeated giving = "keep giving us." For the wondrous character of bread in unlikely circumstances, see the feeding of the multitude, 9:12-17.

4. *forgive us our sins*: Luke retains "debtors" in the second clause, but uses "sins" for human offenses against God. The forgiveness of sins, of course, is a major theme of Luke-Acts (1:77; 3:3; 5:20-21, 23-24; 7:47-49; 12:10; 23:34; 24:47; Acts 2:38; 5:31; 10:43; 13:38; 26:18). For God's behavior as the norm for humans, see 6:35-38.

    do not lead us into testing: The petition reflects the conviction that God controls human events (see 1 Cor 10:13). For "testing" as a chronic, as well as an eschatological reality for disciples, see 8:13; 22:28. Particularly pertinent is the later instruction of Jesus in the garden: "pray that you not enter into testing" (22:40, 46).

5. *suppose one of you has a friend*: The translation aims at the hypothetical character of the example, whose Greek form is syntactically complex. As in 7:6 and 7:34, Luke shows a good awareness of the conventions associated with friendship in the Hellenistic world, particularly that "friends hold all things in common," (cf. Diogenes Laertius, *Life of Pythagoras* 8:10).

8. *the man's shamelessness*: The *anaideia* is shown not only by the effrontery of making a demand in the middle of the night, but also of refusing to take "no" for an answer. The self-protection of the donor becomes the motivation for giving. Luke has another striking example in 18:1-8.

9. *so I say to you*: Is literally, "and I say," but the statement obviously follows from the example as its moral. The sayings on asking, seeking, and knocking are paralleled by Matt 7:7-11 and *Gospel of Thomas* 92, 94. Jas 1:5-6 is also similar. This translation supplies "door."

11. *which father among you*: Luke makes the father/son relationship more explicit than Matt 7:9 in order to strengthen the point of verse 13. Whereas Matthew has bread/stone, fish/snake, Luke matches the sequence of 10:19 by having fish/snake, egg/scorpion.

13. *how much more your Father will give*: The phrase *posō mallon* reflects the rabbinic argument *qal wehomer*, also known in Greek rhetoric as "from the lesser to the greater" (cf. Rom 5:9-17; 11:12; Heb 9:14). It appears again in Luke 12:24, 28. The textual evidence concerning the relationship between "your Father" and "from heaven (*ex ouranou*) is mixed. This translation makes "from heaven" an adverbial phrase modifying the giving of the Holy Spirit, rather than an attributive adjective for God, "Father from heaven."

    Holy Spirit from heaven: Placing the phrase "from heaven" with the Holy Spirit makes good sense (cf. 3:21-22; Acts 1:8; 2:33; 10:44). Some MSS have "good gifts" here rather than Holy Spirit, but probably under the influence of Matt 7:11 ("good things," *agatha*).

INTERPRETATION

Luke's way of weaving didactic materials into the Prophet's journey to Jerusalem is again evident in this section. With the exception of the short parable of the "friend at midnight" (11:5-8), all of the material here derives from Q. In Matthew, these sayings are all placed in the Sermon on the Mount (6:9-13; 7:7-11). But Luke gives them a biographically plausible setting, and uses them to highlight aspects of his overall narrative at this point.

Luke has just shown us Jesus in prayer, calling God "Father" and acknowledging his way of bringing about the kingdom (10:21). He concluded that prayer by saying that no one knew the Father but the Son and the one to whom the Son revealed him (10:22). It seems natural, therefore, that as the disciples now observe Jesus praying once again (11:1) that they ask him how to pray. The additional phrase, "just as John taught his disciples" reasserts the line of prophetic authority, and the special knowledge concerning communication with God that a prophet would be expected to have.

Luke's version of the Lord's Prayer is notably sparer than that in Matthew or the *Didache*. Indeed, the case with this prayer is similar to that of the Beatitudes: Matthew's has more members, is more elaborate in language, and tends toward inwardness. Read in isolation, Luke's prayer is an unadorned series of five imperatives. The first two concern the holiness of God and the establishment of his kingdom. The final three ask for necessary provisions, forgiveness of sins, and freedom from testing. A reader who has been following the narrative can easily spot the ways in which the last four petitions express major themes of the Gospel, and will encounter them again shortly. The prayer Jesus teaches his disciples authenticates his prophetic mission, for it shows that what he proclaims and performs in his ministry expresses the deepest reality of his own relationship with God.

The tiny parable of the friend at midnight is another splendid example of Luke's capacity vividly to evoke with a minimum of words the circumstances of real life and social relationships. It reminds us of earlier examples, like the parable of the creditor (7:41-42). We will meet another Lukan parable very much like this one in 18:1-8, "the widow and the unjust judge," where the lesson will once again be the value of importunateness.

The parable gives lively expression to the concluding exhortations on prayer. Now, when the reader is told to "knock and the door will be opened," there is an imaginative picture of the sleepy friend responding to a midnight crisis. But as always, Luke understands God's way of giving as exceeding that between human friends. The last statement reasserts the distance between the "giving of good things" by human parents (wicked as they are) to their children and the "giving of the Holy Spirit from heaven" by God. Like children with human parents, we can trust that our request will not be answered by malice or trickery; we will not find a snake or scorpion where we had expected fish or egg. But what is this "gift of the Holy Spirit to those who ask?" We must read further in Luke's story to find how that promise is made clearer and then fulfilled.

For Reference and Further Study

Brown, R. E. "The Pater Noster As Eschatological Prayer." *New Testament Essays* (Milwaukee: Bruce, 1965) 217–253.

Edmonds, P. "The Lucan Our Father: A Summary of Lucan Teaching on Prayer?" *ExpT* 91 (1979–80) 140–43.

Kraeling, C. H. "Seek and You Will Find." *Early Christian Origins*. Ed. A. Wikgren (Chicago: Quadrangle Books, 1961) 24–34.

Leaney, R. "The Lucan Text of the Lord's Prayer (Lk xi, 2-4)." *NovT* 1 (1956) 103–111.

Martin, A. D. "The Parable concerning Hospitality." *ExpT* 37 (1925–26) 411–414.

33. *The Two Kingdoms* (11:14-26)

14. He was casting out a demon that was mute. When the demon had come out the mute person spoke. The crowd was astonished. 15. But some of them said, "He casts out demons by Beelzebul the ruler of demons." 16. Others put him to the test by asking of him a sign out of heaven. 17. But he knew their thoughts. He said to them, "Every kingdom divided against itself is destroyed, with household against household. 18. If Satan is divided against himself how can his kingdom stand (since you are saying that I cast out demons by Beelzebul)? 19. If I am casting out demons by Beelzebul, by whom are your own people casting them out? On this point, they will be your judges! 20. But if I cast out demons by the finger of God, then the kingdom of God has come. 21. Whenever a strong man is fully armed and guards his palace, his possessions are secure. 22. But when a stronger than him breaks in and wins victory, he strips off the armor on which the man had relied, and distributes his spoils. 23. The person who is not with me is against me. The one who does not join me scatters. 24. Whenever an unclean spirit departs from a person it passes through waterless areas looking for a resting place but finds none. So it says, 'I will go back to the house I left.' 25. When it arrives, it finds the house swept and tidied. 26. Then it goes and assembles seven other spirits worse than itself. They come in and settle down there. The last state of this person is worse than the first!"

NOTES

14. *a demon that was mute*: The adjective *kōphos* includes "deaf" and "dumb," which often go together. So Zechariah is "struck dumb" in 1:22 but in 7:22 the *kōphoi* "hear." Since the sign of healing here is speaking, the translation "mute" is appropriate. The parallel in Matt 12:22 has "blind and deaf."

15. *casts out demons by Beelzebul*: The charge is found in Mark 3:22 and Matt 12:24, but Mark lacks the healing context shared by Matthew and Luke. Luke uses the name Beelzebul only here. It derives ultimately from the Canaanite God Baal, but Luke uses it simply as a synonym for Satan (11:18). The term "ruler" (*archōn*) is sometimes rendered "prince" (cf. also John 14:30; 16:11; 1 Cor 2:6-8; Eph 2:2).

16. *put him to the test*: The translation inverts the syntactical function of the clauses. The participle *peirazontes* should be taken as a purpose clause. Luke adds this line. It connects this passage to the Lord's prayer in the previous passage (11:4), and also heightens the note of hostility with an ironic twist: they "test" Jesus as the devil did (4:2). "Seeking a sign" comes up again in Jesus' prophetic attack of 11:29-30.

17. *knew their thoughts*: This is again a note added by Luke, signifying that Jesus is the prophet (cf. 2:35; 5:22; 7:39).

    kingdom divided against itself: Is literally "divided upon itself"; Luke simplifies the analogy found also in Mark 3:24-25 and Matt 12:25. He shifts the note of "standing" to verse 18, and substitutes "is destroyed" (literally: "is made deserted") in verse 17.

    household against household: The translation reflects two choices: 1) to take *epi* to mean "against" (as in the previous phrase), and 2) to understand *oikos* as a household ("family") as in Acts 10:2; 11:14; 16:15, rather than as a physical "house." Otherwise, the specifying clause would not mean "family fighting against family" but "one building falling against another."

18. *since you are saying*: This parenthetic remark is added by Luke, perhaps on the basis of Mark 3:30.

19. *if I am casting out demons*: The verse is absent from Mark but is found in Matt 12:27. The translation "your people" aims at greater inclusiveness than "your sons" (*huoi hymōn*).

    on this point: Is literally "on this account" (*dia touto*), and one is tempted to translate, "Let them be your judges!" The statement acknowledges the reality of other Jewish exorcisms, but turns their logic back on them. For exorcisms in the area, cf. Lucian of Samosata, *The Lover of Lies* 16.

20. *the finger of God*: Matt 12:28 has "by the Spirit of God," and we would expect the same from Luke, especially in light of 11:13. But the phrase "finger of God" is a deliberate allusion to Exod 8:19. When Aaron on the command of Moses bests the magicians of Pharaoh's court, they are forced to acknowledge, "this is the finger of God." Another Lukan allusion to Jesus as the prophet like Moses.

kingdom of God has come: Luke (and Matt 12:28) uses the aorist of the verb *phthanō*, which has the literal sense of "to overtake," or "reach." For the wonders of Jesus and his emissaries as signalling the arrival (*engizō*) of the kingdom, see 10:9.

21. *whenever a strong man*: Luke's version of this tiny parable is more elaborate than that of Matt 12:29, because of his specific attention to possessions as symbolizing the prior and later stages of the strong man's status. A version is also found in *Gospel of Thomas* 35. The phrase "possessions secure" renders the Greek "in peace" (*en eirēnē*).

23. *not with me is against me*: This is of course the exact opposite of the statement to the disciples in 9:50. In the present context, the idea of "gathering with me" (*synagōn met'emou*) must be taken to mean the joining of the people forming around the prophet; the alternative is to scatter.

24. *whenever an unclean spirit departs*: The noun is articular in Greek, but this is a general example. This rather odd logion may be in this place because of the theme of demonic possession established by 11:14. Matt 12:43-45 has virtually the same version, but separates it from the "strong man" story by a series of statements against "this generation"; thus he also concludes with "this evil generation" which is lacking in Luke.

26. *seven other spirits*: There seems to be no special significance to the number seven, although that is also the number driven out of Mary Magdalene in 8:2.

INTERPRETATION

The exorcism of the mute demon is brief (11:14) and serves mainly to set up the charge against Jesus that he performed exorcisms under the aegis of the devil himself. The work of the prophet creates a division in the people. Some in the crowd are astonished at what he does (11:14), and we will shortly hear a voice from the crowd praising his birth (11:27-28). But others (and the contrast is deliberately noted) respond negatively. Luke lists two groups. One charges him with collusion with Beelzebul (11:15). The other "tests him" by asking of him a sign from heaven (11:16).

This second group is noted only by Luke, and it gives his version a distinctively ironic edge, for "putting to the test" is the devil's own work, as we learned in 4:2, and the last "sign from heaven" that we heard of in the narrative was that of Satan's falling "like lightning out of heaven" because of the submission of demons to Jesus' seventy emissaries (10:17-18)! The opponents of Jesus are blind to the signs of the kingdom before them, or rather, their vision (we shall learn) is "darkened" (11:33-36). This opening confrontation begins a section of conflict that climaxes with the resolve of the Pharisees and lawyers to make a concerted effort to trap Jesus in his speech (11:53).

Three aspects of Luke's version of Jesus' defense (11:17-20) deserve attention. The first is the way (together with 4:6 and 7:8) it reveals Luke's understanding of how a kingdom is structured. A ruler, we see, exerts power through subordinates who do his will. The conflict Luke sketches is between two very real kingdoms, that of Satan and that of God. When Jesus through his delegates drives out Satan's minions, that is a victory for his kingdom, a sure sign that "the kingdom of God has arrived" (11:20). There is nothing abstract about this; we have seen earlier how healing and exorcism serve as signs that "the kingdom of God has reached you" (10:9). This prophetic discourse serves as a commentary on the narrative of the ministry.

It also provides a polemical contrast to the previous passage in which Jesus taught his disciples to pray (11:1-13). Now, rather asking and receiving the "Holy Spirit from heaven" (11:13), these opponents seek a "sign from out of heaven" (11:16). Rather than praying to God to deliver them from testing (11:4), they deliberately put Jesus to the test (11:16). Rather than ask forgiveness of sins they in effect accuse Jesus of the sin of collusion with Satan (11:4, 15). Rather than recognize in Jesus the one who proclaims the kingdom of the Father (11:2), they accuse him of being a minion of Satan's rule (11:15).

The third aspect of Luke's treatment here is the continued stress on Jesus as prophet. We see again that Jesus "knows their thoughts" (11:17), which we have come to recognize as the sign of a prophet. Even more impressive is the deliberate allusion to the prophetic power of Moses in the expression "finger of God." The phrase occurs only in Exod 8:19. No matter that it is Aaron who does the deed that the Egyptian magicians must recognize in this fashion. Indeed, that is part of the point. Aaron is sent by Moses who is sent by God, just as the seventy have been sent by Jesus who has been sent by God. Acceptance or rejection of the prophet means acceptance or rejection of God (10:16).

The miniature parable of the strong man unveils the violence implicit in this talk of kingdoms and civil wars. There is a battle going on. Luke's version is more elaborate than that of the Synoptic parallels. The strong man has a "palace" and is heavily armed, and because he stands guard his possessions are safe. But his security is illusory. The stronger one conquers him, strips his armor and distributes his things as spoil. Notice the consistent Lukan attention to possessions as symbolizing power and personal relationships. The strong man had "relied" on his possessions, but they needed his protection to be safe! The illusion is revealed when he is stripped and his things distributed.

A stronger ruler than Satan is making war on him and establishing his sovereignty on earth. Thus the jolting application of the parable: if those who listen do not now join the people forming around the prophet, they too will "scatter" (11:23).

The final saying on the exorcised demon who wanders and then returns to his former dwelling (11:24-26) is odd and perhaps intentionally humorous.

This reader, in any case, cannot help but think of a disreputable lodger tossed out for nonpayment of rent, wandering the streets for days, then returning and finding the building empty, clean and tidy, gathering seven of his seediest friends, and sitting with them in rumpled clothes, and stale cigars in an increasingly debris-filled front parlor. But the lesson is chilling: the last state of such a person is worse than the first (11:26). It is not enough to have the power of one ruler routed; one must swear allegiance to the new sovereign, represented by the prophet. One must choose between kingdoms. It is the empty tenement that invites squatters.

FOR REFERENCE AND FURTHER STUDY

Bailey, K. E. *Poet and Peasant: A Literary Cultural Approach to the Parables in Luke* (Grand Rapids: Eerdmans, 1976) 119–141.
Couroyer, B. " 'Le doigt de Dieu' (Exode VIII, 19)." *RB* 63 (1956) 481–495.
Kruse, H. "Das Reich Satans." *Bib* 58 (1977) 29–61.
Légasse, S. " 'L'homme fort' de Luc XI, 21-22." *NovT* 5 (1962) 5–9.
Linton, O. "The Demand for a Sign from Heaven." *ST* 19 (1965) 112–129.

34. *Prophetic Warnings* (11:27-36)

27. As Jesus was saying these things, a woman shouted from the crowd, "Blessed is the womb that carried you and the breasts that fed you." 28. But he responded, "Blessed rather are those who hear the word of God and keep it." 29. As the crowds around him grew larger, he began to declare, "This generation is an evil generation. It seeks a sign. No sign will be given it except the sign of Jonah. 30. Just as Jonah was a sign to the Ninevites so is the Son of Man to this generation. 31. The Queen of the South will rise at the judgment with the people of this generation and she will condemn them. She came from the ends of the earth to hear Solomon's wisdom. Look, something greater than Solomon is here! 32. The Ninevites will rise at the judgment with this generation and will condemn it. They repented at the preaching of Jonah. Look, something greater than Jonah is here! 33. No one lights a lamp and sticks it in a hole or under a basket. It is put on a lampstand so that those entering can see the light. 34. The eye is the body's lamp. When your eye is clear, your whole body is filled with light. But when the eye is bad the whole body is likewise dark. 35. So see to it that you do not turn light into dark. 36. If therefore your whole body is filled with light, with no part of it dark, then it will be completely light, as when the lamp by its shining sheds light on you."

NOTES

27. *blessed is the womb*: The cry is obviously an indirect compliment to Jesus, unique to Luke's Gospel, and the eighth of his macarisms (see 1:45; 6:20, 21 [2], 22; 7:23; 10:23). "That fed you" is literally, "that you sucked." Cf. also *Gospel of Thomas* 79, and the acclamation in Petronius' *Satyricon* 94: "*O felicem matrem tuam quae te talem peperit*," ("how happy your mother who gave birth to such a one as you").

28. *blessed rather are those who hear*: This ninth macarism corrects the earlier one along the lines of Elizabeth's blessing of Mary for believing what was spoken to her by the Lord (1:45). For the "word of God" as the content of Jesus' preaching, see 8:11, and for "hearing the word and keeping it," see esp. 8:21: "my mother and brothers are those who hear the word of God and keep it."

29. *crowds around him grew larger*: Is literally "gathered by him"; Luke alone frames the scene this way. On the journey to Jerusalem, the "crowd" is the most neutral audience, and the one called to repentance by exhortation and warning.
    this generation: For Luke's use of this term, see the note on 7:31. The meaning here is obviously negative as in 9:41; 11:51; 16:8; 17:25 and Acts 2:40. "Seeking a sign" was established by Luke by his insertion in 11:16: "others sought from him a sign from heaven." In Matt 12:39, the adjective "adulterous" is added to "evil generation."
    sign of Jonah: Matt 12:39 adds "the prophet," and explicates the "sign" in terms of Jonah's three day sojourn in the belly of the whale (Jonah 1:17) which is taken as a type of the three-day burial of the Son of Man before the resurrection (Matt 12:40). Luke has nothing of this. He does not call Jonah a prophet, but he obviously exploits exactly that function: Jonah was a "sign to" the Ninevites in his preaching, just as Jesus is a "sign to" this generation. For Jesus as the "sign of contradiction," see the programmatic prophecy of Simeon in 2:35.

31. *Queen of the South*: A reference to the Queen of Sheba who visited the court of Solomon (1 Kgs 10:1-13; 2 Chr 9:1-12). Luke inserts this example between the two references to the Ninevites, but Matthew keeps the characters in sequence (Matt 12:41-42). Note that she came to "hear the wisdom" of Solomon; Jesus proclaims the Word of God and declares blessed those who "hear and keep" it (11:28).
    rise . . . condemn: The contrast between earlier characters in the biblical story and the audience of Jesus is similar to the contrast between Sodom of old and the cities of his day, or the cities of Tyre and Sidon and those of Chorazin and Bethsaida (10:12-15). As with the cities, and as with the examples of Elijah and Elisha in 4:25-27, we notice, those outside Israel are more positively portrayed than those within.

32. *Ninevites . . . repented*: Here and in the previous verse, the translation ignores the explicit masculine noun *anēr* ("men") in favor of inclusive language. In LXX Jonah 3:4-5, the prophet "preaches" (*kēryssein*) and the people "believe" (*enpisteuein*), showing it by sackcloth and ashes. Their response, however, is in the hope that *God* will "repent" (*metanoiein*) of his resolve to punish them (Jonah 3:9).

33. *no one lights a lamp*: Not only is this saying paralleled by Matt 5:15 and Mark 4:21, but Luke himself has an earlier version in 8:16. The words differ slightly but the meaning is the same: light needs to be exposed to be seen. Here, "hole" (*kryptē*) replaces "vessel" (*skeuos*) and "basket" (*modion*) replaces "bed" (*klinē*). The saying is found as well—and connected to preaching—in the *Gospel of Thomas* 33.

34. *eye is the body's lamp*: This complex linking of images is paralleled by a clearer version in Matt 6:22-23. The image works if the eye is taken as the supplier of light rather than the receiver, but is still muddled by the qualification of being "clear" or "bad."

    clear . . . bad: The contrast is between that which can give light fully and that which cannot. The word translated "clear" is literally "simple" (*haplos*), and that translated "bad" is literally "evil/wicked" (*ponēros*). One can scarcely avoid the moral connotations of the last term since it is used immediately before this in the moral sense (11:29).

35. *so see to it*: The verb *skopeō* has the sense of "watch out." The point of the metaphor becomes evident when we realize that responsibility for seeing is the person's—a moral choice is involved. We remember 8:18, "watch how you hear." *turn light into dark*: Is literally "the light in you is not dark," (*mē to phōs to en soi skotos estin*), which must mean "become dark," so the translation simply makes it active in correspondence with "see to it."

36. *lamp by its shining*: The phrase *tē astrapē* is associated with lightning (as in Luke 10:18; 17:24), therefore literally is "by its flashing." The language is labored but the overall point is clear: they are responsible for whether or not they see light truly as it is or turn it into darkness.

INTERPRETATION

It seems at first as though the woman's voice from the crowd blessing Jesus' parentage is an entirely positive response in contrast to the rejection of Jesus by his opponents in the Beelzebul controversy. But Jesus' response to her makes clear that the issue running throughout this narrative of Jesus' journey to Jerusalem is still paramount. It is not enough to respond to Jesus as a person, or indirectly praise him by praise of his mother. Jesus is the prophet who speaks God's word. The response demanded is not admiration of him as a person but the "hearing and keeping of God's word."

As the crowd continues to press on him, therefore, Jesus again issues warnings of the need to repent. Like the stylistically similar sayings of 10:12-15 against Chorazin and Capernaum, these against "the evil generation" compare Jesus' listeners unfavorably with people of the biblical story who were not even part of Israel: the Queen of Sheba came to hear Solomon's wisdom, and the Ninevites believed Jonah's preaching. The crowds, Jesus says, must imitate them and both "hear the word of God and keep it."

The prophetic character of Jesus' speech is especially marked because of the way he uses the example of Jonah. Rather than (as Matthew) make the sojourn of Jonah in the whale's belly a type of Jesus' death and resurrection, Luke points to Jonah's specifically prophetic *function* of preaching God's word. It is in that way Jonah was a "sign to the Ninevites" and in that way Jesus is a "sign to this generation." To accept him, then, as we learn from Jesus' response both to the woman in the crowd and to Martha, is to accept him not just as a person but as a prophet.

He is, however, a "sign of contradiction" (2:35), and the response to him is divided. The sayings on the lamp and the light in this section make sense only if we appreciate the point that the audience can determine how it hears and what it sees. Jesus as prophet is like the lamp that is lit and stood on a stand. Whether they see the light or stay in darkness depends on their choice, and whether their eye is "simple" or "evil." Thus, he tells them to "see to it" that their eye is sound. And when recounting the examples of Solomon and Jonah, he tells them "Look, a greater one is here (vv. 31-32)!"

For Reference and Further Study

Allison, D. C. "The Eye is the Light of the Body (Mt 6:22-23 = Lk 11:34-36)." *NTS* 33 (1987) 61–83.
Benoit, P. "L'oeil, lampe du corps." *RB* 60 (1953) 603–605.
Brown, R. E., et.al, eds. *Mary in the New Testament* (New York: Paulist Press, 1978) 170–172.
Edwards, R. A. *The Sign of Jonah in the Theology of the Evangelists and Q.* SBT 2/18; Naperville, Ill.: Allenson, 1971.
Schmitt, G. "Das Zeichen des Jona." *ZNW* 69 (1974) 123–129.

35. *Attack on Opponents* (11:37-54)

37. As he was speaking a Pharisee asked him to dine with him. He went in and reclined at table. 38. The Pharisee saw him and expressed astonishment that he did not wash himself before the meal. 39. The Lord said to him, "Now you Pharisees clean the outside of the cup and dish. But your insides are full of greed and wickedness! 40. Fools! Didn't the one who made the outside also make the inside? 41. So instead, give that which is inside as alms. And look! Everything is clean for you! 42. But woe to you Pharisees! You pay tithes on mint and rue and every herb, and you pass over justice and the love of God. You ought to have done these things with-

out neglecting the others. 43. Woe to you Pharisees! You love the front seats in synagogues and greetings in the marketplaces. 44. Woe to you! You are like secret graves over which people stroll unaware." 45. One of the lawyers objected, "Teacher, by saying such things you insult us as well!" 46. So he said, "Woe also to you lawyers! You pile loads on people that are hard to carry, and yourselves do not touch the burdens with one of your fingers. 47. Woe to you! You build tombs for the prophets. But your own ancestors killed them! 48. Therefore you are witnesses to and collude with the deeds of your ancestors. They killed them, you build their tombs. 49. For this reason also the Wisdom of God declared, 'I will send to them prophets and apostles, and they will kill and persecute some of them,' 50. so that this generation will be required to answer for the blood of all the prophets shed since the beginning of the world, 51. from the blood of Abel to the blood of Zechariah who perished between the altar and the sanctuary. Yes, I tell you, it will be required of this generation! 52. Woe to you lawyers! You have taken the key of knowledge. You do not enter yourselves, and you close out those trying to enter." 53. When he had left there, the scribes and Pharisees formed a deep resentment against him. They began to draw him out on many issues, lying in wait to trap him in something he might say.

Notes

37. *Pharisee asked him to dine*: This is the second such invitation from a Pharisee, and again an occasion for conflict (cf. 7:36-50). The verb *aristaō* originally meant breakfast (or more than one meal a day) but came to mean a luncheon. Here it could mean any meal, although there are obviously a number of guests present (vv. 39, 45).

38. *did not wash himself*: Luke uses the term *baptizō* for the sort of ritual "dipping" that effected transition from the unclean to the clean. The Pharisee saw Jesus "enter and sit" without this ritual. Matt 15:1-9 and Mark 7:1-9 build a fully developed scene around this issue, but one involving the disciples. In contrast to Luke's three earlier controversies of 5:29–6:5 in which Jesus defends the disciples who have been attacked, Jesus is now the direct target of hostility. For regulations on the washing of hands, see the discussions in *m. Yadaim*, esp. 4:6-8. A description of the Essenes' ritual bathing before meals is found in Josephus *Jewish War* 2:129.

39. *outside of the cup and dish*: For examples of such regulations, see *m.Kelim* 2:1–3:8. Much of the subsequent attack by Jesus is paralleled by Matthew 23. Matthew has Jesus attack "scribes and Pharisees" throughout, whereas in Luke first the "Pharisees" and then (v. 45) the "lawyers" are lambasted.

   your insides: Is literally "the inner of you." The shift from surface of vessels to interior of persons is not entirely without strain. We are to understand: the outside of the plate = external ritual, and the inside of the cup/dish = personal intentions. Cleansing one does not get at the other.

full of greed and wickedness: Matt 23:25 also has *harpagē* ("violent grasping, rape, plunder), but has "uncleanness" (*akrasia*) in place of Luke's more general "wickedness" (*ponēria*). Here we find the second indication after the "woe to you rich" in 6:24 that Luke also uses possessions symbolism negatively for the religious leaders who oppose the prophet; see especially Luke 6:14.

40. *fools*: Is an epithet with roots in the biblical tradition, referring to those who resist the wisdom that comes from God (see e.g., Prov 1:22 and Ps 13:1 [LXX]), but is also a staple of the Hellenistic diatribe (see e.g., Epictetus, *Discourses* 3, 22, 85; 4, 10, 23). Luke uses it again of a rich man in 12:20.

made the outside also make the inside: The reference is clearly now to the person rather than to the vessel. The point is that persons are responsible to God "the maker" for their internal dispositions as much as for outward observance.

41. *give that which is inside as alms*: No fully satisfactory translation is possible for this *crux*. Matthew's version carries on the inside/outside distinctions consistently in terms of cleanness: "cleanse the inside of the cup in order that its outside might also be clean" (Matt 23:26); in other words, internal purity should precede external observance. But the understanding of *ta enonta* ("the inner things") in Luke is more difficult. This translation follows the conviction that Luke uses possessions language consistently to symbolize internal responses. Thus, internal qualities such as righteousness should be expressed by the sharing of possessions. This reading matches the "inner wickedness" of the Pharisees being described as "greed." For the high valuation of almsgiving in Judaism, see Tobit 4:7-12; *Pirke Aboth* 5:2; *bT Sukkah* 49b.

42. *woe to you Pharisees*: In 6:24-26, the woe (*ouai*) was issued against the rich, filled, laughing and well reputed. In 10:13 it was spoken against unconverting cities. Now we find three woes against the Pharisees (11:42, 43, 44) and three against the lawyers (11:46, 47, 52). In the narrative, we have learned, they represent those who oppose the prophets and thereby "God's will for them" (7:29-30). Throughout these woes, the translation omits the Greek connective *hoti* ("because") for a more idiomatic English.

you pay tithes: The offering of a tenth of one's produce or possessions to the Lord is legislated in Deut 14:22-29; 26:12-15; Lev 27:30-33; Mal 3:8-10. The purpose expressed in Deuteronomy is the support of the Levites and the poor in the land: sojourners, orphans and widows. The precise identity of the plants named by Luke is less important than the fact that they represent "seasoning" rather than "staples" such as grain. In fact, Luke may be wrong concerning the laws. *m.She-biith* 9:1 includes rue among the herbs exempt from tithing. For the rabbinic discussions, cf. *m.Maaseroth* and *m.Sheni*, passim.

pass over justice and the love of God: The word *krisis* here actually means "judgment." But Matt 23:23 has *krisis, eleos kai pistis*, all of which are things people do. And although Luke elsewhere uses *krisis* only for the judgment of God (10:14; 11:31, 32), he does include the LXX translation of *mishpat* in Isa 53:8 as *krisis* in Acts 8:33. Furthermore, Luke's conclusion that "you ought to have done these things" without neglecting the others, also implies that *krisis* is something that humans do. In agreement with other contemporary translations, therefore, this version takes *krisis* as meaning "doing justice." In the rabbinic tradition, again, such "doing justice" was equivalent to sharing possessions (see e.g., *bT Baba Bathra* 8b).

43. *front seats in synagogues*: The verb "love" (*agapaō*) here creates a deliberate contrast to the previous verse: they love glory more than God. Matt 23:6 adds, "first seats at banquets," which Luke will supply in his narrative (cf. 14:7). For deference at a synagogue meeting, cf. Jas 2:1-7. Luke also lacks the specification of the greetings in the marketplaces as "Rabbi" (Matt 23:7).

44. *secret graves*: The translation of *adēlos* as "secret" aims at the deliberate concealment suggested. Matt 23:27-28 is more elaborate and less subtle, making the charge of hypocrisy explicit (see Luke 12:1).

45. *you insult us as well*: This ill-timed interjection by a lawyer enables Luke to turn the attack on them. The verb *hybrizō* is strong, connoting maltreatment and damage; a lawyer leaping to a libel charge!

46. *you pile loads on people*: Luke's wording is harsher than Matthew's (23:4), emphasizing both the unsupportability of the legal gravamina, and their refusal to alleviate the loads.

47. *tombs for the prophets*: The same word (*mnēmeia*) is used here and in verse 44 (translated "graves"). The "building" here demands something like "tombs" or "monuments." Matt 23:29-30 is again more elaborate than Luke. The translation "your ancestors" (*pateres hymon*) is more inclusive than the Greek. See the charge made by Stephen, "which of the prophets did your ancestors not persecute?" (Acts 7:52).

48. *collude with*: The translation of *syneudokeō* may be too contemporary, but its legal tone suits the lawyers. The building of tombs to the prophets is twisted here to mean a witness and agreement with their killing. This is because they too persecute the prophets sent by God.

49. *the Wisdom of God declared*: This is an unusual locution, although it has also been used in 7:35. There the reference was to God. Here, it could mean either God or Jesus. The statement is unattested in Scripture. The best explanation for the form of the statement which so much reflects the experience of the early community is that a prophetic utterance was read back into the mouth of the prophet Jesus.

   prophets and apostles: As we have seen repeatedly, for Luke the terms are functionally equivalent. Both are sent out by God to proclaim his word.

   kill and persecute: Matt 23:34 is more explicit and more obviously derived from the experience of the community: "will kill and crucify . . . scourge in synagogues and persecute from city to city." Luke focuses entirely on the theme of killing of the prophets (cf. 13:34!).

51. *the blood of Abel*: The killing of Abel by Cain (Gen 4:1-12) deservedly became proverbial as a sign of envy and murderous rage (cf. Heb 11:4; 12:24; 1 John 3:12; *Testament of Benjamin* 7:5).

Zechariah . . . between the altar and the sanctuary: A priest called Zechariah was struck dead "in the court of the house of the Lord" according to 2 Chr 24:20-22. The identification meant by Luke is confused by Matt 23:25 referring to him as the "son of Barachiah," which would lead us to a prophet by that name in Zech 1:1, but no death is associated with him. The text from Josephus' *Jewish War* 4:335-342 is no real help. Historical identification is in any case secondary to the literary point that the contemporary generation's sanguinary rejection of Jesus and his emissaries places it in a line with previous such rejections. The term "sanctuary" translates *oikos* (literally "house"), which Luke uses in this sense elsewhere (19:46; Acts 7:47).

52. *taken the key of knowledge*: Matt 23:13 has "locked the kingdom of heaven." In Luke the "entry" is left implicit: it could be knowledge itself, or the kingdom, or the people forming around the prophet.

53. *formed a deep resentment*: There is a somewhat surprising shift here to "scribes and Pharisees," after his previous use of "Pharisees and lawyers." The term "draw him out" could mean just the opposite, namely "stifle" (*apostomatizō*), but the context indicates the appropriate translation. The words *enedreuō* ("lie in wait") and *thēreuō* ("entrap") are both hunting terms. They are deliberately stalking Jesus (cf. Matt 22:15).

INTERPRETATION

This extended attack on Pharisees and lawyers is paralleled in Matt 23:1-36 but plays quite a different role in Luke's narrative. Matthew uses the attack on Jewish leaders to distance Jesus and his followers before the secret eschatological discourse (Matt 24–25). Luke in contrast uses this controversy to mark a critical point in the growing hostility between the prophet Jesus and his opponents.

The setting, as so often in Luke, is a meal at which the host Pharisee betrays the genuine spirit of hospitality toward his guest (cf. 7:36-50; 14:1-6). We are reminded of the controversy stories of 5:29–6:5. In them, the disciples were attacked and Jesus defended them. Then, in 6:1-11 and 7:36-50, questions are raised because of Jesus' willingness to heal on the Sabbath or be touched by a sinner, and Jesus defended himself. Now, Jesus is under direct attack for his failure to observe the purity regulations advocated by the Pharisaic party (11:38). Rather than defend himself, he launches a sustained attack on those whom we have already had identified as opponents of God's prophets and rejecters of God's will for them (7:29-30). After this explicit rejection of *them*, the story takes on a darker tone. The opponents, we now know, are intent on trapping him because of their "terrible grudge" against him (11:53).

In the versions of Matthew and Luke alike, the polemic against Jewish teachers follows the conventions of ancient rhetoric between Hellenistic philosophical schools. Slander was commonplace not only between members of rival schools such as the Stoics and Epicureans (e.g., Plutarch, *On Stoic Self-Contradictions*, and *That Epicurus Actually Makes a Pleasant Life Impossible*), but also against all sorts of "false philosophers" (who did not agree with one's own understanding). Such attacks were also levelled by Jewish parties against each other (e.g., *Assumption of Moses*, 7). Every opponent was interested in quibbles and trifles rather than the weightier matters of virtue; was a lover of pleasure, of money, or glory; paraded his virtue and hid his private vice; used his knowledge for unworthy ends (e.g., Dio Chrysostom, *Orations* 32, 33, and 35).

The obvious use of such conventions suggests that Jesus' speech, whether or not it derives from his historical mission, is also marked by the experience of the early Church as it confronted its near and bitter rival within developing Judaism, the Pharisaic party, which, after the definitive split with the messianists, became what we have come to call rabbinic Judaism. The clearest evidence of this community shaping is the saying of 11:49-51 concerning the persecution and killing of the apostles and prophets sent out by the "Wisdom of God."

Beneath the polemic, however, we do learn some accurate information about the early development of the Pharisaic party and its scribal concerns. Luke may confuse the specific items needing tithing (at least according to the decisions in the *Mishnah* some 150 years later), but from our other earliest sources on the Pharisees (such as *m. Demai* 2) we can recognize their concern for purity regulations and tithing, as well as the interpretation of laws to provide a "hedge around Torah" (*Pirke Aboth* 1:1).

Underlying the specifics of Luke's version, in addition, we detect a central understanding of leadership as service which in his eyes the Pharisees and lawyers have failed. Seeking first places in synagogues and greetings in the marketplaces are only the most obvious symptoms of an attitude of self-aggrandizement. They have taken the key of knowledge, and keep others from entering. Their concern for the minutiae of tithing leads to neglect of the purpose of tithing, the care of the needy (Deut 14:22-29). More strikingly, their concern for outward purity hides a deep rapaciousness within. The "love of God" should lead them to the doing of "justice" by sharing their possessions with others.

We should note above all the *narrative* function of this section. The sayings about "building the tombs of the prophets" or "killing and persecuting the apostles and prophets" fit precisely within the journey of the Prophet toward Jerusalem and his own death. Because Jesus has now made the conflict open, the narrative takes on a new intensity. The rage and watchfulness of the opponents (6:11) has now smoldered into a lingering grudge and the fixed intention to trap their foe (11:53). This context of rejection and hostility, furthermore, colors all of the sayings of the Prophet which follow.

FOR REFERENCE AND FURTHER STUDY

Ellis, E. E. "Luke xi. 49-51: An Oracle by a Christian Prophet?" *ExpT* 74 (1962–63) 157–158.

Johnson, L. T. "The New Testament's Anti-Jewish Slander and the Conventions of Ancient Polemic." *JBL* 108 (1989) 419–441.

Moxnes, H. *The Economy of the Kingdom* (Overtures to Biblical Theology; Philadelphia: Fortress Press, 1988) 109–126.

Neusner, J. " 'First Cleanse the Inside': The 'Halakhic' Background of a Controversy Saying." *NTS* 22 (1975–76) 486–495.

Steele, E. S. "Luke 11:37-54—A Modified Hellenistic Symposium?" *JBL* 103 (1984) 379–394.

36. *Courage in Time of Danger* (12:1-12)

1. Meanwhile as the crowds gathered by the thousands with people stepping on each other, Jesus began to say to his disciples, "Above all, keep away from the leaven of the Pharisees, which is hypocrisy. 2. There is nothing concealed that will not be revealed, nothing secret that will not be known. 3. Indeed, whatever things you say in darkness will be heard in the light, and whatever you whisper in a private room will be proclaimed from the roofs. 4. But I tell you, my friends, don't fear those who kill the body and afterwards can do nothing more. 5. I will show you whom to fear. Fear the one who after killing you has the authority to throw you into Gehenna. Yes, I tell you, Fear that one! 6. Five sparrows are sold for two copper coins, are they not? Yet not one of them does God forget. 7. The very hairs of your head, he counts them all. Do not fear! You matter more than many sparrows! 8. I tell you, everyone who declares for me in front of people, the Son of Man will declare himself for that person in front of God's angels. 9. But the one who denies me in front of people will be denied in front of God's angels. 10. Also everyone who speaks a word against the Son of Man will be forgiven, but the one who speaks slanderously against the Holy Spirit will not be forgiven. 11. Whenever they bring you before synagogues and rulers and authorities, do not be anxious how to defend yourself or what you should say. 12. The Holy Spirit will at that very time teach you what you must say."

NOTES

1. *above all*: The adverb *prōton* is awkwardly placed, but is taken here as the opening of the exhortation rather than as a modifier of Jesus' speech, "he began first to say."

keep away from: The verb *prosechō* has as its ordinary use, "devote oneself to," or "pay attention to," but with the preposition *apo*, it is used to express avoidance (see also 17:3; 20:46; 21:34; Acts 5:35; 8:6, 10, 11; 16:14; 20:28).

leaven of the Pharisees . . . hypocrisy: One could translate more colloquially, "I mean hypocrisy." Luke has entirely removed this saying from its narrative context in Mark 8:15 (Matt 16:6), so that it now functions as a metaphoric summary for the entire attack on the Pharisees and lawyers just concluded. Leaven (*zymē*) works within dough as a hidden yet powerful force; so, we are to understand, is the hidden vice of the opposition beneath their virtuous veneer. Luke also eliminates the other parties (Herodians in Mark, Sadducees in Matthew) to focus exclusively on the Pharisees.

2. *concealed . . . revealed*: This is close to the earlier saying in Luke 8:17, with the same double contrast between the private and public. The earlier version was gnomic. This one is direct exhortation, carrying forward the second person plural imperative of *prosechete*: these statements show why for the disciples hypocrisy won't work.

3. *darkness . . . light*: See the sayings on the lamp and eye, darkness and light, in 11:34-36, and *its* antecedent, 8:16!

   whisper: Is literally "spoken in an ear" which is sometimes used of esoteric teaching (see e.g., *bT Hagigah* 14a).

   private room: Is literally a storeroom or treasury, but it is used in LXX Gen 43:30 and Exod 8:3 in the sense of a bedchamber. Luke gives this saying quite a different meaning than does Matt 10:27.

4. *my friends*: Luke uses friendship language and the conventions associated with that language frequently (e.g., 7:6, 34; 11:5, 6-8), but only here does Jesus call his disciples "friends" (*philoi*), a description otherwise found only in the Johannine literature (John 15:13, 14-15; 3 John 15). For the theme of friendship as antidote to fear in face of danger, cf. Epicurus, *Sovereign Maxims* 23, 24, 28, 39.

   don't fear: With this phrase, the real theme of this section is reached (vv. 4, 5, 7, 32). Fear in this case means not religious awe (as in 1:13, 30, 50; 2:9-10; 5:10; 8:25, 35) but the sort of anxiety that is generated by hostility and the threat to life. The context is set by 11:53.

   can do nothing more: The parallel in Matt 10:28 has, "those who are not able to kill the soul." Luke's periphrasis may reflect a Hellenistic discomfort with the idea of killing what was widely considered immortal.

5. *I will show you*: Is a characteristic Lukan expression, and one at home in Hellenistic paraenesis (see e.g., 3:7; 6:47; Acts 9:16; 20:35).

   throw you into Gehenna: Again, Luke avoids the version in Matt 10:28, "able to destroy both body and soul in Gehenna" (see the note above). The term *gehenna* derives from the Hebrew for "Valley of Hinnom," a deep ravine running below Jerusalem and associated with diverse sorts of burnings (cf. 2 Chr 28:3; 33:6). See Jas 3:6, "a fire lit from Gehenna." In the NT its use is restricted to the Synoptics (Mark 9:43, 45, 47; Matt 5:22, 29, 30; 10:28; 18:9; 23:15, 33), and Luke uses it only here. The point of the saying is that fear of absolute power relativizes other fears; as Prov 1:7 has it, "Fear of God is the beginning of wisdom."

6. *five sparrows . . . two copper coins*: The *assarion* was the smallest denomination of coin, equalling 1/16 a *denarius*. Matt 10:29 has "two sparrows for one *assarion*" but Luke keeps the rough proportion; the point is that they are cheap!

   does God forget: The translation turns the passive voice into the active. In Matt 10:29, the sparrows "fall to earth," but Luke wants to emphasize protection and care.

7. *very hairs of your head*: The colloquialism is found in 1 Sam 14:45 for the protection of one on God's side (cf. also 2 Sam 14:11, and 1 Kgs 1:52). Luke uses it again at 21:18 and Acts 27:34. "You matter" translates *diapherō*, which means "to differ" in the direction of excelling.

8. *everyone who declares*: The form of the statement is similar to that in 9:26, except that here the language of "confession" (*homologeō*) and 'denial' (*arneomai*) is explicit and suggestive of human trials. The confession "before people" will be matched by that at the judgment when the Son of Man "comes in his glory and that of the Father and of the *holy angels*" (9:26). The correlation of confession and denial of the Messiah is found in 1 John 2:22-23. Luke will make "denial" an important aspect of the prophet's first visitation (cf. Luke 22:57; Acts 3:13-14). Matt 10:32-33 is substantially the same except that Luke by the substitution of "angels" effects a literary connection to 9:26.

10. *speaks slanderously against the Holy Spirit*: The term *blasphēmein* refers here to speech because it corresponds to "speak a word against." The word is used this way in LXX Tobit 1:18; Dan 3:29; Isa 52:5. The charge of blasphemy is placed *against* Jesus in 5:21 when he forgives sins. The saying in Mark 3:29 and Matt 12:32 is part of the Beelzebul controversy (cf. Luke 11:15-23). The key to Luke's version is found in the narrative of Acts, when the leaders "resist the Holy Spirit" (see Acts 5:32; 7:51).

11. *synagogues and rulers and authorities*: This saying obviously points forward to the narrative of Acts 4:5-6; 5:17, the future persecution of the apostles in Jerusalem, as well as the troubles to be faced by Paul (Acts 17:1-9).

    do not be anxious: The term *merimnaō* was used of Martha's preoccupations in 10:41. In this context, it is equivalent to *phobeomai* ("fear") and part of the same theme (cf. vv. 22, 25, 26).

    how to defend yourself: The Greek here is awkwardly redundant, literally, "how or what you might make defense or what you might say." The idea of "making a defense" (*apologia*) for one's belief motivates both Jewish and Christian apologetic literature, of which Luke is an example (see introduction). The word recurs in 21:14; Acts 19:33; 22:1; 24:10; 25:8, 16; 26:1-2, 24, as well as in 1 Pet 3:15. Mark 13:11 and Matt 10:19 have only "what to say."

12. *the Holy Spirit will . . . teach you*: Mark 13:11 and Matt 10:20 are stronger: the Holy Spirit actually speaks in their place. In Luke the image of prophecy enables the human speech to *be* that "taught by the Spirit." The contrast in this passage between "slander against the Holy Spirit" and the "Holy Spirit teach-

ing" what should be said in defense, is unique to Luke. Just as the idea of "friendship" employed by Luke close to that in John's Gospel, so is this idea of the Spirit teaching the disciples found in John 14:26. The later parallel in Luke 21:14-15 will be discussed in its place.

INTERPRETATION

The brilliance of Luke's literary device of the prophetic journey to Jerusalem shines through his composition of chapter 12. Some of these materials come from Q and some are Luke's own, but he has arranged them in such fashion that they are both dramatically and psychologically satisfying. He has just had the Prophet attack the Pharisees and lawyers, accusing them of murderous malice against prophets and apostles. The discourse ends with those opponents fulfilling his accusation: they lie in wait seeking to trap Jesus in his speech (11:53). In everything Jesus now says, there is danger for him and for his followers. To heighten the tension, Luke has Jesus surrounded by a crowd so large that people are being trampled (12:1). The atmosphere is electric as Jesus turns to his disciples to teach them.

The instructions on fear and anxiety are in this context psychologically convincing. The reader who has followed the story line recognizes the appropriateness of addressing this issue now. Fear is no longer "religious awe" at the miracles of Jesus, and anxiety is no longer "preoccupation" about the minutiae of hospitality. Now is the time to face terror at arrest and persecution and possibly death.

As so often in Hellenistic protreptic discourses (e.g., Lucian of Samosata, *Nigrinus, Demonax*), the excoriation of the opposition (11:37-52) is turned to positive exhortation. Thus the disciples are to "avoid the hypocrisy" of the Pharisees (12:1). One reason is that for them, hypocrisy would not work. In contrast to these well-respected members of the religious elite whose hidden vice could be camouflaged by outward show, the disciples would be tested by persecution, trials, and the threat of death. They will not be able to hide anything. For *them*, Jesus' sayings make clear, whatever is hidden will be brought to light, whatever whispered will be shouted from the roofs (12:2-3). It follows then that they must be transparent in their convictions.

The way that fear—especially the fear of death—could create cowards was well examined in Hellenistic philosophy (cf. e.g., Aristotle, *Nichomachean Ethics*, 3, 6; Seneca, *Moral Epistles*, 4). Epictetus mocks the way in which fear of death (*Discourses* 3, 24, 38–39) and even fear of disapproval (4, 9, 4–8) can make a person abandon principles. Hypocrisy is rooted in such fear of human judges, and the persuasion that they can be fooled. Epictetus recommends that the philosopher fear something even greater, namely the loss of self-respect and reason (3, 10, 12-20). Luke has Jesus also recommend a higher form of fear to relativize the fear of human disapproval, namely the "fear of God." The thought of betraying the one who can utterly destroy relativizes the fear of those who can kill only the body and nothing more (12:4-5).

The conflict facing the disciples, however, is not one simply between human agents; it involves spiritual forces. Those who oppose the prophets and apostles are "slandering the Holy Spirit," and yet it is the "holy Spirit who will teach" the disciples how to respond. In this arrangement of materials, the reader sees clearly how Luke's compositional plan of including a second volume affects his redaction of the Gospel. The word spoken against the Son of Man, we notice, can be forgiven, but not that against the Holy Spirit. This discrimination accords exactly with the two stages of Luke's narrative. The denial of Jesus as the prophet in the Gospel can be reversed by conversion to the proclamation by his successors in Acts. But the rejection of *their* proclamation in the Holy Spirit leads to a final rejection from the people. In the narrative of Acts 4-5, Luke will show these words of Jesus finding their fulfillment.

FOR REFERENCE AND FURTHER STUDY

Boring, M. E. "The Unforgivable Sin Logion, Mark III 28-29/ Matt XII 31-32/Luke XII 10: Formal Analysis and History of the Tradition." *NovT* 18 (1976) 258–279.
Dupont, J. "l'Après-mort dans l'oeuvre de luc." *RTL* 3 (1972) 3–21.
McDermott, J. M. "Luc xii 8-9: Pierre angulaire." *RB* 85 (1978) 381–401.
Negoita A. and Daniel, C. "L'enigme du levain: ad mc viii, 15; mt xvi, 15; et lc xii, 1." *NovT* 9 (1967) 306–314.

37. *Treasure and the Heart* (12:13-34)

13. Someone from the crowd said to him, "Teacher, tell my brother to divide the inheritance with me." 14. He responded, "Man, who appointed me your judge or executor?" 15. And he told them, "Watch out! Protect yourself from every form of greed! No one's life is based on an abundance of possessions." 16. He told them a parable: "The land of a certain rich man produced a good harvest. 17. So he began to calculate: 'What shall I do? I don't have room to store my crops.' 18. He said, 'I will do this. I will pull down my barns and build bigger ones. I will store in them all my grain and all my good things. 19. Then I will say to myself, "My soul, you have many good things laid up for years to come. Relax, eat, drink, enjoy yourself!"' 20. But God said to him, 'You fool! This very night your life

is demanded of you. These things you have prepared, whose will they be?'
21. Such is the case with the person who builds a personal treasure but
is not rich toward God." 22. He said to his disciples, "For this reason I
tell you: Do not be anxious about your life, what to eat, or your body, what
to wear. 23. For your life is more than food, and your body more than clothing. 24. Watch the ravens. They don't sow. They don't harvest. They don't
have a storeroom. They don't have a barn. God feeds them! You matter
considerably more than birds. 25. Can any of you add a moment to your
life by worrying? 26. If you can't do even the littlest thing, therefore, why
worry about the rest? 27. Watch the lilies. How they grow! They don't work.
They don't spin. But I tell you, not even Solomon in all his glory was garbed
like one of these. 28. And if God clothes in such fashion grass out in the
field that exists today but tomorrow is thrown into the oven, how much
more will he clothe you, people of little faith! 29. Do not keep seeking what
to eat or what to drink. 30. The nations of the world seek all these things.
But your father knows that you need them. 31. Rather, seek his kingdom
and these things will be given as well. 32. Do not fear, my little flock: it
has pleased your father to give you the kingdom! 33. Sell your possessions.
Give alms. Make for yourselves purses that do not age, an inexhaustible
treasure in heaven. No thief can get in there! No moth can destroy there!
34. Where your treasure is, in that place your heart also will be."

NOTES

13. *to divide the inheritance*: The voice from the crowd assumes the setting of 12:1.
We are to picture Jesus, while jostled by a mob, being approached as a rabbi
to settle a dispute over a family estate. The basic inheritance laws are laid down
in Deut 21:15-17 and Num 27:1-11; 36:7-9, with elaboration in *m.Baba Bathra*
8:1–9:10.

14. *Man, who appointed . . . judge or executor*: The vocative *anthrōpe* can scarcely be
translated with inclusive language. The tone is condescending, and often used
in diatribes (e.g., Epictetus, *Discourses* 1, 22, 20; Rom 2:1, 3; 9:20). But cf. also
Luke 22:60. The translation of *meristēs* (lit: "divider") as "executor" depends
on the context of settling an inheritance. The *Gospel of Thomas* 72 has this part
of the logion, separated from the statement on greed, and from the parable of
the rich fool, which it also has in another location (*Thomas*, 63). Mark and Matthew lack both the introductory exchange and the parable.

15. *every form of greed*: The term *pleonexia* ("greed" or "avarice") names the vice
that always seeks more possessions: Plutarch says "*pleonexia* never rests from
acquiring *to pleon* ("more")," *On Love of Wealth* 1 (Mor. 523 E). It is prominently
featured in NT vice-lists (Mark 7:22; Rom 1:29; Eph 4:19; 5:3). Colossians 3:5 flatly
identifies *pleonexia* with idolatry, an equation having much truth.
no one's life: The translation is made difficult by the word order and the exact
syntactical relation between clauses. The basic distinction between life and pos-

sessions is clear enough. Life is a gift of God. No amount of possessions, however abundant, can make it greater or give it security.

17. *began to calculate*: Is literally, "debated within himself," but we have seen that Luke uses *dialogismos* and *dialogizomai* negatively (see 2:35; 5:21-22; 6:8; 9:46-47). Given the fact that the protagonist of the story has already been identified as a "rich man" (and therefore a negative character in Luke's taxonomy), the translation is accurate and appropriate.

19. *I will say to myself*: A difficult problem in translation runs through these verses. Luke uses the term *psychē* in verses 15, 19 (twice) and 20, but with a slightly different sense each time. In verse 15 the contrast is between life (as existence) and possessions. In the present verse 19, the man says to his "self," and addresses it as "soul," so familiarly that one is tempted to render it "old man." In verse 20 again, "soul" equals "life" in contrast to possessions.

    eat, drink, enjoy yourself: The proverbial expression of a hedonism divorced from the expectation of future life or judgment, classically expressed in Qoh 8:15 and Tobit 7:10. Compare Isa 22:13, "eat and drink, for tomorrow we die" and its citation by Paul in 1 Cor 15:32. Luke will shortly condemn a life devoted to such pursuits, 12:29.

20. *your life is demanded*: For the translation of *psychē*, see the note on verse 19. The literal Greek is "they are demanding of you your soul," but the third person plural can stand in for the passive, which in turn probably refers to God's action: "God requires your life of you." The parable's contrast between human scheming for possessions and the transitoriness of life is paralleled in Jas 4:13-16.

21. *builds a personal treasure*: The desire for inclusive language here leads to a somewhat awkward construction. The Greek is literally, "the man who makes a treasure for himself." The contrasting phrase is dense: "rich toward God" is in fact a literal rendering. Wealth with respect to God has two levels of meaning for Luke: the first is the response of faith, the second is the disposition of possessions in accordance with faith, which means to share them with others rather than accumulating them for one's self (see 16:9-13).

22. *for this reason I tell you*: The material in 12:22-34 is loosely paralleled by Matt 6:25-34, but the framing within the journey narrative gives it a distinctively dramatic character in Luke.

    anxious about your life: The connection is drawn explicitly between the "anxiety" for the security and protection of life through the accumulation of possessions, and the fear and anxiety experienced at the threat to life in 12:4 and 11.

24. *watch the ravens*: The verb *katanoeō* means to "draw a leson from" as well as "observe closely." The comparison reminds us of that made to the five sparrows in 12:6, with a similar lesson. This translation omits the Greek conjunctions. Luke characteristically adds *tameion*, which can mean a storeroom or treasury (see also 12:3).

    you matter considerably more: The Greek construction is *posō mallon* ("how much more"), which was used in 11:13 and will be again in verse 28. For *diapherō*, see the very similar statement in 12:7. Matt 6:26 puts the same thought in the form of a question.

25. *moment to your life*: The term *pēchus* properly refers to a measurement of space (a cubit, or about eighteen inches), and *hēlikia* can mean "stature" as well as age. The verse could therefore correctly be translated, "add an inch to your height," but the overall context makes the translation of *hēlikia* as "age" and a transferred meaning of *pēchus* appropriate. Matt 6:27 is basically the same, but Matthew omits the next verse, "if you can't do . . . ."

28. *clothes in such fashion*: This translation of the Greek *houtōs* (literally, "thus") creates a pun in the English, but one not unfaithful to Luke's meaning. The construction here is again "how much more" as in verse 24 above. The expression "people of little faith" (*oligopistoi*) is found only here in Luke, but is characteristic of Matthew (6:8, 30; 8:26; 14:31).

29. *do not keep seeking*: The present negative imperative means "stop seeking." Rather than have the sequence begin with "don't worry" as in Matt 6:31, Luke has the series conclude with "do not worry," using a verb (*meteorizō*) which means to hang in the air, so that a translation "don't be all up in the air" would be accurate.

30. *nations of the world*: Luke adds "of the world" to the version in Matt 6:25; the unfavorable contrast to "the nations" is less natural to Luke than to Matthew for whom the appropriation of the symbols of Judaism is distinctive (compare Luke 22:25 to Matt 5:47; 6:7, 32; 18:17; 20:25).

31. *rather, seek his kingdom*: Luke has two differences from Matt 6:33: he lacks the word "first," and he lacks the phrase "and its righteousness."

32. *my little flock*: The gentleness here matches that of "my friends" in 12:4, and the image of the flock echoes the designation of Israel guided by the Lord (as in Ezek 34:11-24). The disciples represent that "little flock" which forms the nucleus of the restored people forming around the prophet.

    it has pleased your Father: For "pleasure" (*eudokeō/eudokia*) as expressing the divine will, see 2:14; 3:22; 10:21.

    to give you the kingdom: This verse entirely substitutes for Matt 6:34 about the evil of the day being sufficient. The disciples were taught to pray for the coming of the Father's kingdom in 11:2. Here, Jesus tells them that it has been given (the "it pleased" is in the aorist tense) *to them*. Compare 22:29-30, where Jesus gives "rule" (*basileia*) to the Twelve.

33. *sell your possessions*: The instruction is lacking in Matthew and reflects Luke's concern that the response of faith be expressed by the sharing of possessions (see 14:33; 18:22, and the command to the Pharisees in 11:41, "give what is inside as alms").

    make for yourselves purses: Luke's metaphorical language reworks the material shared by Matt 6:19-20. The idea is that the giving away of possessions on earth in the form of alms brings a reward from God. See 6:35, "your reward will be great" and esp. 16:9, which is similar in form: "make friends for yourselves with the mammon of iniquity." The idea that almsgiving brought such a heavenly recompense is standard in rabbinic literature; cf. e.g., *m.Peah* 1:1; *bT Shabbath* 156b; *bT Rosh ha Shanah* 16b; *bT Gittin* 7a-b. A mixed version of this saying is found as well in *Gospel of Thomas* 76.

34. *your heart also will be*: The statement is the same in Matt 6:21, but in Luke it has been prepared for by the frequent connections drawn between human passions (the heart) and possessions (the treasure).

INTERPRETATION

The pattern of alternating audiences that Luke uses throughout the journey of the Prophet toward Jerusalem appears again in this section. We have learned of the massive crowd pressing on Jesus in 12:1, so that they are a silent presence as Jesus addresses his disciples on courage before the threat to their lives. Now, with stunning irrelevancy (but providing a wonderful opportunity to the moralist), a voice from the crowd asks Jesus to mediate in a family inheritance dispute (12:13). Not only does the anonymous questioner reveal inattentiveness to the seriousness of Jesus' discourse, but an unawareness that something more than another "lawyer" is here. In any case, Luke uses this framing device to set up what is in effect a long *qal wehomer* (lesser to the greater) argument, but in reverse. If his teaching to this point has stressed lack of fear before the immediate threat of life, *how much less* should fear generate an obsessive concern with possessions.

Yet, Luke's bringing together of these two themes shows how profoundly he has grasped the symbolic function of possessions in human existence. It is out of deep fear that the acquisitive instinct grows monstrous. Life seems so frail and contingent that many possessions are required to secure it, even though the possessions are frailer still than the life. Only the removal of fear by the persuasion that life is a gift given by the source of all reality can generate the spiritual freedom that is symbolized by the generous disposition of possessions.

So the progression of the argument here: the rejection by the Prophet of a legal role leads to the initial exhortation that sets up all the others: above all things *pleonexia* is to be avoided. But Luke also provides the premise for the constant requirement of more, namely, the notion that life consists in possessions, in "having." Once that connection is cut by the understanding that life cannot be secured by possessions, that existence is a gift outside human control, then the rest of the exhortation can proceed. The parable of the rich fool is both lively and directly to the point as Luke's moral parables always are. The man was rich because he had many crops. He was a fool because he thought they secured his life "for many years to come." When his life ended so were his possessions scattered.

Jesus' exhortation to learn from the birds and the flowers can sound sentimental. In fact, there is a hard realism here: Luke does not deny that birds die or flowers fade. Indeed, the grass is here today and tomorrow thrown into an oven! The point is a deeper one: humans have an eternal destiny. This existence is not their only one: what they do now has consequences for the future. The point is not simply that they should "not worry" about food and clothing, but that they should far more radically "sell their possessions. Give alms."

How can such carelessness be countenanced? Only on the basis of two convictions that no longer seem self-evident to contemporary readers but are essential to the understanding of Luke's argument. The first is that God rewards and punishes in the future life. If God controls history and cares for humans more than flowers and birds, then humans can dispose of their life freely in the expectation that this does "make purses in heaven." The second premise is that the Father has already established his rule among them ("given his kingdom") so that they do not live in a world of chaotic chance, but in a world governed by the gracious gift of God. Only because they have been so fundamentally gifted can they be without fear and therefore can share their possessions with others.

The message here is all the more powerful because of Luke's compositional arrangement. There is no time when humans are likely to grasp more tightly to what they have than when there is an overt threat to their lives. The teaching to the disciples on lack of fear before death and this teaching on a lack of anxiety about possessions are all of a piece, and profoundly challenging.

FOR REFERENCE AND FURTHER STUDY

Degenhardt, H.-J. *Lukas Evangelist der Armen* (Stuttgart: Katholisches Bibelwerk, 1965) 68–93.

Horn, F. W. *Glaube und Handeln in der Theologie des Lukas* (Goettingen: Vandenhoeck und Ruprecht, 1983) 58–88.

Johnson, L. T. *Sharing Possessions: Mandate and Symbol of Faith* (Overtures to Biblical Theology; Philadelphia: Fortress, 1981) 1–78.

Pilgrim, W. E. *Good News to the Poor* (Minneapolis: Augsburg, 1981) 85–146.

38. *Watchfulness and Service* (12:35-48)

35. "Have your belts cinched tight and your lamps lit. 36. Be like people waiting for their master to return from a wedding, so that when he arrives and knocks they can open the door for him immediately. 37. Blessed are the servants whom the master finds awake when he comes. Amen I tell you, he will put on an apron, set you down and serve you! 38. Even if he should come in the second or third night watch and find them so, those servants will be blessed. 39. But know this: if the master of a household knew what time the thief was coming, he would not let him break into his house. 40. You also should stand ready, because the Son of Man is coming at a time you do not expect." 41. Peter said to him, "Lord, are you saying this parable only to us, or also to everyone?" 42. The Lord said, "Who then is the faithful household manager, the sensible one, whom the master will set over his household slaves to give them their rations at the appointed times? 43. Blessed is that servant whom the master will find doing just this when he arrives. 44. Truly I tell you that he will place him over all his holdings. 45. But suppose that slave says in his heart: 'the master is slow in coming.' So he starts abusing the men servants and the women servants. He eats and drinks and gets drunk. 46. The master of that servant will arrive on a day he does not expect and at an hour he does not know. He will cut him off. He will place him among the faithless. 47. And the servant who has known the desire of the master yet has not prepared or done anything in accordance with his desire will be flogged. 48. But the one who does not know yet does things deserving of a whipping will be flogged only lightly. Much will be required of the person to whom much has been given. More will be demanded of the person to whom much has been entrusted."

NOTES

35. *belts cinched tight*: This is a very loose translation of the biblical expression, "let your loins be girded," which derives from Exod 12:11. There it described the readiness required in the Passover: the long robe is cinched up to free the feet for action. Cf. Elijah doing this to outrun the rain in 1 Kgs 18:46, and the challenge to Job in Job 38:3.

36. *people waiting for their master*: The passage has some points of resemblance (lamps/wedding/servants/waiting/night) to the parable of the ten virgins in Matt 24:42-51, though Luke's scene is more determinedly domestic.

37. *amen, I tell you*: For the distinctive use of this locution, see the note on 4:24.
   put on an apron: This is the same verb, *perizōnnymi*, that was translated as "cinching the belt" in verse 35. But here it is closer to the use in Epictetus, *Discourses* 4, 8, 16, referring to an overgarment used for work. The phrase "set you down" is literally, "make you recline" (*anaklinō*).

38. *second or third night watch*: The exact time would depend on whether Luke thinks of a three watch or four watch system, but in any case, it is late!

those servants will be blessed: Following that in verse 37, this is the 11th macarism of Luke's Gospel, and it is quickly followed by the 12th in verse 43.

39. *time the thief was coming*: The comparison of the end-time to a "thief in the night" is found in Matt 24:43, in Paul (1 Thess 5:2, 4), in 2 Peter 3:10, and in Rev 16:15. It is an image so striking as to require no explication. Some MSS have "he would have stayed awake," which would create an agreement with verse 37.

40. *Son of Man is coming*: See also Matt 24:44; with the exception of 9:26 and 12:8, the majority of "Son of Man" sayings in Luke have referred to Jesus' ministry (5:24; 6:5, 22; 7:34; 9:56, 58; 11:30; 12:10) or to his suffering (9:22, 26, 44). From this point on, references to the future coming of the Son of Man as judge predominate (17:22, 24, 26, 30; 18:8; 21:27, 36; 22:69).

41. *only to us or also to everyone*: This interjection by Peter is found only in Luke, and it serves a critical redactional function, making the *following* parable apply to the future leadership of the people, using the image of household management as the metaphor for authority (see 9:12-17).

42. *whom the master will set over*: The verb kathistēmi "appoint" is the same as in Matt 24:45, except that Luke has it in the future rather than the aorist tense. Both he and Matthew have the same verb in verse 44 (Matt 24:47). Luke points forward to the apostles' future role of leadership.

    their rations: In place of "food" (trophē) in Matt 24:45, Luke uses the rare *sitometrion* (literally, "measure of grain"). As with the choice of *therapeia* for "household slaves," Luke seems deliberately to be elevating the language.

43. *that servant*: The household manager (oikonomos) is often translated as "steward." He was himself a slave (doulos) just as those he oversees; despite his relative authority, he is equally subject to the authority of the master (kyrios). This language cannot help but evoke the relationship of Christians to *their* master, the risen *kyrios*.

44. *over all his holdings*: Is literally "possessions" (hyparchonta). Compare the parable of the pounds in 19:15-19, in which the proper disposition of possessions leads to an appointment over cities.

45. *suppose that slave says*: Matt 24:48 calls him a "wicked" servant. This translation uses "slave" as a reminder of his real status. The translation also breaks a long conditional sentence in Greek into several shorter segments introduced by a hypothetical "suppose"; compare the parable of the friend at midnight, Luke 11:5-8.

    abuse the men servants and the women servants: It is typical of Luke to notice both genders; Matt 24:49 has "fellow servants." The abuse (literally "beating," tuptein) precedes the drunkenness, so there is no excuse for the arrogance and cruelty.

    eats and drinks: The terms correspond to the activities of the "rich fool" (12:19) with the added note of excess (methuskein) rather than enjoyment (euphrainein). For the vice of drunkenness and its consequences, cf. Seneca, *Moral Epistles* 83, and in the NT, 1 Cor 5:11; 6:10; Eph 5:18; 1 Thess 5:7.

46. *cut him off*: Is literally "cut him in two" (*dichotomein*). Such a sanguinary response is imaginable in the world of parables; compare the slaughter of the enemies in the parable of the pounds (19:27). This translation shades the meaning in the direction of "dismissal" or "rejection" rather than the softening of many translations, "punish him" (e.g., RSV). That actual dismemberment is not in view is supported by the next phrase: literally his *meros* ("portion") is placed among the faithless. The present translation takes "portion" as metonymy for the steward himself. The "faithless" in this verse contrasts with the "faithful" in verse 42; "trustworthy" and "untrustworthy" would perhaps be even better renderings.

47. *has known the desire of his master*: These sayings spell out degrees of accountability on the basis of knowledge. They have no parallel in Mark or Matthew, but do resemble the series of sayings in Luke 16:10-12. The term "desire" is *thelēma*, which can also be translated "will." The prepositional phrase *pros to thelēma* could also be translated: "against his will."

48. *given . . . entrusted*: The two terms suggest the bestowal of authority and act as morals to the preceding parable: leaders in the community are held to higher account because of their added responsibility. For the third person plural of *aiteō* used as a passive, compare 12:20.

INTERPRETATION

Jesus' discourse on fear and anxiety leads naturally to a direct consideration of "whom they should fear," namely the judgment of God that will be carried out at the coming of the Son of Man (12:40). The shift to an eschatological perspective is anticipated earlier in the references to the "One who can throw you into Gehenna" (12:5), and the threat that denial of Jesus now will lead to being denied "before God's angels" (12:9), as well as in the command to "make . . . an inexhaustible treasure in heaven" (12:33). Now, the eschatological judgment becomes the explicit framework for instruction, as we can observe as well from the fact that the few parallels to these materials in Matthew and Mark occur in the eschatological discourses of their Gospels (Mark 13; Matt 24).

The coming of the Son of Man is mentioned explicitly only in 12:40, and only with the caution that the time of his coming will be sudden and unexpected "like a thief in the night." But the theme of "returning" and "coming" runs through these sayings (vv. 35, 37, 38, 39, 40, 43, 45, 46). All of Christian existence therefore stands within an expectation. Its fulfillment may be sure, but its timing is unknown. Therefore the attitudes of watchfulness are required, even if the return of the master appears "delayed" (12:45). The reality of the judgment, we learn, is not simply temporal but existential. God judges humans at every moment, and knows whether they have "given rations at the appointed times" or have fallen to beating the servants.

Several features of Luke's composition are striking. We note first the wonderful image of the master coming home, finding his servants awake and waiting for him, and then—in a reversal entirely unexpected in that hierarchical world—himself putting on an apron and serving his servants as a servant (12:37). The reversal is surprising in this place, and must be understood in the light of Jesus' declaration about himself at the Last Supper, "I am among you as one who serves (22:27). Authority is here expressed in table service.

It is this part of the speech Luke has Peter respond to with his question in 12:41, for Luke has already shown the Twelve and the readers how spiritual authority is to be symbolically expressed by the waiting on tables—in the story of the feeding of five thousand (9:12-17). Peter therefore is made to ask whether that image applied to all who followed Jesus or only the Twelve (whom we must understand as the "us" of Peter's question). Rather than answer directly, Luke has Jesus answer parabolically.

The role of the household manager or steward is well fitted to Luke's understanding of authority in the community. His role was to direct the affairs of the other slaves, to see they did their work, but also to serve their needs. The steward was answerable (in fidelity) to the master who appointed him, as well as answerable (in fidelity) to the other slaves. He could not be faithful to one while being abusive to the other. Luke will in fact use the same household situation again in 16:1-9.

Once more, the image of authority is one of service to others. Yes, this applies in a special way to the Twelve as the leaders of the restored Israel. Whereas all the servants were to stand in readiness for their master, and do their work in a pleasing fashion, the leaders are responsible not only for their work but also for the work of the community as a whole. If they do their work well, they will receive the reward of still greater authority. But if they abuse their privilege, they will be cut off completely.

It is easy to see here not only an anticipation of the Twelve's later role in the Jerusalem community, but also an implied warning against the present leaders of the people, a warning that will become much clearer in the parables of the pounds (19:11-27) and the vineyard (20:9-18): those who abuse their authority over the people will be cut off utterly. As the final sayings make clear, the greater the gift given, the greater the responsibility and the greater the judgment.

FOR REFERENCE AND FURTHER STUDY

Dodd, C. H. *The Parables of the Kingdom.* Rev.ed. (New York: Charles Scribner's Sons, 1961) 122–139.

Jeremias, J. *The Parables of Jesus*. Rev.ed. (New York: Charles Scribner's Sons, 1963)
    48–66.
Schneider, G. Parusiegleichnisse im Lukas-Evangelium (SBS 74; Stuttgart:
    Katholisches Bibelwerk, 1975) 20–37.
Tannehill, R. *The Narrative Unity of Luke-Acts* (Foundations and Facets; Philadelphia:
    Fortress Press, 1986) 240–253.

39. A Call for Decision (12:49-59)

49. "I came to throw fire on the earth. And what do I wish? That it were
already blazing! 50. I have a baptism to undergo, and how distressed I am
until it can be accomplished! 51. Do you think that I am here to bring peace
on earth? Not at all, I tell you, but rather division. 52. From now on five
people in one household will be divided, three against two and two against
three. 53. Father will be divided against son and son against father, mother
against daughter and daughter against mother, mother-in-law against
daughter-in-law and daughter-in-law against mother-in-law." 54. He also
said to the crowds: "When you see a cloud rising in the west you say at
once, 'A storm is coming!' And so it does. 55. And when you see the south
wind blowing you say, 'There will be terrible heat!' And so it is. 56. You
hypocrites! You know how to interpret the face of the earth and sky. Why
don't you know how to interpret this present season? 57. Why don't you
judge for yourselves what is right? 58. As you go to a magistrate with an
adversary, try to make things up with him while still on the road. Otherwise he might drag you before the judge and the judge will hand you over
to the bailiff and the bailiff will throw you into jail. 59. I tell you, you will
not leave there until you pay the last penny."

NOTES

49. *throw fire on the earth*: The term translated "earth" (*gē*) could as easily be "land"
here and in verse 51. The image recalls the prophet Elijah who drew down fire
from the Lord against the prophets of Baal (1 Kgs 18:36-40) and also on the soldiers of King Ahaziah (2 Kgs 1:10, 12, 14). Jesus' disciples wanted to exercise
this sort of retaliation on the Samaritans (9:54) but he did not allow it. If the
prophetic background governs the saying (found only in Luke and in a different form in *Gospel of Thomas*, 10), then Jesus desires the eschatological judgment
that was promised by John: the tree not bearing fruit is to be thrown in the fire
(3:9), the chaff is thrown into unquenchable fire (3:16). Fire as the instrument
of judgment recurs in 17:29. On the other hand, Luke also associates it with
the gift of the Spirit (3:16; Acts 2:3).

what do I wish: The question form makes the sentence more intelligible. The noun phrase following, "that it might already be blazing" is introduced by *ei* ("if") which sometimes happens with verbs expressing strong emotion.

50. *a baptism to undergo*: The phrase is literally, "I have a baptism to be baptized." The verb translated "I am distressed" is *synechō*, which has the sense of "enduring," as in 9:41 (another expression of impatience). As in the previous verse, the reference could be double: to Jesus' death (following the meaning of baptism in Mark 10:38), or to the "baptism in the Spirit" at Pentecost. Either would fit the other key verb "accomplish" (or: fulfill, *teleō*).

51. *peace on earth*: The same ambiguity is found in the term *gē* here as in verse 49; it could be translated, "peace on the land." The saying is the same in Matt 10:34, except that Matt has "sword" rather than "division" (*diamerismon*). This is the clearest statement in Jesus' own mouth of the division created in the people by the prophet (see 2:35). More surprising is the apparent contradiction of the infancy account's promise that Jesus would bring peace (1:79; 2:14, 29). The answer, of course, is that those who accept the prophet have this peace (7:50; 8:48; 10:5-6), but they are then separated from those who reject the prophet's message. If we were to take *gē* as meaning "land," furthermore, the saying (like v. 49) could be taken as referring specifically to the upheaval in the land caused by the prophetic visitation.

52. *from now on . . . in one household*: The statement in Matt 10:35-36 is similar, with these exceptions: a) Luke opens with a thematic statement concerning the household (compare the analogy to Satan's kingdom in 11:17-18); b) he has a series of matched pairs; c) Matthew concludes with servants against masters, which Luke omits. Cf. also *Gospel of Thomas* 16.

53. *father . . . against son*: Most remarkable here is the reversal of the promise made concerning the mission of John by Gabriel, that like Elijah, he would "turn the hearts of fathers to their children" (1:17).

54. *when you see*: Luke has a different meteorological analogy from Matt 16:2-3, but the basic point is the same in both. Luke adds the charge of hypocrisy, which makes the reader think that this is addressed to the opponents rather than to the crowd. The charge of hypocrisy is a little odd since, unlike Matthew, Luke says they do not *know how* to interpret the season, whereas a hypocrite would know how but choose not to. The term "season" is *kairos*, and for "interpret," *dokimazō*. Another version of this saying is in *Gospel of Thomas* 91.

57. *judge . . . what is right*: This question forms a bridge between the saying concerning "judging the season" and that concerning "being brought before a judge." It demands of the listeners a personal decision. *They* must judge what is the "right thing."

58. *try to make things up*: Is literally, "put labor into getting released" (*apallassō*), that is, reaching a settlement out of court. In Matt 5:25-26, the saying is a straightforward moral exhortation. In Luke it is parabolic.

INTERPRETATION

Having begun this section with an exhortation to courage in the face of tribulation, and continued with a warning against avarice in the face of fear, Luke has Jesus finish his sayings to the disciples with parables that explicitly raise the issue of judgment. Although he does not identify the audience for the sayings now being considered, they work best as addressed to the crowd as a whole, for they are in effect strong prophetic warnings. The crowds are called to conversion before it is too late.

The sayings on the fire that Jesus wishes to cast on the earth and the baptism he must undergo are sufficiently obscure as to leave open their precise point of reference: they could refer to the coming judgment of the Son of Man (see 12:40), or to the eschatological gift of the Spirit in fire at Pentecost (Acts 2:3). In either case, Jesus' declaration suggests a prophetic passion and urgency.

The effect of his mission, he declares, is not the sort of peace by which domestic tranquillity is undisturbed. Indeed, the precise point of the prophetic challenge is to divide the people. Here the programmatic prophecy of Simeon in 2:35 is given its explicit fulfillment in the mouth of the prophet himself: he divides households and creates a division in the people.

The division is created by the diverse decisions made in response to the prophet himself and his message about the kingdom of God. Is he, are his works of healing, the signal from God that a rule more powerful than that of Satan has come to free humans? Or is he a minion of Satan, a charlatan, a deceiver of the people? Those who see him must not have blinders, so that "the light in them turns to darkness" (11:35); those who hear him must "watch how they hear" (8:18). They must discern the signs and decide.

But, says the prophet, they seem not to know how to interpret "this present season" although they are adept at detecting the signs of weather all about them. Why is this? By calling them "hypocrites," Luke suggests that they share the blindness of the lawyers, who have "taken away the key of knowledge, not entering themselves and stopping others who would enter" (11:53). So he concludes by saying that they must "decide for themselves what is right!"

The final saying is a wonderful example of how Luke uses Q material in a distinctive fashion. In Matt 5:25-26, the exhortation to make things up with an adversary before going to trial is a teaching to the disciples on fraternal relations. But in Luke, it is parabolic for this moment in the narrative of the Prophet's progression to Jerusalem. They are the ones "on the road" (13:58) who must make their decision now, before it is too late. If they do not "settle things" now with their adversary—in this instance the Prophet himself who calls them to conversion—then it will be harder for them in the judgment to come.

FOR REFERENCE AND FURTHER STUDY

Black, M. "Uncomfortable Words: II, The Violent Word." *ExpT* 81 (1969–70) 115–118.
Bruston, C. "Une parole de Jésus mal comprise." *RHPR* 5 (1925) 70–71.
Caird, C. B. "Expounding the parables: I. The Defendant (Matthew 5:25f, Luke 12:58f)." *ExpT* 77 (1965–66) 36–39.
Delling, G. "*Baptisma Baptisthēnai.*" *NovT* 2 (1958) 92–115.
Jeremias, J. *The Parables of Jesus.* Rev.ed. (New York: Charles Scribner's Sons, 1963) 43–44.

40. *Warnings to Repent* (13:1-21)

1. Some were then present who reported to him about the Galileans whose blood Pilate had mingled with their sacrifices. 2. He answered them, "Do you think these Galileans were worse sinners than all other Galileans, and that's why they suffered this way? 3. No, I tell you! But if you do not repent, you will perish in the same way. 4. Or those eighteen people on whom the tower in Siloam fell and were killed: do you think they were more due for punishment than all the people who live in Jerusalem? 5. No, I tell you! But if you do not repent, you will all perish in the same way." 6. And he told them this parable: "A certain man had a fig tree planted in his vineyard. He went out to look for some fruit on it. He did not find any. 7. He said to the vinedresser: 'Look, I have been coming out here to find fruit on this fig tree for three years. Yet I find none. So cut it down. Why waste the space?' 8. He answered, 'Master, let it be for this year. I will dig around it and fertilize it. 9. Perhaps it will bear fruit in the coming year. If not, then cut it down.' " 10. He was teaching on the Sabbath in one of the synagogues. 11. There was a woman present who for eighteen years had a spirit of weakness. She was all bent over and completely unable to straighten up. 12. When Jesus saw her he called out to her, "Woman, you have been freed of your weakness." 13. He placed his hands on her. At once she straightened up and glorified God. 14. The ruler of the synagogue was irritated because Jesus had healed on the Sabbath. He responded by telling the crowd that there were six days on which one must work. "So come on those days to be healed, not on the Sabbath day!" 15. The Lord answered him, "Hypocrites! You all untie your ox on the Sabbath, or take your donkey from the manger and lead it to water, don't you? 16. This woman is a daughter of Abraham! Satan has bound her for, look, eighteen years. Is it not necessary to relieve her of this enslavement on the Sabbath day?" 17. When he said these things, his enemies were put to shame, but the whole crowd rejoiced at the wonders he was doing. 18. He therefore began to say, "What is the kingdom of God like? To what shall I compare it? 19. It is like a mustard seed that someone took and planted in the garden. It grew

into a tree, and the birds of the sky made nests in its branches." 20. He also said, "To what shall I compare the kingdom of God? It is like yeast that a woman takes and sticks into flour; three small measures leavens the whole."

NOTES

1. *whose blood Pilate had mingled*: The two incidents related in 13:1-5 are unique to Luke. None of the accounts concerning Pilate's penchant for punishing Jews exactly matches this rendition, though they support the picture of him as an administrator who reached quickly for violent solutions (Josephus, *Antiquities* 18:85-89; *Jewish War* 2:169-177). The point of Luke's recital is less the history of Pilate's reign than of the need to repent.

2. *worse sinners*: Is literally "became sinners more than (*para* + acc.) all the Galileans."
   that's why they suffered: Translates a *hoti* clause ("because they suffered"). In popular piety (based on the Deuteronomic promises [see Deut 28–30]), disaster is taken as a punishment for sin (cf. Job 4:17; Ezek 18:26), and this conviction is reflected in John 9:2-3, as well as the healing stories of Luke (e.g., 5:20-24). Jesus does not dispute the equation but simply questions whether they were more egregious sinners than others.

3. *if you do not repent*: His listeners cannot be content with the thought that they are less public in their sins than others. All are called to repentance by the Prophet, who here sounds like John in 3:7-9, 16-17, as well as Isa 3:1-26. "The same way" means suddenly and without preparation.

4. *tower in Siloam*: The term *pyrgos* refers to the sort of tower that was on a city wall. John 9:7, 11 mentions the pool of Siloam as a part of Jerusalem, and the same area is undoubtedly meant here. In his description of the Temple walls, Josephus describes the most ancient wall (going back to David) as having one section "turning southwards above the fountain of Siloam" (*Jewish War* 5:145).
   more due for punishment: The translation tries to capture the sense of *opheiletai*, which literally means "debtors"; the phrase "for punishment" is supplied by the translation.

6. *fig tree planted in his vineyard*: Mark 11:12-14 and Matt 21:18-19 each have a story about *Jesus* and a fig tree in direct narrative: Jesus finds a tree that does not bear fruit and curses it. Luke's parable may derive from the same tradition, but he turns it in quite a different way. The fig tree (*syke*) and the vine (*ampelos*) are found together in Mic 4:4 and Joel 2:22 as signs of God's blessings.

7. *coming out here to find fruit*: In contrast to Mark 11:13 where Jesus does not find fruit "because it was not the season," this man has been coming out regularly to check his tree. The three years do not lend themselves to an allegory of Jesus' ministry since Luke gives no indication that he thought Jesus' ministry was that length.
   why waste the space: Is literally "the earth" or "ground" (*ge*).

9. *if not, then cut it down*: The addition of "then" in this translation imitates the balance of the Greek sentence with its well balanced *men/de* clauses.

11. *there was a woman present*: The story is unique to Luke. The translation weakens the idiomatic force of Luke's biblical diction: "behold (*idou*) a woman." The phrase "spirit of weakness" is understood by verse 16 to be the result of demonic possession. The eighteen years of the sickness match the eighteen people killed by the tower of Siloam. Compare the use of the number twelve in 8:40-48 and 9:1-17.

12. *you have been freed*: Uses the passive perfect tense as in Jesus' statements concerning the forgiveness of sins in 5:20, 23; 7:47-48: God has made her strong.

13. *placed his hands on her*: A characteristic gesture of healing by Jesus (4:40; 5:13; 8:54).
    glorified God: For "glorifying God" (*doxazō*) as a response to miracles, see 2:20; 5:25-26; 7:16.

14. *ruler of the synagogue was irritated*: The verb *aganaktein* is found only here in Luke. It is attributed to Jesus and the disciples by Mark 10:14, 41 and Matt 20:24; 26:8, and to the Jewish leaders by Matt 21:15. The *archisynagōgos* in 8:49 was favorably inclined to the prophet, but that was in Galilee. The charge of hypocrite (v. 15) is deserved at least because the leader does not confront Jesus himself with his irritation but instead harangues the crowd, a classic ploy of deflected anger. For the consistent forbidding of anything resembling healing on the Sabbath, compare the discussions in *bT Shab.* 18a; 53b; 75b; 108b; 111a; 128a; 140a; 147a–148a.

15. *ox . . . donkey*: Deut 5:14 forbids any work by ox or ass on the Sabbath. In Deut 22:1-4, one is allowed to return a stray animal, and if ox or ass has fallen, to lift them again. For the Pharisaic regulations on work forbidden on the Sabbath, cf. *m.Shab.* 5:1-4; for untying knots, *m.Shab.* 7:2; 15:1; for leading to water, *m.Erub.* 2:1-4. Cf. also the regulations at Qumran in *CD* 11:2-21.

16. *a daughter of Abraham*: The argument is obviously one of *qal wehomer*: if you release an animal from restraint and give it relief, how much more ought you to do for a human. For "daughter," see 1:5; 2:26 and 8:42, 48. Zacchaeus is called "son of Abraham" in 19:9, and Paul greets his audience in Antioch of Pisidia as "sons of the family of Abraham" (Acts 13:26). She is, in short, at the very least a "neighbor" for whom compassion should obtain.
    Satan has bound her: For the rule of Satan as chief of the demons and ruler of the kingdom opposed to God, see 10:18 and 11:18. Luke uses *deō* ("bind") in this metaphorical sense only here, but the notion of being bound by evil is obviously present in "release of captives" (4:18), exorcism of the violent demoniac (8:26-39) and the dumb demoniac (11:4) as well as in the "release" of sins (5:20, 23; 7:47). This connection is important, for the essence of the Sabbath was to be a "rest," that is a time of "liberation" as the notion of the Sabbath year indicated, when debts were redeemed and slaves were freed.

17. *his enemies were put to shame*: The term translated "enemies" is literally "those opposing him" (*antikeimenoi*), which occurs again of those opposing the disciples in 21:15. Compare again 2:35, the "sign of contradiction (*sēmeion antilegomenon*)."

but the whole crowd rejoiced: The context suggests that the connective "and" (*kai*) be read here as adversative, since the contrast between opponents and crowd is so firmly drawn.

the wonders he was doing: The term *endoxos* means literally "held in high repute" and by extension, "notable things." Luke uses the adjective in 7:25 of rich people's clothes; compare the use of *paradoxa* in 5:26.

18. *he therefore began to say*: The connective *oun* ("therefore") invites the reader to tie these two short parables as a commentary to the previous discourse and story.

19. *grew into a tree*: Luke omits the emphasis on the seed's smallness which is critical to the point in Mark 4:31 and Matt 13:32, as well as *Gospel of Thomas* 20. There is a possible allusion to Ps 104:12 [LXX] and Dan 4:10-12, but it is too obscure to be exploited as part of Luke's point.

20. *kingdom of God*: This parable is shared with Matt 13:33 and *Gospel of Thomas* 96 but is lacking in Mark. The size of the three measures is not significant. The contrast between small beginnings and powerful influence is, as in the previous parable, obvious.

INTERPRETATION

Luke combines material shared with the other Synoptists (a version of the fig tree and the parables of yeast and mustard seed), together with stories derived from his own sources or composition (the healing of the infirm woman and the reports of disasters in Jerusalem) into another dramatic stage in the Prophet's progression to Jerusalem.

Luke has Jesus respond to these reports of death in the city in classic prophetic style: they are turned to warning examples for his listeners. The people who died were not more deserving of death than others. One cannot argue from sudden and violent death to the enormity of sin. Indeed, Jesus himself will suffer a death that appears to be as much a punishment for sin. But the prophet's point is that death itself, with the judgment of God, is always so close. It can happen when engaged in ritual. It can happen standing under a wall. And when it happens so suddenly, there is no time to repent. Rabbi Eliezer had declared that a person should repent the day before death (*Pirke Aboth* 2:10). But his disciples said that a person could die any day, therefore all of life should be one of repentance (*bT Shab.* 153a). The repentance called for by the prophet Jesus, of course, is not simply a turning from sin but an acceptance of the visitation of God in the proclamation of God's kingdom.

For the reader, however, these death notices serve as a reminder that the Prophet himself is heading inexorably toward the city where such terrible things are likely to happen, a reminder that will be made even more explicit in 13:31-35. The fact that this is the second time the name Pilate occurs in the story (after 3:1), and that he is now identified as a murderer of Galileans can scarcely be accidental.

Luke's use of the fig tree tradition (13:6-9) is particularly interesting. Matthew and Mark relate an encounter between Jesus and a fig tree bearing no fruit. But in Luke, it is a parable that clearly has the function of interpreting this section of his narrative. The fig tree is *not* summarily cut down. It is allowed to have time; indeed, it has already had time to bear fruit. The comfort to Jesus' listeners is that the Prophet is still on his way to the city; there is still time to respond. The warning is that if they do not, they will surely be cut off.

The healing of the bent woman in the synagogue (13:10-17) comes as a surprise in the midst of all these sayings. The last miracle worked by Jesus was the exorcism of the dumb demoniac in 11:14, and only a single line was devoted to that deed, an obvious set-up for the controversy over Jesus' apparent collusion with Satan. In contrast, the present healing/exorcism is fully developed. It is found only in Luke, and again creates a conflict over the legitimacy of healing on the Sabbath. In the earlier healing of the man with a withered hand, Jesus had asked the ''scribes and Pharisees'' who observed him whether one could do good or evil on the Sabbath, give life or destroy it (6:9). In this case, the deflected objection of the synagogue ruler leads Jesus to a more direct charge of hypocrisy: the allowances made for the ''loosing'' of animals on the Sabbath to give them relief is a light thing, compared to the heavy matter of ''loosing'' a human person (and a ''daughter of Abraham'') from the bondage to Satan. Indeed, faced with such a human need, it is *necessary* to heal on the Sabbath!

The responses to Jesus' words are what the reader has come to expect in this journey narrative: the crowd rejoices, but the opponents are ''put to shame,'' and, we understand, grow even more bitter in their fixed grudge against Jesus (cf. 11:53).

It is at this point that Luke appends the two small parables of growth: the mustard seed and the yeast (13:18-21). His compositional placement invites speculation. Matthew and Mark put these tiny parables in the midst of longer parabolic discourses (Mark 4:30-32; Matt 13:31-33). Luke puts them within a highly charged situation of conflict. And he does so deliberately, for he introduces them after the conclusion of the healing: ''*therefore* he began to say.'' We are asked to read these parables as commentaries on the story preceding it. Both parables contrast small beginnings with powerful results: the seed shoots into a tree; the yeast leavens a whole lump. Both parables contrast as well the hidden with the manifest: the seed is planted but becomes visible in the plant; the yeast is hidden in the flour and is known only because of the growth it gives. So, we are to understand, is the case with the kingdom of God proclaimed by Jesus. In just such small and hidden acts of liberation as he has worked in this synagogue is the victory over

Satan's kingdom being won, and the prophetic mission to "proclaim liberty to captives" (4:18) being fulfilled.

Does Luke insinuate still subtler signals into the text? Are we to connect the eighteen people on whom the Temple wall fell with the eighteen years the daughter of Abraham remained bent under the bondage of Satan? And if so, is her "standing up straight" a minor variation of Luke's theme of the rise and fall of many in Israel (2:35)? Perhaps so, just as her standing to glorify God will remind us of the saying about the return of the Son of Man in 21:28: "when these things begin to happen, stand up straight, lift up your heads, for the time of your liberation has come."

For Reference and Further Study

Crossan, J. D. "The Seed Parables of Jesus." *JBL* 92 (1973) 244–266.
Dahl, N. A. "The Parables of Growth." *ST* 5 (1951) 132–166.
Dupont, J. "Les paraboles du sénevé et du levain." *NRT* 89 (1967) 897–913.
Funk, R. W. "Beyond Criticism in Quest of Literacy: The Parable of the Leaven."
    Int 25 (1971) 149–170.
Wilkinson, J. "The Case of the Bent Woman in Luke 13:10-17." *EvQ* 49 (1977) 195–205.

41. *Prophetic Pronouncements* (13:22-35)

22. He was travelling through cities and villages, teaching and making his way toward Jerusalem. 23. Someone said to him, "Lord, are those who are being saved few in number?" He said to them, 24. "Struggle to enter through the narrow door. I tell you that many will seek to enter and they will not be able. 25. From the time the master of the house rises and shuts the door, you will begin to stand outside and knock on the door. You will say, 'Lord, open to us!' He will answer you, 'I do not know you, where you are from.' 26. Then you will say, 'We ate and drank in your presence. You taught in our streets!' 27. And he will say to you, 'I do not know you, where you are from. Depart from me all you workers of wickedness!' 28. When you see Abraham and Isaac and Jacob and all the prophets in the kingdom of God, but you are thrown outside, there will be weeping and grinding of teeth! 29. Indeed they will come from east and west, from north and south, and they will recline in the kingdom of God. 30. Look, those who are last will be first and those who are first will be last." 31. At that time, some Pharisees came up to him and said, "Go away. Leave this place! Herod seeks to kill you." 32. He told them, "Go tell that fox, 'Look, I am casting out demons and performing cures today and tomorrow. On the third day I reach my goal.' 33. But it is necessary for me to go forward today

and tomorrow and the following day, for it is not possible for a prophet to perish outside Jerusalem. 34. Jerusalem! Jerusalem! Killer of the prophets and stoner of those sent to her! How often I wanted to gather your children the way a hen gathers her brood beneath her wings. But you did not want it. 35. Look, your house is being left. And I tell you, you will not see me until the time comes when you will say, 'Blessed is the one who is coming in the name of the Lord.' "

NOTES

22. *teaching and making his way*: By means of such transitions, Luke maintains the reader's attention on the overall theme of this section: the prophet is travelling toward Jerusalem and his *exodos*. As he goes, his main activity is prophetic teaching.

23. *someone said to him*: As in other instances on the journey, a statement from the crowd enables Jesus to deliver a prophetic pronouncement (cf. 9:57; 10:25; 11:15, 27, 45; 12:13, 41; 13:1).

    those who are being saved: The present participle of *sōzō* demands the progressive "being saved," which points us to the mission of Jesus himself. The questioner may intend it to be hypothetical (as "who is my neighbor" in 10:29), but Jesus turns it to a personal challenge: act in such a way as to be one who is saved.

24. *struggle to enter*: The term *agōnizomai* suggests that "the few" will have to contend with "the many" (*hoi polloi*) for entry through a space too narrow in a time too short.

    narrow door: Although Luke has "the" narrow door, the implied contrast is lost because he does not have the "wide gate" and "narrow gate" found in Matt 7:13 and probably in his Q source.

25. *rises and shuts the door*: This note is lacking in the Matthean parallel (Matt 7:13-14) and recalls Matthew's parable of the foolish virgins (Matt 25:10-12) where we find the call to open and the answer, "I do not know you." Two problems in this verse: the first is the relationship of clauses in the Greek, since the temporal introduction is vague. The second is assessing the import of "rising" (*egerthē*). Does it have the sense of the biblical idiom "rise and do something" (cf. 1:39; 4:29; 6:8), or does it mean "rise up"? Luke uses *anistēmi* for the former idiom, and *egeirō* for the latter (cf. 11:8). In the prediction of the resurrection, he uses *egerthēnai* (9:22). Is this then intentionally an allegory?

    know you, where you are from: Both here and in verse 27 (where the MS tradition is shakier), the two phrases are unrelieved by conjunction, and the second seems to add nothing to the first. The lesson concerning knocking on the door is less optimistic than in 11:9-10.

26. *then you will say*: Luke uses the same introductory verb *archomai* ("to begin") with the infinitive here as in verse 25. It is one of his favorite constructions (see 4:21; 5:21; 7:24, 38, 49; 9:12; 11:29, 53; 12:1, 45). Sometimes it demands being translated (as in v. 25) and sometimes not (as here).

you ate and drank with us: In the context of Luke's narrative there is some irony here. His opponents accused him of "eating and drinking" with tax-agents and sinners (7:34), but in the narrative itself Jesus has (with whatever breaches in hospitality) eaten as often with the Pharisees (7:36; 11:37).

taught in our streets: Notice the way this connects to the transition sentence in 13:22. Matt 7:22-23 has quite a different version, geared to the realities of internal ecclesial tension: the criers-out claimed to have prophesied and exorcised in his name.

27. *depart from me*: Both Matt 7:23 and Luke depend on Ps 6:9 [LXX], each with variations: Luke retains the adjective "all" (*pantes*) in contrast to Matthew; he replaces the participial construction "those who are workers" with the noun "workers" (*ergatai*); and he replaces "lawlessness" (*anomia*) with "wickedness" (*adikia*).

28. *when you see*: Luke adds "and all the prophets" to the list of the patriarchs shared with Matt 8:11. This makes the scene echo the Beatitude in 6:23.

   weeping and grinding of teeth: In the Greek text, this clause begins the sentence. The periphrasis, "there will be there (*ekei estai*)" means "you will weep and grind your teeth." The phrase is frequent in Matthew (8:12; 13:42, 50; 22:13; 24:51; 25:30) but is found only here in Luke. It corresponds to the woe in 6:25, *penthēsete kai klausete*, "you will mourn and weep."

29. *come from east and west*: Is paralleled by Matt 8:11, but Luke adds "from north and south." The gathering to Zion of the scattered people of Israel by the Lord is a prophetic motif (see Isa 11:11-16; 60:1-22), which Luke shows as proleptically fulfilled in Acts 2:5-13.

   they will recline: The image is of the kingdom of God as a banquet. For the antecedents, see esp. Moses and the elders eating and drinking in God's presence (Exod 24:9-11). The image is worked out by the prophets: "The Lord of hosts will make for all peoples a feast of fat things" (Isa 25:6-8). The Qumran sectarians imagined a messianic banquet for the end-time (1QSa 2:15-22). In Luke, the banquet is anticipated by the feeding of the multitude (9:12-17), rendered parabolically in 14:15-24, sacramentally in 22:14-30. The meal will continue to be the place where the risen Lord is encountered (24:28-35, 36-43; Acts 10:41).

   look, those who are last: The term *idou* ("behold"), which sometimes need not be translated, here seems particularly graphic: they are asked to contemplate the scene of a banquet in which people from all over participate but from which they are rejected. The saying itself is found also in Mark 10:31 and Matt 19:30. In their Gospels, the saying functions as a warning to Christians against thinking oneself first. In Luke, it fits the narrative pattern of reversal: those not expected to be part of the remnant are included, those who thought themselves holy are not.

31. *some Pharisees came up to him*: This passage is found only in Luke. Luke has consistently identified the Pharisees as opponents of the prophets and of Jesus in particular (5:17, 21, 30; 6:2, 7; 7:30, 36, 39; 11:38, 39, 42, 43). The narrator has told us that the Pharisees have a fixed grudge ("deep resentment") against Jesus and are actively seeking to trap him (11:53). Why should we read their statement as beneficent toward Jesus?

leave this place: Since Jesus is already heading away from Galilee (Herod's fief-dom) toward Jerusalem, it is unclear what they might mean: go even faster? Escape this particular village? Or do they seek to deter Jesus from his prophetic destiny of fulfilling an *exodos* in Jerusalem, so that their message is really "lay low, stop this noise, and you will be safe?"

Herod seeks to kill you: Herod certainly had the will for such decisive elimination of prophets. He imprisoned John (3:19) and had him beheaded (9:9). But we are told by the narrator in 9:9 that although Herod "sought" (same word, *zētein*) Jesus, it was "to see" him. Furthermore, when Jesus is later brought before Herod at his trial, the narrator assures us that Herod "had wanted to see him because of hearing about him and he hoped to see some sign done by him" (23:8). He does not kill Jesus but returns him to Pilate (23:11). The Pharisaic message contradicts the testimony of the reliable narrator and must be evaluated accordingly.

32. *go tell that fox*: Rather than flee, Jesus sends them back. Are they speaking for Herod? Then they can deliver this message back to him. This is, of course, all rhetorical. The fox (*alōpex*) was associated with craftiness and slyness in both Hellenistic (cf. Epictetus, *Discourses* 1, 3, 7–9) and rabbinic literature (cf. *bT Ber.* 61b).

on the third day I reach my goal: The phrase "third day" (*tritē hēmera*) would un-avoidably resonate with Christian readers, suggesting that the goal is resurrection (see 2:46; 9:22). This is only strengthened by the use of *teleioō*, "I am brought to perfection/fulfillment," translated here as "I reach my goal" (as in Acts 20:24). Remember how Jesus was in distress until his baptism was "accomplished" (*telesthai*) in 12:50. The punctuation in the present translation makes Jesus' response to Herod end here. The Greek does not make it clear, and a decision is required.

33. *it is necessary*: Luke's use of the impersonal construction *dei* "It is necessary" here and *ou endexetai* "It is not possible" in the next clause places the activity of Jesus within the divine *boulē* ("will") (see 7:30; Acts 2:23; 4:28). Jesus will "go forward" to Jerusalem because it is his prophetic destiny to die there (as the reader knows on the best authority) and no human plot can hinder that happening. Prophets certainly were killed in Jerusalem (see Jer 26:20-23) but as Luke's earlier reference to Zechariah indicates (11:51), he has a broad and inclusive understanding of the prophets of the past as "suffering" (see 4:24; 6:23; 11:47, 50; 13:28, and esp. Acts 7:52).

34. *stoner of those sent to her*: This lament over Jerusalem is closely paralleled in Matt 23:37-39. In Greek "those sent" is *apestalmenoi* which completes the same pair as in 11:49, "prophets and apostles." The combination "killing and stoning" is found also in Matt 21:35. Stoning as a capital punishment occurs in 1 Sam 30:6; 1 Kgs 12:18 and 21:13. It is enjoined in Torah for several crimes (see Exod 19:13; 21:28; Lev 20:2, 27; 24:14-16; Num 15:35-36; Deut 13:10; 17:5; 21:21; 22:21, 24) and is specifically identified as the penalty for blasphemy in John 10:31-33. Cf. also *bT Sanh.* 43a; 49b-50a.

a hen gathers her brood: An image of care and protection that recalls the description of the Lord with his people, "like an eagle that stirs up its nest, that flutters over its young, spreading out its wings'' (Deut 32:11, RSV), as well as Ps 91:4: ''He will cover you with his pinions and under his wings you will find refuge'' (RSV).

35. *your house is being left*: The translation is very literal here because it is not certain what ''house'' (*oikos*) refers to, or how *aphietai* (''being left'') should be understood. Is the house the Temple (as in Luke 6:4; 11:51 and 19:46), or does it refer to the people (as in Luke 1:27, 33, 69; Acts 2:36)? Should *aphietai* be read as present progressive, so that Jesus' pronouncement is performative, i.e., their rejection will leave them rejected? Or is it a prophetic prediction of the destruction of the Temple? This translation tilts toward house as ''the people'' and ''being left'' as the rejection of the people who reject the prophet, but the other reading is also quite possible.

blessed is the one who is coming: As in the parallel of Matt 21:9, this statement is fulfilled by the entry of Jesus into the city in 19:38 (cf. Matt 23:39). There, Luke will add ''the king'' to the acclamation. For the blessing formula, compare Luke 1:42. Jesus is citing Ps 117:26 [LXX], which shortly before this verse contains the line, ''the stone that the builders rejected has become the cornerstone'' (117:22), which is important for Christian apologists and which Luke cites against the rulers of the people both in 20:17 and in Acts 4:11.

INTERPRETATION

This section challenges the reader's commitment to Luke as conscious author of his Gospel. No one has trouble spotting 13:22 as a Lukan touch: Jesus is located once more on the journey to Jerusalem. But the rest of this section is made up of two quite different sorts of pronouncement stories. The first has to do with inclusion and exclusion in the banquet which is the kingdom of God (13:23-30); it obviously functions as a prophetic warning to repentance. It also contains material shared with Matthew (through Q) but worked into a distinctive pattern. The second pronouncement is two-fold: a reaction by Jesus to a message from the Pharisees, and a lament over the fate of Jerusalem (13:31-35). This scene is found only in Luke. The real issue for the reader is how seriously one is to take Luke's compositional signals. Do we meet here a deft and deliberate crafter of the story, or only a clumsy editor? At stake is the interpretation of the passages themselves.

The question put to Jesus is cast in the distinctive Christian language of ''salvation,'' but it derives from a central preoccupation of Jews in the first century concerning the relationship of historical Judaism to the people of God. Were all those calling themselves Jews really part of the chosen people? The concept of a *remnant* chosen by God from a larger population is found clearly in the writings of the Essenes who saw themselves as that ''saved'' group (cf. CD 1:4) and who scorn other Jews, the ''ungodly of the covenant" (*1QM* 1:2). We can find the same perception in writings more frequently associated with the Pharisees, as in 4 Ezra 8:1: "This age the Most High has made for many, but the age to come for few." Such discussions about who will find their way into the age to come are continued in *m.Sanhedrin* 10:1-6, and *bT Sanh.* 99b; 105a.

It was entirely logical, then, for the question to be posed concerning the repentance demanded by this prophet. John had enjoined them to flee the wrath to come (3:7) and had warned of a pruning of the people (3:9) and a winnowing (3:17). So has Jesus delivered oracles of warning, the latest of which was the threat of sudden death unless they repented (13:1-5). The question therefore of how many would be saved is pertinent. It is characteristic of Luke, however, to have Jesus turn a theoretical question into an existential challenge (cf. 10:37). Jesus' listeners are to "struggle" within the time available to squeeze past *hoi polloi* ("the many") to be among those who are saved.

It is difficult to avoid the impression that Luke's further elaboration has some allegorical features. The master of the house who shuts the door has "arisen" to do so, and is called "Lord." Those who join the banquet come from every direction and recline at table with the patriarchs and "all the prophets." Those who did not enter before the door was shut stand outside in bitter frustration and sorrow. A restored people of God enjoys the banquet of the kingdom of God. And some Jews do not take part in it!

This is a prophetic warning that fits precisely within the context of the prophet's first visitation to the people. They must join this remnant people forming around the prophet now. Later may be too late. At this point not even we as readers know that a second chance will be offered. The allegorical character of the pronouncement is accented by the citation from Ps 6:9 in the mouth of the Lord: "depart from me all you workers of wickedness." The psalm concerns a righteous person beset with enemies, and suffering because of them. But the Lord hears the righteous person's prayers, and the enemies are put to shame. The passage offers a narrative interpretation of the psalm, and together they offer an interpretation of the Gospel.

The second pronouncement by Jesus is in response to the message from the Pharisees that Herod seeks to kill him. Our reading of this passage demands an even clearer commitment to the basic rules of literary analysis. Frequently this passage is taken as an indication that Luke's view of the Pharisees was less hostile than that in the other Synoptics. Were they not looking out for his welfare? This position seems to gain strength from the fact that, like so many scenes of Jesus dining with Pharisees, this encounter is unique to Luke. But as we have pointed out before and will see again shortly, the dining scenes are deceptive, for in fact the Pharisees betray hospitality by their hostile attitudes toward Jesus, and the meals inevitably turn into scenes of conflict.

The basic problem for interpretation is evaluating the character of the Pharisees' report. Up to this point, our reliable narrator has given us *no* indication that the Pharisees (as literary characters) have any interest in Jesus. Quite the opposite; they do not accept him as a prophet, and after his attack on them, have a "deep resentment" against him which they put into action by seeking to trap him in what he says (11:53). Furthermore, neither before this scene or after are we given any indication that Herod wants to kill Jesus. Just the opposite: he "seeks to see him." In light of these characterizations, it is imperative that we take the Pharisaic message as intended hostilely, however difficult that may make it for us as readers. If we do not, then we have betrayed the only reliable guide we have to the story as a whole, which are the authorial directions given by the narrator, and must resign ourselves to viewing Luke as a clumsy editor who does not control the very material that he alone chose to include in his narrative.

When we place the encounter within the overall narrative, however, its functions become clear. Just as Luke had reminded us of the violent death Jesus would meet in Jerusalem by mentioning Pilate's murder of Galileans in 13:1, so here he reminds us of the other "king of the earth" (Acts 4:26) who will figure in Jesus' trial. The encounter also prepares for the climactic role to be played by Jerusalem in the story, with the first explicit announcement that it would in fact reject the prophet's visitation, and would therefore also suffer rejection, the abandonment of its house.

Most of all, however, it shows us how emphatically Luke wants the reader to perceive Jesus as "the Prophet" who must meet his death in that city. As the lawyers have been implicated in the death of "prophets and apostles" (11:47-51), so also the city is condemned as "killer of the prophets and stoner of those sent to her (*apestalmenoi*)."

And in this connection, precisely, we discover the malice and hypocrisy of the Pharisaic message. If Jesus "must" (*dei*) suffer in the city, that means it is God's plan, and that he is a prophet. But we have already learned about the lawyers and Pharisees that they reject prophets and "reject God's plan" (7:30). So the message about Herod is in reality a test. If Jesus does seek to save himself, he is exposed as a fraudulent prophet. If he does go on to the city, they will indeed need to confront his claims explicitly and reject them explicitly. Like the ruler of the synagogue who attacks the people for seeking to be healed rather than attack Jesus for healing them, this message is a helpful ploy. They may yet turn Jesus from his appointed path. They do not, of course, succeed.

But in their attempt, we see another decisive stroke in the portrait of these leaders as implacably resistant to this prophet. Jesus' final saying is again a citation from a psalm, this time Ps 117:26 [LXX], which will be fulfilled in his entrance into the city. That psalm will be quoted twice more in the story. Its critical verse, "the stone which the builders rejected has become the cornerstone" will be cited by Jesus (20:17) and also by Peter (Acts 4:11), as sayings of rejection against "those builders" who are leaders of the people.

FOR REFERENCE AND FURTHER STUDY

Denaux, A. "l'Hypocrisie des Pharisiens et le dessein de Dieu: Analyze de lc, xiii, 31-33." *L'Evangile de Luc.* Ed. F. Neirynck (Gembloux: J. Duculot, 1973) 245-285.

Gaston, L. *No Stone on Another: Studies in the Significance of the Fall of Jerusalem in the Synoptic Gospels.* NovTSupp 23; Leiden: Brill, 1970.

Hoffmann, P. "*Pantes ergatai adikias*: Redaktion und Tradition im Lc 13, 22-30." *ZNW* 58 (1967) 188-214.

Weinert, F. D. "Luke, the Temple, and Jesus' Saying about Jerusalem's Abandoned House." *CBQ* 44 (1982) 68-76.

Zeller, D. "Das Logion Mt 8,11f/Luke 13,28f und das Motiv des 'Völkerwallfahrt.' " *BZ* 15 (1971) 222-237; 16 (1972) 84-93.

42. *Conflict at Table* (14:1-14)

1. He went into the house of one of the rulers of the Pharisees on a Sabbath to eat a meal. They had him under close scrutiny. 2. There was in front of him a certain man with dropsy. 3. Jesus responded by saying to the lawyers and Pharisees, "Is it allowed to heal on the Sabbath or not?" 4. But they were silent. Taking hold of the man he healed him and released him. 5. He said to them, "If a child or an ox of any one of you happens to fall into a pit on the Sabbath, won't you immediately pull it out?" 6. They were not able to reply to these things. 7. He began to speak parabolically to the guests, since he had noticed how they chose the first places. He said to them, 8. "Whenever you are invited by someone to a wedding feast, do not recline at the first place. Perhaps he has invited someone more honorable than you, 9. and the one who invited you both will approach you to say, 'Give your place to this person.' Then with shame you will take the last place. 10. Instead, whenever you are invited, go recline at the last place. Then when your host enters he will say to you, 'My friend! Come up to a higher place!' Then you will enjoy respect in the eyes of all your fellow-guests. 11. For everyone self-exalting will be humbled. Everyone self-humbling will be exalted." 12. He also said to his host, "Whenever you give a luncheon or dinner, stop inviting your friends or your brothers or your family or your rich neighbors. Perhaps they will themselves invite you back, and you will have had repayment in kind. 13. Instead, whenever you give a reception, invite poor people, crippled people, lame people, blind people. 14. And you will be happy that they are not able to repay you, for you will be repaid in the resurrection of the righteous."

NOTES

1. *rulers of the Pharisees*: In Luke-Acts, the "rulers" (*archontes*) form the broadest category of those who oppose the prophet (see 23:13, 35; 24:20; Acts 3:17; 4:5, 8, 26; 13:27). This is the only time the term is used of a Pharisee, and probably refers only to a leader in that sect.

   Sabbath to eat a meal: Is literally, "to eat bread." The setting of the meal has been used for conflict stories before (5:29; 7:36-50; 11:37-53), and the Sabbath has also been a cause of conflict with Pharisees (6:1-5, 6-11) and with the "ruler of the synagogue" (13:10-17). If Jesus eats a meal with a Pharisee on the Sabbath, there surely will be conflict!

   close scrutiny: The verb *paratēreō* has the nuance of "hostile observation," which is clearly the case here and in 6:7; 20:20 and Acts 9:24.

2. *man with dropsy*: This healing story is unique to Luke. The Greek sentence begins with "Behold" (*idou*), which functions here exactly as it does in 2:25; 5:12, 18; 7:12, 37; 10:25; 13:11. The English word "dropsy" derives from hydropsie, which is straight from the Greek word *hydrōpikos*. The condition is a swelling due to an excess of fluid, now more commonly called edema.

   lawyers and Pharisees: The adversarial character of the scene is immediately apparent from this full listing (see 7:29-30, and esp. 11:37-54).

3. *is it allowed*: The form of the question is similar to that in 6:9, except that there it was posed in terms of life and death; see also 13:10-17.

4. *they were silent*: The verb used is *hēsychazō*, "to remain quiet." The response is strange not only because silence was generally taken for consent in legal affairs (Cicero, *De Inventione* 1, 32, 54: "*taciturnitas imitatur confessionem*"), but also because the rabbinic testimony is quite clear in disallowing healing on the Sabbath (compare the note on 13:14).

5. *child or an ox*: This translation changes the order of clauses in the Greek. The listing of a "child" (literally, "son," *huios*) here is puzzling. Why would the case of a child be linked with that of an ox, especially since the ass (*onos*) and ox (*bous*) are so often linked in legal consideration (see the note on 13:15)? Early copyists saw the problem and corrected the text to "ass." But the principles of text criticism demand taking the reading of the earliest and best manuscripts as well as the "hardest" reading (the one least likely to be the result of scribal correction). For better or worse, then, the translation follows the best critical text, with "child." The rendering "happens to fall" aims at capturing the future tense in the Greek.

   immediately pull it out: The discussion in *bT Shab.* 117b is ambiguous concerning what should be done if an animal and its young fall into a pit on the Sabbath. The rabbis agree that the older animal can be taken out at once, and be slaughtered. Some disagreement exists on whether the young one must be kept in the pit and cared for until the Sabbath is over, or whether it can be taken up as well. The Qumran sect was more decisive: "No man shall assist a beast to give birth on the Sabbath day. And if it should fall into a cistern or pit, he shall not lift it out on the Sabbath" (*CD* 11:13-14).

7. *began to speak parabolically*: Is literally, "he began to speak a parable (*parabolē*) to them"; what follows, however, is not a narrative (or at least not until 14:16), but an apparent direct discourse with a deeper level of meaning.

   since he had noticed: The participle *epechōn* is causal: since he "grasped [with his mind] how." Both parties are obviously observing closely!

   chose the first places: Here is the part of the attack on the Pharisees that Luke omitted in 11:43, although it is present in Matt 23:6: *prōtoklisias en tois deipnois* ("first places at banquets"). Luke uses the same term here, *prōtoklisia*, and may have worked up this scene on the basis of the saying he found in Q.

   he said to them: That is, the guests (*hoi keklēmenoi*). We are to understand that they are the "lawyers and Pharisees" identified in 14:3.

8. *wedding feast*: The kind of feast is apparently not significant, since Luke uses *gamous* here, *aristos* and *deipnon* in 14:12. In the parable that follows, Luke will again use *deipnon*, whereas Matt 22:2-14 has *gamous*. The sentence beginning "perhaps" breaks up a Greek dependent clause beginning with *mēpote*, "lest."

9. *with shame*: The concepts of "shame" (*aischynē*) and "honor" (*doxa*) are profoundly important in Hellenistic culture and a strong motivation for action (e.g., Epictetus, *Discourses* 3, 7, 27–36; 3, 18, 6–7; *Frag.* 14). For the significance of assigning places at a banquet, compare *The Letter of Aristeas* 183–187; Plutarch, *Table-Talk* 1:2 (*Mor.* 615–619); Petronius, *Satyricon* 38, 70; Juvenal, *Satires*, 5:16-19; 11:129-132; Jas 2:1-3.

10. *my friends*: As so often in his narrative, Luke appreciates the subtleties of the conventions of friendship in the Hellenistic world. To be greeted as "friend" and invited higher suggests a special intimacy and, more than that, equality with the host (cf. Aristotle, *Nichomachean Ethics* 8, 5, 5).

11. *everyone self-exalting will be humbled*: Making this statement gender inclusive creates some awkwardness but no loss in accuracy. As with other such formulations, the passive voice suggests, in the biblical idiom, "God will humble." Lowly mindedness or humility (*tapeinophrosynē*) was regarded by Hellenistic moralists as a vice not a virtue (e.g., Epictetus, *Discourses* 1, 9, 10; 3, 24, 56). It is a distinctively Christian virtue widely attested in the NT writings (cf. Matt 11:29; Rom 12:16; Eph 4:2; Phil 2:3; Col 3:12; 2 Cor 11:7; Acts 20:19; Jas 4:6), reflecting the experience of a lowly Savior (Phil 2:8). Some version of this idea of "being humbled in order to be exalted" is found in Matt 18:4 and 23:12; Jas 4:6 and 10; 1 Pet 5:6. It has particular thematic force within Luke-Acts as part of the divine reversal (Luke 1:48, 52; 3:5; 10:15; 14:11; 18:14; Acts 2:33; 5:31).

12. *stop inviting your friends*: This is said to the host, whom we know is a chief Pharisee. We should therefore take the negation of the present imperative seriously as a correction: *stop* inviting.

    perhaps they will themselves invite you back: The construction in Greek is the same as in verse 8, *mēpote* with the subjunctive: "lest they invite you." The "themselves" is awkward but the *autoi* is intensive and balances the *antikaleō* ("invite back").

repayment in kind: Translates *antapodoma soi* ("a reward for you" or "a gift back to you"). The translation captures the spirit of the *do ut des* character of Hellenistic social life.

13. *instead, whenever you give a reception*: Luke uses still a fourth term for a gala in addition to *gamous, aristos,* and *deipnon*. Now it is *dochē*, which is properly a reception. No distinction between the terms seems intended.

    invite poor people: The word "people" is supplied for each phrase by the translation. The poor (*ptōchous*), crippled (*anapeirous*), lame (*chōlous*) and blind (*typhlous*) will reappear in the parable that follows (14:21). The lame, blind and poor are also in the list of 7:22. The lame, blind, and crippled, in turn, are excluded from the priesthood by Lev 21:17-21. At Qumran, these disqualifications were extended to exclusion from the Holy War of the end-time (1QM 7:4) and even from participation in the eschatological banquet (1QSa 2:5-6). Note that Luke uses "poor" as a blanket term for all those marginalized in the people.

14. *happy that they are not able to repay*: This is the 13th occurrence of a macarism in Luke's Gospel, but this time it is better translated as "happy" than "blessed" because of the way it introduces the noun clause, "that they are not able." Care for the outcast is a reason for reward in the future age. For the resurrection of both righteous and unrighteous, see Dan 12:2-3. Belief in the resurrection was a Pharisaic tenet, as we learn from Josephus, *Jewish War* 2:163, as well as Acts 23:6. In Acts 24:15, Luke has Paul declare that belief in the resurrection of the "just and unjust" was held by the Jews who opposed him. Note the pertinence of the remark concerning the future judgment after the eschatological saying in 13:29. The point of this saying is the same as in 6:32-35.

INTERPRETATION

One of the common settings for philosophical discussions in Hellenistic literature was the banquet. From the time of Xenophon and Plato, the *Symposium* became in effect a literary form; the eating and drinking provided only the context for sometimes serious and sometimes frivolous discussions of life. The tradition is carried on in the six books of *Table Talk* by Plutarch (*Mor.* 612C-748D). In Jewish literature the form is represented by the *Letter of Aristeas*, with this difference: that the sages are Jewish teachers and their wisdom is illustrated by their devotion to Torah. It is part of Luke's presentation of Jesus as a philosopher as well as a prophet, therefore, to have him so often at table. The fullest expression of this presentation is in the present chapter, although the Lukan version of the Last Supper (22:14-38) also shows traces of the symposium tradition.

In contrast to the normal philosophical drinking party, however, the scene Luke draws is more somber. First of all, we see that he is eating with a chief Pharisee, and that his fellow guests are "lawyers and Pharisees." The fact that the meal takes place on the Sabbath also alerts us to trouble. And in case we do not pick up these signals, the narrator informs us that the guests had Jesus "under close scrutiny," an expression that connotes a hostile preparedness. We are asked to remember that it was precisely these people who had a fixed grudge against Jesus and were lying in wait to trap him in what he said (11:53-54). As in the "warning" to Jesus in the previous pericope (13:31-35), therefore, this pharisaic "invitation" is hypocritical.

The possibility for conflict is set at once with the appearance of a man suffering from dropsy. Once more Jesus is faced with the issue of healing on the Sabbath (cf. 13:10-17). Was this person a guest, or someone who happened by? The story does not tell us, although we might suspect that if his edema was so obvious as to be noticed, he would be regarded as impure because of the Levitical strictures concerning "swellings" that were associated with leprosy (Lev 13:2). When Jesus poses the question of healing on the Sabbath, his fellow-guests—lawyers, remember—express no opinion.

So Jesus heals, then poses the legal argument to them: if their halachic practice allows them to help an animal in a pit on the Sabbath, why can't they respond to a person in need? Their response, of course, would be much like that of the ruler of the synagogue: the man's condition was chronic, not acute; he could come other days to be healed; the Sabbath is too important to break for such nonemergency healings. But they do not answer, and instead of continuing to flail at that issue (on which the positions had been closed anyway from the beginning), Jesus turns to the attack as he had in 11:37. Because of the conflict established by the introduction and this opening story, it is impossible to read what follows as purely neutral "table talk." We are asked to read between the lines of apparently banal advice to discover a prophetic message.

In fact, the narrator helps us evaluate the tone of Jesus' words by his introduction (14:7). Jesus began speaking about places at table because he saw their practice of seeking the first places. Because of the advantage given by our Synoptic analysis, we can recognize that Luke has transposed to narrative the attack on "lawyers and Pharisees" (found in Matt 23:6) that they sought the "first places at banquets."

At first Jesus' words seem to fit within the common sense wisdom of the ancient world concerning etiquette. Proverbs 25:6-7 advises, "Do not put yourself forward in the king's presence or stand in the place of the great; for it is better to be told, 'Come up here' than to be put lower in the presence of the prince" (see also Sir 3:17-20 and *Aboth de R. Nathan* 25). The advice Jesus gives appears only to add the peculiarly Hellenistic resonances of "shame" and "honor." And if we were to stop at this point, we might rightly view this wisdom teaching of Jesus as utterly banal, a minor bit of advice within an accepted cultural system.

It is only when we come to the concluding line that we recognize the subversive and indeed "parabolic" character of Jesus' words: when read in the context of Luke's Gospel as a whole, with its consistent theme of divine reversal, they take on a much more powerful significance: all those who exalt themselves will be humbled, and all those who humble themselves will be exalted. It is not the *appropriate way to get exalted* that Jesus addresses, but the frame of mind that seeks exaltation in any fashion. His advice therefore is "parabolic" because it parodies the "good advice" of worldly wisdom only to subvert it by the more radical demand of the kingdom. His advice to these Pharisees (whom Luke has already identified as "seeking to justify themselves" in 10:29 and will do so again in 16:15) is parabolic/parodic precisely because it issues only in "respect in the eyes of all your fellow guests." But the passives of "will be humbled" and "will be exalted" indicate the action of God, not of other humans.

This challenge to conventional patterns of reciprocity is made obvious in Jesus' rebuke to their habit of inviting to banquets those who could respond in kind (14:12-14). Jesus proposes instead the measure of the kingdom. The Gospel is proclaimed to the outcast, the blind, lame and poor (7:22). These are the people they should invite. They are to "be compassionate as your father is compassionate" (6:36). And if they are, then they will be rewarded by God rather than by other humans. This "measure of the kingdom" that Jesus imposes on their practice of hospitality provides the transition to the next section.

FOR REFERENCE AND FURTHER STUDY

Degenhardt, H.-J. *Lukas Evangelist der Armen* (Stuttgart: Katholisches Bibelwerk, 1965) 97–113.

Malina, B. J. *The New Testament World: Insights from Cultural Anthropology* (Atlanta: John Knox Press, 1981) 25–50.

de Meeus, X. "Composition de Luc XIV et genre symposiaque." *ETL* 37 (1961) 847–70.

Moxnes, H. *The Economy of the Kingdom* (Philadelphia: Fortress, 1988) 127–138.

Smith, D. E. "Table-Fellowship As a Literary Motif in the Gospel of Luke." *JBL* 106 (1987) 613–638.

Ziesler, J. A. "Luke and the Pharisees." *NTS* 25 (1979) 146–157.

43. *Invitations to the Banquet* (14:15-35)

15. One of those reclining at the banquet heard these things and said to him, "Happy is the person who will eat bread in the kingdom of God!" 16. But Jesus said to him: "A certain man gave a great feast. He invited many people. 17. He sent his servant at the time of the banquet to say to those invited, 'Come! It is already prepared!' 18. But every one of them made an excuse not to come. The first said to him, 'I bought a field and must go out and inspect it. I ask you to consider me excused.' 19. Another said, 'I bought five yoke of oxen. I am going to test them. I ask you to consider me excused.' 20. Another said, 'I have married a wife. For this reason I cannot come.' 21. The servant returned. He announced these things to his master. Then the master of the household grew angry. He said to his servant, 'Go out quickly into the streets and lanes of the city. Bring the poor people and the crippled people and the blind people and the lame people here.' 22. The servant said, 'Master, what you have ordered has been done. But there is still room.' 23. So the master said to the servant: 'Go into the roads and the paths and make people come, so that my house will be full. 24. For I tell you, none of those men I first invited will taste my banquet.' " 25. Now considerable crowds were accompanying him. He turned and spoke to them: 26. "If anyone comes toward me and does not hate father and mother and wife and children and brothers and sisters—even one's own life, that person cannot be my disciple. 27. Whoever does not bear one's own cross and come after me cannot be my disciple. 28. For who of you wishing to build a tower does not first sit down and figure out the price, to see if there are enough funds to complete the work? 29. Otherwise, if one lays the foundation but is not able to finish, everyone seeing it will begin to mock that person. 30. They will say, 'This person began to build but was not able to finish!' 31. Or what king going out against another king to engage in battle will not sit down first to deliberate whether it is possible with ten thousand soldiers to engage the one coming at him with twenty thousand? 32. And if not, he sends a delegation while his opponent is still far off to arrange a truce. 33. Such therefore is the case with all of you. If you do not relinquish all your possessions you cannot be my disciple. 34. Salt therefore is a good thing. But if even the salt goes insipid, with what will it be seasoned? 35. It is fit neither for the ground nor for the manure pile. It is tossed out. Let the one with ears to hear listen."

NOTES

15. *happy is the person who will eat bread*: That is, take part in the eschatological banquet, mentioned already in 13:29. "Happy" picks up the *makarios* ("blessed") in verse 14 and is in some sense a response: but whereas Jesus had spoken of a reward given to those who invite outcasts, this guest (by context one of the Pharisees) speaks with the assurance of a participant.

16. *gave a great feast*: The same word, *deipnon*, underlies both "feast" and "banquet" in the translation. The parable of 14:16-24 is paralleled by Matt 22:1-14 (in which it is a wedding feast for a king's son), and the *Gospel of Thomas* 64 (in which it is an attack against "buyers and sellers").

18. *made an excuse*: Just as the servant is sent out three times (vv. 17, 22, 23), so Luke has three examples of excuses. In Matt 22:3-4 there is a first refusal, then a series of excuses which ends with the murder of the servant.

    I bought a field: In Deut 20:5-7, there are three legitimate reasons listed for not participating in a holy war: building a house and not yet inhabiting it (20:5); planting a vineyard and not yet tasting its fruit (20:6); and marrying without yet having consummated the marriage (20:7). These excuses are elaborated in *m.Sotah* 8:1-6. Here, the purchase of the field is roughly equivalent to the second of these reasons.

19. *I bought five yoke of oxen*: This is not one of the reasons listed in Deut 20:5-7. The most striking element in this excuse is the wealth of the person making it, for ten oxen represented a great investment.

20. *I have married a wife*: This is the one excuse that matches perfectly the reason given in Deut 20:7 (and again in Deut 24:5) for not attending a holy war.

21. *master of the household grew angry*: The anger (*orgistheis*) is found also in Matt 22:7, but there it is expressed by the king's destroying "those murderers" and burning their city. This gives Matthew's version a political note similar to that found in Luke's parable of the pounds (19:11-27).

    poor . . . crippled . . . blind . . . lame: These are the same categories of people Jesus told the Pharisees they ought to start inviting to their banquets (14:13). Matt 22:9 has only "invite whomever you may find." The list is also lacking from *Gospel of Thomas* 64 and reflects Luke's thematic interests. The "streets and lanes" translate *plateiai kai rhymai* which appear together also in Isa 15:3.

23. *roads and the paths*: Without the modifier "of the city" as in the previous command, we picture these people in more rural regions. The term *phragmos* properly denotes a fence or hedge (as in Mark 12:1; Matt 21:33; Eph 2:14), thus the frequent translation, "hedgerows." The servant is literally sent out to fetch the "street people" without discrimination.

24. *will taste my banquet*: The word "taste" (*geusetai*) in the future echoes "eat bread" in the future tense (*phagetai*) in verse 15. From this point on, Matthew's parable goes in a completely different direction (Matt 22:11-14). Since the Greek text has *andres* ("men"), the translation follows suit.

25. *considerable crowds*: Luke uses the plural of *ochlos* ("crowd"). As in 12:1, the size of the following populace is emphasized, pointing the way toward the entry into Jerusalem.

26. *hate father and mother*: The language here is very strong, and Matt 10:37 softens it to "love more than." The term "hate" (*misein*) is the opposite of "love" (*agapaō*; cf. 1:71; 6:23, 27). The terms denote attitudes and modes of action, not emotions. The point is not how one feels toward parents and family but one's effec-

tive attitude when it comes to a choice for the kingdom; the choice involved in the terms is clear from 16:13. Note as well that this list includes those invited by Pharisees to their banquets (14:12). The point of the extended list is much like that in the saying concerning division in households (12:49-53). See also the demands of discipleship in 9:59-62, with the note there.

even one's own life: Luke uses *psychē* (literally "soul") here in the way he does in 12:20-24. Matt 10:37 omits this element in his parallel version of the saying.

27. *bear one's own cross*: The awkward use of "one" throughout this saying represents a compromise for the sake of inclusive language; the Greek has "his" throughout. Luke's version here has two special points of emphasis. The use of the term "bear" (*bastazō*) rather than Matthew's "accept" (*lambano*) stresses the continuing character of discipleship. Compare "the cross every day" in 9:23. Similarly, Luke uses *heautou* ("one's own"), stressing the need for a personal acceptance of the role.

cannot be my disciple: Matt 10:38 has "is unworthy of me," but Luke throughout this section emphasizes the notion of "discipleship." Note the use of *mathētēs* in 9:14, 16, 18, 40, 43, 54; 10:22, 23; 11:1; 12:1, 22).

28. *to build a tower*: This parable is found only in Luke's Gospel. The calculation of cost is perfectly suited to the point of the previous saying: don't start if there is not a willingness to expend all one has, including life itself.

31. *king going out against another king*: This parable also is found only in Luke, and recalls the "battle between kingdoms" suggested by 11:18-20. The point is slightly different: calculate the chances of success before starting.

arrange a truce: Is literally "ask for the things leading to peace" (*eirēnē*).

33. *such, therefore, is the case*: The translation breaks up a longer Greek sentence, maintaining the second person in the second sentence rather than shifting to the third person as the second clause in Greek does.

relinquish all your possessions: The verb is literally "bid farewell to" as in 9:61. For "possessions" (*ta hyparchonta*), see also 8:3; 11:21; 12:15, 33, 44; 16:1; 19:8). "You cannot be my disciple" precisely echoes verse 26.

34. *salt therefore is a good thing*: This translation takes seriously the "therefore" (*oun*) as a deliberate connection to the foregoing sayings. As in 11:33-36, Luke adds a saying that in Matthew forms part of the sermon on the mount (Matt 5:13; cf. also Mark 9:49-50), as a commentary on his own previous discourse. The parabolic character of the statement is revealed by the concluding admonition, "let the one with ears to hear listen" (compare 8:8).

goes insipid: Is *mōranthē*, which means literally to "grow foolish." Salt is to food as wisdom is to life.

35. *it is fit*: Meaning it cannot be put to any useful purpose. Salt has a specific function; when it loses its ability to season it is good for nothing.

it is tossed out: Is literally "they throw it out," which uses the third person plural for the passive, as in 12:20. Note again how Luke ends with his characteristic warning of rejection.

INTERPRETATION

This passage is really part of the same scene as 14:1-14, and is discussed separately only for the practical purpose of keeping units of analysis manageable. Jesus is still at table with his foes; he has finished rebuking them for their practices concerning choosing seats and inviting guests, reminding them that the kingdom holds them to a higher standard. The transition to the present section is made by the exclamation by one of the Pharisees (as we must understand him to be from the context) concerning the "happiness" of those who participate in the eschatological banquet. Rather than confirm that judgment, Jesus turns it into another parable of rejection. Nothing at this meal can go right for the Pharisees!

Since some version of this parable is shared by Matthew and the Coptic *Gospel of Thomas*, we able are by means of comparison to see more clearly what Luke's precise purposes are. The version in *Gospel of Thomas* 64, of course, lacks any narrative context, since the Gospel consists only of sayings. The theme of possessions is there very much to the forefront: four excuses are given, and all but one involve some entanglement in monetary matters; the master sends the servant out to the streets to invite "whom you find" to the banquet. The parable appropriately concludes with the statement that "buyers and merchants will not enter the places of my Father." The moral immediately raises the story to the level of a commentary on Jesus' message from God.

In Matthew, as the notes have indicated, a king gives a wedding feast for his son. The excuses are less elaborated, and the focus clearly is on the overall rejection of the invitation, which leads to massive retaliation by the king. Because those first invited "were not worthy," the servants were sent to gather "as many as you find." Most strikingly, Matthew includes a second scene in which those included in the feast are once more judged on the basis of whether they wore a wedding garment (Matt 22:11-14). Although this appendix serves as a teaching to the Matthean Church, it is clear from Matthew's placement of the parable that he too regards the whole as a parable of rejection aimed at those who rejected Jesus (notice the framing in Matt 21:45 and 22:15).

In Luke's version, the reader's attention is caught by the threefold excuses and the threefold invitations. Consideration of these patterns brings us closer to Luke's point. What is the background and what is the nature of the excuses made by those first invited? The background may be provided—as has often been suggested before—by the notion of holy war in Israel. Those who had just planted a vineyard or built a house or married a bride were excused from participation in a holy war, according to Deut 20:5-7. The fit is not perfect in Luke's parable, but it is suggestive, particularly since in 14:13 the list of those "poor, crippled, blind, lame" to be in-

vited to the banquet are listed in the Qumran writings as excluded both from
the eschatological holy war and from the eschatological banquet.

But if Jesus is imaging the banquet which is the kingdom of God, then
these excuses are in any case inappropriate. Even the *m.Sotah* which
elaborates these reasons for not going to war concludes by making a distinction between wars of free choice and a holy war in which all must go,
"even the bridegroom out of his chamber and the bride out of her bride
chamber" (*m.Sotah* 8:7). If it is truly the call of God, in other words, such
excuses do not apply. Furthermore, this is not a war or a banquet that they
are being invited to, but the kingdom itself.

This then brings us to the nature of the excuses. They reveal an entanglement in one's own possessions and relationships that closes one even
to a prophetic imperative. They had been invited; they had agreed to come;
now the feast is ready, and they beg off. Not for reasons of compelling urgency, but because they are looking to their own interests rather than the
call from the Other.

The threefold invitation, in turn, makes the parable a fairly transparent
allegory of Luke's narrative as a whole. The first invitation we are to understand as coming to the "righteous" ones of the people. But it turns out they
"already have their consolation" (6:24), and find their own pursuits more
important than the prophet's call. The second invitation goes out to the "outcast of the people," the same blind, lame, crippled and poor people that
Jesus has identified in 7:22 as the special targets for the proclamation of the
good news. But there is still room, so the invitation goes beyond "the city"
to the byways of a wider region. By this we must understand the extension
of the invitation to become part of God's people to the Gentiles, which will
unfold in the narrative of Acts. Thus will the banquet be made full. We find
here the same point as in the previous parable of the banquet in 13:28-30.
People will come from every corner to recline with the patriarchs at the banquet, "but you will be cast out."

It is worth emphasizing here, however, that "those men first invited"
who will not taste the banquet in Luke's version (14:24) must be understood
as the Pharisees and lawyers who actively reject the prophet. This is not
a parable of the rejection of the Jews as such, because the "poor and outcast" who come into the banquet are themselves Jews, however much they
have been marginalized. It is a parable of rejection told to the leaders and
intended for the leaders.

We have seen that it is Luke's consistent pattern in this journey of the
Prophet to Jerusalem to alternate sayings of rejection, with calls to conversion, with teachings on discipleship. Having told this parable of rejection
to the leaders in which an overinvolvement with possessions and relationships closes those invited to the call of God, Luke has Jesus "turn to the
crowds" (14:25) and repeat the same warning for those who would wish

to follow him. The need to relativize all relationships is stated in 14:26 (corresponding to the man who married a wife and could not come in 14:20), and the requirement of "relinquishing all possessions" is stated in 14:33 (corresponding to those who refused the invitation because of field and cattle in 14:18-19). Between these stark statements, Luke includes the two parables (unique to his Gospel) of the careful calculators. The lesson of each is accessible: don't start if you can't finish. And heading these parables, the most fundamental demand of all: what is required of discipleship is bearing one's own cross and following in the path of the prophetic Messiah (14:27).

The parable of the banquet and the demands of discipleship together make the same point: the call of God issued by the prophet must relativize all other claims on life. The parable shows how entanglement with persons and things can in effect be a refusal of the invitation. The demands make clear that the choice for discipleship demands precisely the choice against a complete involvement in possessions or people. There is little that is gentle or reassuring in this. But as the final saying on salt suggests, any mode of discipleship that tries to do both things, tries to be defined both by possessions and by the prophet's call, will be like salt without savor, fit for nothing much. "It is tossed out."

For Reference and Further Study

Bailey, K. E. "The Great Banquet (Luke 14:15-24)." *Through Peasant Eyes: More Lukan Parables* (Grand Rapids: Eerdmans, 1980) 88-113.

Ballard, P. H. "Reasons for Refusing the Great Supper." *JTS* 23 (1972) 341-50.

Dupont, J. "Renoncer à tous ses biens (Lc 14, 33)." *NRT* 93 (1971) 561-582.

Nauck, W. "Salt As a Metaphor in Instructions for Discipleship." *ST* 6 (1952) 165-178.

Sanders, J. A. "The Ethic of Election in Luke's Great Banquet Parable." *Essays in Old Testament Ethics*. Eds. J. L. Crenshaw and J. T. Willis (New York: KTAV, 1974) 245-271.

Thackeray, H. St-J. "A Study in the Parable of the Two Kings." *JTS* 14 (1913) 389-399.

44. *Parables of Lost and Found* (15:1-32)

1. All the tax-agents and the sinners were coming to hear him. 2. But the Pharisees and the scribes complained. They said, "This person welcomes sinners and eats with them." 3. He spoke this parable to them: 4. "Which one of you having a hundred sheep but losing one of them will not leave the ninety-nine in the open and go after the lost sheep until he finds it? 5. Once he has found it, he puts it on his shoulders rejoicing. 6. He goes to his house and gathers his friends and neighbors. He says to them: 'Rejoice with me! I have found my lost sheep!' 7. In the same way, I tell you, there will be more joy in heaven at one sinner's repentance than at ninety-nine righteous people who do not need repentance. 8. Or suppose a woman has ten drachmas and loses one of them. Will she not light a lamp and sweep the house and search carefully until she finds it? 9. And when she finds it, she gathers her women friends and neighbors. She says, 'Rejoice with me! I have found my lost drachma!' 10. Such, I tell you, is the joy among God's angels at the conversion of a single sinner." 11. He also said, "A certain man had two sons. 12. The younger one said to his father, 'Father, give me the share of the property coming to me.' So he divided the property between them. 13. Not many days later, the younger son gathered everything together and left the country for a distant region. In that place, because he lived without control, he went through all of his possessions. 14. When he had spent everything, a powerful famine fell over that land. He himself began to grow hungry. 15. He hired himself out to one of the citizens of that region who sent him to the fields to tend the pigs. 16. He longed to be filled from the husks that the pigs were eating! But no one gave him any. 17. He came to his senses and said, 'All my father's workers have more than enough food, yet here am I perishing in a famine. 18. I will get up, go to my father and say to him, "Father, I have sinned against heaven and before you! 19. I am no longer worthy to be called your son! Treat me as one of your workers!" ' 20. So he went towards his father. While he was still a long way off, his father saw him. He was moved with compassion. He ran out and embraced him and kissed him. 21. His son said to him, 'Father, I have sinned against heaven and before you. I am no longer worthy to be called your son.' 22. His father said to his slaves, 'Quick, take out the best robe and put it on him! Put a ring on his finger! Put sandals on his feet! 23. Take out the fatted calf and kill it! Let us eat and celebrate! 24. This is my son! He was dead and has come back to life! He was lost and has been found!' So they began to celebrate. 25. Now his older son was in the field. As he approached the house, he heard music and dancing. 26. He called over one of the servants and questioned him what might these things be. 27. He said to him, 'Your brother has come! Your father has killed the fatted calf because he has welcomed him back safely.' 28. He grew angry and did not even want to go in. But his father went out to him. He comforted him. 29. But he answered his father, 'Look, I am slaving for you all these years, and I never ignored your rules. Yet you never even gave me a goat that I might celebrate with my friends! 30. But when

your son here comes, who has devoured his livelihood with whores, you kill the fatted calf!' 31. But he said to him, 'My child, you are always with me and everything that is mine is yours. 32. But it was necessary to celebrate and rejoice, because this brother of yours was dead and has come back to life, was lost and has been found.' "

NOTES

1. *tax-agents and sinners*: For these characters, see especially the note on 7:29-30. The opening sentences set the framework for the entire chapter. The purpose clause, "to hear (*akouō*) him" identifies this group as responding to the final challenge in the previous chapter, "let the one with ears to hear listen (*akouō*)" (14:35). For "hearing" as a sign of conversion, see 5:1, 15; 6:17, 27, 47, 49; 7:29; 8:8-18, 21; 9:35; 10:16, 24, 39; 11:28, 31. These outcast ones are becoming members of the restored people by responding to the prophet.

2. *Pharisees and scribes*: Luke often uses "lawyers" with the "Pharisees" (see 14:3 above), but sometimes uses the traditional combination. These verses recapitulate 7:29-30: sinners and tax-agents "hear" the prophet, while "scribes and Pharisees" complain about him. The scribes and Pharisees were shown "grumbling" (*gonguzō*) against Jesus' disciples in 5:30; they "observed Jesus suspiciously" (*paratēreō*) in 6:7 and 14:1; they "formed a deep grudge" against him in 11:53. The term used here, *diagonguzō*, (also in 19:7), suggests a public remonstrance as well as a private grumble, especially recalling the complaints of the wilderness generation against Moses and Aaron (see Exod 15:24; 16:2, 7-8; 17:3; Num 14:2, 36; 16:11; Deut 1:27; cf. also 1 Cor 10:10).

   welcomes sinners and eats with them: Luke uses the term *prosdechomai* only in a positive sense. Elsewhere it refers more to *expecting* God's visitation (cf. 2:25, 38; 12:36; 23:5; Acts 24:15). The charge of eating and drinking with tax-agents and sinners was first voiced by the Pharisees in 5:30 and is reported again by Jesus in 7:34. For the implication of the charge in the ancient world, see the note on 5:30.

3. *this parable to them*: The first of these three parables is paralleled by Matt 18:12-14 and the *Gospel of Thomas* 107.

4. *losing one of them*: In Matt 18:12 it is the sheep who "wanders off" (*planaō*), but in Luke the key terms "losing" (*apollymi*) and "finding" (*heuriskō*) run through all three parables. Luke has the rest of the flock left "in the open" (*erēmō*) rather than on the mountain, and has the shepherd seek "until he finds it," whereas Matthew makes the finding more hypothetical (18:13). In *Gospel of Thomas* 107 the sheep that went astray is "the largest," which supplies a motivation for the search. This translation keeps the masculine pronouns because the second parable matches the male example with a female one.

5. *puts it on his shoulders*: Matthew lacks this picturesque note which may reflect actual practice as shown in some examples of ancient statuary. Here and in the following stories, Luke shows a strong tactile awareness.

6. *gathers his friends and neighbors*: This also is lacking in Matthew's version. Notice how this picks up "friends and rich neighbors" in the previous passage (14:12). In *Gospel of Thomas* 107, the shepherd addresses the sheep itself, "I love you more than the ninety-nine." The exhortation to others is also repeated in the following parables (15:9, 23-24). The joy in human fellowship mirrors that in heaven.

7. *righteous people who do not need repentance*: For repentance or conversion (*metanoia*) as a theme in Luke-Acts, see the note on 3:3. Jesus expresses his mission in 5:32 as "I did not come to call righteous people, but sinners to repentance." The same terms are used as in this verse. Matt 18:14 concludes with, "it is not the will of your Father that any of these little ones be lost." The note of repentance is distinctive to Luke.

8. *or suppose a woman*: The translation turns a question, "what woman having ten drachmas . . ." into a hypothetical statement in order to break up the complex Greek sentence. It is typical of Luke to match a male example with one involving a woman (cf. 1:6-7; 2:36-38; 4:25, 38; 7:11-15, 36-50; 8:1-3, 19-21, 43-56; 10:38-42; 11:27; 13:10-17). The story is not found in the other Gospels. Luke's characteristic attention to the use of possessions is also obvious.

   until she finds it: The structure of the story is exactly the same as the first: the losing, the search, the finding, the calling of friends and neighbors (female in this case), the invitation to rejoice.

10. *among God's angels*: Is the equivalent of "in heaven" in the previous story (v. 7). The "angels of God" are pictured as part of the heavenly court also in 2:13-15; 9:26; 12:8-9. In Luke's story, they mainly function as messengers from God to humans (1:11, 26; 2:9; 22:43; 24:23; Acts 8:26; 10:3; 12:7; 27:23).

11. *a certain man had two sons*: This extended parable, virtually a novella, is unique to Luke's Gospel. It amplifies the basic point of the two previous parables. Matthew has a parable of "two sons" that has some thematic resemblance (Matt 21:28-31) but does not really form a parallel version.

12. *share of the property*: Is literally, "the share (*meros*) of the property (*ousia*) that falls (*epiballon*) to me." He is asking for an early distribution of the inheritance (compare 12:13). The basics of Jewish inheritance law are found in Lev 27:8-11 and 36:7-9. For the rabbinic discussion of these, see e.g., *m.Bekh.* 8:1-10, *m.Bab.Bath.* 8:1-9:10. The legal niceties of inheritance here are secondary to storytelling.

13. *left the country for a distant region*: Luke uses the same expression (*chōra makra*), "a distant region" in the parable of the pounds (19:12).

    because he lived without control: The participle is here translated in a causal sense: the way he lived led to his impoverishment. The term *asōtōs* has the sense of carelessness but does not by itself suggest sexual excess, in contrast to the interpretation of the elder brother (15:30).

    went through all of his possessions: The best MSS read *ousia*, "property," here, the same as in verse 12. The action of "scattering" (*diaskorpizein*, cf. 1:53), corresponds to that of "gathering together" (*synagein*) in the previous sentence.

14. *a powerful famine*: Biblical literature suggests that this was a frequent occurrence in an area in which agriculture was always a hazardous enterprise (see LXX Gen 12:10; 26:1; 41:27-47; 42:5; 43:1; 47:4; Ruth 1:1; 1 Kgs 18:2; 2 Kgs 4:38; cf. Luke 4:25 and Acts 11:28).

15. *to tend the pigs*: As in the story of the Gadarene demoniac (8:32), the herd of pigs represents something unclean for Jews (see Lev 11:7; 14:8). Not eating pork becomes a test of fidelity to Torah in the time of the Maccabees (see 1 Macc 1:47; 2 Macc 6:18; 7:1). To tend the pigs of a Gentile is about as alienated as a Jew could imagine being. In the Mishnah, raising pigs is forbidden to Jews (*m.Bab.Qam.* 7:7). The attitude toward Samaritans and pigs alike is captured by the saying of Eliezer, "He that eats the bread of the Samaritans is like to one that eats the flesh of swine" (*m.Shebi* 8:10). One rabbi, at least, considered the craft of shepherding to be equivalent to "the craft of robbers" (*m.Qidd.* 4:14), a view reflected in the legislation of *m.Bab.Qam.* 10:9.

16. *filled from the husks*: The verb *chortazō*, ("fill") is used in the Beatitude of 6:21 and the feeding story of 9:17. The word translated "husks" is *keratia*, literally "little horns," which is the name for the fruit of the carob tree. Some MSS have a longer version, "fill his belly."

17. *came to his senses*: Is literally "came to himself," and the expression means the same as it does in current parlance.
    more than enough food: The verb *perisseuein* is used as it was in 9:17 and 12:15 in the sense of "abounding."

18. *against heaven and before you*: The son repeats the phrase in 15:21. As in 15:7, "heaven" refers to God (see also 6:23; 12:33), and the preposition *eis* is taken to mean "against." The repentance from sin which was the *moral* attached to the first two parables is now *thematic*. The son's statement also nicely captures the way in which the relationship with God and with humans is interconnected, even though we might expect "against you before heaven!" Notice, however, that the son does not specify the nature of his sin, which the elder son is more than eager to do (15:30).

19. *treat me as one of your workers*: The contrast here is between a member of the family (and heir to property) and a *misthios*, a hired laborer with no claim of permanence. Torah required the payment of wages to such workers (Lev 19:13), but not a personal relationship. But even as he requests this lesser status, the son uses the greeting, "Father," which evokes quite a different sort of response.

20. *moved with compassion*: Luke uses the same verb (*splangnizomai*) as was attributed to Jesus in 7:13 and the good Samaritan in 10:33. The initiative is shifted to the father. He sees, feels, runs, embraces and kisses his son. The embrace (literally "fell on his neck") and kiss recall the recognition scene in Gen 45:14-15, where Joseph embraces and kisses Benjamin as his brother, and Gen 46:29 where he greets Jacob as his father. The same gesture occurs in Acts 20:37.

22. *quick, take out the best robe*: These extravagant gestures of acceptance (robe, ring, feast) are initiated by the father *before* the son has time to complete his speech. He does not have the chance to say, "treat me as a worker" (although some

MSS do supply that phrase). At the words "father" and "son," the parent moves into action!

23. *the fatted calf*: Is literally "the grain-fed" (*sitos*). In contrast to the cattle left to graze on grass, the beast destined for special feasts is stuffed with grain to put on extra weight and tenderness. It is a mark of great esteem to spend this valuable possession for a celebration. The phrase occurs in the LXX of Judg 6:25, 28 and Jer 46:21.

   eat and celebrate: Compare the statement of the rich fool in 12:19. The verb *euphrainō*, to celebrate or make merry, runs through the rest of the story (15:24, 29, 32).

24. *dead . . . back to life . . . lost . . . found*: The implications of being lost and found as dying and rising were pointed out in the interpretation of the finding of Jesus in the Temple (Luke 2:46). The theme echoes the two previous parables (15:6, 9). A "son" who dies and is found again cannot but have had deeper resonances for early Christian readers.

27. *welcomed him back safely*: Is literally "in good health" (*hygiainōn*). There is a subtle touch in the phrasing, "your father."

28. *angry and did not even want to go in*: Luke shows considerable psychological sensitivity here. The elder son's anger is expressed by the refusal to go in; the father's love is expressed by his coming out also to meet this elder son.

   comforted him: The verb *parakaleō* has a wide range of possible meanings, from "exhort" (Lk 3:18; Acts 14:22), to "plead" (7:4; 8:31), to "comfort" (16:25; Acts 20:2). The rendering "plead" here makes good sense, especially since the elder son "answers" (15:29). The translation "comforted" emphasizes the emotional note already struck by "felt compassion."

29. *look, I am slaving for you*: The Greek present tense is retained in the translation to give the sense that the son *still* feels bound in slavery. The choice of *douleuō* reveals great bitterness. This son feels lower than the hired hands (*misthioi*); he sees himself as a "slave."

   never ignored your rules: Tries to keep the translation within the bounds of the story, even though the Greek is literally "transgressed your commandments (*entolai*)," which breaks into the allegory implicit throughout this part of the story: the elder son is like righteous Jews who do not "need repentance."

   gave me a goat: The language is again quite bitter; in contrast to the fatted calf is the *eriphos*, ("kid"), a much more common and cheaper commodity. But notice as well that he wanted it to celebrate with "his friends"—not with his father. He is alienated even though he never left home!

30. *your son here*: Is once more very angry in tone and distancing. He does not say, "my brother." The Greek is literally, "this son of yours here, the one who . . .".

   devoured his livelihood with whores: The term *bios* ("livelihood") means roughly the same as *ousia* ("property"): the "means of life." Most remarkable here is the imagination of the elder son, who supplies a lurid version of the younger son's life which the narrative itself had not given. Is there once again something of an echo of the charge made against Jesus, that he also consorted with such folk (7:34, 39)?

31. *everything that is mine is yours*: The father is identifying the elder son as a "friend" with whom everything is held in common (cf. Aristotle, *Politics* 1257a who images the family as a "community of possessions," but even in that context recognizes the difficulties of having common property, 1263a). See also Acts 4:32. The ideal of sharing in this fashion is foreign to the rabbinic tradition. *Pirke Aboth* 5:10, for example, lists four types of people, and the one who says, "what is mine is thine and what is thine is mine" is dismissed as "an ignorant man," literally, an *am-ha-aretz*.

32. *it was necessary*: The same construction is used in 13:16 for the need to liberate the daughter of Abraham who was bound by Satan. For Luke, the recognition of human need and circumstance places an obligation superior to that of law.

    celebrate and rejoice: The addition of *chairō*, "rejoice," links this story once more to the "rejoicing" in the previous two (15:5, 10). Notice as well that the father's use of "this brother of yours" represents a subtle correction of "this son of yours."

INTERPRETATION

The necessary framework for understanding these three parables of the lost is provided in 15:1-2. These verses recapitulate the narrative theme established by 7:29-30 concerning the division within the people in response to the prophet. The tax-agents and sinners represent the outcast and the poor who respond positively. They not only eat with Jesus, they approach to "hear" the prophet. They are becoming part of the people. The Pharisees and scribes (or lawyers) represent those who are powerful and "rich" who reject the prophet's call. We were shown just this in the previous narrative where they turned hospitality into hostile surveillance. In response, Jesus had told them the parable of rejection (14:1-35).

Now, in response to the complaint of the leaders concerning the accessibility of the prophet to these "lost ones," Luke has Jesus tell three stories. They are among the most beautiful in the Gospel tradition, puzzling only because they have both the distinctive note of originality that we associate with Jesus, and the distinctive literary sensibility of Luke. It is however impossible entirely to disentangle tradition from redaction, precisely because Luke covers the traces of his sources so thoroughly. We know, for example, that at least the parable of the lost sheep was part of the shared tradition (Q), since it is found also in Matthew. The parables of the lost coin and the lost son, in contrast, are unique to Luke. But even the story of the lost sheep is different from the version told by Matthew, and fits the precise pattern of the other two stories told by Luke! We cannot, therefore, know whether or to what degree he may have reworked sources for these last two stories.

What we can observe and appreciate are the signs of literary skill now evident in the stories as Luke has arranged them. The first two stories form a perfectly matched pair, in which the theme of losing/finding/rejoicing is identical, and in which the joy of a shepherd finding the lost sheep and the joy of a woman finding her lost money stand as a direct rebuke to the "grumbling" of the scribes and Pharisees concerning Jesus' receptivity to the lost among God's people: they should be joining in the celebration! The contrast between the "joy in heaven" (that is, God's joy), and this human grudging is for the moment left only implicit.

Luke enlivens these examples with wonderful touches. It is characteristic of Luke not only to provide a female example matching that of the male shepherd, but also to have her friends and neighbors who are called to celebrate with her be women. The "lighting of the lamp," and "sweeping the floor," enable the reader to appreciate the anxiety felt at the loss of a carefully amassed treasure.

The shepherd in turn not only finds the lost sheep, he lifts it on his shoulders and carries it home. With this small detail, Luke evokes both the Hellenistic pastoral tradition and the biblical imagery of the shepherd who cares for the sheep (see Ps 23:1-6). This image is sketched most dramatically by the prophet Ezekiel (34:1-24), who castigates the "shepherds of Israel" who do not care for the people, and declares in the voice of the Lord, "Behold, I myself will search for my sheep and seek them out. As a shepherd seeks out his flock when some of his sheep have been scattered abroad, so will I seek out my sheep; and I will rescue them" (34:11). The prophet further promises that God will "set up one shepherd, my servant David, and he shall feed them: he shall feed them and be their shepherd" (34:23).

These two stories build toward the long parable of the lost son, surely with the parable of the good Samaritan among the most interpreted and best loved parables in the Gospels. Rather than focus on the loss and restoration of material possessions, this complex tale concerns personal relationships, with possessions language continuing to provide a symbolic underpinning. Because it gets those relationships so right, with such psychological and spiritual penetration, the parable invites interpretation at many levels.

As in the previous two stories the main character is the one who has experienced the loss, in this case the father. Although he seems a strangely passive and reactive character, and the vividness of the two sons draws us into the complexities of their personal struggles, the structure of the story demands our perception of the father as the main figure. He experiences the loss and the restoration; it is his even-handed compassion and concern that extends to both children. It is he who allows one son to withdraw physically with property, taking the risk that both child and property will be lost forever. It is he also who allows the other son to stay on the land but with bitter alienation, a loss of another sort, harder yet to regain. It is the father whose mercy and openness to both children stands as the emblem of Jesus' prophetic mission from God to restore the people with an open invitation to all.

The first part of the story fits perfectly the pattern of the previous two: the son is lost and found; the father and the household rejoices. What gives the story its peculiar depth is the way Luke invites us into the emotional drama of parent-child conflict. The younger son is heedless, seeking only what is "his own." He takes it without thought for what this might do to others, or to the failure to "honor father and mother" that his departure signifies. Luke also suggests that the dispersal of his possessions in a far land was a loss of himself. His alienation is masterfully suggested by his hiring himself out to be a herder of pigs. His "coming to himself" (a note of interiority so characteristic of the Lukan parables) means a return home.

At this point Luke shifts our attention to the father. He does not abuse the son for his carelessness and selfishness. Indeed, he does not even wait passively for the son to arrive. He runs out to meet him. He embraces and kisses him, recognizing him as son even before the child has a chance to state his repentance. And the father interrupts the careful speech of repentance; at the words "father" and "son," he is already in action, bestowing the choicest signs of honor on the returned son: sandals, robe, ring, fatted calf. So eager, Jesus suggests, is God to receive back those who have wandered from covenant with him. This aspect of the return is made explicit by the use of "dying and rising" language.

What gives this story its true poignancy, however, is the final scene between the father and the elder son. We discover through the dialogue that this son, too, has been alienated from his father, perhaps for an even longer time. He has "slaved" for his father for years. He has never transgressed his commands. But he has also never felt rewarded. And he deeply resents the father's joy at his prodigal brother's return. His rage is expressed in every word and gesture: the refusal to enter the house, the questioning of a servant, his response to his father's attempt at comfort. The anger he has toward the father is deflected onto the younger son, whom he regards as privileged although unworthy. So he exaggerates the younger brother's sin, imagining him as consorting with prostitutes! His language is remarkably revealing of his anger. He has "slaved"; his father never even gave him a "goat" so he could celebrate with "his friends"; whereas "this son of yours" gets all the reward!

The tragedy of the older son is not only that he has failed to recognize his constant position of privilege with his father, that all the time they were together, "they shared goods in common," but also that he is blind even now to the fact that his father extends to him the same constant care and concern as toward the prodigal. But the father comes out to him as well, and comforts him.

If the first part of the story is pure gospel—the lost are being found, the dead rising, and sinners are repenting because of the call of the prophet—then the last part of the story is a sad commentary on the Pharisaic refusal out of envy and resentment to accept this good news extended to the outcast. The allegorical level of meaning is irresistible: they, like the elder son, had stayed within covenant and had not wandered off; they had never broken any of the commandments. But (the story suggests) they regarded themselves not as sons so much as slaves. And they resented others being allowed into the people without cost. The son refusing to come into the house of singing and rejoicing is exactly like those who stand outside the heavenly banquet while many others enter in (13:28-30). And if this all were not obvious from the wording of the final scene, then Luke's compositional frame makes it unmistakable: he told these stories to righteous ones who complained about the prophet accepting sinners (15:1-2).

For Reference and Further Study

Bailey, K. E. *Poet and Peasant: A Literary Cultural Approach to the Parables in Luke* (Grand Rapids: Eerdmans, 1976) 142-206.

Cantinat, J. "Les paraboles de la miséricorde (Lc 15:1-32)," *NRT* 77 (1955) 246-264.

Carlston, C. E. "Reminiscence and Redaction in Luke 15:11-32," *JBL* 94 (1975) 368-390.

Cerfaux, L. "Trois rehabilitations dans l'évangile." *Receuil Lucien Cerfaux* (Gembloux: J. Duculot, 1954), 2: 51-59.

Crossan, J. D., ed., *Polyvalent Narration* (complete issue of *Semeia* 9 [1977] devoted to the parable of Luke 15:11-32).

Jeremias, J. "Tradition und Redaktion in Lukas 15." *ZNW* 62 (1971) 172-189.

45. *Possessions in Parable and Paraenesis* (16:1-13)

1. He began to speak also to the disciples: "There was a certain rich man. He had a household manager who was reported to him as having squandered his possessions. 2. He summoned the manager and said to him, 'What is this I hear about you? Give an account of your administration, for you cannot continue as manager.' 3. The household manager said to himself, 'What shall I do now that my master is taking away from me the administration of the household? I am not strong enough to dig. I am ashamed to beg. 4. I know what I shall do, so that when I am removed from management people will receive me into their homes.' 5. He summoned each one of his master's debtors. He said to the first, 'How much do you owe my master?' 6. He said, 'One hundred containers of oil.' He said to him, 'Take your bill. Sit down quickly. Write fifty!' 7. Then he said to another, 'How much do you owe?' He said, 'One hundred bushels of grain.' He said to him, 'Take your bill. Write eighty!' 8. The master praised the wicked household manager because he acted cleverly. Indeed the children of this age are more clever towards their own generation than are the children of light. 9. I also say to you, make friends for yourselves from the mammon of wickedness so that when it fails they will receive you into eternal tents. 10. The person who is reliable in something tiny is reliable in something greater. The one who is wicked in something tiny is wicked also in something greater. 11. If therefore you have not become reliable in your use of wicked mammon, who will entrust you with the genuine thing? 12. And if you have not become reliable in what belongs to another, who will give you what is your own? 13. No household servant is able to serve two masters. Either a person will hate one and love the other, or will cling to one and despise the other. You cannot serve both God and Mammon."

NOTES

1. *speak also to the disciples*: The previous three parables had been addressed to Jesus' opponents; it is characteristic of Luke's journey narrative that he has Jesus turn to the disciples for instruction. The parable that follows is unique to Luke's Gospel.

household manager: The *oikonomos* is sometimes translated as "steward." He was often himself a slave (cf. 12:42) who managed the household for a "master" (*kyrios*) or "master of the household" (*oikodespotēs*). In this case, the "rich man" of verse 1 is also the "master" of verses 3, 5, 8.

squandered his possessions: As the rest of the story makes clear, this manager had control over the finances of an estate, and is accused not of dispersing his own funds but those of the master. The term *diaskorpizein* is the same one used of the younger son in 15:13. As in the previous story as well, the crisis and need for decision are created by the mismanagement of possessions.

244 *The Gospel of Luke*

2. *give an account of your administration*: The same term, *oikonomia*, is translated here by "administration" and "management." The dismissal is not punitive; an owner cannot afford to have his financial affairs handled by one who has lost money. "Give an account" (*dos logon*) is a frequently used idiom (see Plutarch, *Sayings of Kings and Commanders* Alcibiades 4 [Mor 186E]). The manager has to produce the books for audit.

3. *what shall I do*: Echoes the internal questioning of the rich fool in 12:17-18. See also the question posed by the crowds to John in 3:12 and to Peter in Acts 2:37, "what shall we do?" This is the question Luke thinks appropriate to a crisis. The phrase "now that my master" is literally "because (*hoti*) my master."

4. *people will receive me*: The translation supplies "people" to the third person plural verb; the construction is echoed in 16:9. Notice how the Hellenistic notion of reciprocity of benefit is operative here as in 6:32-35 and 14:12-14.

5. *his master's debtors*: In 7:41, Luke told the short parable of a moneylender (*danistēs*) who forgave two debtors (*chreopheiletai*), the same words as used here. Since we are not informed of the exact relationship of creditor to debtor, we cannot be sure what the manager's actions signified. Were the debtors men who leased land from the master? Or had they taken out a loan which needed repaying? Uncertainty on these points makes an interpretation based solely on later Jewish law—or even customary practice—hazardous.

6. *take your bill . . . write fifty*: The plural form *grammata* (literally "letters") was used for various official forms including title deeds and bills. The adverb "quickly" (*tacheōs*) here perhaps suggests something surreptitious in the manager's maneuvers. This translation uses general terms for the quantities, for the precise amounts are not pertinent to the point of the parable. Is the manager acting in a shady fashion? This depends to some extent on whether his action deprives the master of further funds owed him, which in turn depends on whether he was reducing the principle amount owed, or, as some scholars have suggested, his customary cut. What is certain is that the amount the debtors have to pay is less, and they will therefore be forced to reciprocate his "gift," and therein lies the "cleverness."

8. *the master praised the wicked household manager*: Two problems are evident here: first, is the *kyrios* who approves the manager the "master" of the parable, or Jesus (cf. the use of *kyrios* in the narrative at 10:1; 11:39; 12:42)? In the light of verse 9's "I also say to you," it would seem to be the master of the parable who is meant here. Second, the phrase *oikonomos tēs adikias* (literally, "manager of wickedness") is rather strange. Does it stand for the adjective *adikos* "wicked"? Or does it anticipate the phrase "mammon of wickedness" in verse 9? This translation takes the most natural path of using it as an adjective. Thus Jesus as narrator of the parable, expresses *his* judgment on the character or action of the manager, whatever the legality of his activity may have been.

because he acted cleverly: The term *phronimōs* ("cleverly") is cognate with the Greek term "prudence" (*phronēsis*), which Aristotle defined as a kind of practical wisdom: "Hence men like Pericles are deemed prudent because they possess a faculty of discerning what things are good for themselves and for mankind; and that is our conception of an expert in domestic economy (*oikonomikous*) or political science (*politikous*)" *Nichomachean Ethics* 8, 5, 5. In other words, the manager is praised for having the qualities of a manager! He responded to a crisis appropriately to his circumstances. It is this quality of responsiveness rather than the possible morality of the action that is the object of praise.

children of this age: Could also be translated "children (literally, "sons" *huioi*) of this world (*aiōn*)." Luke uses the term in the sense of "age" in 18:30 and 20:34, but the sense of "world" is well attested in the NT (Rom 12:2; 1 Cor 1:20; 2:6; 3:18, etc.). The "children ["sons"] of light" are the members of the community. We find the self-designation at Qumran in contrast to the "children of darkness" (as in *1QS* 1:9; 2:16; *1QM* 1:3), and as a designation of Christians in 1 Thess 5:3; Eph 5:8 and John 12:36. This is the only use in the Synoptic tradition. The point of the analogy is made even clearer: the people of "this age" are more clever (*phronimōteros*) with respect to their own crises than are the children of light with regard to the crisis facing them, namely the visitation of God's prophet and its demands for repentance.

9. *make friends for yourselves*: The form of this statement follows that of 12:33, "make for yourselves purses that do not grow old," and the thought is similar as well. Just as "friends hold all things in common," so that sharing possessions symbolizes unity of outlook (see e.g., Cicero, *De Amicitia* 6:20), so does the sharing of possessions mean a step toward friendship. The use of possessions symbolizes interior self-disposition.

mammon of wickedness: The term *mammon* is not found in the OT, but is found at Qumran (*1QS* 6:2; *CD* 14:20) in the sense of "property." It has much the same neutral sense in *Pirke Aboth* 2:12. In *Targum Onqelos* on Gen 37:26 it refers to the wicked "gain" of Joseph's brothers; in *Targum Onqelos* on Exod 18:21 the honest judge is one who "abhors mammon." In the NT the word is used only in Matt 6:24 (which parallels the concluding statement here, Luke 16:13) and in the present passage. The genitive "of wickedness" is again basically adjectival, equalling "wicked mammon." Since Luke clearly thinks that possessions can be used positively (such is the whole point here), the reason for the designation "wicked" is: a) the use made by the manager, or b) the potential for money to become idolatrous, as in 16:13.

when it fails: Or, "when it runs out"; money is transitory and something that can be used only in this life or "this age," so that life and possessing, however incommensurate, end at the same time.

they will receive you into eternal tents: The third person plural is equivalent to the divine passive. The notion of "friends" is carried over from the parable, but the idea is: "God will receive you" (see the similar construction in 12:20; 14:35). Thus also, the "eternal tents" match the "homes" of the parable; compare the idea of "treasure in heaven" in 12:33-34. The statement advocates almsgiving, and the conviction that such sharing of possessions has a heavenly reward is well attested in the Rabbinic literature (see the note on 12:33 and *Exodus Rabbah*, Mish.31f.).

10. *reliable in something tiny*: The term *pistos* (literally "faithful") is translated "reliable" because that term better catches the meaning in context. The saying is

a perfect illustration of *qal wehomer* (light and heavy): behavior in the small is
even more so in the great. "Tiny" here is literally "smallest thing" (*elachistos*).
The implied contrast is between the lesser thing which is the use of money and
the greater thing which is the response to God.

11. *reliable in your use of wicked mammon*: Again, the word *pistos* ("faithful"), but the
    contrast in the second clause is striking. First it is in the form of a question. Sec-
    ond, the verb "entrust" is cognate with *pistos* ("faithful"), but now from an-
    other; reliability engenders trust. Third, the contrast is between the "wicked
    mammon" and "the real thing" (*to alēthinon*). There is a sort of Platonism here:
    the temporal and transitory is less "real" than that which comes by gift from
    the Eternal.

12. *what belongs to another*: Is a literal rendering of *tọ allotriọ*. Once more, the clauses
    divide between one's own attitude and the response from another. Once more,
    the second clause is in the form of a question. This time, however, the contrast
    concerns ownership. "What is another's" may refer to the conviction that "pos-
    sessions" are always to some degree external and fictive; all things are really
    in God's possession. If we are not faithful with "God's things," then God will
    not give us "our thing" which is our life (see 12:15). This line is cited in 2 *Clem*
    8:5-6, applied to the keeping of the flesh pure so that eternal life might be gained,
    but this does not seem to reflect Luke's own understanding.

13. *no household servant*: The saying is paralleled with remarkable fidelity by Matt
    6:24, in the context of the Sermon on the Mount. The only difference between
    the two is Luke's addition of the word *oiketēs*, "household servant," which ties
    the moral more closely to the parable. The version of *Gospel of Thomas* 47 is in
    this case part of a conflated saying.

    both God and Mammon: The capitalization is required here because the form of
    the statement as well as the reaction to it in 16:14 demand that "Mammon" be
    taken as an idolatrous power that can compete with God for human allegiance.
    This saying as well is quoted by 2 *Clem* 6:1.

INTERPRETATION

Three major problems face the interpreter of this passage. So difficult
is the solving of them that the "parable of the wicked household manager"
with its attendant sayings has generated a disproportionate amount of scholarly discussion. Although the basic point being made is in truth not terribly
complicated, making all the details fit together is. We are given no help by
Synoptic comparison since nothing in this section except the final logion
has a parallel.

The first problem is determining where the parable ends and where the
moral lessons begin. Since the rich man in the parable has been identified
as "master" (*kyrios*) and since Jesus in Luke's narrative has been identified

as *Kyrios* as well, one can understand why 16:8a should create some puzzlement: "the *kyrios* praised the wicked manager because he acted cleverly." Does this end the parable in the voice of Jesus, or does it begin the interpretation put in the mouth of Jesus by the narrator? The issue was troublesome especially to readers who thought that if it were Jesus who approved the cleverness, this would constitute an approval of the man's immoral behavior.

That leads to the second problem: what was the nature of the household manager's action? Did he continue his fraudulent ways for his own advantage and the continued cheating of his master? Or did he sacrifice something of what was legally owed him as agent in order to secure grateful clients for himself? In either case, was his behavior within the bounds of conventional expectations and legality? Was he wicked in the first instance (wasting the master's money) and only "clever" in the second? Or was his "cleverness" also wicked?

The final problem concerns the relationship of the sayings in 16:9-13 to the parable and its first moral (16:8b) as well as to each other. If they were originally discrete logia brought together because of mnemonic linkages (most evident in the recurrence of the word "faithful" or "reliable" and the word "mammon") do they then amount only to a loosely joined series of observations, or is there an internal logic linking them? Do they with the parable make one or more connected points, or a whole series of random ones?

The best reading of the section is the one that pays least attention to the technical problems of tradition and redaction (what came from Jesus and what from Luke) and gives careful consideration to the way in which Luke the author has arranged these materials in this place, as well as the consistent themes of his narrative that appear again in this passage.

Most important, then, is to place these sayings in narrative context. Jesus has turned from controversy with the Pharisees and scribes (15:1-32) to teach his followers. If his usual pattern holds true, some of the elements of the earlier section will reappear in this one, but now by means of positive paraenesis rather than as polemic. We see, furthermore, that this passage is followed by the Pharisees "mocking" what Jesus teaches (16:14), so they are to be imagined as overhearing this instruction of Jesus' disciples.

The manager's trouble began with the way he used possessions, the goods which belonged to "another," his master. He scattered the possessions over which he had control (16:1). When his master discovers this the crisis begins. He is called to account (16:2). The crisis character of the story is essential. It is the manager's ability to respond to this crisis, literally a "visitation of his Lord," which is the point of the story, the reason for the master's admiration, and the example for the disciples. His cleverness consisted in continuing to disperse possessions (by reducing the amounts owed)! But now the dispersal does not result in his rejection (the loss of his position) but in his acceptance (by the new friends from which he can expect *quid pro quo,* 16:4).

Of the two morals directly attached to the parable, the first picks up on the cleverness of the manager's response itself: The children of light should be so discerning in their response to the "visitation of *their* Lord." The second moral flows from the first but now picks up the use of possessions. As the manager used possessions to secure a place for himself, so should the disciples. In the light of Luke's language elsewhere about laying up treasure in heaven (12:33) there can be no doubt that this saying refers to almsgiving.

The three sayings in verses 10-12 will never be entirely clear, although their general import is straightforward. Each of the sayings has a contrast between something lesser and greater. In verse 11, the contrast is specified in terms of possessions. We can, in fact, understand each of them in these terms: the lesser reality refers to possessions, the greater to the disposition of the self before God. Thus, possessions as such are "tiny," but reliability or wickedness in their use indicates reliability or wickedness in the response to God (v. 10). The failure to dispose of "wicked mammon" reliably will lead to one's not being entrusted with what is genuine (v. 11). Lack of reliability in what is "another's" means that what properly belongs to the self will not be given (v. 12). The sayings are obscure and even paradoxical. If the etymology of "mammon" as "something to rely on" is correct, then the real key to the conjunction of sayings may be a bilingual pun on "mammon/faith," which is no longer entirely available to us. What does emerge is that the disposition of possessions, while in some fashion exterior to the self, less important than the self, and perhaps even to some degree unworthy of the self, is nevertheless regarded by Luke as of critical importance for expressing the disposition of the self.

The final saying shows the profound seriousness with which Luke regards this symbolic use of possessions. "Mammon" in 16:13 is personified as an idol, the service of whom is the rejection of God. If giving away possessions in almsgiving secures a place with God, the worship of possessions and a clinging to them as ultimate means separation from God.

FOR REFERENCE AND FURTHER STUDY

Bailey, K. E. *Poet and Peasant: A Literary Cultural Approach to the Parables in Luke* (Grand Rapids: Eerdmans, 1976) 86–110.

Degenhardt, H.-J. *Lukas Evangelist der Armen* (Stuttgart: Katholisches Bibelwerk, 1965) 114–131.

Derrett, J. M. D. "Fresh Light on St. Luke xvi. I: The Parable of the Unjust Steward." *NTS* 7 (1960–61) 198–219.

Feuillet, A. "Les riches intendants du Christ (Luc xvi, 1-13)." *RSR* 34 (1947) 30–54.

Fitzmyer, J. A. "The Story of the Dishonest Manager (Lk 16:1-13)." *TS* 25 (1964) 23–42.
Hickling, C. J. A. "A Tract on Jesus and the Pharisees? A Conjecture on the Redaction of Luke 15 and 16." *HeyJ* 16 (1975) 253–265.

46. *The Claims of Moses and the Prophets* (16:14-31)

14. The Pharisees were money lovers. They heard these things and mocked him. 15. He said to them, "You justify yourselves in people's eyes. But God knows your hearts. What is exalted in human sight is an abomination in God's sight. 16. The law and the prophets continue up to John. From then on, the kingdom of God is being proclaimed, and everyone is being urged to enter it. 17. But it is easier for heaven and earth to pass away than for a single letter of the law to fall. 18. Everyone who divorces his wife and marries another commits adultery, and the one who marries a woman divorced from her husband commits adultery. 19. There was a certain rich man. He was clothed with purple and fine linen. Every day he feasted extravagantly. 20. But a poor man named Lazarus sat at his gates covered with sores. 21. He longed to be filled from what fell off the rich man's table. Instead the very dogs would come and lick his sores. 22. The poor man died. He was carried off by the angels to Abraham's bosom. The rich man also died and was buried. 23. While he was in Hades suffering torments he lifted his eyes. From a long way off he saw Abraham and Lazarus in his bosom. 24. He called out, 'Father Abraham, have mercy on me! Send Lazarus to dip his finger into water and cool my tongue. I am suffering in this flame!' 25. Abraham said, 'Child, remember that you received good things during your life. Lazarus in the same way received evil things. And now here he is being comforted, but you are suffering. 26. And in all these things there is a great divide set up between us and you people, so that those wishing to cross over from this side to you people cannot do so. Neither can any cross over from there to us.' 27. But he said, 'I ask you then, Father, to send him to my father's house, 28. for I have five brothers. He can bear witness to them so that they also will not come to this place of torment.' 29. But Abraham said, 'They have Moses and the Prophets. Let them listen to them.' 30. He said, 'Surely not, Father Abraham! But if someone should come to them from the dead they will repent.' 31. And he said to him, 'If they do not listen to Moses and the Prophets neither will they be convinced if someone rise from the dead!' "

NOTES

14. *Pharisees were money lovers*: The translation makes a participle into an independent clause and puts it in a position of prominence. *philargyria*, or "love of money"

was one of the standard vices in Greek moral teaching (Dio, *Oration* 4, 84; 1 Tim 6:10), and commonly found in the rhetoric of polemic against opposing teachers, who were always "lovers of money" (see Dio, *Oration* 32:9; 35:1; Epictetus, *Discourses* 1, 9, 19-20; Lucian, *Timon* 56; 2 Tim 3:2). For a bitter attack on such avarice as the root of social evils in the Empire, see Juvenal, *Satires* 14:173-178. At issue here is not historical accuracy, but Luke's literary/religious intentions: the Pharisees play the literary role of opponents of the prophets. If those who accept the prophets are "the poor," then the opponents will be both "rich" and avaricious (cf. esp. 11:39).

they heard these things and mocked him: The Pharisees were last directly addressed in 15:1-32. We are to picture them overhearing Jesus' teaching of the disciples (16:1) on possessions which concludes with the statement that it is impossible to serve both God and Mammon. The verb "mock" (*ekmykterizō*) is used of the righteous one reviled by enemies in LXX Ps 21:7; 39:16, and recalls the scornful "laughter" (*gelōn*) of 6:25.

15. *justify yourselves in people's eyes*: We recognize the characterization of the lawyer in 10:29 and (in slightly different form) of the Pharisees in 18:9. In contrast to sinners and tax-agents who "justified God" by their positive response to the prophets (7:29), these seek instead human approval and glory. Note the "leaven of the Pharisees that is hypocrisy" in 12:1.

God knows your hearts: The implication is that their inward dispositions do not match their outward show. Remember again the inside/outside of the cup in 11:39-41, when the contrast was also between rapaciousness and the giving of alms. God is the "knower of hearts" in Acts 1:24 and 15:8, and we have seen that as prophet, Jesus reveals the thoughts of hearts (2:35; 5:22; 9:47).

an abomination in God's sight: The contrast between what is "exalted" (*hypsēlos*) and "low" is typical of Luke, but in this case, the language is stronger: the "abomination" (*bdelygma*) occurs in Gen 43:32; Exod 8:26; Lev 5:2; 7:21; 11:10-42; Deut 17:1 as something utterly reprehensible or "unclean" in thing or act. In Deuteronomy, it is mainly associated, however, with *idolatry* (see Deut 7:25; 12:31; 18:12; 27:15; 29:17; 32:16), and that association is continued in Isaiah (2:8, 20; 17:8; 41:24; 44:19). In Dan 9:27; 11:31 and 12:11, the "abomination of desolation" is the supreme representation of idolatry (cf. also Mark 13:14 and Matt 24:15). The word choice by Luke, in short, corresponds to the portrayal of Mammon in 16:13 as an idol competing for human allegiance against God, which portrayal the Pharisees mock. In light of the sayings which follow, it is instructive to note that the term *bdelygma* is also used to designate sham outward worship (Isa 1:13 and 66:3), immoral financial dealings (Deut 25:16), and the remarrying of a divorced wife (Deut 24:4)!

16. *Law and the Prophets continue up to John*: The verb "continue" is supplied from the preposition phrase *mechri Iōannou*. The temporal meaning is obscure, since *mechri* could either include or exclude John, and the other phrase "from then on" (*apo tote*) could do the same. Any attempt to build an elaborate temporal scheme on such a fragile basis would be doomed. The expression "Law and Prophets" occurs in 24:44 and Acts 13:15; 28:23 for the testimony of the Scriptures. Indeed, the parallel in Matt 11:13 adds "prophesied."

kingdom of God is being proclaimed: This activity characterizes Jesus' ministry rather than that of John (4:43; 8:1; 9:2, 11, 60) and continues into Acts through Jesus' prophetic successors (Acts 1:3; 8:12; 19:8; 20:25; 28:31).

everyone is being urged to enter it: The translation of *biazomai* here is notoriously difficult. It could mean "seize forcefully" or "take by force." This is clearly Matthew's understanding, since in his parallel version he adds "men of violence take it by force" (Matt 11:12, RSV). But it could also be taken in the sense of "being forced." This translation tries to hit the middle ground. The sayings on the narrow door in 13:24 support the first meaning: "struggle to enter." But the adjective "all" in this passage makes it probable that the reference here is to the force of Jesus' preaching: all are being urged to enter, and many in fact are doing so. Either translation is possible, and even if "all are forcing themselves in" is adopted, the sense would be the same in this context, for the "all" is the determining factor.

17. *but it is easier . . . to pass away*: The most obvious problem here is deciding how to treat the particle *de*. Does the saying set up an opposition, "but," or a continuation, "and"? The saying itself is equivalent to "it is impossible" as the use of *eukopōteron* ("it is easier") in 18:25 suggests. See also the parallel in Matt 5:18.

    single letter of the Law to fall: The word "letter" is *keraia* which refers to part of a Hebrew letter (see the parallel in Matt 5:18). "To fall" means to come to an end or fail (see 10:18; 11:17). The term "law" (*nomos*) by itself is used rarely in Luke. After the frequent use in the infancy stories (2:22, 23, 24, 27, 39), it is used in the absolute only here and in 10:26. This makes determining Luke's intended meaning all the more difficult.

18. *everyone who divorces his wife*: The saying is paralleled by Mark 10:11-12 and Matt 19:9 (and 5:32). Mark 10:2-9 counters the Mosaic allowance of divorce (in Deut 24:1-4) with the order of creation described in Gen 1-2, and includes the divorcing of husbands by wives as well. Matthew has only the man divorcing, but follows Deuteronomy by allowing divorce for reasons of sexual immorality (*porneia*). Luke's prohibition has no qualification, and no rationalization. It forbids husbands divorcing and remarrying, as well as marrying a divorcee. The real problem is determining how Luke sees this as a statement concerning the perdurance of "law." Torah forbade adultery absolutely, to be sure (Exod 20:13; Deut 5:18), but nowhere connected divorce to adultery. As the Mishnah tractate *Gittin* shows, a large amount of legislation was devoted in rabbinic Judaism to divorce, some of it quite liberal. Thus, although the School of Shammai would allow divorce only on grounds of fornication, the School of Hillel would allow it simply because the husband found another woman more attractive (*m.Git.* 9:10). Like Jesus, the Qumran sect had a far stricter view of marriage (*CD* 4:20-5:1).

19. *a certain rich man*: This parable is found only in Luke's Gospel. Like the "rich fool" (12:16-21), he is not a sympathetic character. His splendid clothing recalls the description of the wealthy in 7:25. "Purple and fine linen" describe the accoutrements of the royal and wealthy (see Judg 8:26; Sir 45:10; Esth 1:6; 8:15). The traditional name "Dives" derives from the Latin translation of "rich man," although some early MSS supply the name "Nineveh."

feasted extravagantly: The adverb *lamprōs* denotes brilliance and splendor. The term *euphrainō* ("feast," or "celebrate") is used in 12:19 and 15:23-32 of special occasions. But this man does it every day! Each detail suggests the sort of opulence and overdone sumptuousness found in Amos 6:4-7 or "the Dinner at Trimalchio's" in Petronius' *Satyricon*; cf. also Juvenal, *Satires* 11:120-160 and Lucian of Samosata, *The Dream* 7–15.

20. *poor man named Lazarus*: The use of *ptōchos* ("poor") in such close conjunction with *plousios* ("rich") alerts us to the fact that this parable provides a narrative rendering of the first Beatitude and woe of 6:20-24. The name "Lazarus" is the Greek form of Eliezer, "My God helps."

21. *longed to be filled*: Just as Luke masterfully sketched the rich man's careless affluence, so he luridly paints the poor man's condition. He is "dumped" at the rich man's door, so is probably crippled. He is covered with sores. He is hungry. Rather than receive help from the rich man's table, his sores are licked by dogs. This is not a sentimental touch; things associated with dogs were unclean, so this is another sign of the man's outcast condition (see Exod 22:31; 1 Kgs 21:19, 24; LXX Ps 21:16; Matt 15:26-27; Mark 7:27-28; cf. also *m.Kil.* 1:6; 8:6; *Ned.* 4:3; *Sot.* 9:15; *Toh.* 3:8; 4:3; 8:6).

22. *by the angels to Abraham's bosom*: This translation retains the traditional "bosom" for *kolpos*, although as in 6:34 the English word "lap" (cf. the use of *kolpos* in Acts 27:38 for a "bay") might be better. In John 1:18 and 13:23, a place by the bosom denotes intimacy. The expression "bosom of Abraham" is found only in Luke's Gospel, and may derive from the ancient biblical idea of "being gathered to one's people" at death (Gen 49:33; Num 27:13; Deut 32:50; Judg 2:10). Abraham functions here as the "father" of this people (see also 1:73; 3:8; 13:16, 28; 19:9).

23. *while he was in Hades*: For Luke's use of "Hades," see the note on 10:15. Its rough equivalence to *sheol* is indicated by the citation of LXX Ps 16:10 in Acts 2:27. The Greek sentence neatly contrasts the man "in torments" to Lazarus "in the bosom," indicating already the reversal of their conditions.

24. *father Abraham, have mercy on me*: The rich man uses this title here and in verse 30. But John the Baptist had already indicated that it was not enough to claim "we have Abraham as our father"; they must "do the fruits required of repentance" (3:8). The cry "have mercy on us" will be addressed to Jesus in 17:13 and 18:38-39. The irony of the story is that he now requests "mercy" (*eleos*) who did not show mercy in almsgiving (*eleēmosynē*) to the poor man.

25. *good things during your life*: In this case, Luke's theme of the divine reversal is worked out in terms of individual eschatology: the "good things during his life" are matched now by "suffering pain" (*odynaomai*; see 2:48 and Acts 20:38). In contrast, the "evil things" (*kaka*) experienced by Lazarus are replaced by a "present consolation" (*nyn hōde parakaleitai*), which once more echoes the language of the woe against the rich who "have their consolation" (*paraklēsin*, 6:24). For an outspoken depiction of the contrast between the very wealthy and the destitute in the Empire, see Juvenal, *Satires* 1:130-144.

26. *in all these things*: Is a very literal rendering of the Greek *en pasi toutois*. Some translations (RSV, Fitzmyer) treat it as a grammatical transition, "besides all this," which is possible. But it could equally be a statement about "all these matters" of eschatology. In every respect, namely, there is the great divide between the rewarded and the punished. Notice that in Greek the pronouns are plural at this point; the gulf is fixed between "us" and "you people." For the vision of the afterlife here, see the very similar picture in *1 Enoch* 18:11-16; 21:1-10; 22:1-14, and Matt 25:31-46.

27. *can bear witness to them*: The sense is "to warn," but *diamartyromai* is used consistently by Luke throughout Acts for "bearing witness" to one raised from the dead (Acts 2:42; 8:25, 40, 42; 18:5; 20:21, 23, 24; 23:11; 28:23) and fits the *double entendre* of "one returned from the dead" in this passage.

29. *Moses and the prophets*: The phrase refers to the Scriptures in their prophetic force. Above all, in this context (cf. 16:16), to their demand that the poor be cared for in the land (e.g., Exod 22:21-22; 23:9; Lev 19:9-10; 19:33; 23:22; Deut 10:17-19; 14:28-29; 15:1-11; 16:9-15; 24:17-18; 26:12-15; Amos 2:6-8; Hos 12:7-9; Mic 3:1-3; Zeph 3:1-3; Mal 3:5; Isa 5:7-10; 30:12; 58:3; Jer 5:25-29; 9:4-6). This fundamental obligation of covenantal fidelity is the unmistakable teaching of Torah in each of its parts.

    listen to them: "Hearing" the prophet is a fundamental theme both in the Gospel (5:1, 15; 6:17, 27, 47-49; 7:29; 8:8-15, 18, 21; 9:35; 10:16; 11:28; 14:35; 19:48; 21:38) and Acts (2:22, 37; 3:22-23; 4:4; 7:2; 15:7; 18:8). In this connection "hearing" includes "obeying."

30. *they will repent*: The word used is *metanoein*, which describes the proper response to the hearing of God's word through a prophet (see 10:13; 11:32; 13:3-5; 15:7-10). The use of the term implies that the rich man's fate was not simply the result of a mechanical reversal, but was a punishment for *not* heeding the prophets and "repenting" during his lifetime.

    come to them from the dead: Luke stays within the framework of the story, not using the explicit language of "resurrection." For the authority given to such post-mortem appearances, see 1 Sam 28:7-20; Cicero, *Republic* 6:9-26; Philostratus, *Life of Apollonius of Tyana* 8:31.

31. *neither will they be convinced*: The verb *peithō* means "to convince" (see Acts 13:43; 14:19; 17:4; 18:4). In the passive, "be convinced," it is close to "believe," or "rely on" (11:32; 18:9; 20:6; Acts 5:36-37), so some mss in this place have "believe." The verb "rise" (*anistēmi*) is one used frequently by Luke for the resurrection of Jesus (9:22; 18:33; 24:9, 46; Acts 2:24, 32; 3:22, 26; 13:32). Some mss have *egeirō* ("raise") which Luke uses just as often in the same connection (7:14; 9:7, 22; 20:37; 24:6, 34; Acts 3:7, 15; 4:10; 5:30; 10:40; 13:30, 37). The meaning and allusion are in either case the same; the statement points beyond the parable to Jesus as the prophet whom God raised up, proclaimed in the narrative of Acts.

INTERPRETATION

As with the first half of this chapter, the bulk of the material here comes from Luke, with only the sayings in 16:16-18 finding any parallel in the other Synoptic Gospels. As the material is Luke's own, so does it serve his narrative purposes. It is easier, in fact, to make sense of the overall narrative function of this section than it is to figure out how its pieces fit together with internal logic.

Throughout this journey section we have noticed how Luke has Jesus alternate his sayings between the crowds, opponents and disciples. In chapters fifteen and sixteen, the impact of this alteration is particularly strong. Jesus had told the parables of the lost (15:3-32) to the lawyers and Pharisees who complained because he accepted the outcast (15:1-2). Then, Luke had Jesus turn to his disciples with a warning about the appropriate use of possessions (16:1-12), stressing that service both of God and Mammon was impossible (16:13). It is in response to these teachings that the Pharisees mock Jesus (16:14). All his subsequent statements in chapter 16 are to be regarded as a response to this attack (16:15-31), before Jesus turns again in 17:1 with a teaching of his disciples. It is appropriate to see in this exchange, therefore, a continuation of the theme of the rejection of the prophet by the religious leaders, with Jesus' response suggesting as well their own rejection by God.

We notice in this regard that the money-loving Pharisees do not only reject his teaching, they mock *him*. And in his response, Jesus makes clear that they are an "abomination" before God, no matter how much they justify themselves (16:15). So much is clear. But why should Luke at this point include the statements concerning the Law? In particular it is difficult to understand how these sayings fit with each other, or what they are doing in this context. Some patient disentangling may be needed.

The statement in 16:16 is itself obscure enough. Is Jesus contrasting periods in the history of salvation, so that an age of "law and prophets" is succeeded by the age of "kingdom proclamation," with John the Baptist as the turning point? As suggested in the notes on 16:16, if that were the point, one would have wished it be be made with greater clarity. Or is he demarcating those periods in order to assert that "the Law" remains in effect even in this time of the kingdom which is open to "all?" Taking the two statements this way, we would read "the Law and Prophets" in verse 16 as Scripture in its prophetic meaning which is being fulfilled in the proclamation of the kingdom, and verse 17 as stating the enduring normativity of the Law as guide to morality.

But if that is the case, why should Luke include the statement on divorce in 16:18? It pops up in the text without any apparent motivation. What does divorce have to do with the proper use of possessions, or for that matter with idolatry? Worse, the saying seems to stand at least in tension if not in contradiction to verse 17, for Jesus' absolute and unequivocal prohibition of divorce cannot be taken as an affirmation of "law" in any obvious sense, for Moses had clearly allowed divorce in Deut 24:1-4.

As a first point of entry into these sayings, we can observe that the combination of elements found in them is not altogether unprecedented. When discussing 16:9-12, we suggested that a bilingual pun on Mammon/faithful could account for the collocation of disparate sayings. Perhaps something similar is at work, here. Notice the oddness of the term *bdelygma,* or "abomination." Its first and most obvious reference is to "idolatry" in the biblical tradition (see notes). But the term is also used in two other important connections in Torah, once in condemning financial misdealing (Deut 25:16), and once in condemning a divorced man cohabiting again with his former wife (Deut 24:4). Idolatry, money, and divorce are joined by the term *bdelygma.*

That this is not entirely fanciful is suggested by a very similar triad in the Qumran writings. In an interpretation of Isa 24:17, the author of the *Damascus Rule* identifies the "three nets of Satan" that entrap Israel as three sham forms of righteousness: "the first is fornication, the second is riches, the third is profanation of the temple." Fornication is further explained as an interpretation of divorce more liberal than that of the sect, and profanation of the Temple as not observing purity regulations (in sexual situations) (CD 4:14-5:10). Once more, idolatry, divorce, and possessions are joined. Some such precedent may underlie Luke's combination as well.

In Luke's narrative context, of course, the point of these sayings is polemical: the Pharisees pretend to a piety concerning the Law, and on that ground "justify themselves." They complain when "all are urged to enter" the kingdom—or when "anyone can force" themselves into it (16:16). And the basis of their complaint is that such people are not righteous by the Law (15:1-2). Jesus' rejoinder not only calls their criticism a matter of self-inflation, but provides a transition to a parable which questions whether those who are "lovers of money" (16:14) can themselves be "hearing Moses and the Prophets."

The parable of the rich and poor men has some parallels in ancient literature. The theme of fortunes being reversed after death finds splendid expression, for example, in Lucian of Samosata's *Dialogues of the Dead.* The eschatological scenario, however, and especially the negative attitude toward the oppressive rich are best paralleled by the Jewish apocalyptic writing, *1 Enoch* 94-99. This "woe," in *1 Enoch* 94:8 can stand as a commentary on Luke's parable: "Woe to you, ye rich, for ye have trusted in your riches, and from your riches shall ye depart, because ye have not remembered the Most High in the days of your riches."

Indeed, Luke's parable in 16:19-31 provides the perfect narrative expression of his own Beatitudes and woes in 6:20, 24. The characters are simply types, "a certain rich man," a "certain poor man." No moral attributes are given to either directly. The story is simply one of a dramatic reversal of fortunes, which reaches a satisfying climax in verses 25-26. The one who had enjoyed "good things" in life is now tormented; the one who had only "evil things" has now a "consolation." No moralism, only the divine reversal promised in the Sermon on the Plain.

But as in the parable of the lost son, there is an appendix which complicates the simple story and gives it a polemic sting. The rich man asks for Lazarus to be sent as a warning to his brothers. This plea not only reveals the man's continuing arrogance—he wants Lazarus to cool his own tongue, as though he were a servant, and to be sent as a messenger to his brothers!!—but suggests to the reader that there was, in fact, a moral reason for this reversal. This man had not only been rich and extravagant, he had been hard of heart. His wealth had made him insensitive to the demands of the Law and Prophets alike that the covenant demands sharing goods with the poor (see notes). The concrete expression of his rejection of the Law was his neglect of the poor man at his gate. There is a saying in the Talmud, in fact, that "whoever turns away his eyes from one who appeals for charity is considered as if he were serving idols" (*bT Bab.Bat.* 10a). So Abraham's response, "they have Moses and the Prophets. Let them listen to them," applies in the first instance to *this* rich man. We understand that if he had fed the poor man who "longed to be filled from what fell from the table" he could have avoided his present condition.

The words of Abraham suggest that the situation of this man as well as of his brothers is hopeless. They are equally locked into their rejection of the Law and Prophets, for they live as heedlessly as he had. They will not convert on the basis of hearing the Scripture (16:30). The final words of the parable seal their rejection: even if someone came back from the dead, they would not listen (16:31).

The parable is therefore one of rejection. By having Jesus tell it to Pharisees whom he has characterized as "money-lovers," Luke makes it apply directly to their own rejection. As the rich man had scorned the demands of the Law and Prophets to give alms, so have they "mocked" Jesus' teaching on almsgiving (16:9-13). And in spite of their claim to hold the demands of the Law, they reject the outcasts among the people (15:1-2), just as the rich man had rejected Lazarus. Therefore as the rich man is rejected from a place in the people ("the bosom of Abraham"), so are they to be rejected from the people. Finally, the parable points beyond itself to the larger narrative of Luke-Acts. The reader cannot miss the reference in 16:31 to the resurrection of Jesus, whom the leaders will reject yet another time when they refuse to hear the words of the apostles in the narrative of Acts.

For Reference and Further Study

Cortes, J. B. and Gatti, F. M. "On the Meaning of Luke 16:16." *JBL* 106 (1987) 247–259.

Dupont, J. *Les Béatitudes* (Paris: J. Gabalda, 1973) III: 162–182.

Evans, C. "Uncomfortable Words—V: Neither Will They Be Convinced." *ExpT* 81 (1969–70) 260–264.

Moxnes, H. *The Economy of the Kingdom* (Philadelphia: Fortress, 1988) 139–150.

Nickelsberg, G. W. E. "Riches, the Rich, and God's Judgment in *1 Enoch* 92–105 and the Gospel according to Luke." *NTS* 25 (1978–79) 324–44.

Wilson, S. G. *Luke and the Law* (SNTMS 50; Cambridge: University Press, 1983) 43–51.

47. *Teaching and Healing* (17:1-19)

1. He said to his disciples: "It is impossible for scandals not to happen. But woe to the person through whom they happen! 2. It is better for that person to have a millstone hung around the neck and be thrown into the sea, than to cause one of these little ones to stumble. 3. Pay attention to yourselves! If your brother sins, rebuke him. If he repents, forgive him 4. Even if he sins against you seven times a day, yet turns to you and says, 'I repent,' forgive him." 5. The apostles said to the Lord, "Give us faith." 6. But the Lord said, "If you had faith the size of a mustard seed, you could say to this mulberry tree, Be uprooted and be planted in the sea! And it would obey you! 7. Does any of you have a slave who has come in from the field fresh from plowing or tending a herd, say to him, 'Come in at once and sit down?' Don't you say instead, 'Prepare something for me to eat! Put on an apron, wait on me until I finish eating and drinking! After doing these things you can eat and drink.' 9. You don't say 'Thanks' to a slave, do you, for doing what was commanded? 10. The case is the same with you. When you have done everything that has been commanded you, say, 'We are useless slaves! We have done what we were supposed to do!' "
11. He was on his way to Jerusalem. He was passing through an area between Samaria and Galilee. 12. As he came into a certain village ten men who were lepers met him. They stood a long way off 13. and shouted, "Jesus, Master, have mercy on us!" 14. When he saw them, he said to them, "Go! Show yourselves to the priests!" As they were on their way, they were made clean. 15. One of them, when he saw that he had been healed, turned back. He glorified God with a loud cry 16. and he fell at his feet thanking him. And this man was a Samaritan. 17. Jesus responded, "Were not ten people cleansed? Where are the other nine? 18. Were none found to return and give glory to God except this foreigner?" 19. He said to him, "Get up. Go. Your faith has saved you."

Notes

1. *it is impossible*: Luke shares the saying on scandal with Mark 9:42 and Matt 18:6-7. Only Luke and Matthew include the generalized statement, with Matthew asserting that it is "necessary" for scandals to occur, and Luke only that they are impossible to avoid. The term *skandalon* means first of all a trap or snare (as in LXX Ps 68:22; Josh 23:13), and then something over which one could stumble (as in LXX Ps 118:165; Lev 19:14). The NT uses it with reference to the cross as a "stumbling block" to belief in Jesus as Messiah (1 Cor 1:23; Rom 9:33; 11:9; 1 Pet 2:8), and to offenses within the community which cause a brother or sister to "stumble" in their commitment (1 Cor 8:13; Rom 14:13, 21). Luke uses the term in the first meaning in 7:23, "Blessed is the one who does not find me cause to stumble," and in the second meaning here.

   woe to the person: This is the eleventh "woe" (*ouai*) in Luke's Gospel, and the first that appears to be addressed to disciples. It is found also in the parallel of Matt 18:7.

2. *it is better*: All three Synoptists agree on the millstone around the neck and being plunged into the sea. But they differ in the rest of their wording to an unusual degree.

   cause one of these little ones to stumble: The verb "cause to stumble" (*skandalizō*) is cognate with "scandal" (*skandalon*) in the previous verse. Matt 18:6 and Mark 9:42 have this in a conditional sentence. Luke makes it a comparative statement. The other Synoptists also supply "little ones who believe." The expression "little ones" for members of the community is a favorite of Matthew's (10:42; 18:6, 10, 14), but is found only here in Luke.

3. *pay attention to yourselves*: Luke uses *prosechō* with the reflexive pronoun also in 12:1; 21:34; Acts 5:35; 20:28. In 12:1 the warning was to keep away from the hypocrisy of the Pharisees; here it is a call to avoid scandal and to forgive. Their behavior must be consistent with their convictions, as was suggested also by the similar warning, "watch how you hear" (8:18). For consistent action as the criterion of wisdom, cf. Seneca, *Moral Epistles* 20:1; *The Sentences of Sextus* 177.

   if your brother sins: The term "brother" (*adelphos*) here logically includes "sister" as a fellow member of the community. The saying is paralleled by Matt 18:15. In Luke it serves as a positive application of the parable of the lost son. The verbs "sin" (*hamartanō*) and "repent" (*metanoeō*) point unmistakably back to that passage (15:11-32). They are to "be compassionate as your father is compassionate" (6:36).

   forgive him: The future tense "you will forgive" has the force of the imperative. In Matt 18:21, the saying responds to a question from Peter as to how many times one was required to forgive, and Jesus responds "seventy times seven." Luke lacks the hyperbole, but with the phrase "a day" stresses the quotidian character of discipleship, as he does also in 9:23 and 14:27. For the use of correction and reproof in the NT, see e.g., 2 Tim 4:2; Eph 5:11; 1 Tim 5:20; Titus 1:9, 13; 2:15; Jude 15. In the theme of forgiveness, Luke is entirely within the framework of Jewish piety, for which the forgiveness offered by God to those who repent is endless, and demands similar forgiveness of the neighbor (cf. e.g., *Aboth de Rabbi Nathan* 41); for the combination of reproof and forgiveness, cf. *bT Arak.* 16b.

5. *give us faith*: Literally this reads, "add faith to us," which could be translated, "increase our faith." Since the sentence uses the dative case of the personal pronoun rather than the genitive, the absolute form of the request is preferred in this translation. The parallel saying in Matt 17:20 comes after the disciples' failure to exorcise the possessed (Matt 17:14-18), and addresses their lack of faith (17:19). This is the first appearance of the apostles since 9:10 (see also 11:49), and the interjection of Peter in 12:41. No reason is given for the request. Its presence here may be due in part to the presence of the "sea" in both this saying and that in verse 2. For the use of "Lord" (*kyrios*) here, compare 10:1, 41; 11:39; 12:42; 13:15.

6. *faith the size of a mustard seed*: Is literally, "like a mustard seed"; as in 13:19 the point of comparison is the smallness of size. The first part of this statement makes us expect a straightforward hypothetical: if this, then that. But the construction of the apodosis is that for an "unreal conditional," suggesting that in fact the apostles do not have such faith.

   you could say to this mulberry tree: Since the construction here implies that they do not have such faith, the conclusion "it would obey you" is much less forceful than in the parallels, which promise the capacity to move mountains by faith (cf. Matt 17:20; 21:21; Mark 11:22-23).

7. *does any of you have a slave*: The translation alters the syntax slightly from "which of you having a slave . . . will say to him . . ." Once more we find Luke's favorite household analogy of master/slave (compare 12:35-40, 42- 48; 13:25-27; 14:16-24; 16:1-13). The translation of *doulos* by "slave" helps make intelligible the harshness of the social arrangements and attitudes. The saying is unique to Luke's Gospel. For the slave eating after the master, see Petronius, *Satyricon* 74.

9. *you don't say 'thanks'*: The phrase *charin echein* means "give thanks," as in 1 Tim 1:12; 2 Tim 1:3. The point is not good manners, but social obligation and expectation. The structure of the Greek question demands the answer "no," and the translation makes that explicit.

10. *the case is the same with you*: Is literally, "thus also you," with Luke using *houtōs* in the same way as in 12:21; 14:33; 15:7, 10, in order to point out the moral of the story.

    useless slaves: Matt 25:30 has a servant who is literally "unprofitable" (*achreios*) because he does not increase the money left him on deposit. Here the term is the same as "humble," or "good for nothing." In the eyes of the master, they are dispensable, interchangeable for the fulfilling of these tasks. For a similar sentiment, see the saying in *Pirke Aboth* 1:3: "Be not like servants who serve the master for condition of receiving a gift, but be like servants who serve the master not on condition of receiving a gift. And let the fear of heaven be upon you"; cf. also *bT Ab.Zar.* 19a.

11. *an area between Samaria and Galilee*: There are several variant readings in the MSS, showing that even early scribes were troubled by this geographical reference. Luke's grasp of geography seems less physical than theological (see the note on 4:44). Luke uses this transition verse to establish two literary points: a) to remind the reader that the Prophet was still on his way to Jerusalem, after a section of discourse stretching from 14:1 to 17:10; b) to prepare for the healing story involving a Samaritan leper (17:12-19).

12. *ten men who were lepers*: This healing story is unique to Luke's Gospel. The requirement that lepers stay outside the encampment is found in Num 5:2-3, and that they should shout to warn others away from them, in Lev 13:45-46. Here they shout, but for help.

13. *master, have mercy on us*: This is the only time Jesus is called "master" (*epistatēs*) by someone not a disciple (cf. 5:5; 8:24, 45; 9:33, 49). The cry "have mercy," echoes that of the rich man to Abraham (16:24). Jesus will hear it again in 18:38-39. The showing of "mercy" (*eleos*) to the people is part of the expectation concerning the visitation of God (see 1:50, 54, 58, 72, 78).

14. *show yourselves to the priests*: The command is the same as in the first healing of a leper, except in the plural (see the note on 5:14 for the background).

15. *he glorified God*: A standard response in Luke-Acts to the working of a wonder (5:25-26; 7:16; 13:13; 18:43; Acts 4:21; 11:18; 13:48); for "falling on the face" (that is, prostration), see 5:12, and for Luke's use of "at the feet," see 7:38; 8:35, 41; 10:39. The passage provides a cluster of typical Lukan expressions. Only the presence of "giving thanks" (*eucharistein*) is surprising.

16. *this man was a Samaritan*: Like the hero of the parable in 10:33, the Samaritan gives a positive example, this time of faith rather than love. The shock is that it is given by one regarded as an "outcast," only marginally part of "Israel." For Luke's special interest in Samaria, see 9:52; 10:33; 17:11; Acts 1:8; 8:1, 5, 9, 14, 25; 9:31; 15:3.

18. *except this foreigner*: Luke uses the term *allogenēs*, the only time it is used in the NT (see Lev 22:10-13, 25); he uses *allophylēs* to the same effect in Acts 10:28. All the lepers were outcast, but none more so than this foreigner; yet he is the one to recognize the visitation of God in the prophet.

19. *your faith has saved you*: Luke uses the same phrase to conclude a healing in 7:50; 8:48 and 18:42. Notice the contrast to the request put by the apostles in 17:5.

INTERPRETATION

In 16:14-31, Luke had Jesus respond to the mocking of the Pharisees with a series of sayings and a parable that together indicted them of a false legal piety; they did not keep the deep moral demands of the law and prophets even as they posed as their protectors. Since they were money-lovers (16:14) they tried to serve both God and Mammon, but ended by "hating and despising" the commandments that demanded the sharing of possessions (16:13). Now Luke has Jesus turn to his disciples with positive instruction on the demands of discipleship (17:1-9).

The four pronouncements are not joined in any obvious fashion. The first (17:1-2) warns against causing "one of these little ones" to stumble. The second demands forgiveness when a brother or sister sins and repents (7:3-4). The third states the power of faith and suggests that perhaps those who ask for it may not have it (17:5-6). The fourth draws a lesson from the social expectations of the master/slave relationship: the disciples should not expect thanks for doing simply what they have been commanded (17:7-10).

When read in this specific narrative context, however, an implicit thematic thread may be detected which draws these statements closer together. First, the reader has been schooled by this point to identify with "the poor" who are called into the kingdom. The reader's natural temptation is to assume that one is "Lazarus" to the enemy's "rich man." The rich man of the story "stumbled" over the demand to share possessions, and did not repent. The community of the poor can easily see itself as pure victim. But the saying on scandal and repentance turn the ethical demand on this community as well. Even in the kingdom there is opportunity for scandal and the need for repentance and forgiveness. The demand placed by Jesus on his followers is that they are themselves responsible for both; they cannot plead innocence because they are oppressed by others. If they cause scandal, they will be punished for it. If they are sinned against, they must forgive.

Second, these demands represent the absolute minimum for life in the kingdom. The final statement about "useless servants" throws light on the first three sayings: they have done nothing extraordinary when they avoid giving scandal, when they forgive someone seven times a day, when they have faith. They are to avoid the "self-justifying" posture of the Pharisees in 16:14 who preen themselves as defenders of God's word while not fulfilling its most basic demands.

In a word, these sayings addressed to the Prophet's followers are not comforting but demanding. They are, indeed, deflating. And this may provide a clue to the inclusion of the next healing story immediately following these statements (17:12-19). Luke introduces it with one of his reminders that the Prophet was continuing his journey toward Jerusalem, and with whatever damage to his reputation as a geographer, places Jesus in the territory between "Galilee and Samaria" (17:11). The healing is found only in Luke, and represents an expansion of the cleansing of the leper in 5:12-16. Besides the difference in number, however, this story focuses our attention on two features. The first is Jesus' power to heal which now appears to need not even a formal declaration. The second—and the real point of the story—is the response of those healed. They all required some faith, after all, to leave to show the priests. They all were in fact cleansed. But only one returned to praise God and thank the one who healed him. And he was an outsider.

The healing of the Samaritan leper provides Luke with a transition in his story of the Prophet heading toward his death. The story points back to the instructions to the disciples: they were all as outcast as the Samaritan; they were all forgiven, cleansed, healed. They cannot assume another status than that of those who are gifted. They are not to expect thanks, but rather are to give thanks to the one who has saved them. The "faith that saves" of the Samaritan reminds the apostles—for whom the temptation to assume the role of "master" rather than of "slave" is endemic—of the absoluteness of the faith that has been given them (17:5-6): so dramatic has been the turn in their own lives that they are like trees that have been uprooted and transplanted in the sea. For this they can never stop giving thanks to the master, never arrogate to themselves the status of master.

The story of the Samaritan leper also points forward to the next encounter with the Pharisees in 17:20, for when they ask about the coming of the kingdom, Jesus can tell them, in effect, "look around you, here it is." In Luke, the performance of healings is the effective sign of the kingdom.

FOR REFERENCE AND FURTHER STUDY

Betz, H. D. "The Cleansing of Ten Lepers (Luke 17:11-19)." *JBL* 90 (1971) 314–328.
Glombitza, O. "Der dankbare Samariter, Luk. xvii 11-19." *NovT* 11 (1969) 241–246.
Minear, P. "A Note on Luke 17:7-10." *JBL* 93 (1974) 82–87.
Ward, A. M. "Uncomfortable Words: IV. Unprofitable Servants." *ExpT* 81 (1969–70) 200–203.

48. *The Kingdom and the End-Time* (17:20-37)

20. He was asked by the Pharisees when the kingdom of God was coming. He answered them: "The kingdom of God does not come by close scrutiny. 21. Neither will they say, 'Look! Here it is!' or 'There it is!' For look, the kingdom of God is among you." 22. And he said to the disciples, "Times are coming when you will desire to see one of the days of the Son of Man and you will not see it. 23. They will say to you: 'Look there! Look here!' Don't leave. Don't follow. 24. For the Son of Man will be like this in his day: like lightning that flashes and shines from one end of the sky to the other! 25. But first he must suffer many things. He must be rejected by this generation. 26. The situation in the days of the Son of Man will be just as in the days of Noah. 27. Those people ate, they drank, they married, they were given in marriage, until the day when Noah went into the ark. The flood came and destroyed them all. 28. Similarly it will be as in the days

of Lot. People ate, they drank, they bought, they sold, they planted, they built. 29. But on the day Lot left Sodom fire and sulphur rained down from heaven and destroyed them all. 30. It will be the same way on the day when the Son of Man is revealed. 31. On that day the person who is on the roof but has belongings inside the house should not go down to get them. The person who is in the field should likewise not turn back for the things left behind. 32. Remember Lot's wife! 33. Anyone seeking to hold life as a possession will lose it. Whoever loses it will keep it alive. 34. I tell you: on that night there will be two sleeping on a single bed. One will be taken and the other left. 35. Two women will be grinding together. One woman will be taken and the other left." 37. They responded to him: "Where will it be Lord?" He said to them, "Where the body is, there the vultures will gather!"

NOTES

20. *when the kingdom of God was coming*: The reader does not by this time expect a neutral question from the Pharisees who have consistently been portrayed as opponents of the Prophet; all their questions up to this point have had a hostile intent (5:21, 30; 6:2; 10:29). In the narrative context, the question is particularly obtuse since the whole burden of Jesus' proclamation is that "the kingdom of God has arrived" (or: approached, *engiken;* 4:43; 6:20; 8:1; 9:2; 10:9-11; 16:16). See especially the reassurance to followers, "it has pleased the Father to give you the kingdom" (12:32) and the response to opponents, "the kingdom of God has come upon you" (11:20).

    does not come by close scrutiny: The phrase *meta paratēreseōs* has two levels of meaning. The most obvious is that the kingdom of God comes with inexorable power and not by the careful analysis of subtle signs. The second level of meaning derives from Luke's use of *paratēreō* in the narrative, for the Pharisees have twice been identified as "keeping Jesus under close scrutiny" (6:7; 14:1). The response contains a subtle rebuke to the Pharisees' own approach: they do not perceive the kingdom because they are not open to it.

21. *neither will they say*: The force of this is "they will not *need* to tell you"; the kingdom is not a territory but the effective rule of God established among a people.

    the kingdom of God is among you: This saying is unique to Luke and has been interpreted in several ways. The critical problem is the understanding of *entos hymōn*. Some read this as "within you" as though the rule of God were a spiritual awareness. This fits the sense of the Greek adverb (cf. e.g., Matt 23:26), but it does not do as well with the plural pronoun "you," or the narrative context of Luke, in which such a statement to the Pharisees would be unthinkable. The present translation follows the majority opinion that the adverb *entos* with the plural pronoun should have the sense of "among you." This makes good sense of the narrative context: Jesus tells the Pharisees that the kingdom is forming around the prophet even in their midst, yet they cannot see it for what it is.

22. *days of the Son of Man*: In contrast to the statement to the opponents, this teaching for the disciples emphasizes the fact that the kingdom proclaimed by Jesus

is not yet the end-time. For Luke's use of "the day" compare 5:35; 10:12; 12:46, and in connection with the "Son of Man" compare 11:30; 12:8-10, 40. The tension between "desire to see" and "will not see" makes clear that the disciples have a period to wait between the initiation of the kingdom and its full realization at the "revelation of the Son of Man" (17:30).

23. *Don't leave. Don't follow*: Notice how the invitations echo what was said to the Pharisees in verse 21. This saying is paralleled by Mark 13:21 and Matt 24:23, except that in them it is "the Christ" who is identified as being "here or there," and the disciples are told "do not believe." Some of the MSS of Luke's Gospel lack "don't leave," but the balanced phrases are typical of Luke. Throughout these sayings, Luke's emphasis is on practical responses, and he uses much spatial imagery. Notice as well that he lacks any reference to "false messiahs" or "false prophets" such as are found in Mark 13:22.

24. *will be like this in his day*: The translation reverses the order of the Greek clauses ("like lightning . . . thus will be"). Most important, however, is the connective *gar* ("for"), which explains why the disciples need not go out in response to reports: his coming will be overwhelmingly obvious to all.
    like lightning that flashes: Jesus compared Satan's fall to that of "lightning from heaven" in 10:18. Here, Luke uses cognate terms: "lightning that lightens." Matt 24:27 also has this comparison. The participle "flashing" will occur again with reference to the clothes of the witnesses to Jesus' resurrection (24:4).

25. *first he must suffer many things*: This is the second of the passion prophecies revealed to the disciples, and it fits the pattern of "first suffering, then glory" typical of Luke (see 24:26). Luke uses *dei* ("it is necessary") for critical moments in God's visitation (4:43; 9:22; 13:33; 22:37; 24:7, 26, 44; Acts 1:16; 3:21; 9:16; 14:22; 17:3).
    rejected by this generation: The unwillingness of "this generation" to receive the prophets is stated in 7:31. For further negative characterizations, see 9:41; 11:29, 30, 31, 32, 50-51. The word "reject" (*apodokimazō*) is used as well in the passion prediction of 9:22 and recalls the "stone the builders rejected" of LXX Ps 117:22, quoted by Luke in 20:7.

26. *just as in the days of Noah*: This statement is found as well in Matt 24:37-39, except that Matthew uses (here and in his v. 27) the term *parousia* ("arrival"), which Luke never uses. The story of Noah is turned to paraenetic purposes also in Heb 11:7; 1 Pet 3:20; 2 Pet 2:5. The phrase, "thus will it be" (*houtōs estai*) is the same as in verse 24.

27. *those people ate, they drank*: The four activities listed here are found also in Matt 24:38. Luke lacks Matthew's emphasis on their "ignorance" of the coming flood (Matt 24:39). "Eating and drinking" appear as signs of eschatological heedlessness in 12:19, 29, 45. "Marrying and being given in marriage" define earthly as opposed to heavenly activities in Luke 20:35.

28. *as in the days of Lot*: The translation supplies the words "it will be." This example is found only in Luke, and is the basis for the warning in verse 32. Luke refers to the "Sodomites" in an eschatological context earlier in 10:12. The de-

struction of the cities of Sodom and Gomorrah (Gen 19) is used (usually as a moral example) in Matt 10:15; Rom 9:29; 2 Pet 2:6; Jude 7, but Lot is mentioned by name only here and in 2 Pet 2:7.

bought . . . sold . . . planted . . . built: In addition to the activities "eating and drinking," which are repeated from the "days of Noah," these four activities have to do with the use of possessions. The involvement with relationships and things reminds us of the parable of the great feast (14:15-24).

29. *fire and sulphur*: The words *ebrexen pyr kai theion ap' ouranou* form an unmistakable verbal allusion to the destruction of Sodom in Gen 19:24 (cf. also Ezek 38:22). The phrase, "and destroyed them all" is the same as in verse 27.

30. *the same way*: Luke uses this same idiom (*kata ta auta*) with reference to examples again in 6:23 and 26 (cf. also Acts 14:1). In the parallel saying, Matt 24:39 uses the term *parousia*, whereas Luke uses the verb "is revealed" (*apokalyptetai*).

31. *should not go down to get them*: Mark 13:14 precedes this saying with one about the "abomination of desolation." Both Mark 13:15 and Matt 24:17 have only a general reference to what is in the house, but Luke specifies *ta skeuē*. The image is one of people rushing into a house during a disaster to save what is precious to them. Likewise those caught in the field; they are not to turn back for the "things left behind" (*eis ta opisō*). The reader is reminded of the rebuke of the would-be disciple in 9:62.

32. *remember Lot's wife*: This exhortation is unique to Luke and is connected to the example only he includes. According to Gen 19:26, Lot's wife "turned back toward what was left behind," using the same words as here in verse 31. Luke attaches the loss of life to the desire for possessions. Reminding someone of past examples is one of the staples of Hellenistic paraenesis; cf. e.g., Lucian of Samosata, *Demonax* 1-3; *Nigrinus* 6 and 26. In the NT, see especially 2 Timothy and 2 Peter.

33. *hold life as a possession*: This is a very literal rendering of *peripoiein*, which has the sense of "acquiring" or "having as a possession." Luke uses the verb also in Acts 20:28 but this is its only appearance in the Gospels. The saying is similar to that in 9:24, and finds parallels in Mark 8:35; Matt 16:25 and 10:35, as well as John 12:25. The choice of verbs in both clauses, however, gives Luke's version particular force within this context.

will keep it alive: Once more, the choice of *zōogoneō* is unusual. It literally means to "give life" (see 1 Sam 2:6; 1 Tim 6:13), but Luke uses it in Acts 7:19 in the sense of "preserve alive" (as in Exod 1:17; cf. 1 Kgs 20:31; 2 Kgs 7:4).

34. *on that night*: The shift here to night is somewhat surprising, after the constant iteration of "day" in 17:24, 27, 29, 30, 31. Of course, "night" fits the first example of people sleeping on a bed, and perhaps the saying about the Son of Man coming "like a thief in the night" (1 Thess 5:2; Matt 24:43; Luke 12:33; Rev 3:3) had some influence as well.

two sleeping on a single bed: Matt 24:40 has the same combination of male and female pairs from which one is taken and the other left. Very little can be read into the verbs "taken" and "left." Functionally they are equivalent to "saving or losing" one's life, but the point of these examples is the suddenness of the end-time. And for Luke, we have seen, the death of an individual has eschatological significance (12:20; 16:19-31). Critical editions and most contemporary translations omit verse 36 about "two in a field," since the best and most ancient MSS lack it, and it is present in Luke by assimilation from Matt 24:41.

37. *where the body is, there the vultures will gather*: The parallel in Matt 24:28 has *ptōma* ("fallen body" = "corpse") rather than Luke's *sōma* ("body"). The *aetoi* may mean "eagles" (as in Exod 19:4; Jer 4:13; Rev 4:7; 12:4), but the carrion metaphor here seems to demand the translation "vultures," especially since the birds fit broadly into the same category (see Lev 11:13; Deut 14:12).

INTERPRETATION

Typical of the arrangement of materials in this travel section, there is a rapid turn here from the exchange with the opponents, found only in Luke's Gospel (17:20-21), to the teaching of the disciples, in which distinctive Lukan elements are interwoven with materials shared with Matthew and Mark (17:22-37). The character of Jesus' sayings is appropriate to each audience.

Given the narrative presentation of the Pharisees up to this point, it is unlikely that their question concerning the coming of the kingdom could be sincere. The whole point of Jesus' proclamation is the arrival of the kingdom as signalled by his healings and those of his apostles. Immediately before this question, Jesus has healed a Samaritan and dismissed him with the words "your faith has saved you" (17:19). The problem Jesus had with the other nine who were healed, however, is that they did not recognize the significance of what had been done for them, or recognize the one who had done it. Exactly the same point is made by his response to their question in 17:20. By stating that the kingdom does not arrive "by close scrutiny," he is condemning by implication their own suspiciousness toward him (see notes). But in a more obvious sense, he reminds them that in fact the kingdom is forming around him "among them." As the Prophet moves toward Jerusalem, those who accept his challenge join the people and become disciples. The "kingdom of God" that is God's rule over a faithful people is being initiated in the deeds of the Prophet. The fact that the Pharisees do not—cannot—perceive this is self-condemning.

In the teaching of the disciples which follows, Luke takes advantage of this context to include a clarification of the relationship between the kingdom of God as proclaimed by Jesus and the full realization of that kingdom in history. The question of the Pharisees, in fact, provides the perfect foil for his own instruction. The Pharisees were undoubtedly identifying the "kingdom of God" with the eschatological age. But Luke makes a fundamental distinction between the two.

The kingdom announced by Jesus is real. It is not merely a matter of "internal awareness." It is expressed in the healings and exorcisms, and indeed by the conversion of the people. Thus Luke can have Jesus speak of the kingdom of God "reaching" them (11:20) and "being given to them" (12:32). We shall see, shortly, that Jesus is proclaimed as a king (19:38), and disposes of rule within the kingdom (22:29); he dies as a king (23:38) and provides a place in his kingdom (23:42-43). He continues to instruct his followers about the kingdom of God after his resurrection (Acts 1:3), and his resurrection is an enthronement by God (Acts 2:34); people can in fact "enter the kingdom" (Acts 14:21).

But this kingdom is not to be equated absolutely with the end-time when the rule of God will be established, and the Son of Man will serve as "judge of the living and the dead" (Acts 17:31). For Luke's readers, that is still in the future. There is continuity between the two moments, but also a critical distinction. For the kingdom proclaimed by Jesus, there is no need to say "here it is or there" because it is manifest in Jesus' deeds of power. In the case of the coming of the Son of Man, there is no need to go "there or here" because his coming will be as sudden and obvious as lightning that sheets the whole sky.

The instructions concerning response to this final "visitation" of God are therefore consistent with those required by the present "visitation" through the prophet. As those called to discipleship cannot "look back" either at the pleasures ("eating and drinking") relationships ("marrying and being given in marriage") or possessions ("buying, selling, planting, building") they are leaving to follow the prophet, so must those caught in the final cataclysm be willing to lose the "life" located in such "having" in order to save it. Luke's addition of the example of Lot and Lot's wife is particularly pointed. Jesus tells the disciples: "Remember Lot's wife!" (a touch found only in Luke). The point clearly is—in Luke's understanding—that Lot's wife identified her life with her possessions. Looking back at what she had "lost," she "lost her life."

The question of "when" the kingdom will come is therefore entirely inappropriate. For Luke, the call of God, the visitation of God, is constant for every life, as close as death itself. The point is not chronology, but conversion. Those who would obey God must travel with sufficient lightness to be able to respond. The final question of the disciples, "where Lord?" is almost as obtuse, for the kingdom of God is not a place, but a rule. Jesus' answer is therefore parabolic but precise. Vultures gather wherever there is carrion. The kingdom is wherever the people are gathered by God's word.

FOR REFERENCE AND FURTHER STUDY

Feuillet, A. "La venue du règne de Dieu et du Fils de l'Homme (d'apres Luc xvii, 20 a xviii, 18)." *RSR* 35 (1948) 544–565.

Leaney, R. "The Days of the Son of Man (Luke xvii, 22)." *ExpT* 67 (1955–56) 28–29.

Leon-Dufour, X. "Luc 17, 33." *RSR* 69 (1981) 101–112.

Noack, B. *Das Gottesreich bei Lukas: Eine Studie zu Luk. 17, 20–24.* SymBU 10; Lund: Gleerup, 1948.

Schlosser, J. "Les jours de Noe et Lot: a propos de Luc xvii, 26–30." *RB* 80 (1973) 13–36.

49. *Parables on Prayer* (18:1-14)

1. He told them a parable with the point that it is necessary to continue praying always without giving up. 2. He said, "There was a judge in a certain city. He did not fear God. He had no regard for people. 3. There was a widow in that city. She kept coming to him and saying, 'Vindicate me against my opponent!' 4. And for a long time he was not willing to do it. But after this kept up, he said to himself, 'It's true I do not fear God or have any regard for people. 5. But this widow gives me so much trouble that I will give her justice! Otherwise she will keep coming and end up giving me a black eye!" 6. The Lord said, "Listen to what the unjust judge says. 7. Will God not do justice for his elect ones who are crying out to him day and night, and show patience toward them? 8. I tell you that he will do justice for them quickly. But when the Son of Man comes, will he in fact find faith on earth?" 9. And he told this parable to certain people who trusted in themselves as being righteous and scorned others: 10. "Two men went up to the temple to pray. One was a Pharisee. The other was a tax-agent. 11. The Pharisee stood and prayed these things to himself: 'God, I thank you that I am not like the rest of people. They are rapacious. They are unrighteous. They are adulterers. Or they are even like this tax-agent! 12. I fast twice a week. I donate tithes from everything I possess.' 13. But the tax-agent stood a long way back. He did not even want to raise his eyes toward heaven. Instead he beat his breast and said, 'God, have mercy on me. I am a sinner.' 14.. I say to you, this man went back down to his house justified rather than that other, because everyone self-exalting will be humbled. And everyone self-humbling will be exalted."

NOTES

1. *a parable with the point that*: The two parables which follow are found only in Luke, and the introduction to each is unusually explicit. This translation supplies the sense of *pros to dein*, which is literally "toward the necessity."

   to continue praying always: Because of the adverb *pantote*, the continuous sense of the present tense of *proseuchesthai* ("pray") is made explicit. The parable itself makes clear that "always" does not support any technique of "perpetual

prayer" or method of mysticism, but rather *consistency* and *perseverance* in praying. Luke-Acts emphasizes not only the prayer of Jesus but also that of the disciples (6:28; 11:1-2; 22:40, 46; Acts 1:14; 2:42; 3:1; 6:4, 6; 10:4, 9, 30-31; 12:5,
12; 16:13, 16, 25; 20:36; 21:5; 22:17; 28:8).

without giving up: The verb *enkakein* means to grow remiss in something, or culpa-
bly omit something. In the NT it predominantly has the meaning of "giving up"
because of discouragement (see 2 Thess 3:13; Eph 3:13; Gal 6:9; 2 Cor 4:1, 16).
The sense of the term here is made clear by the context.

2. *judge in a certain city*: Luke uses the indefinite twice: "a certain judge in a certain
city." He is meant to be a stock character. Except when the designation of *kritēs*
is applied to Jesus as "judge of the living and the dead," (Acts 10:42), Luke
uses the term for local magistrates (12:14, 58; Acts 18:15; but cf. 24:10).

fear God: Prov 1:7 considers "fear of the Lord" to be the beginning of wisdom,
and "fearing the Lord" is regularly used to describe the pious in the Psalms
(LXX 14:4; 21:23; 24:12; 32:18, etc.). Luke uses the expression "God-fearers" for
Gentiles attracted to Judaism in Acts 10:2, 22, 35; 13:16, 26. In effect, the man
is not religious and has no scruple.

no regard for people: The construction uses the middle voice of the verb *entrepo*
and suggests someone incapable of shame (see also 1 Cor 4:4; 2 Thess 3:14; Titus
2:8; Matt 21:37; Mark 12:6).

3. *a widow in that city*: The choice of character automatically heightens pressure on
the judge. In Israel as in every patriarchal, agriculturally based economy, certain classes of people were endemically vulnerable: the orphans, the sojourners, and the widows. Any "God-fearing" jurist would feel obliged by Torah
to take special care of her (see Deut 10:18; 14:29; 16:11, 14; 24:19-21; 26:12-13).
In particular there is the plain command, "you shall not prevent the justice due
the sojourner or the fatherless, or take a widow's grant in pledge" (Deut 24:17).
There is also this curse: "cursed be he who prevents the justice due to the sojourner, the fatherless, and the widow" (Deut 27:19). Doing justice for widows
becomes shorthand for covenantal loyalty among the prophets (Mal 3:5; Isa 1:17,
23; 10:2; Jer 5:28 [LXX]; 7:6; 22:3; Ezek 22:7; Ps 93:6). In contrast to those who
fail this obligation, God is the judge who will come to the aid of widows (LXX
Ps 67:5; 145:9). This motif is developed fully in Sirach 35:14-18, which some readers think underlies the present parable. For the rabbinic legislation on the main-
tenance of widows, see *m.Ket.* 4:12; 11:1-6; 12:3-4; *Git.* 5:3.

kept coming to him and saying: The imperfect *ērcheto* must be translated as iterative in order to catch the point of the story. She made the request over and over
again.

vindicate me against my opponent: The technical language of the court is used. *Endikeō* means to decide for someone, or to punish someone or take vengeance.
The *antidikos* is the opposing party, whether plaintiff or defendant.

4. *but after this kept up*: The Greek phrase is *meta tauta*, ("after these things"). Luke
uses the expression in 5:27; 10:1; 12:4; 17:8; Acts 13:20; 18:1, as a rather vague
temporal transition. The context here suggests the translation given.

It's true: Is literally "even if"; the translation replaces an awkward conditional sentence with a structure more idiomatically English.

5. *gives me so much trouble*: in light of the next sentence, one is tempted to render this, "giving me such a beating," for *kopos* has that literal meaning. In a broader sense it connotes trouble or suffering; cf. Luke 11:7, "don't bother me."

   otherwise she will keep coming: The translation once more makes an independent statement out of a Greek dependent clause, literally "lest she keep coming . . ." The judge will do one thing to prevent another. As in verse 3, the phrase, "keep coming" derives from the iterative sense of the present participle.

   end up giving me a black eye: In this case, the literal rendering of *hypōpiazō* maintains the delicious ambiguity of the original. She may in fact give him a sock in the eye! The term can also mean to damage the reputation, as it does in English. Although the judge has "no regard for humans," he may depend on some sort of reputation to continue being a judge.

6. *listen to what the unjust judge says*: Notice the similarity to the end of the parable in 16:8: the "Lord" delivers the moral of the story, and he designates the protagonist as "unjust," using the genitive form *adikias* as an adjective.

7. *do justice for his elect ones*: The verb *endikeō* is the same as is used in verses 3 and 5. In the LXX, the term refers to the vengeance that God will take for the righteous oppressed (see Deut 32:34-38; Ps 17:47; 93:1; 149:7). Luke uses "elect ones" (*eklektoi*) only here, although he speaks of the "elect Messiah" in 23:35 (cf. 9:35), and uses the verb form for the selection of persons for service in the community (6:13; Acts 1:2, 24; 6:5; 15:7, 22, 25). The idea of the "chosen people" is found e.g., in Deut 4:37; 7:7; 10:15; 14:2, and the expression "elect ones" recurs in LXX Pss 77:31; 88:3; 104:6, 43.

   crying out to him day and night: The verb *boaō* is used often in the LXX for appealing to God for help (Exod 8:12; 15:25; Num 12:13). Note in particular the threat in Deut 15:9 concerning the poor man who is given nothing "and he will cry out to the Lord against you and it will be sin in you." The expression "day and night" means continually, as in LXX Ps 1:2; 31:3; 41:3; 54:10. Luke uses it in 2:37; Acts 9:24; 20:31; 26:7. See also 1 Thess 2:9; 3:10; 2 Thess 3:8.

   show patience toward them: The way to understand *makrothymeō* here is much debated. The mood of the verb shifts from the subjunctive to the indicative. Some think the phrase should be treated as a separate question, with *makrothymeō* meaning "shall he delay"? (RSV, Fitzmyer). The next verse would then supply a negative answer: he will do justice quickly. The combination of verbs in Sir 35:14-18 has influenced this reading. But the overwhelming use of *makrothymeō* and its cognates is within the context of judicial restraint and long-suffering, or tolerance (cf. e.g., Jer 15:15; Prov 19:11; Sir 29:8). It is a quality most associated in the LXX with God (see Sir 18:11), so that *makrothymos kai polyeleos* ("long-suffering and rich in mercy") are regular attributes of the Lord (e.g., Exod 34:6; Num 14:18; Neh 9:17; Pss 7:11; 85:15; 102:8; 144:8; Wis 15:1). Luke nowhere else uses this vocabulary, but the dominant NT usage supports the reading in the translation (cf. Matt 18:26-29; 1 Thess 5:14; Jas 5:7-8; Rom 2:4; 9:22; Eph 4:2; 1 Tim 1:16; 1 Pet 3:20; 2 Pet 3:9, 15).

8. *do justice for them quickly*: Is literally, "accomplish their vindication" (*ekdikēsis*). For "quickly" (*en tachei*) see also Acts 12:7; 22:18; 25:4. The perceived contrast between "patience" (or: "delay") and "quickly" may be a false one, if "quickly" means not "after a short time" but rather "suddenly." It is possible, in other words, for God to wait for what seems a long time—as did the judge—and then decide "quickly" to act—as did the judge.

will he find faith: The image of the Son of Man coming to judge continues the discourse of 17:22-37. The particle *ara* gives the question a tentative, even troubled, character which the translation seeks to capture by the phrase "in fact." Perhaps "even" would be better. The question is particularly plaintive in light of the apostles' plea in 17:5, "give us faith."

9. *trusted in themselves as being righteous*: For the use of *peithō*, ("trust"), see 11:22; Acts 5:36-37. For "trusting in themselves" contrast Paul's statement in 2 Cor 1:9. The phrase "as being righteous" (*dikaioi*) could be translated "that they were," or "because they were"; the same ambiguity is in the Pharisee's prayer in verse 11. The characterization tells us at once that the audience is made up of Pharisees, even without the identification in the parable (cf. 10:29; 16:15).

and scorned others: The verb *exoutheneō* means to hold in contempt or reject (see e.g., 1 Sam 2:30; 8:7; 10:19; Pss 14:4 [LXX]; 21:24; 50:17; 52:5). Luke uses it of Herod's mockery of Jesus in 23:11, and of the "stone rejected by the builders" (in an adaptation of Ps 117:22) in Acts 4:11. The phrase translated "others" is literally "the rest" (*hoi loipoi*), which occurs also in the parable (v. 11), and says everything essential about the elitist claim: there are those who are righteous and "the rest" of the world.

10. *went up to the Temple to pray*: For the Temple as a place of prayer in Luke-Acts, see Luke 1:9; 19:46; 24:53; Acts 2:46; 3:1; 22:17.

Pharisee . . . tax-agent: With this identification, the reader is prepared for the reversal accomplished at the end, for the tax-agents (and the sinners) have consistently been portrayed in the narrative as open to the prophet and conversion, thereby "justifying God" (7:29; also 3:12; 5:27, 29, 30; 7:34; 15:1), whereas the Pharisees (with the lawyers/scribes) have just as consistently been portrayed as "rejecting God's will for them" (7:30) by "justifying themselves" (10:19; 16:15; also 5:21, 30, 33; 6:2, 7; 7:39; 11:38-39, 42, 43, 53; 12:1; 13:31; 14:1-3; 15:1-2; 16:14; 17:20).

11. *prayed these things to himself*: The phrasing in Greek is awkward. How should one render the preposition *pros* + the accusative? One reading is neutral: he prayed quietly to himself. Two readings are negative: he prayed to himself rather than to God; or, he prayed "with reference to himself" but with an eye on the tax-agent!

like the rest of people: The translation "other people" would be more idiomatic, but *hoi loipoi* has the elitist edge of contrast noted in verse 9. The verb "I give thanks" (*eucharistō*) is a staple of NT prayer (e.g., Rom 1:8; 7:25; 16:4; Phlm 4). The same problem of rendering the *hoti* clause is found here as in verse 9. It can mean "because I am not" or "that I am not"; it comes to much the same thing.

rapacious . . . unrighteous . . . adulterers: The Pharisee's prayer is not only self-aggrandizing; it is, on the terms of the narrative, false. The Pharisees have been declared by Jesus to be "on the inside full of rapacity (*harpage*) and evil" (11:39). They are termed "money-lovers" (*philargyroi*) in 16:14, and this was joined by implication to the charge of adultery in 16:18. Finally, although they justify themselves, Jesus has declared such self-exaltation to be an "abomination (*bdelygma*)" before God (16:15).

even like this tax-agent: The pharisaic animus against the tax-agents (*telonai*) is recorded in 5:30; 7:34; 15:1. The Pharisee gives a portrait of prayer with peripheral vision.

12. *I fast twice a week*: The Pharisees are said to fast "frequently" in Luke 5:33. Luke also seems to regard fasting as a common feature of Jewish piety (2:37) and as a practice continued in the Church (Acts 13:2-3; 14:23). Matt 6:16-18 has Jesus giving advice about fasting in contrast to "the hypocrites," by whom Matthew means the Pharisees. The evidence internal to the rabbinic tradition suggests a concern more for the proper observance of public fast days such as were prescribed for the day of atonement (Lev 16:29-31; Num 29:7); the Mishnah tractate *Ta'anith* does not specify days of private fasting for sages. In *bT Ta'anith* 12a, the days Monday and Thursday are given as examples of a private pledge to fast, but in general the tradition is cautious concerning private fasting as it is about other forms of asceticism. This Pharisee was boasting, in other words, of an asceticism beyond the norm.

    I donate tithes from everything I possess: The basic institution of tithing (Deut 14:22-29) was greatly elaborated by the pharisaic *ḥaburah* ("fellowship"). One of the distinguishing marks between "associates" and the *am-ha-aretz* ("people of the land," that is, not members of the Pharisaic group), was the careful observance of first and second tithes (cf. *m.Demai* 2:2-3). Once more, this Pharisee is claiming a very high standard of observance beyond the legal requirements. That Luke is not entirely caricaturing the prayer of the pious can be seen from the example of a rabbinic prayer in *bT Ber.* 28b.

13. *God have mercy on me. I am a sinner*: Four aspects of the tax-agent's humility are briefly indicated by Luke: 1) he stood far off; 2) he kept his eyes lowered; 3) he beat his breast (as a sign of repentance, cf. Luke 23:48); 4) he cries out for mercy (cf. 17:13). Luke makes the tax-agent different from the Pharisee in two obvious respects. Rather than suggest that he is *dikaios*, much less give evidence for it, he declares himself to be exactly what the Pharisee considered him a sinner (*harmartolos*). Furthermore, rather than speak to God with reference to the Pharisee (with peripheral vision), he straightforwardly begs for mercy. The imperative of *hilaskomai* is used; the verb is predominantly used in contexts of the propitiation of sins (cf. LXX Pss 24:11; 64:3; 77:38; 78:9; cf. also Rom 3:25; Heb 2:17; 1 John 2:2; 4:10).

14. *justified rather than that other*: The verb *dikaioō* is here used in the perfect passive, making it clear that it is God who does the justifying: God considers him righteous.

    everyone self-exalting: This is exactly the same statement made by Jesus in 14:11

at the banquet when the Pharisees sought the best seats. It expresses the Lukan theme of the divine reversal. See the note on 14:11 for the parallel passages.

INTERPRETATION

The two parables that follow Jesus' eschatological discourse in 17:22-37 are found only in Luke. As usual, they serve a narrative function beyond their self-contained message. The first is told to the disciples, the second to those unmistakably identifiable as Pharisees. We recognize at once Luke's alternating pattern, and fully expect the story told the disciples to be one of positive exhortation, and the one told the opponents to be a story of rejection.

The parable of the widow and the unjust judge is brilliantly placed immediately after the discourse in which Jesus makes clear that the kingdom he proclaims is not yet the end-time, that there must be a period in which the disciples will "long to see one of the days of the Son of Man and will not see it" (17:22). A parable told with the point that "it is necessary to pray constantly without giving up" is particularly appropriate. The readers can all too easily see themselves as the widow, subject to oppression and delayed retribution, and by losing hope and courage become those who "have faith for a time but in a season of testing fall away" (8:13). The parable makes its point so forcefully and humorously that little comment is required. Contemporary readers can easily imagine an enraged bag lady hitting the negligent magistrate over the head and literally "giving him a black eye." We are meant, I think, to laugh.

Just as the introduction to this parable is unusually explicit (though no more so than the one following), its moral is made explicit as a logion of "the Lord" (18:6). As with the parable of the household manager, it is the parabalist himself who identifies the central character as "unjust," and invites the hearer to a *qal wehomer* conclusion: God's patience is greater, and God's response to prayer is faster for his elect. But the final question puts a twist on the assurance: God's mercy and long-suffering are not in doubt. But are there any "widows" among the listeners who "cry out to him day and night?" Will the Son of Man find faith on earth?

The parable of the Pharisee and tax-agent is also given an introduction that directs the reader's perception. From the narrative descriptions before this, we know that "those who trust in themselves that they are righteous and scorn others" can only mean the Pharisees and lawyers. This is not to suggest that readers could not make their own further applications to themselves or persons in the community of similar spiritual physiognomy—though to do so risks replicating the parable itself with an unintended irony—but it is to suggest that its narrative function is clearly to show once again the pattern of divine reversal in the story of the Prophet and the people. No less than the parables of the "lost and found" in Luke 15:2-34 are these parables polemical instruments.

The parable itself is one that invites internalization by every reader because it speaks to something deep within the heart of every human. The love of God can so easily turn into an idolatrous self-love; the gift can so quickly be seized as a possession; what comes from another can so blithely be turned into self-accomplishment. Prayer can be transformed into boasting. Piety is not an unambiguous posture. The literary skill revealed by the story matches its spiritual insight. The pious one is all convoluted comparison and contrast; he can receive no gift because he cannot stop counting his possessions. His prayer is one of peripheral vision. Worse, he assumes God's role of judge: not only does he enumerate his own claims to being just, but he reminds God of the deficiency of the tax-agent, in case God had not noticed.

In contrast, the tax-agent is utter simplicity and truth. Indeed, he is a sinner. Indeed, he requires God's gift of righteousness because he has none of his own. And because he both needs and recognizes his need for the gift he receives it.

The parables together do more than remind us that prayer is a theme in Luke-Acts; they show us *why* prayer is a theme. For Luke, prayer is faith in action. Prayer is not an optional exercise in piety, carried out to demonstrate one's relationship with God. It *is* that relationship with God. The way one prays therefore reveals that relationship. If the disciples do not "cry out day and night" to the Lord, then they in fact do not have faith, for that is what faith does. Similarly, if prayer is self-assertion before God, then it *cannot* be answered by God's gift of righteousness; possession and gift cancel each other.

For Reference and Further Study

Bailey, K. E. *Through Peasant Eyes: More Lucan Parables, Their Culture, Their Style* (Grand Rapids: Eerdmans, 1980) 127–156.

Descamps, A. *Les Justes et la Justice dans les évangiles et le christianisme primitive hormis la doctrine proprement paulinienne* (Gembloux: J. Duculot, 1950) 96–98.

Freed, E. D. "The Parable of the Judge and the Widow (Luke 18:1-8)." *NTS* 33 (1987) 38–60.

Jeremias, J. *The Parables of Jesus.* Rev. ed. (New York: Charles Scribner's Sons, 1962) 153–157, 139–144.

Spicq, C. "La parabole de la veuve obstinée et du juge inerte, aux decisions impromptues (Lc xviii, 1–18)." *RB* 68 (1961) 68–90.

50. *Entering the Kingdom* (18:15-34)

15. People were even bringing infants to him so that he might touch them. When the disciples spotted this, they began rebuking them. 16. But Jesus summoned them. He said, "Allow the little children to come to me. Stop preventing them, for the kingdom of God is made up of such as these! 17. Amen I tell you, whoever does not accept the kingdom of God as a child will not enter it." 18. A certain ruler asked him, "Good Teacher, What should I do to inherit eternal life?" 19. Jesus said to him, "Why do you call me good? No one is good except one, God. 20. You know the commandments: 'Do not commit adultery. Do not kill. Do not steal. Do not give false testimony. Honor your father and mother.' " 21. He said, "I have kept all these since youth." 22. When Jesus heard this, he said to him, "One thing remains for you to do: sell everything you possess. Give it to the poor. You will have treasure in heaven. And come, follow me!" 23. When he had heard these words, he became extremely sorrowful, for he was extremely wealthy. 24. When Jesus saw that he had grown sorrowful, he said, "How difficult it is for those who have money to enter the kingdom of God! 25. It is in fact easier for a camel to enter the eye of a needle than for a rich person to enter the kingdom of God." 26. Those who heard this said, "Then who can be saved?" 27. And he said, "Things that are impossible for people are possible for God." 28. Peter said, "Look, we left our own things and followed you!" 29. He said to them, "Amen I tell you, there is no one who has left home or wife or brothers or relatives or children for the sake of the kingdom of God 30. who will not receive many times over in this time and eternal life in the age that is coming." 31. He gathered the twelve and told them: "Look, we are going up to Jerusalem. And everything written by the prophets about the Son of Man will be fulfilled. 32. He will be handed over to the Gentiles. He will be ridiculed. He will be insulted. He will be spat upon. 33. They will flog him. They will kill him. On the third day he will rise again." 34. But they understood nothing of these things and this saying was hidden from them. They did not know what he was saying.

NOTES

15. *even bringing infants*: This incident has a parallel in Mark 10:13-16 and Matt 19:13-15. In contrast to the *paidia* ("little children") in their versions, Luke uses *brephē* ("infants"), and the *kai* is emphatic (perhaps because of this word choice). Like the parallels, Luke uses *paidia* in the next verse. The reader remembers the earlier account of the child who is received in Jesus' name (9:48). The touch of Jesus is sought in Luke 6:19; 8:44, and Jesus heals by touching in 5:13 and 7:14. Matt 19:13 adds, "pray for them."

began rebuking them: The imperfect tense of *epitimaō* expresses a reaction that Jesus cuts short. The verb is used for Jesus' rebuke of demons (4:35, 41; 9:42), fever

(4:39) and wind (8:24), but also of the disciples in 9:21 and 9:55. The antecedent of "them" is not entirely clear: it could be the children or those who brought them forward.

16. *Jesus summoned them*: The *auta* makes clear that it is the children and not the parents or disciples that he calls to himself. Mark 10:14 has Jesus embrace the children.

    allow the little children: As so often in pronouncement stories, it is the saying by Jesus that remains the most constant element in all three Synoptists, with only an alteration of word order in Matt 9:14. The verb *aphiēmi* is used here in the same way as in 6:42; 9:60; 13:18. The negation of the present imperative demands the translation "stop preventing," rather than the generalized "don't prevent." The language is closely paralleled in the incident of the nondisciple exorcist in 9:49-50, and the charge against the lawyers in 11:52.

    made up of such as these: The translation of the genitive is particularly difficult: it could be rendered, "theirs is the kingdom," but Luke clearly does not mean that they possess it; God does. He means, rather, that such as children are the members of the kingdom, they "make up" its membership. The genitive, therefore, is strictly a "material genitive" although it is odd to think of people that way. This whole section of the narrative is dominated by language concerning the *basileia tou theou* ("kingdom of God").

17. *accept the kingdom of God as a child*: The wording is exactly the same as in Mark 10:15. The similar saying in Matt 18:3 has, "whoever does not turn and become as a child will not enter the kingdom of heaven." Matthew therefore makes "like a child" to be the subjective attitude of one who hears the preaching of the kingdom and accepts it simply. Luke may mean that, but it is more likely that he means that the kingdom is like a child whom one must accept. See the interpretation which follows.

    will not enter it: The verb *eiserchomai* ("enter") is used in a similar sense (and with "prevent") in 11:52. In 13:24 the disciples are encouraged to "struggle to enter" through the narrow door. The parable of the banquet also uses the image of "entering" (14:23), and it will be used again below in 18:25.

18. *a certain ruler asked him*: Although the form of the question is the same as in Mark 10:17 and Matt 19:16, Luke has changed the character of the story by identifying the questioner as a "ruler" (*archōn*) and therefore one who in the narrative stands opposed to the prophet (see 14:1; 23:13, 35; 24:20; Acts 4:5, 8, 26; 13:27). Note as well that the question is the same as that asked by the lawyer in 10:25. See the note on that verse for the background of "eternal life."

19. *why do you call me good*: Luke and Mark 10:18 phrase the question identically. Matt 19:17 has, "why do you ask me about the good?" The statement that God alone is good probably derives from the piety of the psalms, where the affirmation of God as "good" (*agathos*) occurs in LXX Pss 53:6; 72:1; 134:3; 135:1, and especially in the refrain "because he is good" in Pss 117:1, 2, 3, 4, 29. Jesus' response is the reflex deflection of human praise in favor of God as source of all being and goodness.

20. *you know the commandments*: The response is similar to the one given the lawyer in 10:26. Rather than the combination of Deut 6:5 and Lev 19:18, however, we find here five of the ten commandments. With the exception of "honor your father and mother" (which should precede the others), they follow the order of Deut 5:16-20 rather than that of Exod 20:12-16. The negative *mē* is used rather than the *ou* of the LXX (in contrast to the citations in Rom 13:9 and Jas 2:11 but like the parallels in Mark 10:19 and Matt 19:18-19). Matt 19:19 adds to this list the commandment of love from Lev 19:18.

do not commit adultery: This appeared as part of the Pharisees' prayer in 18:11, and as an example of the law of God that remained eternally in force, in 16:18.

honor your father and mother: The verb *timaō* ("honor") in this commandment connotes an obligation of financial assistance (cf. Tob 4:3; Sir 3:3-16). The seriousness of the obligation is suggested by its frequent repetition in the NT writings (see Matt 15:4; 19:19; Mark 7:10; 10:19; Eph 6:2; 1 Tim 5:8). In the rabbinic literature, the commandment occurs less frequently than one might expect; although it is recognized as one of the commands (like that of almsgiving) for which there is a reward in the future life (*m.Peah* 1:1; *bT Hul.* 142a), and that therefore an earthly court could not levy penalties for nonobservance (*bT Hul.* 110b), the commandment is considered of less importance than that of Sabbath observance (*bT Yeb.* 5b; *Bab.Mez.* 32a), and of no greater significance than the study of Torah (*bT Shab.* 127a; *Ker.* 28a). One isolated saying even declares the study of Torah superior to the honoring of father and mother (*bT Meg.* 16b). This relativization is significant because it is the same demanded by Jesus in this passage.

21. *I have kept all these since youth*: The verb "to keep" (*phylassō*) means the same as "perform" in this context (see 11:28). In contrast to Luke and Mark 10:20, Matthew calls the questioner a "youth" (*neaniskos*, 19:20). There is no suggestion of this in Luke, for whom the man is a "ruler." Luke also lacks the positive Markan element of Jesus' "gazing at him and loving him."

22. *sell everything you possess*: This command—including the notion of having treasure in heaven—is basically the same as that given to the disciples in 12:33, except that this version has "give it to the poor" rather than "give alms." The poor, of course, are those repudiated by the powerful but special recipients of the good news about the kingdom (4:18; 6:20; 7:22). By telling this ruler to "give to the poor everything you own," Jesus invites him to a fundamental reversal of his own status. It is a conversion call even more radical than that addressed to the Pharisees, that they should invite the poor to their banquets (14:13). This is a call to discipleship, which demands giving up all one's possessions (14:33). For Luke, this is fundamental, rather than a mark of "perfection" as in Matt 19:21.

come, follow me: The invitation to discipleship demands a higher degree of commitment than keeping the ten commandments. It means leaving relationships and possessions (5:11, 28) and taking up one's own cross (9:23). For this man it means as well leaving the seat of power as a "ruler of the people."

23. *became extremely sorrowful*: This is the only time Luke uses *perilypos*, which connotes an deep level of distress, in this case caused by grief at the prospect of

losing wealth. The translation deliberately supplies "extremely" to the first adjective to capture its force and to balance the "extremely" (*sphodra*) Luke applies to the wealth. By using the word *plousios* ("wealthy"), Luke doubly identifies this man as one closed to the call of God; power and possessions prevent a response to the prophet. In contrast to Mark 10:22 and Matt 19:22, however, the ruler is not said to "go away." This means that Jesus' subsequent pronouncement is not only an instruction of the disciples but a rebuke to the rich ruler.

24. *enter the kingdom of God*: In contrast to Mark 10:23 and Matt 19:23, Luke has the present tense rather than the future; the focus therefore is on the kingdom—the people of God—forming around the prophet Jesus, rather than on the future life. The rich and powerful cannot respond to the prophet's call within the narrative—or so it seems to this point (cf. Zacchaeus, in the next story). Luke's version of Jesus' pronouncement can be easily generalized, however, since he does not speak only of "the rich" but of "those who have money"—no matter how little.

    a camel to enter the eye of a needle: Despite all attempts to soften this saying, it resists reduction to something less paradoxical (cf. 6:41 for similar hyperbole, and 16:18 for the form "it is easier"). The camel is a real camel, the needle a real needle. It is meant to be impossible, otherwise the following statement (about what is "possible" in v. 27) would have no point. This translation maintains the balance in the Greek between the two uses of "entering," even though "passing through the eye of a needle" sounds better.

26. *then who can be saved*: The conjunction *kai* ("and") is treated as inferential. The question itself is similar to the one posed by 13:23, "are a few being saved?" The disciples' question here serves to set up the response. Luke omits the element of astonishment found in Mark 10:24 and Matt 19:25.

27. *impossible . . . possible*: Luke generalizes the statement of Mark 10:27 and Matt 19:26 by using the plural "things" rather than the singular. Both the parallels also add the statement "all things are possible for God." In Luke, this sentiment is found not in Jesus' mouth but in the message of the angel to Mary, "Nothing is impossible for God" (1:37; cf. Gen 18:14). Jesus' response here makes clear in any case that "salvation" is something that comes from God's power received by faith (see 7:50; 8:12, 48, 50; 9:24, 56; 17:19).

28. *left our own things*: Peter's use of *ta idia* ("own things") rather than "all things" (*ta panta*) as in Mark 10:28 and Matt 19:27 is strange, particularly because he has shown the disciples "leaving all things" to follow Jesus (5:11 and 5:28). The choice of words may anticipate the language of sharing possessions in Acts 4:32, where the believers are said to "call nothing their own thing (*idion*)."

29. *home or wife or brothers*: The list of relationships and possessions to be left is slightly different than the parallels in Matt 19:29 and Mark 10:29. Luke adds "wife" (cf. 14:20, 26), but omits "sisters." He replaces "mother and father" with "relatives" (perhaps conscious of the closeness of "honor father and mother" immediately above?), and he omits "fields."

    for the sake of the kingdom of God: Luke makes this saying consistent with the entire narrative logic. Matt 19:29 has "for the sake of my name" and Mark 10:29

has "for my sake and for the sake of the Gospel." These expressions leap beyond the narrative framework more obviously than Luke's.

30. *receive many times over*: In contrast to Mark 10:30, which provides a point-by-point replacement of what was given up in Mark 10:29, Luke (and Matt 19:29) use a general expression for an abundant recompense (in Luke, *pollaplēsiona*). The emphasis of course is on receiving rather than grasping.

    in this time: The word used is *kairos*, which has the sense of "season" or "set period of time" (see 12:56; 19:44). Here because of the implied contrast with the "coming world," it is equivalent to *ha olam ha zeh* ("this present world"). This is the only time Luke uses the expression "coming world" (found also in Mark 10:30 but absent in Matt 19:29), although he uses "that age" of the resurrection in 20:35, and speaks of the people of "this age" in 16:8 and 20:34. The language of "this world" and "the world to come (*ha olam ha ba*)" is part of the apocalyptic (4 Ezra 7:47; 8:1) and rabbinic (*Pirke Aboth* 2:8) world-view. For "eternal life," see the note on 10:25.

31. *we are going up to Jerusalem*: This is one of the editorial reminders Luke uses to structure the journey narrative (9:31, 51, 53; 13:4, 22, 33-34; 17:11).

    everything written by the prophets: Although this passion prediction is shared with Matt 20:17-19 and Mark 10:32-34, Luke alone has the characteristic emphasis on the fulfilling of prophecy which will be echoed in the resurrection accounts (24:27, 44).

32. *handed over to the Gentiles*: Luke omits here the reference to the "high priests and scribes" found in Mark 10:33 and Matt 20:18. The agent of the handing over is left obscure; it could even be read as a "divine passive."

    will be ridiculed: The verb *empaizō* means to "make mock" of someone. It is fulfilled in Luke's passion narrative both before Herod (23:11) and the soldiers (23:36). Luke adds the words "be insulted" (*hybrizein*, cf. 11:45). With Mark 10:34, he has "spat upon" (*emptyō*), although unlike both Matthew and Mark, Luke has no reference to the spitting in his passion narrative.

33. *flog him . . . kill him*: The *verberatio* or scourging was a common feature of Roman punishment (e.g., Acts 22:24) and sometimes preceded crucifixion (Josephus, *Jewish War* 2:306). John's passion narrative shows Pilate handing Jesus over to be scourged (*mastigoō*, 19:1). In Luke, Pilate twice threatens to "discipline" (*paideuō*) Jesus but the deed itself is not described (23:16, 22). The image of the Suffering Servant who is flogged and spat upon lies in the background (see Isa 50:6). In Matt 20:19, the verb "crucify" (*stauroō*) is used rather than "kill" (*apokteinō*).

    third day he will rise: Compare the statements in 9:22 and 13:22, as well as 24:7, 21, 46; Acts 10:40.

34. *they understood nothing*: Luke repeats the point in three different forms. In his narrative, it is not the identity of Jesus as Messiah that forms the mystery, but the necessity of the Messiah to suffer (see 24:25-26).

INTERPRETATION

Already in Luke's source (the Gospel of Mark) the two pronouncement stories of the children and the wealthy would-be disciple are deliberately joined together in order to form a contrast (Mark 10:13-31). Already in Mark, these pronouncements concerning discipleship are connected to the final prediction of the passion (Mark 10:32-34). The great Lukan interpolation now rejoins the Markan narrative. Our reading of Luke once more demands careful attention to the way he both accepts and alters his source, retains the basic message of Mark yet shapes it to his own narrative ends. And because we have available to us also Matthew's reading and revision of Mark, our analysis of Luke's particular emphasis gains in precision.

In Mark, the stories are linked by the theme of "entering the kingdom": the children who are led to Jesus are received by him despite the protestations of the disciples, and his action of accepting them is the occasion for the lesson: they must accept the kingdom as a child. What does this mean? In context, it means that the kingdom of God proclaimed by Jesus is "made up of" just such helpless, useless types as children: the poor, the lame, the blind, the sinners.

In contrast to Matthew's interiorizing of Jesus' pronouncement, by which the disciples are told to "become like children," so that one must supply some quality of openness or trust supposedly typical of children, Luke maintains Mark's more objective reading of the tradition, and indeed sharpens it by calling the children in the first instance *brephē*, that is infants, who can scarcely have any atttitude at all. In Luke, therefore, the *hōs paidion* refers not to the spirituality of the one entering the kingdom, but rather to the character of the kingdom: hospitality and the reception of the outcast are essential to the kingdom ruled by the compassionate God.

Already in Mark, the story of the rich man stands as a contrast to that of the children. Their youth is a contrast to his maturity (only in Matthew is the rich man a *neaniskos* [youth]; in Mark and Luke he keeps the commandments "since youth," and there is no reason to think of him as a "young man"); their passivity to his aggressive questioning; their poverty to his wealth; their "having the kingdom" to his "lacking one thing." And Luke deliberately accentuates the contrast, by making the rich man a "ruler" (*archōn*). This small touch changes the character of the story, for in Luke, the rulers are steadfastly against the prophet. Rather than a sincere request to learn about discipleship—to which Jesus responds with "love" as in Mark—we recognize the sort of testing question posed by the lawyer in 10:25. This man is exceedingly wealthy, he has kept all the laws, and he is a ruler: the portrait of those closed to the prophet's visitation is complete.

Rather than have the man leave sorrowfully, therefore, as a "failed disciple," as in Matthew and Mark, Luke keeps him on the scene to hear the prophet's hard words concerning those who cannot respond to the call of God, just as the lawyer who earlier asked this question about "eternal life" and was answered in terms of "the commandments" but who needed further advice, was required to listen to the story of the good Samaritan before being told, "Go and do the same" (10:37).

For those who "rely on themselves that they are righteous," and who "justify themselves" and who are "lovers of money" in Luke's narrative, it is indeed "humanly impossible" to enter this kingdom; trust in mammon for security in one's existence, even when mammon is one's self-attributed righteousness, makes it impossible to "sell everything and give it to the poor." The rich ruler is not only asked to strip himself of his protection, but to join the ranks of those who must rely entirely on the mercy of God—like children. He cannot accept that challenge. The sheer greatness of his wealth generates the greatness of his "sorrow."

The disciples' question concerning who can be saved is appropriate, given Jesus' stark statement of the camel and the needle. The point of the comparison is precisely its impossibility; no need to seek, as so many have, for a softening (as though Jesus were really talking about a small gate in the city walls). But what is humanly impossible is possible for God. The kingdom proclaimed by Jesus is entirely about the power of God at work to heal and liberate and empower, not about humans accomplishing things for themselves. The point of the rich man's disposal of his property was *not* another "good work" or observance of Torah, but precisely to abandon all possessions in order to receive the good news as one who was poor. We will see in the subsequent stories of 18:35–19:10, how "faith saves" and how the reception of the prophet can enable even a wealthy sinner to dispose of possessions.

But the best evidence for the work God is doing in this visitation is the fact that the disciples themselves have left their possessions to follow Jesus. The pronouncement had not said that "the wealthy" found it difficult to enter the kingdom, but "those who had possessions." It is just as hard to leave family and friends and boats and tax collector's booth, as it is to leave "great wealth" when it means throwing one's life completely over to God in faith. The words of promise concerning those who have left all such things, therefore, stands as surety for what was told the ruler: giving away possessions makes a "treasure in heaven."

The pattern of "giving away/getting back more" is particularly pertinent to Jesus' next words, the final prediction of the passion. Although this is the third "formal" passion prophecy (see 9:22, 44), Luke has added many other allusions and informal predictions to his narrative (see 9:31, 51; 13:33; 17:25). This is by far the most elaborate in its details. But notice that the listing of humiliations matches in detail the listing of "things given up" by those who follow Jesus. Likewise, the "being raised up on the third day" matches the "in the age to come, eternal life" of his promise.

The way of discipleship, Luke has often told the readers, follows the path of the Messiah. Only after the resurrection will the disciples understand how "it was necessary for the Messiah to suffer these things and enter into his glory" (Luke 24:26) and that the suffering of Jesus *did* "fulfill everything written in the prophets" (18:31; 24:27, 44). But on this side of the resurrection, the necessity of suffering remains as dark to the disciples as the giving up of possessions does to the rich ruler. They do not understand (18:34; cf. 9:45).

For Reference and Further Study

Degenhardt, H.-J. *Lukas Evangelist der Armen* (Stuttgart: Katholisches Bibelwerk, 1965) 136–159.

Dupont, J. *Les Béatitudes* (Paris: J. Gabalda, 1973) III: 153–160.

Johnson, L. T. *The Literary Function of Possessions in Luke-Acts* (SBLDS 39; Missoula: Scholars Press, 1977) 144–145.

Légasse, S. *Jésus et l'enfant: "Enfants," "petits" et "simples" dans la tradition synoptique* (EBib; Paris: J. Gabalda, 1969) 36–43; 195–209; 326–333.

Tannehill, R. *The Narrative Unity of Luke-Acts*. Vol.I: The Gospel According to Luke (Foundations and Facets; Philadelphia: Fortress, 1986) 120–121; 186–187.

51. *Saving Faith—Again* (18:35–19:10)

35. As he approached Jericho there was a certain blind man. He was sitting beside the road begging. 36. As the crowd was passing through he heard it. He asked what was happening. 37. They told him that Jesus the Nazorean was passing by. 38. So he shouted out, "Jesus, Son of David! Show mercy to me!" 39. Those in front began to rebuke him into silence, but he shouted even more, "Son of David! Show mercy to me!" 40. Jesus stood still. He ordered that the man be brought to him. When he had come close, he questioned him: 41. "What do you want me to do for you?" He said, "Master, I want to see again." 42. Jesus said to him, "Regain your sight. Your faith has saved you." 43. Immediately he could see again, and he began following him, glorifying God. When all the people saw it they gave praise to God. 19:1. Jesus entered Jericho and was passing through it. 2. There was a man there named Zacchaeus. He was a chief tax-agent. And he was wealthy. 3. He was trying to see who Jesus was but he could not see over the crowd, since he was so short. 4. He ran to the front and climbed up a sycamore tree that Jesus was about to pass by, in order to see him. 5. When he reached the spot, Jesus looked up. He said to him, "Zacchaeus, hurry down from there! For I must stay in your house today!" 6. He quickly climbed down and joyfully welcomed him. 7. When everyone saw this they began grumbling. They said that he was going to lodge with a man who was a sinner. 8. Zacchaeus stopped and said to the Lord, "Look, Lord, I am giving half of my possessions to the poor. And if I have cheated some one of something, I make fourfold restitution." 9. Jesus said to him, "Today salvation has happened in this house, because he too is a child of Abraham. 10. For the Son of Man came to seek and save what was lost."

NOTES

35. *as he approached Jericho*: Luke shares this story with Mark 10:46-52 and Matt 20:29-34, each of whom places the story at Jesus' departure from the city. Luke has it at the entrance in order to fit in his second story about Zacchaeus (19:1).

a certain blind man: Mark 10:46 calls him "Bartimaeus son of Timaeus," which is an identification and translation at once. Matthew typically doubles the characters (two blind men) as in fact he doubles the story itself, having given an earlier version in Matt 9:27-31.

beside the road begging: Luke uses the participle *epaitōn*, whereas Mark 10:46 identifies him simply as "a beggar (*prosaitēs*)." The blind man is obviously one of the poor and therefore one of the outcast of the people (see 4:18; 7:22; 14:13, 21). In both Mark and Luke the story provides a contrast to the rich ruler (Mark 10:17-22; Luke 18:18-23). Begging was as much a cause of shame in that world as in our own, as shown by the reflection of the dishonest manager, "I am ashamed to beg." See also Epictetus, *Discourses* 3, 22, 89: "A Cynic who excites pity is regarded as a beggar; everybody turns away from him, everybody takes offense at him."

36. *what was happening*: Is literally, "what this might be," using the optative mood (cf. 1:29; 8:19). Luke uses the same construction with this verb *punthanomai* ("inquire") in 15:26 and Acts 21:33.

37. *Jesus the Nazorean*: Mark 10:47 has "the Nazarene" (*nazarēnos*) as does also Luke in 4:34 and 24:19, which is clearly a reference to Jesus' hometown. But here Luke uses the form *nazōraios*, found also in Matt 2:23; 26:71 and John 18:5-7; 19:19, but otherwise used only in Luke-Acts (here, and Acts 2:22; 3:6; 4:10; 6:14; 22:8; 24:5; 26:91). The origin and original meaning of the designation are obscure. Does it have some connection to the idea of being dedicated to God, or to the shoot (in Heb. *nezer*) from the root of Jesse in Isa 11:1, and therefore have a messianic nuance? Since the blind man here calls him "Son of David," it is possible, but we cannot tell if the term meant anything like this to Luke himself.

38. *so he shouted out*: As often in narrative, the conjunction *kai* ("and") asks to be treated responsively, as "so": he shouted because of what he heard about Jesus. Luke's replacement of Mark's *krazō* (which he retains in v. 39) with *boaō* may be influenced by the saying of Jesus in 18:7, "he will speedily do justice for those who cry out (*boaō*)."

    Jesus, son of David: Mark 10:47 and Luke supply the name "Jesus" which Matt 20:29 lacks. The twofold repetition here is the first use of this designation in Luke's Gospel, although it is obviously implied by 1:27, 32, 69; 2:4, 11; 3:31, and will be picked up by the controversy story in 20:41-44. The title is used far more extensively in Matthew (see 1:1, 20; 9:27; 12:23; 15:22; 20:30-31; 21:9, 15).

    show mercy to me: Given the fact that he is a beggar, his cry for "mercy" (*eleos*) could be heard as a request for alms (as in Acts 3:2-10), which also may be why bystanders tried to silence him. His subsequent response to Jesus' question shows that he desired "mercy" at a more fundamental level (see 16:24; 17:13). For the seriousness of the obligation to give charity to beggars, cf. *bT Bab.Bat.* 10a.

39. *those in front*: Is literally "those going ahead" (*hoi proagontes*). It is probably intended in the spatial sense, but one is tempted to treat it as "leaders," since they will again shortly try to silence a crowd's response to Jesus (19:39).

40. *that the man be brought*: Jesus' authority is obvious within this group, which responds to his directions. Luke omits the direct discourse of Mark 10:49, "courage, get up, he is calling you," as well as the picturesque detail of the man taking off his garment as he got to his feet (10:50).

41. *Master, I want to see again*: In the context of this healing story, the designation *kyrios* should be taken in its full sense (as in Matt 20:33; cf. Luke 5:12; 7:46), especially in light of the distinction to be made shortly between "Son of David" and "Lord" (20:41-44). Mark 10:51 has the man call Jesus *rabbouni* ("my teacher").

42. *your faith has saved you*: This reassurance is characteristic of the Lukan healing stories (7:50; 8:48, 50; 17:19). The note of "salvation" will be picked up in the next story as well.

43. *immediately he could see again*: Luke often uses *parachrēma* ("immediately") to signal the sudden results of a miracle (4:39; 5:25; 8:44, 47, 55; 13:13; Acts 3:7; 5:10;

13:11; 16:26). Equally typical is the response of "glorifying God" (2:20; 4:15; 5:25-26; 7:16; 13:13; 17:15).

19:1. *entered Jericho and was passing through*: By this spatial rearrangement, Luke manages to include both the previous story and this one within the environs of Jericho. The story of Zacchaeus is found only in Luke's Gospel.

2. *a chief tax-agent*: By calling him an *architelōnēs* (the only usage in the NT), Luke establishes a parallel to the *archōn* of 18:18. Like that earlier ruler, this man also is wealthy (*plousios*). The name Zacchaeus appears only here in the NT and otherwise in the Bible only at 2 Macc 10:19.

3. *trying to see who Jesus was*: The translation of *zēteō* as "try" fits the immediate context, but it should be noticed that Luke sets up by means of this word a verbal link with the conclusion of the story: the Son of Man "seeks and saves" that which is lost. Zacchaeus seeks to see and does not know that he is being sought after and saved.

5. *must stay in your house today*: At one level, the statement is entirely pedestrian. At another level, Luke suggests broader literary and religious themes of his Gospel. The word "today" (*sēmeron*) will portentously be repeated in 19:9 with regard to salvation, as it does other times in the narrative (2:11; 4:21; 5:26; 13:32-33). The impersonal verb *dei*, as we have often noticed, also is used to designate important turning points in the story as directed by God (2:49; 4:43; 9:22; 13:16, 33; 17:25; 21:9; 22:37; 24:7, 26, 44, and often in Acts). In his instructions to missionaries, Jesus stresses the importance of "remaining" (*menō*) at a host's house (9:4; 10:7). The verb here therefore suggests that Zacchaeus is being provided the opportunity to welcome the Prophet and his message about the kingdom of God.

6. *joyfully welcomed him*: Again the note of hospitality is obvious, since Luke uses the same verb (*hypodechomai*) as for Martha's reception of Jesus (see also [with *dechomai*] 2:28; 8:13; 9:5, 48, 53; 10:8, 10; 16:9; 18:17). The participle *chairōn* is here translated as an adverb, "joyfully." It suggests the deeper resonances of messianic joy (1:14; 2:10; 6:23; 8:13; 10:17, 20). Notice especially how the motif of "joy" is associated with repentance in 15:5, 7, 10, 32.

7. *they began grumbling*: The reaction is so typical of the scribes and Pharisees within Luke's narrative (5:30; 7:34, 39; 15:2) that the reader is surprised not to find them identified; rather "everyone (*pantes*) who saw" responded this way, which would include the disciples and the crowd and the opponents whom Luke always pictures accompanying Jesus on the way to Jerusalem.

   a sinner: For the meaning of "sinner" and its thematic connection to the tax-agents, see the notes on 3:12 and 5:8.

8. *stopped and said to the Lord*: The verb *statheis* is literally "stood," suggesting that Zacchaeus halted in their progress toward the house to deliver this statement publicly; for the narrator's use of *kyrios* ("Lord"), see 7:13, 19; 10:1, 39, 41; 11:39; 12:42; 16:8; 17:5-6; 18:6; 22:61.

   I am giving half of my possessions to the poor: In both sentences, Zacchaeus uses the present tense, which is here translated as present progressive in order to indicate that he describes repeated, customary practice, rather than a single spontaneous act of generosity. He has clearly not impoverished himself (half a bundle can still be a bundle). But he gives alms, which for Luke is the true sign of righteousness (6:30-31, 38; 11:41; 12:33; 16:9; 18:22, 29).

If I have cheated someone: John told the soldiers "not to shake down anyone or extort from anyone" using the same verb, *sykophanteō*, as here (3:14). John also told tax-agents to take no more than what was owed them (3:13). The form of Zacchaeus' conditional sentence does not imply that he did commit extortion; the sense is "if I discover I have . . ." A fourfold restitution for stolen sheep is demanded by Exod 22:1. In Lev 6:5 and Num 5:6-7 there is a demand for a full restitution "plus a fifth" for anything stolen. The Mishnah tends to limit the applicability of fourfold restitution in favor of twofold restitution (cf. *m.Ket.* 3:9; *m.Bab.Kam.* 7:1-5). At worst, Zacchaeus observes the most stringent demands of the Law in this regard.

9. *salvation has happened in this house*: The construction of the sentence (with *egeneto*) is somewhat awkward, which accounts for the frequent "improved" translation, "come to this house" (RSV). For the emphatic use of *sēmeron* ("today"), see the note on verse 5, above. This is the only use of "salvation" (*sōtēria*) after the infancy account (1:69, 71, 77), although the use of "save" in connection with Jesus' wonders has been frequent (6:9; 7:50; 8:12, 48, 50; 9:24, 56; 17:19; 18:42). Salvation "happens" in this instance in the reception of the prophet's visitation and the disposition of possessions for the poor (cf. esp. 9:24).

he too is a child of Abraham: Is literally "son" (*huios*); Jesus' statement includes Zacchaeus among the people of the blessing (1:55; Acts 3:25), even though by his trade he is despised by many fellow Jews. His actions show him to be a person open to the kingdom, and as John announced early, it is the "fruits of repentance" that matter, for "God can raise up children for Abraham from these stones" (3:8). Notice that there is a shift in the middle of this sentence. Jesus says "to him" that salvation has happened, but the explanation "because he too" is in the third rather than the second person. We are to picture Jesus turning to the crowd with this last part of the pronouncement.

10. *seek and save what was lost*: For statements about Jesus' "coming" for some purpose, see 5:32; 7:34; 9:56; 12:49; 18:8. The closest parallel is the one in 5:32, "I did not come to call righteous people but sinners to repentance." The language of seeking what was lost reminds the reader in particular of the parables of repentance in 15:3-32.

INTERPRETATION

The first of these two stories is shared with Mark and Matthew, the second is unique to Luke. Together they answer the question posed by the disciples in 18:26, "then who can be saved?" That question had been generated by the rich ruler's inability to sell his possessions in order to follow Jesus, and the pronouncement concerning the difficulty for those with possessions to enter the kingdom of God (18:18-25). Luke shows the readers how the poor blind beggar is "saved by faith" (18:42) and how "salvation happens" to the rich tax-agent because of his reception of the prophet and the disposition of his possessions (19:9).

In some ways the story of the blind beggar matches that of the children brought to Jesus in 18:15-17. Like them, the man is helpless, like them, he is brought to Jesus; and as in the case of the children, some would prevent his "bothering" Jesus (18:38). But Jesus receives him, recognizing in his cry for mercy and in his candid statement of his desire, the faith that brings salvation.

Even more obviously, the story of Zacchaeus (19:1-9) is meant to contrast with that of the ruler in 18:18-23. Both men were powerful, both wealthy. The first kept all the commandments, and could be considered as righteous. But he could not do the "one thing remaining," which was to hand over his life utterly to the prophet, and to signal that commitment by selling his possessions and giving them to the poor. Zacchaeus, in contrast, was regarded as a "sinner" by those accompanying Jesus because of his occupation as chief tax-agent. But he is eager to receive the prophet "with joy" and he declares his willingness to share—indeed if this reading of the story is correct, his regular practice of sharing—his possessions with the poor, not as a single gesture but as a steady commitment. And far from being "rapacious," when he finds any profit made on the basis of shady practice, he pays it back at the maximum demanded by Torah.

The most obvious moral lesson taught by the juxtaposition of these stories is that appearances can deceive. Everything about the ruler suggested piety. But he was closed to the call of the prophet. Everything about the tax-agent would suggest corruption. But he is righteous in his deeds, is, as Jesus declares, a "child of Abraham."

Within Luke's narrative, of course, the lesson taught by this juxtaposition is not simply moral. The four stories in sequence say something about the Prophet who makes his way to death and the people forming around him. The good news continues to reach the poor and the outcast: the kingdom is made up of people like the helpless children; the blind beggar's reception of sight fulfills the messianic announcement of 4:18; those who are "lost" are being "sought out and saved." The prophet receives all these, and they accept him. It is in this hospitality which is faith that salvation comes, and it is expressed with "glorifying God," and "giving praise," and "glad welcome." Only the rich ruler whose piety was perfect but whose possessions closed him to the possibility of a new life turns aside, and with great sorrow. Luke reminds his readers once again that the disposition of the heart is symbolized by the disposition of possessions. The one who clings to his wealth is equally closed to the prophet's call. The one who shares generously with the poor can welcome the prophet gladly.

FOR REFERENCE AND FURTHER STUDY

Hamm, D. "Luke 19:8 Once More: Does Zacchaeus Defend or Resolve?" *JBL* 107 (1988) 431–437.
Loewe, W. P. "Towards an Interpretation of Luke 19:1-10." *CBQ* 36 (1974) 321–331.
Meynet, R. "Au coeur du texte: Analyse rhetorique de l'aveugle de Jéricho selon saint Luc." *NRT* 103 (1981) 696–710.
O'Hanlon, J. "The Story of Zaccheus and the Lukan Ethic." *JSNT* 12 (1981) 2–26.
Tannehill, R. *The Narrative Unity of Luke-Acts: A Literary Interpretation* Vol.I: The Gospel According to Luke (Foundations and Facets; Philadelphia: Fortress Press, 1986) 122–125.

52. *The Kingship Parable* (19:11-27)

11. While they were listening to these things he spoke an additional parable, because he was getting close to Jerusalem and because they were thinking that the kingdom of God would immediately appear. 12. He therefore said: "A certain nobleman went off to a distant country to receive a kingdom for himself and then return. 13. He summoned ten of his own slaves. He gave them ten minas. He told them, 'Do business while I am travelling.' 14. But his fellow citizens hated him. They sent a legation after him to say, 'We do not want this man to rule over us!' 15. After he got his kingdom, he returned. He ordered those slaves to whom he had given the money to be summoned, so that he could learn what profit they had made. 16. The first approached and said, 'Master, your mina has yielded ten minas.' 17. So he said to him, 'Well done, good slave! Because you have been reliable in a tiny thing, take charge of ten cities!' 18. The second came and said, 'Master, your mina has made five minas.' 19. He said also to this one, 'You take over five cities!' 20. The other came and said, 'Master, here is your mina. I hid it in a kerchief 21. out of fear of you, for you are a severe man. You withdraw what you have not deposited. You reap what you have not sown.' 22. He said to him, 'I shall condemn you with your own words. You knew that I am a severe man, that I withdraw what I did not deposit, that I reap what I have not sown? 23. Then why didn't you put my money in a bank? When I came I could claim it with interest.' 24. To those standing in attendance he said, 'Take the mina away from him. Give it to the one who has ten minas.' 25. They said to him, 'Master, he has ten minas!' 26. 'I say to you: to everyone who has will something be given; from the one who does not have even what he has will be taken away. 27. Now bring in here those enemies of mine who did not want me to rule over them. Slaughter them in my presence.' "

NOTES

11. *he spoke an additional parable*: The introduction is awkwardly worded. We are meant to imagine the crowd still surrounding Jesus and Zacchaeus (19:7) as having heard Jesus' last words about seeking and saving that which was lost (19:10). Now Jesus "adds" (*prostheis eipen* is literally "adding he said") a parable. For Luke's distinctive use of *prostithēmi*, cf. 3:20; 12:25, 31; 17:5; 20:11-12; Acts 2:41, 47; 5:14; 11:24; 12:3; 13:36. The parable itself—often called "the parable of the pounds"—is paralleled by Matt 25:14-30 and perhaps by the skeletal version of Mark 13:34.

    getting close to Jerusalem: The journey of the Prophet towards Jerusalem is the main organizing device of the central portion of Luke's Gospel (see 9:31, 51, 53; 13:22, 33-34; 17:11; 18:31), and it is now nearing its climax (19:28).

    they were thinking that: The natural antecedent for the implied subject is the accompanying crowd made up of followers, opponents, and "the rest." The verb *dokeō* is sometimes taken to represent a false opinion, but in fact Luke uses it neutrally (1:3; 10:36; 22:24; Acts 15:22, 25, 28, 34; 25:27; 26:9) as often as to designate erroneous perceptions (8:18; 12:40, 51; 13:2-4; Acts 12:9; 17:18). The verb itself does not tell us whether we are to take the parable as a correction or confirmation of their opinion.

    kingdom of God would immediately appear: For Luke's use of *parachrēma* ("immediately"), see the note on 18:43. The thematic importance of the "kingdom of God" in this section of the narrative has been frequently pointed out; see, e.g., the note on 18:17. What does Luke mean by *anaphainō*? The verb is used in the NT only here and in Acts 21:3, where it means "come into sight." Although its dominant meaning in Greek writings is "to appear," it can mean as well "to demonstrate or make known" (Philo, *On Rewards and Punishments* 44), and "to declare" (Philo, *Life of Moses* 2:228). The precise weight to be given it here is discussed in the interpretation which follows.

12. *he therefore said*: The adverb *oun* ("therefore") is used here in a responsive sense: their expectations have generated this response. The closest parallels to this usage in Luke are in 3:7, 18 and 7:31.

    a certain nobleman: The adjective *eugenēs* literally means "of noble birth" (cf. Acts 17:11; 1 Cor 1:26).

    receive a kingdom for himself: We are to picture a local eminence like Herod the Great who received dominion from the imperial patron by travelling to Rome and petitioning for it (Josephus, *Antiquities* 14:370-389). Such a trip might be arduous, but would not take a terribly long time. In Luke, everything is carried out with dispatch; only in Matthew is there an emphasis on time passing, "after a long period of time" (Matt 25:19). It should be noted that this *political* setting of Luke's story is essential to it, but is totally absent from Matthew.

13. *gave them ten minas*: The word *mna* (usually translated as "pound") means a coin equalling approximately 100 drachmas or denarii. It is a considerable though not an enormous sum of money (the women in the parable of 15:8-9 had ten drachmas). Matthew's "talents" are a much larger denomination, with each ta-

lent equalling sixty minas. Matt 25:15 gives each slave a different amount (five, two, or one), whereas Luke gives each of the ten one mina (see vv. 16, 18, 20).

do business while I am travelling: The nobleman makes his expectation concerning the money clear: *pragmateuomai* means to "engage in business" (it is used only here in the NT). "While I am travelling" aims at the sense of a construction that is somewhat ambiguous in Greek.

14. *his fellow citizens hated him*: In Greek moral philosophy, *misos* ("hatred") is often associated with envy, *phthonos,* and like it tends toward the harming of another (cf. Plutarch, *On Envy and Hate* (Mor. 536E-538E)). The new king will call them his "enemies" (*echthroi*) in verse 27. They send a delegation (*presbeia*) to the emperor who is the nobleman's patron, hoping to dissuade him from granting the dominion. For the sending of such a body of representatives on another matter, compare Philo, *The Embassy to Gaius.* Josephus tells of precisely such a delegation of fifty Jews to Augustus to protest against Archelaus, and indeed the motivation of some, according to the author, was hatred (Josephus, *Antiquities* 17:299-314).

15. *he returned*: The nobleman was successful in getting his dominion, and returns to deal with affairs in his new realm: first the household, then the political enemies. Matthew fills in this space with a direct narrative of the disposition of the talents (Matt 25:16-18), and extends the period between the master's departure and return (25:19).

    learn what profit they had made: Luke uses *diapragmateuomai* which intensifies the verb *pragmateuomai,* used in verse 13. We are reminded of the explicit directions the nobleman had left his slaves.

16. *your mina has yielded ten minas*: The proportionate yield here is more impressive than in Matt 25:20, where the slave doubled his five talents. Likewise the man with two talents doubles them, whereas Luke's second slave made five minas from the one assigned him (v. 18).

17. *reliable in a tiny thing*: The translation deliberately echoes 16:10 for the rendering of *elachistos* as "tiny" and *pistos* as "reliable."

    take charge of ten cities: Here and in verse 18 the reward for the reliable use of possessions is political: rule within the kingdom. In this case it is ten cities, and in verse 18, five cities, corresponding to the amount earned. The translation "take charge of" is a bit stronger than the periphrastic Greek, "be having authority over . . ." Once more, Matt 25:21 lacks this political dimension of the story.

20. *the other came and said*: The Greek *ho heteros* is a bit confusing, for the story began with ten servants and this is just the third heard from; the three responses fit the Matthean framework much better. Some MSS correct to "another." This slave hid the coin in a cloth (*soudarion,* see Acts 19:12; John 11:44; 20:7) rather than in the earth (*gē*) as in Matt 25:18, 25. The English phrase "here is" translates *idou* (literally, "behold").

21. *out of fear of you*: This portion of the story is both like and unlike Matt 25:24-25. The ideas are the same, but the diction is almost completely different. Note that: a) Luke has only this report and not the earlier narrative account (Matt 25:18)

and then this report (Matt 25:25); b) Luke has the king as a "severe" (*austēros*) rather than "hard" (*sklēros*) man; c) the accounts share the statement that he "reaps what he has not sown" but Matthew then has "gather what he has not scattered"—continuing the agricultural image—whereas Luke uses the image of banking, "withdrawing/depositing." This better fits the exhortation to use a banker in verse 23, but may also be proverbial: in Plato's *Laws* 913C, the expression describes one who ignores ancestral laws, and in Josephus, *Against Apion* 2:216 it is also listed as a crime. The phrase therefore suggests one who is so "hard" that he ignores conventional piety in his quest for power and possessions.

22. *I shall condemn you*: This could also be translated "I condemn you," since the verb *krinō* could be either future or present, depending on how it is accented. The meaning is much the same in either case. "With your own words" is literally "out of your mouth."

23. *put my money in a bank*: The servant is "wicked" (*ponēros*) because by refusing to "do business" with the master's money—notice the "my money"—he explicitly disobeyed the master. The phrase is literally "give my silver on a table," meaning the moneylenders' table (see Matt 21:12; John 2:15). Matt 25:27 explicitly has "bankers" (that is, "table-men" *tois trapezitais*).

    claim it with interest: The verb *prassō* sometimes has the sense of "claiming payment," as here. The noun *tokos* derives from "offspring," since interest is the "offspring" of money! The taking of interest on loans (usury) is forbidden by Exod 22:25; Lev 25:36-37; Deut 23:19, but the Mishnah distinguishes usury and "increase," with more liberal regulations governing relations with Gentiles (cf. *m.Bab.M.* 5:1-6).

24. *standing in attendance*: Is literally "those standing by," but a royal entourage is clearly intended: compare Luke 1:19 and Acts 23:2 with LXX Pss 2:2; 44:9; Prov 22:29. Matthew lacks this lively and characteristic detail.

    to the one who has ten minas: The transfer of money has less impact here than in Matt 25:28, where the sums are greater and the rule over cities has not been involved. Still, it helps make the point of the pronouncement that follows. So does the objection of the bystanders in verse 25 (unique to Luke's version, and of some debatable textual status). Of more significance to the overall evaluation of Luke's version is the fact that the last slave is not punished; he is merely excluded from political rule.

26. *to everyone who has will something be given*: Who says this? It is not clear whether it is the king in the story, or an interjection by Jesus into the parable. The translation supplies the word "something." This pronouncement is found also in Matt 25:29; 13:12; Mark 4:25; and earlier in Luke 8:18, with the difference that in the earlier version, Luke has "what he *thinks* he has."

27. *not want me to rule over them*: The dominant political framework of this parable is reasserted at the end. The slaughter of enemies is shocking but no more so than the dismemberment of a slave (cf. 12:46). Indeed, the *realpolitik* of the ancient world has precedents for just such harsh measures (Josh 10:16-26; 1 Sam 15:32). The closest parallel is that of Herod's murder of forty-five rivals (Josephus,

Antiquities of the Jews 15:6). They are called "enemies" because "they did not want me to rule (*basileusai*) over them." This theme will be worked out shortly in the narrative, and anticipates what will be said of Moses in Acts 7:27, 35.

INTERPRETATION

This commentary has consistently taken a literary approach to Luke's narrative, seeking to understand the form and the function of specific passages within the larger literary and religious concerns of the narrative. The present passage provides an excellent test for this approach, for the simple reason that if it is followed, a reading results which opposes a broad consensus in scholarship.

Any interpretation must take seriously the difficulties presented by the internal structure of Luke's parable, especially in comparison to the parallel version in Matthew 25:14-30; the relationship between the parable itself (19:12-27) and its long but not entirely clear introduction (19:11); and, the placement of the parable in this precise narrative context by Luke rather than in some other. In order to make the reading adopted here as clear as possible, we will review quickly the important aspects of each of these elements (leaving detailed discussion to the notes), offer the dominant understanding of the passage, and then argue for another interpretation.

First, then, the distinctive elements in Luke's story. It is properly called "the Lukan kingship parable," because in contrast to Matthew's "parable of the talents," the possessions motif is here a subsidiary to a political one. The story is about a king who goes to get a kingdom, gets it despite opposition, and returns to establish that rule by getting rid of his rivals for power and placing in positions of authority over cities the slaves who have shown themselves trustworthy. The parable is therefore "about" the successful establishment of a kingdom. The possessions motif fits well within this framework but is entirely shaped by it: the reward for those reliable is a place in the rule of the kingdom; the slave who did not perform financially is not punished (as in Matthew) but only excluded from ruling power. It is also important to observe that Luke's story takes place with great dispatch. There is no hint—in contrast to Matthew's version—of a long delay between the nobleman's departure and his return as king.

The second factor requiring attention is the relationship between the parable and its long introduction in 19:11. Luke says Jesus tells the parable because he was approaching Jerusalem and they thought that the kingdom of God was going to appear immediately. But nothing in the language of this introduction or Luke's usual practice tells us whether the parable is intended to counter or confirm this expectation, or in what respect.

The third factor to take into account is the context of the parable in Luke's narrative. It is obvious that Luke could have had Jesus tell the parable anywhere. Indeed, Matthew's version is told in the setting of a series of eschatological parables (the ten maidens, the talents, the sheep and the goats) that follow Jesus' eschatological discourse in chapter 24, and clearly fit within the framework of expectation of the Son of Man's return (25:1-46). But Luke has Jesus tell the story at the climax of his journey to Jerusalem.

What events has Luke himself placed immediately before and after this story to shape his reader's perception? Before this story, the theme of the kingdom of God as preached by Jesus and present in his deeds has grown in intensity (the term occurs twenty-one times between 9:1 and 19:11: see esp. 11:2, 20; 12:22; 13:18-21; 17:20-21). Furthermore, immediately *after* this parable of a nobleman who becomes a king, Jesus is himself proclaimed as king (19:38), accused of claiming to be messiah-king (23:2), castigated as such on the cross (23:37, 38), begged there for a place in his kingdom (23:42), and at the Last Supper bestows rule (*basileia*) on the Twelve, a rule which he declares he had received from the Father (22:29).

The usual interpretation of this parable takes it as an allegory that is only incidentally connected to the Lukan narrative, and to be understood within the framework of early Christian ideas about the end-time. Specifically, Luke has Jesus tell the story to teach something about the *parousia*, that is, the second coming of the Son of Man as judge. The nobleman is Jesus who "goes away" to become king. He is opposed by the Jews. He entrusts the Church to the disciples. When he returns, he bestows authority on those who were trustworthy. He punishes those who opposed his rule.

Why did Luke have Jesus tell the parable here? In order to correct the expectation that the entry of Jesus into the city was the final "establishment of God's kingdom." In short, it is an allegory that tells Christians to wait patiently for the final appearance of Jesus and to deal faithfully with their possessions in the meantime.

The difficulties facing this interpretation should be obvious. It makes Luke work against himself as an author. It is not clear in the first place why Luke's *readers* (as opposed to the characters in the story) should need any such correction; surely they already knew that Jesus' proclamation as king in Jerusalem was only the first stage toward the full realization of the kingdom. And if Luke intended to downplay the significance of the entry of Jesus as king, he made a thorough mess of it, for it is precisely the parable and its introduction that draws maximum attention to the proclamation of Jesus as king in the story which follows (a proclamation, by the way, that Luke makes more explicit than any other evangelist).

The traditional interpretation also fails to deal with the particular shape of Luke's version. The kingship theme is not incidental, it is essential. There is no hint of a long passage of time to make the reader think (if not influenced by Matthew's version) of the "delay of the parousia." The conventional interpretation can find no place for the installation of the slaves as participants in ruling within the kingdom, or the fact that the unreliable slave is not punished, only kept from ruling. It cannot face squarely the plain implication that those who reject the king will be cut off utterly.

It is better, therefore, to take the parable as an integral part of Luke's literary work, and not seek immediately to understand it outside the narrative as a response to a theological problem. In fact, the parable is best read— as so often with Luke's parables and speeches—as an authorial commentary on the narrative. The parable does not refer to the end-time, but to the events unfolding in Luke's own story. As Luke's narrative reaches its climax in the Jerusalem account of the Prophet's rejection, installation in power, and second offer of salvation to the people through the apostles (see introduction), he provides the reader with a parable that serves to interpret that larger story.

Who is the nobleman who would be king, and who in fact gets *basileia* so that he can not only exercise it but also bestow it on followers? It is obviously Jesus himself, who will immediately be hailed as king, dispose of *basileia* to his followers, grant entrance to the thief, and as risen Lord, continue to exercise authority through his emissaries' words and deeds. Who are the fellow citizens who do not wish to have this one as their ruler, who protest it, and then defeated, are "cut off"? They are the leaders of the people who will decry the proclamation of Jesus as king, accuse him of royal pretensions in his trial, mock him as king on the cross, reject his mission as prophet, persecute his apostles, and find themselves at last because of all this, "cut off from the people." Who are the servants whose faithful use of possessions is rewarded by *exousia* ("authority") within the realm of this king? The Twelve, whom we shall see in the narrative of Acts exercising just such authority over the restored people of God.

When will all this occur? In the course of the story Luke is telling, beginning "immediately" (19:11) with the kingly proclamation of Jesus in 19:38. In fact, the parable confirms the expectation expressed in 19:11. This is preeminently the Lukan kingship parable, the author's own reliable guide to the story that follows.

For Reference and Further Study

Dupont, J. "La parabole des talents (Mat 25:14-30) ou des mines (Luc 19:12-27)." *RTP* 19 (1969) 376–391.

Johnson, L. T. "The Lukan Kingship Parable (Luke 19:11-27)." *NovT* 24 (1982) 139–159.

Schneider, G. *Parusiegleichnisse im Lukas-Evangelium* (Stuttgart: KBW Verlag, 1975) 38–42.

Tiede, D. *Prophecy and History in Luke-Acts* (Philadelphia: Fortress Press, 1980) 79–80.

Weinert, F. D. "The Parable of the Throne-Claimant (Luke 19:12, 14-15a, 27) Reconsidered." *CBQ* 39 (1977) 505–514.

Zerwick, M. "Die Parabel vom Thonanwärter." *Bib* 40 (1959) 654–674.

V. THE PROPHET IN JERUSALEM

53. *Entering Jerusalem* (19:28-48)

28. After he said these things he continued forward, going up to Jerusalem. 29. As he approached Bethphage and Bethany at the mountain called the Mount of Olives, he sent out two of his disciples. 30. He said, "Go into the village over there. When you enter you will find in it a colt tied up which no one has ever ridden. Untie it. Bring it here. 31. If anyone asks you, 'Why are you untying it,' say this: 'The Lord has need of it.' " 32. Those who had been sent went off and found things to be as he had told them. 33. As they were untying the colt, its owners said to them, "Why are you untying the colt?" 34. They said, "Because the Lord has need of it." 35. They led it toward Jesus. They threw their garments over the colt and seated Jesus on it. 36. As he was setting out, people were spreading their garments on the road. 37. Already as he neared the slope of the Mount of Olives the whole multitude of disciples with full voice began joyfully to praise God for all the powerful deeds they had seen. 38. They said, "Blessed is the King who comes in the name of the Lord! Peace in heaven! Glory in highest heaven!" 39. Some of the Pharisees from the crowd said to him, "Teacher, rebuke your disciples!" 40. He answered them, "I tell you, if these people are silent the stones will cry out." 41. And as he approached, he saw the city. He wept over it. 42. He said, "If you—even you—had known on this day the things that make for peace! But now they are hidden from your eyes. 43. Because days will come upon you when your enemies will throw up ramparts around you. They will encircle you and press on you from every side. 44. They will throw down you and the children within you. They will not leave a stone upon a stone within you—because you did not recognize the time of your being visited." 45. When he had gone into the temple he began to cast out those who were engaged in selling. 46. He said to them, "It stands written, 'My house will be a house of prayer,' but you have made it 'a robber's cave.' " 47. He was teaching every day in the temple. But the chief priests and scribes and leaders of the people were seeking to destroy him. 48. And they could not find the thing that they could use, for the whole people was clinging to him, listening.

NOTES

28. *going up to Jerusalem*: The account of Jesus' entry into the city is shared by Matt 21:1-9; Mark 11:1-10, and John 12:12-19. Luke makes the most explicit connection to the words Jesus had just spoken (namely the kingship parable!), underlining once more their importance for understanding the events to follow.

29. *mountain called the Mount of Olives*: Only Luke adds the qualifying word "called." The mountain is named in Zech 14:4 in a prophecy about the Lord's coming. Neither of the towns mentioned here, Bethphage or Bethany, appears in the OT. Bethphage is named only in this passage (cf. Matt 21:1; Mark 11:1). But Bethany is the scene of Jesus' baptism according to John 1:28, and the place where Lazarus, Martha and Mary lived (John 11:1, 18). In Mark, Jesus returns to Bethany after his first inspection of the Temple (Mark 11:11-12). And in Matt 26:6; Mark 14:3; and John 12:1, Bethany is named as the place of the anointing of Jesus, a story not related by Luke (see the interpretation of Luke 7:36-50). Luke does make Bethany the place of Jesus' ascension in the Gospel account (24:50).

    sent out two of his disciples: Luke here uses *apostellō*, as often in his narrative, of being sent on a mission, however menial this one might be (see 4:18, 43; 7:20, 27; 9:2, 48, 52; 10:1, 3, 16; 11:49, etc.). The disciples are not named here, but in 22:8, Luke will name Peter and John as the two sent to prepare the Passover.

30. *a colt tied up*: Luke follows Mark 11:2 closely here. Matt 21:2 (and 21:7) combines an "ass" (*onos*) tied up with "her colt" (*pōlos*), clearly because Matthew wants to show a literal fulfillment of the prophecy from Zech 9:9, which he cites in 21:5.

31. *the Lord has need of it*: This could also be read "his master has need," but Luke's general use of *chreian echei* has the genitive of the thing required (cf. 5:31; 9:11; 10:42; 15:7; 22:71), and in the next verse we read "his lords." The ambiguity of the use of *kyrios* in both cases cannot entirely be resolved. This translation chooses the highest designation for Jesus, and the specification of "owners" for *kyrioi* in verse 32.

32. *to be as he had told them*: This small Lukan notation (Mark 11:4 lacks it and Matt 21:6 has "they did as Jesus commanded") serves as his characteristic literary connection, showing the fulfillment of prophecy: as Jesus spoke, so it happened (compare 2:20). The sentence also enables Luke to abbreviate Mark's lively details in 11:4.

35. *threw their garments*: Luke replaces Mark's *epiballō* with the rarer *epiriptō* (cf. 2 Sam 20:12; 1 Kgs 19:19; [LXX]= Ps 54:22 and 1 Pet 5:7). The garments (*himatia*) are the outer garments (cloak or robe; see 5:36; 6:29; 7:25; 8:44).

    seated Jesus on it: By adding "Jesus," Luke makes the action clearer. He also uses the term *epibibazō* instead of *kathizō* (in Mark 11:7), a term used also in 10:34 and Acts 23:24 for the providing of a mount.

36. *as he was setting out*: Luke helpfully supplies this genitive absolute which keeps the action moving forward (cf. 19:28).

    people were spreading their garments: The translation supplies the noun "people" for the third person plural verb. Luke uses the imperfect, suggesting a process and movement (in contrast to the aorist tense used by Mark 11:8 and Matt 21:8). Luke omits any mention of the waving of branches (described with different words in Mark 11:8; Matt 21:8; John 12:13), possibly because of their association with national hopes (cf. 2 Macc 10:7). On the other hand, he does not in any sense diminish the royal tone of the entry. The spreading of garments under Jehu's feet (2 Kgs 9:14), for example, is accompanied by the declaration, "Jehu is king" (LXX, *ebasileusen Iou*).

37. *whole multitude of disciples*: Luke uses the term *plēthos* ("multitude") here as in 2:13; 5:6; Acts 2:6; 5:14; 14:1, to indicate a large number of people, rather than in the more technical use of "assembly" (as in 8:37; 23:1; Acts 6:2, 5; 15:12). The phrase here is similar to that in 1:10; 6:17 and 23:27. Notice that Luke has in the course of Jesus' journey created the impression of growth, beginning in 8:1-3 with a small band of followers, and ending here with a "multitude of disciples."

    joyfully to praise God: The participle *chairontes* is translated as an adverb, "joyfully." For "rejoicing" as a response to God's visitation, see 1:14; 2:10; 6:23; 8:13; 10:17, 20; 13:17; 19:6; and, for "praising God," see 2:13, 20; 18:43; 24:53; Acts 2:47; 3:9.

    powerful deeds they had seen: This is found only in Luke and makes the greeting also a recapitulation of the narrative. For the deeds of power (*dynameis*), see 4:14, 36; 5:17; 6:19; 8:46; 9:1; 10:13, 19. In Acts 2:22, Peter will speak of Jesus as a man certified by "deeds of power, wonders, and signs." Notice as well Luke's emphasis on eyewitnesses who stand behind the tradition (1:2).

38. *blessed is the King*: The acclamation is from LXX Ps 117:26. Four verses before this is the line about "the stone which the builders rejected," to be cited by Jesus very shortly in 20:17. Luke omits the cry of "hosanna" found in Mark 11:9; Matt 21:9, and John 12:13. He places the title *ho basileus* ("the king") more emphatically into the heart of the citation than the other evangelists. Mark 11:10 has "and the coming kingdom of our father David," and Matt 21:9, "Hosanna to the Son of David," while John 12:13 adds "and king of Israel." This emphasis on Jesus as king in Luke's version must be understood in light of the kingship parable of 19:11-27.

    peace in heaven! glory in highest heaven: Mark 11:10 and Matt 21:9 have only "hosanna in the highest," but Luke shapes the cry to make it echo the angelic song of 2:14, "glory in the highest to God, and peace on earth."

39. *Pharisees from the crowd*: Although no Pharisee has been explicitly mentioned since 18:10-11, we are to assume their continued presence, which has been suggested in places such as 18:18-21, 39; 19:7. This is also the last explicit mention of the Pharisees in the Gospel (although see the discussion of 20:20, below), and their objection is typical of their stance throughout the narrative.

    teacher, rebuke your disciples: Jesus is addressed as "teacher" (*didaskalos*) by a Pharisee in 7:40, by a lawyer in 10:25; 11:45, and by the rich ruler in 18:18. He will be called this again in the hostile questioning of 20:21, 28, 39. They want Jesus to "rebuke" (*epitimaō*) his disciples (cf. 18:15, 39). They object to the proclamation of Jesus as king, and thereby identify themselves as the ones "who would not have him rule over them" (19:14, 27).

40. *stones will cry out*: The exchange is unique to Luke (although Matt 21:14-16 has one similar in substance). This is the first of a series of sayings in which "stones" (*lithoi*) will figure prominently (19:44; 20:17, 18; 21:5-6; 24:2; cf. Acts 4:11). The reader hears echoes of the saying in 3:8, that God could raise up children to Abraham "from these stones." And the present statement will find eloquent shading in the prediction in 19:44 that Jerusalem's enemies will not "leave stone upon a stone" within her. The point of the saying here is that Jesus *is* king, and no silencing of the disciples can deflect that fact.

41. *wept over it*: The weeping of Jesus is a sign of sorrow over the city's present blindness and its future fate (see 6:21, 25; 7:13; 8:52). For the weeping over the city as a prophetic gesture, (cf. Neh 1:4; LXX Ps 136:1; Jer 9:1; 13:17; Lam 1:1 [LXX], 16). The account of Jesus' weeping and prediction is unique to Luke's Gospel.

42. *if you—even you—had known*: The form of the conditional sentence expresses a wish—would that you had known! The phrase which the translation places between dashes—even you—is also awkwardly placed and has led to a number of scribal corrections in the MSS.

    this day the things that make for peace: The day of Jesus' arrival in Jerusalem is the "time of its visitation" (*kairon tēs episkopēs*). God's visitation has already been associated with "peace" (*eirēnē*) in 1:79; 2:14, 29. Jesus sends away those he has forgiven or healed "in peace" (7:50; 8:48), and his entry into the city has just been acclaimed as a bringing of "peace" (19:38). Yet he is a sign of contradiction (2:35), and he creates a division, so that he is not "peace" for everyone (12:51). But like the general in the parable who saw a more powerful force coming towards him, this city should have recognized the Prophet and "sued for peace" (14:32).

    hidden from your eyes: This line presents a difficult problem of translation and interpretation. If one follows the path of critical Greek editions (as the translation does), then the things hidden from the eyes are "the things that make for peace." This is possible. But it makes harder the meaning of the *hoti* which follows. This translation again follows the lead of precedents and makes it a causal clause, "because . . ." even though the syntactical connection is not altogether clear. If, however, one ignored the period and treated the *hoti* as a noun clause, the whole sentence would read smoothly, "But now *it* is hidden from your eyes *that* days will come upon you . . ." In this case, the final clause of verse 44, introduced by *anth'hōn*, would provide the cause of all the disasters that will befall the city.

43. *days will come upon you*: For similar prophetic pronouncements about the future days, see 5:35; 10:12; 12:46; 17:22, 26, 31; 21:6, 22, 23. For "days are coming" as a standard prophetic locution, cf. Joel 9:7; Amos 4:2; 8:11; 9:13; Zech 14:1; Mal 4:1; Isa 39:6; Jer 19:6.

    throw up ramparts against you: Luke uses the language of Hellenistic warfare. A *parembolē* is an armed camp (see Acts 23:10, 16), and the phrase used here, *paremballō characha* means to set up an encampment surrounded by a wall or palisade, such as would be used in a long siege against a city (cf. Isa 29:3; Ezek 4:2; 21:22; 26:8). The verb translated here "encircle" (*perikukloō*) is also used in military contexts (Num 21:4; Josh 6:13; 7:9; 2 Kgs 6:14; 17:15), as is "press upon" (*synechō*, see 1 Sam 23:8). As these biblical references suggest, Luke could have garnered all this vocabulary from the LXX and need not have relied on or even known the descriptions of Titus' siege of Jerusalem (cf. Josephus, *Jewish War* 5:466-472; and 5:502-510).

44. *throw down you and the children within you*: The Greek word *edaphos* means ground or foundation, and the verb *edaphizō* has as its first meaning the pounding of the ground to make it level. It is used in LXX Ps 136:9 for the "dashing the children [of the enemy Babylon] against the rocks"; it is used for the killing of mothers in Hos 10:14 and again for the killing of children in Nah 3:10.

stone upon stone within you: A form of this saying is in Matt 24:2 and Mark 13:2, and it will be repeated in Luke 21:6. It obviously refers to the destruction of the city; for the imagery applied to just such a disaster, compare 2 Sam 17:3; Mic 1:6. Both Jer 7:30-34 and Mic 3:9-12 utter prophecies against the city which spell out the destruction of city and Temple alike.

time of your being visited: The *kairos* ("time") here means specific season (as in 4:13; 12:42, 56); notice its use in the next parable (21:10). The "season of visitation" (*kairos tēs episkopēs*) occurs in Jer 6:15 and 10:15 to mean God's punishment (see also Deut 28:25; Sir 23:24; Isa 24:22). *Episkopē* can also refer to God's intervention to save (as in Gen 50:24-25; Exod 3:16; 13:19), or neutrally as his coming as judge (Sir 16:18; 18:20; Isa 10:3; 29:6); see the language of "visitation" also at Qumran, as in CD 1:7; 7:21-8:3. The cognate verb *episkeptomai*, however, is used in the LXX more positively for God's saving intervention (see the note on 1:68, 78; 7:16, and the use in Acts 6:3; 7:23; 15:14, 36). Here, the term is double-edged. The prophet's arrival should be God's visitation for peace. But because he is not recognized as such, his rejection becomes a "visitation" of punishment.

45. *gone into the Temple*: The wording here is simple, but the careful reader would hear an echo of Mal 3:2: "the Lord whom you seek will suddenly come to his Temple . . . but who can endure the day of his coming . . . he is like a refiner's fire . . ." This is Jesus' first visit to the Temple since 2:46, when he engaged the teachers in discussion; he will do the same now, after he performs a prophetic cleansing of the Temple precincts (*ieron*, not *naos*).

cast out those who were engaged in selling: The verb for "cast out" is *ekballō*, which is used in exorcisms (9:40, 49; 11:14, 15, 18, 19, 20; 13:32), suggesting that the money changers are roughly equivalent to unclean spirits who profane the holy place. Luke greatly reduces the complexity of this scene, compared to the parallels (Mark 11:15-17; Matt 21:12-13; John 2:13-17). As an international cult center (Acts 2:5-11), the Temple was also inevitably also a center of finance. Pilgrims from abroad brought or sent their yearly Temple tax (*shekel*) as an act of piety (cf. Philo, *Embassy to Gaius* 216, 313). Pilgrims could also purchase animals needed for sacrifice (Luke 2:24) and pay other expenses (Acts 21:24). To facilitate all such transactions, currency required exchange. The Mishnah is unapologetic about the tables of the moneychangers (*m.Shek.* 1:3), and the complex machinery of finance in the Temple precincts. According to *m.Shek.* 6:4-5, there were thirteen tables in the Temple and thirteen chests for funds. The Qumran sect, in contrast, took offense at such financial dealing, calling it a profanation of the Temple (*CD* 6:15-16; 4QpHab 9:1-7).

46. *a house of prayer*: Luke cites Isa 56:7 loosely. The LXX reads, "for my house will be called a house of prayer for all nations." Mark 11:17 retains this last phrase which Matthew and Luke omit. The elimination of this phrase is important for grasping Luke's view of the Temple. It has a significant role for Judaism and for the first Jerusalem community, but not an enduring role for the Gentiles.

made it a robber's cave: The allusion is to Jer 7:11, which occurs in the middle of a long speech (Jer 7:3-20) attacking those who trust in the Temple without converting their hearts (7:8) and promising its destruction (7:14, 20), as well as the "casting out" of "all your kinsmen" (7:15).

47. *teaching every day in the Temple*: This transitional note is found only in Luke, and makes clear that for him, the cleansing of the Temple by the Prophet was a preparation of it for his own teaching (20:1, 28, 39; 22:53) and for that of his apostles after the resurrection (Acts 5:21, 25).

chief priests and scribes and leaders of the people: These are the characters who take the place of the "Pharisees and lawyers" as the main opponents of Jesus all through the Jerusalem narrative. The "chief priests" (*archiereis*) were first mentioned in the passion prediction of 9:22. Now they figure prominently (20:1, 19; 22:2, 4, 50, 52, 54, 66; 23:4, 10, 13; 24:20; Acts 4:1, 6, 23; 5:17, 21, 24, 27; 7:1). The "scribes" (*grammateis*) also appeared in the passion prediction of 9:22, but were earlier sometimes teamed with the Pharisees (5:21, 30; 6:7; 11:53; 15:2). Now they are listed with the chief priests (20:1, 19, 39, 46; 22:2, 66; 23:10; Acts 4:5; 6:12; 19:35; 23:9). Another designation *not* listed in this verse is that of the "elder" (*presbyteros*). We met them first in a positive function in 7:3, but they are also in the first passion prediction of 9:22, and play a role in the passion and persecution of the first believers (20:1; 22:52; Acts 4:5, 8, 23; 6:12). All of these may in some sense be subsumed under the rubric of "rulers" (*archontes*; cf. 23:13, 35; 24:20; Acts 3:17; 4:5, 8, 26; 13:27), just as is Luke's final category in the present list, *hoi prōtoi tou laou* "leaders of the people" (see 19:47; 20:29; Acts 13:50; 25:2). Luke shares with Mk 11:18 the statement "they sought to destroy him"; for the build-up to this resolution, see 6:11; 11:53-54. Jesus "sought to save what was lost" (19:10); these "sought to destroy."

48. *the whole people*: We have seen throughout the narrative that Luke has established a division within Israel determined by response to God's visitation in the prophet. On one side are the leaders who reject the Prophet and God's will for them (7:30); on the other side are the "people" who accept the Prophet and justify God (7:29). Luke is fond of the designation "people" (*laos*), and uses it often in the passion account to distinguish those who do not seek to destroy the Prophet but hear him gladly (see 20:1, 6, 9, 19, 26, 45; 21:38; 22:2; 23:27, 35; 24:19).

INTERPRETATION

Luke's placement of the kingship parable in 19:11-27 becomes more obviously pertinent as we read his version of Jesus' entry into the city. It becomes clear that by providing his own parabolic interpretation of the events Luke not only guides the reader's perceptions but makes the account of the Prophet's visitation of the city a fulfillment of Jesus' own implicit prophecy.

For the most part, Luke follows his Markan source closely—indeed there is considerable agreement between all the evangelists throughout the Jerusalem section of the Gospel story. Luke follows Mark in having Jesus send disciples to find the colt, in the ride to the city with its acclamation, and in the cleansing of the Temple. But Luke has also made significant alterations in his source, and these deserve particular consideration since the whole logic of Luke's narrative since 9:51 when Jesus began his journey toward Jerusalem has prepared for this climax. By observing what he has omitted, added, and altered, we can better grasp Luke's shaping of this important moment.

Luke lacks the explicit citation from Zechariah found in Matt 21:4-5, and the waving of branches found in all the other Gospels (Mark 11:8; Matt 21:8; John 12:13). He thereby eliminates what might be perceived as the nationalistic implications of Jesus' kingship. Luke emphatically asserts this title of "king" by placing it within the citation from LXX Ps 117 itself, but the kingdom ruled by Jesus is not simply that of the Jewish nation. It is the rule of God over the people of God.

Luke also eliminates the complex intertwining of Temple and fig tree that he found in Mark 11:12-14 and 20-25. By his placement of the cursing of the fig tree, the cleansing of the Temple, and then the withering of the fig tree (11:12-25), Mark foreshadowed the destruction of the Temple. Matthew uses this story from Mark, although he presents the entire fig tree story in sequence, so that it less obviously connects to the Temple (Matt 21:18-22). Luke however has Jesus utter his lament over the city before entering it (19:41-44). This lament provides an authoritative commentary (by Jesus himself) on the significance of his arrival in the city, and a reminder of important literary themes: Jesus' arrival is the visitation of God that offers peace; the rejection of the Prophet will lead to destruction; this first rejection is one that is carried out in ignorance (Acts 3:17). We are reminded of the parable about the king who "sued for peace" because he recognized that he was being attacked by a superior force (14:31); Jerusalem lacks this recognition, and so faces destruction.

Most of all, by ordering the materials the way he has, Luke enables Jesus' entrance of the city, cleansing of the Temple, and occupation of it to take place in one uninterrupted sequence. The reader truly sees in this unified flow the fulfillment of the prophecy of Malachi: "the Lord whom you seek will suddenly come to his temple" (Mal 3:1). The expulsion of the sellers from the Temple is taken care of in one line; Jesus simply clears out the bad to make room for himself. And in his citation from Isaiah, Luke deliberately drops the phrase "for all nations." The Jerusalem Temple is indeed intended to be a place of prayer, but it does not have a future significance for the Gentiles. It reaches its final significance as the place where the good news is taught and preached to the people, first by Jesus and then by his prophetic successors. Everything in Luke's arrangement pushes the reader to this final point: he was in the Temple every day, teaching (19:47), fulfilling the destiny foreshadowed in 2:49 of "being involved in his father's business."

At the acclamation of Jesus by "the whole multitude of the disciples" Luke had Pharisees from the crowd object (19:39). The theme of the divided people continues. And now that the Prophet has made the Temple the place for his own proclamation, Luke reminds the reader again that the rejection of the Jewish populace—even in this city—is by no means complete. As Jesus teaches in the Temple, Luke shows not a uniformly hostile, but a divided people. Indeed, "the whole people" clung to him, listening. It is still only the leadership of scribes, chief priests and "leaders of the people" (now absent the Pharisees) that intensifies its opposition and indeed actively seeks to kill him (19:47b-48). With only the smallest possible exception (23:13), throughout this Jerusalem account Luke will portray the populace as a whole as positive toward Jesus, and place responsibility for his death squarely and exclusively on the leadership (see esp. 24:20).

For Reference and Further Study

Dupont, J. "Il n'en sera pas laissé pierre sur pierre (Marc 13,2; Luc 19,44)." *Bib* 52 (1971) 301–320.

Gaston, L. *No Stone on Another: Studies in the Significance of the Fall of Jerusalem in the Synoptic Gospels.* NovTSuppl 23; Leiden: Brill, 1970.

George, A. "La royauté de Jésus selon l'évangile de Luc," *ScEccl* 14 (1962) 57–69.

Kodell, J. "Luke's Use of *laos*, 'People,' especially in the Jerusalem Narrative." *CBQ* 31 (1969) 327–343.

Rese, M. *Alttestamentliche Motive in der Christologie des Lukas* (SNT 1; Gütersloh: G. Mohr, 1969) 196–199.

54. *Conflict with Leaders* (20:1-19)

1. On one of the days that he was teaching the people in the Temple and preaching the good news, the chief priests and scribes came up with the elders. 2. They said to him, "Tell us, by what authority are you doing these things or who has given you this authority?" 3. He answered them by saying, "I too will ask you something, and you tell me! 4. Was John's baptism from heaven or from humans?" 5. They consulted with each other. They said, "If we say from heaven, he will say, Why didn't you believe in him? 6. But if we say, from humans, the whole people will stone us, for they are convinced that John was a prophet." 7. So they answered that they did not know where it was from. 8. Jesus said to them, "Neither do I tell you by what authority I am doing these things." 9. He began to tell the people this parable: "A certain man planted a vineyard. He leased it to farmers and left the country for a considerable period of time. 10. At the appropriate season he sent a slave to the farmers so that they could give him the vineyard's produce. But the farmers beat him and sent him away with nothing. 11. So he sent another slave. They beat that one also, and after abusing him, sent him away with nothing. 12. He sent still a third. But they wounded him and cast him out. 13. The master of the vineyard said, 'What shall I do? I will send my beloved son. Perhaps they will respect him.' 14. But when the farmers saw him they plotted with each other. They said, 'This is the heir! Let us kill him so that the inheritance might be ours.' 15. They cast him out of the vineyard. They killed him. Now what will the owner of the vineyard do to them? 16. He will come and destroy these farmers. And he will give the vineyard to others." When they heard this, they said, "May it not be!" 17. But he stared at them and said, "Why then does this stand written, 'a stone which the builders rejected, this one has become the cornerstone?' 18. Everyone falling against that stone will be broken. On whomever it falls it will crush." 19. The scribes and the chief-priests sought to lay hands on him at that moment for they knew that he had spoken this parable against them. But they were afraid of the people.

Notes

1. *teaching the people*: Although Luke shares this verse with Mark 11:27 (and the story as a whole with Mark 11:27-33 and Matt 21:23-27, with a variant also in John 2:18-22), he modifies it in three important ways: a) he links it directly to 19:47 where Jesus was shown "teaching every day in the temple"; b) he identifies Jesus' audience explicitly as "the people" (*laos*) whom we recognize as those eager to hear Jesus' words (see the note on 19:47); c) he adds the participle, "preaching the good news" (*euangelizomai*) which shows that this activity is in continuity with Jesus' activity throughout the narrative (4:18, 43; 7:22; 8:1; 9:6; 16:16).

2. *by what authority*: The question distances the leaders from the people who ac-knowledge Jesus' authority—by proclaiming him as king and listening to him—and also the reader, who knows that Jesus resisted the *exousia* ("authority") offered him by Satan (4:6), and showed in his own works and words the *exousia* of the kingdom (4:32, 36; 5:24), which he could indeed bestow on others as well (9:1; 10:19).

3. *and you tell me*: As in the parallels, Luke uses the noun *logos* ("word"), here translated as "something." Luke omits the further statement, "and I will tell you by what authority I do these things," found in Mark 11:29 and Matt 21:24, undoubtedly because Jesus, in fact, does *not* tell them (20:8)!

4. *from heaven or from humans*: Is literally "out of heaven" (meaning: from God), or "out of a human being (*anthrōpos*)." It is not simply John's "baptism" that is at issue, but the authority for his prophetic mission. Is John really a prophet?

5. *consulted with each other*: Luke uses the verb *syllogizomai* ("to reason" or "to cal-culate") rather than *dialogizomai* which he has used previously, and which is used by Mark 11:31 and Matt 21:25.

   why didn't you believe in him: It is assumed here that the chief priests, scribes and elders did *not* believe in John as a prophet, although the narrative never explicitly says so. Clearly, Luke intends the reader to connect these leaders to the earlier representatives of unbelief, the lawyers and Pharisees (see 7:30).

6. *whole people will stone us*: The verb *katalithazō* is found only here in the NT, although *lithazō* is used elsewhere. For stoning as the customary punishment for blas-phemy, see the note on 13:34. For the same fear of being stoned by the people, see Acts 5:26. It is a remarkable indication of the leaders' alienation from the populace. Luke uses *laos* ("people") here rather than *ochlos* ("crowd") as in Mark 11:32 and Matt 21:26.

7. *they did not know*: Perhaps no story in the Gospel more clearly suggests the self-serving calculation called "hypocrisy" (12:1). The leaders refuse to take a posi-tion on an issue that by nature demands a decision (compare Gamaliel in Acts 5:38-39).

9. *tell the people this parable*: The framing of the parable is unusual, since it is told "to the people," but points to the leaders' rejection, and Luke notes (v. 19) that the leaders themselves understood it to be directed against them. The parable of the vineyard is found also in Mark 12:1-12 and Matt 21:33-46, with a much shorter version also in the *Gospel of Thomas* 65.

   planted a vineyard: Matt 21:33 makes him a "master of a household" (*oikodespotēs*). Both Matt and Mark 12:1 use the very words of LXX Isa 5:2 in their descriptions of the vineyard, making the allusion to Isaiah and therefore to understanding the vineyard as "the house of Israel" (Isa 5:6) even more explicit.

   leased it to farmers: The noun *geōrgos* means generally a farmer or husbandman, and when the planting is vines, a "vinedresser." The translation uses the generic term simply because it is more widely recognizable. Note that having left out of the kingship parable any reference to a long lapse of time, Luke here inserts it where Mark 12:1 and Matt 21:33 do not: the man goes away "for a considerable period of time."

10. *the appropriate season*: The noun *kairos* is translated in its full sense. Notice the "time (*kairos*) of visitation" in 19:44. While Luke and Mark have a single slave sent, Matt 21:34 has "slaves."

   sent him away with nothing: Is literally "sent him away empty" (*kenos*). Luke follows Mark 12:3 closely. Matt 21:35 has one of the slaves killed and the other stoned.

11. *abusing him, sent him away*: Matt 21:36 has "more slaves than at first." Mark 12:4 has simply "another slave," and he is "beheaded and dishonored." Luke has him "abused" (*atimazō*) and sent away "empty" (*kenos*) like the first.

12. *sent still a third*: Here and in verse 11 Luke uses *prostithēmi* with the infinitive (for his use of this verb, see the note on 19:11). Mark 12:5 has the third slave killed, and then others sent, some of whom are beaten and others killed. The third slave sent in Luke is not killed, only "wounded" and expelled.

13. *master of the vineyard*: Luke's use of *kyrios* makes for difficulty in translation. Within the story itself, the translation "owner" is correct, as in 19:33. On the other hand, in Greek *kyrios* would have an obvious allusion to Isaiah 5:7, "for the vineyard of the Lord (*kyrios*) of Sabaoth is the house of Israel." Note also that the question, "what shall I do" (*ti poiēsō*) is not only a Lukan favorite (cf. 3:10, 14; 10:25; 12:17; 16:4; 18:18; Acts 2:37; 4:16), but also echoes the question of the Lord of the vineyard in Isa 5:4.

   send my beloved son: The reader recognizes in the *huios agapētos* the figure of Jesus (see 3:22 and possibly 9:35). The designation recalls Isaac (Gen 22:2, 12, 26). Most suggestively, it recalls the opening of the "song of the vineyard" in Isa 5:1, "Let me sing for my beloved (*tǭ agapēmenǭ*) a song of the beloved (*asma tou agapētou*) concerning his vineyard." Note also the repetition of "beloved" (*agapēmenǭ*) in Isa 5:7.

   perhaps they will respect: The adverb *isōs* appears only here in the NT; it expresses uncertainty—"maybe so, maybe not." The middle voice of the verb *epitrepō* expresses respect for someone or something (cf. LXX Exod 10:3). Cf. Luke's earlier use for the "unjust judge" (18:2, 4).

14. *plotted with each other*: Only Luke uses the verb *dialogizomai*, which throughout the narrative describes evil designs and calculations (2:35; 5:21-22; 6:8; 9:46-47; 12:17). Despite the shift in verbs, the similarity to the action of the leaders in the story just preceding (20:5) is clear.

   this is the heir: The noun *klēronomos* ("heir") is used only here by Luke (as also by Mark 12:7; Matt 21:38), although Paul uses it in Romans (4:13-14; 8:17) and Galatians (3:29; 4:1, 7, 30) with reference to the Abraham story (see also Heb 1:2; 6:17; 11:7). This is the obvious connection, since Isaac, "the beloved son" was also to be the heir of the promise (Gen 15:7; 21:10; 22:17).

   inheritance might be ours: The logic of this statement is not altogether clear. How could killing the son give them the property, unless *agapētos* ("beloved") is understood here also as "only" son (Hebrew *yaḥid*; see the note on 3:22), and killing him would make them the heirs of the owner? The term "inheritance" (*klēronomia*) is also intimately connected to Abraham and especially the promise of possessing the land; see the note on 10:25.

15. *cast him out . . . killed him*: Luke and Matt 21:39 reverse the order of events in Mark 12:8, so that the son is first driven out of the vineyard, then killed, perhaps to reflect the tradition concerning Jesus that he was killed "outside the camp" (Heb 13:12-13). The deed described corresponds to the intention attributed to the leaders in 19:47.

    do to them: The question echoes that in verse 13 and also that of Isa 5:4-5. Mark has only "what will the Lord of the vineyard do" (12:9). Luke adds "to them," and Matt 21:40 adds "to those farmers," having also added "when therefore he returns."

16. *come and destroy those farmers*: The sequence is like that in the kingship parable: the king returns and slaughters his enemies (19:27). Here, the verb *apollymi* echoes its use in 19:47. What the leaders plan to do to Jesus will happen to them; rejection leads to rejection of the rejecters.

    give the vineyard to others: The demonstrative "these" farmers, which Luke adds to Mark 12:9 is deliberate, providing a contrast to "others." Matt 21:41 again expands to "who will give to him the produce in their seasons."

    may it not be: Only Luke has this interjection between the parable and the Scripture citation. It enables him to contrast the pious exclamation of the people (20:9) to the murderous resolve of the leaders at whom the parable is directed (20:19). The phrase *mē genoito* ("may it not be") is found only here in the Gospels. It is an exclamation found in diatribal literature (see Epictetus, *Discourses* 1, 1, 13; 1, 8, 15) and is used by Paul (e.g., Rom 3:4, 6; 6:15; 7:7; 11:11).

17. *stared at them*: The verb *emblepō* denotes a direct and intense gaze (see 22:61) which commands attention. Only Luke has this detail. Its effect is to force the audience and reader to focus particular attention on the following question.

    why then does this stand written: *Ti* is here taken as the interrogative adverb "why," as in 2:49; 5:22; 6:2, 41, 46; 12:57; 18:19. The translation "what then is this" is possible, but is less responsive to the people's exclamation. Luke has the Scripture citation respond to their perplexity and concern (compare Mark 12:10; Matt 21:42).

    stone which the builders rejected: The citation is *verbatim* from LXX Ps 117:22. He omits the following verse "this was done by the Lord and it is a marvel in our eyes" (Ps 117:23) which is cited by both Mark 12:11 and Matt 21:42. Luke thereby focuses entirely on the rejection motif, as he does also with the same citation in Acts 4:11. Coming after the use of Ps 117:26 "Blessed is he who comes" in the entry (19:37), the citation has a particular edge. If we take seriously the allusion to the Isaiah "song of the vineyard," which identifies the vineyard with "the house of Israel" (Isa 5:7), then the "builders of the house" in this citation can refer only to the leaders of the people.

18. *falling against that stone*: Only Luke adds this to the previous "stone" saying. The allusion is to the "stone of stumbling" in Isa 8:14, which was to be a trap for "the house of Jacob" and a snare to "the inhabitants of Jerusalem" and those

who would fall on it would be crushed. Luke's use of the phrase "that stone" reminds us of the *catenae* of texts involving "stone" in Rom 9:32-33 and especially 1 Pet 2:4-8, which combine Isa 8:14, 28:16, and Ps 117:22. Distinctive to Luke's version is the combination of "falling on it" and "it falling." The verb in this second phrase is *likmaō* which often appears in texts speaking of the crushing of grain and its scattering, in the process of winnowing (see e.g., Isa 17:13; Ezek 26:4).

19. *scribes and the chief priests*: Luke identifies those who seek to kill Jesus, the same characters as in 19:47, and gives their motivation: they knew that the parable was told against (*pros*) them. They wanted to act at once, but were restrained by their fear of the populace (see 20:6; 22:2 and Acts 5:26). The division in the people continues.

INTERPRETATION

The Prophet has entered the city and has taken possession of the Temple. He teaches boldly in its precincts, proclaiming the good news. The populace hangs on his words. The leaders seek to destroy him but fear the reaction of the people. Luke has brought all of the elements of his story of Prophet and people to a sharp focus in this Jerusalem narrative. Here is the heart of his story, the spot toward which his narrative has tended, the place of pivot. From chapter 20 of the Gospel through chapter 7 of Acts, all the action takes place in Jerusalem and centers on the basic issue of the acceptance and rejection of God's Prophet.

The way is prepared for the first murderous rejection by a series of controversies between Jesus and the leaders in the city. Luke follows his Markan source in presenting several short encounters between various representatives of the Jewish leadership. The reader is to imagine something like a public debate taking place in the Temple precincts.

Jesus teaches the people in public, like a prophet, yes, but also like a philosopher. As he teaches he is approached by opponents from other "philosophical schools." Such public debates were common in the Hellenistic world (see Acts 17:18-34!), so common that they could be easily satirized (see e.g., Lucian of Samosata, *Zeus Rants*, 4; *Alexander the False Prophet*, 44-46). When reduced to literary form, these controversies were read by adherents of a particular school not only to discover the errors of opponents but to understand more deeply the truth of their own position (e.g., Plutarch, *Reply to Colotes in Defense of the Other Philosophers*).

For Christian readers, these confrontations between Jesus and the Jewish leaders enabled them not only to perceive the authority of Jesus as prophet and philosopher, but also to situate their understanding of Torah within the spectrum of diverse Jewish views of the late first century. They also serve Luke, as they did Mark, as a way of building narrative suspense and providing plausible motivation for the plot against Jesus. As Jesus repeatedly bests each group that questions him, the growing resentment at such public skewering is easily grasped. The threat posed by the Prophet is now located in the Temple itself and directed against the entrenched leadership. Jesus is not a passive figure: as we see in the two encounters presently being discussed, he is aggressive, and the force of his challenge will be met by violence.

The first encounter (20:1-8) is paradigmatic both in form and substance. In form, we see the challenge put to Jesus in terms of a question, and his response in the form of still another question to which he demands an answer. This form of controversy is often associated with rabbinic discussions, and is indeed found frequently in them: a question is "answered" by another question (e.g., *Lev.Rab.* 34,3; *bT Shab.* 101a; 119a). But it is also common in other Hellenistic controversy forms, especially those of the diatribe (e.g., Epictetus, *Discourses* 2, 23). By being able to deflect a hostile question with one of his own, Jesus is recognizable as a sage of that world.

In substance, the encounter is paradigmatic because it focuses on the central issue of Jesus' "authority" (*exousia*) for doing and saying the things he does: is he a prophet or only a troublemaker? The authorities are clever enough. They are the only ones who could give "human authority" to teach in the Temple. They seem to force Jesus into a claim to "divine authority" that they could use against him on a charge of blasphemy.

Jesus' response is more than clever; it is a prophetic challenge. By forcing them to deal with the prophetic ministry of John, he shifts attention from his own credentials to the issue of their openness to God's visitation. As the reader would expect in the light of the entire narrative to this point (see esp. 7:29-30) their mutual consultation reveals that they are indeed not open to the prophetic call. Their refusal to answer, "we do not know where it was from," is terribly ironic, for neither now "do they know the time of their visitation," (19:44) which will lead to their destruction.

The second encounter (20:9-19) is indirect. Jesus goes on the attack by telling the parable of the vineyard. Although he tells it to the people as a whole (20:9), the leaders overhear it and recognize it as having been directed against them (20:19). For the most part, Luke follows Mark's version of the parable itself. This means that (in contrast to the version of the story in *Gospel of Thomas*, 65) he takes over (with approval) the allegorical connection of this story to that of the "vineyard of the beloved" in Isaiah 5:1-7. In Luke's version, therefore, the identification of the vineyard with the "house of Jacob," that is, Israel, is unmistakable.

Because the reader already recognizes Jesus as "the beloved son" (3:22), the parable unavoidably functions also as an allegory of the sending of Jesus to the people Israel. The demand for the fruits of the vineyard echoes John's demand for the "fruits of repentance" (3:8) and Jesus' demand for "good fruit" (6:43). The "season" of this demand is like the "season of visitation" brought by the prophet. Above all, of course, the plot to kill the heir and the carrying out of that murder point directly to the rejection of Jesus and his execution. In fact, because of Luke's framing of the parable, it functions as a sort of "self-fulfilling prophecy" (see introduction): even as he finishes speaking, the leaders who recognize the parable as directed against them fulfill its message by seeking to kill him (20:19).

As in the other Synoptics, Luke's parable of the vineyard is a parable of rejection. Indeed, Luke has sharpened this element by the combination of scriptural allusions he uses to close the parable. He not only cites from Ps 117:22 (LXX)—leaving out the triumphant note of verse 23 included by Matthew and Mark and thereby heightening the aspect of rejection—but he includes an allusion to the "stone of stumbling" passage of Isa 8:14, making it, if anything, more threatening: this stone is not simply a passive block against which one may stumble—it can fall on someone!

It is equally important to note, however, how Luke has made this rejection apply to the leaders rather than to the people as a whole. The people greet the parable with dismay: "may it not be!" It is only the leaders who hear it and then proceed to enact it. The psalm verse tells us that it is "the builders of the house" who reject the stone (a point made even more emphatically in Acts 4:11). If the vineyard is to be read as "the house of Jacob," then the builders must be the leaders. They will be destroyed because of their rejection of the heir. But the vineyard itself will remain and be given over to other leaders (20:16). In Luke's story, the present leadership over Israel of the chief priests, scribes and elders will be replaced by that of the Twelve, a development we will observe in the narrative of Acts.

For Reference and Further Study

Bultmann, R. *The History of the Synoptic Tradition.* Rev. ed. Trans. J. Marsh (New York: Harper and Row, 1963) 39–51.

Crossan, J. D. "The Parable of the Wicked Husbandmen." *JBL* 90 (1971) 451–465.

Jeremias, J. *The Parables of Jesus.* Rev. ed. (New York: Charles Scribner's Sons, 1963) 70–77.

Nestle, E. "Lk 20, 18." *ZNW* 8 (1907) 321–22.

Schramm, T. *Die Markus-Stoff bei Lukas: Eine literarkritisches und redaktionsgeschichtiche Untersuchung* (SNTMS 14; Cambridge: University Press, 1971) 149–167.

Shae, G. S. "The Question on the Authority of Jesus." *NovT* 16 (1974) 1–29.

55. *Debates with Leaders* (20:20–21:4)

20. So they kept him under close scrutiny. They sent as spies those who pretended to be righteous. They were to catch him in his speech so they could hand him over to the rule and authority of the prefect. 21. They questioned him: "Teacher, we know that you speak and teach correctly. You are impartial and teach the way of God in truth. 22. Is it allowed for us to pay a tax to Caesar or not?" 23. He recognized their deceptiveness. He said to them, 24. "Show me a Denarius. Whose image and inscription does it have?" They said, "Caesar's." 25. And he said to them, "Therefore pay back to Caesar the things that are Caesar's, and to God the things that are God's." 26. They were not able to trap him verbally in front of the people. They were astonished at his answer and fell silent. 27. Some of the Sadducees approached. They deny that there is a resurrection. They questioned him: 28. "Teacher, Moses wrote for us, If someone's brother has a wife and dies childless, let the brother marry his wife and produce children for his brother. 29. Now there were seven brothers. The first married a woman and died childless. 30. Both the second 31. and the third married her, and in the same manner also the seven. They died and did not leave children. 32. Finally the woman too died. 33. In the resurrection, therefore, whose wife will the woman be? For the seven men had her as wife!" 34. Jesus told them, "People in the present world marry and are given in marriage. 35. But those who have been considered worthy of reaching that world and the resurrection of the dead neither marry nor are given in marriage. 36. For neither are they still able to die. For they are like angels. And because they are children of the resurrection they are children of God. 37. But even Moses has shown that the dead are raised, as he says at the bush, 'The Lord, the God of Abraham and the God of Isaac and the God of Jacob.' 38. Now, he is not a God of dead people but of living people, because for him all are alive." 39. Some of the scribes responded, "Teacher, you have spoken well!" 40. For they were no longer daring to question him. 41. But he said to them, "How do they say that the Messiah is David's son? 42. For David himself says in the Book of Psalms, 'The Lord said to my Lord, sit at my right hand until I put your enemies as a footstool for your feet.' 44. David therefore calls him Lord, so how is he his son?" 45. While all the people were listening, he said to his disciples: 46. "Stay away from the scribes! They want to walk in robes. They love greetings in the marketplaces and first places in synagogues and first couches at banquets. 47. They swallow the houses of widows. And for show they make long prayers. These will receive a harder judgment!" 21:1. Looking up, he saw rich people throwing their gifts into the treasury. 2. And he saw there a certain poor widow throwing in two copper coins. 3. He said, "I tell you truly: this poor widow has contributed more than all of them. 4. For all these gave their gifts out of their abundance. But this woman contributed out of her poverty everything that she had to live on."

NOTES

20. *under close scrutiny*: The circumstantial participle *paratērēsantes* could be taken as expressing purpose: "in order to keep him under close scrutiny." The term *paratēreō* was used earlier for hostile observation by Jesus' opponents (6:7; 14:1; cf. 17:20). This controversy story is paralleled by Mark 12:13-17 and Matt 22:15-22.

as spies: Since the subject of "sent" is not given it must refer to the leaders last mentioned in 20:19. They could not act openly but sent spies. The term *enkathetos* means someone lying in wait (cf. Gen 49:17; Job 31:9) but is used by Josephus in the sense of spies (*Jewish War* 6:286).

those who pretended to be righteous: This phrase is different from Mark 12:13 and Matt 22:15-16, where the questioners are identified as Pharisees and Herodians. Luke clearly wants the reader to recognize them as Pharisees since this is his earlier description of them (16:15; 18:9). He may have eliminated the explicit designation out of concern for what he considered the proper sequence in opponents beginning with the Jerusalem narrative. The verb "pretend" (*hypokrinomai*) is cognate with "hypocrisy" (*hypokrisis*), as in Sir 1:29; 32:15; 33:2; 2 Macc 5:25; 4 Macc 6:15, 17. For the "hypocrisy of the Pharisees," see Luke 12:1.

catch him in his speech: Is literally "lay hold of his word," with the sense of "entrapping" him. Luke uses a variant phrase in verse 26 which this translation renders "trap him verbally." This attempt continues the effort begun by the scribes and Pharisees in 11:53-54.

rule and authority of the prefect: The reader is reminded of the last passion prediction in 18:32, which spoke of the Prophet's being "handed over to the Gentiles." The prefect (*hēgemōn*) is of course Pontius Pilate (cf. 3:1), whose bloody tendencies have been adumbrated (13:1-5). Luke emphasizes more than the parallels do the essentially *political* motivation of Jesus' opponents.

21. *you are impartial*: The literal Greek phrase, "receive the face" (*prosōpon lambanein*) is closer to the LXX idiom in Luke than in the parallels. It derives from the context of judgment, and refers to the fairness of the judge who is not swayed by "appearance" (*prosōpon*) and cannot be bribed (see Lev 19:15; Deut 1:17; 10:17; 16:19). There is wonderful irony here, for they are obviously trying to bribe him with their praise, even though Luke reduces the fulsomeness of Matt 22:16 and Mark 12:14.

22. *allowed for us to pay a tax to Caesar*: Luke adds the words "for us," which shifts the question from a general proposition to one of practical pertinence. Is this "king" one who refuses to recognize the emperor of the *oikoumenē*, now mentioned for the third time in the narrative (see 2:1; 3:1)? The issue of what is "allowed" (*exestin*) refers what is demanded by Torah and therefore covenantal loyalty to God (see 6:2, 4, 9; 14:3; Acts 16:21), a difficult issue for all Palestinian Jews living under Roman occupation. The question is designed to place Jesus in an impossible situation, for Jews themselves were hotly divided over just such points of tension between religious and political loyalties. The context for the issue was set by the taxation of Judea under Quirinius (see Luke 2:2) which is repeatedly mentioned by Josephus as the cause for the revolt led by Judas the

Galilean, in which submission to Rome was regarded as treason against the people (Josephus, *Antiquities* 18:1-10, 23-25; 20:102; *Jewish War* 2:117-118; 7:253-258).

23. *their deceptiveness*: Luke uses *panourgia*, which has a more specifically rhetorical flavor appropriate to spies; it has the sense of "cleverness in speech," as in Plato, *Laws* 474C, Aristotle, *Nichomachean Ethics* 6, 12, 9; Sirach 1:6; compare "evil" in Matt 22:18 and "hypocrisy" in Mark 12:15.

24. *whose image and inscription*: The answer, of course, is "Caesar's," specifically: "Tiberius Caesar, Son of the Divine Augustus, Augustus." Not only the image of a face but also the designations "divine" and "augustus" bring the coinage into the realm of idolatry. The fact that they had a coin to produce shows that they used the currency and therefore were as much implicated by its suggestions of idolatry as if they paid the tax.

25. *therefore pay back*: The verb *apodidōmi* can mean simply to "give" (as in 4:20; 9:42; Acts 4:33; 7:9) or to "pay back" in the sense of "pay what is owed" (see 10:35; 12:59; 16:2). Either sense fits here: what is appropriate to each is to be given.

    things that are God's: The phrase *ta tou theou* is a pregnant expression (cf. 1 Cor 2:11). Obviously, if "the world and all that are in it are the Lord's" (Ps 24:1-2), then "all things" are owed to God. And that is the subtle point: allegiance to God is not on the same plane as political allegiance. Caesar may call himself "Augustus," and issue a coin with that on it, but letting him have that coin back does not mean we recognize the claim, only that we allow the idolatrous circle to close. Allegiance to God has the demand of absolute devotion of the mind, the heart, and the strength (10:27). The version of this saying in *Gospel of Thomas* 100 adds "and give to me what is mine."

26. *fell silent*: Compare the response of the opponents in 14:4, and for "astonishment," the response of the Pharisees in 14:38.

27. *some of the Sadducees approached*: This is the only mention of the Sadducees in Luke's Gospel, although they reappear in Acts 4:1; 5:17; 23:6-8. In the parallel versions of this controversy (Mark 12:18-27; Matt 22:23-33), the opponents are also Sadducees. The Jewish sect took its name from Zadok, David's priest (2 Sam 8:17). Josephus describes them as one of the "philosophical schools" in Judaism. He says they belong to the wealthy aristocracy, and hold only to the written Scriptures, rejecting the oral tradition of the Pharisees (*Antiquities* 13:297-298; 18:17). Consequently, they were conservative in their belief, rejecting the existence of angels as well as of the resurrection of the dead (*Antiquities* 18:16; *Jewish War* 2:165). Since the Sadducees disappeared after the destruction of the Temple, they are treated rather shabbily in the rabbinic sources: cf. *Psalms of Solomon* 4:1-20; *m.Ber.* 9:5; *m.Nid.* 4:1; bT *Erub.* 1101a; bT *Yom.* 4a.

    deny that there is a resurrection: Explicit belief in the resurrection developed late (see Dan 12:2-3; 2 Macc 7:9, 11, 14, 23), and although it was firmly held by Pharisees (Josephus, *Jewish War* 2:163; 1 *Enoch* 91:10; 2 *Baruch* 49-52) and in some fashion by the Essenes (*Jewish War* 2:154-157), the Sadducean position could claim to be more traditional. Luke uses the disagreement between Pharisees and Sadducees on this point to set off an argument in Acts 23:7-10.

28. *Moses wrote for us*: Notice how the "for us" has the same personalizing effect as verse 22. The actual citation is a loose reworking of Deut 25:5 concerning the "levirate" ("brother-in-law") marriage, except for the final phrase, "produce children for his brother" (literally, "raise up a seed"), which paraphrases slightly the statement of Judah to Onan in Gen 38:8.

33. *whose wife will the woman be*: There are many minor textual variants in this short but complex puzzler, indicating the desire of scribes to be helpful. Luke considerably shortens Mark 12:20-22 and the effect is not altogether smooth. The intricacies of the levirate law in practice are well demonstrated by the Mishnah tractate *Yebamoth* 1:1-4. For a situation similar to the one posed here, cf. *m.Yeb.* 2:2. The Sadducees naturally heighten the *reductio ad absurdum*: one is tempted to translate: "Remember, all seven had the same wife!" Their point is the impossibility of a physical resurrection. For a similar *reductio*, compare the passage in *bT Nid.* 70b, where "Alexandrians" ask a rabbi whether corpses in the next life will need to be ritually sprinkled! The question is categorized as "sheer nonsense."

34. *people in the present world*: For Luke's distinction between the present world (or age: *aiōn*) and "that world" in verse 35, see the note on 16:8 and 18:30. Luke strikingly eliminates the charge in Mark 12:24, "are you not on this account deceived, since you do not know the scriptures or the power of God?" (also Matt 22:29).

35. *worthy of reaching that world*: Is found only in Luke and is wonderfully circumspect: entering "that world" is not something that can be grasped or assumed, but comes from God's judgment of one's worthiness; the passive reflects the action of God. For *kataxioō*, see Acts 5:41, and for the idea, see Acts 13:46. By adding the phrase "and the resurrection of the dead," Luke defines the "age to come" in terms of the resurrection life.

    neither marry nor are given in marriage: For this combination, see 1 Cor 7:38-39, and Luke's allusion to the "day of the Son of Man" in 17:27. Jesus' statement suggests a qualitative difference between the normal functioning of bodies now and in the resurrection. Above all, sexual activity is geared toward the perpetuation of life because of human mortality. If "they are no longer able to die," the purposes for which marriage exists no longer obtain.

36. *they are like angels*: The compound *isangeloi*, "like" or "equal to" angels, occurs only here in the NT. Mark 12:25 and Matt 22:30 use *hōs angeloi*. That the angels ("messengers") of God were spiritual is suggested by LXX Ps 103:4: "he has made his angels spirits (*pneumata*), and his ministers a burning fire" (cf. Heb 1:7), and is developed in such apocalyptic texts as *1 Enoch* 15:6-12. The state of those in the future resurrection is stated by *2 Baruch* 51:10 as "they shall be made like unto the angels, and be made equal to the stars, and they shall be changed into every form they desire." Compare as well Paul's statement on the discontinuity between "flesh and blood" and the glorified resurrection body in 1 Cor 15:35-50.

    children of God: Is literally "sons (*huioi*) of God" and "sons of the resurrection." Compare "sons of peace" in 10:6, and "sons of light" in 16:8. The phrase "sons of God" is applied to angels in Gen 6:2 and LXX Ps 29:1, but the more pertinent connection is to Paul's speaking of Jesus as "Son of God" in virtue of the resurrection (Rom 1:4).

37. *even Moses has shown . . . as he says at the bush*: The verb *emēnysen* could also be rendered, "made known" or "revealed." This is an abbreviated allusion by Luke; "the bush" refers to the voice from the burning bush in the great theophany of Exod 3:6 and 3:15. The citation here includes "the Lord" which is absent from Exod 3:6 but is in 3:15, but excludes "God of your fathers" which is in both the Exodus passages. This story is cited again by Luke in the all-important speech of Stephen in Acts 7:32 (see introduction, pp. 19–20). For Moses as prophetic authority, see 16:29, 31; 24:27, 44; Acts 3:22; 26:22.

38. *not a God of dead people but of living people*: The particle *de* (translated as "now") is important for the argument, for God had said "I am the God" (*egō eimi ho theos*) of men who had historically died (the patriarchs). If God remains *their* God in the time of Moses, then in some sense they must still be alive. This way of reading the text may appear specious to us, but would not to Jesus' or Luke's contemporaries, for the tenses of verbs and the smallest grammatical points were constantly exploited for interpretative leverage; compare, e.g., *Exodus Rabbah* III, 1–7.

    because for him all are alive: This is a Lukan addition. The connective *hoti* indicates that this clause explains the previous one. But how? The difficulty comes in the dative of the pronoun "him" (*autō*). Does it mean "for him" in the sense of "in his eyes" (so that the point is that God is eternal and all temporal realities are irrelevant—all past figures are present to him)? Or does it mean "in him" (with the point being that those who die rise by his power)? The logic of the passage seems to demand the last option, but the first was certainly within Luke's Hellenistic range. There is quite possibly also a parallel here to 4 Macc 7:19 and 16:25, where the Jewish martyrs are confident that they "like our patriarchs Abraham and Isaac and Jacob live to God (*zōsin tō theō*)." Cf. also the phrase in Rom 6:10.

39. *some of the scribes responded*: This ending is peculiar to Luke, and at first glimpse is odd, because the scribes are never positively portrayed by him. The context is important: a) the "they" who no longer question Jesus (v. 40) are not the scribes themselves, but the Sadducees whom Jesus has just rebutted; b) the response of the scribes derives from the end of Mark's version of the "greatest commandment" controversy (Mark 12:28-34) which Luke omits here, having given his own version in 10:25-28; c) the apparently benign response is used by Luke as a transition to an attack on the scribes themselves in 20:41-47, the "them" (*autous*) in 20:41 being the scribes.

41. *they say that the Messiah is David's son*: "They" are the scribes of verse 39 (cf. Mark 12:35); Matt 22:41 has the Pharisees as the interlocutors for this controversy. There is an obvious sense in which Luke agrees that the Messiah is "Son of David" (1:32, 69; 2:11; 3:31; 18:38-39). The issue is whether the Messiah is *only* an earthly descendant of David.

42. *David himself. . . in the Book of Psalms*: For David as prophet, see Acts 1:16; 2:25; 4:25; 13:36, and for the psalms as prophetic, see Luke 24:44; Acts 1:20. Rather

than Luke's designation, "Book of Psalms," Mark 12:36 has "in the Holy Spirit," and Matt 22:43, "in the Spirit calls him Lord." The citation in all three Synoptists is from LXX Ps 109:1, an important proof-text for the resurrection of Jesus (see Acts 2:34; 1 Cor 15:25; Heb 1:3, 13).

44. *David therefore calls him Lord*: Luke states the same idea somewhat differently than does Mark 12:37 and Matt 22:45. The psalm verse is taken as pointing not only to an earthly descendant (lesser than David), but a resurrected Lord (and greater than David, since the prophet David calls *him* "Lord"); it points, therefore, to Jesus. This king will inherit not only "the throne of his father David," but "will rule over the house of Jacob forever and his rule will have no end" (Luke 2:32-33). See the very similar argument in Acts 2:25-34.

45. *said to his disciples*: Luke nicely edits this transition statement (cf. Mark 12:37-38; Matt 23:1) so that the people overhear, the disciples are instructed and the opponents are condemned: the same pattern as in the journey narrative! This makes clear that the positive response of the scribes in verse 39 is being used by Luke literarily to set up this attack.

46. *stay away from the scribes*: Luke uses this same construction, *prosechete apo* with reference to the Pharisees in 12:1. In the present polemic, Luke follows Mark 12:38-39 very carefully, adding only "they love" before "greetings in the marketplaces." Matthew at this point has expanded the passage into his sustained attack on scribes and Pharisees (23:1-36) which is partially paralleled by Luke 11:37-52. In 11:43, Luke also charged the Pharisees with "loving the first seat in synagogues and greetings in the marketplaces," and adds the charge of "seeking first places at banquets" to the Pharisees' actual practice at the banquet of 14:7.

47. *swallow the houses of widows*: As always, Luke portrays widows as particularly vulnerable and in need of protection within a patriarchal society in which they are chronically impoverished (cf. 2:37; 4:25-26; 7:12; Acts 6:1; 9:39, and especially the story that follows immediately in 21:1-4). For the special claims widows should have within the legislation of Torah, see the note on 18:3. We do not know how Luke sees the scribes as "swallowing" the widows' houses; the polemic is as stereotypical as the charge that the Pharisees are "lovers of money" (16:14).

for show they make long prayers: Here again is a parallel to the behavior of the Pharisees, who are said to cleanse the outside of the cup (that is "for show") while being avaricious within (11:39). Note also the prayer of the Pharisee in 18:11.

a harder judgment: Is literally a "greater judgment," with *krima* being understood in the sense of "condemnation." For similar statements by Jesus, see 10:14; 11:31-32, 51.

21:1. *gifts into the treasury*: The noun *gazophylakaion* is found in the NT only here, Mark 12:41-43, and John 8:20. For the presence of a treasury in the Temple precincts, see Neh 10:38, and Josephus, *Jewish War* 6:282. In the Mishnah, *m.Shek.* 5:6 refers to the "chamber of secrets" in the Temple as the place where "the devout used to put their gifts in secret and the poor of good family receive support therefrom in secret." It was, therefore, a mechanism for the collection and distribution of alms; cf. also *Sifre on Deuteronomy* 15:10.

2. *a certain poor widow*: In this verse, Luke uses the adjective *penichos,* and in the next, *ptōchos.* In Prov 28:15 and 29:7 they are virtually interchangeable, and Luke may change them only for the sake of stylistic variety (cf. also Exod 22:25; 23:11). The widow provides an obvious contrast to the scribes who "swallow widows' houses" (20:47), and exemplifies the righteous poor who receive the good news (4:18; 6:20; 7:22; 14:21; 16:20), as shown by her response of disposing of her own possessions. The "two copper coins" (*lepta*) are the smallest coins then in circulation.

4. *gave their gifts*: Is awkward in Greek, literally "threw into their gifts," by which Luke must mean the Chamber of Secrets (see note on 21:1); he has considerably abbreviated Mark 12:43-44.

out of their abundance . . . out of her poverty: These two phrases balance each other: "abundance" is literally "out of what exceeds" (*ek tou perisseuontos*; cf. 9:17; 12:15; 15:17); "out of her poverty" is literally "out of her lacking" (*ek tou hysterēmatos autēs*; cf. 15:14).

everything that she had to live on: Is literally "all the life (*bios*) that she had," with *bios* here being understood as "means of subsistence" as in 8:43; 15:12, 30, and I John 3:17.

INTERPRETATION

After the opening skirmish between the leaders and Jesus in the Temple (20:1-19), Luke presents a series of controversy stories between the Prophet and various representatives of the Jewish "philosophical schools." The nature and function of such controversy stories was discussed in the interpretation of the previous section. In order to appreciate the distinctive Lukan version of this public debate in the Temple, it may be helpful to begin by observing his arrangement of materials in sequence.

In the main, Luke follows Mark's order carefully: he has the controversy about paying taxes to Caesar (20:20-26; Mark 12:13-17), about the resurrection (20:27-40; Mark 12:18-27), about David's Son (20:41-44; Mark 12:35-37a), the polemic against scribes (20:45-47; Mark 12:37b-40), and the story of the widow (21:1-4; Mark 12:41-44). He has, however, eliminated the controversy concerning the greatest commandment (Mark 12:28-34; Matt 22:34-40). Two things about its placement in Mark may have bothered Luke: the relative neutrality of the question (as opposed to the clear malice involved in the others), and the approbation of the scribe found in Mark 12:32 (Jesus declares that he is not far from the kingdom). Luke therefore moved his version of this controversy to 10:25-28, portraying in the process Jesus' lawyer interlocutor as self-justifying, and the commandment fulfilled by a Samaritan (10:30-37). The result of Luke's rearrangement here is a more logical narrative development: each of the present stories serves to reveal consistently the division between Jesus and his opponents.

By comparing Luke's use of Mark with Matthew's use of the same source, we can also observe some of the choices Luke did not make, also sharpening our perception of his literary method. First, Luke retains Mark's story of the widow's contribution (21:1-4) which Matthew omits. Second, Luke follows Mark's short polemic against the scribes in 20:45-47, rather than expand it with material from Q into a full-fledged attack on the Pharisees and scribes together, as Matthew does (Matt 23:1-36).

Much of Matthew's material is included by Luke in his polemic against lawyers and Pharisees in 11:39-52, and in the lament over Jerusalem in 13:34-35. But by keeping to Mark's sequence, Luke is able to accomplish two goals of his own. He is able first to level in an abbreviated form exactly the same charges that he placed against the "lawyers and Pharisees"; by so doing he shows that although the names may have changed, the character of Jesus' opponents in this Jerusalem narrative remains the same. He is also able to make a final contrast between the "oppressive rich" (the scribes who swallow the houses of widows) and the "righteous poor" (the impoverished widow who donates her entire livelihood in alms), so that immediately before the passion narrative the theme of division in the people can be sounded one more time.

Each of these controversy stories is rich in detail, informing us with considerable accuracy about controversies within first-century Judaism and about Christianity's emerging self-understanding within that setting. Luke has also taken particular care to shape these stories to his own literary purpose. Notice in the controversy over taxes to Caesar how Luke not only makes the political motivation of these Pharisaic spies explicit, but prepares the way for the distorted statement of Jesus' position as a charge at the trial (23:2). Notice also how he has the questioners themselves ready to supply a coin on demand, showing the reader that they actually use the coinage of Caesar, a small redactional touch that accentuates both their personal hypocrisy and their rhetorical *panourgia* ("deceptiveness").

Likewise in the controversy with the Sadducees about the resurrection, Luke modifies his Markan source to bring out some distinctive points important for his own story. The tiny detail about the resurrected being "like the angels" is not only a subtle dig at another belief not held by the Sadducees, but prepares for the near riot over the issue of the resurrection in Acts 23:6-9. The fact that "Moses revealed that the dead are raised in the story of the bush" is also of importance for Luke, since he uses precisely that story from Exodus 3 in his own version of the Moses story in Acts 7:30-34. This finding of the teaching of resurrection in "Moses," furthermore, anticipates the argument of Paul in Acts 26:22-23.

But it is by taking these controversy stories as a whole that we begin to recognize that the point made partially by each is made fully and forcefully by them all together. That point is the radical discontinuity between the good news of the kingdom of God proclaimed by Jesus the Prophet, and the messianic expectations and religious concerns of the Jewish leaders. The discontinuity is all the sharper, of course, because it is seen from the other side of the resurrection experience and years of reflection within the Christian community on the meaning of Jesus as Messiah.

In the controversies, we see in Jesus' opponents a perception of "the kingdom of God" as politically structured, so that allegiance to God must have a direct political expression in allegiance to a Jewish king, or at the least, rebellion against the emperor in however symbolic a fashion. We see an understanding of "life before God" as consisting only in this present earthly existence with no hope for a blessed resurrection, and with God's blessings for the righteous therefore necessarily being spelled out in terms of earthly prosperity, long life, and children, an understanding rooted in a conviction, furthermore, that God's revelation is closed once for all in a book. We see the expectation of a Messiah who is a descendant of the ruler who symbolizes the nation's glorious past, and who by being nothing more than such a descendant holds out a hope for no greater realization of "God's rule" than safe borders and prosperity. Finally, we see the symbolic expression of such a closed-horizon religion: the professional religionists who find their reward in earthly recognition in public acclaim and prestige, but who cannot be content with that, and oppress others even as they parade a public piety.

Against such a perception, we find the words of Jesus expressing the deepest convictions of the Christian community concerning its understanding of the kingdom of God. God owns "all things" and "all things" must be given back to God, but this allegiance is not spelled out in terms of a specific political commitment; rather it transcends every political expression. No king, not even a Jewish king, not even David's son, can receive the devotion of "all the heart and soul and strength and mind" (10:27), but only God.

God is, furthermore, infinitely rich in life, alive himself and giving life to all. God's revelation does not stop with Moses but continues in the experience of humans. God raises the dead to life as easily as God gives life in the first place. And this resurrection life is radically different from the present one. The "children of the resurrection" are "children of God" and share God's own life. Not only lack of faith in God but an impoverished imagination insists on portraying such a hope in terms of earthly preoccupations about descent and property!

The source of this resurrection life for Christians is, furthermore, obviously not one who is simply a "son of David," but the one who is "life-giving Spirit," (1 Cor 15:45), who is "Son of God in power according to the Spirit of holiness by his resurrection from the dead, Jesus Christ our Lord" (Rom 1:4). The kingdom shaped by such a Lord is therefore entirely new with the newness of God's own life; it is not simply the perpetuation of a national dream of sovereignty, but hope of eternal life for all humans.

Finally, this kingdom is symbolized by the widow, who though left all alone in human terms, is not only herself alive but capable of giving life by sharing "all her living" with others.

FOR REFERENCE AND FURTHER STUDY

Cassidy, R. *Jesus, Politics and Society: A Study of Luke's Gospel* (Maryknoll, N.Y.: Orbis, 1978) 55–61.
Charpentier, E. "Tous vivent pour lui: Lc 20, 27-28." *AsSeign* n.s. 63 (1971) 82–94.
Degenhardt, H.-J. *Lukas Evangelist der Armen* (Stuttgart: Katholisches Bibelwerk, 1965) 93–97.
Fitzmyer, J. A. "The Son of David Tradition and Mt 22:41-46 and Parallels." *Essays on the Semitic Background of the New Testament* (SBS 5; Missoula: Scholars Press, 1974) 113–126.
Giblin, C. H. " 'The things of God' in the Question concerning Tribute to Caesar." *CBQ* 33 (1971) 510–61.

56. *Prophecies about Jerusalem* (21:5-24)

5. And when some of them were talking about the temple, how it was adorned with beautiful stones and votive offerings, he said: 6. "These things you are looking at—days will come when there will not be left a stone upon a stone that will not be torn down!" 7. They began to ask him: "Teacher, when therefore will these things be? What will be the sign that these things are about to happen?" 8. He said: "Watch out! Don't be deceived! For many will come in my name. They will say, 'I am he!' and, 'The time is near!' Do not follow them. 9. And when you hear of wars and revolutions, do not panic. For these things must happen first, but the end is not immediate." 10. Then he told them: "A nation will rise against a nation, a kingdom against a kingdom. 11. There will be great earthquakes, and in various places there will be famines and plagues. There will be terrors and great signs from heaven. 12. But before all these things they will lay hands on you and persecute you. They will hand you over to synagogues and prisons. They will lead you away to kings and governors on account of my name. 13. It will turn out to be a chance for you to bear witness. 14. Therefore put it in your hearts not to prepare ahead of time your defense. 15. For I will give you speech and wisdom such that all those opposing you will not be able to resist or contradict. 16. But you will be handed over by parents and brothers, by relatives and friends. And they will kill some of you.

17. You will be hated by all on account of my name. 18. And not a hair from your head will be lost! 19. You will gain possession of your lives by your endurance. 20. But when you see Jerusalem surrounded by an army encampment, then you will know that its devastation is near. 21. Then those in Judaea should flee into the mountains. Those in the middle of the city should get out of it. Those in the countryside should not go into it. 22. Because these are the days of judgment to fulfill all things written. 23. Woe to those who are pregnant and those nursing infants during those days! For there will be great distress over the land and a wrath shown toward this people. 24. People will fall by the edge of the sword. They will be taken as prisoners into every nation. And Jerusalem will be ground under the heel of the Gentiles until the times of the Gentiles are completed."

NOTES

5. *some of them*: In context, these would be the disciples whom Jesus last addressed in 20:45.

beautiful stones and votive offerings: The Temple was one of Herod the Great's major building projects; for admiring descriptions, see Josephus, *Jewish War* 1:401; 5:184-227; *Antiquities* 15:380-425. The term *anathēma* means "what is set up," and it refers to votive offerings ("memorials") made by the wealthy devout for the adornment of the Temple; see e.g., the pledge made by Antiochus in 2 Macc 9:16 and the report about Ptolemy in 3 Macc 3:17. Luke's language here is terse and accurate; compare Mark 13:1.

6. *these things you are looking at*: The sentence is anacolouthic (there is a break in the Greek syntax), indicated in the translation by a dash. Luke adds the phrase "days are coming," which echoes his earlier sayings on the future (17:22, 25; 19:43).

stone upon a stone: This pronouncement is basically the same as that in Mark 13:2 and Matt 24:2, except that in Luke it picks up his earlier statement in 19:44, with two differences: a) the first prediction dealt with Jerusalem itself and this one with the Temple; b) this one adds the emphatic "pulled down" (*katalythēsetai*).

7. *will these things be*: Note the setting for the following discourse: Luke has Jesus continue to speak in the Temple, rather than withdraw to the Mount of Olives (cf. Mark 13:3; Matt 24:3).

sign that these things are about to happen: In Luke, the "sign" is limited to the destruction of the Temple and city, in striking contrast to Mark 13:4, "the signs when all these things will be completed," and even more, Matt 24:3, "the sign of your coming and the completion of the ages."

8. *watch out! don't be deceived*: The translation divides into two imperatives a single Greek sentence, "beware lest you be deceived." Cf. the warning in 8:18. In Mark 13:5 and Matt 24:4, the deception is personalized: "beware lest *someone* deceive you."

I am he . . . the time is near: Like the parallels, Luke pictures these coming "in my name" (see 9:48-49). Matthew expands the "I am" of Mark (and Luke) into "I am the Messiah." Only Luke, on the other hand, has the additional clause, "the time is near," perhaps because an obvious concern in his redaction is to avoid precipitous panic. The most obvious referent for *kairos* ("time") is the "time of visitation" in 19:44. For a similar warning, see 2 Thess 2:1-2.

do not follow them: Is literally "go after them." Luke does not want his readers to respond to the claims of prophets concerning imminent doom. For the presence of such prophetic voices in the actual siege of Jerusalem, cf. Josephus, *Jewish War* 6:285-287; 6:300-309. Luke replaces with this command the statement in Mark 13:6 and Matt 24:5, "they will deceive many."

9. *do not panic*: Luke uses the stronger verb *ptoeō* ("strike with panic") rather than that in Mark 13:7 and Matt 24:6, *throeomai* ("be troubled"); cf. 2 Thess 2:2. Luke's verb is found in Exod 19:16 and Deut 31:6. He also replaces "rumors of wars" in the parallels to "revolutions" (*akatastasia*), possibly to reflect the turbulence of the imperial court after Nero, but possibly because the term is naturally linked with *polemos* ("war") in the literature (e.g., Jas 3:16; 4:1).

these things must happen first: For Luke's use of *dei* ("it is necessary"), see 2:49; 4:43; 9:22; 17:25. He adds the adverb "first" (*prōton*) and changes the "not yet" of Mark 13:7 and Matt 24:6 to "not immediately" (*eutheus*). Luke wants to show a necessary progression of events, and "the end" (*to telos*) is not, as in Mark, "the end of all things," but simply the end of the city of Jerusalem.

10. *a nation . . . against a nation*: The translation emphasizes the anarthous nouns, which enables the reader to understand, not a gnomic utterance, but a prediction of the Jewish revolt against Rome. The language of the prophecy is similar to that in 2 Chr 15:6, although the verb "will rise up" echoes as well a similar prediction in Isa 19:2.

11. *earthquakes . . . famines and plagues*: In this rapid-fire list of disasters, Luke expands the "earthquakes" of Mark 13:8 to "great earthquakes," and the "famines" (*limoi*) to "famines and plagues" (*loimoi*); for this combination, see *Testament of Judah* 23:3. By adding the words "in various places," Luke generalizes the prediction. An earthquake is to precede the "Day of the Lord" in Zech 14:5, and is an instrument of divine punishment in Isa 29:6 and Ezek 38:19. The earthquake is part of the theophany in Ezek 3:12-13. Famine frequently figures in divine punishments (see Amos 8:11; Isa 14:30; 51:19; Ezek 36:29-30.

terrors and great signs from heaven: The term *phobētron* ("terror") occurs in Isa 19:17. Luke has replaced the "beginnings of the birth pangs" of Mark 13:8 (Matt 24:8) with this much less explicitly apocalyptic designation (for birth pangs, see 1 Thess 5:3). A dreadful apparition over Jerusalem at the time of Antiochus Epiphanes is reported by 2 Macc 5:24, and Josephus describes heavenly portents during the siege of Jerusalem in the war with Rome (*Jewish War* 6:288-300). Luke may have had some such event in mind. Notice, however, that the combination of "terrors and signs" (*terata kai sēmeia*) will recur in Acts 2:19.

12. *but before all these things*: This is a key editorial insertion, enabling Luke to place Jesus' predictions of his followers' sufferings *before* the fall of the city. In Mark 13:9 they are part of the "birth-pangs" signalling the end-time. Matthew in-

cludes part of this material in 10:17-22 and part of it in the present discourse, 24:9-14.

hand you over: The fate of Jesus to "be handed over" (9:44; 18:32) will be his disciples' fate as well (see Acts 8:3). In general, these predictions find their literal fulfillment in the narrative of Acts about the first Christians. For the (violent) laying on of hands, see Acts 4:3; 5:18. For "persecuting" (*diōkō*, not found in Mark 13:9), see Acts 9:4; 22:4. For the synagogues (instead of the "Sanhedrins" of Mark 13:9 and Matt 10:17), see Acts 9:2; 26:11. For prisons (added to Mark and lacking in Matthew), see Acts 5:19; 8:3; 12:4; 16:23.

kings and governors: The noun *hēgemōn*, translated here as governor, could also be "prefect," as in 20:20. As Jesus is to be "led away" (22:26), to appear before the king Herod (23:6-12) and the prefect Pilate (23:1-5, 13-25), so are the disciples to face "kings" (Acts 12:1; 25:13) and "governors" (Acts 23:24, 26; 26:30). For the phrase "on account of my name," see 6:22; 9:48, and its fulfillment in Acts 4:7, 10, 17-18; 5:28, 40.

13. *chance for you to bear witness*: The translation is fairly loose, to get at the sense. The verb *apobainō* used in this sort of construction means "to turn out to be"; the phrase *eis martyrion* is expanded into "a chance to bear witness." Once more, the fulfillment is literally carried out in Acts 3:15; 4:33; 5:32; 20:26; 26:22. Luke omits Mark 13:10 "and first the gospel must be preached to all the nations" (Matt 10:18 has, "witness to them and to the nations"), since that is a theme developed in Acts (see esp. Acts 1:8).

14. *put it in your hearts*: Is a call to attention and memory; compare the similar exhortations in 1:66 and 9:44.

15. *I will give you speech*: These words parallel the earlier instructions to the disciples on their behavior in persecution (12:11-12). That passage promises that "the Holy Spirit will teach [them] what they must say." Here, Jesus himself will give speech (literally, a "mouth," *stoma*) and wisdom. That the Holy Spirit is the Spirit of Jesus is made explicit in Acts (3:12-13; 4:7-10, 29). For the prophecy's fulfillment, see Acts 6:3 and 6:10.

to resist or contradict: The line is found only in Luke, and reaches its literal fulfillment in Acts. In the story of Stephen, his opponents are "not able to resist his wisdom," (Acts 6:10) and the leaders confronted by John and Peter "had nothing to contradict" (Acts 4:14).

16. *you will be handed over*: The agents of betrayal are now supplied in place of the indefinite third person plural verb of verse 12. The list of "parents, brothers, relatives and friends" partly resembles the list of those invited to banquets (14:12) and partly those left behind for the sake of discipleship (18:29): the people close to them are the ones who will hand them over, again just as Jesus is to be handed over by one of the Twelve (6:16; 22:3), his "family" (8:21). On the other hand, Luke particularizes Mark 13:12 ("they will kill them") to "they will kill some of you," which also finds fulfillment in the murder of James (Acts 12:1-2).

17. *hated by all*: Luke's saying is exactly matched by Mark 13:13, and echoes the final Lukan beatitude, "when people hate you" (6:22). Matt 24:9 adds, "hated by all the nations."

18. *hair from your head*: Another line unique to Luke, which picks up an earlier statement to the disciples in 12:7: "the hairs of your head are all counted." See the note on that verse for the background. Here, the assurance seems to contradict what goes before it, but in reality it does not. What is at issue is the "possession of their souls (lives)" with God, and that is assured by resurrection.

19. *gain possession of your lives*: Some MSS have the imperative mood here, and some the future indicative. In context, the meaning is much the same either way. The verb *ktaomai* has a commercial ring appropriate to this evangelist who plays off the relationship between "life" and "possession" so frequently (9:24-25; 12:15, 33-34; 14:33; 18:29). "Endurance" or "patience" (*hypomonē*) is frequently connected in the NT to the experience of persecution (cf. Rom 5:3-4; 8:25; 2 Cor 1:6; Col 1:11; 1 Thess 1:3; 2 Thess 1:4; Heb 10:36; 12:1; Jas 1:3-4; Rev 13:10). Compare "bearing fruit by endurance" in Luke 8:15.

20. *when you see Jerusalem surrounded*: Luke now shifts back to the "wars and revolutions" he had left behind in 21:10-11 in order to describe the time of Christian persecution (21:12-19). Luke makes abundantly clear that these are signs not of the end of time but of the end of a Temple and city. Notice that he changes the "abomination of desolation" (*bdelygma tēs erēmōseōs*) in Mark 13:14 and Matt 24:15 (deriving from LXX Dan 9:27), to "its desolation" (*erēmōsis*), namely Jerusalem's. The "encirclement" (*kukloō*) echoes the prediction of 19:43 (*perikukloō*). The *stratopedon* could mean either "army" or "army encampment" (cf. 2 Macc 8:12; 9:9; Josephus, *Jewish War* 5:47-50).

21. *should flee into the mountains*: This verse is taken from Mark 13:14 unchanged (cf. also Matt 24:16), but Luke adds the further admonition to avoid the city, which is advice appropriate for a state of siege (cf. Josephus, *Jewish War* 4:377-389; 5:317-330). To accomplish this, he also omits the instructions of Mark 13:15-16, which he includes in his earlier discourse of 17:31.

22. *these are the days of judgment*: The term *ekdikēsis* can mean "vindication" or "retribution," depending on the context. In Luke 18:3-5, the widow demands *ekdikēsis* from the judge, and in the sayings following that parable, Jesus says that God will speedily give *ekdikēsis* to those who pray (18:7-8). In the present context, the term undoubtedly means "punishment" coming to Jersualem for having failed to recognize the "time of her visitation" (13:35; 19:44).

    to fulfill all things written: Here is the characteristic Lukan emphasis on the fulfillment of prophecy, although this is the only time he uses the verb *pimplēmi* in this connection. The prophets of Israel certainly issued many such warnings concerning the Temple and city (see Jer 7:14-26, 30-34; 16:1-9; 17:27; 19:10-15; Mic 3:12; Zeph 1:4-13), a fact recognized also by Josephus, who interpreted the Temple's fall as a punishment preordained by God (*Jewish War* 6:110; 6:250); this motif played an important role in early Christian apologetic against the Jews: cf. Justin's *Dialogue with Trypho* 16, 92, 110, 115; Tertullian, *Against the Jews* 13.

23. *woe to those who are pregnant*: Is literally "who have in the belly," an idiom of the LXX (Gen 16:4; Judg 13:3; 2 Sam 11:5); see also Luke 1:31; 1 Thess 5:3; Rev 12:2. For the horrible experience of pregnant women in a siege or attack, see LXX Hos 14:1; Amos 1:3, 13; for those nursing infants, see LXX Lam 2:11-12, 20;

4:4, and Jesus' lament over the city in Luke 19:44. The grisly details of the actual siege of Jerusalem are graphically displayed by Josephus, *Jewish War* 4:326-333; 5:420-438; 5:512-518. For Luke's use of "woe" (*ouai*), see the note on 6:24.

great distress over the land: The term *anankē* means "need" or "necessity," but can mean, as here, violence and distress (cf. LXX Ps 106:6; Zech 1:15; 2 Macc 6:7). The term "wrath" (*orgē*) is frequently used of the divine punishment (see Mic 5:15; Zeph 1:15, 18; Zech 1:2; Isa 26:20-21; cf. Luke 3:7; Rom 1:18; 1 Thess 1:10). Luke has considerably altered Mark 13:19, emphasizing the fate of the people (*laos*) rather than the signs.

24. *fall by the edge of the sword*: Is literally, "mouth (*stoma*) of the sword." For this language in prophetic statements, see Isa 3:25; 13:15; 65:12; Jer 14:12-18; 16:4. Cf. Josephus, *Jewish War*, 5:516-518.

taken as prisoners into every nation: This verse is unique to Luke. Once more, the theme of exile and captivity is a common one in the prophetic warnings (Mic 1:16; Ezek 12:3; 39:23; Zech 14:2; Jer 15:2; 20:6; 22:22; Isa 5:13). And once again, it is part of the historical reality of the fall of the city as reported by Josephus, *Jewish War*, 6:414-419.

ground under the heel of the Gentiles: As always, it is difficult to know whether to translate *ethnē* as "Gentiles" or "nations." In the present case, "nations" might be better, and in the next verse, "Gentiles," but for the sake of consistency, "Gentiles" is used for both. The verb *pateō* is used for treading grapes in Joel 3:13 and in Amos 2:7 for "trampling the head of the poor into the dust," and in Zech 10:5 for "trampling the foe into the mud of the streets." Likewise, Lam 1:15 has "the Lord has trodden us as in a winepress, the virgin daughter of Judah" (that is, Jerusalem).

times of the Gentiles are completed: Or: "the seasons of the Gentiles are fulfilled." This temporal reference is only in Luke and replaces the assurance in Mark 13:20 about the times being shortened for the sake of the elect.

INTERPRETATION

The long discourse of Jesus about the future will be considered in two sections for the sake of ease in reading. The discourse itself is a coherent literary whole, with three main parts which are somewhat difficult to disentangle because of Luke's use of an excursus: He begins with talk about the times before the fall of the Temple (21:5-11), but interrupts this with a consideration of what could be expected even before those events (21:12-19), before returning with a full description of the fall of the city (21:20-24), and then a glimpse at the days of the Son of Man (21:25-38). The arrangement obscures a decisive threefold temporal division: a) the times of persecution facing the Christians; b) the times of the destruction of the city; c) the times of the Son of Man.

When considering this material, it is important to maintain a steady focus. As everywhere else in this commentary, we are seeking to grasp the part within the whole, to find the function of a specific passage within Luke's general literary and religious purposes. This requires of us a steadfast refusal to speculate (as millenarians do) about the fulfillment of Jesus' words in our contemporary world, as well as a refusal to speculate (as historians do) about what was possible for Jesus to have said, as opposed to what reflected the hindsight of the community.

A properly literary focus on this material asks what image of Jesus Luke was portraying, and what functions this discourse has within his overall narrative.

The first and most obvious thing to observe is that Luke portrays Jesus as a prophet. In this instance, being a prophet means not only being God's spokesperson, but one who predicts the future. Luke is about to show in his narrative how Jesus' predictions about his own fate were coming true in his rejection by the leadership and his being handed over to death. But in this discourse the words of Jesus embrace a more public drama.

The Hellenistic reader could not miss the significance of one standing in a temple, discoursing about the fate of this very temple and of the city enclosing it. Predictive prophecy was highly esteemed in the Mediterranean world, whether connected with Oracle Shrines (such as Delphi), as in Herodotus, *The Persian Wars* I, 46–50; Plutarch, *The Oracles at Delphi* 9–11 (*Mor.* 398C–399E), or individuals (cf. Cicero, *On Divination* 1:1-2; Philostratus, *Life of Apollonius,* 1:2). Best of all, when prophecies were fulfilled, the authenticity of the prophet was proven, as we see in Philo's elaboration of Moses as prophet (*Life of Moses* 2:45–51).

There was still an older tradition of such prophecy in Israel, whose great prototype was Jeremiah in his speech against the Temple in Jerusalem (Jer 7). Jeremiah's prophecy came true, and by the standards of Torah itself (Deut 18:21-22) this showed the validity of his prophetic word (Jer 28:7-9). Thus, any part of Jesus' prophecies known by the readers to have been already fulfilled could only heighten trust in his word for what still was to happen.

Such is the real significance of parts one and two of Jesus' prophetic discourse in Luke 21. Luke shows how the first part has already been fulfilled, suggests that the second has, as well, and thus creates confidence in the expectation of what is predicted (very generally, to be sure) about the days of the Son of Man.

How does Luke accomplish this restructuring of the "eschatological discourse" that he inherited from Mark? Very subtly, indeed. He first eliminates much of the explicitly "eschatological" language from the first part of the discourse, leaving out Mark's language about the "birth pangs" and the "abomination of desolation," and certainly not heightening this element as Matthew does by referring to the time "of your *parousia* (coming)." He then carefully shades the language he does take over from Mark in the direction of specific historical incidents rather than the end-time.

Most impressively, he focuses on the suffering of his followers in the period *before* the fall of Jerusalem, and uses language which (as the notes indicate) is echoed consistently in the narrative about Jesus' followers in Acts. For the reader of Luke-Acts, therefore, these first predictions of Jesus about the future are now clearly past, and have been shown to have reached fulfillment—in Luke's own narrative! Luke not only thereby strengthens the literary unity of his two-volume work, and accomplishes once more a literary "prophecy and fulfillment," but most significantly, he has enhanced the presentation of Jesus as the Prophet.

The same is true of the second set of predictions concerning the fall of the Temple and city. As the notes demonstrate, the language used by Luke is found both in the biblical prophets and in Josephus. No conclusion can be drawn as to whether Luke may have used Josephus or some other source in his description, since the language was already so thoroughly stereotyped. What is more significant is that by the time Luke-Acts was published, the events surrounding the fall of the city were almost certainly already in the past. This is the case even if, as with this commentary, a conservative estimate of dating and authorship is maintained. Luke is certainly circumspect in his description, so much so that one is not compelled to assert that the city had already fallen. For most of Luke's readers, however, the fact that these events had occurred, and in a way consistent with the words of Jesus, must have had a powerful impact. In the first place, it demonstrated graphically how the rejection of the Prophet *did* lead to the rejection of the rejectors, and thus validate Jesus' prophetic claims. In the second place, it lent more weight to the predictions concerning the coming of the Son of Man. If what the prophet predicted about their past came true, his words about our future can be trusted.

FOR REFERENCE AND FURTHER STUDY

Braumann, G. "Die lukanische Interpretation der Zerstörung Jerusalem." *NovT* 6 (1963) 120–127.

Carroll, J. T. *Response to the End of History: Eschatology and Situation in Luke-Acts* (Atlanta: Scholars Press, 1988).

Dupont, J. "Les épreuves des chrétiens avant la fin du monde: Lc 21, 5-19." *AsSeign* n.s. 64 (1969) 77–86.

Geiger, R. *Die lukanischen Endzeitsreden: Studien zur Eschatologie des Lukasevangelium* (Bern: H. Lang, 1973) 149–258.

Kaestli, J.-D. "Luc 21: 5-36: l'Apocalypse synoptique." *L'Eschatologie dans l'oeuvre de Luc* (Geneva: Labor et Fides, 1969) 41–57.

Tiede, D. *Prophecy and History in Luke-Acts* (Philadelphia: Fortress, 1980), 65–96.

57. *Preparation for the Son of Man* (21:25-38)

25. "There will also be signs in the sun and moon and stars. And on the earth there will be anxiety among nations, with confusion caused by the sound and surging of the sea. 26. People will collapse from fear and from dread of the things that are coming upon the inhabited world. For the powers of heaven will be shaken. 27. And then they will see the Son of Man coming on a cloud with power and great glory. 28. When all these things start to happen, stand up! Lift up your heads, because your liberation is coming near!" 29. He also told them a parable: "Look at the fig tree and all the trees. 30. As soon as they have put out shoots, you can see and know for yourselves that summer is already near. 31. The same is the case for you. When you see these things happening, know that the kingdom of God is near. 32. Amen I tell you that this generation will not pass away until all things happen. 33. Heaven and earth will pass away. But my words will not pass away. 34. Pay attention to yourselves! Don't let your hearts be weighed down by dissipation and drunkenness and the distractions of daily life, so that day comes on you suddenly 35. like the snap of a snare. For it will come on everyone inhabiting the earth. 36. Keep awake in every season. Keep praying that you have the strength to flee all these things and can stand before the Son of Man." 37. He was in the temple teaching during the day. But he would go out and spend his nights at the Mount of Olives. 38. And the whole people would get up early in the morning and come to the temple to hear him.

NOTES

25. *signs in the sun and moon and stars*: The reader remembers that Jesus' opponents had asked for a "sign from heaven" (11:16) and the disciples had asked for the "sign" that these things were about to happen. The repetition of *sēmeion* here marks the shift to the properly eschatological section of Jesus' discourse. Note that in Acts 2:19 the citation from Joel 2:30 is altered to make the *sēmeia* occur "on earth below." Luke reduces Mark 13:14-15 and Matt 24:29-31, each of whom contain an allusion to Isa 13:24-25 on the signs accompanying "the day of the Lord."

anxiety among nations, with confusion: The noun *synochē* means "constraint" and is used in LXX passages such as Mic 5:1 and Jer 52:5 for a siege. Here, as in 2 Cor 2:4, it points to a state of internal distress. Likewise *aporia* here means the confusion accompanying panic (cf. 21:9). By shifting attention to cosmic signs and the panic "among nations," Luke introduces a larger end-time drama than that involving Jerusalem.

26. *collapse from fear*: The entire line is absent from the parallels. Fear (*phobos*) and dread (*prosdokia*, literally, "expectation") will be so great that people will "expire"; the verb *apopsychō* can mean to "faint away" or literally "to die" (as in 4 Macc 15:18). The cause of such dread is the "sound and the surging of the sea" (cf. Jer 51:16), the translation trying to catch some of the assonance of the

Greek. Note again that the use of *oikoumenē* ("inhabited world") expands this discourse beyond the confines of Palestine (see Luke 2:1; 4:5; Acts 11:28).

powers of heaven will be shaken: This is the same as in Mark 13:25 (Matt 24:29), and may pick up a textual variant in the LXX of Isa 34:4 (cf. also Joel 2:10; Hag 2:6, 21, and especially Heb 12:26-27). By using the connective "for" (*gar*), Luke provides the basis for the previous sentence found only in his Gospel.

27. *the Son of Man coming*: Is an explicit allusion to Dan 7:13, complete with attendant cloud (*nephelē*). Daniel has him coming in "authority" (*exousia*) and "glory" (*doxa*). All the synoptics have "power and glory" (*dynamis kai doxa*), with Luke and Matt 24:30 changing Mark's "great power and glory" to "power and great glory." Luke has carefully prepared for this "coming of the Son of Man" in 9:26; 11:30; 12:8, 40; 17:22, 24, 26, 30; 18:8.

28. *stand up . . . lift up your heads*: Luke omits entirely the line in Mark 13:27 concerning the sending of the angels to gather the elect (cf. Matt 24:31). Instead, he has this direct command to courage and hope. The verb *anakyptō* echoes the description of the crippled woman in 13:11 who could not "stand up straight" because she was "bound by Satan."

your liberation is coming near: The term *apolytrōsis* is cognate with *lytrōsis*, a redemption from slavery. For the theme in Luke, see 1:68; 2:38; 24:21; Acts 7:35).

29. *fig tree and all the trees*: Luke introduces this as a "parable," one of the many short ones in his Gospel (4:23; 5:36; 6:39). This one echoes the parable on the fruitless fig tree in 13:6-9. Luke generalizes the lesson to include "all trees," in contrast to Mark 13:28 and Matt 24:32, just as in his version of the parable he avoided connecting the fig tree to the destruction of the Temple.

30. *see and know for yourselves*: Luke's editing makes it clear that the visible emergence of the leaves makes it possible for anyone to draw the proper conclusion about the coming of summer.

kingdom of God is near: The obvious tension in Luke's Gospel concerning this term is again suggested; the kingdom is present in the words and works of Jesus (10:9, 11), but it has not yet realized itself fully (see below, 22:16-18). It is important to note that Luke has fundamentally altered Mark 13:29 (Matt 24:33), who referred the simile directly to the coming of the Son of Man: "he is at the gates."

32. *this generation will not pass away*: The predominant use for "this generation" (*genea*) in Luke is as evil and resistant to the prophet (see 7:31; 9:41; 11:29, 30, 31, 32, 50, 51; 16:8; 17:25). The statement here therefore is less directly temporal than it might at first appear.

33. *my words will not pass away*: This statement certifies the predictions, and is basically the same here as in Mark 13:21 and Matt 24:35. Luke does eliminate, however, the reference to the Son's ignorance of the "day or hour" (Mark 13:32; Matt 24:36).

34. *pay attention to yourselves*: This is the fourth time Luke has used *prosechete* to the disciples (see 12:1; 17:3; 20:46; see also Acts 5:35; 20:28). In Greek the exhortation introduces a subordinate clause, "lest you . . .," which this translation turns into an independent command.

dissipation and drunkenness and the distractions of daily life: Luke alone has this line, which quite typically gives his eschatology a quotidien aspect. For "hearts weighed down," see Exod 7:14; 9:7, 34; Zech 11:8. The term translated "dissipation" is *kraipalē*, occuring only here in the NT. It is literally a "drinking-bout." For "drunkenness" (*methē*) see the warnings against the vice in Tob 4:15; Sir 28:8; Eph 5:18; Rom 13:13; see also *Testament of Judah* 14:1-8; Plutarch, *On Talkativeness*, 4 (Mor. 503E-504C). Of direct interest is Paul's description of the end-time in 1 Thess 5:7, and the behavior of the household manager who thought his master was delayed in Luke 12:45. The "distractions of daily life" (*merimnais biōtikais*) are what Luke says chokes the word of God in 8:14; see also 10:41; 12:22, 25, 26.

comes on you suddenly: The adverb *aiphnidios* "suddenly" is used together with "come upon" (*epistamai*) in the eschatological saying of 1 Thess 5:3; cf. also the use in Wis 17:15; 2 Macc 14:17.

35. *snap of the snare*: The translation tries to get at the suddenness of a "trap" (*pagis*) springing; for the term, see Ps 34:7-8; 69:23; 118:110; Prov 12:13; Wis 14:11, and in an explicitly eschatological context, Isa 24:17-23.

everyone inhabiting the earth: The phrase is literally "sitting on the face of the earth," but *kathēmai* can be used in the sense of "dwelling" (cf. Neh 11:6; Jdt 5:3). As in verses 25 and 26, Luke emphasizes the universality of these events.

36. *awake in every season*: For wakefulness as an eschatological stance, see Eph 6:18. With the saying, "Watch, keep awake," Mark 13:33-37 picks up the general theme of this command, along the lines of Luke 12:40 and Matt 24:46-51. The phrase "in every season" recalls the expression "in season out of season" in 2 Tim 4:2.

keep praying: The present participle dependent on the the verb "keep awake" in Greek is here translated as a separate imperative. The verb *deomai* ("pray") is used by Luke uniformly of the prayer of petition (5:12; 8:28, 38; 9:38, 40; 10:2; 22:32; Acts 4:31; 8:22, 24, 34; 10:2; 21:39; 26:3).

flee all these things: Echoes the question of John the Baptist in 3:7, "who taught you to flee the coming wrath?" The stance of "standing up (*stathēnai*) before the Son of Man" fits the body language commanded in 21:28.

37. *teaching during the day*: Luke reminds his readers that Jesus continues his ministry in the Temple and in fact has delivered this entire discourse within its precincts (see 21:5). He withdraws to the Mount of Olives only at night (compare John 8:1-2). This statement also prepares for his withdrawal to that location in 22:39. Once more in verse 38 Luke emphasizes the fundamentally positive—indeed eager—reception of Jesus by the "people" (*laos*) in contrast to the leaders.

INTERPRETATION

We have seen how in the first part of Jesus' discourse, Luke has shaped the Prophet's words so that they can be perceived by the reader as having been already fulfilled, first in the experience of persecution by the first Christians (recounted in Luke's own narrative of Acts in words directly derived from this discourse), and secondly in the events surrounding the fall of the Temple and the city Jerusalem. An even greater confidence is thereby engendered in these final words which concern the true eschatological event, the coming of the Son of Man, which Luke suggests is the "fulfillment" of the kingdom of God, the moment when God's rule becomes definitive.

The transition to this third part of the discourse is unobtrusive, marked mainly by the repetition of the term "sign" from 21:7 in 21:25. It quickly becomes clear, however, that the things now being described no longer concern the history of the believers or the fate of the city, but the world-wide experience of humans at the judgment: Luke speaks of the "distress and confusion among the nations" (v. 25), the things that are coming on "the inhabited world" (*oikoumenē*, v. 26), on "everyone inhabiting the earth" (v. 35). And if these indications were not clear enough, his description of "signs" are no longer those of wars and revolutions (v. 10) or even of earthquakes, famines, plagues and portents in the sky (v. 11) or armies around the city (v. 20), but entirely of cosmic events in sun, moon and stars (v. 25), the tumult of the ocean (v. 25), shaking of the heavenly powers themselves (v. 26).

There are two remarkable aspects of this final stage of the prophecy. The first is that it entirely lacks any temporal reference or time-table. Even the statement concerning the Son's ignorance of the time of the end in Mark and Matthew is eliminated. The parable of the fig tree and all the trees functions simply to remind them that the signs will be so obvious that they will be able "to see and know for themselves" what is happening. The time of final judgment is left completely undetermined and unattached to any tumultuous events in Palestine.

The second striking feature is the attention given to moral exhortation. The advice about fleeing into the mountains or not going in and out of the city concerned the fall of the city, just as the exhortation to "gain their lives by endurance" (v. 19) and to make suffering a chance to bear witness (v. 13) concerned the time of persecution in the Church's early days. But in the possibly long period of time before the coming of the Son of Man, more general advice is required: They are to stay awake (to be sure) and remain alert. They are to keep praying. But they are also to maintain hearts free of the burdens of dissipation, drunkenness and daily distraction. The reader is reminded of the fate of the household manager in 12:45 who concluded by his master's delay that he was not coming at all and, growing drunk, abused the slaves. We are reminded as well of Luke's interpretation of the parable of the sower, in which the "cares of daily life" smothered the growth of God's word (8:14).

The final word of this prophecy is a good word, indeed good news. Those who endure, who bear witness, who remain alert in prayer, have nothing to fear from the coming of the Son of Man. For them there is not distress or confusion or dread. For them it is the time of "liberation." And they can therefore stand up straight, hold their heads high in happy anticipation before the Son of Man.

FOR REFERENCE AND FURTHER STUDY

Carroll, J. T. *Response to the End of History: Eschatology and Situation in Luke-Acts* (Atlanta: Scholars Press, 1988).
Dupont, J. "La parabole du figuier qui bougeonne (Mc xiii, 28-29 et. par.)." *RB* 75 (1968) 526–48.
Ellis, E. E. *Eschatology in Luke* Facet; Philadelphia: Fortress, 1972.
George, A. "La venue du fils de l'homme. Lc 21, 25-28, 34-36," *AsSeign* n.s. 5 (1969) 71–78.
Schneider, G. *Parusiegleichnisse im Lukas-Evangelium* (Stuttgart: Katholisches Bibelwerk, 1975) 55–61; 62–66.

VI. THE SUFFERING OF THE PROPHET

58. *The Plot at Passover* (22:1-13)

1. The feast of unleavened bread which was called Passover was drawing near. 2. The chief priests and the scribes were looking for a way they could eliminate him, for they were afraid of the people. 3. And Satan entered into Judas who was called Iscariot. He was one of those numbered as the Twelve. 4. He went off to speak with the chief priests and officers how he might hand him over to them. 5. They were delighted and came to an agreement to give him money. 6. He consented and looked for a good time to hand him over to them apart from the crowd. 7. But the day of unleavened bread arrived, when it was required to sacrifice the paschal lamb. 8. Jesus sent out Peter and John. He said, "Go prepare the Passover meal for us to eat." 9. They said, "Where do you want us to prepare it?" 10. He told them, "Look, when you are entering the city, a man carrying a waterpot will meet you. Follow him to the house he enters. 11. Then you will say to the master of the house 'The teacher says to you, "Where is the guest room where I might eat the Passover with my disciples?'" 12. That man will show you a large upstairs room furnished with couches. Prepare the meal there." 13. When they had gone out they found things just as he had told them, and they prepared the Passover meal.

NOTES

1. *feast of unleavened bread which is called Passover*: The feast of *Pesach* was celebrated on 14 Nisan. It was one of the three ancient pilgrimage feasts (with Weeks and Booths). It combined agricultural (elimination of yeast) and nomadic (killing of first lamb) elements of apotropaic ritual with the historical remembrance of the Exodus (see Exod 12:1-28; Num 9:2-14). Luke eliminates the temporal reference "after two days" in Mark 14:1 and Matt 26:1-2.

2. *a way they could eliminate him*: Matt 26:3 has a more elaborate version of this verse; the verb *anairō* ("eliminate") can also be translated simply as "kill."

    for they were afraid of the people: By eliminating the calculations of the leaders concerning the feast in Mark 14:2, Luke's explanatory clause loses some of its clarity. On the other hand, it repeats one of his constant themes of the division between leaders and people (20:19). For the historical reality of huge crowds in Jerusalem for this feast, cf. Josephus, *Jewish War* 6:425-426, who estimates 2 1/2 million. Josephus tells us further that the crowds on such feasts were particularly volatile and given to violence (*Jewish War* 1:88-89), an observation he supports with the description of riots at Passover (2:8-13; 2:223-227) and Pentecost (2:43). Unrest was particularly acute during the time Pilate was prefect (2:169-174).

3. *Satan entered into Judas*: Luke shares with John 13:27 the conviction that Judas' betrayal of Jesus was caused by Satan (see also 22:31 and Acts 5:3). He is also more explicit in his emphasis on Judas being "one of the number of the Twelve," a description important because of the symbolic significance of the Twelve as the leadership of the restored Israel (cf. 22:30, 47, and esp. Acts 1:15-26).

4. *chief priests and officers*: These are the ones who, with the elders, come to arrest Jesus in the garden (22:52). The term *stratēgos* means a leader of troops but can be used more widely of an administrator. In 22:52, Luke supplies the qualifier "of the Temple," and it is this designation that carries over into Acts 4:1; 5:24. Josephus has the "guards" (*phylakes*) of the Temple report to a *stratēgos* (*Jewish War* 6:294). We are to picture a sort of sanctuary security force.

    hand him over: Uses the verb *paradidōmi*, which is used several times of Jesus' fate (9:44; 18:32; 20:20). The "delight" (*chairein*) of the leaders is ironic, since throughout the Gospel the term has been used to describe the positive response to God's visitation through the prophet (8:13; 10:17; 13:17; 19:6, 37).

5. *came to an agreement*: In this case, the Greek vocabulary is richer and more suggestive than the possibilities for English translation. Literally "they put in with him to give money," or "they put in to give him money," (using *syntithēmi*). Judas' "agreement" uses the verb *exhomologeō* which usually means "to confess" or to "profess."

6. *apart from the crowd*: This picks up the leaders' "fear of the crowd" in 22:2, and continues the theme of the division between leaders and people. Jesus must be handed over in secret or the crowd favorable to him will protest.

7. *required to sacrifice the paschal lamb*: Luke dates this simply as "the day of unleavened bread," in contrast to "the first day of unleavened bread" in Mark

14:12 (Matt 26:17). For the command to sacrifice (*thuō*) the animal (here *pascha* refers to the beast itself) on 14 Nisan, see Exod 12:6, and esp. 12:21: *thusate to pascha.* Compare also 1 Cor 5:7, *pascha hēmōn etutheto christos*, "Our passover lamb, the Messiah, has been sacrificed."

8. *sent out Peter and John*: The translation supplies the name "Jesus" to clarify the antecedent of "he" in the Greek. The initiative here is taken entirely by Jesus and is not a response to disciples' questions as in Mark 14:12 (Matt 26:17). For a command of a master to a slave "go sacrifice for me" at Passover, see *bT Pes.* 88b. The entire incident resembles that of the getting of the colt for the entry into the city: the sending, the description of events, the outcome as Jesus had foretold (Luke 19:28-34). In the earlier account the disciples are not named. Here, Peter and John, already singled out in the narrative (8:51; 9:28), assume the place they will play through the rest of the Jerusalem narrative (22:8; Acts 3:1, 3, 4, 11; 4:13, 19; 8:14).

prepare the Passover meal: In this context, *pascha* means the ritual meal that was to be celebrated this first evening of the feast. In the Synoptic Gospels, the last meal of Jesus with his disciples is unambiguously and emphatically described as a Passover meal. In John's Gospel, the last meal takes place a day earlier, and Jesus' death on the cross is synchronized with the killing of the lambs on the day of preparation for the feast (John 19:31-37). A confused independent testimony to the connection of Jesus' death with the passover celebration is given by a *baraita* in *bT Sanh.* 43a: "Joshua was hanged on Passover eve."

11. *the teacher says*: The presentation of Jesus here is as of a rabbi with his students. The Passover was a family feast, with "a lamb for each household" (Exod 12:3), but the size of the "family" was flexible (Exod 12:4; cf. the discussion of the make-up of groups in *bT Pes.* 91a-b). Josephus says that a group had to consist in at least ten, and could go as large as twenty, so that "a little fraternity, as it were, gathers around each sacrifice" (*Jewish War* 6:423). There are clear indications that rabbinic students celebrated the feast with their teachers in *bT Pes.* 89b, 102a, 103b, 108a. For the "rented room" (*katalyma*), see the note on 2:17.

12. *large upstairs room*: The *anagaion* is found in Luke and Mark 14:15 but is absent from Matt 26:18. In Acts 1:13, the disciples again gather in an "upper room" (*hyperōon*). The adjective "furnished" translates the Greek *estrōmmenon*, literally "strewn" (probably with couches for reclining).

13. *just as he had told them*: Luke follows Mark 14:16. As in 19:32, this comment validates the predictions of Jesus. With the concluding remark, "they prepared the Passover (meal)," Luke has repeated an allusion to the feast six times in thirteen verses. The symbolic importance of this meal is unmistakably being underscored.

INTERPRETATION

With the notice concerning the Passover celebration in 22:1, the passion narrative properly begins. It is appropriate to provide some perspective on this part of Luke's story before beginning a detailed discussion. The place to start is with the nature of the passion accounts in general. The reader will remember in the discussion of the infancy accounts that several pieces of evidence pointed to the conclusion that the infancy accounts were the last part of the Gospel composed. These were the facts: that the early epistolary literature ignored Jesus' childhood, that two of the Gospels (John and Mark) lacked infancy accounts entirely, that the infancy accounts of Luke and Matthew were almost entirely disparate. As a corollary to that observation, we suggested as well that the ratio of imagination to history in that part of the story was tilted in favor of imagination, or interpretation.

The same sort of argument points in the opposite direction for the suffering and death of Jesus. The epistolary literature preceding the composition of the gospels indicates that the problem of a crucified Messiah was the most critical one for the first Christians to resolve: how could Jesus be the life-giving Spirit, when his death was one that according to Torah was cursed by God? The Cross was a stumbling block not only to Jews and Greeks who chose not to believe, but also for Jews and Greeks among the believers (cf. 1 Cor 1:18-31; Gal 3:1-29). From the first, therefore, the death of Jesus demanded interpretation, simply because as historical fact it was so problematic.

The present condition of the four Gospels supports the suggestion that the passion account was the first part of the Jesus story to reach a settled state of composition (whether oral or written). Each of the canonical Gospels has a passion account. They are of disproportionate length, in comparison to the rest of the Gospel narrative. They are highly detailed in their references to times and places, in contrast with the earlier segments of the story. They are each sequentially coherent, with careful connections made between incidents, in contrast to the (apparently) more casual linking of events in the ministry of Jesus. Most impressively, there is the highest degree of agreement between the Gospels at this point in the story, not only between the Synoptics, which we might expect because of their literary relationship, but between the Synoptics and John as well.

There is, therefore, a considerable weight of tradition controlling the composition of each evangelist. This part of the story is both too well known and too important for excessive literary license. This part of the story has also been extensively interpreted before it reaches Luke. Luke's most important source remains the Gospel of Mark, although he is more independent than Matthew in his use of Mark. Attempts to locate a separate written Lukan source for the passion have not proven successful.

The specific elements that Luke has omitted from Mark's version, or added to it, as well as his specific alterations, will be noted in the notes and interpretation on each section. Two overall impressions left by his multiple small touches can, however, be stated at once. First, Luke has shaded the presentation of Jesus so that he appears more like the Hellenistic *sophos* or philosopher: Jesus engages in discourse at the Last Supper like Socrates before his death; he is courageous in his suffering in contrast to his followers; he expresses not anguish or despair at the moment of death, but resignation, acceptance and forgiveness; he suffers as the righteous one. Second, Luke does everything he can to shift the burden of responsibility for Jesus' death from the populace as a whole to the leaders, an emphasis all the more impressive since it resisted the tendency of the tradition.

The passage we consider now sets the stage for the suffering of the Messiah, providing at once a contrast between the outer plot (the machinery of betrayal) and the inner story (the meaning of the events). The chief priests and Temple officers enter into a financial agreement with Judas. They will pay him if he hands Jesus over. Luke notes that they are "delighted," and the reader is not in the least surprised, since from the start of Jesus' ministry the leadership has been opposed to him, and since his arrival in Jerusalem has actively been seeking his removal. But how can we understand Judas' betrayal?

Luke does not in the least soften the enormity of the act. Indeed, he shifts a fuller account of the betrayal and of Judas' death to the beginning of Acts, as the first thing required by the community to interpret and correct, even before Pentecost (Acts 1:15-26). And instead of attributing Judas' act to greed (cf. John 12:6), or entering into Judas' psychology of betrayal (cf. Matt 27:4), Luke starkly credits the adversary Satan. Satan enters Judas (22:3), as Jesus will state shortly, as a way of seeking the surrender of the disciples, to "sift them like wheat" (22:31). We understand, therefore, that more than a power struggle between Jewish religious leaders is at work. This is a battle between good and evil, and for this space, the conflict is dominated by evil: "this is your hour, and the power of darkness" (22:53).

But even as the process of "handing over" the Prophet begins, we are shown another dimension of the story. In thirteen verses, Luke manages to tell the reader six different times that Jesus was to celebrate the Passover with his disciples. He especially notes that "it was the day when it was required to sacrifice the paschal lamb" (22:7). By so doing, he begins to invite the reader into the understanding of Jesus' death not as a meaningless accident of human greed or as the triumph of evil in the world, but as the fulfillment of God's plan for the Messiah. The connection of Jesus' death with the Passover is historical, attested to even by the Talmud (cf. *bT Sanh.* 43a). And it was thoroughly interpreted within the symbolism of the feast already by Paul who declared, "our passover lamb, the messiah, has been sacrificed" (1 Cor 5:7). It will remain for the evangelist to spell out some of the implications of this convergence.

One of them is suggested immediately: Jesus is not a passive victim, but the prophet who anticipates his own death and interprets its meaning for his followers. At the deepest level, Jesus exercises direction. The small incident of choosing a room for the celebration becomes in the telling, like the incident of finding a colt for the entry to the city, a reinforcement of the portrayal of Jesus as prophet: "they found things just as he had told them" (22:13).

FOR REFERENCE AND FURTHER STUDY

Blinzler, J. "Passionsgeschichte und Passionsbericht des Lukasevangelium." *BK* 24 (1969) 1–4.

Brown, S. *Apostasy and Perseverance in the Theology of Luke* (AB 36; Rome: Pontifical Biblical Institute, 1969) 82–97.

Green, J. B. "Preparation for the Passover (Luke 22:7-13): A Question of Redactional Technique." *NovT* 29 (1987) 305–319.

Karris, R. J. *Luke: Artist and Theologian: Luke's Passion Account as Literature* (New York: Paulist, 1985) 5–15.

Osty, E. "Les points de contact entre le récit de la passion dans saint Luc et dans saint Jean." *RSR* 39 (1951) 146–154.

59. *The Passover Meal* (22:14-23)

14. When the hour came, he reclined at table, and the apostles were with him. 15. He said to them, "I have longed eagerly to eat this Passover meal with you before I suffer. 16. For I tell you, I will certainly not eat it until the time when it is fulfilled in the kingdom of God." 17. He took a cup. After he gave thanks, he said, "Take this and divide it among yourselves. 18. For I tell you that I will certainly not drink from the fruit of the vine from now until the kingdom of God comes." 19. He also took bread. After he gave thanks, he broke it and gave it to them. He said, "This is my body which is being given for you. Keep doing this as a remembrance of me." 20. He did the same with the cup after the meal. He said, "This cup is the new covenant in my blood which is being poured out for you. 21. Now look, the hand of the one betraying me is with me on the table. 22. The Son of Man is going as it has been determined. But woe to that person through whom he is being handed over." 23. And they began to dispute with each other about who from among them could do this thing.

NOTES

14. *the apostles were with him*: Luke makes three subtle but significant alterations to Mark 14:17: a) rather than "when evening came," he has "the hour" (*hōra*),

which has a more solemn tone (cf. 1:10; 2:38; 7:21; 10:21; 12:12, 39, 40, 46; 13:31), especially in the light of 22:53: "this is your hour and the power of darkness"; b) he uses "apostles" (*apostoloi*) rather than "the twelve," possibly because of his sensitivity to Judas' betrayal and the desire to minimize his presence, or because of his desire as elsewhere to connect apostleship to service at meals (9:10; 12:41); c) he has the apostles recline "with him" rather than he "with them," emphasizing the central role of Jesus as teacher and host.

15. *I have longed eagerly*: In Greek, *epithymia epethymēsa* is "I have desired with desire," using a construction frequent in the LXX (see Gen 31:30; Num 11:4; Ps 105:14). The term *pascha* is here translated as "Passover meal": note that these introductory remarks in Luke are quite different from those in Mark 14:18-21 and Matt 26:21-25. Those Gospels begin with the prediction of the betrayal and lead to the questioning by the disciples concerning the betrayer's identity. They also put the statement about not drinking again *after* the words spoken over the cup (Mark 14:25; Matt 26:29). Luke, in turn, puts the statement about the betrayal after the words over both bread and cup (22:21).

before I suffer: This constitutes a reminder to the reader of the meal's deeper significance, and is unique to Luke. For Jesus' "eagerness" for everything to be accomplished, compare the saying in 12:50.

16. *it is fulfilled in the kingdom of God*: The natural subject of "to be fulfilled" (for *plēroō*, see 1:20; 4:21; 7:1; 9:31; 21:24) is the Passover meal itself. How will it be fulfilled in the kingdom of God? There are two possibilities Luke may have had in mind: a) the eschatological banquet suggested by 13:29 and 14:15-24; since the *Passover Haggadah* interprets the feast as one of "liberation," this meal could point forward to the time of full "liberation" in the coming of the Son of Man (21:28); remember in this connection the Essene vision of the eschatological banquet presided over by the Messiah at which "new wine" would be drunk (*1QSa* 2); b) alternatively, the celebration of meals by the first Christians (Acts 2:41-47) at which the risen Lord was present (Luke 24:30, 42; Acts 10:41).

17. *after he gave thanks*: Here and in verse 19 Luke uses *eucharisteō*, "give thanks," which refers to the *berakah* or blessing formula spoken over the elements at all Jewish meals, including the Passover; at the feeding story of 9:12-17, Luke used the term *eulogeō*, "bless."

take . . . divide it among yourselves: At this point, Luke's Gospel presents a major textual difficulty. The problem is mainly that Luke has two blessings over a cup, one before and one after the breaking of the bread (vv. 17, 20), whereas the parallels have a single blessing of the bread and cup in that order (Mark 14:22-23; Matt 26:26-28). There is impressive external MS support for the "longer reading" adopted here. The shorter versions, indeed, testify by their variety to the attempts by scribes to "correct" Luke, either by eliminating the first blessing over the cup or the second, or inverting the order so that the sequence better matches that of Mark and Matthew. According to the most ancient discussion of the Passover meal in *m.Pes.* 10:1-7, there are four cups of wine at the Passover. Each has its own blessing, with the second (as here in Luke) bearing the words of interpretation, "why is this night different from other nights" (*m.Pes.* 10:4).

18. *I will certainly not drink*: This saying appears to repeat the earlier statement of
verse 16, another reason why scribes might view it with suspicion. But there
are subtle differences. In this statement, the expression "fruit of the vine" is
used, which recalls the blessing to be said over the cup at the Passover (cf. *Passover Haggadah*, "Blessed art thou, O Lord our God, king of the universe, creator
of the fruit of the vine"). And instead of speaking of the "fulfillment in the kingdom," this statement has "until the kingdom of God comes." Another prayer
in the *Passover Haggadah* echoes the same theme: "The compassionate one—
may he reign over us for ever and ever." This statement, finally, explains why
("for," *gar*) they are to divide the cup among themselves; see the interpretation
which follows.

19. *took bread . . . gave thanks . . . broke . . . gave*: The sequence of gestures reminds
the reader of the feeding of the multitude in 9:16 (cf. also the reference to David's
feeding in 6:4). Luke's version is identical to the parallels in Mark 14:22 and Matt
26:66, except that he uses *eucharisteō* ("give thanks") rather than *eulogeō* ("bless").
Matthew also adds "to his disciples." Luke's version is even closer, however,
to that of Paul in 1 Cor 11:24, who also uses *eucharisteō*.

my body which is being given for you: Luke omits the "take" from Mark 14:22 (cf.
"take, eat" in Matt 26:26). He is once more closer to Paul in 1 Cor 11:24. Like
Paul, he has "for you," but Paul lacks the participle *didomenon*, "being given."
According to *m.Pes*. 10:4, the haggadic recital of the meaning of the Passover
meal was to take place after the second cup of wine is poured but before it is
drunk. This would include the recitation of the words interpreting the unleavened
bread, the *matzah*, "because our fathers were redeemed from Egypt." Jesus' interpretative words have an obvious twofold symbolism. The bread is being given
"for them" as it is broken and distributed at table: Jesus is the one among them
who serves. The bread also points to his body which is "being given" for their
sake in death.

keep doing this as a remembrance of me: the present imperative of *poieō* is translated
strictly as a command to continued practice. The term *anamnēsis* ("remembrance")
means "to bring to mind" in something more than a mechanical way; it is a
form of presence (see Plato, *Phaedrus* 72E, 92D). In the LXX, the verbs *anamimn-
ēskō* and *mimnēskō* translate the Hebrew *zakar*, and their respective noun forms
the Hebrew *zikron*, and have this strong sense of "keeping in mind" (e.g., Gen
8:11; 9:15; 19:29; Exod 2:24; 6:5; Neh 1:8; 9:17; 2 Sam 18:18; Ezek 21:23; 29:26;
33:3; Tob 1:12; 2:2). It is therefore easily transferred to the language of sacrifice
as something that makes God "remember" the people as well as the people
"remember" the Lord (Lev 24:7; Num 5:15; 10:9-10; Ps 19:3; cf. also Heb 10:3).
What is to be "remembered" here by the repetition of the ritual act is Jesus.
The fact that this line is found only in Luke's Gospel and 1 Cor 11:24 made it
suspect to some copyists. For the notion of the *zikron* at the Passover meal, see
Deut 16:3, "that you may remember the day of your exodus from Egypt," and
the *Passover Haggadah*.

20. *the cup after the meal*: Of the Synoptics only Luke has the adverb *hōsautōs* ("in
like manner") and the phrase "after the meal." Since these are found also in
1 Cor 11:25, the possibility of an interpolation bothered some copyists and the

editors who prefer the "shorter reading." According to *m.Pes.* 10:7 there are two cups at the end of the meal. Over one the meal blessing is said. Over the other the Hallel (passages of song from Pss 113–118) is sung. The adverb "in the same way" leads us to see Jesus taking the cup, offering it to them, and saying words over it, just as with the bread.

this cup: The symbolism of "sharing" is built into the ritual of "drinking from the same cup" (cf. 1 Cor 10:16; 12:13). Although the "cup" (*potērion*) in the OT could mean a sharing in consolation (Jer 16:7), its overwhelming use is in reference to "God's wrath" coming on humans as a punishment for sin (LXX Ps 74:8; Isa 51:17, 22; Hab 2:16; Jer 25:15, 17, 28; 51:7; Lam 4:21; Ezek 23:31-33). Still another level of symbolism is suggested by LXX Ps 115:14: "I will lift the cup of salvation and call on the name of the Lord," which continues in the next verse, "precious in the eyes of the Lord is the death of his saints" (Ps 115:15).

is the new covenant: The covenant (*berith/diathēkē*) is a binding relationship. It is the central concept for the bond of loyalty and love between God and the people. The covenant with Noah (Gen 6:18; 9:9-17) was succeeded by that with Abraham (Gen 15:18), enacted by the splitting of victims ("cutting a covenant"), and having as its symbol the "spilling of blood" in the rite of circumcision (17:2-21). The Exodus story begins with God "remembering his covenant" (Exod 2:24), and the giving of Torah on Sinai was another articulation of that covenant (Exod 19:5) that the people were to observe (Exod 23:22). The covenant regulates relations. God "remembers the covenant" (LXX Ps 104:8; 105:45; 110:5) when he acts with fidelity and compassion, and the people "remember his covenant" when they keep his commandments (LXX Ps 131:12; Amos 1:9; Mal 2:10; Jer 11:2 10; 22:9). The promise of a "new covenant" written in human hearts is initiated by Jeremiah (Jer 31:31-34), and becomes a fundamental category for Christians to express their sense of a new relationship with God through Jesus (see 2 Cor 3:6; Gal 3:15; 4:24; Heb 7:22; 8:8-10; 9:15; 10:16; 12:24; Rev 11:9). Although Mark 14:24 and Matt 26:28 have "covenant" here, only Luke has "new covenant," which provides another point of contact with 1 Cor 11:25.

my blood which is being poured out: The ability of wine to symbolize blood is patent, and in the symbolism of Torah, blood signifies life: when blood is poured out, therefore, life is lost. Lev 17:11 states: "the life of all flesh is in its blood." And the logic of sacrifice is therefore: "it is the blood that makes atonement by reason of its life." Shedding blood therefore constitutes the offering of life to God (Lev 16:1-34). Hebrews states the principle: "without the shedding of blood there is no forgiveness of sins" (Heb 9:22) referring to the covenant on Sinai which was sealed in blood. Moses sprinkled the book of the covenant and the people with blood, saying, "behold the blood of the covenant" (Exod 24:8). The verb used here by Luke (*enkunnō/enkeō*) is used throughout Torah in sacrificial contexts (e.g., Lev 4:18, 25, 30, 34; 8:15; 17:4).

for you: The sacrifice is vicarious. The phrase *hyper hymōn* ("for you") is found in verse 19 and is repeated here; it means both "in place of you" and even more "in your behalf" (cf. Acts 5:21; 8:24; 9:16; 15:26; 21:13, 26). With reference to Jesus' death in the sense Luke uses it here, compare Rom 8:32; 1 Cor 15:3; 2 Cor 5:14-15, 21.

21. *the hand of the one betraying me*: Luke handles this moment delicately and far more indirectly than Mark 14:18-21; Matt 26:21-25; John 13:21-30. As noted above, Mark and Matthew place the prediction of betrayal at the start of the meal and make clear that the betrayer is present (cf. Mark 14:18, "the one eating with me"). Given the biblical sense of "hand" (*cheir*) as "power" (Exod 3:8; 7:4; 15:6; 1 Sam 4:3; LXX Ps 9:35; 30:15), Luke's statement need not even require Judas' physical presence, and simply indicate how the fact of the betrayal overshadows the meal.

22. *going as it has been determined*: The translation drops the Greek *hoti* ("because/for"). Jesus has made clear the necessity (*dei*) for the Son of Man to suffer (9:44; 17:25). The perfect participle of *orizō* shows that it is not Judas' perfidy but God's will that directs events; this has all been preordained (cf. Rom 1:4, and especially Acts 2:23; 10:42; 17:26, 31, for the sense of *orizō*).

    woe to that person: For the use of "woe" (*ouai*), see the note on 6:24. Luke softens the harsh statement of Mark 14:21 and Matt 26:24 that it would be better for the betrayer not to have been born.

23. *they began to dispute*: For *sunzētein*, see 24:15; Acts 6:9; 9:29; there is a genuine note of fractiousness in the description, but Luke is again remarkably circumspect. He omits the questioning of Jesus and his response identifying Judas (most direct in Matt 26:25 and John 13:20-30). Luke keeps the debate restricted to the apostles themselves. Once more he has removed the name and even the presence of Judas as much as he is able.

INTERPRETATION

The account of Jesus' last meal with his disciples has had such an obvious and overwhelming importance for the Christian community—providing the foundation story for its Eucharistic celebration and much of its understanding of the meaning of the Messiah's death—that a straightforward literary analysis is difficult. The reader must let go of fascinating and in their own right important issues in order to confront the passage as part of Luke's larger story.

One distracting issue is the meaning of Jesus' words for the sacramental life of the Church, a disputed question that much preoccupied the interpreters of the medieval and Reformation period alike. Another is the question concerning what sort of meal Jesus might have been sharing with the disciples, and the difference that might make for understanding his last hours. Was it a Passover meal or a fellowship meal or both? Was it celebrated on the first day of the feast (as the Synoptics have it) or the day before (as John has it)? Connected to these questions is the issue of what Jesus thought or intended by his words and gestures at the meal.

However interesting and important these questions, they are not immediately germane to the understanding of Luke's Gospel. It is obvious, first of all, that Christian liturgical practice is not based directly on this text but rather on a complex development of ritual traditions that look back to the Gospels only for legitimation after the fact.

Less obvious but no less true is the fact that it is impossible to settle definitively what kind of meal Jesus celebrated. This is only partly because the Gospels disagree on important aspects of the event. Equally problematic is any attempt to reconstruct the Jewish Passover meal in first century Palestine in all its details. Our earliest Jewish liturgical text of any completeness is the *Seder Rav Amri Gaon*, which comes from the ninth century. It does correspond in important ways with the very partial treatment of the Passover meal in the Mishnah tractate *Pesachim*.

But two further factors complicate matters considerably: the first is that for the parts of the meal that most concern us, the Babylonian Talmud's tractate *Pesachim* has practically nothing to add to the unsatisfying treatment in the Mishnah. What information it does contain, furthermore, suggests both a variety of practice and a lively dispute concerning exactly the same details that preoccupy scholars trying to pin down the historical actions of Jesus (see e.g., *bT Pes.* 103a-108a and especially 114a). One passage of the Talmud, indeed, forbids a Passover assembly being made up entirely of proselytes because they would be too preoccupied with the precise details of the ritual and would detract from the celebration (*bT Pes.* 91b)! In the light of these realities the attempt to determine the historical Jesus' exact intentions is an even more fugitive enterprise.

We are able to see clearly, however, how Luke understood this meal and its significance. He emphasizes in every way that it was a Passover meal, so we are justified in picking up the various allusions that this setting provides. He also stresses the special relationship between Jesus and his followers. To some extent this emphasis is found not only in what Luke includes, but what he excludes. Notice how he omits all but the barest mention of betrayal, and saves it for after the meal shared with his apostles. Judas is never named, and may as well not even be present. The result is a focus on the positive relationship between Jesus and those he has chosen, at least for this first portion of the meal.

Nowhere in Luke's story is there such a weight of interpretation given to every gesture, and nowhere is this interpretation so thoroughly self-referential as here. Note, for example, Jesus' first statement over the cup (22:17). He blesses the cup. He passes it to his apostles, telling them to "divide among yourselves," since he will not drink it again until the kingdom of God comes. The symbolism of sharing implicit in drinking from the same cup is here exploited to signify, in a truly complex fashion, the role of the disciples after Jesus' death. They are to "divide among themselves": at one level, this is an implicit bestowal of authority and fellowship, for such was the status of those who drank from the same cup as the king (cf. the implication of verses 29-30, below). The apostles are to continue Jesus' authority after the resurrection.

At another level, sharing equally in the cup signifies as well a sharing in the suffering of the Messiah, for as we shortly learn, this is the cup of suffering in which his blood is being poured out for them. This destiny as well the apostles will fulfill in the narrative of Acts, when they "suffer for the name" of the Messiah (5:41). It is also, in a very real sense, through the fellowship meals of believers that Jesus as the resurrected one will share again in the fruit of the vine in the kingdom of God. The time of final "liberation" will come only with the return of the Son of Man (21:28); but in the meals of the community, the "liberation" accomplished by Jesus will be realized.

A similarly dense symbolism pervades the ritual action regarding the bread. Jesus' physical gestures mimic those used in the feeding of the multitude in 9:10-17. That feeding too, had been shadowed on one side by the proclamation of the kingdom in healings and power (9:6, 11) and the coming of the death of the Messiah (9:22). Now as the disciples (and readers) see Jesus repeating the same actions, they perceive not only that Jesus is a prophet whose words reach fulfillment, but also the true meaning of the feeding: Jesus is the servant who gives his life for others. And as the bread must be broken to be shared, so is his body to be broken in death so that the life-giving spirit might be given to them. When they in turn "do this as a remembrance of him" in their "breaking bread" together (Acts 2:46; 20:7), he will be present not as a fond memory but as a powerful and commanding presence (24:44).

Nowhere are the symbolic resonances more richly overlayered than in Jesus' words over the cup. The "cup of blessing" is central first of all to the Passover celebration itself. Each of the four cups is the occasion for what are in effect, "toasts" to God. The *berakoth* (blessings) mingle praise of the Lord and petition for the people. Both remembrance and hope revolve around the primordial experience of liberation that was the Exodus. It was more than an escape from Egypt. It was God's formation of a people by the giving of Torah and the establishment of the covenant, sealed by the sacrificial blood sprinkled alike on the book of the covenant and the people. Luke therefore portrays the cup given by Jesus in equally "foundational" terms. The restoration of Israel by the prophet Jesus is equally sealed by sacrificial blood. But now the blood is not of animals, but of the Prophet himself. It is by the giving of his life in sacrifice—donation to God for the sake of others—that a regeneration of the people can take place.

This is why the moment of solemn announcement by Jesus is followed immediately by reference to the betrayal. Luke is extraordinarily circumspect. He does not identify Judas as the betrayer or draw attention to him. The one who has invited Satan into his heart will not dominate this meal (22:3).

But he must make mention of the "hand of the betrayer at the table," because in narrative terms this is how the sacrifice of the prophet will be accomplished. Because this covenant is being established anthropologically—in the very fabric of human freedom—the offer of the gift and the rejection of it as well must be carried out in the messy tangle of human decisions, and the decision of Judas to "hand over" Jesus is pivotal. Yet Luke also makes clear that even Judas' decision is part of the larger process that no human agency controls. The Son of Man moves toward a destiny determined by God. As Jesus will shortly say, "everything written about me has a fulfillment."

FOR REFERENCE AND FURTHER STUDY

Bacon, B. W. "The Lukan Tradition of the Lord's Supper." *HTR* 5 (1912) 322–348.

Jeremias, J. *The Eucharistic Words of Jesus* (Philadelphia: Fortress, 1977).

Karris, R. *Luke: Artist and Theologian: Luke's Passion Account as Literature* (New York: Paulist, 1985) 47–78.

Sparks, H. F. D. "St. Luke's Transpositions." *NTS* 3 (1956–57) 219–233.

Wanke, J. *Beobachtungen zum Eucharistieverständnis des Lukas auf Grund der lukanischen Mahlberichte* (Leipzig: St. Benno Verlag, 1973).

60. *Teachings at Table* (22:24-38)

24. They began to argue competitively among themselves: who seemed to be the greatest of them? 25. So he said to them: "The kings over nations rule by dominating. Those who exercise authority among them are designated benefactors. 26. But it is not to be that way with you. Instead, the greater among you is to become as the younger. And the one who governs is to be as one who serves. 27. For who is greater, the one who reclines at table or the one who serves at table? Is it not the one who reclines at table? But I am in your midst as the one who serves at table. 28. You are the ones who have remained with me in my trials. 29. And I bestow on you just as my father bestowed on me, a kingly authority, 30. so that you might eat and drink at my table in my kingdom, and sit on thrones judging the twelve tribes of Israel. 31. Simon, Simon! Look, Satan has asked for you all so that he can sift you out like wheat. 32. But I have prayed for you that your faith not fail. And when you turn back, you are to strengthen your brothers." 33. But he said to him, "Lord, I am ready to go with you both to prison and to death!" 34. So he said, "I tell you, Peter, this day a rooster will not crow before you will three times deny knowing me! 35. And he said to them, "When I sent you out without a purse or bag or san-

dals, did you lack anything?" And they said, "Nothing." 36. So he told them, "But now, let the one who has a purse take it along, and a bag as well! And let the one who does not have a sword sell his robe and buy one! 37. For I tell you that this scripture must find its fulfillment in me, 'He was reckoned with the lawless.' For that which is written about me has a fulfillment." 38. They said, "Look, Lord, here are two swords!" And he said to them: "Enough."

NOTES

24. *argue among themselves competitively*: The translation aims at the sense of the sentence which is literally: "there happened a rivalry (*philoneikia*) among them" (cf. 1 Cor 11:16). The phrasing and the location of this conflict are unique to Luke, but the substance is found in Mark 10:33-34 and Matt 18:1, and there is an earlier version in Luke 9:46. The tendency of the Pharisees and scribes to "seek first places" (14:7; 20:46) is here attributed to the disciples as well.

25. *kings over nations rule by dominating*: Is literally "dominate them (viz. "nations")." The basic point is paralleled by Mark 10:41-45 and Matt 20:24-28, although Mark has those who "think to rule" and Matthew "the rulers." Translating the verb *kyrieuō* is difficult. It is not as harsh as the *katakyrieuō* of Mark 10:42 (Matt 20:25). In the LXX, for example, *katakyrieuō* is used for "subdue the earth" (Gen 1:28), whereas *kyrieuō* is used for "he will rule over you" (Gen 3:16). Luke recognizes the dominance without insisting on suppression.

    those who exercise authority: The Lukan redaction is subtle but significant. Mark 10:42 (Matt 20:25) has "their great ones (*megaloi*) exercise authority (*katexousiazō*)," with the definite sense of domination in the choice of words. Luke's "those who exercise authority" (cf. Neh 5:15; 9:37; 1 Cor 6:12; 7:4) is more neutral. He shows his genuine Hellenistic sensitivities when he adds, "are designated benefactors (*euergetai*)." The term occurs only here in the NT and its cognates only in 1 Tim 6:2; Acts 4:9 and 10:38. The basic pattern of the "benefactor/client" relationship, however, is very much part of the symbolic world of the NT. Cf. e.g., Wis 3:5; 7:22; 11:5, 13; 19:14; Esth 8:13. Josephus calls Vespasian "benefactor" in *Jewish War* 3:459 as he does Titus in *Jewish War* 4:113. He even claims to have been given that title himself (*Life* 47; 50; 259). In this relationship the one who gives gifts is adequately rewarded by the title, with the glory (*doxa*) that goes with it.

26. *not to be that way with you*: The Greek is cryptic: "but you not thus." The following statement has the third person imperative, "let him become" rather than the indicative "will be" of Mark 10:43 and Matt 20:26.

    greater . . . younger: The first of these oppositions is striking for its displacement of the expected "lesser" with "younger" (*neōteros*). The parallels have "servant" (*diakonos*). Luke's language recalls the earlier dispute over greatness, which Jesus answered with reference to a child (9:47). It also reminds us of the biblical theme of the younger one who is favored (see Gen 27:15, 36; 37:3; 42:13; 48:14, 19; 1 Sam 17:14; cf. Luke 15:11-32).

governs . . . serves: Luke replaces "the one who wishes to be first (*prōtos*)" of Mark 10:44 and Matt 20:27—with its slightly negative overtones—with the more matter-of-fact *hēgoumenos* (from *hēgeomai*, "lead"). He uses the same term in Acts 7:10; 14:12; 15:22; 26:2. The verb *diakoneō* derives from a down-to-earth context, and in Luke-Acts never entirely loses its sense of "waiting on tables" (see 4:39; 8:3; 10:40; 12:37; 17:8; Acts 1:17, 25; 6:1, 2, 4; 11:29; 12:25; 19:22; 20:24; 21:19).

27. *who is greater*: The question picks up the dispute of verse 24 except that it asks who is *really* greater, as opposed to who "seems" to be. The question is phrased so as to demand the affirmative response. For the contrast between the one who "reclines" and the one who "serves," see especially the example given by Jesus in Luke 17:7-10.

in your midst as the one who serves: For the phrase "in your midst" (*en mesǭ hymōn*), see 2:46; 10:3; 21:21; 24:36; Acts 1:15; 2:22; 17:22, 33). The definite article is important in this context: by giving the bread and the wine, Jesus is literally "the one who serves," and the spiritual resonances build on that practical reality. In the parallels of Mark 14:45 and Matt 19:28, the saying concerns the Son of Man who "came not to be served but to serve and to give his life as a ransom for many." Luke's version is at once simpler and more directly an example for leaders.

28. *remained with me in my trials*: The verb *diamenō* has the sense of "enduring," and this saying is clearly appropriate for the apostles as those who are "still persevering" through this period of testing (*peirasmoi*)—notice the difference from Matt 19:29, "I say to you who have followed me." The saying's significance is given by Luke's interpretation of the parable of the sower: those who fall away in testing do not bear fruit, and those who persevere bring fruit to maturity (8:12, 15). This recognition of fidelity is the prelude to the bestowal of authority on the apostles in the following verse. And in fact, Luke does not have the apostles abandon Jesus the way Matthew and Mark do.

29. *I bestow . . . a kingly authority*: The statement is unique to Luke and reveals his distinctive understanding of Jesus as already proclaimed king (19:38) of the kingdom that it has pleased the Father to give them (12:45). The term *diatithēmi* means to dispose (as of property). Here, what the Father has given to Jesus, he gives to them; the legal tone is unmistakable. The anarthous *basileia* has the sense of "reign," or (in this context), "royal/kingly authority." The gestures of "the man who became king" in the Lukan kingship parable (19:11-27) are here enacted.

30. *eat and drink at my table*: The image is that of the king's closest associates sitting at privileged places at the kingdom banquet (cf. 13:29; 14:16-24), at the very table of the king himself. We are reminded of the elders of Israel who ate and drank in the presence of God with Moses (Exod 24:11). The saying also anticipates the presence of Jesus at the post-resurrection meals of the disciples (Luke 24:36-43; Acts 10:41).

judging the twelve tribes of Israel: Luke decisively alters the reference point for this prediction. In Matt 19:28 it refers to the "rebirth when the Son of Man sits on the throne of his glory." But in Luke the saying points forward to the role that the apostles will have within the restored Israel in the narrative of Acts. Like those in the kingship parable who are given authority within the kingdom, so will these followers exercise effective rule within the people gathered by the power of the resurrected prophet (see e.g., Acts 5:1-11).

31. *has asked for you all*: This strange verse is found only in Luke. The verb *exaiteō* often has the sense of "seeking the surrender" of someone. The translation supplies "all," to make clear that the personal pronoun "you" is plural rather than singular. The statement shows that they are in a period of "testing" (*peirasmos*) just like that experienced by Jesus at the beginning of his ministry (4:1-13); for the disciples, this is the "season" (*kairos*) Satan was waiting for (Luke 4:13). He has sifted out Judas by entering his heart (22:3); will he succeed with the rest?

32. *but I have prayed for you*: In this saying, the personal pronoun "you" is in the singular, referring specifically to Peter rather than to the disciples as a group. See the note on 21:36 for Luke's use of *deomai*, which means the prayer of petition. The repetition of "Simon" is striking, particularly since this name has not been used for Peter since 6:14. Jesus' prayer is that his faith not "run out" (cf. *ekleipō* in 16:9). Even if he fail, he can return and help the others.

    when you turn back: The verb *epistrephō* is used frequently for "conversion" (see Neh 1:9; Hos 3:5; 5:4; 6:1; Amos 4:6; Joel 2:12; Isa 6:10; 9:13; Jer 3:10). In Luke-Acts, see 1:16-17; 17:4; Acts 3:19; 9:35; 11:21; 14:15; 15:19). Jesus implicitly predicts Peter's rehabilitation after his moral collapse, and his role in "strengthening" (*stērizō*, cf. 9:51 and esp. Acts 18:23), which Luke will show dramatically in Acts 1:15-26.

33. *both to prison and to death*: Luke slightly softens Peter's statement from Mark 14:29 and Matt 26:33, where he denies that he will be "scandalized," even though everyone else is. Luke is closer to John 13:37, where Peter declares his willingness to "follow now; I will give up my life for you." As the narrative will show, Peter is not yet "ready" (*hetoimos*) for either sacrifice, although he will eventually be shown offering the first (Acts 4:3-22; 5:18-21; 12:3-12) and possibly even the second (by implication in Acts 12:17?).

34. *will three times deny knowing me*: Luke once more softens this slightly by inserting "knowing me" rather than the absolute "denying me" of Mark 14:30; Matt 26:34 and John 13:38.

35. *when I sent you out*: This is found only in Luke. The oddity of the question is that it asks of the Twelve details found not in the instructions to them (9:1-6) but in the instructions given to the Seventy (10:4). The point is not the details but the negative response which the form of the question demands. They lacked nothing because they were received by the hospitality of believers; precisely that context of hospitality can no longer be assumed.

36. *let the one who has a purse take it*: The details are less significant than the point about the changed circumstances for their work. They are entering into the same context of rejection being experienced by the Prophet; as his prophetic successors, they will experience such rejection directly. Luke consistently uses possessions to symbolize the larger patterns in the story of the Prophet and the people.

buy one: The Greek is ambiguous; it could mean either that a person who had no *purse* should sell a cloak and buy a sword, or (as here) that the one who had no sword should sell a cloak to get one. In either case, the hyperbole of the statement should be obvious. Selling one's outer garment for a sword has not a literal but a symbolic point: they are entering a state of testing in which they will be without external resources and in danger.

37. *this Scripture must find its fulfillment in me*: Jesus opened his ministry with the statement that "this Scripture" (*graphē*) of Isaiah 61:1; 58:6 "was fulfilled" (*peplērōtai*, 4:21). At the end, he declares that "this Scripture (*touto to gegrammenon*) must be completed in me (*telesthēnai en emoi*). And once more, the text in question is from one of the Servant songs of Isaiah.

reckoned with the lawless: Luke has *meta* ("with") rather than the *en tois* ("among") of the LXX, but otherwise, this citation is the LXX of Isa 53:12. The full sentence in the LXX reads, "On this account he will inherit many and will share in the goods of the powerful ones, because his life was handed over (*paredothē*) to death, and he was reckoned among the lawless. But he himself bore the sins of many and on account of their sins he was handed over (*paredothē*)." This Suffering Servant song of Isaiah plays a particularly important role in Luke's interpretation of Jesus, as can be seen from Acts 8:32-35. Here, the citation has three functions: a) it interprets Jesus' death in terms of the fulfillment of God's will expressed in Scripture rather than the machinations of humans; b) it interprets that death as one of vicarious suffering *for* the lawless and the sinners although he himself is innocent; c) it shows that Scripture foretold that Jesus would be "reckoned" (*elogisthē*) as lawless by outsiders.

that which is written about me has a fulfillment: The Greek is very cryptic: "for that about me has a *telos*"—which term can mean "goal" or "end." But it is clearly meant to complement the verb form *teleo* in the previous verse, and should be taken to mean "fulfillment." Luke's conviction is that all the Scripture points to the suffering and glory of the Messiah (Luke 24:27, 44; Acts 1:16). In the narrative, the prediction of being placed among the lawless is fulfilled by Jesus' being arrested as a *lēstēs* (22:52) and his being crucified between two *kakourgoi* (23:32).

38. *here are two swords*: This misunderstanding of Jesus' statement about swords reveals just how "unready" the disciples are to follow where Jesus must go—in fact they will use the sword violently in the garden (22:50); they do not understand the meaning of the Scriptures despite Jesus' instruction (cf. 9:45). Jesus' exasperated termination of this discussion ("enough," *hikanon estin*) here is matched by his chagrin when the sword is actually used (*eate eōs toutou*, "enough of that")! Jesus' speech about being "reckoned among the lawless" and being arrested as a *lēstēs* is ironic; they are not meant to *act* like such people!

INTERPRETATION

Luke's account of Jesus' last meal is distinctive because of the way it combines the elements of the Passover meal with a farewell discourse by Jesus.

The other Synoptics have the meal but not the discourse; John's Gospel has all discourse and only the merest mention of a meal (John 13–17). When reading Luke's presentation of Jesus at table with the Pharisees (14:7-24), we saw that he deftly appropriated the Hellenistic literary conventions of the *symposium*, with its traditions of philosophic discourse. We observed that although this genre began with Plato and Xenophon, it found its way into Jewish literature as well. This section of the Last Supper shows another such literary convention being used by Luke.

At least since Plato's *Phaedo*, which described the last moments of Socrates with his disciples, the Hellenistic world was familiar with a genre of writing that scholars now call the "farewell discourse" or "testament." Portrayals of the death of a soldier or sage would often include certain stereotypical elements: a statement concerning one's own life; a prediction of future events; a bestowal of authority or blessing on one's attendants (e.g., Diogenes Laertius, *Life of Epicurus* 10:15-22).

Jewish traditions could claim at least equal antiquity. At the end of Genesis, we find the patriarch Jacob predicting the future for his sons and blessing them (Gen 49:1-28), a passage that was not only considerably expanded in the *Palestinian Targum*, but inspired the most literarily elaborate example of this genre, *The Testaments of the Twelve Patriarchs*. Not only Jacob, but also Moses was a hero of the past whose last words were particularly deserving of remembrance and ornamentation. Torah itself portrays Moses before his death delivering a classic version of a farewell discourse (Deut 31; cf. Philo, *Life of Moses* 2:290-292), and we are not surprised to find at least one *Testament of Moses* among the extant Jewish literature from the first century.

Since Luke has consistently portrayed Jesus as both prophet and philosopher, indeed a "prophet like Moses," it is entirely consistent that he appropriate this testamentary tradition in his version of the Last Supper. As with other such conventions, however, Luke's use of it is both flexible and creative. His capacity for concision is remarkable, for he suggests far more than he states. In twenty-three verses (22:14-37) he provides virtually all the elements of the Hellenistic farewell discourse, but with complete naturalness and apparent spontaneity.

The reason why such a literary convention developed in the first place, of course, was because the final words of a person are considered to be particularly significant as the seal and symbol of a life. In the case of a philosopher, the last words communicated to followers are treasured as clues to the meaning of the sage's message. Then, all that was required was to die in a manner fitting the words (cf. Plato, *Phaedo* 117A–118A). Luke has therefore reshaped elements from the tradition to interpret Jesus' relationship with his closest followers.

The dimensions of that relationship are determined largely by the character of Jesus' ministry. As in the instructions on discipleship in 9:44-62 the nature of discipleship and leadership within the community are conformed to the pattern of the Messiah. Three aspects of his identity and work are emphasized. The first is his authority as king over the people Israel. In the trial that follows, this title will be twisted into a political threat against Rome (23:2). But with his followers, Jesus acknowledges that his father has given him *basileia*, "kingly rule," over the people (22:29). The second point made about Jesus is that his authority is exercised by means of service: he is "among them as the one who serves" (22:27). The most obvious proof of this is the fact that he has "waited at table," that is, passed to them the cups of wine and the bread (22:17-20); the deeper meaning is that he "gives his life for them" as a servant. The third point made about Jesus is that he is now entering into a time of acute "testing" (*peirasmos*), when he will be rejected by the leaders, and counted among "the lawless" (22:37).

Corresponding to this portrayal of Jesus is the instruction to the apostles who are to continue Jesus' prophetic ministry after his resurrection in the narrative of Acts. First, Jesus bestows on them *basileia*: they are to "judge the twelve tribes of Israel," (22:30), an exercise of authority that Luke will show being fulfilled in the apostolic ministry of the Jerusalem Church (Acts 1-6).

Second, their exercise of authority is also to be carried out as a practical service to others. The wrangling over status (*philoneikia*, 22:24) is entirely inappropriate. They are neither to dominate nor to regard themselves as benefactors (22:26). Like their teacher, they are to serve humbly those they teach. Luke will again show us this dimension of the apostolic authority exemplified in Acts, when the apostles stand at the middle of the community of possessions and wait on tables (Acts 4:32-37; 6:1-2).

Third, they too are going to share the fate of Jesus, and be subjected to "testing" even greater than that they have already endured (22:28). The power of Satan (22:3), the authority of darkness (22:53) is at work in the arrest and death of the Messiah, and these who share Jesus' table will also be violently "sifted" by these events (22:31). Judas had already fallen away, and broken the apostolic circle. Despite his protestations, Peter also will deny Jesus (22:34). But as Jesus prophesies, and as the narrative of Acts 1:15-26 will show, Peter will turn back and "strengthen his brothers" (22:32). Nevertheless, the apostles will never again be able to rely upon the gift of hospitality to supply their needs; they are entering with the Messiah into a period of danger that will not soon end (21:12-19), and their use of possessions must reflect these changed circumstances (22:35-36).

Finally, Luke shows the disciples (and the reader) that all of these things are in fulfillment of prophecy. This stark statement stands as a summary of Luke's view concerning Jesus: "that which is written about me has a fulfillment" (22:37).

FOR REFERENCE AND FURTHER STUDY

Danker, F. *Benefactor: Epigraphic Study of a Greco-Roman and New Testament Semantic Field*. St. Louis: Clayton, 1982.

Dupont, J. "Le logion des douze trônes (Mt 19, 28; Lc 22, 28-30)." *Bib* 45 (1964) 355–392.

George, A. "La royauté de Jésus selon l'évangile de Luc." *ScEccl* 14 (1962) 57–69.

Kurz, W. S. "Luke 22:14-38 and Greco-Roman and Biblical Farewell Addresses." *JBL* 104 (1985) 251–268.

Lull, D. J. "The Servant-Benefactor as a Model of Greatness (Luke 22:24-30)." *NovT* 28 (1986) 289–305.

Minear, P. "A Note on Luke xxii, 36." *NovT* 7 (1964–65) 128–134.

Neyrey, J. "Jesus' Farewell Speech." *The Passion According to Luke: A Redaction Study of Luke's Soteriology* (New York: Paulist, 1985) 5–48.

61. *The Time of Testing* (22:39-53)

39. He left and went as usual to the Mount of Olives with the disciples also following him. 40. When he had come to the place, he told them, "Pray not to enter into testing." 41. He himself withdrew about a stone's throw. He went to his knees and prayed. 42. He said, "Father, if you will it, take away this cup from me. Nevertheless, let not my will but yours be done." 43. An angel from heaven appeared to him, strengthening him. 44. And entering the struggle, he continued to pray even more eagerly. His sweat was like drops of blood falling to the ground. 45. Rising from prayer, he went to his disciples. He found them sleeping because of their sorrow. 46. He said to them, "Why are you sleeping? Get up! Pray that you not enter into testing." 47. While he was still speaking, a crowd appeared. One of the Twelve named Judas led them. He drew near to Jesus to kiss him. 48. But Jesus said to him, "Judas, are you handing over the Son of Man with a kiss?" 49. When those who were around him saw what was about to happen, they said, "Lord, should we strike with the sword?" 50. And one of them struck the slave of the chief priest and cut off his right ear. 51. Jesus responded, "Enough of that!" Touching the ear, he healed it. 52. Jesus said to the chief priests and Temple officers and elders who had come up to him, "You have come out with swords and clubs as though to capture a bandit! 53. While I was with you day by day in the Temple you did not lift your hands against me. But this is your hour and the power of darkness."

NOTES

39. *went as usual*: Luke had established in 21:37 that Jesus was spending his nights on the Mount of Olives. For the phrase "according to custom," see Luke 1:9;

2:42. Luke omits the place-name "Gethsemane" in Mark 14:32 (but not in Matt 26:36), as well as the specification that it was a "garden" (*kēpos*) as in John 18:1. He refers to it in the next verse only as "the place" (*topos*).

40. *pray not to enter into testing*: There are two significant alterations in Luke's version: a) he tells the disciples to pray, rather than to wait while he goes to pray (Mark 14:32; Matt 26:37); b) he does not single out Peter, James, and John (Mark 14:33; Matt 26:37), but deals with the disciples as a whole. The focus therefore remains on Jesus himself. His command echoes the Lord's Prayer, "lead us not into testing (*peirasmos*)" (11:4), as well as Jesus' statements at the table about fidelity in testing (22:28-38).

41. *he went to his knees and prayed*: The description emphasizes Jesus' control and lack of emotional turmoil. He drops from Mark 14:33 (Matt 26:37) the terms describing Jesus' extreme state of psychic distress, as well as the request that the disciples "watch with him." Luke simply has Jesus withdraw, and rather than "fall on the ground" (Mark 14:35) or "fall on his face" (Matt 26:39), he has Jesus simply sink to his knees.

42. *if you will it, take away this cup from me*: This is simpler than the parallels, with "Father" rather than "abba, Father" (Mark 14:36) or "my Father" (Matt 26:39), and with no preliminary statement about all things being possible to God (see rather Luke 1:37). The cup is his suffering, as his words at supper made plain (22:17, 22).
not my will: The contrasting word *plēn* ("nevertheless") is quite strong. Luke uses the substantive *thelēma* ("will") rather than "what I will" (Mark 14:36; Matt 26:39), bringing Jesus' prayer closer to the one he taught the disciples, "Father, let your will be done" (11:2).

43. *an angel from heaven appeared to him*: There is some doubt as to whether the next two verses are originally part of Luke's composition. The MSS evidence is split fairly evenly with perhaps a slight tilt (according to the rules) against inclusion. Omitting the verses would obviously yield a "shorter reading," which is usually to be preferred. The third basic rule of text criticism is that the "harder reading" is to be preferred, and in this case, the determination of which is "harder" is not clear. Those arguing against inclusion say that it was included to protect Jesus' divinity against the scandal of his distress. But the appearance of an angel at this point in the narrative is obviously "harder" in other respects, as the tendency of contemporary readers to dismiss it attests. The decision rests on thematic plausibility, and on this criterion, the verses appear to be Lukan. Certainly "strengthening" (*enischuō*) is part of Luke's vocabulary (see Acts 9:19). As for the appearance of a heavenly visitor, no one should be surprised at that anywhere in Luke's narrative (see 1:11, 13, 18, 26; 2:9-10, 13; 4:3; 9:30-31; 24:23; Acts 5:19; 8:26; 10:3, 22; 11:13; 12:7-15; 27:23)! Note also that the idea of angels "ministering" to Jesus at a time of testing is found elsewhere in the tradition (Mark 1:13).

44. *entering the struggle*: The term *agōnia* derives from *agōn* which refers to the sort of struggle in which wrestlers engage; the cognate verb *agōnizesthai* has the same sense. This is the only occurrence of *agōnia* in the NT. In 2 Macc 3:14, 16; 15:19,

it occurs with the meaning "anguish of soul." But Luke uses the verb form (*agōnizesthai*) to mean "struggle" in Acts 13:24, and this is the dominant meaning of the term in the NT (cf. John 18:36; 1 Cor 9:25; Col 1:29; 1 Tim 4:10; 6:12; 2 Tim 4:17). Notice in particular Col 4:12, "always struggling for you in prayer." The term *agōn* is used in Phil 1:30; Col 2:1; 1 Thess 2:2; 1 Tim 6:12; 2 Tim 4:7. Nowhere does it reflect an emotional tension or anguish of soul (cf. also the use of *agōnizesthai* in LXX Dan 6:14; 1 Macc 7:21; 2 Macc 8:16, and especially Sir 4:28, "strive even to the point of death for truth, and the Lord God will fight for you," which sounds like a gloss on this verse in Luke).

pray even more eagerly: The comparative of the adjective *ektenōs* is used here as a comparative adverb; we are to understand the greater energy as a response to the strengthening by the angel.

sweat was like drops of blood: The text does not say that Jesus had a "bloody sweat" as a sort of physiological reaction to stress, but makes a comparison (*hōsei*) between the profuseness of the sweat (in its huge drops) and globules of blood. For the sweat of athletes in the *agōn* as a sign of their effort, cf. Epictetus, *Discourses* 1, 24, 1–2.

45. *sleeping because of their sorrow*: Notice that *lypē* is attributed to the disciples, not Jesus, in contrast to the *perilypos* ascribed to Jesus by Mark 14:34 and Matt 26:38. Luke is sensitive to the negative associations of *lypē* for Hellenistic readers. It is an emotion that is always connected to envy (Aristotle, *Rhetoric* 1387B; Diogenes Laertius, *Life of Zeno* 7:111) or cowardice/fear (Philo, *On the Migration of Abraham* 60; Epictetus, *Discourses* 3, 11, 1–2; 3, 24, 90). In his discussion of *lypē*, in fact, Diogenes Laertius speaks of its "weighing down" someone (*Life of Zeno*, 7:112). We remember that when Jesus was in prayer an earlier time with Elijah and Moses, discussing the *exodos* he was to fulfill in Jerusalem, Peter, John and James were similarly "weighed down with sleep" (9:32). Singularly lacking in Luke's description of Jesus is fear (*phobos*) which again indicates that he faces his death as a philosopher should (Epictetus, *Discourses* 2, 1, 8–20), that is, with "courage" (*andreia*; see Aristotle, *Nichomachean Ethics* 3, 6, 8–10).

46. *why are you sleeping*: Luke reduces the entire scene involving the disciples, omitting the threefold failure and accusation in Mark 14:37-42 (Matt 26:40-46).

47. *one of the Twelve named Judas led them*: Like Mark 14:43 and Matt 26:47, Luke has a crowd (*ochlos*) come to get Jesus, and identifies Judas as one of the Twelve (see 6:16). But in contrast to the parallels, he has Judas leading them (*proērcheto*), and makes clear below that the "crowd" is actually made up of Jesus' official opponents rather than the "people" (*laos*). Luke also omits the description of the swords and clubs which the others include at this point (Mark 14:43-45; Matt 26:47-49).

drew near to Jesus to kiss him: In contrast to the parallels, no sign of identification has been worked out; indeed, Luke does not actually have Judas kiss Jesus, only make the attempt. Neither does Judas call Jesus "Rabbi"; he is not given the dignity of speech in Luke's Gospel.

48. *handing over the Son of Man*: The language is shaped by the passion predictions, and is unique to Luke (see 9:44; 18:32; 20:20; 22:4, 6, 21-22).

49. *should we strike with a sword*: For the construction with *ei*, see 13:23. This element of the tradition is found in all four Gospels, although only Luke has prepared for it with the saying on the sword at table (22:36). All the Gospels agree that the ear of the chief priest's slave was cut (Luke alone specifying the *right* ear; cf. John 18:10; Mark 14:47; Matt 26:51). Only John identifies the sword wielder as "Simon Peter" and the slave's name as Malchus. Only Luke introduces the act with a question, apparently to connect the incident to the earlier misunderstanding about the sword (22:38).

51. *enough of that*: The construction, like that in 22:38, is cryptic, literally "allow up to this" (*eate heōs toutou*). The point is clear enough: they are to stop any such violent resistance. Matthew at this point includes the logion about those who use the sword "perishing by the sword" (Matt 26:52-54), and John 18:11 has Jesus ask a rhetorical question about drinking the cup given by the Father.

    touching the ear, he healed it: The gesture is found only in Luke. Not only does it show the continuation of the ministry of healing that has accompanied Jesus' proclamation of the good news from the beginning (4:23; 5:17, 31; 6:18-19; 7:7; 8:47; 9:2, 11, 42; 13:32; 14:4; 17:15), but it shows Jesus exemplifying the attitudes of forgiveness and compassion toward those "who hate him" that he had enjoined on his followers (6:27-36). The way a philosopher faced death revealed whether his own teachings worked (cf. Plato, *Phaedo* 118A, and the account of the death of Zeno of Elea in Diogenes Laertius, *Lives of Philosophers* 9:26-28).

52. *chief priests and Temple officers and elders*: These are now shown to be the ones making up the "crowd" (*ochlos*) led by Judas. No others are identified. Once more, therefore, Luke separates the leaders who aggressively try to do away with Jesus from the populace who have no role in this venture.

    as though to capture a bandit: There is some humor in Jesus' observation, since there is obvious overkill involved in their coming out with clubs and swords against a teacher. It also makes them look undignified in contrast to the philosophical calm of Jesus. The translation expands on the Greek *epi lēstēn*. The same term is in Mark 14:48 and Matt 26:55. The term is used of bandits and highwaymen and pirates (see LXX Obad 1:5; Sir 36:31, and Luke's parable of the good Samaritan, 10:30, 36). Luke had earlier accused those in the Temple of turning it into a "robber's cave" (*spēlaion lēstōn*, 19:46). Josephus associates the *lēstai* with revolutionaries armed against the Romans in *Jewish War* 2:57; 2:229; 2:264.

53. *day by day in the Temple*: This reminds us of the series of conflicts in the Temple precincts between Jesus and the leaders that built toward this confrontation (19:47-48; 20:1, 19).

    this is your hour: Compare the use of *hōra* in 2:38; 7:21; 10:21; 12:12, 39, 40, 46; 13:31; 22:14, and especially 20:19, "they wanted to put hands on him in that very hour."

    the power of darkness: The term translated "power" is *exousia*, ("authority"); the reader remembers 20:20, "to deliver him to the power and authority of the prefect." The word "darkness" (*skotos*) can suggest evil or the time of secret deeds; note that at the death of Jesus there is "darkness over the whole land" (23:44).

INTERPRETATION

The two scenes at the Mount of Olives provide the narrative transition from the supper which celebrates the inner meaning of Jesus' gift of himself, to the trial and death which carry out that sacrifice. The moment of Jesus in prayer (22:39-46) draws us even further into the mystery of Jesus' obedient faith, revealing the internal disposition of the one who is about to die. The moment of Jesus' arrest (22:47-53) leads us toward the machinery of death itself, revealing the poison of betrayal and deception contained in the cup of the Messiah's suffering. The way Luke reshapes the traditions available to him in these scenes testifies both to his literary skill and his cultural sensitivity.

That Jesus went through a powerful testing of his faith and obedience before his death is firmly rooted in the tradition. The Letter to the Hebrews says that Jesus "offered up prayers and supplications, with loud cries and tears, to him who was able to save him from death and he was heard for his godly fear. Although he was a son he learned obedience through what he suffered" (Heb 5:7-8). John lacks any scene of prayer in the garden, but does have Jesus cry out in public, "Now is my soul troubled. And what shall I say? Father, save me from this hour? No, for this purpose I have come to this hour" (John 12:27). And of course, Mark and Matthew each show us a Jesus riveted with fear and sorrow, asking his disciples to wait with him while he prays, and begging his Father repeatedly that the cup pass from him, even while accepting the Father's will (Mark 14:32-42; Matt 26:36-46). The element of emotional turmoil is a common feature in each of these accounts.

Luke's reworking of the tradition moves into two related directions. The first is to place the entire focus on Jesus rather than on the disciples. He omits the request that they watch with him, the repeated visits and exhortations. Because of this important omission, the reader's attention is fixed on Jesus. Related to this is his shaping of the image of Jesus. He removes from him the need for companionship and the terrible fear and grief emphasized by Mark. Why? Because these are understood by him (and his Hellenistic readers) to be signs of vice rather than virtue, and Luke is concerned to show that Jesus is not only prophet but true philosopher (*sophos*).

We notice, therefore, that the emotion of "sorrow" (*lypē*) which is associated in Hellenistic moral literature with fear and cowardice as well as envy, is shifted from Jesus to the disciples. They fail to pray as he has told them, because their "sorrow" (read: fear/anxiety/cowardice) has weighed them down with sleep. In contrast, Luke presents Jesus as the spiritual athlete. He enters the *agōn* of prayer before God, bringing his mind and will into line with that of the Father, releasing his deep desire to live and avoid suffering, and accepting what has been determined for him.

In just such fashion would Epictetus portray the philosopher's struggle for virtue in terms of an athletic contest (cf. *Discourses* 2, 18, 28; 3, 22, 59; 3, 25, 1-4). The angel strengthening Jesus is like a trainer, urging on his "eager prayer." The profuse sweat falling to the ground in globules so great they foreshadowed the blood he was to shed tells us that this prayer/wrestling is an anticipation of a still harder victory the next day on the cross.

It would be a complete and insensitive misreading to think that Luke has "diminished the humanity" of Jesus by this portrayal, or engaged in a sort of docetism. Indeed, he portrays Jesus as engaging in the most fundamental sort of struggle for the human will. Like Jacob wrestling all night with the angel (Gen 32:24-32), Jesus "enters the struggle" against the power of darkness, and in his prayer, accepts his destiny.

The scene of the arrest shows us the *sophos* whose acceptance of God's will stands steady and unshaken in the midst of turmoil. Everything around Jesus is chaotic and out of control. The leaders coming as a mob with weapons; Judas lunging forward to kiss Jesus; the disciples brandishing the sword and slashing at the chief priest's slave. Jesus stands as a still center. The leadership's loss of dignity and loss of credibility with the people is revealed by the quiet humor of Jesus' observation: "you have come out as for a bandit," when they could have taken him any time during the day. Why do they need such weapons and the cover of night? Likewise, the meretriciousness of Judas' kiss is deflected by the ironic question: "do you hand over the Son of Man with a kiss?"

That Jesus is not lacking in power is demonstrated not only by his self-control, but also by his control of his disciples: at his word, they cease resistance. Most of all, it is demonstrated by his action of healing the ear of the slave. What Jesus was from the beginning he remains to the end: a bringer of healing. It is demonstrated, finally, by his quiet recognition that this power to heal is useless in a situation dominated by deception, betrayal, and violence: "this is your hour and the power of darkness" (22:53). A greater sacrifice is required of the Son of Man, who must now "go as it was determined for him" (22:22).

For Reference and Further Study

Ehrmann, B., and M. Plunkett "The Angel and the Agony: The Textual Problem of Luke 22:33-34." *CBQ* 45 (1983) 401-416.

Feuillet, A. "Le recit lucanien de l'agonie de Gethsemane (lc xxii. 39-46)." *NTS* 22 (1975-76) 397-417.

Larkin, W. J. "The Old Testament Background of Luke xxii, 43-44." *NTS* 25 (1978-79) 250-254.

Lescow, T. "Jesus im Gethsemane bei Lukas und im Hebräerbrief." *ZNW* 58 (1967) 215–239.

Neyrey, J. "Jesus in the Garden (Lk 22:39–46)." *The Passion according to Luke: A Redaction Study of Luke's Soteriology* (New York: Paulist, 1985) 49–68.

62. The Sanhedrin Hearing (22:54-71)

54. They arrested and led him off. They brought him to the house of the chief priest. Peter followed at a distance. 55. He sat in the midst of those who gathered in the courtyard around a fire they had lit. 56. A certain woman slave saw him as he was sitting toward the light. She stared at him closely. She said, "This man was also with him." 57. He denied it. He said, "Woman, I do not know him!" 58. A short time later another person noticed him. He said, "You are also one of them." Peter said, "Man, I am not!" 59. About an hour later, another man kept insisting, "It's true. This man was also with him, for he is a Galilean!" 60. But Peter said, "Man, I don't know what you are talking about!" Immediately, while he was still speaking, a rooster crowed. 61. The Lord turned and looked straight at Peter. Peter remembered the word of the Lord, how he had told him, "Before a rooster crows today you will deny me three times." 62. He went outside. He wept bitterly. 63. Those who held Jesus kept mocking him. They struck him. 64. They blindfolded him and questioned him: "Prophesy! Who is it that has struck you?" 65. They spoke harshly against him in many other ways. 66. As day came, the board of elders of the people, chief priests, and scribes, gathered together. They led him away to their Sanhedrin. 67. They said: "Are you the Messiah? Tell us!" But he told them, "If I tell you, you will certainly not believe. 68. And if I ask you, you will certainly not answer. 69. But from now on the Son of Man will be sitting on the right hand of the power of God." 70. They all said to him, "Are you therefore the Son of God?" He said to them, "You are saying that I am." 71. So they said, "What further need do we have of testimony? For we have ourselves heard it from his mouth!"

NOTES

54. *they arrested him*: Luke uses *syllambanō* (as does John 18:12) as part of the narrative, rather than as a question put by Jesus to the crowd as in Mark 14:48; Matt 26:55. Compare the summary in Acts 1:16, "Judas was the leader of those arresting Jesus."

to the house of the chief priest: Luke is very spare. Matt 26:57 and John 18:13 identify him as Caiaphas (cf. Josephus, *Antiquities* 18:35). Matt 26:57 and Mark 14:53 also have Jesus brought to the chief priest rather than simply to his house.

Peter followed at a distance: The adverb *makrothen* means "far off." John 18:15-16 expands this short notice by introducing the beloved disciple as the means of entry into the courtyard.

55. *in the courtyard around a fire*: The *aulē* ("courtyard") could be a yard or hallway or even a palace (see 11:11; Rev 11:2; also Jer 37:21; 38:26; 39:14). The parallels are more expansive: they note that Peter was with the "servants" (*hyperētai*, John 18:18; Mark 14:53; Matt 26:58). Mark and John have Peter seeking warmth; John adds that it was cold; and Matthew that Peter wanted to "see the outcome (*telos*)."

56. *woman slave saw him*: All the Gospels agree that the first challenge was posed by a woman slave (*paidiskē*). Luke adds that Peter was sitting toward the light, to explain her ability to study his features. The major difference in the accounts is an important one: Luke tells the entire story at once, whereas the parallels all interject between the placement of Peter in the courtyard and his subsequent denials an account of Jesus' hearing before the chief priest.

stared at him closely: The verb *atenizo* is a favorite of Luke's (see 4:20; Acts 1:10; 3:4, 12; 6:15; 7:55; 10:4; 11:6; 13:9; 14:9; 23:1).

this man was also with him: In contrast to the other Gospels, Luke has the first charge levelled indirectly, "this man," rather than the "you" of John 18:17; Mark 14:67; Matt 26:69. Mark further specifies, "Jesus the Nazarene," and Matthew, "Jesus from Galilee."

57. *woman, I do not know him*: Only Luke uses the vocative *gynai* here for colloquial vividness, just as he uses "Man," (*anthrōpe*) in verses 58 and 60, below. Even a gender-inclusive translation can tolerate such harmless stylistic touches, particularly when they are so nicely and deliberately balanced.

58. *another person noticed him*: In context the aorist participle *idōn* has the sense of "caught sight of him"; the substantive *heteros* is masculine, and Peter will address him as "man" (*anthrōpe*). Mark 14:69 has the same *paidiskē* (woman slave) accost him a second time, and Matt 26:71 has another woman slave (*allē*) pose the challenge; John 18:25 has "they." Note that in this challenge, Peter is not accused of being "with him," but rather of being "from among them" (*ex autōn*).

59. *about an hour later*: The fact that Luke uses a genitive absolute construction (*diastasēs hōras*) rather than the prepositional phrases of Mark 14:70 and Matt 26:73 is less significant than the fact that this is a fine example of the way the passion accounts pay much closer attention to temporal relationships than do the other parts of the Gospels.

for he is a Galilean: The charge is again Peter's association with Jesus, tipped off by his Galilean appearance or speech (cf. Matt 26:73). The connection to Galilee reminds the reader of the chilling report in 13:1-2, and points forward as well to Pilate's attempt to shuffle Jesus to Herod because of his Galilean provenance (23:6). The Galilean character of the first community in Jerusalem is emphasized by Luke (Acts 1:11; 2:7). John makes this final accusation come from someone who had seen Peter in the garden (John 18:26).

61. *turned and looked straight at Peter*: This dramatic moment is only in Luke. The verb *emblepō* means to look at someone straight in the face, as Jesus does with his audience in 20:17; here the gaze balances that of the woman slave in verse 56. The title *kyrios* ("lord") here and in the following line obviously heighten the pathos. For Luke's narrative use of the title, see the note on 7:13.

remembered the word of the Lord: The gist is the same in all three Synoptics, but Luke's use of "word of the Lord" gives a special *prophetic* coloration to the incident (for *logos tou kyriou* as the signature of the prophet, see Hos 1:1; 4:1; Amos 5:1; 7:16; Mic 1:1; 4:2; Joel 1:1; Jon 1:1; Zech 1:1; Hag 1:1; Zeph 1:1; Isa 1:10; 28:14; Jer 1:4; 2:31). The literal fulfillment of Jesus' prediction is in Luke's narrative just another of many prophecies that reach fulfillment (cf. introduction, pp. 15–17).

62. *he wept bitterly*: If the best MSS preserving this verse are correct, here is a case in which Luke and Matt 26:74 agree against Mark 14:72 in having the adverb *pikrōs* ("bitterly"). The phrase "weep bitterly" occurs in LXX Isa 22:4; 33:7 and Ezek 27:30 as a response to defeat, failure, ruin and loss.

63. *those who held Jesus*: The translation supplies the name of Jesus for clarity. For the use of *synechō*, "hold" or "surround," see 8:45; 19:43 (and the note there). Luke makes the people mocking Jesus the same as those who arrested him, therefore the leaders. In Mark 14:65 and Matt 26:67 the mocking takes place after the hearing, not before it as in Luke.

kept mocking him: The verb *empaizō* is in the imperfect, denoting continuing action. There was an precedent for such treatment of a prophet. The court prophet Zedekiah struck Micaiah (who had opposed him) on the cheek, saying, "how did the spirit of the Lord go from me and speak to you?" (1 Kgs 22:24). Captives in the ancient world were not necessarily treated with respect; see e.g., 2 Macc 7:1, 7, 13, 15; Acts 16:22-23. Luke omits the "spitting" found in Mark 14:65 and Matt 26:67, and replaces it with "beating" (*derontes*), echoing the treatment of the messengers to the vineyard (20:10-11; cf. also 12:47-48). The mocking of Jesus explicitly fulfills his prophecy of the passion in 18:32.

64. *prophesy*: The readers of course know that Jesus is the prophet who brings God's visitation, so this mockery is particularly ironic. Jesus not only knows who is striking him (in Luke's narrative it is clearly the same group that arrested him), but he has already "prophesied" that this would happen to him. It is, as we have seen repeatedly, characteristic of the leaders to reject and refuse to recognize God's prophets (7:29-30).

65. *spoke harshly against him*: The line is only in Luke, and reads literally, "they were saying many other things against him, blaspheming." The term *blasphēmeō* can mean (as in this translation) scornful or slanderous speech, but it can also bear the weightier religious sense of "blasphemy" (see 5:21; 12:10; Acts 13:45; 18:6; 19:37). In light of Luke's deliberate use of *kyrios* for Jesus in this context, the meaning of "blaspheme" may be intended. The passion prediction of 18:32 said

that the Son of Man would be "insulted," (*hybrizō*), and this passage fulfills the prophecy.

66. *board of elders of the people*: Luke's phrasing is a bit unexpected. Mark has the "council" (*symboulion*) made up of chief priests, scribes and elders (Mark 15:1; see also 14:33). Matthew also has the *symboulion* of "chief priests and elders of the people" (Matt 27:1). Luke's use of *presbyterion*, "board of elders," (see Acts 22:5; 1 Tim 4:14) is more or less in apposition to "chief priests and scribes." However awkwardly, Luke appears to mean the makeup of the Jewish Sanhedrin (*synedrion*) that ruled in religious matters under the hegemony of the empire, and was made up of elders, priests, and scribes (Josephus, *Antiquities* 12:142). For a fascinating account of the Sanhedrin's dealings with a well-known miscreant, cf. *Antiquities* 14:167-184. According to *m.Sanh.* 1:6 the full Sanhedrin was made up of seventy-one members, who sat in a semicircle (*m.Sanh.* 4:3).

67. *they said*: Luke's version is very different from that of Mark 14:55-64 and Matt 26:59-66: a) as noted above, he reverses the order of events, having this incident follow Peter's betrayal in the courtyard; b) he omits all mention of false witnesses against Jesus concerning the destruction of the Temple; these he shifts to the charges against Stephen in Acts 6:12-15; c) he has the question put to Jesus come from all of them rather than simply the chief priest (the participle *legontes* is plural). The result of these alterations is a notably spare hearing, scarcely a "trial."

are you the Messiah: Luke omits the additional epithet of Mark 14:61, "the Messiah the Son of the Blessed one," followed by Matt 26:63, "Messiah son of God." Luke separates the two titles, with the result that the charge against him by the leaders in 23:2 appears especially deceptive. Luke has been extremely careful in his use of the title "Messiah" after the infancy account (2:11, 26), using it only at 4:41 and 9:20. The reason is precisely the political ambiguity that the leaders will now exploit.

if I tell you: Jesus' answer is deflective. They obviously will not listen to an affirmative answer *on his terms*, but will insist on interpreting any claim to be "anointed one" on their own terms, as they show in the sequel; furthermore, if he tries to open a discussion, they will not answer. Communication has clearly been broken already if he has been blindfolded, beaten, and mocked as a false prophet!

69. *from now on*: As with other Lukan uses of the phrase *apo tou nyn* (1:48; 5:10; 12:52; 22:18), this does not mean an immediate change, but rather a new possibility. The use of this phrase places the next statement in the context of history rather than of eschatology.

sitting at the right hand of the power of God: The basic statement is shared with Mark 14:62 and Matt 26:64, but Luke's small alterations give it a startlingly different meaning. Like the parallels, he combines the saying about the Son of Man from Dan 7:13 with the image of one "sitting at the right hand" which derives from LXX Ps 109:1. Unlike them, however: a) Luke drops the "you will see" (which the tradition probably had derived by midrash from Zech 12:10); in Acts, only Stephen will so see the Son of Man (Acts 7:55-56); b) Luke adds "of God" to the phrase "right hand of power," which also brings this prediction more in line with Acts 7:55-56; c) Luke omits the phrase "coming on the clouds of heaven," so that the statement refers not to the "coming of the Son of Man" at the end-time (see 11:30; 12:8, 40; 17:22, 24, 26, 30; 18:8; 21:27), but to the resurrection of Jesus.

70. *are you therefore the Son of God*: Luke has "all of them" ask this. As noted above, he deliberately separates this question from that in verse 67 concerning messiahship. For Jesus as "son of God" in the narrative, see 1:32, 35; 3:22, 23; 4:3, 9, 41; 8:28; 10:22, and Acts 8:37; 9:20; 13:33. Much more explicitly than with the title "Messiah," this designation involves a special relationship with God, bringing it within the framework of possible blasphemy. According to *m.Sanh.* 7:5, the blasphemer "must pronounce the name itself," meaning the tetragrammaton. For the charge of blasphemy against Jesus because he called God his Father, see John 10:31-39.

you are saying that I am: In contrast to Mark 14:62, which has "I am," and Matt 26:64, which has Jesus respond, "you say it," Luke has Jesus answer still more equivocally: the personal pronouns "you" (*hymeis*) and "I" (*egō*) put the burden on the questioners, while not altogether denying the assertion. The reader schooled in the LXX would be delighted to find the irony of the chief priest inadvertently terming Jesus *egō eimi* (the "I am" of the revelation from the bush to Moses in Exodus 3:14, *egō eimi ho ōn*).

71. *we have ourselves heard*: Luke omits the rending of the garments by the chief priest (Mark 14:63; Matt 26:65) with the designation of Jesus' answer as "blasphemy." Indeed, Luke has already called their speech toward Jesus "blaspheming" (22:65). Rather than ask what need there is for more witnesses (since he has had none), Luke changes *martyres* to *martyria* (testimony). He omits as well the determination that Jesus was worthy of the death penalty (*enochos thanatou*) which is found in Mark 14:65; Matt 26:66.

INTERPRETATION

Precisely the same difficulties facing the reader of Luke's account of the Last Supper must be dealt with again in this passage. So important are the historical issues surrounding Jesus' death, that close attention to the narrative of each evangelist is difficult to achieve. The nagging question of "what really happened" is closely connected to the question, "who really was responsible for Jesus' death?" The present passage, which shows Jesus undergoing a hearing in front of the Sanhedrin before being handed over to the Roman prefect, has been exhaustively analyzed from the perspective of historical accuracy.

Analysis even of the most exhaustive sort does not, alas, necessarily yield certainty. Once more, the problem is not simply that the Gospels themselves differ in important details. The more serious issue is that our sources concerning the central issues of the Sanhedrin procedures, especially as they pertain to the carrying out of the death penalty, are sparse and ambiguous.

Some scholars argue that the Sanhedrin had the right to levy the death penalty for blasphemy and other religious crimes (cf. *m.Sanh.* 7:1-10), but that the penalty for these crimes was stoning (*m.Sanh.* 7:4). If Jesus was executed by the Roman penalty of crucifixion, therefore, he must have been killed for a specifically political crime, not a religious one. A further implication would be that the Jewish court had nothing to do with Jesus' death; it was the Romans who were responsible for killing him.

They further point out that the Sanhedrin was forbidden to hold capital trials on the eve of a Sabbath or a festival (*m.Sanh.* 4:2). The reason was that in cases of a guilty verdict, capital sentencing had to wait at least a full day after the verdict (*m.Sanh.* 4:2; 5:5). This suggests to some scholars that the Synoptic account of a trial at which Jesus was declared worthy of death was a fiction created to blame the Jews for the death of Jesus. Finally, they observe that the Sanhedrin rules demanded that witnesses agree, and that contradictory evidence is invalid (*m.Sanh.* 5:2); the implication, again, is that the Synoptic account is fictional.

The difficulty of judging the Gospels on the basis of these sources, however, is severe. First, the rabbinic law codes were compiled in their present form up to a hundred and fifty years after the events here described; later regulations do not necessarily correspond to earlier historical events. Second, people do not always follow their own rules, or even their own idealized version of their authority. Josephus reports on the difficulties the Sanhedrin had in another case exercising its prerogatives under a Roman prefect (*Antiquities* 20:197-207), as well as what could happen to a religious troublemaker in a tumultuous city (*Jewish War* 6:300-309). He tells us as well of the way in which a local Jewish court (*gerousia*) operated with a keen eye on Roman responses to their internal conflicts, as in the incident concerning *sicarii* (revolutionaries) in Alexandria (Josephus, *Jewish War* 7:412-413).

Even the notice in the Babylonian Talmud about the death of "Joshua" on the Passover testifies to the ambiguity of the historical situation: it claims that a period of forty days passed during which any one could defend Jesus and no one did (obviously and understandably a defensive statement against Christian charges), but it also vacillates between whether Jesus was "stoned" or "hanged" (*bT Sanh.* 43a; cf. *m.Sanh.* 6:4).

But even if all historical questions were capable of resolution, an obsessive preoccupation with them could blind us to the particular shaping of the account by each evangelist. It should be obvious that Luke had available to him neither the minutes of Jesus' hearing (if there was a hearing), nor the highly systematized rules from the Mishnah that would not find written form until a century after Luke's death. Luke had before him Mark, and possibly other traditions (from "eyewitnesses and ministers of the word," 1:2). Most of all, he had his own imaginative grasp of Jesus' significance, and it is this above all which shapes his narrative.

It is in this light that we turn to the three scenes making up this part of the passion account: the denial by Peter, the mocking of Jesus, the questions put by the council. We ask not about the facts of history but about the meaning of narrative.

The most noteworthy feature of Peter's denial is the way Luke has changed the order of events. Mark's Gospel makes a powerful literary point (found in Matthew and John as well) by alternating the scenes of Peter's denial and Jesus' nighttime confession before the chief priest. The contrast is obviously to Peter's disadvantage! Consistent with Luke's gentler treatment of the apostles (who must, after all, function as Jesus' prophetic successors after the resurrection), Peter's denial is not so vividly intertwined with the trial of Jesus. The impact is still considerable: the reader now recognizes the emptiness of Peter's boast at table (22:33), and the cowardice that the "sleep because of sorrow" signified (22:45). But most of all, the reader once more perceives Jesus as the prophet, whose predictions unfailingly come true. Indeed, Luke calls his prediction "the word of the Lord" (22:61). Consistent with this presentation is the distinctive Lukan ending of the story. Jesus had foretold that "after Peter turned" he would strengthen his brothers (22:32). Peter's restoration begins immediately after his fall, when Jesus "turns toward him" and gazes intently at him. As he is seen and known by the prophet, Peter remembers the prophet's word and recognizes the truth about himself: his bitter tears are the start of repentance.

The second scene shows us the prophet being even more directly rejected. Luke again changes the order of events. Mark and Matthew have the mocking after the condemnation of Jesus. The point of putting it first is not that this is the way it happened historically—who could know? The point is to show how the leadership of the people (and they are the ones in Luke's version who are the mockers) explicitly fulfill what was said about them throughout the narrative (see esp. 7:29-30): they reject God's prophets and God's will for them. If the reader had not realized before now that Jesus was the prophet, the closing of the Peter incident would have made it obvious. The leadership may blindfold Jesus in mockery, but it is they who are blind.

The third scene shows us the prophet being examined—challenged—by the leadership in the Sanhedrin. Luke's version is distinctive most of all for what it omits: he has no succession of false witnesses, for example, with their charge about the destruction of the Temple. He has no rending of the garments by the chief priest, or cry of blasphemy, or statement that Jesus deserves death. In fact, Luke's version is remarkably pared down. His creative shaping of the incident is found in three small but telling details.

The first is that he involves the whole Sanhedrin in the questioning:

"they" ask Jesus. The point here is that the rejection of the Prophet is not the work of the whole people (*laos*); they are sympathetic to him. But neither is it the work of the chief priest alone. The leadership that consistently opposed Jesus is involved as a whole in his final rejection. The second detail is that the questions concerning Jesus' messiahship and sonship are separated rather than combined (as in the parallels). There is a double effect: Jesus does not assent to the title Messiah, and there can be no misunderstanding of that; consequently, the charge made by the leadership before Pilate that he "called himself Messiah, a King" (23:2) is at the very least deceptive. The third detail is that Jesus' response concerning his being Son of God is answered not in terms of the parousia, but in terms of his resurrection. The leaders will not see him, but the apostles and the readers will "see Jesus" at the right hand of God.

FOR REFERENCE AND FURTHER STUDY

Blinzler, J. *The Trial of Jesus*. Westminster: Newman, 1959.
Lampe, G. W. H. "St. Peter's Denial." *BJRL* 55 (1972-73) 346-68.
Miller, D. L. "*empaizein*: Playing the Mock Game (Luke 22:63-64)." *JBL* 90 (1971) 309-313.
Neyrey, J. "The Trials of Jesus in Luke-Acts." *The Passion according to Luke: A Redaction Study of Luke's Soteriology* (New York: Paulist, 1985) 69-107.
Tyson, J. B. "The Lukan Version of the Trial of Jesus." *NovT* 3 (1959) 249-258.
Walasky, P. W. "The Trial and Death of Jesus in the Gospel of Luke." *JBL* 94 (1975) 81-93.

63. *Delivered to Prefects and Kings* (23:1-12)

1. Their whole assembly got up and led him to Pilate. 2. They began to level a charge against him. They said: "We have found this man to be leading our nation astray, and he forbids paying taxes to Caesar, and he says that he is Messiah, a king." 3. Pilate questioned him. He said, "Are you the king of the Jews?" And he answered him, "You are saying it." 4. Pilate said to the chief priests and the crowds, "I find in this man no proof of the charge." 5. So they pressed their case: "He is stirring up the people through all of Judaea by his teaching, beginning in Galilee and ending up here." 6. When Pilate heard this, he inquired whether the man was a Galilean, 7. and having determined that he belonged to Herod's jurisdiction, sent him to Herod, who was also in Jerusalem at that time. 8. Herod was very glad when he saw Jesus. He had been wanting to see him for

a long time, for he had heard about him. He hoped to see some sign performed by him. 9. He questioned him at length, but he gave no answer. 10. But the chief priests and scribes stood up and accused him vigorously. 11. Herod joined with his soldiers in treating him with contempt. They mocked him by putting a splendid robe on him, and returned him to Pilate. 12. That day Herod and Pilate became friends. They had been enemies before this.

Notes

1. *their whole assembly*: Because of the way he has arranged the order of events, Luke is able to make a quick transition to the hearing before Pilate. Mark 15:1 and Matt 27:1-2 have a further "plan" formed by the Sanhedrin. The term *plēthos* is translated here as "assembly," rather than as "multitude," because it refers to this specific group as a representative body (cf. 2:13; Acts 6:2, 5; 14:4; 15:12, 30). This leadership group has been the active agent since 22:47.

   led him to Pilate: Luke omits the detail of "binding" in Mark 15:1 and Matt 27:2. This is the first mention of the Roman prefect by name since 13:1, where the reader learned that Pilate had murdered Galileans. The prophecy that the Son of Man would be "handed over to the Gentiles" is now being fulfilled.

2. *began to level a charge*: Is literally, "accuse," using the technical legal term (see LXX Dan 6:5; 1 Macc 7:6, 25; 2 Macc 4:47; 10:13). Notice that it is brought by the leadership itself, in line with the two previous occurrences of the term in Luke's Gospel, 6:7 and 11:54. They have now "found a charge," and are using it (see also Acts 22:30; 24:2). Only Luke has this verse, which greatly intensifies his presentation of the *leaders* as responsible for Jesus' death.

   leading our nation astray: The term *diastrephō* has the nuance of perverting something or someone. The charge is similar to that made in *bT Sanh.*43a concerning Jesus.

   forbids paying taxes to Caesar: This part of the charge is manifestly a distortion of Jesus' statement in 20:25. The extent of the opposition's *panourgia* (20:23) is now becoming apparent.

   Messiah, a king: Or, "an anointed king." Although Jesus did not respond affirmatively to the question put to him, whether he was the Messiah (22:67), and that claim is never put in Jesus' mouth by the narrator, the leaders make it something that he himself is claiming. The charge does of course reflect a reality: the people did proclaim Jesus as a king (19:38), as he had spoken of himself in terms of kingship (19:11-27). But the phrasing of the charge translates the ambiguous religious/political designation "Messiah" into the politically unambiguous reduction, "king," that the Roman authorities could not utterly ignore.

3. *the king of the Jews*: Pilate's question is virtually identical in all four Gospels (Mark 15:2; Matt 27:11; John 18:33), and probably reflects some nucleus of historical fact, as does the inscription on the cross (23:38). In John, this question is part of a long discussion between Jesus and Pilate (18:29-38).

you are saying it: Is similar to Jesus' response to the Sanhedrin (22:70): not a denial but neither a straightforward acknowledgement. It is at this point in Mark 15:3 and Matt 27:12 that the parallels have the chief priests (in Matthew the elders as well) accuse Jesus, together with Pilate's query to him why he does not respond.

4. *no proof of the charge*: The term *aition* has the same legal sense as *aitia* ("cause") in Acts 10:21; 13:28; 22:24; 23:28; 25:18, 27; 28:18, 20. Pilate's statement is literally, "I have found no cause," which means that he found no evidence to support the charge as made. Notice here that the "crowd" is included in the process for the first time.

5. *they pressed their case*: Is literally, "they kept growing strong in saying." The combination of participle with imperfect creates a sense of urgency.

stirring up the people . . . teaching: The verb *anaseiō* literally means to "shake up" physically, but in this context it means to rile or work up the populace. The circumstantial participle "teaching" is taken as the means by which Jesus is creating the disturbance. This is a clever move which creates a new situation for Pilate. Whether or not Jesus claimed personally to be a king, if his teaching created unrest against Rome, he would be practicing *lèse majesté*. The more fiercely the Jewish leaders pursue this point, the more a prefect would be forced to respond. In that politically charged atmosphere, anyone encouraging such revolt could be executed simply as a warning to others. Prefects in imperial provinces such as Palestine had a rather wide discretionary power over the *ius gladii* (death penalty). No matter what the formal charge or its merits, if a situation developed that threatened public order, the prefect could eliminate the problem any way he saw fit.

beginning in Galilee and ending up here: The geographical description corresponds to the plan of Luke's narrative, suggesting that the previous phrase "all of Judaea" means the whole of Palestine ("land of the Jews"). Luke's geographical sense is not always clear to us (cf. 4:44; 17:11). In narrative terms, this statement presents Pilate both with a problem and a possible solution. The problem is the extent of the unrest Jesus is accused of creating; if this is not a local commotion at the feast, but a deliberate program of propagandizing, Pilate must take it more seriously into account. On the other hand, the mention of Galilee provides him a possible way of avoiding the issue by shifting the venue of the hearing!

7. *Herod's jurisdiction*: Is literally "authority (*exousia*) of Herod." We learned that Herod Antipas was tetrarch of Galilee in 3:3 (see also Josephus, *Jewish War* 1:664). The entire episode which follows is unique to Luke's Gospel.

in Jerusalem at that time: Josephus, *Jewish War* 2:344 mentions a "palace of the Hasmoneans" in Jerusalem, and in *Jewish War* 5:176-183 describes the magnificence of Herod's palace. "At that time" is literally "in those days," probably referring to the period of the feast (1:23; 2:43; 22:7; Acts 2:1; 20:16).

8. *Herod was very glad*: Is literally, "he rejoiced (*echarē*) exceedingly"; the fact that Herod wanted to see Jesus was established in 9:9, as was the fact that he had

"heard about him" in a confused report (9:7). He had at that time asked, "who is this about whom I am hearing" such things (9:9).

hoped to see some sign: Herod's earlier report had included the works being done through the Twelve (9:7), together with the supposition that Jesus was John the Baptist raised from the dead (9:8). Herod was undoubtedly expecting to see a thaumaturge who could perform on command. For the "seeking of a sign," see 11:16, 29-30.

9. *questioned him at length*: Is literally, "with many words." Notice that Jesus' refusal to answer is placed by Mark 15:4 and Matt 27:14 in the context of the questioning by Pilate.

10. *accused him vigorously*: The adverb *eutonōs*, like the term *epischuō* in 23:5, points to an all-out effort. The verb *katēgoreō*, "bring a charge against," is the same as was used before Pilate (23:2).

11. *treating him with contempt*: The term *exoutheneō* was used for the way the Pharisees treated others (18:9), and is used in Acts 4:11 as a variant for the citation from Ps 117:22 about the stone "despised" by the builders.

mocked him: Luke strings together participial phrases dependent on the main verb "sent him back"; the translation attempts a more idiomatic English sentence structure. The same verb *empaizō* ("mock") is used here as in 22:63, and like it helps fulfill the passion prophecy of 18:32. The clothing of Jesus in a "splendid robe" is probably a parody of kingship; cf. Acts 12:21, where Herod the king is dressed in *esthēta basilikēn*, and the characterization of the clothes of those in king's palaces (7:25). The adjective *lampros* can mean "white" or "radiant" (Acts 10:30; 26:13), but also simply "magnificent" (Jas 2:2-3), as in the adverbial form used to describe the feasting of the rich man (16:19).

12. *became friends*: Luke is unusually familiar with the conventions of friendship in the Hellenistic world (see the notes *passim* on 7:6, 34; 11:5-8; 12:4; 14:10-12; 16:9). He is undoubtedly aware that one of the axioms concerning friends is that they are equals; see Aristotle, *Nichomachean Ethics* 9, 4, 5: *philotēs isotēs*, "friendship is equality." Pilate's recognition of Herod's *exousia* ("authority")—however useful it was for himself—signified a recognition of him as "equal," and therefore capable of being a "friend."

INTERPRETATION

Hellenistic readers were accustomed to stories of noble endings for philosophers. Since the profession was an intrinsically perilous one— challenging the mighty as well as the lowly—many philosophers had the chance to show the authenticity of their teaching about virtue and self-control at a trial with their very life at issue. The tradition is given literary expression already in Plato and Xenophon, each of whom portrayed their teacher Socrates in a stirring *Apology* before the Athenian judges, demonstrating his fearlessness and philosophical composure. Even more dramatic was the response of the Stoic philosopher Zeno when called before the tyrant; according to diverse traditions, he either bit off the ear of his judge, or bit off his own tongue and spit it at the judge, rather than betray his fellow conspirators against tyranny (Diogenes Laertius, *Life of Heraclitus* 9:26). The tradition was more ambiguously present in a figure like Apollonius of Tyana, who managed to avoid a real showdown with the emperor; but the inclusion of a defense speech in his biography indicates how necessary the inclusion of such an element was considered (Philostratus, *Life of Apollonius of Tyana* 7:14).

Those schooled in Torah had no lower expectations. The image of Moses boldly confronting Pharoah was a powerful one (Exod 5-11); not less stirring was the noble courage of Daniel (Dan 5:17-28; 6:16-24). And in the Maccabbean martyrs, Jews could find unparalleled examples of fortitude and courage in the face of death, expressed with great eloquence (2 Macc 6-7; 4 Macc 5-14). This tradition also would be extended into the portrayal of the martyrdom of Rabbi Aqiba in the Bar Kochba revolt (*bT Ber.* 61b).

Measured against this literary standard, the Gospels' portrayal of Jesus' death could only be perceived as disappointing. Jesus makes no long defense of his actions or philosophy. He makes no dramatic gesture of contempt toward his judges. He was for the most part silent. And although taciturnity was highly regarded by the ancients in some contexts, it was expected of a philosopher to give expression in some fashion, verbal or symbolic, to his convictions at the end. Testimony to this perception is given by the pagan critic of Christianity Celsus, who in his *True Word* (an extended attack on Christianity) criticized this very silence by Jesus (Origen, *Against Celsus* 2:35).

Within the early Christian community, of course, Jesus' silence (which surely had a historical basis, otherwise it would present no problem requiring interpretation) was understood in light of the Suffering Servant of Isa 53:7: "He was oppressed and he was afflicted, yet he opened not his mouth; like a lamb that is led to the slaughter, and like a sheep that before its shearers is dumb, so he opened not his mouth" (see 1 Pet 2:22-25).

Luke explicitly builds on this interpretation by citing this very passage from Isa 53:7 in Acts 8:32-35 as the basis for preaching Jesus. It is a good sign of Luke's deepest allegiance that despite his sensitivity to Hellenistic cultural norms (nowhere more obvious than in his delicate portrayal of Herod and Pilate in this section) and his shading of the portrayal of Jesus in the direction of a *sophos* elsewhere in the passion account, he remains so close to his source in this scene, resisting the temptation to elaborate a defense speech for Jesus.

The main Lukan shaping of this section is found in his addition of the hearing before Herod, and in his portrayal of the Jewish leaders. Herod had played a role earlier in the narrative that foreshadowed this passion account (9:7-9; 13:31-33). His role in the trial sequence is found only in Luke, and serves several literary functions. It shows how the Scriptures were fulfilled concerning "God's anointed" as the interpretation of Ps 2:1-2 in Acts 4:25 indicates: "both Herod and Pontius Pilate, with the Gentiles and the peoples of Israel" gathered together "against your holy servant Jesus whom you anointed" (Acts 4:27). Together with the hearing before Pilate, it also fulfills the prophecy of Jesus about the suffering of the Son of Man, that he would "be delivered to the Gentiles, mocked and shamefully treated" (18:32), since it is above all Herod who mocks and abuses Jesus. The mockery of Jesus, particularly his being dressed in a splendid robe, continues the parodic rejection of the claims made for him in the narrative, that he is prophet and king. None of those "seated upon thrones" accept the rule of God that he announces (Luke 1:52). At the same time, Herod also helps to certify Jesus' innocence of the charge brought against him, since despite extensive questioning (23:9) he finds nothing deserving of punishment more severe than mockery. Pilate will later cite Herod's sending Jesus back to him as evidence that he had found him innocent (23:15).

Most of all, the behavior of Pilate and Herod alike throw into even greater relief the malice and deception of the Jewish leaders who are intent on getting rid of Jesus. Three aspects of Luke's depiction are striking. The first is that the charges brought against Jesus before Pilate are plainly deceptive. The title of Messiah, which Jesus refused to acknowledge unequivocally before the Sanhedrin (22:67), is not only reported as his own claim but is cast in its politically most dangerous form: Messiah, a king (23:2). The report that he forbade payment of taxes to Caesar is a plain lie (20:25). And when these fail to persuade Pilate, they invoke the charge that he "stirs up the people," clearly to force Pilate's hand as keeper of the imperial order (23:5).

The second aspect of Luke's portrayal of the Jewish leaders is by way of contrast to Pilate and Herod. Luke has introduced both to the reader earlier in the narrative. Each was mentioned in particularly and arbitrarily murderous contexts. Herod acknowledged beheading John the Baptist (9:9). Pilate was described as the murderer of Galileans (13:1-2). But now, they are astonishingly reluctant to murder Jesus when they have the legal opportunity to do so! Pilate finds nothing to support the charge (23:4) and avoids the leaders' importunateness by shifting Jesus over to Herod. And Herod does nothing but mock him. At this point, the reader should remember the difficult passage in 13:31, and the debate whether the Pharisees were being helpful to Jesus or not. The present passage tells us that they were lying then when they told Jesus, "Herod seeks to kill you," for now, when he has every opportunity—and the plain permission of the prefect—he does nothing of the sort.

This brings us to the final aspect of Luke's portrayal of the Jewish leaders, which is their insistence. When their first charge against Jesus fails, they "press their case" (23:5) and shift to the more generalized and dangerous accusation of causing insurrection. When Jesus is brought before Herod and after Herod's lengthy questioning yields no reason to punish him, the leaders then "stand up and accuse him vigorously" (23:10). Finally, as we shall see in the next section, they will carry the crowd with them in a violent rejection of Jesus (23:18-23).

FOR REFERENCE AND FURTHER STUDY

Creed, J. M. "The Supposed 'Proto-Luke' Narrative of the Trial before Pilate: A Rejoinder." *ExpT* 46 (1934-35) 378-379.

Dibelius, M. "Herodes und Pilatus." *ZNW* 16 (1915) 113-126.

Sherwin-White, A. N. "The Trial of Christ in the Synoptic Gospels." *Roman Society and Roman Law in the New Testament* (Oxford: Clarendon, 1963) 24-47.

Soards, M. L. "Tradition, Composition and Theology in Luke's Account of Jesus before Herod Antipas." *Bib* 66 (1985) 344-364.

Verral, A. W. "Christ before Herod (Luke xxiii, 1-16)." *JBL* 10 (1908-9) 321-353.

64. *Condemnation to Death* (23:13-31)

13. Pilate called together the chief priests and the rulers and all the people. 14. He said to them, "You brought me this man as one who was leading the people astray. Now look, I have examined him in your presence. I have found in this man no basis for the things you charge him with. 15. But neither did Herod, for he sent him back to us! And look, nothing deserving of death has been done by him. 16. After disciplining him, therefore, I will release him." 17, 18. And the whole assembly cried out. They said, "Take away this man! Release Barabbas to us!" 19. (He had been thrown in prison because of a certain disturbance in the city, and murder.) 20. But again Pilate cried out to them. He wanted to release Jesus. 21. But they kept calling out, "Crucify! Crucify him!" 22. Still a third time he said to them, "What evil thing has this man done? I have found in him no basis for the death sentence. I will therefore discipline him and release him." 23. But they kept insisting, demanding with loud roars that he be crucified. And their cries grew even louder. 24. Pilate decided that what they demanded should be done. 25. He released the man imprisoned because of riot and murder for whom they asked. But Jesus he handed over to their will. 26. As they led him away, they seized Simon, a certain Cyrenean, as he was coming from

the field. They put the cross on him to carry behind Jesus. 27. A great gathering of the people was following him. There were also women beating their breasts and wailing for him. 28. Jesus turned toward the women. He said, "Daughters of Jerusalem! Stop weeping over me. Weep instead over yourselves and over your children. 29. For, look! Days are coming when people will say, 'Blessed are the barren and the wombs that have not born children and the breasts that have not fed them!' 30. Then people will start to say to the mountains, 'Fall on us!' And they will say to the hills, 'Cover us!' 31. For if they are doing these things in the green wood, what will happen in the dry wood?"

NOTES

13. *chief priests . . . rulers . . . all the people*: Pilate now holds an open-air hearing. He intends it to be an announcement of his decision and a dismissal. But the crowd turns it into another sort of situation. The presence of "the people" (*ho laos*) at this place is surprising, since otherwise Luke has worked so hard to remove them from participation in the proceedings against Jesus. There is no MS support for a suggested emendation to "leaders of the people," but the mere attempt indicates how striking and bothersome this exception is. Because of it, the outcry in verse 18 should probably be read as including the people as well. Certainly, despite his redactional efforts, Luke recognizes the tradition that the populace had some role to play in Jesus' death, since he reports it in Acts 2:23; 3:13-14, even while mitigating it by the theme of "ignorance" (Acts 3:17).

14. *leading the people astray*: This announcement by Pilate in which he summarizes the charge, is unique to Luke. He alters the *diastrephonta* to *apostrephonta*, and *ethnos* to *laos*, but otherwise faithfully repeats the substance of 23:2. The notion of "leading the people astray" is found frequently in the OT, associated especially with idolatry and the teachings of false prophets (see Exod 5:4; Num 15:39; Ezek 13:18, 22).

    no basis for the things you charge him with: Luke again uses *aition* ("cause") as in 23:4, but this time connects it to the charges they have brought (*hōn katēgoreite kat'autou*). Pilate's failure to "find" (*heuron*) contradicts their "we have found" in 23:2.

15. *sent him back to us*: The prefect uses the royal plural. The connective "for" (*gar*) is in this case significant: the fact that Herod sent Jesus back is taken as proof that he had no reason to put Jesus to death, either.

    nothing deserving of death has been done by him: This represents still another expansion from 23:4 and 14, and introduces the first mention of "death" into Luke's account (he has omitted that statement by the Sanhedrin).

16. *after disciplining him*: The term *paideuō* (literally, "educate") here and in 23:22 refers to a disciplinary action such as whipping (see 1 Kgs 12:11, 14; 2 Chr 14:12; 2 Cor 6:9), intended by Pilate to be the full punishment rather than as a prelude to crucifixion. For such flogging as a possible consequence of a philosopher's life, see Epictetus, *Discourses* 3, 22, 54–56.

I will release him: Since under examination he was found guiltless of the charge brought against him, this is the proper move. In some MSS another verse is here inserted (v. 17): "he was required to release to them one person on the feast." Although there is good external attestation for the verse, the oldest and best MSS omit it, and the MSS including it have significant variations in wording as well as in placement. It may have been a gloss borrowed from Mark 15:6 and Mt 27:15 inserted into the text to explain the cry for release in verse 18. For a similar example, cf. the expansion of John 5:3.

18. *the whole assembly cried out*: Luke uses *panplēthei* adverbially: literally, "as a whole crowd." Does he intend the *plēthos* here to mean the assembly of the leaders, as in 23:1? Possibly, but see the note on 23:13.

   release Barabbas to us: in Aramaic, the name means "son of the father"; it occurs in the NT only in this part of the Gospel narrative (Mark 15:7-15; Matt 27:16-26; John 18:40), and nothing is known about him apart from it. Matt 27:16 calls him a "notable prisoner." John identifies him as a *lēstēs* (see the note on Luke 22:52). Mark says he was "with rebels who committed murder in the riot (*stasis*)" (Mark 15:7). Luke makes the reference less specific, perhaps with an interest in minimizing the political overtones of any upset created in the city by Jesus. He acknowledges that Barabbas committed murder (*phonos*), but separates this from "a certain disturbance." The fact that Barabbas was a murderer is repeated in 23:25, and is taken up by the kerygmatic statement in Acts 3:14.

21. *crucify him*: Luke uses the present imperative of *stauroō* rather than the aorist of Mark 15:13. The verb occurs in the OT only in LXX Esther 7:9; 8:13. It was a typical though not exclusively Roman means of execution (see Petronius, *Satyricon* 111; Josephus, *Jewish War* 5:449; *Antiquities* 17:295); it was also practiced by non-Romans (Josephus, *Jewish War* 1:97). It has often been asserted that the Jews did not practice crucifixion, but the contemporary evidence is not altogether clear on the point (cf. Josephus, *Antiquities* 13:381). Certainly, the Mishnah tractate *Sanhedrin* speaks of certain crimes being punished by "hanging on a tree," but this refers to the corpses of those previously stoned (*m.Sanh.* 6:4). At Qumran, the difficult passage in *4QpNah* 3–4 appears to condemn those who "hang men alive [a thing never done] formerly in Israel," but the condemnation itself may serve as evidence for the practice among those "who seek smooth things" (the opponents of the sect). The evidence in the Qumran *Temple Scroll* 64:7-12 is also ambiguous.

22. *still a third time*: The translation renders the conjunction *de* as "still" in order to follow Luke's emphasis on "third." In this last attempt at placating the crowd, Pilate asks what evil thing (*kakon*) Jesus had done—now there is no legal charge, just *any* reason for his being killed. The phrase "no basis for the death sentence" is literally "no cause for death" (*ouden aition thanatou*).

23. *kept insisting*: Luke uses the imperfect tense of *epikeimai*, "to be urgent," "press upon" (see 5:1; Acts 27:20). The participle of *aiteō* is therefore translated as "demand" rather than "ask." Likewise, the noun *phōnē* is translated as "roar" and "cry" according to the sense given by this riotous context.

25. *released the man . . . for whom they asked*: Luke repeats that he was a rioter and murderer. In Acts 3:13-14, this sequence is used as an accusation against the whole populace: "whom you delivered up and denied in the presence of Pilate, when he had decided to release him. But you denied the holy and righteous one and asked for a murderer to be granted to you." It should be noted as well that Luke omits the mocking by the soldiers that is included by Mark 15:16-20; Matt 27:27-31; John 19:2-3. Remarkably, this omission has the effect of making the Jews themselves appear as the ones who carry Jesus off to crucifixion rather than the Roman soldiers in 23:26. Pilate has capitulated to what has become a mob action.

26. *a certain Cyrenean*: Luke retains the detail from Mark 15:20 that Simon was coming from the field, but omits the fact that he was the father of Alexander and Rufus. Cyrene in North Africa was a major center of Judaism in the first century (Josephus, *Jewish War* 7:437-450). Luke shows Jews from Cyrene present in Jerusalem at Pentecost (Acts 2:10), as among those opposing Stephen (Acts 6:9), and active as Christian missionaries in Antioch (Acts 11:20; 13:1).

    to carry behind Jesus: By using the present infinitive of *pherein* and by adding the words "behind Jesus" (*opisthen Iēsou*), Luke subtly alters Mark 15:20 (in the aorist tense) from a flat historical report to a lesson in discipleship (cf. Luke 9:23; 14:27).

27. *a great gathering of the people*: For the possible translations of *plēthos* ("multitude"), cf. 23:1. Here, "the people" (*ho laos*) provide a contrast to those who have agitated for Jesus' death.

    there were also women: The translation breaks an awkward Greek sentence into two. The response of women to Jesus has been highlighted throughout the narrative, since they are included in a special way among the outcast of the people (4:39; 7:11-17, 36-50; 8:43-56; 10:38-42; 11:27-28; 13:10-17; 21:1-4). For beating the breast as a sign of sorrow, see 8:52; 18:13; 23:48; for "wailing" (*thrēnein*), see Judg 11:40; Joel 1:5, 8; Zech 1:11; Lam 1:1; Ezek 8:14. The combination of "beating breast and wailing" is found in Mic 1:8. See also Luke 7:32; John 16:20.

28. *turned toward the women*: The use of the aorist participle *strapheis* here is precisely the same as in 22:61, where Jesus "turns to" Peter.

    daughters of Jerusalem: Is an idiom equivalent to "sons of Abraham," that is, "women inhabitants of Jerusalem." In biblical literature, however, the "daughters of Zion" or "daughters of Jerusalem" came to represent the city itself, as is the case here (e.g., LXX Ps 9:14; 72:28; Mic 1:8, 13, 15; 4:8, 10; Zech 3:14; Zeph 2:10; 9:9; Isa 6:23; 16:1; 62:11; Jer 6:2). Once more, Luke makes Jesus' speech prophetic even in its form.

    weep . . . over yourselves . . . your children: For weeping in Jerusalem, see Joel 1:5; 2:17; Isa 30:19; Jer 9:1; Lam 1:2. Jesus had wept over the city in 19:41, contemplating its fate because it would reject him. The present statement is a reprise of the earlier one: Now the time of reversal is near. Those who were involved in the rejection will themselves face disaster, and it will spill over onto all the city's inhabitants. As in any such catastrophe, women and children are the most vulnerable not only physically but also because of their emotional ties.

29. *days are coming*: We recognize Luke's characteristic prophetic introduction (see 5:35; 17:22; 21:6), and are reminded in particular of the laments over the city in 13:35 and 19:43.

    blessed are the barren: This is a deeply bitter rendition of the macarism (*makarioi*, see the note on 6:20): the objective woes will be so great that happiness will consist simply in avoiding them. Notice how this saying exactly reverses the macarism of the woman from the crowd in 11:27, "blessed is the womb that bore you and the breasts that fed you." Sterility and barrenness are classic expressions of failure and of God's disfavor rather than blessing (see Gen 15:2; 16:1-6; 1 Sam 1:2-11; and Luke 1:25). For a tradition in which having children is the quintessential blessing of God (Gen 15:5; Deut 30:5-10), a situation in which the barren are blessed is indeed grievous. For the fate of women and children in times of siege and warfare, see the note on 19:44.

30. *say to the mountains, fall on us*: This is a citation from the LXX of Hos 10:8, except that the substantives are reversed. Hosea has "hills fall on us, mountains cover us." The line in the prophet occurs in the context of a prediction of punishment for Israel (and in particular of Samaria) for idolatry. The same text from Hosea is used (with still further variation) in Rev 6:16, in the context of divine wrath. The point seems to be that those in the siege would find it better to be killed quickly by avalanche than to face the terrible slow sufferings of starvation.

31. *doing these things in the green wood*: The saying is parabolic, but the meaning is clear. The green wood means the present time and circumstances, the dry wood is the future circumstances of the city. If the people of Jerusalem (that is, its leaders) are capable of such violence against a prophet of peace now, what will they be capable of in the future when the city is under siege by the Romans? Indeed, Josephus reports terrible events in those circumstances (e.g., *Jewish War* 4:326-333; 5:420-438).

INTERPRETATION

This section of Luke's narrative carries the reader from the brief moment of Jesus' encounter with the political powers (the Sanhedrin hearing, the questioning by Pilate and Herod) to the even briefer moment of his death on the cross, a transition in which the major themes running through Luke's account of the passion are clearly stated.

The first theme is that of Jesus' innocence. Pilate had already declared Jesus innocent of the original charge (23:4). Now, in this open-air meeting before the crowd, Luke has him repeat that declaration twice more (23:13, 22), so that the Roman prefect officially declares Jesus' innocence three times. Each declaration, furthermore, becomes ever more general. The first declares him innocent of the charge brought by the Jews. The second declares him innocent of leading the people astray. The third declares him innocent of any wrongdoing deserving of death, and is introduced by the almost plain-tive question, "what evil thing has he done?" In addition to his own decla-rations, Pilate reports the implication of Herod's sending Jesus back to him: this too is a sign of Jesus' innocence (23:15). Pilate wants only to "discipline" Jesus and dismiss him (23:16, 22). It is the turbulent insistence of the crowd that drives him to "hand over Jesus to their will" (23:25).

This threefold declaration of innocence by the Roman authorities is im-portant not only for Christian apologetic purposes (neither Jesus nor the messianic movement has the political goal of overthrowing Rome and this was recognized from the beginning by the authorities on the spot), but also for the Christian self-understanding of Jesus as the suffering righteous one, whose death is not one of punishment for his own crimes but one of sacri-fice for others. It also throws into even greater relief the second major Lukan theme: the responsibility of the Jews for Jesus' death.

We have seen how Luke has shaded the narrative so that the major re-sponsibility for the proceedings against Jesus falls on the leadership that has opposed him from the beginning. He cannot, however, completely change the tradition of the people's involvement. In Acts 3:13-14, the re-sponsibility of the people as a whole is emphasized, even though it is ex-cused on the grounds of "ignorance" (Acts 3:17). In the present scene, it is just possible that Luke intends the reader to continue to see the leaders as the main actors, as they have been up to this point. Certainly, they are the ones who bring the charge against Jesus, and twist it into an ever more provocative form (23:2-5). But in the last analysis, it seems clear that Luke involves the people at least passively (23:13). Indeed, in Acts 3:13-14, their desire to have released to them a murderer rather than the "pioneer of life" (Acts 3:15) forms the basis for the call to their repentance. What is more, by eliminating the account of the Roman soldiers mocking Jesus after his sentencing, Luke creates the effect that the Jews themselves take away Jesus to be killed "by their will" (23:25-26).

Yet the theme of the division within the people continues despite that critical scene. Immediately as Jesus is put on his way to the place of death, Luke shows us another dimension. A Jew from the Diaspora, Simon of Cyrene, has the cross put on him to "carry after Jesus," and Luke's word-ing unmistakably identifies this as an act of discipleship (cf. 9:23). Further-more, there is a great crowd of "the people" (*ho laos*) whom Luke has always portrayed as positive in their response to the Prophet. They "follow" (*akoloutheō*) Jesus (23:27), another term that suggests discipleship (see Luke 5:11, 27, 28; 9:11, 23, 49, 57, 59, 61; 18:22, 28, 43; 22:39, 54). Finally, there is the group of women, who have also been consistently positive in their response to the Prophet, and who now "beat their breasts and wail over him" (23:27). Although Jesus delivers his prophecy to them, it is clear that they are not to be seen as the perpetrators but as the victims of violence.

Finally, Luke continues to portray Jesus as the sage and prophet. Even as he goes toward his death, he can "turn toward" the women and deliver his somber prediction; he is capable even in this moment of greatest vulnerability to perceive the larger meaning of events and declare them: the violence done to him the messenger of peace, will be visited on those who do this violence, and in such terrible fashion that even the innocent will suffer as a result.

For Reference and Further Study

Karris, R. *Luke: Artist and Theologian; Luke's Passion Account As Literature* (New York: Paulist, 1985) 5–46.

Käser, W. "Exegetische und Theologische Erwägungen zur Seligpreisung der Kinderlosen, Lk 23:29b." *ZNW* 54 (1963) 240–254.

Neyrey, J. "The Trials of Jesus in Luke-Acts," and "Jesus' Address to the Women of Jerusalem." *The Passion according to Luke: A Redaction Study of Luke's Soteriology* (New York: Paulist, 1985) 69–107, 108–128.

Rau, G. "Das Volk in der lukanischen Passionsgeschichte, eine Konjektur zu Lc 23:13." *ZNW* 56 (1965) 41–51.

Soards, M. L. "Tradition, Composition, and Theology in Jesus' Speech to the 'Daughters of Jerusalem,' (Luke 23:26-32)." *Bib* 68 (1967) 221–244.

65. The Death of the Prophet (23:32-46)

32. They took two other criminals along with him to be executed. 33. When they came to the place called Skull, they crucified him there, and the criminals, one on the right side the other on the left. 34. Jesus said, "Father, forgive them, for they don't know what they are doing." They cast lots in order to divide up his garments. 35. The people stood watching. But the leaders kept mocking. They said, "He saved others. Let him save himself if this is God's Messiah, the elect one!" 36. The soldiers also approached and mocked him. They offered him vinegar 37. and said, "If you are the king of the Jews, save yourself!" 38. There was indeed even an inscription over him: "This is the King of the Jews." 39. One of the criminals who was crucified was speaking to him abusively. He said, "Aren't you the Messiah? Save yourself and us!" 40. But the other responded by rebuking him. He said, "Don't you even fear God? For you are under the same sentence! 41. In our case, it is just, for we are receiving what we deserve for our actions. But this man has done nothing wrong." 42. And he said, "Jesus, remember me when you enter your kingdom!" 43. He told him, "Amen, I say to you, you will be with me in paradise today." 44. It was already

about the sixth hour, and darkness was over the whole land until the ninth hour, 45. because the sun failed. And the curtain of the sanctuary was split down the middle. 46. Crying out with a loud voice, Jesus said, "Father, into your hands I entrust my spirit." When he said this, he died.

NOTES

32. *two other criminals*: The term *kakourgos* is generic, meaning one who is a malefactor, especially under the law. It occurs in Esth 8:13; Prov 21:15; Sir 11:13. Luke typically prepares for the scene on the cross by interjecting this identifying notice. In Mark 15:27 and Matt 27:38, the men are called *lēstai* ("bandit/revolutionary"), a term foresworn by Jesus in Luke 22:52, and one Luke apparently wanted to avoid in any connection with Jesus.

33. *place called Skull*: Luke omits the Semitic equivalent (John 19:17, "in Hebrew"), Golgotha (Mark 15:22; Matt 27:33), just as he had the name Gethsemane. The nickname for the place probably derived from its physical shape.

    crucified him there: Luke omits the giving of wine mixed with myrrh that is found (with some variation) in Mark 15:23 and Matt 27:34. All of the evangelists are extremely brief in this most terrible part of the story, in sharp contrast to the graphic descriptions of religious martyrs already popular in Judaism (e.g., 2 Macc 7:3-19). Crucifixion was considered one of the worst possible forms of execution (Josephus, *Jewish War* 7:203), since it combined torture (the wrenching of the limbs, even when roped rather than nailed—as Jesus was according to John 20:25 although the Synoptics do not mention it), and slow asphyxiation caused by the inability—because of pain and fatigue—to draw the body up and fill the lungs with air.

34. *Father, forgive them*: The verse is missing in important MSS, and appears to interrupt the flow of the narrative. If the issue of its inclusion were to be decided on thematic grounds, however, there is every reason to consider it authentic: a) it confirms the image of Jesus as *sophos* who demonstrates virtue until the very end of his life; b) it matches Luke's version of the Lord's Prayer (11:4); c) it fits within Luke's narrative schema: in the time of the prophet's first sending the people reject him because of their "ignorance" (Acts 3:17; 7:25; 13:27); d) it establishes in Jesus' own practice the legitimation for the proclamation of "repentance for the forgiveness of sins" which describes the apostolic mission (24:47; Acts 2:38; 5:31; 10:43; 13:38; 26:18).

    to divide up his garments: Luke uses the participle *diamerizomenoi* to express purpose, in an allusion to LXX Ps 21:19 which is extensively employed by the Synoptics for their interpretation of Jesus' death, though less in Luke than in the others (cf. Mark 15:24, 29, 34). The psalm describes a righteous person unjustly afflicted by enemies who in the end is vindicated by God. Compared to Mark 15:22-26, Luke shortens the allusion and also omits the phrase "who would get them." For the "casting of lots" see Acts 1:17, 26.

35. *the people stood watching*: Luke distinguishes carefully between the response of the *laos* and the leaders. The people do *not* actively mock Jesus. In 23:48, Luke describes the crowds as having come "for the spectacle," and will indicate that they repent. In contrast, Mark 15:29 has "the passers-by blaspheming" Jesus (as does Matt 27:39).

but the leaders kept mocking: In contrast to the people, the leaders (*archontes*) actively mock Jesus. Luke heightens the contrast by using an emphatic *kai* which is almost untranslatable. The term used for mocking (*ekmykterizō*) is the same attributed to the Pharisees in 16:14. Mark 15:31 and Matt 27:41 specify the members of the Sanhedrin (in Mark, "chief priests/scribes," and Matthew adds "elders"), but neither distinguishes their response from that of the people as Luke so carefully does.

saved others . . . save himself: Mark 15:31 and Matt 27:42 have, "he *cannot* save himself." In Luke, we are reminded of the proverb quoted by Jesus in Nazareth, "Doctor, heal yourself" (4:23). After all Jesus has said and done, the same gibe is made. This is the first of three slurs involving "saving" (cf. vv. 36, 39). The reader knows the truth of the statement, "he saved others" (7:50; 8:48; 17:19; 18:42), and that he is "Savior" (2:11; Acts 5:31; 13:23), but knows as well that those he saved were saved "by faith," as is Jesus himself in these last moments. But the leaders in the narrative think only in terms of physical survival.

God's Messiah, the elect one: In contrast to Mark 15:32, which has "Messiah king of Israel," and Matt 27:42, which has "king of Israel," Luke uses the same phrasing as in Peter's confession, "Messiah of God" (*christos tou theou*). Rather than the designation "king" which will be picked up in the next slur, Luke adds *ho eklektos* ("the elect one"), which echoes the voice at the transfiguration (*ho eklelegmenos*). For the background of the term, see the note on 9:35. Mark and Matthew add the challenge to come down from the cross so that they might believe in him.

36. *soldiers also . . . mocked*: Luke eliminated the mocking of Jesus by soldiers after his sentencing, as well as the flogging (cf. Mark 15:16-20; Matt 27:27-31). So he includes this bit of tradition here. The offering of vinegar (*oxos*, actually a sour wine, Num 6:3) forms an allusion to LXX Ps 68:22, "In my thirst they gave me vinegar to drink," although the allusion is less obviously intentional in Luke than in Mark 15:35-36 (Matt 27:47-48). In Luke, the gesture could function as a parody of the kingly table at which the disciples shared the cup (Luke 22:17, 29-30).

37. *if you are the king of the Jews*: Their cry picks up from the *epigraphē* calling Jesus that (in the next verse), and forms the second challenge to save himself (cf. v. 35).

38. *indeed even an inscription*: The translation tries to do justice to the combination of *de kai* in connection with the soldier's taunt in the previous verse, which the inscription seems to have motivated. The *epigraphē* was a standard element of an execution (Suetonius, *Life of Caligula* 32:2). Luke follows Mark 15:26 in calling it an *epigraphē*, whereas Matt 27:37 is more periphrastic. John 19:19 says that Pilate wrote the charge, creating the occasion for a debate with the Jews as to its appropriateness (John 19:20-22), as well as the information that it was writ-

ten in Hebrew, Latin, and Greek. This last element filtered into the Lukan MSS tradition, but has little to recommend it as part of Luke's original text.

this is the King of the Jews: All the Gospels have this as the charge with some small variations: John 19:19 has "Jesus the Nazorean, the King of the Jews." Mark 15:26 has, "the King of the Jews." Matt 27:37: "this is Jesus the King of the Jews." Luke's version is closest to Mark's, except for sharing with Matthew the demonstrative "this" (*houtos*), albeit at the end rather than at the beginning. Why would Pilate place such a charge if he had declared Jesus was not guilty of it? Three reasons suggest themselves: a) to protect himself from the later charge that he had merely given way to a mob's desire; b) to mock Jesus in order to please the Jewish leadership; c) to provide a warning against any other would-be revolutionaries against the empire: "this is what happens to those calling themselves King of the Jews."

39. *speaking to him abusively*: Mark 15:32b and Matt 27:44 note only that 'those (Matthew "bandits") crucified with him were reviling him." Luke expands this into a distinctive account (vv. 39-43). The numerous textual variants for the passage as well as *The Gospel of Peter* 10–16 show an even further expansion of the tradition.

save yourself and us: Like the leaders, the criminal assumes a connection between being Messiah and the ability to "save/liberate." Understandably, the executed man's own interest is more personal.

40. *under the same sentence*: The word *krima* can mean "judgment" or "sentence," so that this statement can be read at two levels: they are all three suffering under the same sentence of death, but at the same time they are all three under God's judgment as they face death. "Fear God" is therefore appropriate. The rebuke is a call to authentic acceptance of his own destiny and need for decision, rather than a distancing and alienating sarcasm.

41. *this man has done nothing wrong*: This is now the fourth declaration of Jesus' innocence (cf. 23:13-23), made by a wrongdoer who can contrast his own deeds for which the death penalty is deserved, and the lack of wrongdoing (*atopos* = "out of place") in Jesus.

42. *remember me when you enter your kingdom*: For the understanding of "remember," here, see the note on 22:19. Two of the textual variants point toward the eschaton: one has the criminal asking Jesus to remember him "when you come in your kingdom," and another, "remember me in the day of your coming." In a sense the criminal utters a version of the Lord's Prayer, "Your kingdom come" (11:4). The use of the personal name "Jesus" is striking; it is used otherwise in Luke only by demoniacs or others seeking healing (4:34; 8:28; 17:13; 18:38). The name itself, of course, means "the Lord saves."

43. *be with me in paradise today*: For "today" (*sēmeron*) compare 2:11; 4:21; 5:26; 13:32-33; 19:9; 22:34, 61; in each case, the word signifies a special moment of revelation or salvation. What is meant by "paradise" (*paradeisos*)? This is one of only three uses in the NT. Both 2 Cor 12:4 and Rev 2:7 refer to the garden prepared by God for the first humans (Gen 2:8), the most noteworthy feature of which was the "tree of life" (Gen 2:9). It was a garden of joy and pleasure

(*tryphē*, Gen 2:15). Other references to *paradeisos* in the LXX derive from this original meaning. Before the catastrophe, Sodom was "like the *paradeisos* of God" (Gen 13:10). Balaam's view of Israel was as a "*paradeisos* upon the river" (Num 24:6). See also Cant 4:13; Sir 24:30; 40:17, 27; Joel 2:3; Isa 1:30; Ezek 28:30; 31:8-9. Isaiah begins to image the restoration of the people in terms of "paradise." See Isa 51:3, "he will make her wilderness like *paradeisos*" (cf. also Ezek 31:8-9). This future reference is highly developed in Jewish literature contemporaneous with and later than the Gospels (e.g., *Testament of Levi* 18:10-14; *Psalms of Solomon* 14:2; *1 Enoch* 60:8; 61:12; *Leviticus Rabbah* XXVI, 7). A remarkable passage in *bT Ber.* 12b, in discussing forgiveness, says, "How do we know that heaven had forgiven him (i.e., Saul)? Because it says, 'And Samuel said . . . Tomorrow shalt thou and thy sons be with me' and R. Johanan said, 'with me' means in my compartment in paradise."

45. *because the sun failed*: The time span is the same as in Mark 15:33 and Matt 27:45. Luke adds the genitive absolute to account for the darkness. The verb *ekleipō* ("fail/run out") is used in the same sense as in 16:9 and 22:32. Some MSS replace it with "and the sun was darkened."

curtain of the sanctuary was split down the middle: This is the second wonder accompanying the death of Jesus. The problem is determining what Luke understands it to mean. Mark 15:38 has the specification, "from the top to the bottom," while Matt 27:51 combines "in two" and "from top to bottom." All three use the word *naos* rather than *ieron*, indicating that it is the sanctuary and not just the Temple precincts that is meant (cf. 1:9, 21, 22). If we knew which curtain Luke had in mind, determining the significance might be easier. There was a curtain before the holy place (Exod 26:36; Josephus, *Jewish War* 5:212) and also one separating the holy place from the "holy of holies" (Exod 26:31-33; Josephus, *Jewish War* 5:219). All of these are possible: a) the rending of the veil signifies the punishment to come to the Temple because of the rejection of the Prophet (13:35; 19:44; 21:6); b) the rending of the veil signifies the end of the old covenant of atonement through animal sacrifice and the beginning of the "new covenant in the blood poured out" for them (22:20; cf. Heb 9:11-14, 23-28); c) the rending of the veil could symbolize the end of the division separating Jew and Gentile, giving all equal access to God (cf. Eph 2:14-21). It is impossible to decide whether Luke had any or all of these in mind.

46. *into your hands I entrust my spirit*: Luke omits the frantic action around the cross in these last moments, and the cry of desolation from LXX Ps 21:1, "My God, My God, why have you forsaken me" (Mark 15:34-37; Matt 27:46- 49). Jesus cries with a "loud voice" (as in Mark 15:37; Matt 27:50), but his final word is a citation from LXX Ps 30:6. Psalm 30 equally portrays the rejection of the righteous one by adversaries (11-18, 22), but breathes throughout a quiet confidence in God's saving power. It concludes, "have courage and let your hearts take strength, all you who hope in the Lord (30:25). In the verse cited by Jesus, "hands" obviously refers to God's "power" (see the note on 22:21), into which Jesus entrusts (*paratithēmi*) his life (see 12:48; Acts 14:23, and esp. 20:32). In *bT Ber.* 5a, this verse from the psalm is cited as the sort of "verse of supplication" that even a scholar should recite on the deathbed.

when he said this, he died: Is literally, "he expired" (*exepneusen*), following Mark 15:37. Matt 27:51 has "he gave up the spirit," and John 19:30, "handed over the spirit." The verb *ekpneuō* can mean simply "exhale" but is used for the "last breath" as well. It does not occur in the LXX. The significant thing about Luke's phrasing is that it emphasizes Jesus' self-control. He says his prayer, then he dies.

INTERPRETATION

In his description of Jesus' death, Luke continues to shape the tradition in a distinctive fashion, exercising much more liberty with his Markan source than Matthew does. His changes, furthermore, serve to advance major themes of his entire work.

It is immediately striking, for example, that he so carefully distinguishes the leaders of the people and the soldiers, who actively mock Jesus, and the people, who only stand watching. Even at this point of the prophet's rejection, and even in the face of the tradition that involves all of the people in the proceedings, Luke struggles to maintain the division within the people. In fact, he exploits the presence of two other criminals being executed to make that division even more dramatic: one of the criminals joins the leaders and the soldiers in their mockery of him. But the other makes a confession of faith and asks to be remembered in Jesus' kingdom.

The second theme is that of Jesus as Savior. Luke develops this theme ironically. Each of those mocking him combines a title and the challenge to save himself. The "leaders" mock his being Messiah of God and "elect one"; the soldiers his being called "King of the Jews"; the criminal, his being "the Messiah." It is obvious that for each of them, "saving himself" means to come down from the cross, to escape death. This is made most obvious by the criminal who adds to "save yourself" the rider, "and us." The distance between Jesus as the proclaimer of God's kingdom and his opponents has never been clearer, for they can understand no salvation except that involving the perpetuation of this human existence.

But as the reader of the Gospel to this point well understands, it is through faith that God has brought salvation in the words and deeds of Jesus. The reader has also learned that salvation does not consist in political liberation or the perpetuation of life, but rather in the restoration of God's people through the forgiveness of sins. The irony of Luke's portrayal therefore is obvious, when Jesus is shown extending forgiveness to his executioners, even as their mocking shows them incapable of receiving it (23:34). And to the criminal who responds to Jesus in faith, asking to "be remembered" in the kingdom, Jesus responds with the promise of a place with him in paradise (23:43).

Luke's portrayal of Jesus as Prophet is enhanced because everything that has happened to him in the passion narrative is in fulfillment of his own predictions (9:22, 44; 17:25; 18:31-32). To the very end, furthermore, Luke has Jesus maintain his philosophic composure and self-control. Luke's account is notable as much for what it omits from the death scene as for what it includes. First, he reduces the cosmic wonders accompanying the death to a minimum. He explains the darkness over the land as an eclipse (the word "eclipse" comes from the Greek word used here, *ekleipō*), and the allusion to the sanctuary curtain is so overdetermined that it almost misses saying anything certain. The effect, however, is to focus our attention on the person of Jesus as he dies rather than on accidental side effects. Second, Luke omits the cry of anguish from the cross, and the accompanying confusion over whether he was calling Elijah. Again, the effect is to remove attention from the bystanders and their misunderstanding, and place attention on the death of Jesus. Finally, Luke shows Jesus in utter control. He forgives his executioners. He promises paradise to the repentant criminal. And having done these things, he entrusts his spirit to his Father in prayer, and dies. His death is shown to be utterly consistent with his life, his life an enactment of his teaching. He is Philosopher, Prophet, Lord of God's kingdom.

For Reference and Further Study

Daube, D. " 'For They Know Not What They Do,' Luke 23, 34." *Studia Patristica* 4 (TU 79; Berlin: Akademie-Verlag, 1961) 58–70.

Ellis, E. E. "Present and Future Eschatology in Luke." *NTS* 12 (1965–66) 27–41.

Fitzmyer, J. A. "Crucifixion in Ancient Palestine, Qumran Literature, and the New Testament." *CBQ* 40 (1978) 493–513.

Karris, R. J. "Luke 23 and Luke's Thematic Christology and Soteriology." *Luke: Artist and Theologian; Luke's Passion Account As Literature* (New York: Paulist, 1985) 79–119.

Neyrey, J. "The Crucifixion Scene: The Saved Savior." *The Passion According to Luke: A Redaction Study of Luke's Soteriology* (New York: Paulist, 1985) 129–155.

66. *Responses to the Prophet's Death* (23:47-56)

47. When the centurion saw what had happened, he glorified God. He said, "This man was truly righteous." 48. And when all the crowds that had gathered in order to observe this spectacle saw the things that had happened, they turned back beating their breasts. 49. All of his acquaintances stood a long way off. The women who had together followed him from Galilee witnessed these things. 50. And there was a man named Joseph who was a member of the assembly. He was a good and righteous person. 51. He had not agreed with their decision or action. He was from Arimathea, a city of the Jews. He was awaiting the kingdom of God. 52. This man approached Pilate. He requested the body of Jesus. 53. After taking it down, he wrapped it in a cloth. He placed it in a tomb cut into the stone. No one had yet been placed in it. 54. It was the day of preparation and the sabbath was about to begin. 55. The women who had together come with him from Galilee followed after. They observed the tomb and how the body was placed. 56. They went back and prepared aromatic oils and myrrh. And on the sabbath they rested according to the commandment.

NOTES

47. *this man was truly righteous*: Luke's version is simpler than the parallels: Mark 15:39 has the centurion "see how Jesus died" and respond, "This man was a son of God." Matt 27:54 has the centurion and his companions observe all the wonders that had happened, and *they* declare, "this was truly a son of God." Luke's centurion simply "sees what had happened." His declaration could be translated "innocent" (RSV); certainly Jesus' innocence is a major theme of the passion narrative (23:4, 14, 15, 22, 41). But the term *dikaios* has the deeper religious significance of "righteous," and this is the sense Luke clearly wants the reader to take. Notice how this is picked up in the kerygmatic statement of Acts 3:14: "you denied the holy and righteous one."

48. *in order to observe this spectacle*: The term *theōria* together with the verb *theōrein* in verses 35 and 48 suggest a spectacle or entertainment (cf. 2 Macc 5:26; 3 Macc 5:24, Epictetus, *Discourses*, 3, 24, 12).

    turned back beating their breasts: The spectacle turned sour; when they saw what had happened, the crowds experienced remorse. The term "turn back" (*hypostrephō*) literally means to return to the city, but it echoes the consistent LXX translation of the Hebrew term *shub*, which is used for repentance (*teshubah*). For "beating the breast" as a sign of grieving, see 23:27. Luke shows a populace only marginally involved in the death of the prophet now stunned and remorseful, ready to respond to the call to conversion in Acts 2:37-41.

49. *all of his acquaintances*: Is literally "those known (*gnōstoi*) to him"; for the construction, see 2:44. Luke has omitted the earlier scene of the disciples' abandoning Jesus in the garden (cf. Mark 14:50; Matt 26:56); instead, he had Peter

following Jesus "from afar" (*apo makrothen*, 22:54). So also we are probably to picture this group watching "from afar" (*apo makrothen*) as including the disciples. *women who had together followed him*: Luke makes three important points about these women: a) although they are distinguished from the apostles, they are not distinguished from disciples; they have "followed together"; b) they have come from Galilee; the reference is to 8:1-3, and the women who supported Jesus and the Twelve from their resources; they are part of the nucleus of the Galilean community that will be the first Church in Jerusalem (Acts 1:14); c) they are eyewitnesses to the events of Jesus' ministry (8:1-3), death and burial (v. 55), and the resurrection (24:1-8).

50. *a good and righteous person*: Joseph of Arimathea figures in all the Gospels (Mark 15:42-47; Matt 27:57-61; John 19:38-42) as the one who buries Jesus. His status and actions are diversely described. Matthew makes him a wealthy man who was a disciple. John makes him a "secret disciple for fear of the Jews." Luke follows Mark in making him a well-intentioned member of the council: "he did not agree with their decision or action." And by adding that he "awaited the kingdom of God" as well as being good and righteous, Luke portrays him as a member of the faithful "people of God" like the characters in the infancy account (1:6; 2:25, 37).

52. *requested the body of Jesus*: Luke's version is again simpler than Mark's, and even more so than John's account. Mark 15:44-45 has Pilate interrogate the centurion to see if Jesus is really dead. John 19:39 reintroduces Nicodemus (from John 3:1) for the actual burial.

53. *placed it in a tomb*: Luke agrees with Mark 15:46 in having the tomb cut out of rock, but omits any mention of a large stone rolled to its entrance. Matt 27:60 includes Mark's elements and adds that it was a "new" tomb. Only Luke and John 19:41 add that "no one had been placed in it." For the presence of tombs in the vicinity of an execution spot and soldiers standing guard, cf. Petronius, *Satyricon* 111. For the problem of hewing a new tomb on the festival, cf. *m.M.Qat.* 1:6.

54. *day of preparation*: This note is lacking in Mark and Matthew. John 19:42 says that it was the day of preparation but may mean for the day of Passover (cf. 19:31). Luke makes clear he means the Sabbath day by using the term "dawning" (*epiphōskō*) in a transferred sense to mean the evening onset of the Sabbath observance. According to *m.Sanh.* 6:5, bodies were not to be left overnight without burial, so there was need for haste.

55. *they observed the tomb*: As in verse 49, Luke emphasizes the fidelity and function of the women from Galilee. They "follow after" Joseph of Arimathea as he buries Jesus, and they observe the tomb. Most of all, "they had followed together from Galilee"; they are thus authentic eyewitnesses to Jesus as he was and as he now is, and as he will be. They provide the essential "chain of evidence" for the Christian claims about Jesus. They embody those who were "eyewitnesses become ministers of the word" after Jesus' resurrection (see 1:2).

56. *prepared aromatic oils*: For the use of unguents in preparing a body for burial, see *m.Ber.* 8:6 and *m.Sheb.* 23:5. Luke has the women return to prepare the oils, whereas Mark 16:1 has them go buy them.

rested according to the commandment: Only Luke has this characteristic notice. At the end as at the beginning of the story, those around Jesus show the piety desired by Torah (1:6; 2:22, 23, 27, 39).

INTERPRETATION

At the crucifixion scene, Luke showed Jesus surrounded by those who rejected him and his message. With only the exception of the criminal who asked to be remembered in the kingdom, everything said to Jesus by the leaders, the soldiers and the other criminal was filled with parody, mocking, and abuse. The titles of Messiah and elect one were thrown at him abusively. He was taunted to save himself in order to prove his identity. The crucifixion showed the climactic moment of the first rejection of the Prophet.

But as soon as Jesus entrusts his spirit to God and dies, Luke shows the reader four other responses, each of them in its way positive and preparing for the next part of the story.

He begins with those standing closest to the cross. The centurion proclaims that Jesus was truly a righteous person (23:47). Although the translation "innocent" is possible, and even captures one of the major themes in Luke's passion account, it misses the richness of the centurion's declaration. For Luke, Jesus is more than simply "innocent" in the juridical sense. He is even more than "just" in the philosophical sense of being virtuous—although Luke has also portrayed Jesus in that fashion throughout this narrative.

He is God's "righteous one" (Acts 3:14), the Messiah who through his life and death brings healing and salvation to the people. The centurion's statement must be read—Luke surely wants us to read it—as a confirmation of the (parodic) taunt of the leaders that Jesus was "the elect one," for it is as the suffering servant prophesied by Isaiah that Luke wants Jesus' death to be understood (Acts 8:32-35), the "righteous one, my servant, [who will] make many to be accounted righteous" (Isa 53:11). Nor is it an accident that this declaration is made by a Gentile soldier, who on seeing Jesus die, "glorifies God" (23:47). Like a centurion earlier in the narrative (7:1-10) and like another centurion later in the narrative (Acts 10-15), he provides a glimpse of the "God-fearing" Gentiles who will become members of God's restored people.

The second response is that of the people of the city. We have seen how Luke has tried—despite the weight of the tradition—to keep them removed from participation in the rejection and death of the Prophet. At the crucifixion scene, he distinguished their silent watching from the mockery of the officials. Now, Luke has them as well react to "what they had seen." In two short phrases he indicates their remorse and readiness for conversion. They "beat their breasts" and they "return." These elements are only in Luke. They not only indicate his preoccupation with Israel and his understanding of the messianic movement as the restoration of God's people, but his literary concern to prepare the reader for later narrative developments. The implications of this short scene will not be understood by the reader until Peter's preaching at Pentecost.

The third response is by Joseph of Arimathea, who seeks Jesus' body and buries it in a new tomb. In contrast to other Gospels (Matthew and John) Luke does not portray Joseph as a secret disciple, which makes his response all the more interesting. By calling him good and righteous and expecting the kingdom of God, Luke identifies him as part of pious Israel. By showing reverence for the body of Jesus, he responds positively to the Prophet. But more significantly, he himself was a "leader of the people," since he was a member of the council (23:50). By emphasizing that he had not gone along with the council's decision or action (23:51), Luke does more than secure the righteousness of this individual; he shows as well that even the leadership of the people was not uniformly rejecting of the Prophet. As with the account of the divided response by the two criminals executed with Jesus, Luke extends and refines the theme of the divided Israel.

Finally, there is the response of the women. All the Gospels say that they prepared ointments for Jesus' body. But only Luke has paid such attention to another function of the women: their role as eyewitnesses. He reminds us twice that these women had come up as a group with Jesus from Galilee (23:49, 55). He notes explicitly that they observed the things that happened at Jesus' death (23:49), and his burial (23:55). He will shortly show us how they become the first witnesses to the resurrection (24:10) and are part of the community that receives the Holy Spirit (Acts 1:14). For Luke, the women are uniquely faithful to Jesus, and function as the eyewitness link between these critical events.

FOR REFERENCE AND FURTHER STUDY

Kilpatrick, G. D. "A Theme of the Lucan Passion Story and Luke xxiii, 47." *JTS* 43 (1942) 34–36.

Neyrey, J. "Jesus' Faith: Our Salvation." *The Passion according to Luke: A Redaction Study of Luke's Soteriology* (New York: Paulist, 1985) 156–192.

Schreiber, J. "Die Bestattung Jesu: Redaktionsgeschichtliche Beobachtungen zu Mk 15, 42-47, par." *ZNW* 72 (1981) 141–177.

Zehnle, R. "The Salvific Character of Jesus' Death in Lukan Soteriology." *TS* 30 (1969) 420–444.

VII. THE PROPHET IS RAISED UP

67. *The Empty Tomb* (24:1-12)

1. On the first day of the week, when it was very early, they came to the tomb, bringing the aromatic oils they had prepared. 2. But they found the stone rolled away from the tomb. 3. When they had entered they did not find the body of the Lord Jesus. 4. As they were puzzling over this, two men stood by them. They were in shining clothes. 5. The women grew frightened. They bowed their faces to the ground. The men said to them: "Why are you seeking among the dead the one who lives? 6. He is not here, but has been raised! Remember how he spoke to you while he was still in Galilee: 7. He said, 'The Son of Man must be handed over into the hand of people who are sinners, be crucified, and on the third day rise.' " 8. And they remembered his words. 9. When they had returned from the tomb, they reported all these things to the eleven and all the rest. 10. The women were Mary Magdalen, Joanna, Mary the mother of James, and the rest of the women with them. They began to tell these things to the apostles. 11. But these words seemed in their view to be so much nonsense. They refused to believe the women. 12. But Peter got up and ran to the tomb. He looked in. He saw only the burial cloths. He went away marvelling to himself.

NOTES

1. *on the first day of the week*: This is the day after the Sabbath on which they had rested. All the Gospels emphasize the earliness of the hour (Mark 16:2; Matt 28:1; John 20:1). Since the women bring the ointments they had prepared, the body of Jesus had not yet been anointed but only wrapped in cloths and laid in the tomb over the Sabbath.

2. *stone rolled away from the tomb*: Luke is like John 20:1 in the brevity of his account. Like John, he mentions the stone being rolled back without having first established its presence—an unusual lapse in narrative anticipation. Mark 16:3 is more profuse, having a discussion among the women concerning who would roll the stone back for them (looking back to Mark 15:46). Matt 28:2 is still more dramatic, as it is throughout this last part of the Gospel, by having an earthquake occur and an angel of the Lord rolling back the stone.

3. *find the body of the Lord Jesus*: Only Luke has this most telling detail, which then is reported in 24:12, 23, 24. The body was not there! Also important is the detail that "they went in" to see for themselves, as Peter later does as well (24:12). The title "Lord Jesus" is omitted in some MSS, but is probably original. Luke likes to use "Lord" of Jesus in the narrative (e.g., 10:1; 11:39). The title *kyrios*

is particularly associated with the resurrection in early Christianity (e.g., 1 Cor 12:3; Phil 2:11), as we see from Acts 2:36. Luke will use "Lord Jesus" again in Acts 1:21; 4:33; 8:16.

4. *as they were puzzling over this*: The verb *aporeō* denotes mental confusion or perplexity (cf. the use of *aporia* in 21:25). Luke uses the cognate *diaporeō* in 9:7; Acts 2:12; 5:24; 10:17. Note that the *fact* of the empty tomb does not itself lead to faith. It must be interpreted.

two men stoood by them: The translation retains "men" because the *andres* is definite, but drops the characteristic biblicism *kai idou* ("and behold"). The verb *ephistēmi* sometimes has the sense of "sudden appearance," as in Luke 2:9; 21:34; Acts 12:7. Mark 16:5 has a *neaniskos* ("young man") at the tomb, pointing back to the *neaniskos* who fled naked in the garden at the arrest (Mark 14:51). Matt 28:2 has the angel who had rolled back the stone.

in shining clothes: Luke does not identify the two witnesses, but wants them to be understood as supernatural figures, as the participle of *astraptō* suggests (see 10:18; 11:36; 17:24); in 24:23, in fact, they are referred to as "angels." Most intriguing in this connection is Luke's use of *exastraptō* for the clothes of Jesus at the transfiguration (9:29), when he was "in glory" (*doxa*). In that scene as well there were "two men" (*duo andres*), as there are here. They were Moses and Elijah. They spoke to Jesus about the *exodos* he was to "fulfill" in Jerusalem (9:30). In strictly literary terms, Luke would seem to want the reader to make this connection (see also Acts 1:10).

5. *seeking among the dead the one who lives*: The translation reverses the order of phraces to capture the proper emphasis. In contrast to Mark 16:6 and Matt 28:6, which have the messenger identify the object of their quest as "Jesus (Mark: the Nazarene) who was crucified," Luke's two men issue what is in effect a rebuke leading into a reminder.

6. *not here, but has been raised*: Luke shares this line with Matthew and Mark, but reverses the clauses. He also omits their additional phrase, "see the place where they laid him," since he has already told the reader that the women had seen just that. Matt 28:6 has "just as he said" (*kathōs eipen*), which functions the same way as Luke's expanded note on the fulfillment of prophecy.

remember how he spoke to you: For the meaning of "remember" (*mimnēskomai*), see the note on 22:19. Here we meet one of the distinctive elements of the Lukan resurrection accounts, the way they recapitulate the earlier story and show how Jesus' words had been fulfilled. Rather than being told to go tell Peter and the disciples that Jesus went before them to Galilee (Mark 16:7; Matt 28:7), which looks forward, Luke turns the women and the reader backwards to remembrance of what he had said in Galilee. No command is given them to tell the others.

7. *Son of Man must be handed over*: In the light of the event, the passion prophecy of 9:22 is made more specific: rather than naming "elders, chief priests and scribes," we have the moral evaluation: people who are sinners! Rather than "killed," we now have "crucified." Although a different verb is used for "rise" (9:22 *egerthēnai*, 24:7 *anastēnai*), the detail of "the third day" remains constant.

8. *remembered his words*: Like the rehearsal of the prophecy itself, this is unique to Luke's account. Something more than "prophecy/fulfillment" is at work here. The words of Jesus are regarded as critical for understanding the events, providing a first interpretation that shapes their very perception.

9. *reported all these things*: Even though they were not ordered to do so, the women report their experience. This is in sharp contrast to Mark 16:8, which says the women out of fear told no one. Matt 28:8 has the women run with great joy to tell the apostles, but then as they go, have them encounter Jesus who tells them himself to "tell my brothers" to meet him in Galilee (Matt 28:9-10). The way Luke relates this, we are reminded of the eager response of the shepherds to the angelic announcement of Jesus' birth (2:20).

    to the Eleven and all the rest: Luke carefully notes the rupture in the apostolic circle of Twelve caused by the apostasy of Judas (see also 24:33, Acts 1:26). "The rest" (*hoi loipoi*) are those disciples other than the apostles who make up the core of the Galilean community (cf. Acts 1:14).

10. *the women were Mary Magdalene, Joanna*: Compare the lists in Mark 16:1 and Matt 28:1, which are given before the women come to the tomb. The first two names are in the list of women given in 8:1-3 as those ministering to Jesus and the Twelve. "Mary the mother of James" is added to this list (and is found in Mark 16:1; Matt 28:1 has "the other Mary"). On the other hand, "Susanna" was in the earlier list (8:3), but does not appear here. Mark 16:1 also has "Salome," whom Luke omits. The point is given not by the specific names (as the addition "the rest of the women" shows), but by the fact that those who had followed from Galilee and had seen Jesus die and be buried, were now the ones who reported this experience. These are the first witnesses.

11. *to be so much nonsense*: Although it resembles the theme of the incredulity of Thomas in John 20:24, this note is distinctive to Luke, as is the strange remark in 24:41 that they "disbelieved for joy." The term *lēros* ("nonsense") could scarcely be more condescending. It forms the basis for the English word "delirious." There is a definite air of male superiority in this response. We remember from 9:45 that the disciples could not grasp the fact that Jesus had to suffer, and were afraid even then to ask Jesus about "his word" (*rhēma autou*), just as now they refuse to hear "these words" (*rhēmata tauta*).

12. *Peter got up and ran to the tomb*: This verse is omitted by a number of important MSS (probably because it was considered an interpolation from John 20:3, 5, 6). The overwhelming majority of MSS, however, include it. Nor does it seem that the verse would have been interpolated to provide a basis for 24:34, "The Lord has appeared to Peter," for there is no appearance here. Nor does this properly provide a basis for 24:24, for in that verse, "some of our number went to the tomb" is in the plural, rather than just Peter. Although this account shares with John the words "run," "see," and "burial cloths" (*othonia*), each has distinctive elements: a) John has "the other disciple" with Peter; b) John's account is considerably longer and more complex; c) Luke has "burial cloth only" in contrast to John's "burial cloth lying"; d) Luke has Peter "marvelling to himself" which is absent from John. For "marvelling (*thaumazō*) as a typically Lukan

word to describe response to wondrous events, see 1:21, 63; 2:18, 33; 4:22; 7:9; 8:25; 11:4, 38; 20:26; Acts 2:7; 4:13).

INTERPRETATION

The resurrection of Jesus is the starting point of Christian faith. In the earliest Christian writings, the conviction that Jesus was alive in a new and more powerful fashion was connected to the experience of the Holy Spirit, so that having this Spirit and being able to confess "Jesus is Lord" went together (1 Cor 12:1-3). Faith in Jesus as Lord was based on a continuing, transforming experience of transcendent power in communities, and not simply on experiences that people had on Easter day.

Nevertheless, the traditions concerning the first encounters between the risen Lord and his followers were handed on from the first as historical validation for the spiritual transformation (1 Thess 1:9-10; 1 Cor 9:1; 15:3-8; Gal 1:15-16). And although the Christian conviction concerning Jesus' resurrection is not to be equated with the *narratives* about that event, each of the Gospels contains diverse traditions concerning the resurrection, shaped by the continuing experience and reflection of communities over a period of years.

Such "after-death" stories were not unknown in Hellenistic culture, whose understanding of the world made the passage between the human and the divine more accessible and common. Stories of heroes becoming immortal or ascending (apotheiosis) were in circulation (cf. Ovid, *Metamorphoses* 14:805-851; Diodorus Siculus, *Library of History* 4, 38, 3-5), as were accounts of missing tombs (Philo, *Life of Moses* 2:291; Philostratus, *Life of Apollonius* 8:31), and of the dead visiting the living in vision or dream (Cicero, *The Republic*, 6, 9-26; Philostratus, *Life of Apollonius*, 8:31). Even within the stricter framework of monotheism, Torah contained the accounts of those who had been "translated" into heaven, like Enoch (Gen 5:24) and Elijah (2 Kings 2:9-12), making them available for future revelations and visitations. Although the philosophically sophisticated of that age, like ours, might scoff at such notions (Acts 17:32; Lucian of Samosata, *The Lover of Lies*, 24–32), they nevertheless enjoyed great circulation and prestige among the many.

By comparison with such Hellenistic after-death stories, two elements common to the Christian accounts about Jesus should be noted. The first is that the Jesus of the resurrection accounts is not vestigially or marginally visible but is rather emphatically *present* in a more powerful way than ever. The most consistent feature of the Christian resurrection accounts is the commanding word of the Lord. Correlative to that is the second feature, which is the communal character of these stories. It is not simply that the stories about Jesus for the most part involve more than scattered individuals, but more importantly, they bring a community into existence.

The canonical Gospels differ considerably in their use of such traditions about Jesus. The so-called "shorter ending" of Mark (16:1-8) has only an empty-tomb account. Mark's "longer ending" (Mark 16:9-20) appears to be a composite of other appearance traditions. Matthew has an empty-tomb account (28:1-8), a very short notice of an appearance to the women (28:9-10), and the final commission by Jesus to the Eleven in Galilee (28:16-20). John has a long empty-tomb account different in character from that in the Synoptics (20:1-10), a separate appearance to Mary Magdalene (20:11-18), two appearances to the collected disciples, one without Thomas (20:19-23), and one with him (20:26-29). Finally, in his appendix, John has an extended account of Jesus appearing to the disciples in Galilee (21:1-23). In the so-called gnostic gospels, in turn, the resurrection sometimes becomes the *mise-en-scene* for the entire gospel, as the resurrected Jesus reveals secret knowledge to his followers (cf. e.g., *Gospel of Thomas, Pistis Sophia*).

Within this spectrum, Luke-Acts has a rich collection of stories: an empty-tomb account (24:1-12); a "recognition story" in the appearance to the two disciples on the road to Emmaus (24:13-35); an appearance to all the disciples gathered together (24:44-49); an ascension story in the Gospel narrative (24:50-52); and another ascension account in the beginning of Acts (1:9-11). These are the main elements; he includes as well reports of other appearances (24:34; Acts 1:3), and descriptions of the "resurrection" experiences of Stephen (Acts 7:55-56) and Paul (Acts 9, 22, 26).

Before turning to the first of these accounts, Luke's version of the empty-tomb story shared with Matthew and Mark, we can note some of the characteristic features of all of Luke's resurrection/ascension stories. First, he continues his geographical concentration on Jerusalem. Not only are there no appearances or promises of appearances in Galilee, the concentration on Jerusalem and its environs is emphatic, leading in the last Gospel appearance to a command from Jesus to stay in the city (24:49). Second, Luke's accounts combine the mysterious with the matter-of-fact: Jesus can appear as an ordinary traveller on the road and not be recognized. On the other hand, he is not a wraith or ghost: he eats bread and grilled fish, and declares that he has "flesh and bones." Third, Luke's accounts all involve the theme of prophecy and fulfillment: the words of Jesus prophesying his suffering and death are explicitly recalled in the light of the events; the words of Torah as well are shown to have predicted these things. Fourth, the appearance accounts look forward to the narrative of Acts and the ministry of the apostles in that part of the story. Fifth, in all of these, we find Luke showing a community in the process of formation from eyewitnesses to ministers of the word (1:2). They begin to understand the meaning of this first part of the story, and need only be empowered by Jesus' own prophetic Spirit before beginning to proclaim it themselves.

We can see many of these concerns expressed in the empty-tomb story, and the more impressively since Luke derives this story from his Markan source and therefore has less freedom for invention. We have noted how Luke emphasizes the role of the women as eyewitnesses. They have followed the story every step of the way. Luke eliminates completely any negative nuance concerning the women he might have found in Mark. They are not commanded to tell anyone, yet they report everything they have experienced. The problem of disbelief is not that of the women but of the men, the "Eleven and the rest" who with obvious condescension regard their report as delirium. Even when Peter confirms the "facts" of the case, he does not yet believe, but only walks back full of wonder.

We can see as well how Luke manages to secure both his geographical interest and his prophecy/fulfillment theme in his redaction of the empty-tomb story. He eliminates the promise that Jesus would appear in Galilee, and instead has the women remember *what Jesus had said in Galilee*! As a result, he not only invites the reader to remember the course of Jesus' ministry, but also once more certifies the role of these women: they could remember because they had been there. The words they are to remember is the prophecy Jesus had made concerning his own suffering, death, and resurrection. This is not the fulfillment of Scripture, we notice, but the fulfillment of Jesus the Prophet's words. If they can but remember, Jesus' own words provide the authoritative interpretation of this otherwise puzzling event of his bodily disappearance. By telling us that the women *do* remember, Luke informs the reader that the women have come to belief, and the proper understanding of the event.

For Reference and Further Study

Dillon, R. J. *From Eye-Witnesses to Ministers of the Word: Tradition and Composition in Luke 24.* AnBib 82; Rome: Biblical Institute, 1978.

Dupont, J. "Les discours de Pierre dans les Actes et le chapitre xxiv de l'évangile de Luc." L'évangile de Luc. Ed. F. Neirynck. BETL 32; Gembloux: Duculot, 1973.

Leaney, A. R. C. "The Resurrection Accounts in Luke (xxiv, 12–53)." *NTS* 2 (1955–56) 110–114.

Schmitt, J. "Le récit de la resurrection dans l'évangile de Luc: Etude de critique littéraire." *RevScRel* 25 (1951) 119–137, 219–242.

Schubert, P. "The Structure and Significance of Luke 24," *Neutestamentliche Studien für R. Bultmann.* Ed. W. Eltester (BZNW 21: Berlin: Töpelmann, 1954) 165–186.

68. *Appearance to Two Disciples* (24:13-35)

13. On that very day two of them were on their way to a village called Emmaus, about seven miles outside Jerusalem. 14. They were talking together about all these things that had happened. 15. As they were talking and discussing, Jesus himself drew near and walked with them. 16. But they were prevented from recognizing him. 17. He said to them, "What are these words that you are exchanging as you walk?" They stood there sorrowfully. 18. One of them, named Cleopas, answered. He said, "Are you the only person staying in Jerusalem who doesn't know the things that have happened in it during these days?" 19. He said to them, "What kind of things?" They told him, "Those concerning Jesus of Nazareth. He was a prophet, a man powerful in deed and speech before God and all the people. 20. The chief priests and our leaders handed him over to the sentence of death, and they crucified him. 21. Now we had hoped that he was the very one who was going to liberate Israel. But also, together with all this, it is the third day since these things happened. 22. But also certain women from our group startled us. They had gone early to the tomb, 23. but since they did not find his body, they came back saying that they had seen a vision of angels who declared that he was alive. 24. And some of those with us went off to the tomb and found it just as the women said. But him they did not see." 25. Jesus said to them, "O you foolish people, so reluctant to believe everything that the prophets said! 26. Was it not necessary for the Messiah to suffer these things and enter into his glory?" 27. And beginning from Moses and from all the prophets, he interpreted for them the things concerning himself in all the scriptures. 28. They approached the village to which they were going, and he made as if to keep going further. 29. They began to urge him: "Stay with us, for evening is near and the day is almost over." He went in to stay with them. 30. As he was reclining at table with them, he took bread. He blessed and broke it. He gave it to them. 31. Their eyes were opened and they recognized him. And he disappeared. 32. They said to each other, "Were our hearts not burning within us as he spoke to us on the road, as he opened the scriptures to us?" 33. They got up at once and turned back to Jerusalem. They found the Eleven and those with them gathered together, 34. declaring, "The Lord has truly been raised!" and, "He has appeared to Simon!" 35. They related what had happened on the road and how they recognized him in the breaking of the bread.

Notes

13. *two of them*: Refers back to "the rest" who were with the Eleven in 24:9. Notice that they are able to relate the women's experience as reported to them (24:22). This entire story is unique to Luke's Gospel, with no real point of contact with other canonical appearance accounts except for the brief notice (possibly a summation) in the "longer ending" of Mark 16:12-13: "after this he appeared in

another form to two of them, as they were walking into the country. And they went back and told the rest, but they did not believe them."

about seven miles outside Jerusalem: The location is uncertain. The Greek is literally "about sixty *stadia*" which translates to approximately seven miles. The place itself has significance only because it is in the environs of Jerusalem, the location for all Luke's appearance accounts and all the major events of the narrative between chapter 19 of the Gospel and chapter 8 of Acts.

14. *talking together*: The verb *homileō* (see 20:11; 24:26) means to be in conversation with someone; it is used here in the imperfect to suggest an extended discussion. In the next verse, the verb *suzētein* has much the same sense, with the added nuance of "inquiring" or "examining." We are to picture the two disciples trying to figure out the meaning of the events.

all these things that had happened: Luke uses *symbainō* in the perfect participle, meaning "the things that have come together," or occurred (see Acts 3:10; 20:19; 21:35). By using the phrase "all these things" Luke invites the reader to review the previous narrative sequence.

15. *Jesus himself drew near*: The *autos* is emphatic: it *was* Jesus! The personal name is also striking. Remarkably, this is the last time that his name occurs in the direct narrative, although it is picked up in the disciples' recital in verse 19.

16. *prevented from recognizing him*: Is literally, "their eyes were held (*krateō*) in order that they might not recognize (*epiginōskō*) him." This condition will be reversed in verse 31. For Luke's use of "recognize" (*epiginōskō*), see 1:4, 22; 5:22; 13:7.

17. *stood there sorrowfully*: The verb *histēmi* ("stand") has the sense here of coming to a stop on the road, as in 8:44. The adjective *skythrōpos* can mean to be sad or angry—in Matt 6:1 it describes the "long face" of the fasting Pharisees—and here it takes on the sense of "sorrow" from the context (cf. Gen 40:7; Neh 2:1, and esp. Sir 25:23). This is one of many "novelistic" touches in the story which give it vividness and psychological plausibility.

18. *one of them, named Cleopas*: This is the only mention of a disciple by this name in the NT. Like the names of Simon of Cyrene's sons Rufus and Alexander in Mark 15:21, such details can be regarded as the sign of reliable tradition or inventive storytelling.

only person staying in Jerusalem: The verb *paroikeō* has the technical sense of a person residing among others as an alien or stranger (see e.g., Gen 17:8; 26:2; Deut 5:14; Josh 24:20; Heb 11:9); see also the cognate *paroikos* ("sojourner") in Acts 7:6, 29; 13:17. In context, the term is used appropriately for those who were staying in the city for the days of the festival, "during these days." Notice the repetitive reminder of "Jerusalem" as the place where the events took place, stressed again by the phrase "in it" (*en autē*).

19. *concerning Jesus of Nazareth*: Luke thus begins a recital that will become, with the explicit addition of the resurrection event, the *kerygma* ("proclamation of good news"). If the best MS witnesses are correct, Luke uses *Nazarene* (translated "of Nazareth") here (as in 4:34) rather than his usual *Nazaraios* (18:37; Acts 2:22; 3:6; 4:10; 5:14; 22:8; 24:5; 26:9).

he was a prophet: The argument throughout this commentary, that Luke's shaping of Jesus in the image of the prophet like Moses, goes far beyond the explicit use of the term *prophētēs*. This is fact is one of the most important uses of the title (see also 4:24; 6:23; 7:16, 39; 13:33-34; Acts 3:22-23; 7:37), coming as it does at a point in the story where the significance of Jesus' ministry is being interpreted. The description by Cleopas, it should be noted, agrees with the narrator's own perceptions.

powerful in deed and speech: The term "powerful" (*dynatos*) picks up the narrative emphasis on the *dynamis* at work in Jesus (4:14, 36; 5:17; 6:19; 8:46; 9:1; 10:13, 19; 19:37), and it will be echoed by Peter's Pentecost speech in Acts 2:22. Note further that the final appearance account tells the disciples that they will be "clothed with power (*dynamis*) from on high" (24:49), and that Moses in Acts 7:22 is described in exactly the same terms as "powerful in words and deeds."

before God and all the people: Just as the previous phrase picks up the "signs and wonders" associated with Moses the prophet (Deut 34:11), so does the present phrase recall the description of Moses as one who knew God "face to face" and worked wonders "before all of Israel" (Deut 34:10-12).

20. *chief priests and our leaders handed him over*: The wording recalls the passion prophecy of Jesus in 9:22, 44, and 18:32, as well as its recapitulation in the empty-tomb story, 24:7. Notice the emphasis on "our leaders," which will be contrasted to "we" in the next verse. Luke repeats his theme of the divided populace. The leaders are blamed for what happened to Jesus; indeed, the syntax of the sentence would even allow them to be seen as the ones who crucified him! As in 24:7, the verb *stauroō* is used to describe the manner of the Prophet's death (see also Acts 2:36; 4:10). Luke is sometimes characterized as minimizing the significance of the Cross, but in terms of simple usage, he uses the verb *stauroō* seven times (compared to eight times in Paul's letters), and the noun *stauros* three times (compared to ten times in Paul's letters).

21. *now we had hoped*: The conjunction *de* is translated as "now," in an attempt to capture the strong opposition between "our leaders" and "we" built in to the Greek syntax. The people had placed their hope in Jesus. Luke did not make a major theme out of "hope" in the Gospel (only at 6:34 and 23:18), but develops it further in the second volume (Acts 2:26; 23:6; 24:15; 26:6; 28:20), mostly in terms—as here—of the "hope of Israel."

going to liberate Israel: This expectation picks up the theme begun in 1:68 and 2:38 concerning "redemption" (also Acts 7:35). As in the earlier statements, the concern is for "Israel" understood in spiritual terms as the restored people of God (1:16, 54, 68, 80; 2:25, 32, 34; 4:25-27; 7:9; 22:30; Acts 1:6; 2:36; 4:10; 5:31; 7:23, 37, 42; 9:15; 10:36; 13:17). See especially Acts 13:23: "according to his promise, God brought to Israel a savior, Jesus."

it is the third day: The sentence is clear in intent, but difficult to translate exactly: a) the connecting phrase *alla ge kai* intends a contrast to what went before; the translation treats it somewhat woodenly as "but also" both here and in the next verse; b) the phrase "with all this" (*syn pasin toutois*) is awkwardly placed but has something of a summary effect; c) the combination of the accusative of time "how long" in *tritēn hēmeran* with the impersonal verb *agei* is difficult to put together. The emphasis of the sentence, in any case, is on the "third day" as in 9:22 and 24:7.

22. *women from our group startled us*: Is literally "from among us" (*ex hēmōn*), a characterization consistent with the vagueness in 23:55; 24:9, 10, 23. The verb *exhistēmi* ("startle") is a strong one (see 2:47; 8:56; Acts 2:7, 12; 8:9, 11, 13; 9:21; 10:45; 12:16). The sense is that they were both surprised and confused.

23. *a vision of angels*: It is difficult to know whether this is meant to be a straightforward report or a condescending parody, since these men had not believed the women's report. Notice that the two men in radiant garments (24:4) have now become *angeloi* ("angels"). This could mean only "messengers' (Luke 7:24) in the way that Epictetus speaks of the Cynic as a "messenger (*angelos*) sent (*apostellō*) from Zeus" (*Discourses* 3, 22, 23), but it probably means "angels" (see e.g., 1:11, 13; 2:9, 13; Acts 5:19).

declared that he was alive: This makes a little more specific the double statement of 24:5, "why do you seek among the dead the one who lives" and 24:6, "he is not here, he has been raised."

24. *found it just as the women had said*: In contrast to the notice about Peter in 24:12, this speaks of "some from among us" in the plural. This mention of the tomb now makes the eighth time it has been identified; the narrative is circling back over the critical event of the first discovery, and preparing the way for this "appearance." The motif of "finding just as it was said" is found as well in 19:32 and 22:13.

25. *O you foolish people*: The epithet *anoētai* (literally "lacking sense") is frequently used by philosophers for those without proper understanding (e.g., Philostratus, *Life of Apollonius*, 8:7; Josephus, *Against Apion* 2:255; Rom 1:14; Gal 3:1, 3; 1 Tim 6:9; Titus 3:3).

reluctant to believe: Is literally "slow (*bradeis*) of heart to believe"; a typical Lukan biblicism, with the "heart" signifying the center of intelligence and will (see also 1:17, 51, 66; 2:19; and esp. 21:14, "put therefore in your heart," and 21:34, "so that your hearts not grow heavy"). The translation "reluctant" tries for the implication of moral failure. Luke uses the construction *pisteuein epi* ("to believe upon") as in Acts 9:42; 11:17, 21; 16:31.

everything that the prophets said: Two things about this statement should be noted: a) to believe in Jesus is connected with the proper understanding of the Scriptures; b) Luke understands this as "all the prophets," implying that all the Scripture bears a prophetic, messianic significance.

26. *was it not necessary*: The form of the question demands the affirmative answer. For Luke's use of *dei* ("it is necessary") as a shorthand reference to God's plan in history, see 2:49; 4:43; 13:14, 33; 21:9; 22:37. With reference specifically to the suffering (*paschein*) of the Messiah, see 9:22; 17:25; 24:7; Acts 17:3. Although the *Targum Jonathan* interprets Isa 52–53 in terms of the Messiah, it does not make the critical connection to the suffering of the Messiah, and Jewish literature contemporary to the NT (the Targum may actually reflect considerably later tradi-

tion) lacks the notion of a "suffering Messiah." The ability of Christians to find this in the texts of Torah does not derive from a standard view within Judaism but from their experience of a crucified and raised Jesus.

and enter into his glory: The verb *eiselthein* is the same used of "entering the kingdom" (13:24; 18:17, 25; and 23:42). For the background to the term "glory" (*doxa*), see the note on 2:9. Luke uses the term especially with regard to kingly rule and authority (2:14; 4:6; 9:26, 31; 19:38; 21:27), which Jesus, by virtue of his resurrection, has now taken possession of (Acts 2:35-36; 7:55). A remarkably similar perception concerning the Messiah is found in 1 Pet 1:11.

27. *beginning from Moses and all the prophets*: Luke uses this same phrase in 16:29-31 with reference to the ones the rich man should have heeded during his life. He uses it again in Acts 26:22 and 28:23 with reference to the Scriptures which spoke about Jesus. Although the phrase is expanded in 24:44 to include "the psalms," it is clear that Luke basically means here all of Torah; notice how the verse continues, "in all the Scriptures." There is another level at which the phrase can be understood: Moses and the other prophets reveal the pattern of rejection and acceptance that is essential to understanding the mission of Jesus (see Acts 7 and the introduction).

interpreted for them: The verb *diermēneuō*, like its cognate *hermēneuō* (which some MSS have here) means "to translate" (as in Acts 9:36) or "interpret" (as in 1 Cor 12:30; 14:5, 13, 27). In this case, Jesus shows them "the things concerning himself," that is, how he "brought to fulfillment" the meaning of Scripture (see 22:37: "that which is about me has a fulfillment"). Luke shows the risen Jesus teaching the Church the proper way to read the texts of Torah, that is, messianically.

28. *made as if to keep going further*: The verb *prospoieō* means to "pretend" or to "affect" something; thus the translation "made as if to." Like the disciples' "standing sorrowfully" in verse 17, this is simply a narrative device meant to bring liveliness and humanity to the story.

29. *they began to urge him*: The only reason for taking note of this is that the verb *parabiazō* is cognate with *biazō* used in 16:16. It too can mean "force." But as it is used here and in Acts 16:15, it clearly means "urge," and this helps support the reading this commentary gives to the difficult passage in Luke 16:16.

30. *as he was reclining at table with them*: The translation supplies "at table." Luke uses *kataklinō* as in 7:36; 9:14-15; 14:8.

took . . . blessed . . . broke . . . gave: These words obviously recall the feeding of the five thousand (9:16) and the Last Supper (22:19). In both accounts as here, Jesus "took" bread (*lambanō*). Here and in 9:16, he "blesses" (*eulogeō*), whereas in 22:19 he "gives thanks (*eucharisteō*). As in 22:19, he breaks the bread (*klaō*). But rather than the imperfect *edidou* of 9:16 or the aorist *edōken* of 22:19, Luke here uses the imperfect of the compound form *epididōmi*, "to hand over" (4:17; 11:11-12).

31. *their eyes were opened*: The passive construction corresponds to verse 16, "their eyes were bound." They do not "see" Jesus, but rather "recognize" (*epiginōskō*)

him. For Luke's use of "recognition," see 1:4, 22; 5:22; 23:7; Acts 3:10; 4:13. The phrase echoes the biblical language used of Adam and Eve in Gen 3:7, "the eyes of the two were opened and they recognized that they were naked."

he disappeared: Is literally, "he became invisible from them"; the adjective *aphantos* appears only here in the NT.

32. *were our hearts not burning*: Probably because they sensed a conflict of fact, some Latin MSS change "burning" to "veiled" or "blinded," but that is to miss the psychological point of the recollection. The notion of "burning" (*kaiomenē*) is sometimes associated in Greek literature with emotions such as love (Plato, *Laws* 783A), and such seems to be the basic sense here as well, although in the LXX, the verb is often used with reference to the presence of the Lord (see Exod 3:2; Deut 4:11; 9:15; Ps 49:3; Sir 48:1; Isa 30:27; 62:1).

as he opened the Scriptures to us: Luke uses the same word (*dianoigō*) for the "opening" of the texts as for the "opening" of their eyes in verse 31. As they perceived the true, messianic meaning of the Scripture, they were also able to "see" Jesus in the breaking of the bread. Luke uses *graphē* here and in verse 27 for Scripture, otherwise using the term only in 4:27, and in the scene that follows this one, 24:45 (but see Acts 1:16; 8:32, 35; 17:2, 11; 18:24, 28).

33. *Eleven and those with them gathered together*: As in 24:9, Luke uses this awkward phrasing to remind the reader that the apostolic circle of the Twelve is still broken, and that the messianic community is made up of others as well. The verb *athroizō* is used only here in the NT, but in the LXX is used for the gathering of Jacob's sons at his death (Gen 49:2); the joining together of Israel against Moses (Num 20:2); the gathering of Israel at Mizpah under Samuel (1 Sam 7:5); and of the military gathering of Judas Maccabeus (1 Macc 3:13, 44; 9:28).

34. *truly been raised*: The adverb *ontōs* represents the shift from incredulity on the part of the assembly (reported in 24:11). The title "Lord" (*kyrios*) is used absolutely (cf. "Lord Jesus" in 24:3 and "Jesus" in 24:15). Now, the message of the men in 24:6 that "he has been raised" (*egerthē*) has become the conviction of the community; or perhaps better, it becomes a community as it shares this conviction.

has appeared to Simon: Luke gives us no report of a separate appearance to Peter, although one is noted by Paul in 1 Cor 15:5. In 24:12 (with its textual difficulties) Peter is only said to run and view the tomb. Here, he is called "Simon," as in 4:38; 5:3-10; 6:14; 22:31. The aorist passive of the verb *horaō* ("to see") is *ōphthē*, and appears in a number of NT reports of appearances (1 Cor 15:3-8; Acts 9:17; 13:31).

35. *they related what had happened on the road*: Luke uses *exēgeomai* (Acts 10:8; 15:12, 14; 21:19) in much the same way as *diēgeomai* (1:1; 8:39; 9:10; Acts 12:17), for the *narration* of events. The most striking use may be Acts 9:27, where Barnabas speaking up for Paul "related to them how he had seen Jesus on the road" (*en tē hodō*, as here).

in the breaking of the bread: See 22:19; 24:30. Luke here uses the phrase *klasis tou artou*, which recurs in Acts 2:42 as the ritual meal of the community (see also Acts 2:46; 20:7, 11; 27:35).

INTERPRETATION

Luke's storytelling ability is beautifully displayed in this appearance story. He provides a sense of particularity by the rich use of detail: the name of the village and its distance from the city, the name of the disciple, the gestures of hospitality. The story is full of emotions subtly sketched: the men stopping in sorrow, their report that the women had "stunned" them, their recollection of how their "hearts had burned" while in conversation with Jesus.

And after the tumultuous movement of the previous section, there is an almost pastoral quality to this story. It has the feel of an evening spring walk in the country and a quiet conversation and a spiritual presence. No wonder monks prayed at the end of day in words taken from the disciples, "*Mane nobiscum Domine, quoniam advesperascit*"—"Stay with us Lord, for the evening falls."

The Hellenistic reader would find nothing strange in this account of appearance and disappearance, for such stories were in circulation about figures such as Romulus. As Ovid reports in *Fasti* 2:489, "Romulus was seen, standing in the middle of the road . . . he gave the order and he vanished into the upper world from Julius' eyes" (cf. also Livy, *Roman History* 1:16; Philostratus, *Life of Apollonius* 8:5). The freshness of Luke's account, however, is impressive. He combines the elements of a "recognition story" with a sensitivity to genuine human emotion. At the same time, he provides a subtly shaded interpretation of the *mode* of Jesus' presence to humans after his resurrection: he can really appear in the guise of a stranger on the road in the midst of human dialogue; he can be recognized in the ritual gestures of the community fellowship meal.

We can note in particular three literary and religious functions that this story serves within Luke's composition. First, this story provides an easy transition from the empty-tomb account to the appearance of Jesus in the full gathering of disciples. Luke has provided, by the very detail and length of this story, an emotionally satisfying bridge between the shock of absence (the tomb) and the shock of full presence (the appearance to the community). The very indirection of speech and gesture employed throughout the story admirably accomplishes this purpose.

Second, Luke demonstrates one of his most remarkable narrative skills, that of gathering a number of disparate stories into a single narrative. He is fond of repeating an account several times, and with each telling, adding some further level of meaning or shade of interpretation. The most obvious example of this technique is the threefold recital of Paul's conversion in Acts 9; 22, and 26. But the sequence most resembling the present one is the story of Cornelius' conversion and how that becomes the basis for a community decision, in Acts 10–15. In those chapters, Luke intertwines experience and narration by several characters, moving progressively and dramatically toward the creation of a community narrative that is the basis for discernment. Something very much like that happens here: Luke tells a story of men on the road, who tell what had happened in the city, who relate what was related to them by women, who have a further experience of Jesus' words and actions, and who then report *this* to the assembled community, which tells *them* in turn, of further such events. Beneath the calm and almost matter-of-fact simplicity of this story, a complex process of narration is in process.

Third, this narrative process is connected to Luke's broader thematic interests. As people tell the story to each other, they also interpret the story. Luke shows us a process of community interpretation. This is the true significance of Jesus' speech to the men on the road: the words that he spoke to them "while still with them" (we have learned from 24:6-7) interpret his death and resurrection. But there is an even broader framework within which the "necessity of the Messiah to suffer and enter his glory" is to be understood: the writings of Torah, and the pattern of prophetic sending and rejection to be found in those writings.

In a remarkably down-to-earth fashion, Luke shows us narratively the process by which the first believers actually did learn to understand the significance of the events they had witnessed, and to resolve the cognitive dissonance between their experience and their convictions. The resurrection shed new light on Jesus' death, on his words, and on the Scriptures. The "opening of the eyes" to see the texts truly and the "opening of the eyes" to see Jesus truly are both part of the same complex process of seeking and finding meaning. Without "Moses and the prophets" they would not have had the symbols for appropriating their experience. Without their experience, "Moses and the prophets" would not have revealed those symbols. Luke shows us how the risen Lord taught the Church to read Torah as prophecy "about him."

Finally, Luke shows us how the process of telling and interpreting these diverse experiences begins not only to build a community narrative, but actually begins to create the community itself. The scattered fragments that have whirled in different directions (the women, Peter, those who had run to the tomb, the men on the road) are being gathered together in one place with one shared story, which is, "the Lord has truly risen." They are ready for the full encounter.

For Reference and Further Study

Betz, H. D. "The Origin and Nature of Christian Faith according to the Emmaus Legend (Luke 24:13-32)." *Int* 23 (1969) 32–46.

Dillon, R. J. *From Eyewitnesses to Ministers of the Word: Tradition and Composition in Luke 24* (AnBib 82; Rome: Biblical Institute, 1978) 69–155.

Ehrhardt, A. "The Disciples of Emmaus." *NTS* 10 (1963–64) 182–201.

Walker, W. O. "Post-Crucifixion Appearances and Christian Origins." *JBL* 88 (1969) 157–165.

Wanke, J. *Die Emmauserzählung: Eine redaktionsgeschichtliche Untersuchung zu Lk 24, 13-35.* (Leipzig: St. Benno-Verlag, 1973).

69. The Community Is Gathered (24:36-53)

36. As they were saying these things, he stood in their midst and said to them, "Peace to you!" 37. They were terrified, however, and fearful. They thought that they were seeing a spirit. 38. So he told them, "Why are you disturbed? Why do you have these doubts? 39. Look at my hands and my feet. I am myself! Touch me and see: a spirit doesn't have flesh and bones the way you see I have them!" 40. Saying this he showed them his hands and feet. 41. But since they were still disbelieving and marvelling because of their joy, he said to them, "Do you have some food here?" 42. They gave him a piece of grilled fish. 43. He took it and ate it in their presence. 44. And he said to them, "These are my words which I spoke to you while I was still with you: that everything written concerning me in the law of Moses and the prophets and psalms must be fulfilled." 45. Then he opened their mind so they could understand the scriptures. 46. And he told them, "Thus it is written that the Messiah suffers and rises from the dead on the third day, 47. and in his name repentance will be proclaimed to all nations for the forgiveness of sins. 48. Beginning from Jerusalem, you are witnesses of these things. 49. And look! I am sending the promise of my Father upon you. You are to remain in the city until the time you are clothed with power from on high." 50. He led them outside as far as Bethany. He lifted his hands. He blessed them. 51. And as he was blessing them, he withdrew from them and was carried up into heaven. 52. They worshipped him, and returned with great joy to Jerusalem. 53. They stayed constantly in the temple blessing God.

NOTES

36. *peace to you*: Some MSS add "It is me, do not fear," but the support is not overwhelming, and it could well have infiltrated from John 6:20. The greeting "peace" (Greek, *eirēne*; Hebrew, *shalom*) is traditional (see Judg 6:23; 18:6; 19:20; 1 Sam 16:5; 29:7; 1 Kgs 2:13; 2 Kgs 9:11; Judg 8:35). The greeting is used by Jesus in two of John's appearance accounts (John 20:19, 26). In Luke's narrative, the greeting has an additional resonance because Luke has portrayed Jesus as the prophet whose visitation of the people is a proclamation of peace (1:79; 2:14, 29; 7:50;

8:48; 19:38, 42; cf. Acts 10:36). As he enters their presence, he greets them in the fashion he taught them to greet the households they were to visit (10:5-6).

37. *terrified . . . fearful*: The first of these terms is a verb (*ptoeō*) that Luke uses to describe the terror caused by war (21:9); in the LXX it is used for the response of the people to the theophany on Mt. Sinai (Exod 19:16) and the response of the people of Ai at the conquest by Joshua (Josh 7:5). The second term (*emphobos*) is used of the women at the tomb (24:5).

seeing a spirit: One important MS (D) tries to make this clearer by using *phantasma* ("ghost") rather than *pneuma* ("spirit"), but Luke is scarcely using technical philosophical language. As the rest of the passage shows, he is simply trying to assert the *reality* of Jesus' personal presence. For the "ghostly" appearance of the dead, see 1 Sam 28:8-14; for the physical touch as reassurance that an appearance is not a ghost, cf. Philostratus, *Life of Apollonius* 8:12).

38. *why are you disturbed*: The only other time in the Gospel that Luke uses the verb *tarassō* (here in the perfect participle) is to describe Zechariah's response to the angel Gabriel's appearance; see also Acts 15:24; 17:8, 13.

have these doubts: Is literally, "why do thoughts (*dialogismoi*) arise in your hearts?" Luke uses "heart" (*kardia*) as the center of consciousness, as in 24:25. The translation of *dialogismoi* as "doubts" derives from the context. The term has a predominantly negative connotation in Luke; for the noun, see 5:22; 6:8; 9:46-47, and for the verb *dialogizomai*, see 5:21-22; 12:17; 20:14. More neutral examples are found in the response of Mary to the angel's announcement (1:29) and the response of the people to John the Baptist's preaching (3:15). The fact that Jesus can read their "hearts" is not a function of his resurrected state, but is a sign that he is a prophet, as we have seen throughout the narrative in fulfillment of Simeon's prophecy that he would "reveal the *dialogismoi* of many hearts" (2:35).

39. *look at my hands and my feet*: in John's appearance accounts (John 20:20, 25, 27), Jesus shows his hands and feet to show the marks of the nails. Luke makes no mention of this, just as he does not of the fact that Jesus was nailed to the cross in the first place. If the reader stays within Luke's version, therefore, the feet and the hands serve to demonstrate the physical reality ("flesh and bones"), but not necessarily the marks of crucifixion.

I am myself: Is literally, "see that I am myself," with the intensive *autos*. The showing of hands and feet prove that this risen Lord is the same person whom they knew before.

touch me and see: The verb *pselaphaō* means to touch physically (see Isa 59:10) or to examine closely. In this case, the physical touch amounts to an examination. The LXX uses the verb for the "touch" of blind Isaac as he tries to identify his son Esau (Gen 27:12, 21-22).

flesh and bones: The biblical idiom derives from "bone of my bone and flesh of my flesh" in LXX Gen 2:23, so that "flesh and bones" suggests not only being human, but the sharing of a common humanity; thus it is frequently used for kinship relations (2 Sam 5:1; 19:12-13; 1 Chr 11:1). This translation makes an independent sentence out of a *hoti* clause that could be rendered either as "*that* a spirit does not have," or "*because* a spirit does not have." They amount to the same thing.

41. *still disbelieving and marvelling*: The translation puts together two participles that in Greek are separated by the prepositional phrase "from joy" (*apo charas*). The verb *apisteuō* ("disbelieve") was used for the response to the women's announcement of the empty tomb in 24:11 (cf. also Acts 28:24). The verb "marvel" (*thaumazō*) was used of Peter in his return from the tomb (24:12), and throughout the narrative as a response to wonders (see the note on 24:12). Most difficult here is how to understand "from joy." Luke uses *apo* to express cause in 21:26 and 22:45. But "joy" is otherwise almost entirely associated with the response of positive acceptance in Luke (1:14; 2:10; 8:13; 10:17; 15:7, 10). How is it the cause of "unbelief"? Two points can be made: a) Luke is portraying a purely *emotional* response which is so powerful that they are too overwhelmed to really "believe" it in the sense of committing themselves to its reality; b) once more, we see how "fact" or "experience" is itself insufficient for faith; the interpretive word is also required.

42. *a piece of grilled fish*: As with the breaking of bread in 24:30, this detail reminds the reader of the feeding of the multitude in 9:16. In John 21:13, the risen Jesus shares both bread and fish with his disciples. The point of having Jesus eat "in their presence" (*enōpion autōn*), of course, is to make them "eyewitnesses" of the resurrection (see 1:2).

44. *these are my words*: Jesus now shows them the significance of the story. The phrase should be understood as "this is the *meaning* of my words." He refers first of all to passion prophecies made during his ministry (9:22, 44; 18:32-33), "while still with them." The oddness of this last phrase indicates the difficulty for the narrator, who must at once emphasize the fact that Jesus is truly "present" to them, and also that he is not "with them" in the same way he was before the resurrection.

   must be fulfilled: Here at the end of the Gospel story we find the components of "prophecy and fulfillment": a) the Scriptures speak of Jesus (*peri emou*); b) there is a divine necessity (*dei*) to the events of his ministry, death and resurrection; c) this divine necessity expresses itself in a "fulfillment" of the meaning of the texts of Torah; d) Torah includes the Law of Moses, the Prophets, and the "Writings" (Psalms).

46. *thus it is written*: Having sketched the *formal* elements in the prophecy/fulfillment schema, Luke now supplies its *material* content: these are the things "about him" (and, as we shall see, "about them") that the Scripture speaks. In the first place are the events of his suffering and resurrection from the dead. Each of Luke's resurrection accounts recapitulates Jesus' prophecy predictions, stressing that they reached fulfillment.

47. *in his name repentance will be proclaimed*: Luke now makes the decisive turn toward his second volume. Having shown how the prophecies of Scripture and the prophecies of the Messiah about himself have reached fulfillment, Luke has Jesus now utter a "programmatic prophecy" (see Introduction, pp. 16–17) that

anticipates the narrative to follow and places it, too, under the guidance of the Scripture: a) the proclamation (*kērysso*), Acts 8:5; 9:20; 19:13; 20:25; 28:31; b) of repentance (*metanoia*), Acts 5:31; 11:18; 13:24; 20:21; 26:20; c) for forgiveness of sins (*aphesis tōn hamartiōn*), Acts 2:38; 5:31; 10:43; 13:38; 28:18; d) in Jesus' name (*onomati autou*), Acts 2:38; 3:6, 16; 4:7, 10, 12, 30; 5:28, 40-41; 8:16; 9:15-16, 27-28; 10:43, 48; 15:14, 26; 16:18; 19:5, 17; 21:13; 22:16; e) to all the nations (*panta ta ethnē*), Acts 9:15; 10:35, 45; 11:1, 18; 13:46-47; 14:16, 27; 15:3, 7, 12, 14, 19; 17:26; 18:6; 21:25; 22:21; 26:23; 28:28.

48. *beginning from Jerusalem*: There is some textual confusion concerning the number and case of the participle; this translation takes the nominative plural *arxamenoi* as the best reading and has it modify those who are witnessing; this best corresponds with Acts 1:8. As the Gospel narrative moved toward Jerusalem, the narrative of Acts will move out from it, in accord with the programmatic prophecy here and in Acts 1:8. The entire first eight chapters of Acts center in the city, and even after the mission moves outward, it circles back to its starting point (Acts 11:2; 12:25; 15:2; 18:21; 19:1, 21; 20:16, 22; 21:13).

witnesses of these things: As they proclaim the good news they will be more than "eyewitnesses," they will be "ministers of the word" (1:2). The category of "witness" (*martys*) is one applied to all the protagonists of Acts (1:8, 22; 2:32; 3:15; 5:32; 10:39-41; 13:31; 22:15, 20; 26:16). See also the cognates *martyromai* (Acts 20:26; 26:22), *martyrion* (Acts 4:33) and *martyreō* (Acts 6:3; 13:22; 14:3; 23:11).

49. *I am sending the promise of my Father*: The verb *apostellō* ("I am sending") is particularly striking, since it reminds us both of Jesus' "being sent" as prophet by God (4:18, 43), and of his "sending" his emissaries (9:2, 48; 10:1, 3, 16; 11:49). The term "promise" (*epangelia*) is picked up again in Acts 1:4. The language of promise is much more prominent in the NT than in the LXX. Like Paul (Gal 3:16, 18; Rom 4:13-14; 15:8), Luke associates the idea with Abraham, and makes it roughly equivalent to the "blessing" made by God to Abraham (Acts 2:39; 3:24-26; 13:32; 26:6). Also like Paul (Gal 3:14), Luke identifies this blessing/promise not in terms of land or Temple or king or offspring or prosperity but in terms of the Holy Spirit (Acts 2:33).

clothed with power from on high: The command to stay in the city obviously reflects Luke's geographical interest; see also 24:52. The "power (*dynamis*) from on high" refers to the Holy Spirit, as Luke's use in 4:14 and especially in the sequel, Acts 1:8, makes clear. The phrase is exegetical to "promise of the Father" as in Acts 2:33. Notice how this promise of the power from on high at the end of the narrative matches the annunciation scene, where Mary is told "the Holy Spirit will come upon you and the power of the Most High will overshadow you" (1:35). The image of "clothing" with a quality or capacity is common (see LXX Pss 34:26; 92:1; 108:18; 131:9, 16, 18; Prov 31:25; Wis 5:18; 17:3; Rom 13:12, 14; 1 Cor 15:53-54; Gal 3:27; Eph 4:24; 6:11; Col 3:10, 12; 1 Thess 5:8). In 1 Chr 12:18, for example, the Spirit "clothes" Amasai, enabling him to speak.

50. *lifted his hands . . . blessed them*: The phrase "lifting the hands" (*epairōn tas cheiras*) recalls the LXX of Exod 17:11, when Moses lifted his hands to give Israel victory in battle (see also Num 20:11; Ps 133:2). For *eulogeō* ("bless"), see Moses again

in Exod 39:43. The combination is associated with the priests (cf. Simeon in Luke 2:34), as when Aaron raised his hands and blessed the people (Lev 9:22), then joined Moses in blessing them (Lev 9:23; also Num 6:23; Sir 50:20-21).

51. *carried up into heaven*: There are two simultaneous movements, one "away" from them (*dihistēmi*, see 22:59), and the other "carried up" (with the imperfect passive of *anapherō*). Because some MSS lack this phrase and because it seems to duplicate the ascension scene in Acts 1:9-11, some prefer to see this as an interpolation. But the MS evidence for inclusion is good, and it actually makes for a harder reading (and therefore to be preferred on purely textual grounds). In the preface to his second volume (Acts 1:2), Luke refers to Jesus "having been taken up" (*analēmphthē*) even though he has not yet recounted the scene of Acts 1:9-11, so he was aware of his own earlier account. Ancient historians were less fastidious in such matters of overlap than are some contemporary scholars.

52. *worshipped him*: The verb *proskyneō* means literally to prostrate oneself as an act of homage (see Gen 18:2; 19:1; Exod 11:8), but was extended to mean worship, whether of idols (Exod 20:5; 23:24; Acts 7:43) or of the true God (LXX Pss 28:2; 71:11; 95:9; see Luke 4:7-8).

with great joy: As so often in Luke, "joy" (*chara*) signifies a state of messianic exaltation and peace (1:14; 2:10; 8:13; 10:17; 15:7, 10). They show their obedience to Jesus by returning to Jerusalem.

53. *in the Temple blessing God*: This Gospel began in the Temple (1:8) and it ends in the Temple. Jesus had made it his own place of ministry (19:47; 20:1; 21:37-38; 22:53), and the messianists will continue to teach, preach and worship there (Acts 2:46; 3:1-10; 5:20, 25, 42). For "blessing God," see 1:64; 2:28. Other MSS have "praising" or a combination of the two terms, "blessing and praising"; but the reading here adopted seems the best.

INTERPRETATION

Luke brings his first volume to a close with a final appearance account (24:36-49) and a brief description of Jesus' ascension (24:50-53), providing at once a satisfying conclusion to his story of "all that Jesus said and did" (Acts 1:1) and providing a transition to the story of Jesus' prophetic successors that he will relate in the second volume.

Luke's narrative technique (as we observed in the last section) has been to draw the threads of the resurrection story together from disparate witnesses, and as he shapes a shared narrative, shows at the same time a community in the process of formation. The way has been prepared for a final encounter between Jesus and his followers. We know from Acts, of course, that this is not really the end: Acts says that Jesus appeared over a period of forty days to his followers, eating with them and speaking to them of the kingdom of God (Acts 1:3; 10:41). Acts 1:4-8, in fact, provides the last of these scenes, although even after that, the risen Lord is seen by Stephen (Acts 7:55-56) and Paul (Acts 9:1-9, 27). The final scene of the Gospel, then, is intended to serve literary and religious purposes and not simply historical ones.

Luke uses the scene first to remind his readers of the way in which Jesus will be present to the community. At first glimpse the emphasis on touching the hands and feet and eating the fish may appear like crass physicalism. A closer reading, however, reveals that Luke has the delicate task of asserting (through the clumsy mechanism of narrative) both the reality of Jesus' presence and its difference from his former presence. The Emmaus story emphasized the elusiveness and indirection of Jesus' presence: Jesus could appear as a stranger without being recognized. This story emphasizes the other side: he is not a ghost, but a real person: "It is truly myself!"

Yet even with the reassuring touch and bit of fish "taken in their presence," it is obvious that Luke is not portraying a resuscitation but a resurrection. The disciples are filled with a mixture of terror and joy. And when Jesus speaks, it is not simply the same as "when he was with them" (24:44); now he is the commanding Lord. They worship him and he departs for heaven with hands lifted in blessing. Luke teaches the community that from now on, Jesus' presence to them will be at such fellowship meals where they break bread as Jesus had taught them, read the Scriptures that speak of him, and remember his words.

At this final encounter, Luke also pulls together the interpretation of the first part of the story and provides the reader with the framework for understanding the second part. Jesus himself reminds his followers of how his words and those of Scripture serve to interpret these events. Luke builds incrementally: the empty-tomb account showed that Jesus' passion prophecies reached fulfillment; the Emmaus story showed that Moses and the prophets foretold the suffering and resurrection of the Messiah. Now the suffering and resurrection of the Messiah are shown to be the interpretive key both to the words of Jesus and to Law, Prophets, and Writings. It is the risen Lord who teaches the Church to read Torah properly. He "opens their mind to understand the Scriptures." And this is necessary if those who have been "eyewitnesses" are also to be "ministers of the word" (1:2) in preaching these events and interpreting them from Torah.

Thus the seamlessness of the syntax allows us to read the programmatic prophecy that follows in 24:47-48—laying out the basic themes of the apostolic mission in Acts—as events that will not only fulfill the sayings of this prophet, but also fall under the "fulfillment of Scripture." Luke could hardly have provided the reader with a clearer indication of how he wanted the two volumes to be read together as mutually interpretive. The first of these "fulfillment" events, and the one that enables all the others, is the gift of the Holy Spirit, the "power from on high" with which they will be clothed.

The promise of the Holy Spirit is the final statement of Jesus in the Gospel, and is followed immediately by this first account of his ascension. For Luke, these are two moments of the same process: the "withdrawal" of Jesus is not so much an absence as it is a presence in a new and more powerful mode: when Jesus is not among them as another specific body, he is accessible to all as life-giving Spirit.

It is important at this point to recall the prophetic imagery associated with Moses and Elijah which Luke uses so consistently and flexibly. At the transfiguration, Moses and Elijah were "in glory" with Jesus, and spoke to him about the *exodos* (or: departure) that he was to accomplish in Jerusalem (9:30-31). And when Jesus "set his face" for Jerusalem to begin his prophetic journey to the city, it was as "the time for his being taken up" was approaching (9:51). The narrative has prepared us for this departure and for its prophetic significance.

Now if we remember the prophet Moses and Elijah (whose depiction in Torah was surely modelled on that of Moses), we remember how their Spirit was transmitted to their successors at their departure. Joshua "was full of the Spirit of wisdom, for Moses had laid his hands on him: so the people of Israel obeyed him and did as the Lord had commanded Moses" (Deut 34:9). Joshua inherited the Spirit and was able to lead the people into the Promised Land even though Moses could not.

Likewise Elisha before the departure of his master Elijah asked for a double portion of the Spirit (2 Kgs 2:9). When Elijah ascended into heaven, he left the prophetic "mantle" for his successor Elisha to wear (2 Kgs 2:14); so when Elijah had departed, his Spirit was still more actively present in his successor, who at once demonstrated the deeds of a prophet (2 Kgs 2:14-22). Thus the imagery of "being clothed from on high" is particularly fitting. Jesus' followers will receive a double share of the Spirit, and the mantle of his prophecy; they will work signs and wonders in his name, and declare openly what they had once held in silence (9:36).

For Reference and Further Study

Dillon, R. J. *From Eye-Witnesses to Ministers of the Word: Tradition and Composition in Luke 24* (AnBib 82; Rome: Biblical Institute, 1978) 157–225.

Dupont, J. "La mission de Paul d'après Actes 26:16-23 et la mission des apôtres d'après Luc 24:44-49 et Actes 1:8." *Paul and Paulinism.* Ed. M. D. Hooker and S. G. Wilson (London: SPCK, 1982) 290–301.

Fitzmyer, J. A. "The Ascension of Christ and Pentecost." *TS* 45 (1984) 409–440.

Lohfink, G. *Die Himmelfahrt Jesu: Untersuchungen zu den Himmelfahrts-und Erhöhungstetxten bei Lukas* (SANT 26; Munich: Kösel, 1971) 147–176.

Van Stempvoort, P. A. "The Interpretation of the Ascension in Luke and Acts." *NTS* 5 (1958–59) 30–42.

INDEXES

SCRIPTURAL INDEX

INDEX OF ANCIENT WRITINGS

3. Christian Writings

INDEX OF AUTHORS